Exam 70-503: *TS: Microsoft® .NET Framework 3.5—Windows® Communication Foundation Application Development*

Objective	Chapter	Lesson
Creating Services		
Define Service contracts.	1	1
Define Data contracts.	1	2
Define Operation contracts.	1	1
Define Message contracts.	1	2
Process generic messages.	9	1
Exposing and Deploying Services		
Create and configure service endpoints.	2	1
Manage consistency between life cycle, sessions, concurrency, and bindings.	2	2
Host a service in a managed application.	3	2
Host a service on a Web server.	3	1
Create custom behaviors.	2	2
Instrumenting and Administering Services		
Implement end-to-end service tracing.	6	2
Monitor service health.	6	4
Log messages.	6	1
Dynamically configure the service by using the service model.	5	2
Implement inspectors.	6	3
Consuming Services		
Create a service proxy.	4	1
Configure the client endpoint.	5	1
Call a service by using a service proxy.	4	1
Handle exceptions on clients.	9	2
Consume non-WCF services.	4	2
Securing Services		
Implement transport-level security.	7	1
Implement message-level security.	7	2
Authenticate clients.	8	1
Authorize clients.	8	2
Impersonate clients.	8	2
Managing the Service Life Cycle		
Manage instances.	10	1
Manage sessions.	10	1
Manage transactions.	11	1
Manage concurrency.	12	1
Manage consistency between instances, sessions, transactions, and concurrency.	12	1

Note: Exam objectives are subject to change at any time without prior notice and at Microsoft's sole discretion. Please visit the Microsoft Learning Certification Web site (*www.microsoft.com/learning/mcp/*) for the most current listing of exam objectives.

MCTS Self-Paced Training Kit (Exam 70-503): Microsoft® .NET Framework 3.5—Windows® Communication Foundation

Bruce Johnson, Peter Madziak,
and Sara Morgan

PUBLISHED BY
Microsoft Press
A Division of Microsoft Corporation
One Microsoft Way
Redmond, Washington 98052-6399

Library of Congress Control Number: 2008929790

Printed and bound in the United States of America.

1 2 3 4 5 6 7 8 9 QWT 3 2 1 0 9 8

Distributed in Canada by H.B. Fenn and Company Ltd.

A CIP catalogue record for this book is available from the British Library.

Microsoft Press books are available through booksellers and distributors worldwide. For further information about international editions, contact your local Microsoft Corporation office or contact Microsoft Press International directly at fax (425) 936-7329. Visit our Web site at www.microsoft.com/mspress. Send comments to tkinput@microsoft.com.

Acquisitions Editor: Ken Jones
Developmental Editor: Laura Sackerman
Project Editor: Valerie Woolley
Editorial Production: nSight, Inc.
Technical Reviewer: Kurt Meyer; Technical Review services provided by Content Master, a member of CM Group, Ltd.
Cover: Tom Draper Design

Body Part No. X14-15149

About the Authors

Bruce Johnson

Bruce Johnson is a partner at ObjectSharp Consulting in Toronto, Canada. For over 25 years, he has been involved in various parts of the computer industry, starting with UNIX and PL/1, through C++ and Microsoft Visual Basic (pre .NET), and, finally, all manner of Microsoft Windows applications and .NET technologies. His position as a consultant has allowed him to implement consumer-facing Web applications, Windows applications, and the whole gamut of service-based applications (Web Services, .NET remoting, and Windows Communication Foundation [WCF]). As well as having fun working just behind the bleeding edge of technology (you know, the place where stuff actually has to be delivered), he has given more than 200 presentations at conferences and user groups across North America. His writings include magazine columns and articles, a blog (found at *http://www.objectsharp.com/blogs/bruce*), and a number of Microsoft Press training kit books.

Peter Madziak

Peter Madziak is a senior consultant and instructor with Object-Sharp Consulting—a Microsoft Gold Partner based in Toronto, Canada. He is a technical leader with more than 10 years' experience helping development teams plan, design, and develop large software projects. Peter's primary focus over the past few years has been on helping customers understand service-oriented architecture (SOA), Workflow and Business Process Management (BPM), Web Services (both RESTful and WS-*), event-driven architecture (EDA), and, more important, how all these technologies and architectural styles can be reconciled into an architecture that aligns well with business needs.

As an SOA and BPM expert, Peter helps customers implement solutions, using technologies such as WCF, Windows Workflow, Microsoft BizTalk Server 2006, SQL Service Broker, and ASP.NET Web applications. You can visit his blog at *http://www.objectsharp.com/cs/blogs/pmadziak/default.aspx*.

Sara Morgan

Sara Morgan is a robotics software engineer with CoroWare, Inc., (*http://www.coroware.com*) and author of the newly released Programming Microsoft Robotics Studio (Microsoft Press, 2008). In addition to robotics, she has extensive experience with Microsoft SQL Server and Microsoft Visual Studio .NET and has been developing database-driven Web applications since the earliest days of Internet development.

Prior to joining CoroWare, she was an independent author and developer, and her main client was Microsoft. During that time, she co-wrote four training kits for Microsoft Press. Developers use these training kits to study for certification exam; the kits cover topics such as distributed development, Web application development, SQL Server query optimization, and SQL Server business intelligence. Sara has also written several articles for the online development journal, *DevX.com*, concerning Speech Server and the newly released Microsoft Robotics Studio. In early 2007, she was named a Microsoft Most Valuable Professional (MVP) for the Office Communications Server (OCS) group.

Contents at a Glance

Table of Contents

What do you think of this book? We want to hear from you!

Microsoft is interested in hearing your feedback so we can continually improve our books and learning resources for you. To participate in a brief online survey, please visit:

www.microsoft.com/learning/booksurvey/

8   User-Level Security 357

What do you think of this book? We want to hear from you!

Microsoft is interested in hearing your feedback so we can continually improve our books and learning resources for you. To participate in a brief online survey, please visit:

www.microsoft.com/learning/booksurvey/

Introduction

This training kit is designed for developers who plan to take the Microsoft Certified Technology Specialist (MCTS) exam, Exam 70-503, as well as for developers who need to know how to develop Windows Communication Foundation (WCF)–based applications, using Microsoft .NET Framework 3.5. It's assumed that, before using this training kit, you already have a working knowledge of Microsoft Windows and Microsoft Visual Basic or C# (or both).

By using this training kit, you will learn how to do the following:

- Create and configure a WCF service.
- Implement a client for a WCF service, using different transport protocols.
- Provide security to a WCF application, using transport-level and message-level protection.
- Extend WCF by using custom behaviors, including message inspectors, parameter inspectors, and operation invokers.
- Perform end-to-end (E2E) tracing on a WCF application.

Hardware Requirements

The following hardware is required to complete the practice exercises:

- A computer with a 1.6-gigahertz (GHz) or faster processor.
- A minimum of 384 megabytes (MB) of random access memory (RAM).
- A minimum of 2.2 gigabytes (GB) of available hard disk space is required to install Microsoft Visual Studio 2008. Additionally, 75 MB of available hard disk space is required to install the labs.
- A DVD-ROM drive.
- A 1024 × 768 or higher resolution display with 256 colors or more.
- A keyboard and Microsoft mouse or compatible pointing device.

Software Requirements

The following software is required to complete the practice exercises:

- One of the following operating systems:
    - Windows Vista (any edition except Windows Vista Starter)
    - Windows XP with Service Pack 2 or later (any edition except Windows XP Starter)
    - Microsoft Windows Server 2003 with Service Pack 1 or later (any edition)

- ❏ Windows Server 2003 R2 or later (any edition)
- ❏ Windows Server 2008
- ■ Microsoft Visual Studio 2008

NOTE Evaluation edition of Visual Studio included

A 90-day evaluation edition of Visual Studio 2008 Professional edition is included on a DVD that comes with this training kit.

Using the CD and DVD

A companion CD and an evaluation software DVD are included with this training kit. The companion CD contains the following:

- ■ **Practice Tests** You can reinforce your understanding of how to create WCF applications in Visual Studio 2008 with .NET Framework 3.5 by using electronic practice tests that you can customize to meet your needs from the pool of Lesson Review questions in this book. Alternatively, you can practice for the 70-503 certification exam by using tests created from a pool of 200 realistic exam questions, which will give you enough different practice tests to ensure that you're prepared.

- ■ **Practice Files** Most chapters in this training kit include code and practice files that are associated with the lab exercises at the end of every lesson. For some exercises, you are instructed to open a project prior to starting the exercise. For other exercises, you create a project on your own and then reference a completed project on the CD if you have a problem following the exercise procedures. Practice files can be installed to your hard drive by simply copying them to the desired directory. After copying the practice files from the CD to your hard drive, you must clear the *Read Only* attribute to work with the files on your hard drive.

  The instructions in an exercise will look like the following:

  1. Navigate to the *<InstallHome>*/Chapter8/Lesson1/Exercise1/*<language>*/Before directory and double-click the Exercise1.sln file to open the solution in Visual Studio.

     In the path described here, the *<InstallHome>* directory is the one into which you copy the sample files from the CD.

  Many samples require that you either run Visual Studio or the solution's executable files with Administrator privileges. Also be aware that antivirus software can interfere with some samples. As you work through an exercise, you are expected to add appropriate *Imports/using* statements as necessary.

- **eBook**   An electronic version (eBook) of this training kit is included for use at times when you don't want to carry the printed book with you. The eBook is in Portable Document Format (PDF), and you can view it by using Adobe Acrobat or Adobe Reader. You can use the eBook to cut and paste code as you work through the exercises. Command-line commands should be typed directly into a command prompt, because pasting these commands sometimes causes the hyphen (-) to be misinterpreted in the command prompt.
- **Webcasts**   Several webcasts are mentioned throughout this book. The companion CD has links that will take you directly to the webcasts.
- **Sample Chapters**   Sample chapters from other Microsoft Press titles on Windows Communication Foundation. These chapters are in PDF format.
- **Evaluation software**   The evaluation software DVD contains a 90-day evaluation edition of Visual Studio 2008 Professional edition in case you want to use it instead of a full version of Visual Studio 2008 to complete the exercises in this book.

> **Digital Content for Digital Book Readers:** If you bought a digital-only edition of this book, you can enjoy select content from the print edition's companion CD.
> Visit **http://go.microsoft.com/fwlink/?LinkId=124849** to get your downloadable content. This content is always up-to-date and available to all readers.

How to Install the Practice Tests

To install the practice test software from the companion CD to your hard disk, perform the following steps:

1. Insert the companion CD into your CD drive and accept the license agreement that appears onscreen. A CD menu appears.

NOTE   Alternative installation instructions if AutoRun is disabled

If the CD menu or the license agreement doesn't appear, AutoRun might be disabled on your computer. Refer to the Readme.txt file on the CD-ROM for alternative installation instructions.

---

2. Click Practice Tests and follow the instructions on the screen.

How to Use the Practice Tests

To start the practice test software, follow these steps:

1. Click Start and select All Programs and Microsoft Press Training Kit Exam Prep.
   A window appears that shows all the Microsoft Press training kit exam prep suites that are installed on your computer.
2. Double-click the lesson review or practice test you want to use.

Lesson Review Options

When you start a lesson review, the Custom Mode dialog box appears, enabling you to config-ure your test. You can click OK to accept the defaults, or you can customize the number of questions you want, the way the practice test software works, which exam objectives you want the questions to relate to, and whether you want your lesson review to be timed. If you are retaking a test, you can select whether you want to see all the questions again or only those questions you previously skipped or answered incorrectly.

After you click OK, your lesson review starts. You can take the test as follows:

- To take the test, answer the questions and use the Next, Previous, and Go To buttons to move from question to question.
- After you answer an individual question, if you want to see which answers are correct, along with an explanation of each correct answer, click Explanation.
- If you would rather wait until the end of the test to see how you did, answer all the ques-tions, and then click Score Test. You see a summary of the exam objectives that you chose and the percentage of questions you got right overall and per objective. You can print a copy of your test, review your answers, or retake the test.

Practice Test Options

When you start a practice test, you can choose whether to take the test in Certification Mode, Study Mode, or Custom Mode.

- **Certification Mode**   Closely resembles the experience of taking a certification exam. The test has a set number of questions, it is timed, and you cannot pause and restart the timer.
- **Study Mode**   Creates an untimed test in which you can review the correct answers and the explanations after you answer each question.
- **Custom Mode**   Gives you full control over the test options so that you can customize them as you like.

In all modes, the user interface you see when taking the test is basically the same, but different options are enabled or disabled, depending on the mode. The main options are discussed in the previous section, "Lesson Review Options."

When you review your answer to an individual practice test question, a "References" section is provided. This section lists where in the training kit you can find the information that relates to that question, and it provides links to other sources of information. After you click Test Results to score your entire practice test, you can click the Learning Plan tab to see a list of ref-erences for every objective.

How to Uninstall the Practice Tests

To uninstall the practice test software for a training kit, use the Add Or Remove Programs option in Control Panel in Windows.

Microsoft Certified Professional Program

Microsoft certifications provide the best method to prove your command of current Microsoft products and technologies. The exams and corresponding certifications are developed to validate your mastery of critical competencies as you design and develop or implement and support solutions with Microsoft products and technologies. Computer professionals who become Microsoft-certified are recognized as experts and are sought after industrywide. Certification brings a variety of benefits to the individual and to employers and organizations.

MORE INFO List of Microsoft certifications

For a full list of Microsoft certifications, go to *http://www.microsoft.com/learning/mcp/default.mspx*.

Technical Support

Every effort has been made to ensure the accuracy of this book and the contents of the companion CD. If you have comments, questions, or ideas regarding this book or the companion CD, please send them to Microsoft Press by using either of the following methods:

E-mail: *tkinput@microsoft.com*

Postal Mail:

Microsoft Press
Attn: *MCTS Self-Paced Training Kit (Exam 70-503): Microsoft® .NET Framework 3.5–Windows® Communication Foundation* Editor
One Microsoft Way
Redmond, WA, 98052-6399

For additional support information regarding this book and the CD-ROM (including answers to commonly asked questions about installation and use), visit the Microsoft Press Technical Support Web site at *http://www.microsoft.com/learning/support/books*. To connect directly to the Microsoft Knowledge Base and enter a query, visit *http://support.microsoft.com/search*. For support information regarding Microsoft software, please connect to *http://support.microsoft.com*.

Evaluation Edition Software

The 90-day evaluation edition provided with this training kit is not the full retail product and is provided only for the purposes of training and evaluation. Microsoft and Microsoft Technical Support do not support this evaluation edition.

Information about any issues relating to the use of this evaluation edition with this training kit is posted in the Support section of the Microsoft Press Web site (*http://www.microsoft.com /learning/support/books/*). For information about ordering the full version of any Microsoft software, please call Microsoft Sales at (800) 426-9400 or visit *http://www.microsoft.com*.

Chapter 1

Contracts

Windows Communication Foundation (WCF), which is part of the .NET Framework (included in versions 3.0 and 3.5), is a platform developers can use to build service-oriented applications. This book intentionally avoids the term SOA (service-oriented architecture). The term *service-oriented* (SO) *applications* will be used instead to convey the very practical scenario wherein applications are composed of a collection of services that communicate only by exchanging messages. Most would argue that SOA implies further constraints but, for the purposes of this book, you need only know that some services exist, that those services can receive messages to trigger certain business logic, and, finally, that they might return response messages to indicate what they have done. But where does this leave you? How do you know how to format the messages you send to a given service? What will it do when it receives them? What kind of response messages should you expect in return or, if something goes wrong, what kind of a fault does the service issue? Answering these questions amounts to defining a service's contract and is the focus of this chapter.

To answer these questions for the consumers of a service, WCF structures an overall contract with its consumers by defining the following three core contracts:

- **Service contract**   Defines which operations the service makes available to be invoked as request messages are sent to the service from the client
- **Data contract**   Defines the structure of data included in the payloads of the messages flowing in and out of the service
- **Message contract**   Enables you to control the headers that appear in the messages and how the messages are structured

Implicit in these contracts, as you'll see, are which faults might be issued from the service and the message exchange patterns (MEPs) necessary to converse with the service.

Exam objectives in this chapter:
- Define Service contracts.
- Define Data contracts.
- Define Operation contracts.
- Define Message contracts.

Lessons in this chapter:

Before You Begin

Because WCF is a platform for building standards-based Web services, it is in your best interest to have a strong working knowledge of the relevant Web and Web services standards: Extensible Markup Language (XML), XML schema definition (XSD), SOAP, Web Services Description Language (WSDL), and the family of SOAP-based Web services specifications (for example, WS-Addressing, WS-Security, WS-Policy, and so on) known collectively as the WS-* specs.

MORE INFO   **Core Web services standards**

The SOAP 1.2 specification can be found at *http://www.w3.org/TR/soap/*.

The WSDL 1.1 specification can be found at *http://www.w3.org/TR/wsdl*.

The XML Schema primer can be found at *http://www.w3.org/TR/xmlschema-0/*.

WCF does an excellent job of shielding the service developer from the details inherent in all these standards but, as always, a working knowledge of them will help clarify what your services are actually doing out on the network.

In addition to some working knowledge of the Web services standards, to complete the lessons in this chapter, you must have:

- A computer that meets or exceeds the minimum hardware requirements listed in the "Introduction" section at the beginning of the book.
- Any edition of Microsoft Visual Studio 2008 (including Microsoft Visual C# 2008 Express Edition or Microsoft Visual Basic 2008 Express Edition) installed on the computer. Please see the Introduction for installation instructions.
- Access to the Visual Studio solutions for this chapter. You can install the solutions from the companion CD.

Real World

Peter Madziak

When it comes to defining Service contracts, the most important thing to realize is that, as a developer, you have to let go of the object-oriented thinking that might well have colored your thinking for years. Even though, as you'll see in this chapter, WCF enables you to turn a .NET class into a service by simply decorating the class with the appropriate attribute, you have to always remember that sending messages to a service out on the network somewhere is fundamentally different from simply calling a method on an object in the same address space as the caller.

In service-oriented systems, messages are flowing in and out of service endpoints, and it is best to think of the message payloads as business documents that, when received by the service, trigger some sort of business transaction. For instance, you might have a *LoanProcessingService* that would receive *LoanApplication* documents in a message payload, which would in turn trigger the processing of a loan application. Furthermore, the receipt of this *LoanApplication* document might trigger long-running work that must be processed asynchronously. In such cases, a common pattern is for the service to return some form of acknowledgement (or receipt) document that, at the very least, contains an identifier that the consumer can subsequently use to check the status of the loan application. As you'll see in this chapter, this sort of document-centric thinking, which in many ways mirrors the means of conducting business in a paper-based world, should shape how you define your Service contracts.

Lesson 1: Defining Behavioral Contracts

This lesson provides you with the tools you need to start defining WCF services. In particular, it focuses on the .NET attributes you need from the *System.ServiceModel* namespace to specify the behavioral aspects of your WCF services:

- How the service behaves and what operations it exposes
- When the service might issue faults and what kind of faults it might issue
- What are the MEPs required to interact with the service? That is, whether the operation involves a basic request/response interaction, or the operation is one-way, or finally whether some two-way communication is possible between the consumer and the service.

After this lesson, you will be able to:

- Use the *ServiceContract* and *OperationContract* attributes to declare a Service contract.
- Define a service type to implement a Service contract.
- Use the *FaultContract* attribute to declare when a service operation might issue a fault, as well as identify the data that will be included along with the fault.
- Use the *ServiceContract* attribute, the *OperationContract* attribute, or both to define the MEPs for a service.

Estimated lesson time: 50 minutes

Service Contracts and Service Types

For the purposes of this section, *Service contract* means the collective mechanisms by which a service's capabilities and requirements are specified for its consumers. In WCF, these mechanisms take the form of .NET interface (or class) types, operations within that type, and the following three core .NET attributes, which are used to annotate these types and operations: the *ServiceContractAttribute*, the *OperationContractAttribute*, and the *MessageParameterAttribute*. For example, the following is a portion of a sample Service contract for a Task Manager service:

```
' VB
<ServiceContract()> _
Public Interface ITaskManagerService
    <OperationContract()> _
    Function AddTask(ByVal taskDescription As String, _
            ByVal assignedTo As String) As Integer

    ' Etc...
End Interface

// C#
[ServiceContract()]
public interface ITaskManagerService
{
```

```
[OperationContract()]
int AddTask( string taskDescription, string assignedTo);

// Etc...
}
```

The discussion that follows covers these attributes in more detail to show how their properties can be used to gain further control over factors such as how a service's metadata looks and how its messages will be formatted.

WCF and Web Services Standards

Although the details of Web standards are outside the scope of this book, it is at least worth commenting on how the various WCF contracts relate to three of the core Web services standards. The three core types of WCF contracts map directly to a corresponding Web services standard in the following way:

- Service contracts map to WSDL
- Data contracts map to XSD
- Message contracts map to SOAP

In fact, as can be seen from the fact that most of these contract definition mechanisms reside in a namespace called *System.Service*Model, Microsoft as part of its vision of modeling and Domain Specific Languages (DSLs) views these contract-definition languages as .NET-based models that can be used as alternatives to their standards-based counterparts.

No matter which transport protocol, (Hypertext Transfer Protocol [HTTP], Transmission Control Protocol [TCP], named pipes, or Microsoft Message Queuing [MSMQ]), is used to carry messages to and from your service endpoint, the WCF channel-based plumbing layer ends up representing the message in memory as a *Message* object. *Message* is a class defined in the *System.ServiceModel.Channels* namespace, that is, where the channel plumbing resides. *Message* objects are essentially .NET representations of a SOAP message. When sent over the wire, the format of the message will comply with SOAP 1.1 or 1.2 or, possibly, Message Transmission Optimization Mechanism (MTOM), depending on the binding configuration for the endpoint.

These *Message* objects might also hold addressing headers consistent with the WS-Addressing standard, headers that are serialized with the message if the binding supports addressing. When the WCF channels process messages, other WS-* standards that are typically focused on qualities of service might affect how WCF serializes its messages before they go out over the wire. For example, WS-ReliableMessaging, WS-Security, WS-AtomicTransaction, and so on might play a role.

> However, at the final stage of processing, the dispatcher (the last in the chain of channels) translates these *Message* objects into calls on your service instances so that you have to worry very little about how the plumbing is serializing these *Message* objects in accordance with all these standards. As you'll see in later chapters, you will need only to configure your bindings so that the correct plumbing is in place.

The *ServiceContractAttribute*

The *ServiceContractAttribute*, defined in the *System.ServiceModel* namespace, can be applied to either .NET interfaces or .NET classes. It is used to declare the type as a Service contract. This attribute is not inherited, so if the interface or class you are using to define your Service contract inherits from another Service contract, you must explicitly use the *ServiceContract-Attribute* to declare the subtype as a Service contract as well.

NOTE **Always apply the *ServiceContractAttribute* to an interface**
Although the *ServiceContractAttribute* can be applied to classes, it is considered best practice to apply it to an interface and thereby cleanly separate the contract declaration from any implementation details.

The *ServiceContractAttribute* can be declared without any parameters, but it can also take named parameters. Table 1-1 outlines those parameters and provides a description of each.

Table 1-1   Named Parameter Options for the *ServiceContractAttribute*

Named Parameter	Description
Name	Specifies a different name for the contract instead of the default, which is simply the interface or class type name. This contract name is what will appear in the *portType* name when consumers access the WSDL.
Namespace	Specifies a target namespace in the WSDL for the service. The default namespace is *http://tempuri.org*.
CallbackContract	Associates another Service contract as a Callback contract. This sets up the infrastructure for a duplex MEP and thereby allows the service to initiate sending messages to the client. The "Message Exchange Patterns" section of this lesson discusses MEPs in more detail.
ProtectionLevel	Enables the Service contract to specify constraints on how messages to all operations in the contract are protected on the wire, that is, whether they are signed and encrypted. See Chapter 8, "User-Level Security," for more about security.

Table 1-1   Named Parameter Options for the *ServiceContractAttribute*

Named Parameter	Description
ConfigurationName	Specifies the name attribute of the service element in a configuration file. The default is the name of the service implementation class, that is, the service type.
SessionMode	Specifies whether sessions should be enabled by the endpoint exposing this Service contract. See Chapter 10, "Sessions and Instancing," for more about sessions and session management.

The following are a few points to keep in mind about the usage of these parameters when you define your Service contracts:

- Always use the *Namespace* property to provide a Uniform Resource Identifier (URI) that in some way uniquely identifies both your organization and the conceptual or business domain in which the service operates. Furthermore, it is a good idea to adopt the World Wide Web Consortium (W3C) convention of using the year and month to differentiate versions of your service.

- It is good practice to use the *Name* property to remove the leading "I" because the "I" prefix is really more of a .NET idiom than anything else.

With these points in mind then, a slightly improved version of the Task Manager Service contract would be:

```vb
' VB
<ServiceContract(Name:="TaskManagerService", _
    Namespace:="http://schemas.fabrikam.com/2008/04/tasks/")> _
Public Interface ITaskManagerService
    ' Etc...
End Interface
```

```csharp
// C#
[ServiceContract(Name = "TaskManagerService",
    Namespace = "http://schemas.fabrikam.com/2008/04/tasks/")]
public interface ITaskManagerService
{
    // Etc...
}
```

The *OperationContractAttribute*

The *OperationContractAttribute*, also defined in the *System.ServiceModel* namespace, can be applied only to methods. It is used to declare the method as belonging to a Service contract. As with the *ServiceContractAttribute*, the *OperationContractAttribute* can be declared with a variety of named parameters that provide control over the service description and message formats. Table 1-2 outlines those parameters and provides a description of each.

Table 1-2   Named Parameter Options for the *OperationContractAttribute*

Named Parameter	Description
Name	Specifies a different name for the operation instead of using the default, which is the method name.
Action	Controls the action header for messages to this operation.
ReplyAction	Controls the action header for response messages from this operation.
IsOneWay	Indicates whether the operation is one-way and has no reply. When operations are one-way, ReplyAction is not supported. IsOneWay is covered in more detail later in this lesson, in the section called "OneWay," while discussing MEPs.
ProtectionLevel	Enables the Service contract to specify constraints on how messages to all operations in the contract are protected on the wire, that is, whether they are signed and encrypted. See Chapter 8 for more about security. The setting for this property at the operation level overrides the *ProtectionLevel* property of the *ServiceContractAttribute*.
IsInitiating	Indicates whether invoking the operation initiates a new session between the caller and the service. See Chapter 10 for more about sessions and session management.
IsTerminating	Indicates whether invoking the operation terminates an existing session between the caller and the service. See Chapter 10 for more about sessions and session management.

In most cases, the defaults for *Name*, *Action*, and *ReplyAction* are perfectly acceptable and will be what you should use. The most common cases for explicitly using them with values different from the defaults is when the resulting WSDL that the service emits must conform to something very specific, something that might seem out of place in a .NET context.

The *Action* property supports the usage of wildcards. One example of when this is used is to declare one of your service's operations to be a default operation to be called whenever a message comes in with an action it doesn't know about. The following code highlighted in bold shows how this might be done. The *ProcessUnrecognizedMessage* operation is called whenever it receives messages with actions other than what are mapped to the defined operations:

```vb
' VB
<ServiceContract()> _
Public Interface ISomeCrudContract

    <OperationContract( _
        IsOneWay:=True, Action:="urn:crud:insert")> _
    Function ProcessInsertMessage( _
            ByVal message As Message) As String

    <OperationContract( _
    IsOneWay:=True, Action:="urn:crud:update")> _
```

```
Function ProcessUpdateMessage( _
        ByVal message As Message) As String

<OperationContract( _
IsOneWay:=True, Action:="urn:crud:delete")> _
Function ProcessDeleteMessage( _
        ByVal message As Message) As String

' The catch-all operation:
<OperationContract( _
IsOneWay:=True, Action:="*")> _
Function ProcessUnrecognizedMessage( _
        ByVal message As Message) As String

End Interface

// C#
[ServiceContract]
public interface SomeCrudContract
{
    [OperationContract(IsOneWay = true,
        Action = "urn:crud:insert")]
    void ProcessInsertMessage(Message message);

    [OperationContract(IsOneWay = true,
        Action = "urn:crud:update")]
    void ProcessUpdateMessage(Message message);

    [OperationContract(IsOneWay = true,
        Action = "urn:crud:delete")]
    void ProcessDeleteMessage(Message message);

    // The catch-all operation:
    [OperationContract(IsOneWay = true,
        Action = "*")]
    void ProcessUnrecognizedMessage(Message message);
}
```

See Lesson 1, "Dealing with POX," of Chapter 9, "When Simple Is Not Sufficient," for more details and examples about the *Message* class and the use of the *Action* and *ReplyAction* attributes.

The *MessageParameterAttribute*

The *MessageParameterAttribute*, also defined in the *System.ServiceModel* namespace, controls how the names of any operation parameters and return values appear in the service description, that is, how they are emitted as part of the WSDL for the service. This attribute has only one property, the *Name* property.

One concrete case in which this attribute can be useful is when you need to have a .NET keyword or type name for the name of the XML element that is serialized at the wire-level transport layer. In the following code fragment, a *MessageParameterAttribute* is used with this parameter to control how both the parameter and return values are serialized to XML request and response elements at the transport layer. You need to use the *Name* property because the variable name as is cannot be used in the target programming language.

```vb
' VB
<OperationContract()> _
Function SomeOp( _
        <MessageParameter(Name:="String")> _
            ByVal workOrderNumber As Integer) As _
            <MessageParameter(Name:="responseString")> String
```

```csharp
// C#
[OperationContract()]
[return: MessageParameter(Name = "responseString")]
string SomeOp([MessageParameter(Name = "string")]string s);
```

Fault Contracts

This section covers the details around how WCF enables you to specify the fault behavior of your service, that is, when your service might issue faults and what type of information will be sent with the fault when it does issue one.

Faults vs. Exceptions   The first thing to realize is that faults and exceptions are not the same thing. Exceptions, as referred to here, are a .NET mechanism used to communicate problems encountered as a program executes. The .NET languages allow you *throw*, *catch/handle*, and possibly *ignore* exceptions so that they can be further propagated up the call stack. At some point, they should be handled (for instance, logged, warning the users to take some form of a recovery action, and so on) or the .NET run time will terminate the thread in which the exception was thrown.

Alternatively, faults, again as referred to here, refer to the SOAP fault mechanism for transferring error or fault conditions from a service to a consumer. The SOAP specification includes a definition for SOAP faults, providing structure for the contents of the message body when errors occur. This makes it possible for all the different SOAP stacks to issue faults in a standard way.

Exam Tip   Pay close attention to the exact requirements for any given question on the exam. You need to satisfy all the requirements listed in the question and only those requirements. Do not assume anything; pay close attention to exactly what is written.

WCF *FaultException* Class   WCF provides a *FaultException* class (there are actually two versions of it) that is the standard mechanism for translating between the two worlds of .NET exceptions and of SOAP faults. That is, when your service implementation throws a *Fault-Exception*, the WCF plumbing thereafter takes care of serializing that back to the consumer as a SOAP fault. This class comes in two forms:

- *FaultException* Used to send untyped fault data back to the consumer.
- *FaultException<TDetail>* A generic version used to send typed fault data back to the client, where *TDetail* represents the type parameter for the detailed fault information to be serialized back to the consumer as part of the SOAP fault message. If you have some class of objects that you use to bundle up your fault details, you can specify it as the type parameter for this generic exception class. Clients catching the exception can access the detailed fault information by getting it from the exception object's *Detail* property.

The *FaultContractAttribute* The *FaultContractAttribute*, also defined in *System.ServiceModel*, enables a service developer to declare which faults a given service operation might issue if things go wrong. Following are the key pieces of information pertinent to working with the *FaultContractAttribute*:

- The attribute can be applied to operations only.
- The attribute is not inherited.
- The attribute can be applied multiple times; for instance, if your service operation might return different types of faults, you would have a *FaultContractAttribute* declaration for each type of fault.
- The attribute's constructor takes a *Type* object used to reference the .NET type of the *Detail* object, that is, the type of fault information details you want to bundle with your faults.

Putting the Pieces Together So, to put these pieces together, the following code displays an example, first, of how you declare which faults a service might issue as part of its contract and, second, how the service type might create and throw a *FaultException*, basing it on some underlying detail type that represents the type of data you want to package your fault in. Here is the code:

```vb
' VB
<ServiceContract()> _
Public Interface ICalculatorService

    <OperationContract()> _
    <FaultContract(GetType(String))> _
    Function Divide(ByVal numerator As Double, _
        ByVal denominator As Double) As Double

End Interface

Public Class CalculatorService
    Implements ICalculatorService
```

```vb
    Public Function Divide( _
        ByVal numerator As Double, ByVal denominator As Double) _
        As Double Implements ICalculatorService.Divide

        If denominator = 0D Then
            Dim faultDetail As String
            faultDetail = "You cannot divide by zero"
            Dim fex As FaultException(Of String)
            fex = New FaultException(Of String)(faultDetail)
            Throw fex
        End If

        Return numerator / denominator

    End Function
End Class
```

```csharp
// C#
[ServiceContract()]
public interface ICalculatorService
{
    [OperationContract()]
    [FaultContract(typeof(string))]
    double Divide(double numerator, double denominator);
}

public class CalculatorService : ICalculatorService
{
    public double Divide(double numerator, double denominator)
    {
        if (denominator == 0.0d)
        {
            string faultDetail = "You cannot divide by zero";
            throw new FaultException<string>(faultDetail);
        }

        return numerator / denominator;
    }
}
```

A few final comments are apropos before ending this section:

- For simplicity's sake, this simple example used only a string type for its fault detail type because you have yet to learn about Data contracts. In most cases, you would use some form of a Data contract, as shown in the lab for Lesson 2, "Defining Structural Contracts," of this chapter.

- The details of how faults are handled on the client proxy side are covered in Chapter 4, "Consuming Services."

Message Exchange Patterns

MEPs describe the protocol of message exchanges a consumer must engage in to converse properly with the service. For instance, if a consumer sends a message, it needs to know whether it should expect a message back or whether simply sending the request is enough. Further, can the consumer expect unsolicited messages back from the service? WCF supports the following three MEPs, each of which is covered in more detail in this section:

- Request/Response
- OneWay
- Duplex

Request/Response

This is by far the most common MEP and very little has to be done to set it up because the default value for the *IsOneWay* property of *OperationContractAttribute* is *false*. Thus, as long as you don't have *IsOneWay* set to *true*, and you are not in a Duplex channel setting, you are using Request/Response. Note that it doesn't even necessarily mean that you have a non-void return type. That is to say, even with a void return type, if you are using Request/Response, then a response message is still going back to the consumer when the operation is called; it just would have an empty SOAP body. Also, this two-way communication channel enables the service to issue faults (if anything goes wrong), return transaction contexts, or both. (See Chapter 11, "Transactional Services," for transactions.) In the following code sample, both operations are configured to use the Request/Response MEP:

```vb
' VB
<ServiceContract()> _
Public Interface ILogisticsService
    <OperationContract()> _
    Function SubmitWorkOrder( _
        ByVal workOrder As WorkOrder) _
            As WorkOrderAcknowledgement

    <OperationContract()> _
    Sub CancelWorkOrder( _
            ByVal workOrderNumber As Integer)
End Interface
```

```csharp
// C#
[ServiceContract()]
public interface ILogisticsService
{
    [OperationContract()]
    WorkOrderAcknowledgement SubmitWorkOrder(WorkOrder workOrder);

    [OperationContract()]
    void CancelWorkOrder(int workOrderNumber);
}
```

Finally, all WCF bindings except the MSMQ-based bindings support the Request/Response MEP. (See Chapter 2, "Exposing the Services," for more about bindings.)

OneWay

Sometimes, you simply want to send a message off to a service and have it trigger some sort of business logic, and you aren't in fact interested in receiving anything back from the service. In such cases, you might want to use the OneWay MEP, that is, have the consumer simply send one-way messages into the service endpoint without any responses back from the service. This MEP is declared by setting the *IsOneWay* property on the *OperationContractAttribute* to *true*. The following shows an example of this:

```vb
' VB
<ServiceContract()> _
Public Interface ILogisticsService
    <OperationContract(IsOneWay:=True)> _
    Sub CancelWorkOrder( _
            ByVal workOrderNumber As Integer)
End Interface
```

```csharp
// C#
[ServiceContract()]
public interface ILogisticsService
{
    [OperationContract(IsOneWay=true)]
    void CancelWorkOrder(int workOrderNumber);
}
```

However, you must keep the following points in mind when considering whether the OneWay MEP is the right choice for you:

- It cannot be used in conjunction with the *FaultContract* attribute because for a service to issue faults, it must have a two-way channel of some form, which is not the case with one-way messaging. Nor can it return transaction contexts. (Again, see Chapter 11 for transactions.)
- It can be dangerous just to send off a one-way message and not have some assurances that it arrived and was processed. So, with that in mind, if an MSMQ binding is feasible in your environment, you might want to use OneWay messaging only when you can couple it with queued message delivery.
- Note also that, if you want queued message delivery, the OneWay MEP is your only choice, at least as far as the WCF infrastructure is concerned.
- Also be aware that it does not conform to the asynchronous, send-and-forget semantics that one might think it does, given the name "one-way." In other words, given the one-way nature of the channel, one might think that as soon as the consumer sends the

message, it is processed asynchronously from that point on and the client is free to do other things. However, the way the WCF plumbing handles this means that the consumer actually blocks, even after it has sent its one-way message, until the dispatcher on the service side (the last in the chain of channels on the service side) has taken the message off its internal queue and dispatched it to a service instance in the form of a method call on that object. Thus, if the service happens to be backed up in processing messages, your one-way message will sit in its queue until it is processed, thereby blocking the caller until that point in time. This could even be done intentionally, to some extent, due to the throttling settings for the service. See Chapter 12, "Concurrency" for more about concurrency and throttling.

Duplex

The Duplex MEP is a two-way message channel whose usage might be applicable in either of these two situations:

- The consumer sends a message to the service to initiate some longer-running processing and then subsequently requires notification back from the service, confirming that the requested processing has been done.
- The consumer needs to be able to receive unsolicited messages from the service.

Because there are two Service contracts to consider in a Duplex MEP scenario, namely the Service contract and the Callback contract, this MEP is declared by associating the Callback contract with the Service contract. This association is done through the *CallbackContract* property of the *ServiceContractAttribute* that is adorning the service that needs to be capable of calling back to a consumer. For an example of this, consider a simple "Hello World" application, this time where a consumer sends a one-way message to a greeting service, and at some point after that, the service calls back to the consumer and says, "I have processed your greeting request and here it is; I am calling you back with it now." The following code shows not only the Service contract, the Callback contract, and how they are associated but also how the service implementation (that is, the service type) uses the *OperationContext* to ask for a reference to the Callback contract, thereby enabling the service to call back to the consumer. Here is the code:

```vb
' VB
<ServiceContract()> _
Public Interface IGreetingHandler
    <OperationContract(IsOneWay:=True)> _
    Sub GreetingProduced(ByVal greeting As String)
End Interface

<ServiceContract(CallbackContract:= _
                GetType(IGreetingHandler))> _
Public Interface IGreetingService
```

```vb
        <OperationContract(IsOneWay:=True)> _
        Sub RequestGreeting(ByVal name As String)
End Interface

<ServiceBehavior(InstanceContextMode := _
    InstanceContextMode.PerSession)>
Public Class GreetingService
    Implements IGreetingService

    Public Sub RequestGreeting(ByVal name As String) _
            Implements IGreetingService.RequestGreeting
        Console.WriteLine("In GreetingService.RequestGreeting")
        Dim callbackHandler As IGreetingHandler
        callbackHandler = OperationContext.Current.GetCallbackChannel( _
                            Of IGreetingHandler)()
        callbackHandler.GreetingProduced("Hello " + name)
    End Sub
End Class
```

```csharp
// C#
[ServiceContract]
interface IGreetingHandler
{
    [OperationContract(IsOneWay = true)]
    void GreetingProduced(string greeting);
}

[ServiceContract(CallbackContract =
    typeof(IGreetingHandler))]
interface IGreetingService
{
    [OperationContract(IsOneWay = true)]
    void RequestGreeting(string name);
}

[ServiceBehavior(InstanceContextMode =
        InstanceContextMode.PerSession)]
class GreetingService : IGreetingService
{

    public void RequestGreeting(string name)
    {

        Console.WriteLine("In Service.Greet");
        IGreetingHandler callbackHandler =
          OperationContext.Current.GetCallbackChannel<IGreetingHandler>();
        callbackHandler.GreetingProduced("Hello " + name);
    }
}
```

Duplex Channels and Client-Side Proxies

Several more steps are required on the client proxy side for duplex channels to be set up, and Chapter 4 discusses this in further detail.

In the preceding code, don't worry too much about the "instancing mode" option declared within the *ServiceBehaviorAttribute* adorning the service type. For now, just understand that callback channels require a session to be established between the consumer and the service. You'll learn more about sessions, session management, and instancing in Chapter 10.

As with the OneWay MEP, you must consider some points before deciding the Duplex MEP is right for your service operations. The following are just some of the points you should take into account before using the Duplex MEP:

- The Duplex MEP is problematic in the real world because the service needs a connection back to the client, something that is generally avoided for security reasons and often impossible because of intervening firewalls and Network Address Translation (NAT) problems.

- A Duplex MEP doesn't scale very well because, as mentioned previously, its usage depends upon the existence of a long-running session maintained between the consumer and the service, thereby taking you back to the client/server era and all the scaling problems that entailed. Service orientation works best when every single message exchange is an independent event and doesn't depend on any messages that went before it—that is, when it is conversationally stateless.

- You lose interoperability. For instance, as Duplex MEP is implemented today with WCF callback channels, there is no chance at interoperability with clients on other platforms such as Java.

- Threading problems can easily occur when the operations on either end of the callback channel are not one-way. Note that in the example you looked at, all the operations involved were one-way.

NOTE   Request/Response is the most common MEP

The Request/Response MEP should be used in most cases because it is the safest and the most versatile. In most real-world services, even if the incoming request message is intended to trigger long-running work that should happen asynchronously from the consumer's perspective, a best practice is still to return some kind of acknowledgement, usually containing some form of ID with which the consumer can correlate later requests that check on the status of that long-running work.

Quick Check

1. A user has a service with a one-way operation that includes a fault contract, and he gets an exception when he tries to host the service. Why?
2. A user has a service he wants to expose on the Internet, and it needs to send notifications out to its consumers. Would the WCF Duplex MEP be a good choice for implementing this?

Quick Check Answers

1. This happens because, to return faults, the service needs some form of a two-way communication channel in place, which is not the case with one-way operations.
2. No. The WCF Duplex MEP can be problematic to enable, even inside an enterprise. Its implementation depends upon the service establishing a connection back to the consumer, which can't happen in certain scenarios, such as when the client's machine uses NAT behind a firewall. On the Internet, where you are never certain where your consumers are coming from, this type of callback channel would rarely, if ever, work. When you factor in the security risks it could pose and the scalability concerns with the fact that callback channels require the presence of sessions between client and service, it isn't a feasible solution.

Lab: Defining a Service

In this lab, you will use what you have learned to define your first Service contract. Then, just so that you can see it in action, you define a service type that implements that contract. The labs in this book require you to start a WCF service. You need to have the appropriate permissions to do so; therefore, you might want to run Visual Studio as an Administrator. Alternatively, when required to start a service you can browse to the service's .exe and run it as an Administrator.

NOTE   Before and After solutions

Throughout this book, the labs will always be based on a Visual Studio solution that represents a reasonable starting point. The full path indicating where to find these solutions will always include the word *Before*. There will always be a corresponding After solution that represents a final, working solution for the lab. For instance, for this first lesson, you can find the starting point solution at the following location: *<InstallHome>*/Chapter1/Lesson1/Exercise1/*<language>*/Before, where *<language>* represents the programming language of choice between Visual Basic or C#. Similarly, you can find the final solution at: *<InstallHome>*/Chapter1/Lesson1/Exercise1/*<language>*/After.

▶ **Exercise 1   Create the Service Contract and Service Type**

In this exercise, you will define both the contract and the service type.

1. Navigate to the *<InstallHome>*/Chapter1/Lesson1/Exercise1/*<language>*/Before directory and double-click the Exercise1.sln file to open the solution in Visual Studio.

2. The solution consists of two projects:

    ❑ The ServiceConsoleHost project is a simple console application used to host your first service. The details of what is being done here, configuring and hosting WCF services, is covered in Chapter 2 and in Chapter 3, "Deploying Services," respectively.

    ❑ The TaskClient project is a Windows Forms application that enables you to consume your first service. Once again, the details of how the WCF client proxy is created, used, and configured are covered later in Chapter 4.

3. Add a new Class Library project to the solution and call it **Tasks.Services**.

NOTE What project type should be used to define a service?

You could start with a WCF Service Library project, which would take care of some of the details; however, for this first service, you'll start with a regular library project and manually add all the pieces you'll need.

---

4. Add a reference to the *System.ServiceModel* namespace in this new Tasks.Services project.

5. Add a new Interface item to this project and call it **ITaskManagerService.cs** (or **ITaskManagerService.vb**).

6. Edit this new ITaskManagerService file (.cs or .vb as appropriate) to read as follows:

```
' VB
Imports System.ServiceModel
Imports System.Collections.Generic

<ServiceContract(Name:="TaskManagerService", _
    Namespace:="http://schemas.fabrikam.com/2008/04/tasks/")> _
Public Interface ITaskManagerService
    <OperationContract()> _
    Function AddTask(ByVal taskDescription As String, _
            ByVal assignedTo As String) As Integer

    <OperationContract()> _
    Function GetTasksByAssignedName( _
            ByVal assignedTo As String) As List(Of Integer)

    <OperationContract()> _
    Function GetTaskDescription( _
            ByVal taskNumber As Integer) As String

    <OperationContract()> _
    Function IsTaskCompleted( _
            ByVal taskNumber As Integer) As Boolean

    <OperationContract(IsOneWay:=True)> _
```

```
            Sub MarkTaskCompleted(ByVal taskNumber As Integer)

            <OperationContract(IsOneWay:=True)> _
            Sub DeleteTask(ByVal taskNumber As Integer)

        End Interface

        // C#
        using System;
        using System.Collections.Generic;
        using System.ServiceModel;

        namespace Tasks.Services
        {
            [ServiceContract(Name = "TaskManagerService",
                Namespace = "http://schemas.fabrikam.com/2008/04/tasks/")]
            public interface ITaskManagerService
            {
                [OperationContract()]
                int AddTask(string taskDescription,
                                string assignedTo);

                [OperationContract()]
                List<int> GetTasksByAssignedName(string assignedTo);

                [OperationContract()]
                string GetTaskDescription(int taskNumber);

                [OperationContract()]
                bool IsTaskCompleted(int taskNumber);

                [OperationContract(IsOneWay = true)]
                void MarkTaskCompleted(int taskNumber);

                [OperationContract(IsOneWay = true)]
                void DeleteTask(int taskNumber);
            }
        }
```

NOTE   Use of OneWay MEP

Both the *MarkTaskCompleted* and *DeleteTask* operations have been declared to use the One-
Way MEP by using the *IsOneWay* named parameter for the *OperationContractAttribute*. Why?
In both cases, you want the service to carry out an action, but you are not particularly inter-
ested in getting anything back from the service.

7. Rename the Class1.cs (or Class1.vb) file (that was added by default to the Tasks.Services
   project when you created the project) to TaskManagerService.cs (or TaskManagerSer-
   vice.vb). When prompted, click Yes to rename all references to **Class1**.

8. Edit the new TaskManagerService file so that it defines a service type that implements the Service contract you have already defined. The following code shows how this would be done for two of the methods, namely, the *AddTask* and *GetTaskDescription* methods. To complete this solution, the remaining methods must be implemented in a similar fashion. See the *After* solution for details if necessary.

```vb
' VB
Imports System.ServiceModel
Imports System.Linq

Public Class TaskManagerService
    Implements ITaskManagerService
    Public Function AddTask(ByVal taskDescription As String, _
            ByVal assignedTo As String) _
            As Integer Implements ITaskManagerService.AddTask
        Dim taskNum As Integer = s_nextTaskNumber
        s_nextTaskNumber = s_nextTaskNumber + 1
        Dim ti As New TaskInfo(taskNum, taskDescription, assignedTo)
        Console.WriteLine("Adding new task:\n{0}", ti.ToString())
        s_activeTasks.Add(taskNum, ti)
        Return taskNum
    End Function

    Public Function GetTaskDescription(ByVal taskNumber As Integer) _
        As String Implements ITaskManagerService.GetTaskDescription
        If Not s_activeTasks.ContainsKey(taskNumber) Then
            Dim msg As String = String.Format( _
                "No task with number {0}", taskNumber)
            Console.WriteLine(msg)
            Throw New Exception(msg)
        End If

        Dim descr As String = s_activeTasks.Item(taskNumber).Description
        Console.WriteLine("Description for task number {0} is {1}", _
                        taskNumber, descr)

        Return descr

    End Function

    ' Remaining functions omitted...

    Private Shared s_activeTasks As Dictionary( _
        Of Integer, TaskInfo) = New Dictionary(Of Integer, TaskInfo)
    Private Shared s_nextTaskNumber As Integer = 1
End Class

Class TaskInfo
    Public Sub New(ByVal taskNumber As Integer, _
            ByVal description As String, ByVal assignedTo As String)
        _taskNumber = taskNumber
        _description = description
```

```vbnet
                _assignedTo = assignedTo
        End Sub
        Public Property TaskNumber() As Integer
            Get
                    Return _taskNumber
            End Get

            Set(ByVal value As Integer)
                _taskNumber = value
            End Set
        End Property

        Public Property Description() As String
            Get
                    Return _description
            End Get

            Set(ByVal value As String)
                _description = value
            End Set
        End Property

        Public Property AssignedTo() As String
            Get
                    Return _assignedTo
            End Get

            Set(ByVal value As String)
                _assignedTo = value
            End Set
        End Property

        Public Property IsCompleted() As Boolean
            Get
                    Return _isCompleted
            End Get

            Set(ByVal value As Boolean)
                _isCompleted = value
            End Set
        End Property

        Public Overrides Function ToString() As String
            Return String.Format( _
            "Task: {0}\tAssigned to: {1}\tCompleted: {2}\nDescription:\n{3}", _
                    _taskNumber, _assignedTo, _
                    _isCompleted, _description)
        End Function

        Private _description As String
        Private _assignedTo As String
        Private _taskNumber As Integer
        Private _isCompleted As Boolean = False
    End Class
```

```csharp
// C#
using System;
using System.Collections.Generic;
using System.Linq;
using System.ServiceModel;
using System.Text;

namespace Tasks.Services
{
    public class TaskManagerService : ITaskManagerService
    {
        public int AddTask(string taskDescription,
                    string assignedTo)
        {
            int taskNum = s_nextTaskNumber++;
            TaskInfo ti = new TaskInfo(
                    taskNum, taskDescription, assignedTo);
            Console.WriteLine(
                    "Adding new task:\n{0}", ti.ToString());
            s_activeTasks.Add(taskNum, ti);
            return taskNum;
        }

        public string GetTaskDescription(int taskNumber)
        {
            if (!s_activeTasks.ContainsKey(taskNumber))
            {
                string msg = string.Format(
                    "No task with number {0}",
                    taskNumber);
                Console.WriteLine(msg);

                throw new Exception(msg);
            }

            string descr = s_activeTasks[taskNumber].Description;

            Console.WriteLine(
                "Description for task number {0} is {1}",
                taskNumber, descr);

            return descr;
        }
        // Remaining methods omitted...

        private static Dictionary<int, TaskInfo> s_activeTasks =
                    new Dictionary<int, TaskInfo>();
        private static int s_nextTaskNumber = 1;
    }

    // Helper class:
    class TaskInfo
    {
```

```csharp
public TaskInfo(int taskNumber,
        string description, string assignedTo)
{
    _taskNumber = taskNumber;
    _description = description;
    _assignedTo = assignedTo;
}

public int TaskNumber
{
    get
    {
        return _taskNumber;
    }
}

public string Description
{
    get
    {
        return _description;
    }
}

public string AssignedTo
{
    get
    {
        return _assignedTo;
    }
}

public bool IsCompleted
{
    get
    {
        return _isCompleted;
    }

    set
    {
        _isCompleted = value;
    }
}

public override string ToString()
{
    return string.Format(
        "Task: {0}\tAssigned to: {1}\tCompleted: {2}\nDescription:\n{3}",
            _taskNumber, _assignedTo,
            _isCompleted, _description);
}
```

```
        private int _taskNumber;
        private string _description;
        private string _assignedTo;
        private bool _isCompleted = false;
    }
}
```

NOTE   Not a real-world solution

This implementation is not realistic because it stores the tasks it is managing in a volatile, in-memory collection. Any real-world solution would use a database for persistent storage. However, it serves the purpose of easily getting a first service running.

---

9. To the ServiceConsoleHost project, add a project reference to your new service library, namely, **Tasks.Services**.

10. Build the solution and start the service, making sure that the ServiceConsoleHost project is the startup project.

    You can now explore the WSDL this service generates.

11. From the app.config file in the ServiceConsoleHost project, you can see that the service is hosted at *http://localhost:8080/Tasks*. Therefore, you can open your browser to this URI and follow the link to *http://localhost:8080/Tasks?wsdl* to see the WSDL.

    Note that from there, you can progress further to the WSDL imported by this WSDL file, namely, *http://localhost:8080/Tasks?wsdl=wsdl0* to access the WSDL that contains the detailed description for your service.

    At this point, if you want to see the service actually being used, you can leave the service host application running, switch the startup project to the TaskClient Windows Forms application, and run it against your service. To use it, simply enter your name, click View Tasks to invoke the task form, and start creating tasks. Any task you create with your name will show up in your list of tasks. If you assign a task to someone else, the task will show up in that person's list of tasks when he or she invokes the task form. In Chapter 4, you come back to how this application creates, uses, and configures the proxy to your service.

▶ **Exercise 2   Specify Fault Behaviors for the Service**

In this exercise, you will build on the service from the previous exercise and add some fault contracts that show consumers when and what type of faults might be issued by your service. In this case, at the very least, any time a consumer is invoking one of the operations that require a specific task number to identify a task that is currently being managed by the service, there is a chance that the user is submitting a task number not currently being managed by the service. In such a case, the service can issue a fault to the client to let the client know.

1. Navigate to the *<InstallHome>*/Chapter1/Lesson1/Exercise2/*<language>*/Before directory and double-click the Exercise2.sln file to open the solution in Visual Studio.

The solution consists of the three projects you ended with at the end of Exercise 1, "Defining a Service," with the only difference being that the TaskClient project has already been modified to take into account the fault specifications you are about to declare on the service.

2. Define a *FaultInfo* class that you'll use to provide the information to be carried as the fault's payload. To do this, add the following to the *ITaskManagerService* interface file above the interface definition:

```vb
' VB
<DataContract(Namespace:= _
    "http://schemas.fabrikam.com/2008/04/tasks/")> _
Public Class FaultInfo
    <DataMember()> _
    Public Reason As String = Nothing
End Class
```

```csharp
// C#
[DataContract(
    Namespace = "http://schemas.fabrikam.com/2008/04/tasks/")]
public class FaultInfo
{
    [DataMember()]
    public string Reason = null;
}
```

NOTE   More on Data contracts in the next lesson

For now, ignore the *DataContract* and *DataMember* attributes because they are covered in the next lesson. Think of this class as a means of packaging information you want to send as a fault's payload.

3. Declare the fault contract with operations in your Service contract that might issue faults.

For example, the following code shows in bold how this would be done for the *MarkTaskCompleted* operation. To complete this solution, the remaining fault contracts must be declared in a similar fashion. See the After solution for details if necessary.

```vb
' VB
<OperationContract()> _
<FaultContract(GetType(FaultInfo))> _
Sub MarkTaskCompleted(ByVal taskNumber As Integer)
```

```csharp
// C#
[OperationContract()]
[FaultContract(typeof(FaultInfo))]
void MarkTaskCompleted(int taskNumber);
```

CAUTION   The OneWay MEP cannot be used in conjunction with faults

The *MarkTaskCompleted* operation in the previous lesson was declared as one-way, but it can no longer be one-way because you now want to be able to send back faults if one occurs. Returning faults requires at least some form of two-way communication.

4. Change the service type implementation to return faults instead of just using regular .NET exceptions as was done in the previous exercise.

   Once again, to complete this solution, you must perform a similar change on all the operations. See the After solution for details if necessary. For your *MarkTaskCompleted* operation, this would involve the code shown in bold here:

```vb
' VB
Public Sub MarkTaskCompleted(ByVal taskNumber As Integer) _
      Implements ITaskManagerService.MarkTaskCompleted

    If Not s_activeTasks.ContainsKey(taskNumber) Then
        Dim msg As String = String.Format( _
                "No task with number {0}", taskNumber)
        Console.WriteLine(msg)

        Dim fi As FaultInfo = New FaultInfo()
        fi.Reason = msg
        Dim fe As FaultException(Of FaultInfo)
        fe = New FaultException(Of FaultInfo)(fi)
        Throw fe
    End If

    s_activeTasks.Item(taskNumber).IsCompleted = True
    Console.WriteLine( _
        "Marking task number {0} as completed", taskNumber)

End Sub
```

```csharp
// C#
public void MarkTaskCompleted(int taskNumber)
{
    if (!s_activeTasks.ContainsKey(taskNumber))
    {
        string msg = string.Format(
                "No task with number {0}", taskNumber);
        Console.WriteLine(msg);

        FaultInfo fi = new FaultInfo();
        fi.Reason = msg;
        throw new FaultException<FaultInfo>(fi);      }

    s_activeTasks[taskNumber].IsCompleted = true;

    Console.WriteLine(
        "Marking task number {0} as completed", taskNumber);
}
```

5. Build and run the application again to be sure everything is working, making sure *Service-ConsoleHost* is the startup project.

You can also explore the WSDL to see how adding your fault contracts changed the WSDL description of your service. In particular, you'll notice that the WSDL now includes *fault* elements. Also keep in mind that, as mentioned previously, the details of how faults are handled on the client proxy side are covered in Chapter 4.

Lesson Summary

- *ServiceContract* attributes declare types as Service contracts. They should be used with interfaces instead of with classes in the interest of cleanly separating the contract declaration from implementation details.
- *OperationContract* attributes declare the operations a Service contract exposes to its consumers.
- *FaultContract* attributes declare an operation that might issue faults and indicate into which type of object the fault details will be packaged.
- *OperationContract* attributes can declare that the operation uses a OneWay MEP.
- *ServiceContract* attributes are used to set up the Duplex MEP by associating a Callback contract with the service destined to be performing the callback.

Lesson Review

You can use the following questions to test your knowledge of the information in Lesson 1, "Defining Behavioral Contracts." The questions are also available on the companion CD if you prefer to review them in electronic form.

NOTE   Answers

Answers to these questions and explanations of why each answer choice is correct or incorrect are located in the "Answers" section at the end of the book.

---

1. You are about to define a new Service contract. Which of the following represent the .NET attributes from the *System.ServiceModel* namespace that you will need for certain when defining your contract?

   A. The *ServiceContractAttribute* and the *FaultContractAttribute*

   B. The *OperationContractAttribute* and the *FaultContractAttribute*

   C. The *ServiceContractAttribute* and the *OperationContractAttribute*

   D. The *OperationContractAttribute* and the *MessageParameterAttribute*

2. Suppose you have the following .NET interface:

```
' VB
Interface IInventoryService
    Sub RemoveItem(ByVal itemID As String)
End Interface
```

```
// C#
public interface IInventoryService
{
    void RemoveItem(string itemID);
}
```

Now suppose that you are asked to turn this interface into a Service contract in which the resulting service is named InventoryService, the *RemoveItem* operation is part of the contract, and you want to indicate that it might issue faults where the fault information will simply be contained within a string object. Which steps must you perform to turn this interface into a Service contract? (Choose all that apply.)

A. Apply the following contract to the interface:

```
' VB
<ServiceContract( _
    Namespace:="http://schemas.fabrikam.com/inventory/")>
```

```
// C#
[ServiceContract(
    Namespace="http://schemas.fabrikam.com/inventory/")]
```

B. Apply the following contract to the *RemoveItem* operation:

```
' VB
<FaultContract(GetType(String))>
```

```
// C#
[FaultContract(typeof(string))]
```

C. Apply the following contract to the *RemoveItem* operation:

```
' VB
<OperationContract(IsOneWay:=True)>
```

```
// C#
[OperationContract(IsOneWay=true)]
```

D. Apply the following contract to the *RemoveItem* operation:

```
' VB
<FaultContract()>
```

```
// C#
[FaultContract()]
```

E. Apply the following contract to the *RemoveItem* operation:

```
' VB <OperationContract()>
// C# [OperationContract()]
```

F. Apply the following contract to the interface:

```vb
' VB
<ServiceContract(Name:="InventoryService")>
```

```csharp
// C#
[ServiceContract(Name="InventoryService")]
```

G. Apply the following contract to the interface:

```vb
' VB
<ServiceContract(Name:="InventoryService", _
    CallbackContract:=GetType(IInventoryChangedHandler))> _
```

```csharp
// C#
[ServiceContract(
    Name="InventoryService",
    CallbackContract=typeof(IInventoryChangedHandler))]
```

Lesson 2: Defining Structural Contracts

This lesson provides you with the tools to define Data and Message contracts used by your WCF services. When, as a service developer, you are working with .NET types that represent the data your service works with and processes, you will use WCF Data contracts (defined in the *System.Runtime.Serialization* namespace) to declare which elements of that data belong in the structural Data contract from the consumer's perspective as well as which of those elements are required, which are optional, and so on.

If you need further control over what needs to appear in your messages at the SOAP header level, or how your SOAP message structures are packaged as they are serialized out to consumers, you can use the WCF Message contracts, defined in the *System.ServiceModel* namespace.

Finally, because part of your overall Data contract includes how your data is serialized at the wire-level transport layer, this lesson provides you with the tools to gain the appropriate control over serialization that might be required in some situations.

***

After this lesson, you will be able to:

- Use the *DataContract* attribute, along with the *DataMember* attribute, *EnumMember* attribute, or both to define Data contracts that specify the structure of the data in the inbound and outbound messages that your WCF service must process.
- Use the *MessageContract* attribute to control aspects of your messages at the SOAP message level.
- Use collections in your Service contracts.
- Use the *DataContract* and *MessageContract* attributes, along with the *IExtensible-DataObject* interface, to design version-tolerant messages and message payloads.
- Use the *XmlSerializerFormat* and *DataContractFormat* attributes to declare which serializer WCF should use in serializing your data and to control some aspects of that serialization.
- Use the *XmlSerializerFormat* attribute together with the XSD command-line tool to build WCF services, using an XML schema-driven approach.

Estimated lesson time: 50 minutes

***

Data Contracts

Data contracts are the contractual agreement about the format and structure of the payload data (that is, the SOAP body) in the messages exchanged between a service and its consumer. They fill the .NET/WCF role that XSDs fill in the XML world.

NOTE Schema languages for XML

There are alternatives to XSDs in the world of XML: both document type definitions (DTDs) and Relax NG are languages for declaring the structure of XML documents, but XSDs are the de facto choice, especially in the Web services space.

Just as the purpose of an XSD is to define the structure of an XML document, the WCF Data contract language defines the structure of data in your WCF service messages. When that data is sent over the wire-level transport, it might be transmitted as angle-bracket-laden XML text or it might not be. The "Controlling Serialization" section at the end of this lesson discusses this in greater detail.

Data contracts are the preferred WCF way to enable serialization of complex types included in operation signatures, either as parameters or as return values. Do you recall the "Real World" sidebar at the start of this chapter? It discusses the importance of thinking of your service messages as carrying business documents; Data contracts are the WCF mechanism for specifying the structure of the request documents being received by your service as well as of the response documents the service sends back to its consumers.

Consider the code that follows. To embrace the document-centric paradigm fully, always prefer Operation contracts shown for *SomeOp1* over those shown for *SomeOp2*:

```vb
' VB
<OperationContract()> _
Function SomeOp1( _
            ByVal reqMsg As RequestMessageType) _
            As ResponseMessageType


<OperationContract()> _
Function SomeOp2(ByVal element1 As String, _
        ByVal element2 As String) As String
```

```csharp
// C#
[OperationContract()]
ResponseMessageType SomeOp1(RequestMessageType reqMsg);

[OperationContract()]
string SomeOp2(string element1, string element2);
```

Data contracts are declared by applying the *DataContractAttribute* to a .NET type, and you will need to decorate that type's members that you want to include in the Data contract with the *DataMemberAttribute*. This is an optional approach that is independent of the visibility of members (that is, whether they have public, protected, or private visibility). Unless explicitly declared otherwise, the new WCF serializer called the *DataContractSerializer* performs serialization. In the "Controlling Serialization" section at the end of this lesson, you'll look at how you can specify explicitly that the earlier .NET *XmlSerializer* be used.

The following code shows a few Data contract definitions; first, an enumeration and then a class:

```vb
' VB
Public Enum TitleOptions : int
    <EnumMember()> _
    Mr = 0

    <EnumMember()> _
    Ms = 1

    <EnumMember()> _
    Mrs = 2

    <EnumMember()> _
    Dr = 3
End Enum

<DataContract( _
    Namespace:="http://schemas.fabrikam.com/customers/")> _
Public Class ContactInfo
    <DataMember(IsRequired:=False)> _
    Public PhoneNumber As String

    <DataMember(IsRequired:=False)> _
    Public EmailAddress As String
End Class
```

```csharp
// C#
[DataContract(
    Namespace = "http://schemas.fabrikam.com/customers/")]
public enum TitleOptions : int
{
    [EnumMember()]
    Mr = 0,

    [EnumMember()]
    Ms = 1,

    [EnumMember()]
    Mrs = 2,

    [EnumMember()]
    Dr = 3,
}

[DataContract(
    Namespace = "http://schemas.fabrikam.com/customers/")]
public class ContactInfo
{
    [DataMember(IsRequired = false)]
    public string PhoneNumber;
```

```
        [DataMember(IsRequired = false)]
        public string EmailAddress;
}
```

The *DataContractAttribute*

The *DataContractAttribute*, defined in the *System.Runtime.Serialization* namespace, is used to declare a type as a Data contract. When using it, the essential details are as follows:

- It can be applied to enums, structs, and classes only.
- It is not inherited, so your inherited Data contracts must have the attribute applied explicitly.
- It has only two parameters, which are covered in Table 1-3.

Table 1-3   Named Parameter Options for the *DataContractAttribute*

Named Parameter	Description
Name	Determines the type name as it is generated in the resulting schema. The default is the .NET type name as it is declared.
Namespace	Sets the target namespace for the schema. This defaults to *http:// schemas.datacontract.org/2004/07/*[CLR namespace], where [*CLR namespace*] is the namespace in which the complex type is defined.

As with the *ServiceContractAttribute*, always be sure to set the *Namespace* property to be something that identifies both your organization and the conceptual domain of the data and services.

The *DataMemberAttribute*

The *DataMemberAttribute,* also part of the *System.Runtime.Serialization* namespace, is applied only to members and is used to declare that the member should be included in the serialization of the data structure. This attribute provides several parameters for controlling the resulting schema generated for a complex type, each of which is covered in Table 1-4.

Table 1-4   Named Parameter Options for the *DataMemberAttribute*

Named Parameter	Description
Name	Controls the schema element name generated for the member (that is, the field or property) the attribute adorns. The default behavior is to use the field or property name as defined in the .NET type.
IsRequired	Controls the *minOccurs* attribute for the schema element. The default value is *false*, that is, the element is optional, which translates into *minOccurs* = 0.
Order	Controls the order of each element in the schema. By default, if this property is not set explicitly, the data members appear alphabetically, followed by elements for which this property is set explicitly.

Table 1-4   Named Parameter Options for the *DataMemberAttribute*

Named Parameter	Description
EmitDefaultValue	Controls whether default values will be included in the serialization. This property is *true* by default, so that all data members are serialized. If this property is set to *false*, any member that is set to its default value for its type (for instance, *null* for reference types) will not be serialized.

Here are a few points to keep in mind about the usage of these parameters when you define your Data contracts:

- Having the *EmitDefaultValue* property set to *false* can cause problems when the *IsRequired* property is set to *true* because the serializer might emit a default value if it doesn't find something it was expecting when, in fact, the correct behavior might be to throw an exception.

- If you apply the *DataMemberAttribute* to both a property and a field that is associated with calculating the property, you will generate duplicate members in the schema.

NOTE   Be explicit about member optionality

Even though the default value for *IsRequired* is *false*, it is a good practice to be explicit about it in your code by declaring *IsRequired = false*. That way, there is no room for doubt for a developer managing the contract in the future.

The following additional points pertain to the ordering rules for elements in your Data contract:

- If a Data contract type is part of an inheritance hierarchy, data members of its base types are always first in the order.

- Next in order are the current type's data members that do not have the *Order* property of the *DataMemberAttribute* attribute set, in alphabetical order.

- Next are any data members that have the *Order* property of the *DataMemberAttribute* attribute set; these are ordered by the value of the *Order* property first and then alphabetically if there is more than one member with a certain *Order* value. *Order* values can be skipped.

The *EnumMemberAttribute*

The final Data contract–related attribute to consider is the *EnumMemberAttribute*. As the name suggests, it is used to declare that a given element of an *enum* that has been declared with a *DataContractAttribute* should be considered as part of the Data contract. The only property (or named parameter) is the *Value* property, which can be used to provide an enumerated value to be serialized. The default is its actual value within the enumeration.

Opt-In vs. Opt-Out

The *DataContractSerializer*, the new default WCF serializer, operates in an opt-in mode that is the opposite of its predecessor, the *XmlSerializer*. That is, with the *DataContractSerializer*, members that are to be part of the Data contract must be explicitly marked as such, whereas with the *XmlSerializer*, members are assumed to be in the Data contract unless explicitly marked as opting out. For more on working with the *XmlSerializer* in the context of WCF services, see the section, "Controlling Serialization," later in this chapter. The following code uses the opt-out approach of the *XmlSerializer* to prevent the field shown in bold from being serialized:

```vb
' VB
' The opt-out approach:
<Serializable()> _
Public Class ContactInfo
    Public PhoneNumber As String
    Public EmailAddress As String

    <NonSerialized()> _
    Public HomeAddress As String
End Class
```

```csharp
// C#
// The opt-out approach:
[Serializable()]
public class ContactInfo
{
    public string PhoneNumber;
    public string EmailAddress;

    [NonSerialized()]
    public string HomeAddress;
}
```

The preceding code is very much in contrast with the following code, which uses the opt-in approach of the *DataContractSerializer*. The fields shown in bold are serialized.

```vb
' VB
' The opt-in approach:
<DataContract()> _
Public Class ContactInfo
    <DataMember(IsRequired:=False)> _
    Public PhoneNumber As String

    <DataMember(IsRequired:=False)> _
    Public EmailAddress As String

    Public HomeAddress As String
End Class
```

```csharp
// C#
```

```
// The opt-in approach:
[DataContract()]
public class ContactInfo
{
    [DataMember()]
    public string PhoneNumber;

    [DataMember()]
    public string EmailAddress;

    public string HomeAddress;
}
```

Collections

You can use the various collection types in .NET (which means anything that implements the *IEnumerable* or *IEnumerable<T>* interfaces), but the specific collection-type information gets lost in the metadata (WSDL) export, so in terms of how collection types are sent across the wire, they all are represented as arrays. For instance, suppose you have the following contract:

```
' VB
<ServiceContract()> _
Interface ITaskManager
    <OperationContract()> _
    Function GetTasksByAssignedName( _
        ByVal name As String) As List(Of Task)
End Interface
```

```
// C#
[ServiceContract()]
interface ITaskManager
{
    [OperationContract()]
    List<Task> GetTasksByAssignedName( string name);
}
```

After importing the service's metadata, a client would see the contract as follows. (Chapter 4 covers client code generation from a service's metadata.)

```
' VB
<ServiceContract()> _
Interface ITaskManager
    <OperationContract()> _
    Function GetTasksByAssignedName( _
        ByVal name As String) As Task()
End Interface
```

```
// C#
[ServiceContract()]
interface ITaskManager
{
```

```
        [OperationContract()]
        Task[] GetTasksByAssignedName( string name);
}
```

However, there is a caveat: This happens automatically only when the collection in the contract is a concrete collection (that is, not an interface) and is serializable (annotated with the *Serializable* attribute). If that is the case, WCF can automatically serialize the collection as an array of the collection's type as long as the collection contains an *Add* operation. This holds true for both the built-in .NET collections and for any of your own custom collections that implement the *IEnumerable* or *IEnumerable<T>* interface; as long as they are serializable and have an *Add* operation, they can be serialized to arrays automatically.

However, what if your collection does not meet these constraints? Is there still a way to ensure your collection serializes properly? Yes. Specify the *CollectionDataContractAttribute*. You can use this attribute to annotate your own custom collections, and the resulting collection will always be exposed to its WCF consumers as a *List* collection. As an example of how this attribute is used, suppose the following is your Service contract:

```
' VB
<CollectionDataContract(Name:="MyCollectionOf{0}")> _
Public Class MyCollection(Of T)
    Implements IEnumerable(Of T)

    Public Sub Add(ByVal item As T)
        ' Etc...
    End Sub

    Public Function GetEnumerator() _
        As IEnumerator(Of T) _
            Implements IEnumerable(Of T).GetEnumerator
        ' Etc...
    End Function

    Public Function GetEnumerator() _
        As IEnumerator _
        ' Etc...
    End Function

    ' Etc...
End Class

<ServiceContract()> _
Interface ITaskManager
    <OperationContract()> _
    Function GetTasksByAssignedName( _
        ByVal name As String) As MyCollection(Of Task)
End Interface

// C#
[CollectionDataContract(Name = "MyCollectionOf{0}")]
```

```
public class MyCollection<T> : IEnumerable<T>
{
    public void Add(T item) { // Etc...
    }

    IEnumerator<T> IEnumerable<T>.GetEnumerator() { // Etc...
    }

    public IEnumerator GetEnumerator() { // Etc...
    }
    // Etc...
}

[ServiceContract()]
interface ITaskManager
{
    [OperationContract()]
    MyCollection<Task> GetTasksByAssignedName(string name);
}
```

After a proxy is generated on the client, it will see the return type of the *GetTasksByAssigned-Name* operation as:

```
' VB
<CollectionDataContract()> _
Public Class MyCollectionOfTask
    Inherits List(Of Task)
End Class
```

```
// C#
[CollectionDataContract]
public class MyCollectionOfTask : List<Task>
{}
```

Known Types

WCF also supplies you with the *KnownTypeAttribute*, which enables you to designate acceptable derived classes for a given Data contract. It can be used, for example, as shown here.

```
' VB
<DataContract()> _
<KnownType(GetType(LoanApprovalTask))> _
Public Class Task
    ' Etc...
End Class

<DataContract()> _
Public Class LoanApprovalTask
    Inherits Task
    ' Etc...
End Class
```

```
// C#
[DataContract()]
[KnownType(typeof(LoanApprovalTask))]
class Task
{ // Etc...
}

[DataContract()]
class LoanApprovalTask : Task
{ // Etc...
}
```

When working with polymorphic types in your Service contract, the *KnownTypeAttribute* is required because polymorphism is outside the paradigm of service orientation. For example, assume you have the following Service contract:

```
' VB
<ServiceContract()> _
Interface ITaskManager
    <OperationContract()> _
    Function GetTasksByAssignedName( _
        ByVal name As String) As List(Of Task)
End Interface
```

```
// C#
[ServiceContract()]
interface ITaskManager
{
    [OperationContract()]
    List<Task> GetTasksByAssignedName( string name);
}
```

If some of the objects being returned by the *GetTasksByAssignedName* operation are *LoanApprovalTask* objects, the client can know how to deserialize these more specific tasks only if the *KnownTypeAttribute* was used.

CAUTION   Remember to think in terms of documents, not objects

The "Real World" sidebar near the start of this chapter suggests that to do service orientation well, you will have to let go of much of your object-oriented thinking. Polymorphism is at the heart of object-oriented thinking and really shouldn't have much of a place in well-designed Service contracts. Again, think "big, chunky documents" instead of objects and class hierarchies. Use the *KnownTypeAttribute* with caution if at all.

Message Contracts

When developing your WCF services, Data contracts enable you to define the structure of the data that will be sent in the body of your SOAP messages, either in the inbound (request) messages or in the outbound (response) messages. WCF Message contracts take it one step higher, so to speak. That is, when you use a Message contract as both the operation parameter type and the return type, you gain control over the entire SOAP message and not just over the structure of the data in the body. The following are the primary reasons you might want to use Message contracts:

- To control how the SOAP message body is structured and, ultimately, how it is serialized
- To supply and access custom headers

This section covers the attributes needed to define Message contracts and the main reasons for using Message contracts.

Message Contract Attributes

To define Message contracts, use the following attributes: *MessageContractAttribute*, *MessageHeaderAttribute*, and *MessageBodyMemberAttribute*. The following sections cover each of these individually.

The *MessageContractAttribute*   The *MessageContractAttribute* can be applied to classes and structures to define your own message structure. It has several properties, outlined in Table 1-5.

Table 1-5   Named Parameter Options for the *MessageContractAttribute*

Named Parameter	Description
IsWrapped	If *true*, the message body includes a wrapper element named by using the Message contract type or the *WrapperName* if specified. If *false*, the message body is unwrapped, and body elements appear directly beneath it.
ProtectionLevel	Enables the Service contract to specify constraints on how messages to all operations in the contract are protected on the wire, that is, whether they are signed and encrypted. See Chapter 8 for more about security.
WrapperName	Supplies a custom name for the body wrapper element.
WrapperNamespace	Supplies a namespace for the body wrapper element.

The *MessageHeaderAttribute*   The *MessageHeaderAttribute* can be applied to members of a Message contract to declare which elements belong among the message headers. It has several properties, outlined in Table 1-6.

Table 1-6   Named Parameter Options for the *MessageHeaderAttribute*

Named Parameter	Description
Name	Controls the name of the serialized header element.
Namespace	Supplies a namespace for the header element and its children unless otherwise overridden at the type level.

Table 1-6   Named Parameter Options for the *MessageHeaderAttribute*

Named Parameter	Description
ProtectionLevel	Enables the Service contract to specify constraints on how messages to all operations in the contract are protected on the wire, that is, whether they are signed and encrypted. See Chapter 8 for more about security.
Actor	A URI value indicating which actor is the intended target of the header. By default, the receiving service is assumed.
MustUnderstand	Indicates whether the recipient of the header (designated through the *Actor* property) is required to process this header. If this property is set to *true* and the actor doesn't understand the header, the actor should issue a fault.
Relay	Indicates whether this header should be forwarded to the next recipient of the message in the event the message is not being processed by the actor.

The *MessageBodyMemberAttribute*   The *MessageBodyMemberAttribute* can be applied to members of your Message contracts to declare which elements belong within the message body. Recall that if *IsWrapped* is set to *false* on the *MessageContractAttribute*, these elements will be direct children of the SOAP body element. If *IsWrapped* is set to *true*, they will be wrapped within a child element, an element named using either the *WrapperName* property if it is set explicitly or the Message contract name. This attribute, outlined in Table 1-7, contains several properties to provide control over how it is used.

Table 1-7   Named Parameter Options for the *MessageBodyMemberAttribute*

Named Parameter	Description
Name	Controls the name of the serialized body element.
Namespace	Supplies a namespace for the body element and its children unless otherwise overridden at the type level.
ProtectionLevel	Enables the Service contract to specify constraints on how messages to all operations in the contract are protected on the wire, that is, whether they are signed and encrypted. See Chapter 8 for more about security.
Order	Controls the order of each element in the schema. By default, if this property is not set explicitly, the data members appear alphabetically, followed by elements for which this property is set explicitly. The same rules are used to apply ordering as are used with Data contracts. (See the section titled "The DataMemberAttribute.")

Reasons for Using Message Contracts

Now, why might you want to use a Message contract?

Control over Message Body Wrapping   If you don't use any Message contracts in your service operation signatures, the WCF default behavior is to serialize messages so that the SOAP body element contains a child *wrapper* element that exactly matches the operation name and *wraps* any parameters (or return values for a response message). If there aren't any parameters, this element will be empty in the inbound (or request) message; similarly, if the return type is *void*, this *wrapper* element will be empty on the outbound (response) message.

NOTE   Message contracts must be used all or none

There isn't any partial usage of Message contracts. After you introduce a Message contract into an operation's signature, you must use a Message contract as the *only* parameter type *and* as the return type of the operation. This is in contrast with the more typical scenario in which you have a parameter list or return value composed of Data contracts or serializable types.

When you declare a *MessageContractAttribute*, the named parameter *IsWrapped* controls whether this wrapping in an element (named the same as the operation name) should happen. Thus, when you set *IsWrapped* to *false*, this wrapping does not occur, and the child of the SOAP body would simply be the collection of *MessageBodyMember* elements within the Message contract.

Controlling wrapping can be important when interoperating with other platforms because they might serialize their SOAP messages differently from the default way WCF does, which is to wrap them.

Supplying Custom Headers   You might sometimes need to send along private elements in your SOAP messages, and defining Message contracts supports this. Two common reasons for doing this are that:

■ You have your own security mechanism in place, so you need to pass along your own authentication token in a private SOAP header.

■ Consumers of your service might have to include some sort of license key (or developer's key) to access the service at run time. In such cases, a SOAP header is a reasonable place for such a field.

Putting the Pieces Together

Taking what you have learned in the previous few sections, put it all together by examining how Message contracts are used in some sample code. In the interest of keeping things simple, suppose you have a service that has one operation that simply returns some contact info about the service provider. As such, you might propose the following contract:

```vb
' VB
<DataContract()> _
Public Class ContactInfo
    <DataMember()> _
```

```
    Public PhoneNumber As String

    <DataMember()> _
    Public EmailAddress As String
End Class

<ServiceContract()> _
Public Interface ISomeService
    <OperationContract()> _
    Function GetProviderContactInfo() As ContactInfo
End Interface
```

```
// C#
[DataContract()]
public class ContactInfo
{
    [DataMember()]
    public string PhoneNumber;

    [DataMember()]
    public string EmailAddress;
}

[ServiceContract()]
public interface ISomeService
{
    [OperationContract()]
    ContactInfo GetProviderContactInfo();
}
```

However, then suppose that access to your service requires a license key. That is, every message sent to the service must be checked for license key validity. Because a SOAP header is a reasonable place to store a license key, you can rework this Service contract to use Message contracts. The following code does just that by defining both a Request Message contract and a Response Message contract. It even includes a simplistic implementation that validates the license key.

```
' VB
<DataContract()> _
Public Class ContactInfo
    <DataMember()> _
    Public PhoneNumber As String

    <DataMember()> _
    Public EmailAddress As String
End Class

<MessageContract(IsWrapped:=False)> _
Public Class ContactInfoRequestMessage
    <MessageHeader()> _
    Public LicenseKey As String
```

```vbnet
End Class

<MessageContract(IsWrapped:=False)> _
Public Class ContactInfoResponseMessage
    <MessageBodyMember()> _
    Public ProviderContactInfo As ContactInfo
End Class

<ServiceContract()> _
Public Interface ISomeService
    <OperationContract()> _
    <FaultContract(GetType(String))> _
    Function GetProviderContactInfo( _
        ByVal reqMsg As ContactInfoRequestMessage) _
            As ContactInfoResponseMessage
End Interface

Public Class SomeService
    Implements ISomeService

    Public Function GetProviderContactInfo( _
        ByVal reqMsg As ContactInfoRequestMessage) _
        As ContactInfoResponseMessage _
            Implements ISomeService.GetProviderContactInfo

        If reqMsg.LicenseKey <> ValidLicenseKey Then
            Dim msg As String = "Invalid license key."
            Throw New FaultException(Of String)(msg)
        End If

        Dim respMsg As ContactInfoResponseMessage
        respMsg = New ContactInfoResponseMessage()
        respMsg.ProviderContactInfo = New ContactInfo()
        respMsg.ProviderContactInfo.EmailAddress = "sam@fabrikam.com"
        respMsg.ProviderContactInfo.PhoneNumber = "123-456-7890"

        Return respMsg
    End Function

    Private Const ValidLicenseKey As String = "abc-1234-alpha"

End Class
```

```csharp
// C#
[DataContract()]
public class ContactInfo
{
    [DataMember()]
    public string PhoneNumber;

    [DataMember()]
    public string EmailAddress;
}
```

```
[MessageContract(IsWrapped = false)]
public class ContactInfoRequestMessage
{
    [MessageHeader()]
    public string LicenseKey;
}

[MessageContract(IsWrapped = false)]
public class ContactInfoResponseMessage
{
    [MessageBodyMember()]
    public ContactInfo ProviderContactInfo;
}

[ServiceContract()]
public interface ISomeService
{
    [OperationContract()]
    [FaultContract(typeof(string))]
    ContactInfoResponseMessage GetProviderContactInfo(
        ContactInfoRequestMessage reqMsg);
}

public class SomeService : ISomeService
{
    public ContactInfoResponseMessage GetProviderContactInfo(
                    ContactInfoRequestMessage reqMsg)
    {
        if (reqMsg.LicenseKey != ValidLicenseKey)
        {
            const string msg = "Invalid license key.";
            throw new FaultException<string>(msg);
        }

        ContactInfoResponseMessage respMsg =
                        new ContactInfoResponseMessage();
        respMsg.ProviderContactInfo = new ContactInfo();
        respMsg.ProviderContactInfo.EmailAddress = "sam@fabrikam.com";
        respMsg.ProviderContactInfo.PhoneNumber = "123-456-7890";

        return respMsg;
    }

    private const string ValidLicenseKey = "abc-1234-alpha";
}
```

Note that, because you used *IsWrapped = false*, the request and response messages will not be wrapped inside an element named *ContactInfoRequestMessage* in the request and response SOAP bodies. Rather, the children of the *body* element will be the elements in the *ContactInfoRequestMessage* that are annotated with the *MessageBodyMemberAttribute* for the request message. Similarly, with the *ContactInfoResponseMessage*, its members marked with the *MessageBodyMemberAttribute* will be direct children of the body in the response message.

Versioning of Data Contracts

One of the main advantages of service orientation is that it facilitates decoupling a service from its consumers. The primary driver behind this decoupling is that consumers need only know about the XML format of the messages they send to the service; they do not have a binary-level code dependency on the service as there was with component-based middleware technologies of the past, such as .NET Remoting, DCOM, CORBA, and so on. But is this enough? It is if the service never changes, but how likely is that? To be truly decoupled, services should also be version tolerant. Ideally, that means that any version of the client should be able to consume any version of the service. When a service exposes a Data contract, the moment it has its first consumer, the service and consumer share that Data contract thereafter to some extent. As such, the true goal for version tolerance is to enable both the service and the client to evolve their versions of the Data contract separately. To enable such version tolerance, WCF supports what are generally referred to as *backward* and *forward* compatibility.

To explore this notion of version tolerance a little further, and WCF's support for it, subsequent sections look at the following three versioning scenarios:

- New members have been added to a Data contract.
- Members from a Data contract are missing.
- Roundtripping is supported, meaning that when a new version of a Data contract is passed to and from an old version, the transmission requires both backward and forward compatibility.

Adding New Members to a Data Contract

By far the most common version change that occurs with Data contracts is that a new member is added. However, the *DataContractSerializer* will simply ignore any new members when deserializing the type, so both the service and the client can accept data with new members that were not part of the original contract.

Members Missing from a Data Contract

The WCF default policy is to try to allow the service to accept data with missing members or to return data with missing members to the client. How does it do this? Suppose one entity is trying to send data to a recipient (this could be either client to service or service to client), but it is missing a member that the recipient is expecting to find there. It might have done so intentionally (although hopefully not), but the more likely cause is that the sender knows only about an older version of the Data contract while the recipient knows about a newer version, one with new members. What happens in this scenario? For any members that are optional

(*IsRequired* is set to *false*, the default) but are nonetheless expected to be found but aren't, the *DataContractSerializer* will simply go ahead and deserialize them to their default value—that is, *null* for reference types and zero values for value types. For members that are not optional (*IsRequired* is set to *true*), an exception will be thrown.

Is this the desired behavior? Likely, if the element is not required (the *IsRequired* property of the *DataMember* attribute is set to *false*, which is the default). But what if the element is required? Then an exception is probably the best of all possible things to do because, presumably, the element was required for a good reason. However, one should go to all lengths to avoid this scenario; when adding a new field to a Data contract, you should do everything in your power to make the field an optional element (that is, *IsRequired* is set to *false*).

Roundtripping

The situations discussed so far might be adequate in many scenarios, but what if you have a v1.0 client conversing with a v2.0 service that has added new members to its Data contract that the v1.0 client obviously knows nothing about; suppose further that the service returns data (conforming to the new contract) to the client and is expecting the client to modify certain data in the message and, ultimately, send it back to the service. Is there any way the client will be able to successfully return the data it knows about without losing the unknown data it was sent? This new-to-old-to-new interaction is called a versioning roundtrip, and WCF does have some built-in support for it.

This support comes in the form of the *IExtensibleDataObject* interface and how you implement it on your Data contract. Consider how the following Data contract uses this technique:

```vb
' VB
<DataContract(Namespace:= _
    "http://schemas.fabrikam.com/2008/04/tasks/")> _
Public Class Task
    Implements IExtensibleDataObject

    <DataMember(IsRequired:=True, Order:=1)> _
    Public Description As String

    ' Etc...

    Public Property ExtensionData() _
        As ExtensionDataObject _
        Implements IExtensibleDataObject.ExtensionData
        Get
            Return _extensionData
        End Get

        Set(ByVal value As ExtensionDataObject)
            _extensionData = value
```

```
        End Set
    End Property

    Private _extensionData As ExtensionDataObject
End Class
```

```csharp
// C#
[DataContract(Namespace =
        "http://schemas.fabrikam.com/2008/04/tasks/")]
public class Task : IExtensibleDataObject
{
    [DataMember(IsRequired = true, Order = 1)]
    public string Description;

    // Etc...

    public ExtensionDataObject ExtensionData
    {
        get
        {
            return _extensionData;
        }

        set
        {
            _extensionData = value;
        }
    }

    private ExtensionDataObject _extensionData;
}
```

In this code, the _extensionData_ object is simply a placeholder in which the *DataContractSerializer* (because it sees that the contract implements the *IExtensibleDataObject* interface) can package any unknown (or extra) data that it comes across and doesn't know anything about. Thus in a roundtrip scenario, the client could keep this data (unknowingly packaged along with an extensible data object) and, when it sends its message back to the service, the *DataContract-Serializer* will once again come to the rescue by serializing it as part of the message. Because the service knows about this data, it can properly deserialize it and use it intelligently.

Controlling Serialization

This section covers the tools you need to gain control over serialization as is required in some situations. It discusses those situations and explains how you can declare the right serializer to use.

Real World

Peter Madziak

Frequently, you will be defining your services in a domain in which open standards initiatives exist that have worked toward defining XSDs, WSDL, or both, to encourage interoperability among the participants in the given domain. These standardization efforts are aimed at ensuring that, typically within business to business (B2B) scenarios, the providers can rely on the format of the messages being sent and the type of processing that will occur within the service endpoints receiving the messages.

An example of this would be the Open Travel Alliance (OTA), a group consisting of a wide variety of participants from within the travel industry, which has defined XSD request and response schemas for a vast array of business transactions that could occur within the context of B2B travel scenarios. In such cases, it is far better to adopt these standard schema and WSDL definitions and, thereby, help the drive toward true standardization instead of inventing your own standard.

MORE INFO   Open Travel Alliance

For more information on the OTA, see *http://www.opentravel.org/*.

This section discusses how you can use WCF to ensure that your services send and receive messages in the correct XML format when the starting point is a preexisting (hopefully standard) XML schema as opposed to WCF Data contracts.

Serialization vs. Encoding

The terms *serialization* and *encoding* are used in so many different ways in the world of software that it is worthwhile pausing here to clarify how these terms are used in the context of WCF. This will help set the context around the topic of this lesson.

Suppose you have an object—perhaps a Data contract object or a serializable object—that you are working with in the context of a WCF service-type implementation, and you return it from one of your service operations. When this object is passed off to the WCF plumbing, it is serialized to a *Message* object (whose class is defined in the WCF plumbing in the *System.ServiceModel.Channels* namespace). The resulting *Message* object is the WCF way of representing a SOAP message but only in the sense of an abstract XML InfoSet representation of it. Don't think angle brackets because, as you'll see in a moment, the *Message* object might never be represented that way. WCF provides two serializers to do this job of rendering an object graph to a WCF *Message* object:

- The *DataContractSerializer*, new with WCF
- The *XmlSerializer* that has been part of .NET from the outset

At a later stage in the chain of channels comprising the WCF plumbing, there will be an encoder whose job is to encode the *Message* object (the abstract InfoSet representation of the SOAP message) to a byte stream in a particular concrete syntax. The resulting message sent out over the wire might well be the angle bracket–laden XML, but then again, it might not be. WCF provides three encoders out of the box to handle this job of producing a *Message* object as a byte stream to send over the wire: the text encoder to do standard XML text encoding and two others to do MTOM encoding and WCF-to-WCF binary encoding, respectively. Chapter 2 discusses these encoders.

The Format Attributes

WCF provides two attributes, namely *XmlSerializerFormatAttribute* and *DataContractFormat-Attribute*, that you can use to declare that WCF uses a specific serializer, namely the *Xml-Serializer* and the *DataContractSerializer*, respectively. Both of these attributes have a *Style* property that enables you to control which style of SOAP is to be used, *Rpc* (remote procedure call) or *Document*. The *XmlSerializerFormatAttribute* has another property, called *Use*, that enables you to control whether the serializer uses the *Literal* or *Encoded* approach to constructing SOAP messages. Although these attributes can be applied to your Data contracts, the more typical scenario is to apply them at the service level because your Data contracts could be used in more than one service. The following code sample shows in bold two examples of their usage:

```
' VB
<ServiceContract()> _
<XmlSerializerFormat( _
    Style:=OperationFormatStyle.Rpc, _
    Use:=OperationFormatUse.Encoded)> _
Interface ISomeLegacyService
    <OperationContract()> _
    Function SomeOp1( _
        ByVal name As String) As String
End Interface

<ServiceContract()> _
<DataContractFormat( _
    Style:=OperationFormatStyle.Rpc)> _
Interface ISomeRpcService2
    <OperationContract()> _
    Function SomeOp2( _
        ByVal name As String) As String
End Interface

// C#
[ServiceContract()]
```

```
[XmlSerializerFormat(Style=OperationFormatStyle.Rpc,
    Use=OperationFormatUse.Encoded)]
interface ISomeLegacyService
{
    [OperationContract()]
    string SomeOp1( string name);
}

[ServiceContract()]
[DataContractFormat(Style=OperationFormatStyle.Rpc)]
interface ISomeRpcService2
{
    [OperationContract()]
    string SomeOp2( string name);
}
```

Consider the following points in reference to using these attributes:

- For both the *DataContractFormatAttribute* and the *XmlSerializerFormatAttribute*, the default style is *Document*. The *Rpc* style is outdated, so you'll probably never encounter it. However, if you do, WCF can support it.

- The *DataContractSerializer* is the default serializer WCF uses, so you need only use the *DataContractFormat* attribute when you need to specify the *Rpc* style, which should almost never happen.

- The primary usage of these format attributes is to declare explicitly that WCF should use the *XmlSerializer* instead of the *DataContractSerializer*.

- The *XmlSerializerFormat* attribute enables you to specify the *Use* to be either *Literal* or *Encoded*, but again, *Literal* is the default and *Encoded* is an outdated SOAP artifact that you will likely never encounter.

The *DataContractSerializer* vs. the *XmlSerializer*

The *DataContractSerializer* has the following benefits:

- Its opt-in approach provides nice control over Data contracts for developers. Your Data contract classes can be equipped with other elements and validation logic that need not be opted in.

- It is very fast. It is targeted at a very small, simple subset of the XML InfoSet and is focused on speed instead of on being comprehensive.

However, the fact that it targets a small subset of XML also means that there are many complex XSDs for which the *DataContractSerializer* is not well equipped to handle. The *DataContractSerializer* will always be able to serialize to XML; it's just that, in many cases, the structure of the resulting XML might not be acceptable for your needs. However, that is where the *XmlSerializer* comes in. It can be used to work with complex XML schemas, as you'll see in the next section.

MORE INFO The *DataContractSerializer* Support for XSD

Visit *http://msdn2.microsoft.com/en-us/library/ms733112.aspx* for details about the *DataContract-Serializer* support for XSD.

Building XML Schema–Driven Services

Sometimes you might need to start from an existing XML schema. As mentioned in the "Real World" sidebar at the start of the "Controlling Serialization" section, this is often the case when you are working in an industry in which there exist well-defined, open-standard schemas. You can build WCF services in a schema-driven approach if you follow these steps:

- You design your XML schemas or work with existing standard schemas.
- You generate code from the schemas. To generate classes from a schema, you can use the XSD command-line tool, as you'll do in the lab for this lesson.
- You mark your Service contract to use the *XmlSerializer*.
- You declare service operations to:
  - ❏ Receive a single parameter based on the generated type from one of your schema types.
  - ❏ If not one-way, similarly return an object of a class generated from one of your schema types.
- From a client proxy perspective, you will need to use the */serializer:XmlSerializer* option. Chapter 4 returns to this point.

The lab you start next takes you through these steps, working with two schemas from the travel industry.

Quick Check

1. You have a Data contract specifying a *Person* class from which you derive a *Customer* class. Does a *Customer* object automatically have a Data contract as well?
2. Your company has its own proprietary authentication mechanism, and you are required to authenticate every message coming into the service. What is the best way to handle using this mechanism with WCF?
3. Can you support the *Rpc* SOAP style by using the *DataContractSerializer*?

> **Quick Check Answers**
> 1. No. The Data contract is not inherited, so any derived class, such as the *Customer* class, would have to be explicitly declared as having a Data contract as well.
> 2. Likely the best way to handle this would be to design a Message contract that accepts these proprietary authentication tokens in the header.
> 3. Yes. You need only adorn your service with the *DataContractFormatAttribute* and explicitly set the attribute's *Style* property to *OperationFormatStyle.Rpc*.

Lab: Defining Data Contracts and Controlling Serialization

In this lab, you will work with the Data contract–related attributes and use them to define a Data contract. In the second exercise, you will declare that the *XmlSerializer* is to be used in a situation when the *DataContractSerializer* won't emit the XML that is required at the wire-level transport layer. If you have a problem completing the exercises, you can find completed solution files in the /After folder. As with the first lab, this lab requires you to start a WCF service, so you need to have the appropriate permissions to do so. Therefore, you might run Visual Studio as an Administrator.

▶ **Exercise 1   Define and Use an Extensible Data Contract**

In this exercise, you improve upon the Task Manager service built in Lesson 1 by using Data contracts to design extensible message formats to flow in and out of the service as opposed to just taking multiple parameters, as was used in that lesson. Note that this is very much in keeping with the "Real World" sidebar at the start of this chapter, namely, that you want to conceive of services as endpoints out on the network, with business documents flowing into and out of them as the message body. In this case, the Data contracts are the WCF mechanism for describing the structure of these documents. It also gives you a chance to use the *IExtensible-Object* mechanism for handling roundtrip extensibility problems.

1. Navigate to the *<InstallHome>*/Chapter1/Lesson2/Exercise1/*<language>*/Before directory and double-click the Exercise1.sln file to open the solution in Visual Studio.
2. The solution consists of three projects:
   a. The ServiceConsoleHost project, which is a simple console application used to host your first service
   b. The TaskClient project, which is a Windows Forms application that enables you to consume your first service
   c. The Tasks.Services project, which is a class library project that initially contains only an incomplete definition of the Task Manager service
3. Add a new Class Library project to the solution and call it **Tasks.Entities**. This is where you define your Data contracts.

4. Add a reference to the *System.Runtime.Serialization* namespace in this new Tasks.Entities project.

5. Rename the Class1.cs (or Class1.vb) file to **TaskEntities.cs** (or **TaskEntities.vb**). When prompted, click Yes to rename references to **Class1**.

6. Edit this code file to be as follows to define your Data contract.

   The implementation of the *ToString* method is left to you, but anything that captures the essential task data is fine. If you need to, you can examine one possible implementation in the "After" solution.

```vb
' VB
Imports System.Runtime.Serialization

<DataContract(Namespace:= _
    "http://schemas.fabrikam.com/2008/04/tasks/")> _
Public Enum TaskStates
    <EnumMember()> _
    Active = 0

    <EnumMember()> _
    CompletedByDueDate = 1

    <EnumMember()> _
    CompletedPastDueDate = 2

    <EnumMember()> _
    Overdue = 3
End Enum

<DataContract(Namespace:= _
    "http://schemas.fabrikam.com/2008/04/tasks/")> _
Public Class FaultInfo
    <DataMember()> _
    Public Reason As String = Nothing
End Class

<DataContract(Namespace:= _
    "http://schemas.fabrikam.com/2008/04/tasks/")> _
Public Class Task
    Implements IExtensibleDataObject

    <DataMember(IsRequired:=False, Order:=0)> _
    Public TaskNumber As Integer

    <DataMember(IsRequired:=True, Order:=1)> _
    Public Description As String

    <DataMember(IsRequired:=False, Order:=2)> _
    Public TaskState As TaskStates

    <DataMember(IsRequired:=False, Order:=3)> _
```

```vbnet
    Public AssignedTo As String

    <DataMember(IsRequired:=False, Order:=4)> _
    Public CreatedBy As String

    <DataMember(IsRequired:=False, Order:=5)> _
    Public DateCreated As DateTime

    <DataMember(IsRequired:=False, Order:=6)> _
    Public DateLastModified As DateTime

    <DataMember(IsRequired:=False, Order:=7)> _
    Public DueDate As DateTime

    Public Overrides Function ToString() As String
        ' Your own implementation...
    End Function

    Public Property ExtensionData() _
        As ExtensionDataObject _
        Implements IExtensibleDataObject.ExtensionData
        Get
            Return _extensionData
        End Get

        Set(ByVal value As ExtensionDataObject)
            _extensionData = value
        End Set
    End Property

    Private _extensionData As ExtensionDataObject
End Class

<DataContract(Namespace:= _
    "http://schemas.fabrikam.com/2008/04/tasks/")> _
Public Class TaskAcknowledgement
    Implements IExtensibleDataObject

    <DataMember(IsRequired:=False, Order:=0)> _
    Public TaskNumber As Integer

    <DataMember(IsRequired:=False, Order:=1)> _
    Public CurrentState As TaskStates

    <DataMember(IsRequired:=False, Order:=2)> _
    Public Comments As String

    Public Property ExtensionData() _
        As ExtensionDataObject _
        Implements IExtensibleDataObject.ExtensionData
        Get
            Return _extensionData
        End Get
```

```vb
        Set(ByVal value As ExtensionDataObject)
            _extensionData = value
        End Set
    End Property

    Private _extensionData As ExtensionDataObject
End Class
```

```csharp
// C#
using System;
using System.Runtime.Serialization;

namespace Tasks.Entities
{
    [DataContract(Namespace =
        "http://schemas.fabrikam.com/2008/04/tasks/")]
    public enum TaskStates : int
    {
        [EnumMember()]
        Active = 0,

        [EnumMember()]
        CompletedByDueDate = 1,

        [EnumMember()]
        CompletedPastDueDate = 2,

        [EnumMember()]
        Overdue = 3,
    }

    [DataContract(Namespace =
            "http://schemas.fabrikam.com/tasks/")]
    public class FaultInfo
    {
        [DataMember(IsRequired = true, Order = 0)]
        public string Reason;
    }

    [DataContract(Namespace =
                "http://schemas.fabrikam.com/2008/04/tasks/")]
    public class Task : IExtensibleDataObject
    {
        [DataMember(IsRequired = false, Order = 0)]
        public int TaskNumber;

        [DataMember(IsRequired = true, Order = 1)]
        public string Description;

        [DataMember(IsRequired = false, Order = 2)]
        public TaskStates TaskState;

        [DataMember(IsRequired = false, Order = 3)]
```

```
        public string AssignedTo;

        [DataMember(IsRequired = false, Order = 4)]
        public string CreatedBy;

        [DataMember(IsRequired = false, Order = 5)]
        public DateTime DateCreated;

        [DataMember(IsRequired = false, Order = 6)]
        public DateTime DateLastModified;

        [DataMember(IsRequired = false, Order = 7)]
        public DateTime DueDate;

        public override string ToString()
        {
            // Your own implementation...
        }

        public ExtensionDataObject ExtensionData
        {
            get
            {
                return _extensionData;
            }

            set
            {
                _extensionData = value;
            }
        }

        private ExtensionDataObject _extensionData;
}

[DataContract(Namespace =
            "http://schemas.fabrikam.com/2008/04/tasks/")]
public class TaskAcknowledgement : IExtensibleDataObject
{
    [DataMember(IsRequired = false, Order = 0)]
    public int TaskNumber;

    [DataMember(IsRequired = false, Order = 1)]
    public TaskStates CurrentState;

    [DataMember(IsRequired = false, Order = 2)]
    public string Comments;

    public ExtensionDataObject ExtensionData
    {
        get
        {
            return _extensionData;
```

```
        }

        set
        {
            _extensionData = value;
        }
    }

    private ExtensionDataObject _extensionData;
    }
}
```

7. To the Tasks.Services project, add a project reference to the Tasks.Entities project that you have just defined.

8. Edit the ITaskManagerService file (.cs or .vb as appropriate) to be as follows, so that your Service contract now uses your newly created Data contracts.

```vb
' VB
Imports System.ServiceModel
Imports System.Collections.Generic
Imports System.Runtime.Serialization
Imports Tasks.Entities

<ServiceContract(Name:="TaskManagerService", _
    Namespace:="http://schemas.fabrikam.com/2008/04/tasks/")> _
Public Interface ITaskManagerService
    <OperationContract()> _
    Function AddTask(ByVal task As Task) As TaskAcknowledgement

    <OperationContract()> _
    Function GetTasksByAssignedName( _
            ByVal assignedTo As String) As List(Of Task)

    <OperationContract()> _
    <FaultContract(GetType(FaultInfo))> _
    Function GetTask(ByVal taskNumber As Integer) As Task

    <OperationContract()> _
    <FaultContract(GetType(FaultInfo))> _
    Sub MarkTaskCompleted(ByVal taskNumber As Integer)

    <OperationContract()> _
    <FaultContract(GetType(FaultInfo))> _
    Sub DeleteTask(ByVal taskNumber As Integer)

End Interface
```

```csharp
// C#
using System;
using System.Collections.Generic;
using System.ServiceModel;
using Tasks.Entities;
```

```
namespace Tasks.Services
{
    [ServiceContract(Name = "TaskManagerService",
        Namespace = "http://schemas.fabrikam.com/2008/04/tasks/")]
    public interface ITaskManagerService
    {
        [OperationContract()]
        TaskAcknowledgement AddTask(Task task);

        [OperationContract()]
        List<Task> GetTasksByAssignedName(string assignedTo);

        [OperationContract()]
        [FaultContract(typeof(FaultInfo))]
        Task GetTask(int taskNumber);

        [OperationContract()]
        [FaultContract(typeof(FaultInfo))]
        void MarkTaskCompleted(int taskNumber);

        [OperationContract()]
        [FaultContract(typeof(FaultInfo))]
        void DeleteTask(int taskNumber);
    }
}
```

9. Edit the TaskManagerService file (.cs or .vb as appropriate) so that it defines a service type that implements this new version of your Service contract. The following code shows how this would be done for two of the methods, the *AddTask* and *MarkTask-Completed* methods. To complete this solution, the remaining methods must be completed in a similar fashion. See the After solution for details if necessary.

```
' VB
Imports System.ServiceModel
Imports System.Linq
Imports Tasks.Entities

Public Class TaskManagerService
    Implements ITaskManagerService
    Public Function AddTask(ByVal task As Task) _
            As TaskAcknowledgement _
                Implements ITaskManagerService.AddTask
        Dim taskNum As Integer = s_nextTaskNumber
        s_nextTaskNumber = s_nextTaskNumber + 1

        Dim ack As New TaskAcknowledgement()
        ack.TaskNumber = taskNum
        task.TaskNumber = taskNum

        If task.DueDate > DateTime.Now Then
            task.TaskState = TaskStates.Active
        Else
```

```vb
            task.TaskState = TaskStates.Overdue
        End If

        ack.CurrentState = task.TaskState
        If ack.CurrentState = TaskStates.Overdue Then
            ack.Comments = "Warning: task is already overdue!"
        End If

        Console.WriteLine( _
                "Adding new task:\n{0}", task.ToString())
        s_activeTasks.Add(taskNum, task)
        Return ack
    End Function

    Public Sub MarkTaskCompleted(ByVal taskNumber As Integer) _
        Implements ITaskManagerService.MarkTaskCompleted

        If Not s_activeTasks.ContainsKey(taskNumber) Then
            Dim msg As String = String.Format( _
                    "No task with number {0}", taskNumber)
            Console.WriteLine(msg)

            Dim fi As FaultInfo = New FaultInfo()
            fi.Reason = msg
            Dim fe As FaultException(Of FaultInfo)
            fe = New FaultException(Of FaultInfo)(fi)
            Throw fe
        End If

        Dim task As Task = s_activeTasks.Item(taskNumber)
        If DateTime.Now > task.DueDate Then
            task.TaskState = TaskStates.CompletedPastDueDate
        Else
            task.TaskState = TaskStates.CompletedByDueDate
        End If

        Console.WriteLine( _
                "Marking task number {0} as completed", _
                    taskNumber)

    End Sub

    ' Etc...

    Private Shared s_activeTasks As Dictionary(Of Integer, Task) _
                    = New Dictionary(Of Integer, Task)

    Private Shared s_nextTaskNumber As Integer = 1
End Class

// C#
using System;
using System.Collections.Generic;
```

```
using System.Linq;
using System.ServiceModel;
using System.Text;
using Tasks.Entities;

namespace Tasks.Services
{
    public class TaskManagerService : ITaskManagerService
    {
        public TaskAcknowledgement AddTask(Task task)
        {
            int taskNum = s_nextTaskNumber++;

            TaskAcknowledgement ack = new TaskAcknowledgement();
            ack.TaskNumber = taskNum;
            task.TaskNumber = taskNum;

            if (task.DueDate > DateTime.Now)
                task.TaskState = TaskStates.Active;
            else
                task.TaskState = TaskStates.Overdue;

            ack.CurrentState = task.TaskState;
            if (ack.CurrentState == TaskStates.Overdue) {
                ack.Comments = "Warning: task is already overdue!";
            }

            Console.WriteLine(
                "Adding new task:\n{0}", task.ToString());
            s_activeTasks.Add(taskNum, task);
            return ack;
        }

        public void MarkTaskCompleted(int taskNumber)
        {
            if (!s_activeTasks.ContainsKey(taskNumber))
            {
                string msg = string.Format(
                    "No task with number {0}",
                    taskNumber);
                Console.WriteLine(msg);

                FaultInfo fi = new FaultInfo();
                fi.Reason = msg;
                throw new FaultException<FaultInfo>(fi);
            }

            Task task = s_activeTasks[taskNumber];
            if (DateTime.Now > task.DueDate)
                task.TaskState = TaskStates.CompletedPastDueDate;
            else
                task.TaskState = TaskStates.CompletedByDueDate;
```

```
        Console.WriteLine(
            "Marking task number {0} as completed",
            task.TaskNumber);
    }

    // Etc...

    private static Dictionary<int, Task> s_activeTasks =
                    new Dictionary<int, Task>();
    private static int s_nextTaskNumber = 1;
    }
}
```

10. Build the solution and start the service, ensuring that the ServiceConsoleHost project is the startup project.

    As was the case in Exercise 1, "Create the Service Contract and Service Type," in Lesson 1, with the service running, you can both run the TaskClient application to consume the service and explore the WSDL that the service generates. Note the differences in the WSDL between this new version and the version from Lesson 1, noting in particular the richer XML Schema constructs in the WSDL *types* section.

▶ **Exercise 2   Use the *XmlSerializer* with OTA Schemas**

In this exercise, you work with some open standard schemas from the travel industry, namely, the OTA schemas FS_OTA_VehResRQ.xsd and FS_OTA_VehResRS.xsd, for vehicle reservation requests and vehicle reservation responses, respectively.

1. Navigate to the *<InstallHome>*/Chapter1/Lesson2/Exercise2/*<language>*/Before directory and double-click the Exercise2.sln file to open the solution in Visual Studio.

2. The solution consists of three projects:
   a. The ServiceConsoleHost project, which is a simple console application used to host the service.
   b. The OTASample.Vehicles.Service project, which is a class library project that initially contains only an incomplete definition of the OTA-based Vehicle Reservation service, one that in this exercise you enhance just enough to see the WSDL it emits.
   c. The OTASample.Vehicles.Entities project, which is a class library project that, as the name suggests, will contain the entities required by this service. It initially contains only two OTA travel industry standard schemas, namely, FS_OTA_VehResRQ.xsd and FS_OTA_VehResRS.xsd, the schemas for vehicle reservation requests and vehicle reservation responses, respectively.

3. Open a Visual Studio 2008 command prompt and change to the directory for the Entities project, in this case, *<InstallHome>*/Chapter1/Lesson2/Exercise2/*<language>*/Before/OTASample.Vehicles.Entities.

4. Run the following command from the command line to generate classes from these XML schemas, being careful to note that this is all one line; it is formatted on two lines here to fit on the printed page:

```
' VB
xsd /c /l:vb FS_OTA_VehResRQ.xsd FS_OTA_VehResRS.xsd
```

```
// C#\
xsd /c /l:cs /n:OTASample.Vehicles.Entities
        FS_OTA_VehResRQ.xsd FS_OTA_VehResRS.xsd
```

5. Run a second command simply to give the resulting file a friendlier name:

```
' VB
ren FS_OTA_VehResRQ_FS_OTA_VehResRS.vb VehicleEntities.vb
```

```
// C#
ren FS_OTA_VehResRQ_FS_OTA_VehResRS.cs VehicleEntities.cs
```

6. Returning to Visual Studio, add this newly created VehicleEntities (.cs or .vb as appropriate) file to the OTASample.Vehicles.Entities project.

   You now have .NET classes that represent your OTA schemas, so you'll use them in your service, also being sure to declare that the *XmlSerializer* is used instead of *DataContract-Serializer*.

7. Edit the IVehicleReservationService file (.cs or .vb as appropriate) so that it becomes:

```
' VB
Imports System.ServiceModel
Imports OTASample.Vehicles.Entities

<ServiceContract(Name:="VehReservationService", _
    Namespace:="http://www.opentravel.org/OTA/2003/05")> _
<XmlSerializerFormat(Style:=OperationFormatStyle.Document, _
                Use:=OperationFormatUse.Literal)> _
Public Interface IVehicleReservationService
    <OperationContract()> _
    Function ReserveVehicle( _
        <MessageParameter(Name:="OTA_VehResRQ")> _
            ByVal reservationReq As OTA_VehResRQ) As OTA_VehResRS
End Interface
```

```
// C#
using System;
using System.Runtime.Serialization;
using System.ServiceModel;

using OTASample.Vehicles.Entities;

namespace OTASample.Vehicles.Service
{
    [ServiceContract(Name = "VehReservationService",
        Namespace = "http://www.opentravel.org/OTA/2003/05")]
```

```
[XmlSerializerFormat(
    Style = OperationFormatStyle.Document,
    Use = OperationFormatUse.Literal)]
public interface IVehicleReservationService
{
    [OperationContract()]
    OTA_VehResRS ReserveVehicle(
        [MessageParameter(Name = "OTA_VehResRQ")]
            OTA_VehResRQ reservationReq);
}
}
```

You'll implement this service just enough for it to compile successfully; your only goal here is to explore the effects of declaring that the *XmlSerializer* is to be used, and you can explore these effects by simply reviewing the WSDL that the service generates.

8. Edit the VehicleReservationService file (.cs or .vb as appropriate) so that it becomes:

```
' VB
Imports OTASample.Vehicles.Entities

Public Class VehicleReservationService
    Implements IVehicleReservationService

    Public Function ReserveVehicle( _
            ByVal reservationReq As OTA_VehResRQ) _
                As OTA_VehResRS _
                Implements IVehicleReservationService.ReserveVehicle
        Dim resp As New OTA_VehResRS()

        ' In reality we'd build a response but for now
        ' we'll implement this service just enough for
        ' it to successfully compile by returning
        ' an empty response...

        Return resp
    End Function
End Class


// C#
using System;
using System.Xml.Serialization;
using System.Runtime.Serialization;
using System.ServiceModel;

using OTASample.Vehicles.Entities;

namespace OTASample.Vehicles.Service
{
    public class VehicleReservationService : IVehicleReservationService
    {
        public OTA_VehResRS ReserveVehicle(
                OTA_VehResRQ reservationReq)
```

```
        {
            OTA_VehResRS resp = new OTA_VehResRS();

            // In reality we'd build a response but for now
            // we'll implement this service just enough for
            // it to successfully compile by returning
            // an empty response...

            return resp;
        }
    }
}
```

9. Build the solution.

10. If you run this service and then explore the WSDL at *http://localhost:8080/vehicles?wsdl*, drill down in particular to where the XML schemas are declared in the WSDL, which in this case is at *http://localhost:8080/vehicles?xsd=xsd0*. You can go to this directly or drill down to it by first going to *http://localhost:8080/vehicles?wsdl=wsdl0*.

    There you see that the XML schema matches exactly the schema you started with, namely, the OTA Vehicle Reservation request and response schemas.

11. To see the effect of declaring that the *XmlSerializer* is to be used, try running the service again and exploring the WSDL after commenting out the following declaration:

    ```
    ' VB
    <XmlSerializerFormat(Style:=OperationFormatStyle.Document, _
                    Use:=OperationFormatUse.Literal)> _
    ```

    ```
    // C#
    [XmlSerializerFormat(
        Style = OperationFormatStyle.Document,
            Use = OperationFormatUse.Literal)]
    ```

    When you do so, you will see a set of XML schema *complexType* elements that are vastly different from the OTA schemas.

CAUTION   **Be sure to refresh the browser**

If you have kept your browser open during this process, be sure you refresh the page when trying to explore the WSDL after commenting the declaration to use the *XmlSerializer*. Otherwise, the browser might have cached the old page, and you won't see any difference.

Lesson Summary

- *DataContract* attributes declare types that will be used to specify the Data contract with consumers. Your service operations should always opt to use Data contracts over a list of parameters.

- *DataMember* attributes declare which members of your types should be included, or opted in, in the Data contract. *EnumMember* attributes do the same for enumerations.

- You can use serializable collections that implement an *Add* operation in your Service contracts. For other collections not meeting those conditions, you can use the *Collection-DataContract* attribute to ensure that your own custom collections can be serialized as lists.

- *MessageContract* attributes define the structure of the SOAP messages your service processes, including both which custom elements should appear among the SOAP headers and how the SOAP body is structured, for example whether it is wrapped.

- The *IExtensibleDataObject* interface is used to design Data contracts that support both forward and backward compatibility in roundtrip versioning scenarios.

- *DataContractFormat* and *XmlSerializerFormat* attributes control which SOAP style (*Rpc* or *Document*) is used to serialize your SOAP messages. In addition, the *XmlSerializer-Format* attribute can be used to specify whether the SOAP usage will be *Literal* or *Encoded.*

- When building WCF services from an XML schema–driven approach, you might be required to use the *XmlSerializer* to work with objects that will serialize to the desired XML.

Lesson Review

You can use the following questions to test your knowledge of the information in Lesson 2, "Defining Structural Contracts." The questions are also available on the companion CD if you prefer to review them in electronic form.

NOTE Answers

Answers to these questions and explanations of why each answer choice is correct or incorrect are located in the "Answers" section at the end of the book.

---

1. You have the following Data contract:

```vb
' VB
<DataContract( _
    Namespace:="http://schemas.fabrikam.com/customers/")> _
Public Class Address
    <DataMember(IsRequired:=False, Order:=0)> _
    Public City As String

    <DataMember(IsRequired:=False, Order:=0)> _
    Public AddressLine As String

    <DataMember(IsRequired:=False, Order:=1)> _
    Public ZipOrPostalCode As String
```

```
    <DataMember(IsRequired:=False)> _
    Public StateOrProvince As String

    <DataMember(IsRequired:=False)> _
    Public Country As String

    Public ApartmentNumber As String
End Class

// C#
[DataContract(
    Namespace = "http://schemas.fabrikam.com/customers/")]
public class Address
{
    [DataMember(IsRequired = false, Order = 0)]
    public string City;

    [DataMember(IsRequired = false, Order = 0)]
    public string AddressLine;

    [DataMember(IsRequired = false,Order = 1)]
    public string ZipOrPostalCode;

    [DataMember(IsRequired = false)]
    public string StateOrProvince;

    [DataMember(IsRequired = false)]
    public string Country;

    public string ApartmentNumber;
}
```

What is the correct order in which the members of the contract will be emitted when serialized?

- **A.** *Country, StateOrProvince, AddressLine, City, ZipOrPostalCode*
- **B.** *Country, StateOrProvince, AddressLine, City, ZipOrPostalCode, ApartmentNumber*
- **C.** *AddressLine, City, ZipOrPostalCode, Country, StateOrProvince*
- **D.** *Country, StateOrProvince, City, AddressLine, ZipOrPostalCode*

2. You have the following Message contract and Service contract that uses it:

```
' VB
<MessageContract()> _
Public Class GreetingRequestMessage
    <MessageBodyMember(Name:="TheSalutation", _
        Namespace:="http://www.fabrikam.com")> _
    Public Greeting As String

    <MessageBodyMember(Name:="TheName", _
        Namespace:="http://www.fabrikam.com")> _
    Public Name As String
```

```
    <MessageHeader(Name:="TheCustomHeader", _
        Namespace:="http://www.fabrikam.com", _
        MustUnderstand:=True)> _
    Public CustomHeader As String
End Class

<ServiceContract( _
    Namespace:="http://schemas.fabrikam.com/Greetings/")> _
Public Interface IGreeter

    <OperationContract( _
        Action:="http://GreetingMessage/Action", _
        ReplyAction:="http://HelloResponseMessage/Action")> _
    Sub Greet(ByVal msg As GreetingRequestMessage)

End Interface
```

```
// C#
[MessageContract()]
public class GreetingRequestMessage
{
    [MessageBodyMember(Name = "TheSalutation",
        Namespace = "http://www.fabrikam.com")]
    public string Greeting;

    [MessageBodyMember(Name = "TheName",
        Namespace = "http://www.fabrikam.com")]
    public string Name;

    [MessageHeader(Name = "TheCustomHeader",
        Namespace = "http://www.fabrikam.com",
        MustUnderstand = true)]
    public string CustomHeader;
}

[ServiceContract(Namespace = "http://schemas.fabrikam.com/Greetings/")]
interface IGreeter
{
    [OperationContract(Action = "http://GreetingMessage/Action",
        ReplyAction = "http://HelloResponseMessage/Action")]
    void Greet(GreetingRequestMessage msg);
}
```

Which one of the following correctly represents what the incoming SOAP request message would look like if this Message contract were deployed?

   A.   The SOAP message would look most like:

```
<s:Envelope>
    <s:Header>
        <a:Action>
            http://GreetingMessage/Action
        </a:Action>
```

```
                        <h:CustomHeader s:mustUnderstand="1"
                                        xmlns:h="http://www.fabrikam.com">
                            The custom header value
                        </h:CustomHeader>

                        <!-- etc... -->
                    </s:Header>
                    <s:Body etc...>
                        <GreetingRequestMessage
                            xmlns="http://schemas.fabrikam.com/Greetings/">

                            <Greeting xmlns="http://www.fabrikam.com">
                                Hello!
                            </Greeting>
                            <Name xmlns="http://www.fabrikam.com">
                                John Doe
                            </Name>

                        </GreetingRequestMessage>
                    </s:Body>
                </s:Envelope>
```

B.   The SOAP message would look most like:

```
<s:Envelope>
    <s:Header>
        <a:Action>
            http://GreetingMessage/Action
        </a:Action>

        <h:TheCustomHeader s:mustUnderstand="1"
                           xmlns:h="http://www.fabrikam.com">
            The custom header value
        </h:TheCustomHeader>

        <!-- etc... -->
    </s:Header>
    <s:Body etc...="">
        <TheSalutation xmlns="http://www.fabrikam.com">
            Hello!
        </TheSalutation>
        <TheName xmlns="http://www.fabrikam.com">
            John Doe
        </TheName>
    </s:Body>
</s:Envelope>
```

C.   The SOAP message would look most like:

```
<s:Envelope>
    <s:Header>
        <a:Action>
            http://GreetingMessage/Action
        </a:Action>
```

```
        <!-- etc... -->
    </s:Header>
    <s:Body etc...="">
        <GreetingRequestMessage
            xmlns="http://schemas.fabrikam.com/Greetings/">

            <h:TheCustomHeader s:mustUnderstand="1"
                xmlns:h="http://www.fabrikam.com">
                The custom header value
            </h:TheCustomHeader>
            <TheSalutation xmlns="http://www.fabrikam.com">
                Hello!
            </TheSalutation>
            <TheName xmlns="http://www.fabrikam.com">
                John Doe
            </TheName>

        </GreetingRequestMessage>
    </s:Body>
</s:Envelope>
```

D. The SOAP message would look most like:

```
<s:Envelope>
    <s:Header>
        <a:Action>
            http://GreetingMessage/Action
        </a:Action>

        <h:TheCustomHeader s:mustUnderstand="1"
                            xmlns:h="http://www.fabrikam.com">
            The custom header value
        </h:TheCustomHeader>

        <!-- etc... -->
    </s:Header>
    <s:Body etc...="">
        <GreetingRequestMessage
            xmlns="http://schemas.fabrikam.com/Greetings/">

            <TheSalutation xmlns="http://www.fabrikam.com">
                Hello!
            </TheSalutation>
            <TheName xmlns="http://www.fabrikam.com">
                John Doe
            </TheName>

        </GreetingRequestMessage>
    </s:Body>
</s:Envelope>
```

Chapter Review

To further practice and reinforce the skills you learned in this chapter, you can:

- Review the chapter summary.
- Review the list of key terms introduced in this chapter.
- Complete the case scenarios. These scenarios set up real world situations involving the topics of this chapter and ask you to create solutions.
- Complete the suggested practices.
- Take a practice test.

Chapter Summary

- To specify rigorously a service's contract with its consumers requires you to specify many details:
  - ❑ Which operations are available
  - ❑ How the request messages should be structured
  - ❑ How the response messages are structured
  - ❑ What patterns of message exchanges are required to converse with the service
- WCF provides service developers with a rich set of .NET attributes that comprise a model they can use to specify these details in the form of the following contracts:
  - ❑ The Service contract that, like its open-standard counterpart WSDL, enables consumers to access the metadata that describes which operations will be available
  - ❑ The Data contract that, like XSD in the XML space, is used to specify the structure of the data transported along with the service's messages.
  - ❑ The Message contract that, like its open-standard counterpart SOAP, is used to specify which special header elements might be found in the messages and how those messages might be structured

Key Terms

Do you know what these key terms mean? You can check your answers by looking up the terms in the glossary at the end of the book.

- Callback channel
- Callback contract
- Data contract
- Duplex
- encoding

- Fault contract
- fault exception
- Message contract
- Message Exchange Pattern (MEP)
- OneWay
- Request/Response
- roundtripping
- serialization
- service orientation
- service type

Case Scenarios

In the following case scenarios, you will apply what you've learned in this chapter. You can find answers to these questions in the "Answers" section at the end of this book.

Case Scenario 1: First Identifying a Service

Your company has an in-house application the customer service representatives (CSRs) in your call center use to capture possibe sales leads when on the phone with customers. It's a client/server application with a Windows Forms (rich client) front end and a database backend. The situation works up to a point, in that the CSRs are happy with the application. However, you have a Java-based Web application that enables users to request brochures on your products, which amounts to a lead that is not currently being captured in your leads database. The Java-based Web application is not in-house, but the vendors are willing to work with you to integrate their site with your system. Answer the following questions for your manager:

1. How will the leads from the Web application be consolidated best in the database used by your client/server application?

2. Is your solution future-proofed? That is, how well will it fare when you need to design a new leads client because the sales representatives are unable to access their leads when they are on the road with only their mobile devices?

3. Knowing your internal customers as you do, you know that what constitutes a lead in your solution will evolve over time. What is the best way to make certain that the data captured as a lead will support future changes?

Case Scenario 2: Working with Legacy Systems

You have been asked to implement a service to manage product inventory within your orgnization. From the outset, you are told that one of the primary consumers of the service will be a supply-chain system implemented on an old platform whose SOAP support is weak at best. More specifically, it can support only *Rpc/Encoded* SOAP. Answer the following questions for your manager:

1. Can WCF even be used to implement a service that this system can consume?
2. How will you define your service so that it will use the *Rpc/Encoded* SOAP format?
3. Later, you also realize that the system is not capable of wrapping its SOAP messages. How can you turn off the WCF default bevavior, which is to wrap SOAP messages?

Suggested Practices

To help you successfully master the exam objectives presented in this chapter, complete the following tasks.

Build on an Existing Service

Improve the Task Manager service.

■ **Practice**   Improve the task Data contract by adding new members. For instance, consider adding a *Comments* property, *StartDate* property, and a collection of URIs to reference external documents relevant to the task.

Implement the Task Manager service in a more realistic fashion by using a database.

Improve the Service contract by:

❑ Changing the *MarkAsComplete* method to a more generic *Update* operation that can be used to update not just the task's status but any other field. When implementing this update, watch the *LastModified* property (locking it if need be) to make sure your update isn't wiping out someone else's update since you last retrieved the task.

❑ Add other *Get* operations to bypass incomplete status and so on.

Define a New Service Contract

Define a Lead Management service.

■ **Practice**   Define a *SalesLead* Data contract. Instances of this Data contract will be used to store information for actual sales leads that need to be tracked and followed up by sales agents. As such, the contract would likely include, at the very least, the following *DataMember* fields: *DateCreated*, *CreatedBy*, *Notes*, *Priority*, *SalesRegion*, and *SourceOfLead*.

Define operations to store leads; retrieve leads by region, priority, ID, or creation date; update leads; and delete leads.

Take a Practice Test

The practice tests on this book's companion CD offer many options. For example, you can test yourself on just one exam objective, or you can test yourself on all the 70-503 certification exam content. You can set up the test so that it closely simulates the experience of taking a certification exam, or you can set it up in study mode so that you can look at the correct answers and explanations after you answer each question.

MORE INFO Practice tests

For details about all the practice test options available, see the "How to Use the Practice Tests" section in this book's introduction.

Chapter 2
Exposing the Services

In Chapter 1, "Contracts," you learned about service contracts and the operations they expose. For these services to be usable, they must be exposed to clients. Clients must be able to access information to find out how to locate and communicate with these services. This is where the service endpoint comes in. In this chapter, you will learn about what comprises a service endpoint and which methods you can use to define and configure them. You will also learn how to extend endpoints by using custom bindings.

Exam objectives in this chapter:
- Create and configure service endpoints.

Lessons in this chapter:
- Lesson 1: Service Endpoint Basics
- Lesson 2: Customizing and Extending Bindings

Before You Begin

To complete the lessons in this chapter, you must have:

- A computer that meets or exceeds the minimum hardware requirements listed in the "Introduction" section at the beginning of the book.
- Any edition of Microsoft Visual Studio 2008 (including Microsoft Visual C# 2008 Express Edition or Microsoft Visual Basic 2008 Express Edition) installed on the computer.

Lesson 1: Service Endpoint Basics

Exposing one or more endpoints is one of the required tasks associated with service-oriented programming. In this section, you explore the basics associated with creating and configuring service endpoints. This involves defining what constitutes an endpoint and examining the basic rules associated with managing these elements. You also explore the ways you can specify an endpoint through code or configuration.

After this lesson, you will be able to:

- Define the three elements that constitute an endpoint.
- Identify and name the standard bindings provided with Windows Communication Foundation (WCF).
- Specify an endpoint, using configuration (declaratively).
- Specify an endpoint, using code (imperatively).
- Understand how to use multiple bindings.
- Publish service metadata, using an endpoint.

Estimated lesson time: 45 minutes

ABCs of Endpoints

Fortunately, the three elements that constitute an endpoint start with letters that make up a mnemonic phrase, "ABCs of endpoints," which refers to the three principal elements used to form an endpoint. Every endpoint must be associated with an address, a binding, and a contract.

Address

The address for an endpoint is a unique Uniform Resource Locator (URL) that identifies the location of the service. The address should follow the Web Service Addressing (WS-Addressing) standard, which means it might contain the following four parts:

- **Scheme** The top-level portion of the address, this is typically "http" followed by a colon. This is *not* the same thing as a protocol, even though it commonly uses the same letters as the protocol.
- **Machine** Identifies the machine name, which can be a public URL such as "www.contoso .com" or a local identifier such as "localhost".
- **Port** The optional port number, preceded by a colon.
- **Path** The path used to locate the service files. Typically, this is just the service name, but the path can consist of more than one level when a service resides in a directory structure.

An address can vary, depending on whether it is hosted by Microsoft Internet Information Services (IIS) on a public network or hosted locally on an internal network computer. It can also vary, depending on the protocol the binding uses. For example, all the following could be valid addresses:

- *http://www.contoso.com/OrderService/*
- *http://localhost:8000/ServiceModelSamples/OrderService/*
- *net.tcp://localhost:8001/OrderService/*

Binding

The binding determines how the service can be accessed. This means that the binding can specify not only the protocol used to access the service but an encoding method used to format the message contents. The binding can also specify any security requirements such as Secure Sockets Layer (SSL) or SOAP message security.

To make things easier for developers, WCF provides a set of built-in bindings, listed in Table 2-1. Which binding you choose depends on several factors specific to your network and operating environment. For example, if you know the service can reside on a single computer, the *netNamedPipeBinding* would be the most efficient. Alternatively, if you need to communicate across computers, *netTcpBinding* or *netPeerTcpBinding* might work well. If interoperability is critical and you must communicate with non-WCF computers, you need to choose a binding such as *basicHttpBinding* or the *wsHttpBinding*. Finally, if your service requires support for disconnected or queued calls, you must use a binding that supports Microsoft Message Queue (MSMQ).

Table 2-1 System-Provided Bindings

Binding	Description
basicHttpBinding	This interoperable binding is commonly used as a replacement for earlier Web services based on ASMX (Active Server Methods). It supports Hypertext Transfer Protocol (HTTP) and Hypertext Transfer Protocol over SSL (HTTPS) transport protocols as well as text and Message Transmission Optimization Mechanism (MTOM) encoding methods.
wsHttpBinding	This secure and interoperable binding uses SOAP over HTTP and supports reliability, transactions, and security over the Internet. It supports HTTP and HTTPS transport protocols as well as text and MTOM encoding methods.
wsDualHttpBinding	This interoperable binding is commonly used for duplex service contracts because it supports bidirectional communication.
webHttpBinding	This secure and interoperable binding sends information directly over HTTP or HTTPS without creating a SOAP envelope. It is an efficient choice when SOAP is not required by the client.

Table 2-1   System-Provided Bindings

Binding	Description
wsFederationHttpBinding	This secure and interoperable binding supports federated security. It supports HTTP and HTTPS transport protocols as well as text and MTOM encoding methods.
netTcpBinding	This secure binding is used to send binary-encoded SOAP messages from one WCF computer to another. It uses Transmission Control Protocol (TCP) and includes support for reliability, transactions, and security.
netNamedPipeBinding	This secure binding should be used on a single WCF computer. Binary-encoded SOAP messages are sent over named pipes.
netMsmqBinding	This queued binding is used to send binary-encoded SOAP messages over MSMQ. Communication should occur between two computers.
netPeerTcpBinding	This secure binding is used for peer-to-peer communication over TCP. Communication should occur between two or more computers.
msmqIntegrationBinding	This interoperable binding can be used for existing MSMQ applications that use COM and native C++ application programming interfaces (APIs).
basicHttpContextBinding	This binding provides support for HTTP cookies and enables SOAP headers to exchange context.
netTcpContextBinding	This secure binding enables SOAP headers to be used in the exchange of content.
wsHttpContextBinding	This secure and interoperable binding enables SOAP headers to exchange context while also supporting reliability, transactions, and security.

The binding you choose also depends on which message-encoding method is required. Some bindings can be encoded as binary, which can yield better performance results. However, binary encoding is not available with all bindings. For services requiring interoperability, plaintext encoding or MTOM is required. Fortunately, you are able to specify multiple endpoints for a service. This means you are not tied to a single method, and the client can use the best one available.

Contract

The final element in the service endpoint is the contract. This identifies the operations exposed by the service, and it typically refers to the interface name, preceded by the project namespace. By including the namespace, you are using the fully qualified type name for the contract. For example, assume you have a service named MyService, and the interface used to define the service is named *IMyService*. The class file that this service resides within uses the *MyNamespace* namespace. In this case, the contract for this service would be *MyNamespace .IMyService*.

> ### Quick Check
> 1. What does the "ABCs of endpoints" refer to?
> 2. Which standard binding could be used for a service that was designed to replace an existing ASMX Web service?
>
> ### Quick Check Answers
> 1. The ABCs of endpoints refers to the three required elements that comprise a service endpoint: address, binding, and contract.
> 2. The *basicHttpBinding* standard binding was designed to expose a service as if it were an ASMX Web service. This enables you to support existing clients as applications are upgraded to WCF.

Creating an Endpoint by Using a Configuration File

Endpoints can be specified imperatively through code or declaratively in configuration. Anything that can be done in code can be done with a configuration file and vice versa. In this section, you learn how to create an endpoint, using an XML-based configuration file. This could be the web.config file, if your service is hosted in IIS or Windows Application Service (WAS), or the app.config file if your service is hosted independently with a managed application.

NOTE **Always configure endpoints by using a configuration file**

It is considered good practice to use a configuration file when specifying endpoints. This enables you to make changes to the endpoints without a costly code recompile.

Using the *system.servicemodel* Element

The configuration information for a service is contained within a *system.servicemodel* element. This element includes a *services* element, which can also contain one or more *service* elements. This is where the endpoint is defined. You must specify at least one endpoint, or you will receive an error during run time. For example, the following code specifies a single service endpoint for a service named OrderService:

```
<configuration>
  <system.serviceModel>
    <services>
      <service name="MyNamespace.OrderService">
        <endpoint address="http://localhost:8000/OrderService/"
                  binding="wsHttpBinding"
                  contract="MyNamespace.IOrderService" />
      </service>
    </services>
```

```
  </system.serviceModel>
</configuration>
```

The preceding configuration uses *wsHttpBinding* and refers to an interface named *IOrderService*. This configuration represents one of the most basic, but WCF offers you several options when configuring your service.

Real World

Sara Morgan

Even though you have the option of specifying endpoints through code, you should try always to use the configuration file instead. The values assigned to your endpoints are likely to change throughout the development process and even more so when the service is placed into production. Rather than force yourself or someone else to do a code recompile when one of these inevitable changes is needed, it is much better to use a configuration file and make changes dynamically.

For example, it is usually impossible to predict the address for your service when it is in development. In many cases, the people in charge of assigning these addresses are not the same people doing the initial development work. Additionally, network infrastructures tend to be dynamic, and significant changes can occur as your company grows in size. Trust me. It is much easier to make a simple change to an XML-based configuration file than to make a change to the service code.

Using Multiple Bindings

For services exposed to multiple clients, it makes sense to specify more than one endpoint. This enables each client to use the endpoint that is most applicable for that situation. For example, clients accessing the service through HTTP or TCP can use the following configuration:

```
<configuration>
  <system.serviceModel>
    <services>
      <service name="OrderService">
        <endpoint address="http://localhost:8000/OrderService/"
                contract="MyNamespace.IOrderService"
                binding="BasicHttpBinding">
        </endpoint>
        <endpoint address="http://localhost:8000/OrderService/secure"
                contract="MyNamespace.IOrderService"
                binding="wsHttpBinding">
        </endpoint>
        <endpoint address="net.tcp://localhost:8001/OrderService/"
                contract="MyNamespace.IOrderService"
                binding="NetTcpBinding">
```

```
            </endpoint>
          </service>
        </services>
      </system.serviceModel>
    </configuration>
```

NOTE Address must be unique for multiple endpoints

When creating multiple endpoints, remember that the address must be unique. If two endpoints use the same address, an error will be thrown at run time.

The exception to this rule occurs when you use a different contract, such as a service that uses two interfaces. In this case, two endpoints can use the same address and binding, but the contract name must be different.

Using a Base Address

WCF offers two main options for specifying the service address. In the examples provided so far, you have seen the address specified as an absolute address. This method is straightforward and probably the simplest to understand, but when multiple endpoints are involved, it is more efficient to use a relative address method. In this case, you must use a base address to specify the common portion of the address.

Specify the base address within the *host* element for each service. You can specify more than one base address by using the *add* element. For example, in the previous configuration where multiple bindings are specified, there is a common address in the form of *http://local-host:8000/OrderService/*. This portion of the address is used in the first two endpoints from that configuration. If you wanted to use a base address in that same example, the configuration would need to be changed as shown in bold to look like the following:

```
<configuration>
  <system.serviceModel>
    <services>
      <service name="OrderService">
        <host>
          <baseAddresses>
            <add baseAddress="http://localhost:8000/OrderService/"/>
            <add baseAddress="net.tcp://localhost:8001/OrderService/"/>
          </baseAddresses>
        </host>
        <endpoint address=""
                  contract="MyNamespace.IOrderService"
                  binding="BasicHttpBinding">
        </endpoint>
        <endpoint address="secure"
                  contract="MyNamespace.IOrderService"
                  binding="wsHttpBinding">
        </endpoint>
        <endpoint address=""
```

```
                    contract="MyNamespace.IOrderService"
                    binding="NetTcpBinding">
       </endpoint>
     </service>
   </services>
  </system.serviceModel>
</configuration>
```

Notice that in this new example, the address is empty for the first and last endpoints. This means that the corresponding base address itself will be used as the endpoint address. WCF knows to use the HTTP address for the first and second bindings because the *basicHttpBinding* and *wsHttpBinding* use HTTP. For the second endpoint, you just include the ending portion of the address, and the relative address will be a combination of the base address followed by the /secure folder.

NOTE The base address for IIS-hosted services are mapped to the virtual directory

When specifying an endpoint for a service hosted in IIS, the base address is mapped to the virtual directory where the service files reside. In these cases, any base addresses specified in the web.config file will be ignored by WCF.

Creating an Endpoint by Using Code

WCF enables you to specify endpoints programmatically. In this case, an instance of the *Service-Host* object is created, and endpoints are added using the *AddServiceEndpoint* method. This method can be used to create endpoints that are either absolute or relative addresses. For example, if you wanted to use code to specify the same endpoints created in the "Using a Base Address" section, you could use the following:

```
' VB
Dim httpAddress As New Uri("http://localhost:8000/OrderService/")
Dim tcpAddress As New Uri("net.tcp://localhost:8001/OrderService/")
Dim baseAddresses As Uri() = {httpAddress, tcpAddress}

Dim host As ServiceHost = _
    New ServiceHost(GetType(MyNamespace.OrderService), baseAddresses)

Dim basicBinding As New BasicHttpBinding()
Dim wsBinding As New WSHttpBinding()
Dim netBinding As New NetTcpBinding()

host.AddServiceEndpoint(GetType(MyNamespace.IOrderService), _
            basicBinding, _
            "")

host.AddServiceEndpoint(GetType(MyNamespace.IOrderService), _
            wsBinding, _
            "secure")
```

```
host.AddServiceEndpoint(GetType(MyNamespace.IOrderService), _
            netBinding, _
            "")

// C#
Uri httpAddress = new Uri("http://localhost:8000/OrderService/");
Uri tcpAddress = new Uri("net.tcp://localhost:8001/OrderService/");
Uri[] baseAddresses = {httpAddress, tcpAddress};

ServiceHost host = new
        ServiceHost(typeof(MyNamespace.OrderService),baseAddresses);

BasicHttpBinding basicBinding = new BasicHttpBinding();
WSHttpBinding wsBinding = new WSHttpBinding();
NetTcpBinding netBinding = new NetTcpBinding();

host.AddServiceEndpoint(
            typeof(MyNamespace.IOrderService),
            basicBinding,
            "");

host.AddServiceEndpoint(
            typeof(MyNamespace.IOrderService),
            wsBinding,
            "secure");

host.AddServiceEndpoint(
            typeof(MyNamespace.IOrderService),
            netBinding,
            "");
```

In this code sample, multiple base addresses are declared and placed in a *Uri* array. This array is then passed in when declaring an instance of the *ServiceHost* object. Just like with the configuration example, the first endpoint uses the HTTP base address because the *basicBinding* requires this. The second endpoint uses the HTTP base address along with the /secure folder to form a relative address. The last endpoint uses the TCP base address because the *netTcpBinding* requires this.

Publishing Metadata Through Endpoints

WCF enables you to publish service metadata, using the HTTP-GET protocol. Clients can access the metadata using an HTTP-GET request with a *?wsdl* query string appended. You do this by specifying a service behavior either programmatically or through a configuration file. The behavior is then referenced when specifying the service.

Exam Tip   Pay close attention to the steps for exposing service metadata. You should expect at least one exam question on this topic.

You also need to create a metadata exchange endpoint. This special endpoint can append *mex* to the HTTP address the service uses. The endpoint should use the *IMetadataExchange* interface as the contract and *mexHttpBinding* as the binding. Alternatives for the *mex* binding include *mexNamedPipeBinding* and *mexTcpBinding*.

To understand how this works, look at the following configuration code used to specify that OrderService can expose metadata through HTTP-GET:

```
<configuration>
  <system.serviceModel>
    <services>
      <service name="OrderService" behaviorConfiguration="MexGet">
        <endpoint address="http://localhost:8000/OrderService/"
                  contract="MyNamespace.IOrderService"
                  binding="BasicHttpBinding">
        </endpoint>
        <endpoint address="mex"
             binding="mexHttpBinding"
             contract="IMetadataExchange" />
      </service>
    </services>
    <behaviors>
      <serviceBehaviors>
        <behavior name="MexGet">
          <serviceMetadata httpGetEnabled ="True" />
        </behavior>
      </serviceBehaviors>
    </behaviors>
  </system.serviceModel>
</configuration>
```

Alternatively, you can use code to add a new service metadata behavior to the behavior collection for the host while marking the HttpGetEnabled property as *true*. For example, the following code can be used to accomplish this:

```
' VB
Dim host As ServiceHost = _
    New ServiceHost(GetType(MyNamespace.OrderService))

Dim mb As ServiceMetadataBehavior
' Look to see if the service behavior already exists.
' If not, then add it
mb = host.Description.Behaviors.Find(Of ServiceMetadataBehavior)()
If (mb Is Nothing) Then
    mb = New ServiceMetadataBehavior()
    mb.HttpGetEnabled = True
    host.Description.Behaviors.Add(mb)
End If

Dim basicBinding As New BasicHttpBinding()
```

```
host.AddServiceEndpoint(GetType(MyNamespace.IOrderService), _
                        basicBinding, _
                        "http://localhost:8000/OrderService/")
host.AddServiceEndpoint(ServiceMetadataBehavior.MexContractName, _
                        MetadataExchangeBindings.CreateMexHttpBinding(), _
                        "mex")

// C#
ServiceHost host = new ServiceHost(typeof(OrderService));

ServiceMetadataBehavior mb;
mb = host.Description.Behaviors.Find<ServiceMetadataBehavior>();
if (mb == null)
{
    mb = new ServiceMetadataBehavior();
    mb.HttpGetEnabled = true;
    host.Description.Behaviors.Add(mb);
}
BasicHttpBinding basicBinding = new BasicHttpBinding();
host.AddServiceEndpoint(
        typeof(MyNamespace.IOrderService),
        basicBinding,
        "http://localhost:8000/OrderService/");
host.AddServiceEndpoint(
        ServiceMetadataBehavior.MexContractName,
        MetadataExchangeBindings.CreateMexHttpBinding(),
        "mex");
```

Lab: Configuring Services by Using Endpoints

In this lab, you will build on the Visual Studio solution created in Chapter 1. The lab focuses on changing values in the service configuration file to demonstrate the effects of changes to this file.

▶ Exercise   Modify Configuration Properties

In this exercise, you will use an existing solution file that can be installed from the book's CD to alter values in the service configuration file. The service from Chapter 1 was configured to expose the service metadata, using HTTP-GET by using the HttpGetEnabled property. You will first examine the service metadata exposed by the service and then make a change to the HttpGetEnabled property. You will then view the results of changing this configuration.

1. Navigate to the *<InstallHome>*/Chapter 2/Lesson 1/Exercise 1/*<language>*/Before directory and double-click the Exercise1.sln file to open the solution in Visual Studio.

   The solution consists of three projects:

   ❑ The ServiceConsoleHost project, a simple Console application used to host your first service. This is the project you will be editing in this exercise.

❑   The TaskClient project, a Windows Forms application that enables you to consume your service.

❑   The Tasks.Service project, which contains the service code hosted by the Service-
ConsoleHost project.

2.   Build the solution and start the service by pressing F5, making sure that the Service-
ConsoleHost project is the startup project.

NOTE   Run Visual Studio as an Administrator

Make sure that your copy of Visual Studio is set to run as an Administrator. You can check
this by right-clicking the Visual Studio shortcut and selecting Properties. On the Shortcut tab,
click the Advanced button. Make sure the Run As Administrator check box is selected. Alternatively, start Visual Studio from the Start menu by right-clicking the Microsoft Visual Studio
2008 item and choosing Run As Administrator.

You can now explore the Web Services Description Language (WSDL) this service generates. From the app.config file in the ServiceConsoleHost project, you can see that the
service is hosted at *http://localhost:8080/Tasks*. Therefore, you can open your browser to
this Uniform Resource Identifier (URI) and, from there, follow the link to *http://local-
host:8080/Tasks?wsdl* to see the WSDL. The app.config for this project sets the
HttpGetEnabled property to *true*, which exposes the service metadata through HTTP-
GET. In the next steps, you edit the configuration file to see what effect it has on the
exposed metadata.

3.   End the service that is currently running by pressing Shift+F5 in Visual Studio. Open the
app.config file in the ServiceConsoleHost project by double-clicking the file in Solution
Explorer. Edit this file so that the *httpGetEnabled* property is set to a value of *false*.
Remove or comment out the *mex* endpoint. Save the app.config file, which should now
look like the following. (The changes are shown in bold.)

```
<?xml version="1.0" encoding="utf-8" ?>
<configuration>
  <system.serviceModel>
    <services>
      <service name="Tasks.Services.TaskManagerService"
        behaviorConfiguration="Tasks.Services.TaskServiceBehavior">
        <host>
          <baseAddresses>
            <add baseAddress = "http://localhost:8080/Tasks" />
          </baseAddresses>
        </host>
        <endpoint address ="TaskManager"
          binding="basicHttpBinding"
          contract="Tasks.Services.ITaskManagerService" />
        <!-- <endpoint address="mex"
             binding="mexHttpBinding"
             contract="IMetadataExchange" />  -->
```

```
        </service>
      </services>
      <behaviors>
        <serviceBehaviors>
          <behavior name="Tasks.Services.TaskServiceBehavior">
            <serviceMetadata httpGetEnabled="False"/>
            <serviceDebug includeExceptionDetailInFaults="True" />
          </behavior>
        </serviceBehaviors>
      </behaviors>
    </system.serviceModel>
</configuration>
```

4. Rebuild the solution and start the service, making sure that the ServiceConsoleHost project is the startup project.

5. Open a Web browser and go to *http://localhost:8080/Tasks*.

   This time, you will notice that, near the top, the page displays the message, "Metadata publishing for this service is currently disabled." This is because you have set the *httpGetEnabled* property to a value of *false* and commented out the *mex* endpoint.

   End the service that is currently running by pressing Shift+F5.

6. If you want to use this solution as the starting point for the later exercises or for the suggested practices, make sure you return the service to normal. To do so, edit the app.config file and change the *httpGetEnabled* property back to a value of *true*. Save all changes before continuing to the next lesson.

Lesson Summary

- Endpoints enable you to specify where a service is (using the address), how the service should be communicated with (using the binding), and what the service does (using the contract). These three elements form what is known as the ABCs of endpoints.

- WCF includes several standard bindings that can be used to specify the properties associated with a binding easily. Services can be configured with multiple bindings and endpoints as long as the address associated with each endpoint remains unique.

- An endpoint can be added programmatically or with a configuration file. Base addresses can be used when adding multiple endpoints with a common URL.

- Services can be configured to expose metadata by adding a service behavior and setting the *HttpGetEnabled* property to *true*.

Lesson Review

You can use the following questions to test your knowledge of the information in Lesson 1, "Service Endpoint Basics." The questions are also available on the companion CD if you prefer to review them in electronic form.

1.   You need to configure a service that will be hosted on the same computer as the client. Which standard binding would be the most efficient to use?

   A.   Basic binding

   B.   TCP binding

   C.   Peer network binding

   D.   Named pipe binding

2.   You need to configure a service that will replace an existing MSMQ application on a non-WCF computer. Which standard binding should you use?

   A.   Basic binding

   B.   Web service binding

   C.   *msmqIntegrationBinding*

   D.   *netMsmqBinding*

3.   You need to configure a service that will expose its metadata through HTTP-GET. Which of the following properties must be set to enable this?

   A.   *HttpGetEnabled*

   B.   *ServiceMetadataBehavior*

   C.   *AddServiceEndpoint*

   D.   *behaviors*

Lesson 2: Customizing and Extending Bindings

In most cases, you will be able to configure your WCF services by using one of the standard bindings provided. However, there might be cases in which special considerations must be made. In these circumstances, you might need to customize one of the standard bindings or, if necessary, create a custom binding. This lesson discusses how you can both customize a standard binding and create a custom binding from individual binding elements.

After this lesson, you will be able to:
- Customize a standard binding.
- Identify the three methods you can use to create a custom binding.
- Understand the ordering associated with binding elements.

Estimated lesson time: 30 minutes

Customizing a Standard Binding

Each of the standard bindings exposes a number of properties that you can customize. For example, the *wsHttpBinding* binding, which is commonly used to provide HTTP access to non-duplex contracts, exposes the modifiable properties listed in Table 2-2.

Table 2-2   Modifiable Properties Exposed by the *wsHttpBinding* Binding

Property	Description	Default Value
AllowCookies	*Boolean* value that determines whether the client accepts and propagates cookies.	False
BypassProxyOnLocal	*Boolean* value that determines whether to bypass the proxy server for local addresses.	False
CloseTimeout	*TimeSpan* value that indicates how much time should pass while closing a connection before an exception is thrown.	1 minute
HostNameComparisonMode	Determines whether the hostname is used to reach the service when matching the URI.	StrongWildcard
MaxBufferPoolSize	*Long* value that determines maximum amount of memory allocated for the buffer manager.	65,536 bytes
MaxRecievedMessageSize	*Long* value that determines maximum size for a message.	65,536 bytes
MessageEncodng	Determines whether MTOM or Text/XML is used to encode messages.	Text
Name	Name of the binding. Can be helpful if you use multiple versions of a certain binding.	Null reference

Table 2-2 Modifiable Properties Exposed by the *wsHttpBinding* Binding

Property	Description	Default Value
Namespace	Determines the XML namespace for the binding.	http://tempuri.org/
OpenTimeout	*TimeSpan* value that indicates how much time should pass while opening a connection before an exception is thrown.	1 minute
ProxyAddress	Determines the URI address of the HTTP proxy. Property is ignored if *UseDefaultWebProxy* is *true*.	Null reference
ReaderQuotas	Determines the constraints applied to string content within a message. For example, can be used to specify a maximum length for string content.	None
ReceiveTimeout	*TimeSpan* value that determines how long a connection can remain inactive before an exception is thrown.	10 minutes
SendTimeout	*TimeSpan* value that determines how long a write operation can take before an exception is thrown.	1 minute
TextEncoding	Determines the encoding used for message text.	UTF8Encoding
TransactionFlow	*Boolean* value that determines whether the binding should support flowing WS-Transactions.	False
UseDefaultWebProxy	*Boolean* value that determines whether the autoconfigured HTTP proxy should be used.	True

Each of the properties listed in Table 2-2 comes with a default, but you might need to override these defaults for your particular binding scenario. For example, the *wsHttpBinding* sets the timeout for closing a connection (*CloseTimeout*) at one minute. This means that an exception will be thrown if the connection does not close before this time has expired. If something about your environment requires a higher timeout value, you can change this one property.

NOTE Properties apply to *wsHttpBinding* only

The values specified in Table 2-2 apply to the *wsHttpBinding* only. Although other bindings will use properties similar to this one, check the documentation on MSDN if you need to alter properties for a binding other than *wsHttpBinding*.

Properties for the standard bindings can be changed programmatically by using the *binding* class or by using the *bindingConfiguration* property for a configuration file. When using the *bindingConfiguration*, you must specify the property to be changed in the *bindings* section and then refer to the *bindingConfiguration* name in the *endpoint* declaration. For example, if you wanted to change the *CloseTimeout* property for the *wsHttpBinding* to three minutes, you could use the following code:

```
<system.serviceModel>
  <services>
    <service name="OrderService">
      <endpoint address=""
                contract="MyNamespace.IOrderService"
                binding="WsHttpBinding"
                bindingConfiguration="CloseTimeout">
      </endpoint>
    </service>
  </services>
    <bindings>
     <wsHttpBinding>
       <binding name="CloseTimeout" closeTimeout="00:03:00">
       </binding>
     </wsHttpBinding>
    </bindings>
</system.serviceModel>
```

Alternatively, you can make the same customization by using code similar to the following:

```
' VB
Dim host As ServiceHost = _
    New ServiceHost(GetType(MyNamespace.OrderService))

Dim wsBinding As New WSHttpBinding()
Dim ts As New TimeSpan(0, 3, 0)
wsBinding.CloseTimeout = ts

host.AddServiceEndpoint(GetType(MyNamespace.IOrderService), _
                    wsBinding, _
                    "http://localhost:8000/OrderService/")
```

```
// C#
ServiceHost host = new ServiceHost(typeof(OrderService));

WSHttpBinding wsBinding = new WSHttpBinding();
TimeSpan ts = new TimeSpan(00, 03, 00);
wsBinding.CloseTimeout = ts;

host.AddServiceEndpoint(
            typeof(MyNamespace.IOrderService),
            wsBinding,
            "http://localhost:8000/OrderService/");
```

Custom Bindings

For those rare cases in which a standard binding does not meet your needs, a custom binding or user-defined binding is available. Custom bindings can be created in one of several ways. You can create a custom binding based on the *CustomBinding* class, or you can even create an entirely new binding type.

NOTE   Favor customize an existing binding over creating a custom binding

If at all possible, try to customize an existing standard binding rather than create a custom binding. In most cases, application developers don't need to create a custom binding, and creating one just adds to the complexity of your solution.

Bindings are simply composed from one or more binding elements. Binding elements control things such as the protocol, encoding, and transport methods used. Of these elements, the transport and encoding methods are the only required elements. The important thing to remember about creating a custom binding is that elements will be added in layers and that the order of the binding elements is critical. They should be added in the following order:

- **Transaction flow**   The optional transaction flow element enables you to specify a protocol flow for incoming transactions and interrupt the transaction flow at certain points.
- **Reliability**   The optional reliability element specifies sending and receiving channels for reliable sessions. This enables ordered message delivery. This element is available for the *netTcpBinding*, *wsHttpBinding*, and *wsDualHttpBinding* standard bindings.
- **Security**   The optional security element specifies features such as authorization, authentication, protection, and confidentiality.
- **Transport**   The required transport element specifies your own transport or one of the following: TCP, NamedPipes, HTTP, HTTPS, MSMQ, or Peer-to-Peer.
- **Encoding**   The required message encoding element specifies text, binary, or MTOM message encoding methods.

As with all bindings, you can make the changes programmatically or with a configuration file. When creating a custom binding using the configuration file, you create a *customBinding* element in the *bindings* collection. For example, if you want to create a custom binding that sets the *inactivityTimeout* property for the binding's security, you can use the following code:

```
<system.serviceModel>
  <services>
    <service name="OrderService">
      <endpoint address="http://localhost:8000/OrderService/"
                contract="MyNamespace.IOrderService"
                binding="customBinding"
                bindingConfiguration="NewBinding">
      </endpoint>
    </service>
```

```
    </services>
    <bindings>
      <customBinding>
        <binding name="NewBinding">
          <reliableSession />
          <security>
            <localServiceSettings inactivityTimeout="00:10:10"/>
          </security>
          <httpTransport/>
          <textMessageEncoding />
        </binding>
      </customBinding>
    </bindings>
</system.serviceModel>
```

Alternatively, you can accomplish the same result using code, although you would first need to add the following reference to the top of your class file:

```
' VB
Imports System.ServiceModel.Channels
```

```
// C#
using System.ServiceModel.Channels;
```

After you include the namespace reference, you can create your own custom binding by first declaring a *BindingElementCollection* object. You would also create a *SymmetricSecurityBinding-Element*, which contains the *InactivityTimeout* property for the local service settings. After the property is set, it can be added to the binding element collection and then associated with the new custom binding. For example, you can use the following code to create an endpoint that increases the *InactivityTimeout* period to ten minutes:

```
' VB
Dim host As ServiceHost = _
    New ServiceHost(GetType(MyNamespace.OrderService))

Dim bec As New BindingElementCollection()
Dim ssbe As New SymmetricSecurityBindingElement()
ssbe.LocalServiceSettings.InactivityTimeout = New TimeSpan(0, 10, 0)
bec.Add(ssbe)
bec.Add(New TextMessageEncodingBindingElement())
bec.Add(New HttpTransportBindingElement())

Dim customBinding As New CustomBinding(bec)

host.AddServiceEndpoint(GetType(MyNamespace.IOrderService), _
                        customBinding, _
                        "http://localhost:8000/OrderService/")
```

```
// C#
ServiceHost host = new ServiceHost(typeof(MyNamespace.OrderService));

BindingElementCollection bec = new BindingElementCollection();
```

```
SymmetricSecurityBindingElement ssbe = new
        SymmetricSecurityBindingElement();
ssbe.LocalServiceSettings.InactivityTimeout = new TimeSpan(0, 10, 0);
bec.Add(ssbe);
bec.Add(new TextMessageEncodingBindingElement());
bec.Add(new HttpsTransportBindingElement());

CustomBinding customBinding = new CustomBinding(bec);

host.AddServiceEndpoint(
        typeof(MyNamespace.IOrderService),
        customBinding,
        "http://localhost:8000/OrderService/");
```

Lab: Customizing Standard Bindings

In this lab, you will continue to build on the Visual Studio solution created in Chapter 1. The lab focuses on customizing standard bindings by changing values in the service configuration file.

▶ **Exercise   Customize the *basicHttpBinding***

In this exercise, you will alter the configuration file for the service from Chapter 1. After modifying buffer properties in the configuration file, you examine the results by executing the service and its client.

1. Navigate to the *<InstallHome>*/Chapter 2/Lesson 2/Exercise 1/*<language>*/Before directory and double-click the Exercise1.sln file to open the solution in Visual Studio.

    The solution consists of three projects:

    ❑ The ServiceConsoleHost project, a simple Console application that hosts your first service. This is the project you will be editing in this exercise.

    ❑ The TaskClient project, a Windows Forms application that enables you to consume your service.

    ❑ The Tasks.Service project, which contains the service code hosted by the ServiceConsoleHost project.

2. Open the app.config file in the TaskClient project by double-clicking the file in Solution Explorer. Edit this file so that the *maxBufferSize* and *maxReceivedMessageSize* properties are set to a value of 6.

    This represents the allowable number of bytes, which will not be large enough for messages sent from the service.

3. Save the app.config file, which should now look similar to the following (the changes are shown in bold):

    ```
    <?xml version="1.0" encoding="utf-8" ?>
    <configuration>
      <system.serviceModel>
    ```

```
  <bindings>
    <basicHttpBinding>
      <binding name="BasicHttpBinding_TaskManagerService"
          closeTimeout="00:01:00" openTimeout="00:01:00"
          receiveTimeout="00:10:00" sendTimeout="00:01:00"
          allowCookies="false" bypassProxyOnLocal="false"
          hostNameComparisonMode="StrongWildcard"
          maxBufferSize="6" maxBufferPoolSize="524288"
          maxReceivedMessageSize="6"
          messageEncoding="Text" textEncoding="utf-8"
          transferMode="Buffered" useDefaultWebProxy="true">
        <readerQuotas maxDepth="32" maxStringContentLength="8192"
                      maxArrayLength="16384" maxBytesPerRead="4096"
                      maxNameTableCharCount="16384" />
        <security mode="None">
          <transport clientCredentialType="None"
              proxyCredentialType="None" realm="" />
          <message clientCredentialType="UserName"
              algorithmSuite="Default" />
        </security>
      </binding>
    </basicHttpBinding>
  </bindings>
  <client>
      <endpoint address="http://localhost:8080/Tasks/TaskManager"
              binding="basicHttpBinding"
              bindingConfiguration="BasicHttpBinding_TaskManagerService"
              contract="TaskService.Proxy.TaskManagerService"
              name="BasicHttpBinding_TaskManagerService" />
  </client>
 </system.serviceModel>
</configuration>
```

Note that the client configuration specifies the individual properties associated with the *basicHttpBinding*. When the *transferMode* property is set to *Buffered*, the *maxBufferSize* and *maxReceivedMessageSize* properties become applicable. If the message size (in bytes) exceeds the amounts specified in these properties, an exception will be thrown.

4. To see the exception thrown, set the ServiceConsoleHost project as the startup project, and then choose Start Without Debugging from the Debug menu (or press Ctrl+F5).

    After the service is started, you can leave the Console window open and return to Visual Studio.

5. This time, set TaskClient as the startup project, and then choose Start Debugging from the Debug menu (or press F5).

    When the client project starts, it displays the Main form.

6. Type your name and click View Tasks.

    Visual Studio should break execution and bring you to the area of code where the exception has been thrown. The exception should inform you that The Maximum Message

Size Quota For Incoming Messages (6) Has Been Exceeded. To Increase The Quote, Use The MaxReceivedMessageSize Property On The Appropriate Binding Element. Note that the exception was not thrown until you initiated one of the tasks.

Lesson Summary

- All the standard bindings can be customized by altering the properties they expose. You can do this programmatically or by making changes to the configuration file.
- You can create custom bindings when one of the standard bindings fails to provide all the functionality your service requires. You can do this programmatically or by using a configuration file.

Lesson Review

You can use the following questions to test your knowledge of the information in Lesson 2, "Customizing and Extending Bindings." The questions are also available on the companion CD if you prefer to review them in electronic form.

NOTE Answers

Answers to these questions and explanations of why each answer choice is correct or incorrect are located in the "Answers" section at the end of the book.

---

1. You know that your service, which uses the *wsHttpBinding*, will be used to send large messages. You have been told that MTOM is the most efficient encoding method to use for this scenario. Which steps should you take to ensure that your service uses MTOM to encode messages?

   A. Change the binding to *netTcpBinding* because this is the only binding that allows for MTOM encoding.

   B. Change the binding to *netNamedPipeBinding* because this is the only binding that allows for MTOM encoding.

   C. Customize the *wsHttpBinding* by changing the *messageEncoding* property to *Mtom*.

   D. Do nothing because the default encoding method for the *wsHttpBinding* is already MTOM.

2. You have decided to create a custom binding for your service. Which of the following binding elements are required? (Choose all that apply.)

   A. Transport

   B. Encoding

   C. Security

   D. Reliability

Chapter Review

To further practice and reinforce the skills you learned in this chapter, you can:

- Review the chapter summary.
- Review the list of key terms introduced in this chapter.
- Complete the case scenarios. These scenarios set up real-world situations involving the topics of this chapter and ask you to create solutions.
- Complete the suggested practices.
- Take a practice test.

Chapter Summary

- The service endpoint specifies the address, binding, and contract for a service. WCF provides several standard bindings you can use to configure most services.
- To facilitate supporting multiple clients and scenarios, you can specify more than one endpoint for your service. Each endpoint can expose a unique address, binding, or contract combination.
- A service can expose the service's metadata, using HTTP-GET, by providing a metadata exchange endpoint.
- You can change the default values for properties associated with all the standard bindings. You can make these changes programmatically or to the service configuration file. For scenarios in which a standard binding does not provide the functionality required, you can create custom bindings.

Key Terms

Do you know what these key terms mean? You can check your answers by looking up the terms in the glossary at the end of the book.

- federation
- Hypertext Transfer Protocol (HTTP)
- metadata
- Microsoft Message Queue (MSMQ) services
- Message Transmission Optimization Mechanism (MTOM)
- named pipes
- peer-to-peer
- Secure Sockets Layer (SSL)
- SOAP
- Transmission Control Protocol (TCP)

Case Scenarios

In the following case scenarios, you apply what you've learned about how to expose services through endpoints. You can find the answers to these questions in the "Answers" section at the end of this book.

Case Scenario 1: Configuring an Endpoint

You are the lead developer for a financial company that has developed several WCF services to replace a set of previous Web services. Remote employees use the WCF services to retrieve data from a Microsoft SQL Server database. The services have all been tested and are ready to be deployed. You now must decide on the best method of exposing these WCF services. Which of the built-in system bindings would work best for this scenario?

Case Scenario 2: Choosing a Binding

You are the lead developer for the company mentioned in Case Scenario 1. You have been informed that one of the WCF services your company provides must support message reliability to guarantee that messages are delivered in a certain order. In Case Scenario 1, the *basicHttpBinding* was selected as the appropriate binding. Will *basicHttpBinding* still be the best choice, given the new reliability constraint?

Suggested Practices

To help you successfully master the exam objectives presented in this chapter, complete the following tasks.

Configure Using Code and Experiment with Binding Configurations

Perform the following exercises to practice configuring by using code and experimenting with binding configurations.

- **Practice 1**   Modify the ServiceConsoleHost project provided in Lesson 1. Add code to the *Program* class file to specify an endpoint such as the one initially specified in the app.config file. You can then remove the endpoint in the app.config file and save the changes. Try running the project by starting the ServiceConsoleHost project without debugging, letting it remain open, and then starting the TaskClient project. Ensure that you receive no errors.

- **Practice 2**   Modify the different properties associated with the binding in the TaskClient and ServiceConsoleHost projects, and then run the application to see what effects the changes have on the application. For example, try the following:
  - ❑ Change the *messageEncoding* property to a value other than *Mtom* or *text*.
  - ❑ Determine which other values are allowed for the *transferMode* property.

❑ Change the binding to a binding name such as *basicHttpBinding* and see what happens.

❑ Add a new binding, such as *netTcpBinding*, to both the ServiceConsoleHost and TaskClient configurations.

Take a Practice Test

The practice tests on this book's companion CD offer many options. For example, you can test yourself on just one exam objective, or you can test yourself on all the 70-503 certification exam content. You can set up the test so that it closely simulates the experience of taking a certification exam, or you can set it up in study mode so that you can look at the correct answers and explanations after you answer each question.

MORE INFO   Practice tests

For details about all the practice test options available, see the "How to Use the Practice Tests" section in this book's introduction.

Chapter 3
Deploying Services

Now that you have learned the basics of creating and exposing your services, it is time to move on to deploying the service. Services do not function like standalone executables; they require a host process. Windows Communication Foundation (WCF) offers several options regarding service hosting. The host can be a managed application such as a Console application, Windows service, or Windows Forms application. You can also host your service on a Web server, using Internet Information Services (IIS) or Windows Process Activation Service (WAS). With WAS, you have the added benefit of not requiring a Web server. WAS also supports non-HTTP protocols such as Transmission Control Protocol (TCP), Microsoft Message Queuing (MSMQ), and named pipes. Clients can then access service operations, using whichever hosting option you have selected.

In this chapter, you learn the considerations to make when creating and configuring a service host, whether it is hosted from a managed application, IIS Web server, or WAS. You also learn how to create a service host factory. Additionally, you learn about the WCF-provided host (wcfSvcHost.exe). New with .NET Framework 3.5, the WCF-provided host enables you to create a simple host project, using a command-line utility.

Exam objectives in this chapter:
- Host a service on a Web server.
- Host a service in a managed application.

Lessons in this chapter:

Before You Begin

To complete the lessons in this chapter, you must have:

- A computer that meets or exceeds the minimum hardware requirements listed in the "About This Book" section at the beginning of the book.
- Windows Vista or Windows Server 2008 installed.
- Any edition of Microsoft Visual Studio 2008 (including Microsoft Visual C# 2008 Express edition or Microsoft Visual Basic 2008 Express edition) installed on the computer.

Lesson 1: Hosting a Service on a Web Server

One of the simplest ways to host a service is by using IIS or the newly available WAS. The benefit to using either of these methods is that they handle much of the overhead associated with hosting a service. For example, you do not have to write code that handles automatic processes recycling or that ensures that the host process will always be running. You can also take advantage of message-based activation. Services hosted by IIS or WAS are launched automatically upon the first client request. Additionally, WAS is not limited to using the Hypertext Transfer Protocol (HTTP), so you can host services, using the TCP, MSMQ, or named pipes protocols.

> **After this lesson, you will be able to:**
> - Know how to host a service on an IIS Web server.
> - Know how to host a service by using WAS.
> - Know what is required to support non-HTTP protocols.
> - Know how to create a service host factory.
>
> **Estimated lesson time: 60 minutes**

Hosting a Service on an IIS Web Server

Hosting a service on an IIS Web server is very similar to hosting a traditional Web service (with an .asmx file extension). Services exposed this way will be highly available and scalable, but they will require the installation and configuration of an IIS Web server. You can use IIS 5.1, IIS 6.0, or IIS 7.0, but which one you use determines the options available when deploying your service.

Services hosted with IIS 5.1 are limited to using the same port number, thus restricting the number of host processes that can execute concurrently. Services hosted with any version can run side by side with earlier ASP.NET applications and thus be integrated easily with existing Web services. Unfortunately, they are all restricted to using the HTTP protocol.

The easiest way to host a service by using IIS is to use the built-in template with Visual Studio 2008 to create a new Web site. To do this, in Visual Studio 2008, choose New and then Web Site from the File menu. Select WCF Service as the template (as shown in Figure 3-1). Visual Studio creates a virtual directory in which you can place your service code files. The virtual directory maps to a location on the Windows file system for the Web server. The template will also create the subdirectories and configuration files you need.

NOTE Reusing an existing ASP.NET application as the service host

You can also reuse an existing ASP.NET application for your service host. You just need to add an .svc file to the directory where this application is located. You also need to create an App_code subdirectory that will contain your service contract and service implementations.

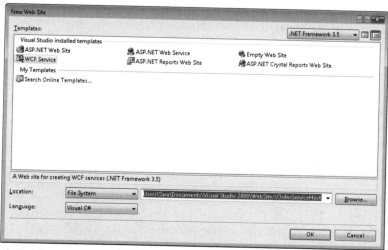

Figure 3-1 Visual Studio 2008 can be used to create a new Web site, using the built-in template

Before creating your Web site, ensure that IIS is installed and configured on the Web server and that the WCF HTTP activation component is installed. If you install .NET Framework 3.5 after IIS is installed, you do not need to perform any additional steps. Otherwise, you must register WCF with IIS and ASP.NET. How you do this depends on your operating system.

MORE INFO **Ensuring that IIS and WCF are correctly installed**

Refer to the following URL for more information about how to ensure that IIS and WCF are correctly installed and registered: *http://msdn.microsoft.com/en-us/library/aa751792.aspx*.

Services hosted in IIS require the creation of a file with an .svc file extension. This is done for you automatically if you use the Visual Studio 2008 WCF Service template. The Service.svc file is an XML-based file that must include an *@ServiceHost* directive. The directive identifies your service, and it should include attributes that identify the service code language and the name of the service. For example, if you wanted to host a service named OrderService that uses C# code, you could use a directive such as the following:

```
<% @ServiceHost Language="C#" Service="OrderService" %>
```

NOTE **Visual Studio 2008 adds a Service.svc file automatically**

If you use the Visual Studio 2008 template to create your IIS service host, a file named Service.svc will be added automatically to the application directory. This file already contains an *@ServiceHost* directive, so you need only edit the attributes to match your environment.

Exam Tip Make sure you understand what information the Service.svc file needs to contain. Even if the file is created for you automatically by Visual Studio, access the file and study the values assigned to the attributes. You are likely to have a question about this on the exam.

The directory in which your Web application resides should include a directory named App_Code. This is where you will place the code files for your service. For example, the code files for the OrderService service would be placed in this subdirectory. This should include both the Service contract and the service implementation. The code should reside in a language-specific file such as OrderService.cs or OrderService.vb. Alternatively, you could compile your service code and place it in a subdirectory named bin.

In addition to the code files, use the application configuration file to specify endpoints used by your service. For services hosted by IIS, the configuration file will be web.config. If you use the Visual Studio template to create the host application, the web.config file should already reside in the application directory. Edit this file so that it includes a *system.serviceModel* section, which specifies the types exposed as services. In most cases, this will be similar, if not identical, to the configuration file created for the service. Refer to Chapter 2, "Exposing the Services," for more information about exposing your *using* service endpoints.

The only thing different about a service hosted in IIS is that you do not have to specify a base address because the address is determined by the virtual directory for the Web site. This rule also applies to services hosted by the other IIS-based platform, WAS.

Quick Check

1. What is the main disadvantage of using IIS to host a service?
2. Which file specifies the types that your service will expose in IIS?

Quick Check Answers

1. Using IIS to host your services means that you will not be able to support non-HTTP protocols such as TCP, named pipes, and MSMQ. You will have access to the many built-in features available with IIS such as process recycling and message-based activation.
2. Service types are exposed through IIS by using the service file. This file must have an .svc file extension and should reside in the application directory for your IIS hosting application. This file will include an *@ServiceHost* directive, which specifies the service name and language for the service code files. These files should be located in an App_Code subdirectory.

Hosting a Service by Using WAS

WAS is a component of IIS 7.0 that enables you to host applications in a similar way to how IIS 6.0 hosts applications. The best part is that you are not limited to using the HTTP protocol. You can also use supported protocols such as TCP, named pipes, and MSMQ. In addition, you do not have to install the entire IIS 7.0 package. You can opt to install just WAS and not include the Web server.

Hosting a service through WAS is similar to hosting it through IIS. You still create a virtual directory that contains a service file with an .svc file extension. The service file will include an *@ServiceHost* directive to specify the service name and code language. The actual code should reside in the App_Code subdirectory or be compiled in the bin subdirectory. Configuration for WAS-hosted services is also handled by the web.config file. All exposed endpoints should be included in the *system.ServiceModel* section of this file.

Hosting a service in WAS means that you rely on a request to come in before the application domain hosting the service is created. By default, the application domain is recycled every 29 hours. This could be an issue if your service relies on in-memory state. For this reason, WAS is more suitable for services that rely on a *PerCall* session mode.

Support for Non-HTTP Protocols

If you plan on supporting non-HTTP protocols, you must configure WAS by using the Windows Features option available with Windows Vista. To begin, click Start, and then click Control Panel. Choose Programs, and then click Turn Windows Features On Or Off under the Programs And Features heading. Expand the node for Microsoft .NET Framework 3.0 and select the Windows Communication Foundation Non-HTTP Activation check box. Click OK, and then close all Control Panel windows.

To handle non-HTTP protocol requests, IIS 7.0 and WAS use a set of long-running Microsoft Windows NT services. These services, which represent listener adapters, are responsible for monitoring ports and receiving requests. The requests are then handled by an external process, SMSvcHost.exe.

Each of the Windows NT services used for non-HTTP protocols must be running on the host computer before you can run any of the non-HTTP samples available on the MSDN Web site. To ensure that they are running, navigate to Services (on Windows Vista, in Control Panel, click System And Maintenance, and then click Administrative Tools. Double-click Services in the right-side pane) and check that the following services are started:

- Net.Pipe Listener Adapter
- Net.Tcp Listener Adapter
- Net.Tcp Port Sharing Service

NOTE You must install the MSMQ core

By default, the .NET MSMQ Listener Adapter is disabled. To enable and start this service success-fully, you must first install the Microsoft Message Queue (MSMQ) server core. You can do so by using Programs And Features; however, it is not necessary to do this to complete the exercises in this book because MSMQ is not used in the exercises.

Configuring Bindings

To enable TCP, MSMQ, or named pipes communication specifically, perform the additional step of configuring support for the associated protocol. For TCP communication, bind the default Web site to a net.tcp port by using the Appcmd command-line utility. Appcmd is an IIS utility that enables you to administer virtual sites, directories, applications, and application pools. For example, if you need to support TCP on port 8080, you could run the following command from a command prompt (with administrative privileges). Note that commands in this chapter are formatted on multiple lines to fit on the printed page, but they should be entered as a single command.

```
%windir%\system32\inetsrv\appcmd.exe set site "Default Web Site"
    -+bindings.[protocol='net.tcp',bindingInformation='808:*']
```

NOTE Options for configuring WAS

Executing the Appcmd utility will make changes to the WAS configuration file. This file is located in the %windir%\system32\inetsrv\config folder, and it is named applicationHost.config. Even though you can edit this XML-based file directly, it is not recommended that you do so.

Also note that it is possible to receive an error message when trying to add support for TCP. The error message will indicate that it cannot add a duplicate collection entry. You can ignore this error.

To support the other protocols, run additional commands that enable those protocols for the default Web site. At this point, you have configured the net.tcp protocol at the site level. To enable TCP communication for a specific application, you must run the Appcmd utility for the application. For example, if your application is named OrderServiceHost, you could run the following command to add support for both HTTP and the net.tcp protocols:

```
%windir%\system32\inetsrv\appcmd.exe set app
    "Default Web Site/OrderServiceHost" /enabledProtocols:http,net.tcp
```

NOTE Protocols are configured on Windows Server 2008 by default

By default, the protocols are configured on computers running Windows Server 2008. You must configure these protocols only if you are using the non-HTTP protocols on a computer running Windows Vista.

Configuring MSMQ Activation

To enable MSMQ communication specifically, you must also create a queue, using the Computer Management snap-in. The queue you create must use the name of the hosting application along with the service file name. For example, if your service host application is named OrderServiceHost and the service file is named service.svc, the queue must be named Order-ServiceHost/service.svc.

By default, the Windows NT service that handles MSMQ activation uses the NETWORK SERVICE Windows account. This account must be granted peek and receive message permissions, which you can do also by using the Message Queuing MMC snap-in (as shown in Figure 3-2).

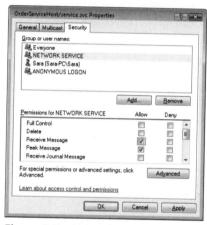

Figure 3-2   Using the Security tab for the queue properties, you can grant receive and peek message permissions to the NETWORK SERVICE account

Finally, you must specify the queue name in the service configuration file. You can do this by adding an endpoint that identifies the name of the private queue. For example, if you created a queue named OrderServiceHost/service.msc, the endpoint declaration would look like the following:

```
<endpoint
    address="net.msmq://localhost/private/OrderServiceHost/service.svc"
    binding="netMsmqBinding"
    contract="IOrderService" />
```

NOTE   Configuring the Client

There also must be a corresponding endpoint for the client application. Because creating a client is covered in Chapter 4, "Consuming Services," creating an endpoint for the client is not covered here. Just note that when you generate the client proxy from metadata, you must add a child element for each protocol supported.

Creating a Service Host Factory

Because WAS and IIS 7.0 support dynamic activation, you have the option of creating a custom service host factory. WCF provides the *ServiceHostFactory* class, by which you can create instances of service hosts dynamically as the requests come in. This gives you access to the extensibility model of WCF and can be beneficial when you need to create event handlers for opening and closing the service. Service host factories can also be beneficial when you must configure a large number of services in a consistent way.

To create a service host factory, you implement the *CreateServiceHost* method by deriving from the *ServiceHostFactory* class. This method is responsible for returning a new instance of the custom host class. You can then create a *ServiceHost*, even though WAS and IIS 7.0 would normally do this for you. For example, if you want to create a *ServiceHost* named *CustomService-Host* to override the *OnOpening* and *OnClosing* methods, you could use something similar to the following:

```vb
' VB
Class CustomServiceHost
    Inherits ServiceHost
    Public Sub New(ByVal serviceType As Type, _
            ParamArray baseAddresses As Uri())
        MyBase.New(serviceType, baseAddresses)
    End Sub

    Protected Overloads Overrides Sub OnOpening()
        'Place code here that should execute before service startup
        MyBase.OnOpening()
    End Sub

    Protected Overloads Overrides Sub OnClosing()
        'Place code here that should execute when service is shut down
        MyBase.OnClosing()
    End Sub
End Class
```

```csharp
// C#
class CustomServiceHost : ServiceHost
{
    public CustomServiceHost(Type serviceType, params Uri[] baseAddresses)
        : base(serviceType, baseAddresses) { }

    protected override void OnOpening()
    {
        //Place code here that should execute before service startup
      base.OnOpening();
    }

    protected override void OnClosing()
    {
```

```
        //Place code here that should execute when the service is shutdown
        base.OnClosing();
    }
}
```

Lab: Deploying a Service by Using a Service Host

In this lab, you use WAS, which is part of IIS 7.0 and available with Windows Vista and Windows Server 2008. You use the same Task Manager service that was used in Chapter 1, "Contracts," and in Chapter 2. Instead of hosting the application by using a Console application, you use WAS to host the service. By doing this, you can support communication over TCP.

Note: You will not be able to complete this exercise unless you are running Windows Vista or Windows Server 2008. If you encounter a problem completing an exercise, refer to the completed project located in the After folder on the companion CD.

Exercise 1   Set Up and Configure WAS

In this exercise, you will set up and configure your computer not only to use WAS but to support the net.tcp protocol. You might be able to skip this entire exercise if you already have WAS installed on your computer. Depending on your operating system, WAS and IIS might already be installed and configured properly.

1. Click Start, and then choose Control Panel.
2. Click Programs. Click Turn Windows Features On And Off under the Programs And Features heading.
3. If Internet Information Services does not have a check mark, expand the Internet Information Services node, and then the Web Management Tools node. Select the IIS Management Console check box.

    Note: You do not have to install the full IIS Web server to use WAS. Select the IIS Management Console check box so that you can use that tool to create the virtual directory in the next exercise.
4. If the Windows Process Activation Service check box is not selected, expand the node and make sure all subnodes are selected.
5. Expand the node for Microsoft .Net Framework 3.0. Ensure that the Windows Communication Foundation HTTP Activation and Windows Communication Non-HTTP Activation check boxes are selected.
6. When you have checked all the nodes, click OK to apply the changes. It might take several minutes for the features to be configured. When complete, close all Control Panel windows.
7. Click Start and type **Services.msc** in the search text box. Press Enter.

8. Scroll through the list of services and locate one named Net.Tcp Listener Adapter. Ensure that this service, along with one named Net.Tcp Port Sharing Service and another named Windows Process Activation Service, have a status of Started.

Exercise 2   Create a Hosting Application

In this exercise, you will create the hosting application that will run using WAS. The hosting application will consist of a virtual directory that also supports the net.tcp protocol.

1. Navigate to the *<InstallHome>*/Chapter 3/Lesson 1/Exercise 2/*<language>*/Before directory and copy the bin folder and all the contents to a new folder named TaskManagerHost on your local hard drive. For example, you can copy the files to a new sub folder within your \Inetpub\wwwroot folder.

   The bin folder should now be a subfolder beneath the TaskManagerHost folder. The bin subfolder contains a compiled version of the TaskManager service introduced in the lab exercises for Chapter 1.

2. Right-click within the TaskManagerHost folder, click New, and then click Text Document. Name the text file **Service.svc** and make sure the file extension is not still .txt. Click OK when warned about changing the file name extension.

3. Open the Service.svc file with any text editor and type the following code; then save and close the file:

   ```
   ' VB
   <% @ServiceHost Language="VB" debug="true"
        Service="Tasks.Services.TaskManagerService" %>
   ```

   ```
   // C#
   <% @ServiceHost Language="C#" debug="true"
        Service="Tasks.Services.TaskManagerService" %>
   ```

4. Right-click within the TaskManagerHost folder, click New, and then click Text Document. Name the text file **Web.Config** and make sure the file extension is not still .txt. Click OK when warned about changing the file name extension.

5. Open the Web.Config file with any text editor and type the following code:

   ```
   <?xml version="1.0" encoding="utf-8" ?>
   <configuration>

     <system.serviceModel>
       <services>
         <service name="Tasks.Services.TaskManagerService"
             behaviorConfiguration="Tasks.Services.TaskServiceBehavior">
           <host>
             <baseAddresses>
               <add baseAddress = "http://localhost/" />
                 <add baseAddress = "net.tcp://localhost:8080/" />
             </baseAddresses>
   ```

```
        </host>

        <endpoint address ="TaskManager"
                binding="wsHttpBinding"
                  contract="Tasks.Services.ITaskManagerService" />

         <endpoint address ="TaskManager"
                  binding="netTcpBinding"
                contract="Tasks.Services.ITaskManagerService" />

        <endpoint address="mex"
                binding="mexHttpBinding"
                contract="IMetadataExchange" />

      </service>
    </services>
    <behaviors>
      <serviceBehaviors>
        <behavior name="Tasks.Services.TaskServiceBehavior">
          <serviceMetadata httpGetEnabled="True"/>
          <serviceDebug includeExceptionDetailInFaults="True" />
        </behavior>
      </serviceBehaviors>
    </behaviors>
  </system.serviceModel>
</configuration>
```

6. Click Start and type **mmc** in the Search text box. Press Enter.

7. In Microsoft Management Console, click the File menu, and then click Add/Remove Snap-in.

8. Select the Internet Information Services (IIS) Manager snap-in and click Add. Click OK to load the snap-in.

9. Click the Internet Information Services node under the Console Root node. Expand the entry listed under the Connections pane. Expand the Web Sites folder.

10. Right-click Default Web Site and choose Add Application.

11. From the Add Application dialog box, type the name **TaskManagerHost** in the Alias text box and click the Browse button to browse to the TaskManagerHost folder that you created in step 1 (as shown in Figure 3-3). Click OK to create the application.

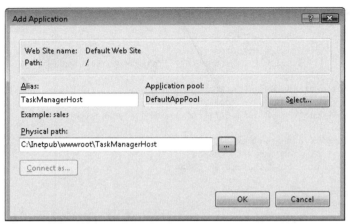

Figure 3-3 Add Application dialog box enables you to add a new Web application to the Default Web Site, using the Internet Information Services Manager console

12. Click All Programs, then Accessories. Right-click Command Prompt and select Run As Administrator.

13. From the command prompt, type the following command:

```
%windir%\system32\inetsrv\appcmd.exe set site "Default Web Site"
    -+bindings.[protocol='net.tcp',bindingInformation='808:*']
```

14. Ensure that the previous command executed successfully, and then type the following command:

```
%windir%\system32\inetsrv\appcmd.exe set app
    "Default Web Site/TaskManagerHost" /enabledProtocols:http,net.tcp
```

15. In Microsoft Internet Explorer, type the following URL:

```
http://localhost/TaskManagerHost/Service.svc
```

You should receive the service confirmation page, which shows that the service is available. You might also receive a prompt from your antivirus software, alerting you about the service being started. At this point, client code can be generated using the svcutil utility. More about using this utility and creating the client will be covered in Chapter 4.

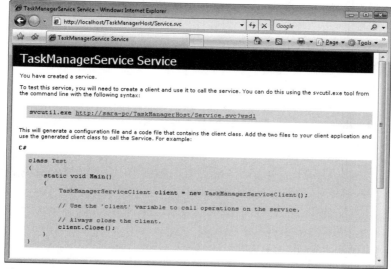

Figure 3-4 The service confirmation page indicates that the service is available

Lesson Summary

- Services can be easily deployed using IIS or WAS. Services hosted by IIS are available through the HTTP protocol only. Services hosted by WAS, a component of IIS 7.0, are available to non-HTTP protocols such as TCP, named pipes, and MSMQ.

- Services deployed through IIS or WAS need only a virtual directory, a service file that contains an *@ServiceHost* directive, a web.config file with defined endpoints, and a service provided either as code in an App_Code subfolder or compiled in a bin subfolder.

- Creating a service host factory enables you to access opening and closing event handlers when handling WAS hosted services. You can also use a service host factory to configure a large number of services in a consistent way.

Lesson Review

You can use the following questions to test your knowledge of the information in Lesson 1, "Hosting a Service on a Web Server." The questions are also available on the companion CD if you prefer to review them in electronic form.

NOTE Answers

Answers to these questions and explanations of why each answer choice is correct or incorrect are located in the "Answers" section at the end of the book.

---

1. You need to deploy a service to a Web server. Which version of IIS supports non-HTTP protocols?
   A. IIS 5.1
   B. IIS 6.0
   C. IIS 7.0
   D. No versions of IIS

2. You have decided to use WAS to host your service because you plan on supporting the TCP protocol. The computer you will use to host the service is running Windows Vista. What must you do before you can set up your Web application?
   A. In Windows Features, you must select the Non-HTTP activation check box for the Windows Activation Services node.
   B. In Windows Features, you must select the Non-HTTP activation check box for the .NET Framework 3.0 node.
   C. In Windows Features, you must select the Non-HTTP activation check box for the Internet Information Services node.
   D. You must add a Service.svc file to your application directory.

3. Your service must support MSMQ, and you plan on using WAS to host the application. You have already configured WAS to support non-HTTP activation. Which additional steps must be performed to support MSMQ activation? (Choose all that apply.)
   A. You must create a private queue, using the Message Queuing snap-in.
   B. You must grant read permissions to the NETWORK SERVICE account for the queue you just created.
   C. You must specify the private queue name in the endpoint declaration.
   D. You must add an MSMQ element to the web.config file.

Lesson 2: Hosting a Service in a Managed Application

WCF enables you to host your service through any managed application. This means you can use a Console application, a Windows service, a Windows Forms application, or even an application built with Windows Presentation Foundation. For users who need to host simple services, WCF provides a built-in host that can be initiated using a command-line utility. Which method you choose depends on how robust your hosting option needs to be. It also depends on what type of client application will be accessing your service.

After this lesson, you will be able to:
- Host a service by using a Console application.
- Host a service by using a Windows NT service.
- Host a service by using the WCF-provided host.

Estimated lesson time: 45 minutes

Hosting a Service by Using a Console Application

As opposed to hosting your service by using IIS or WAS, hosting your service using a Console application involves adding code to manage the host process. For this reason, Console applications can be referred to as self-hosting. In most cases, this type of application is used during the development process. The Console application must specifically create and open an instance of the *ServiceHost* object. The *ServiceHost* then remains open and available until it is no longer needed.

In most cases, you will want to add a Console application project to the solution for your service. In Visual Studio 2008, you do this by right-clicking the solution in Solution Explorer, choosing Add, and then choosing New Project. You then select Console Application as the template and type a name for your hosting application.

You must add code to the *Main* method that creates an instance of the *ServiceHost* object. Opening this object creates an open listener for the service and enables it to start receiving messages. For example, the following code can open an instance of a service named *OrderService* and leave it open until a user presses any key to close the service:

```vb
' VB
Sub Main()
   Using host As New ServiceHost(GetType(OrderService))

      host.Open()

      Console.WriteLine("The OrderService is ready." + _
         vbCrLf + "Press a key to exit.")
      Console.ReadKey()
```

```
      host.Close()
   End Using
End Sub

// C#
static void Main(string[] args)
{
   using (ServiceHost host = new ServiceHost(typeof(OrderService)))
   {
      host.Open();

      Console.WriteLine("The OrderService is ready.\nPress a key to exit");
      Console.ReadKey(true);

      host.Close();
   }
}
```

You must also specify an endpoint for your service host. Just like the service, you can do this programmatically with code or declaratively by using a configuration file. Typically, you add a configuration file named App.config to your Console application project. You should be able to use the same configuration scenario that was used to create the service. Refer to Chapter 2 for more information about configuring the service.

Hosting a WCF Service by Using a Windows Service

Windows services, formerly known as Windows NT services, are useful when dealing with long-running WCF services that do not require a user interface. By using a Windows service, you can be sure that the service host is always available. A Windows service can be configured to start automatically when the operating system loads. It can also be paused, stopped, and restarted by using an MMC snap-in.

You can create a Windows service by using one of the Visual Studio 2008 templates. Just like the Console application, the Windows service project can be added to the solution for your service. In Visual Studio 2008, right-click the solution in Solution Explorer, click Add, and then click New Project. You then select Windows Service, which is located under the category of Windows, as the template and type the name **OrderWindowsService** for your hosting application.

Before you start adding code to the project, you must add a reference to the *System.ServiceModel* component by right-clicking the new project and then choosing Add Reference. Then select System.ServiceModel from the list and click OK. You must also add a reference to the *System.Configuration.Install* component, which is used for the project installer. After the components are selected, add the following directives to the top of the Service1.vb or Service1.cs file:

```
' VB
Imports System.ServiceModel
Imports System.ComponentModel
Imports System.Configuration.Install
Imports System.ServiceProcess
```

```
// C#
using System.ServiceModel;
using System.ComponentModel;
using System.Configuration.Install;
using System.ServiceProcess;
```

OnStart and *OnStop* method handlers are added automatically when you create an application, using the Visual Studio 2008 template. Also, the application class inherits from the *ServiceBase* class. This is essential for the application to be a Windows service. You must add code to the top of your class file, which declares a *ServiceHost* variable. For example, the following code can be added to the Windows service at the end of the class definition:

```
' VB
Dim serviceHost As ServiceHost = Nothing
```

```
// C#
public ServiceHost serviceHost = null;
```

To locate your service in the service Console window, set the *ServiceName* property in the constructor. You must also provide an entry point for your hosting application. For example, you can provide the necessary code for a Windows service named OrderWindowsService by using the following code:

```
' VB
Public Sub New()
    ServiceName = "Order Service Windows Service"
End Sub

Shared Sub Main()
    System.ServiceProcess.ServiceBase.Run(New OrderWindowsService)
End Sub
```

```
// C#
public OrderWindowsService()
{
    ServiceName = "Order Service Windows Service";
}

public static void Main()
{
    ServiceBase.Run(new OrderWindowsService());
}
```

You must also add code to the *OnStart* method that will create an instance of *ServiceHost* and pass in the type for your WCF service. The *ServiceHost* will be opened and thus available to all client applications. For example, you can add the following code to the *OnStart* method to start a WCF service named OrderService:

```
' VB
Protected Overrides Sub OnStart(ByVal args() As String)
    If serviceHost IsNot Nothing Then
        serviceHost.Close()
    End If

    serviceHost As New ServiceHost(GetType(OrderService))

    serviceHost.Open()
End Sub
```

```
// C#
protected override void OnStart(string[] args)
{
    if (serviceHost != null)
    {
        serviceHost.Close();
    }

    serviceHost = new ServiceHost(typeof(OrderService));

    serviceHost.Open();
}
```

The *OnStop* method is responsible for closing the *ServiceHost* instance. For example, the following code can be used for the *OnStop* method:

```
' VB
Protected Overrides Sub OnStop()
    If serviceHost IsNot Nothing Then
        serviceHost.Close()
        serviceHost = Nothing
    End If
End Sub
```

```
// C#
protected override void OnStop()
{
    if (serviceHost != null)
    {
        serviceHost.Close();
        serviceHost = null;
    }
}
```

For the service to be installed as a Windows service, you must create a *ProjectInstaller* class. This class will inherit from the *Installer* class (which is part of the *System.ComponentModel* namespace) and must be marked with the *RunInstaller* attribute. The code for the class can reside in the same Windows service project created previously. For example, you could add the following code below the *OrderWindowsService* class:

```vb
' VB
<RunInstallerAttribute(True)> _
Public Class ProjectInstaller
    Inherits Installer

    Dim process As ServiceProcessInstaller
    Dim service As ServiceInstaller

    Public Sub ProjectInstaller()
        process = New ServiceProcessInstaller()
        process.Account = ServiceAccount.LocalSystem
        service = New ServiceInstaller
        service.ServiceName = "Order Service Windows Service"
        Installers.Add(process)
        Installers.Add(service)

    End Sub
End Class
```

```csharp
// C#
[RunInstaller(true)]
public class ProjectInstaller : Installer
{
    private ServiceProcessInstaller process;
    private ServiceInstaller service;

    public ProjectInstaller()
    {
        process = new ServiceProcessInstaller();
        process.Account = ServiceAccount.LocalSystem;
        service = new ServiceInstaller();
        service.ServiceName = "Order Service Windows Service";
        Installers.Add(process);
        Installers.Add(service);
    }
}
```

Finally, you must add configuration code to the app.config file. The configuration code should include a base address and should specify all endpoints exposed by the WCF service. After this is done, you can compile the application to create a service executable. You can then use the installutil command-line utility to install the Windows service. For example, if you created a service named OrderWindowsService, you can run the following command from a Visual Studio 2008 command prompt:

```
installutil C:\MyProjects\bin\OrderWindowsService.exe
```

When installed, the Windows service is accessible through the Service Control Manager, which is an MMC snap-in. You can access the Service Control Manager by typing **services.msc** from a command prompt. If you have followed all the steps in this section, Order Service Windows Service should appear in the list.

Hosting a Service by Using the WCF-Provided Host

Visual Studio 2008 introduced a new feature known as the WCF-provided host. This built-in host is useful when you need to deploy simple services quickly. This can be especially helpful when you are first learning WCF, because it will free you from having to add Console applications to your service solutions constantly. The WCF-provided host is a command-line utility available through the WcfSvcHost executable.

To get an idea how it works, assume you want to host a service named SimpleService. The contract and implementation classes for this service were compiled into a dynamic-link library (DLL) called SimpleService.dll. The configuration file for the service is named App.config. To use the WCF-provided host, you open a command prompt and type something similar to the following (replacing the path and file names with those specific to your service):

```
WcfSvcHost.exe /service:C:\MyProject\bin\SimpleService.dll
    /config:C:\MyProject\App.Config
```

You should see a message box pop up near your task bar, informing you that WcfSvcHost has been started. You should also get a WCF Service Host dialog box (as shown in Figure 3-5) that displays information about the service that has been loaded. At this point, you can use a client to access the WCF service.

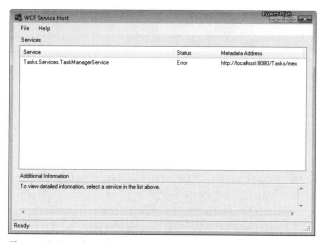

Figure 3-5   The WCF Service Host dialog box appears when you use the WcfSvcHost utility to host your WCF service

Lab: Deploying a Service by Using a Managed Application

In this lab, you will use a Console application to host a WCF service. Once again, you use the Task Manager service as in Chapter 1 and Chapter 2.

Exercise 1   Use a Console Application

In this exercise, you will host an application by using a Console application. This will be the same Task Manager service used in previous chapters.

1. Navigate to the *<InstallHome>*/Chapter 3/Lesson 2/Exercise 1/*<language>*/Before directory.
2. Double-click the Tasks.Services project file for your chosen language to open the project in Visual Studio 2008.
3. Right-click the Tasks.Services solution from Solution Explorer, click Add, and then click New Project.
4. Select the Console Application template, name the project **ServiceConsoleHost**, and then click OK.
5. Right-click the ServiceConsoleHost project and choose Add Reference. Click the Browse tab in the Add Reference dialog box.
6. Browse to Tasks.Services.dll in the /bin/Debug subfolder. Click OK to add the reference.
7. Return to the Add Reference dialog box and, from the .NET tab, scroll through the list of components until you locate System.ServiceModel. Select this component and click OK to add the reference.

   The project should open to the Program or Module1 file.
8. Add the following code to the top of the code file, before the namespace declaration:

   ```
   ' VB
   Imports Tasks.Services
   Imports System.ServiceModel
   ```

   ```
   // C#
   using Tasks.Services;
   using System.ServiceModel;
   ```
9. Add the following code to the *Main* method:

   ```
   ' VB
   Using host As New ServiceHost(GetType(TaskManagerService))
       host.Open()

       Console.WriteLine("The Service is ready. " + _
               vbCrLf + "Press a key to exit.")
       Console.ReadKey()

       host.Close()
   End Using
   ```

```csharp
// C#
using (ServiceHost host = new ServiceHost(typeof(TaskManagerService)))
{
     host.Open();

     Console.WriteLine("The Service is ready.\nPress a key to exit");
     Console.ReadKey(true);

     host.Close();
}
```

10. Right-click the ServiceConsoleHost project, click Add, and then click New Item.

11. Select Application Configuration File and click Add to add the App.config file to your project. In Visual Basic, Application Configuration File is located beneath the General category.

12. Add the following code to the configuration file within the *configuration* element:

```xml
<system.serviceModel>
  <services>
    <service name="Tasks.Services.TaskManagerService"
      behaviorConfiguration="Tasks.Services.TaskServiceBehavior">
       <host>
       <baseAddresses>
         <add baseAddress = "http://localhost:8000/Tasks" />
       </baseAddresses>
       </host>
       <endpoint address ="TaskManager"
              binding="basicHttpBinding"
              contract="Tasks.Services.ITaskManagerService" />

       <endpoint address="mex"
              binding="mexHttpBinding"
              contract="IMetadataExchange" />
    </service>
  </services>
  <behaviors>
    <serviceBehaviors>
      <behavior name="Tasks.Services.TaskServiceBehavior">
      <serviceMetadata httpGetEnabled="True"/>
      <serviceDebug includeExceptionDetailInFaults="True" />
      </behavior>
    </serviceBehaviors>
  </behaviors>
</system.serviceModel>
```

13. Save the Tasks.Services.sln file, and then right-click the ServiceConsoleHost Project and click Build.

14. Click Save to continue.

    The status bar should indicate that the build was successful.

15. Right-click the ServiceControlHost project and choose Set As Startup Project. You can then run the project by pressing F5 or by choosing Start Debugging from the Debug menu.

NOTE Administrator permissions needed

You must have administrator permissions to run this application. Otherwise, you might receive a permissions exception. You can run Visual Studio as an Administrator to execute the DLL with administrator permissions.

Lesson Summary

- Services can also be deployed by using a managed application such as a Console application, a Windows Forms application, or a Windows service. Deploying with a Console application is simple because it does not require a supporting infrastructure such as IIS or WAS.

- Services hosted with a Windows service have the benefit of being able to start automatically when the server starts. You need to add code only to the *OnStart* and *OnClose* methods to open and close your WCF service.

- Visual Studio 2008 includes a WCF-provided host that enables you to host applications easily, using a command-line utility. This frees developers from having to generate repetitive hosting code for simple services.

Lesson Review

You can use the following questions to test your knowledge of the information in Lesson 2, "Hosting a Service in a Managed Application." The questions are also available on the companion CD if you prefer to review them in electronic form.

NOTE Answers

Answers to these questions and explanations of why each answer choice is correct or incorrect are located in the "Answers" section at the end of the book.

---

1. Which of the following methods can you use to host a WCF service in a managed application? (Choose all that apply.)

    A. Windows Forms application

    B. Windows Presentation Foundation UI application

    C. Console application

    D. Windows service

2. You have designed a WCF service and now you wish to host it by using a Windows service. Besides creating the Windows service application, what must you do to load your new Windows service?

   A. Add the application to the machine.config file for your server computer.

   B. Execute the installutil command-line utility to install the service.

   C. Add the application to the app.config file for your WCF service.

   D. Do nothing. All you need to do is create the Windows service application.

Chapter Review

To further practice and reinforce the skills you learned in this chapter, you can:

- Review the chapter summary.
- Review the list of key terms introduced in this chapter.
- Complete the case scenario. This scenario sets up a real-world situation involving the topics of this chapter and asks you to create solutions.
- Complete the suggested practices.
- Take a practice test.

Chapter Summary

- Services can be hosted either on a Web server or in a managed application. Options for hosting on a Web server include hosting with IIS or WAS. When hosting with a managed application, you can use a Console application, a Windows Forms application, a Windows Presentation Foundation UI application, or a Windows service.
- To host simple WCF services, you can use the WCF-provided host. You can use this built-in service host with a command-line utility to host a service quickly, and it requires no extra code or supporting infrastructure.

Key Terms

Do you know what these key terms mean? You can check your answers by looking up the terms in the glossary at the end of the book.

- command-line utility
- Internet Information Services (IIS)
- message-based activation
- virtual directory

Case Scenario

Case Scenario: Upgrading a Series of Earlier Web Services

You are a developer for a large retail food organization that operates hundreds of stores throughout the United States. Additionally, the food chain maintains a retail Web site to accommodate Internet users. The Web site uses a series of Web services, which allow Internet customers to place orders with a particular store and have the food delivered to them. The only clients to access the Web services do so using the ASP.NET application designed by your company.

The Web services are currently hosted on a Web server running IIS 6.0 and Windows Server 2003. At this time, the Web server is running .NET Framework 2.0.

You have been put in charge of converting all the earlier Web services to WCF services. It is critical for the conversion to cause the least amount of downtime for the customer.

1. Which hosting platform should be used to host your new WCF services?
2. What is the best strategy for converting the earlier Web services to WCF services?

Suggested Practices

To help you successfully master the exam objectives presented in this chapter, complete the following tasks.

Hosting Services

Perform these practices to create a service host factory and to host a WCF service by using a Windows service.

- **Practice 1** Create a service host factory by using the *ServiceHostFactory* class. The class should be used to create an event handler that writes a generic message to a log file when the WCF service is started. The WCF service can be hosted in either WAS or IIS 7.0.
- **Practice 2** Host the Task Manager service by using a Windows service. This will involve some of the following steps:
  1. Add a Windows service project to the Task Manager solution that is part of the Lesson 1 lab in this chapter.
  2. Add method handlers to handle the *OnStart* and *OnStop* events.
  3. Add Project Installer code.
  4. Install the Windows service by using the installutil utility.
  5. Start the Windows service by using the MMC snap-in (services.mmc).

Take a Practice Test

The practice tests on this book's companion CD offer many options. For example, you can test yourself on just one exam objective, or you can test yourself on all the 70-503 certification exam content. You can set up the test so that it closely simulates the experience of taking a certification exam, or you can set it up in study mode so that you can look at the correct answers and explanations after you answer each question.

MORE INFO   **Practice tests**

For details about all the practice test options available, see the "How to Use the Practice Tests" section in this book's introduction.

Chapter 4

Consuming Services

Until this chapter, the primary focus of this book has been on building and configuring Windows Communication Foundation (WCF) services. However, the value of service orientation is to make certain capabilities (services) available for use (or consumption) in other programs, so in this chapter, the emphasis shifts to consuming services. The chapter begins with coverage of the mechanics of creating proxies to services and then discusses what you'll need to know to consume services effectively, using those proxies. Because one of the most powerful aspects of Extensible Markup Language (XML)-based Web services is that their consumption does not impose any platform, technology, or operating system constraints, the chapter will close with a look at how WCF can be used to consume services built on other platforms.

Exam objectives in this chapter:
- Create a service proxy.
- Call a service by using a service proxy.
- Consume non-WCF services.

Lessons in this chapter:

Before You Begin

To complete the lessons in this chapter, you must have:

- A computer that meets or exceeds the minimum hardware requirements listed in the "About This Book" section at the beginning of the book.
- Any edition of Microsoft Visual Studio 2008 (including Microsoft Visual C# 2008 Express Edition or Microsoft Visual Basic 2008 Express Edition) installed on the computer.
- Access to the Visual Studio solutions for this chapter included on the companion CD.
- An active Internet connection for the lab following Lesson 2, "Consuming Non-WCF Services."

Real World

Peter Madziak

SOAP-based Web services have really come into their prime over the past few years when it comes to usage inside an enterprise or institution. Many companies are using Web services inside their organization for consumption by rich-client applications inside their enterprise, their own Web applications, and, in many cases, by partners in a business-to-business (B2B) setting. However, what are less common are Internet-facing SOAP services that are available for massive consumption by any number of consumers. They certainly exist; however, to use Gartner's term (see *http://en.wikipedia.org/wiki/Hype_cycle*), they are further behind on the hype cycle than inside-the-enterprise usage of SOAP-based Web services.

Even so, there are many who would argue that all this is about to change. Borrowing from Gartner again, Internet-facing Web services are rapidly approaching the "plateau of productivity". Whenever it happens, all will agree that it will be a fascinating era for software development, an era in which application development teams will be able to assemble applications more rapidly than ever before by consuming best-of-breed services on the Internet in much the same fashion as we consume utilities such as electricity and cable television services today. Central to working in this kind of an environment is being able to consume other services effectively (whether they are WCF services or not), which is the focus of this chapter. In the lab that follows the second lesson of this chapter, the exercise works through the steps of consuming Microsoft MapPoint, an Internet-facing mapping and geolocation Web service. This is an excellent example of a very powerful capability, namely, access to worldwide map images and data, which is available for use in applications more easily than it ever has been before. The true mark of its utility is that most application developers would never dream of trying to build this capability themselves and would be happy simply to consume it as a service offered by someone else.

Lesson 1: Consuming WCF Services

This lesson provides you with the tools you need to start consuming WCF services. Most Web services platforms, WCF included, provide developers with a mechanism for creating an object that can be used to communicate with the service. Such objects are called proxies, or proxy objects, because they are effectively acting as a proxy to the service. In this lesson, the focus is first on the four ways you can create a proxy to a WCF service and then on the details you need to consider to call services in the most effective manner using those proxies.

After this lesson, you will be able to:
- Generate proxy classes to WCF services, using the svcutil command-line utility and Visual Studio.
- Use *ChannelFactory* objects to create proxies dynamically to WCF services.
- Manually define classes whose instances can act as proxies to WCF services.
- Use proxies to call service operations, both synchronously and asynchronously.
- Create and use proxies to communicate with a service over a duplex channel.
- Create and use proxies to communicate with a non-WCF service.

Estimated lesson time: 40 minutes

Creating Proxies and Proxy Classes

WCF provides developers with several mechanisms for creating proxy objects that can be used to communicate with a Web service. This section covers these different approaches.

Generating Proxy Classes from Service Metadata

The most common approach to creating proxies is first to create a class based on the metadata of the service and then instantiate that class to create an actual proxy object. The metadata is typically accessed by engaging in a metadata exchange with the remote service. As Lesson 2 explores further, when the remote service is not a WCF service, the only option for representing that service metadata is through the standard Web Services Description Language (WSDL) approach. If the service is a WCF service, a richer WCF metadata exchange is possible. Either way, there are two ways of exchanging metadata, both of which are covered in this section. In the lab following this lesson, you use these mechanisms.

Using svcutil to Generate a Proxy Class   WCF provides a command-line utility called svcutil that you can use to generate a proxy class to a service. To use it, you must open a Visual Studio command prompt or simply refer to its full path in a regular command prompt. Table 1-1 covers the most commonly used options you will need when using svcutil to generate proxy classes.

Table 4-1 Commonly Used Options for the svcutil Tool

Option	Description
/out:<file>	Specifies the filename for the generated code. Default: derived from the WSDL definition name, WSDL service name, or target namespace of one of the schemas (short form: */o*).
/config:<configFile>	Specifies the filename for the generated config file. Default: output.config.
/mergeConfig	Merges the generated configuration file into an existing file instead of overwriting the existing file.
/language:<language>	Indicates the programming language in which to generate code. Possible language names are *c#, cs, csharp, vb, visualbasic, c++,* and *cpp*. Default: *csharp* (short form: */l*).
/namespace:<targetNamespace, .NETNamespace>	Maps a WSDL or XML schema target namespace to a .NET namespace. Using an asterisk (*) for the target namespace maps all target namespaces without an explicit mapping to the matching .NET namespace. Default: derived from the target namespace of the schema document for Data contracts. The default namespace is used for all other generated types (short form: */n*).
/messageContract	Generates Message contract types (short form: /mc).
/async	Generates both synchronous and asynchronous method signatures. Default: generates only synchronous method signatures (short form: */a*).
/serializer:XmlSerializer	Generates data types that use the *XmlSerializer* for serialization and deserialization.

The following is an example of how you might use the svcutil command to generate a proxy class to an *OrderEntryService* hosted at *http://localhost:8080/orders/*. (The commands are formatted on multiple lines to fit on the printed page.)

```
' VB
svcutil /1:VB /async /config:app.config /mergeConfig
    /namespace:*,SvcUtilProxy /out:ServiceUtilProxy.vb
    http://localhost:8080/orders/
```

```
// C#
svcutil /async /config:app.config /mergeConfig
    /namespace:*,SvcUtilProxy /out:ServiceUtilProxy.cs
    http://localhost:8080/orders/
```

Note a couple of things about this example:

- The default language is C#, so for the Visual Basic version, the language must be specified.

- Asynchronous operations are generated on the proxy because of the */async* option.
- It is common to use a wildcard such as * simply to map all XML namespaces encountered in the service metadata and Data contracts to a single .NET namespace. This is done in the preceding example using the *,*SvcUtilProxy* pair.

MORE INFO More on svcutil

For more information on the svcutil command-line tool, consult the documentation from your local Visual Studio installation or online at *http://msdn.microsoft.com/en-us/library/aa347733.aspx*.

Using Visual Studio to Generate a Proxy Class In Visual Studio, you can add a service reference by right-clicking a project node in Solution Explorer and choosing Add Service Reference, as shown in Figure 4-1.

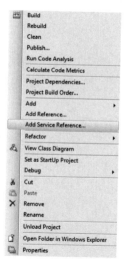

Figure 4-1 Adding a service reference using a context menu

In the resulting dialog box, enter the address of a service endpoint and click Go or click Discover to browse for available services. Click OK to have a proxy class generated for you. Figure 4-2 shows what the Add Service Reference dialog box might look like in the context of using Visual Studio to add a service reference to a task service.

To add asynchronous methods to your generated proxy class and control some of the collection types, first click the Advanced button in the Add Service Reference dialog box. Figure 4-3 shows the resulting Service Reference Settings dialog box.

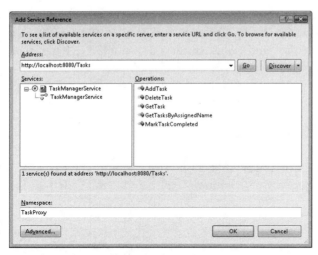

Figure 4-2   The Add Service Reference dialog box

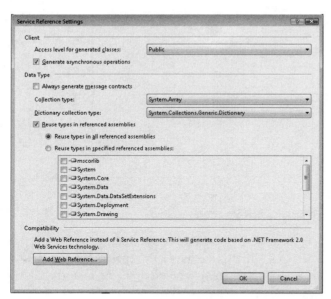

Figure 4-3   The Service Reference Settings dialog box for adding a service reference

Visual Studio uses the same svcutil tool, but it provides you with a friendly interface and takes care of some of the manual steps you need to perform when using svcutil yourself, such as adding the reference to *System.ServiceModel*, adding the resulting proxy code to your project, and so on.

Visual Studio Service Reference vs. svcutil

Which one is the better approach: using Visual Studio or svcutil to create your proxy classes? In many cases, it's a matter of developer preference, but here are a few points to consider:

- Using the svcutil utility gives you the most control.
- Using the svcutil utility requires additional manual steps such as adding the reference to *System.ServiceModel*, adding the resulting proxy code to your project, and so on, that Visual Studio does automatically.
- The svcutil utility can be useful in an automated build scenario in which you want to generate proxy classes as part of the automated build process.

Manually Defining a Proxy Class

As opposed to having a tool generate a proxy class for you, you can manually define a proxy class on your own using the same base classes that the tools use. Suppose you have the following Service contract:

```vb
' VB
<ServiceContract()> _
Public Interface IOrderEntryService
    <OperationContract()> _
    Function SubmitOrder(ByVal order As Order) _
        As OrderAcknowledgement

    ' Etc...
End Interface
```

```csharp
// C#
[ServiceContract()]
public interface IOrderEntryService
{
    [OperationContract()]
    OrderAcknowledgement SumbitOrder(Order order);

    // Etc...
}
```

You could manually define a proxy class based on that contract as follows:

```vb
' VB
Public Class OrderEntryServiceProxy
    Inherits ClientBase(Of IOrderEntryService)
    Implements IOrderEntryService

    Public Sub New(ByVal binding As Binding, _
                ByVal epAddr As EndpointAddress)
```

```
        MyBase.New(binding, epAddr)
    End Sub

    Public Sub New(ByVal endpointConfigurationName As String)
        MyBase.New(endpointConfigurationName)
    End Sub

    Public Function SubmitOrder(ByVal order As Order) _
        As OrderAcknowledgement _
            Implements IOrderEntryService.SubmitOrder
        Return Me.Channel.SubmitOrder(order)
    End Function
End Class

// C#
public class OrderEntryServiceProxy :
        ClientBase<IOrderEntryService>,IOrderEntryService
{
    public OrderEntryServiceProxy(
            Binding binding, EndpointAddress epAddr)
        : base(binding,epAddr)
    {
    }

    public OrderEntryServiceProxy(
            string endpointConfigurationName)
        : base(endpointConfigurationName)
    {
    }

    public OrderAcknowledgement SumbitOrder(Order order)
    {
        return this.Channel.SumbitOrder(order);
    }
}
```

If a callback channel is involved (perhaps the Service contract specifies a Callback contract because at least one of the service operations uses the Duplex message exchange pattern [MEP]), the base class should be *DuplexClientBase* instead of *ClientBase*. There are more steps to setting up a callback channel, as is explained later in this lesson and in the lab that follows.

Dynamically Creating a Proxy

In some cases, you don't need to have a proxy class explicitly defined anywhere because WCF provides the *ChannelFactory* class as a means of dynamically creating a proxy object based on the Service contract alone. Without ever explicitly generating a proxy class or manually defining one, you can create a proxy object, using only the Service contract and the *ChannelFactory* class. The following code shows how this would be done.

```vb
' VB
Dim binding As Binding
binding = New NetTcpBinding

Dim factory As ChannelFactory(Of IOrderEntryService)
factory = New ChannelFactory(Of IOrderEntryService)( _
    binding, "net.tcp://localhost:6789/orders/")

Dim proxy As IOrderEntryService
proxy = factory.CreateChannel()

Try

    Dim order As New Order
    order.Product = "Widget-ABC"
    order.Quantity = 10
    ' Etc...

    Dim ack As OrderAcknowledgement
    ack = proxy.SubmitOrder(order)

    Console.WriteLine( _
        "Order submitted; tracking number: {0}", _
        ack.TrackingNumber)
Catch ex As Exception
    Console.WriteLine("Error: {0}", ex.Message)
End Try
```

```csharp
// C#
Binding binding = new NetTcpBinding();
ChannelFactory<IOrderEntryService> factory;
factory = new ChannelFactory<IOrderEntryService>(
    binding, "net.tcp://localhost:6789/orders/");

try
{

    IOrderEntryService proxy = factory.CreateChannel();

    Order order = new Order();
    order.Product = "Widget-ABC";
    order.Quantity = 10;
    // Etc...

    OrderAcknowledgement ack = proxy.SumbitOrder(order);

    Console.WriteLine(
        "Order submitted; tracking number: {0}",
        ack.TrackingNumber);
}

catch (Exception ex)
{
    Console.WriteLine("Error: {0}",ex.Message);
}
```

BEST PRACTICES   Generate proxy classes from service metadata

One of the tenets of service orientation is that consumers should depend only on a service's schema and not on any of the service's classes. The only way consumers of a service should be coupled to the service is through the schema of the messages they must exchange with the service. That is certainly better than some of the middleware technologies of the past such as DCOM, CORBA, and .NET Remoting, which required consumers to have a code or binary-level dependency on the service and the request and response objects.

If you manually create proxy classes or use the *ChannelFactory* class to create proxy objects dynamically, you need to have access to the WCF Service contract. If you are not getting access to the service contract by generating code from service metadata, that means you must have a code or binary-level reference to the WCF Service contract. Avoid that form of coupling when building services. Always strive to minimize the coupling between a service and its consumers. In short, always generate proxy classes from service metadata, either by using svcutil or by adding a service reference in Visual Studio.

Using Proxies to Call Services

In one sense, using a proxy to call a service is as simple as calling a method on the proxy object, which the WCF plumbing will then translate into a message and send the message to the wire-level transport layer. Suppose you have the following service:

```vb
' VB
<DataContract()> _
Public Class Order
    <DataMember()> _
    Public Product As String

    <DataMember()> _
    Public Quantity As Integer

    ' Etc...
End Class

<DataContract()> _
Public Class OrderAcknowledgement
    <DataMember()> _
    Public TrackingNumber As String

    ' Etc...
End Class

<ServiceContract()> _
Public Interface IOrderEntryService
    <OperationContract()> _
    Function SubmitOrder(ByVal order As Order) _
        As OrderAcknowledgement
```

```vb
        ' Etc...
    End Interface

    Public Class OrderEntryService
        Implements IOrderEntryService

        Public Function SubmitOrder(ByVal order As Order) _
            As OrderAcknowledgement _
                Implements IOrderEntryService.SubmitOrder
            Dim ack As New OrderAcknowledgement
            ack.TrackingNumber = "alpha-bravo-123"
            Return ack
        End Function

        ' Etc...
    End Class
```

```csharp
// C#
[DataContract()]
public class Order
{
    [DataMemberAttribute()]
    public string Product;

    [DataMemberAttribute()]
    public int Quantity;

    // Etc...
}

[DataContract()]
public class OrderAcknowledgement
{
    [DataMemberAttribute()]
    public string TrackingNumber;

    // Etc...
}

[ServiceContract()]
public interface IOrderEntryService
{
    [OperationContract()]
    OrderAcknowledgement SumbitOrder(Order order);

    // Etc...
}

public class OrderEntryService : IOrderEntryService
{
    public OrderAcknowledgement SumbitOrder(Order order)
    {
        OrderAcknowledgement ack = new OrderAcknowledgement();
```

```
        ack.TrackingNumber = "alpha-bravo-123";
        return ack;
    }

    // Etc...
}
```

You could use the proxy to call such a service in a number of ways. First, you could use the *ChannelFactory* class to create a proxy dynamically, as shown here. (In this section, the code that differs among the three methods of using a proxy is shown in bold.)

```vb
' VB
Dim binding As Binding
binding = New NetTcpBinding
Dim factory As ChannelFactory(Of IOrderEntryService)
factory = New ChannelFactory(Of IOrderEntryService)( _
    binding, "net.tcp://localhost:6789/orders/")
Dim proxy As IOrderEntryService
proxy = factory.CreateChannel()
Dim order As New Order
order.Product = "Widget-ABC"
order.Quantity = 10
' Etc...

Dim ack As OrderAcknowledgement
ack = proxy.SubmitOrder(order)

Console.WriteLine( _
    "Order submitted; tracking number: {0}", _
    ack.TrackingNumber)
```

```csharp
// C#
Binding binding = new NetTcpBinding();
ChannelFactory<IOrderEntryService> factory;
factory = new ChannelFactory<IOrderEntryService>(
    binding, "net.tcp://localhost:6789/orders/");
IOrderEntryService proxy = factory.CreateChannel();
Order order = new Order();
order.Product = "Widget-ABC";
order.Quantity = 10;
// Etc...

OrderAcknowledgement ack = proxy.SumbitOrder(order);

Console.WriteLine(
    "Order submitted; tracking number: {0}",
        ack.TrackingNumber);
```

Second, you could manually define a proxy class as follows:

```vb
' VB
Public Class OrderEntryServiceProxy
    Inherits ClientBase(Of IOrderEntryService)
```

```vb
    Implements IOrderEntryService

    Public Sub New(ByVal binding As Binding, _
                   ByVal epAddr As EndpointAddress)
        MyBase.New(binding, epAddr)
    End Sub

    Public Sub New(ByVal endpointConfigurationName As String)
        MyBase.New(endpointConfigurationName)
    End Sub

    Public Function SubmitOrder(ByVal order As Order) _
        As OrderAcknowledgement _
            Implements IOrderEntryService.SubmitOrder
        Return Me.Channel.SubmitOrder(order)
    End Function
End Class
```

```csharp
// C#
public class OrderEntryServiceProxy :
        ClientBase<IOrderEntryService>,IOrderEntryService
{
    public OrderEntryServiceProxy(
            Binding binding, EndpointAddress epAddr)
        :base(binding,epAddr)
    {
    }

    public OrderEntryServiceProxy(
            string endpointConfigurationName)
        : base(endpointConfigurationName)
    {
    }

    public OrderAcknowledgement SumbitOrder(Order order)
    {
        return this.Channel.SumbitOrder(order);
    }
}
```

You would use the manually defined proxy class like this:

```vb
' VB
Dim binding As Binding
binding = New NetTcpBinding
Dim epAddr As EndpointAddress
epAddr = New EndpointAddress( _
    "net.tcp://localhost:6789/orders/")
Dim proxy As IOrderEntryService
proxy = New OrderEntryServiceProxy(binding, epAddr)
Dim order As New Order
order.Product = "Widget-ABC"
order.Quantity = 10
```

```
' Etc...

Dim ack As OrderAcknowledgement
ack = proxy.SubmitOrder(order)

Console.WriteLine( _
    "Order submitted; tracking number: {0}", _
    ack.TrackingNumber)
```

```csharp
// C#
Binding binding = new NetTcpBinding();
EndpointAddress epAddr = new EndpointAddress(
    "net.tcp://localhost:6789/orders/");
IOrderEntryService proxy =
    new OrderEntryServiceProxy(binding,epAddr);  Order order = new Order();
order.Product = "Widget-ABC";
order.Quantity = 10;
// Etc...

OrderAcknowledgement ack = proxy.SumbitOrder(order);

Console.WriteLine("Order submitted; tracking number: {0}",
    ack.TrackingNumber);
```

Finally, if you used either svcutil or Visual Studio to generate a proxy class, you would use the generated proxy class like this:

```
' VB
Dim proxy As OrderEntryServiceClient
proxy = New OrderEntryServiceClient()
Dim order As New Order
order.Product = "Widget-ABC"
order.Quantity = 10
' Etc...

Dim ack As OrderAcknowledgement
ack = proxy.SubmitOrder(order)

Console.WriteLine( _
    "Order submitted; tracking number: {0}", _
    ack.TrackingNumber)
```

```csharp
// C#
OrderEntryServiceClient proxy = new OrderEntryServiceClient();
Order order = new Order();
order.Product = "Widget-ABC";
order.Quantity = 10;
// Etc...

OrderAcknowledgement ack = proxy.SumbitOrder(order);

Console.WriteLine("Order submitted; tracking number: {0}",
    ack.TrackingNumber);
```

Recall that in Chapter 1, "Contracts," it was suggested that to design services well you must let go of many of the concepts of object-oriented programming. This is not only true for the design of the document-centric messages going in and out of your service; you must also always keep in mind what is being done for you by the plumbing. When you make a method call on a proxy, the WCF plumbing translates your method call into a message that it sends over the wire-level transport layer, so you always need to be aware of issues such as:

- How slow that might be in comparison to a normal method call on an in-process object.
- How network communication troubles could result in an inability to communicate with the remote service.

The following sections cover some of the other considerations you need to keep in mind to use proxies effectively to communicate with a service.

Invoking Service Operations Asynchronously

In many cases, a method call on a proxy, which is translated into a message that is sent to a remote service, might take longer than the consuming application can reasonably wait. The reason for the slowness can be poor network bandwidth, large message size, or a combination thereof. In GUI applications, you don't want to keep the UI unresponsive for any length of time while the application waits for a response from the service. In non-GUI applications as well, the call to a service typically must be done as quickly as possible.

A good solution is to invoke the service operation asynchronously. You can use the */async* option on svcutil or in Visual Studio. For the latter, click Advanced in the Add Service Reference dialog box, and then select the Generate Asynchronous Methods check box in the Service Reference Settings dialog box to generate a *Begin-* and *End-* pair of methods for each service operation. The method pairs together support the asynchronous invocation of a service operation.

To show how these method pairs are used, suppose you have generated a proxy to *Order-EntryService* with asynchronous methods. In addition to the *SubmitOrder* operation on the proxy class, there would be a corresponding *BeginSubmitOrder* and *EndSubmitOrder* method pair. This *Begin-* and *End-* method pair could be used as follows to invoke the *SubmitOrder* operation asynchronously:

```vb
' VB
Dim proxy As OrderEntryServiceClient
proxy = New OrderEntryServiceClient()

Dim order As New Order
order.Product = "Widget-ABC"
order.Quantity = 10
' Etc...

Dim cb As AsyncCallback
```

```
cb = New AsyncCallback(AddressOf HandleCallback)

proxy.BeginSubmitOrder(order, cb, proxy)

Console.WriteLine( _
    "Order submitted asynchronously; waiting for callback")
```

```
// C#
OrderEntryServiceClient proxy = new OrderEntryServiceClient();

Order order = new Order();
order.Product = "Widget-ABC";
order.Quantity = 10;
// Etc...

AsyncCallback cb = new AsyncCallback(HandleCallback);
proxy.BeginSumbitOrder(order, cb, proxy);

Console.WriteLine(
    "Order submitted asynchronously; waiting for callback");
```

The *HandleCallback* method, which might be defined as shown here, is called back when the asynchronously invoked operation completes:

```
' VB
Public Shared Sub HandleCallback( _
        ByVal result As IAsyncResult)
    Dim proxy As OrderEntryServiceClient
    proxy = result.AsyncState

    Dim ack As OrderAcknowledgement
    ack = proxy.EndSubmitOrder(result)
    Console.WriteLine( _
        "Order submitted; tracking number: {0}", _
        ack.TrackingNumber)

End Sub
```

```
// C#
static void HandleCallback(IAsyncResult result)
{
    OrderEntryServiceClient proxy =
        result.AsyncState as OrderEntryServiceClient;
    OrderAcknowledgement ack = proxy.EndSumbitOrder(result);
    Console.WriteLine(
        "Order submitted; tracking number: {0}",
        ack.TrackingNumber);
}
```

In the lab that follows this lesson, you use this technique.

Closing Proxies

It is a good practice to close service proxies whenever the client is finished using them. One of the main reasons for doing so is that when a session has been established between the client and the service, closing the proxy not only closes the connection to the service but also terminates the session with the service. The importance of this will become clearer when sessions are covered in Chapter 10, "Sessions and Instancing."

Instead of calling the *Close* method explicitly, you can also use the *Dispose* method, which will close the proxy as well. As usual, the advantage of the *Dispose* method is that you can use it in the context of a *using* statement so that it is called implicitly even if an exception occurs:

```
' VB
Using proxy As MyServiceClient = New MyServiceClient()
    proxy.SomeOp1()
End Using
```

```
// C#
using(MyServiceClient proxy = new MyServiceClient())
{
    proxy.SomeOp1();
}
```

Alternatively, if the object reference's type is the Service contract interface, as opposed to a concrete proxy class, you can use the following variation:

```
' VB
Dim proxy As IMyService
proxy = New MyServiceClient()
Using proxy As IDisposable
    proxy.SomeOp1()
End Using
```

```
// C#
IMyService proxy = new MyServiceClient();
using (proxy as IDisposable)
{
    proxy.SomeOp1();
}
```

Duplex Channels with Proxies

To enable a proxy to communicate using a Duplex, or callback, channel, you must perform the following steps:

- Define a class that implements the Callback contract.
- Construct an instance of the class implementing the Callback contract and pass the instance to an *InstanceContext* constructor.

■ Pass the *InstanceContext* object to the constructor of the proxy class.

■ The proxy class must inherit from *DuplexClientBase* instead of from *ClientBase*.

Typically, the easiest way to handle this is to wrap the autogenerated proxy with another class that deals with the *InstanceContext* details and acts as the callback object (implementing the Callback contract). In Exercise 4, "Consume a Service Using a Callback Channel," of this lesson, you step through this process in greater detail.

Exam Tip   Pay close attention to the base type of your proxy classes. If you are defining a proxy that uses OneWay or Request/Response MEPs, the right base class is *ClientBase<IMyContract>*, where *IMyContract* is your Service contract. If your proxy uses the Duplex MEP, the proxy class must inherit from *DuplexClientBase<IMyContract>*.

Service Agents

It is very common to want to wrap usage of a proxy in another class that has some additional capabilities in terms of interacting with the remote service. The generic term for these more capable objects that facilitate access to a remote service is *service agent*. The following are some reasons you might want to wrap access to a proxy in a service agent:

■ The client might have limited or unpredictable connectivity, or the consumer might simply need to operate in an offline mode.

■ Performance problems associated with service calls might necessitate actions such as client-side caching, request batching, aggregate result disassembly, and so on.

■ A proxy class might be very awkward or inefficient to work with, for example, taking several calls that could be wrapped up into one by an agent.

In Exercise 4 in this lesson, you will see a very simple example of when you might use an agent. In the lab that follows Lesson 2, you will see an even better example of a service agent being used.

Quick Check

1. If you want to generate a proxy class that uses the *XmlSerializer*, which of the four methods for generating a proxy would be best to use?
2. Does it ever make sense to invoke a OneWay operation asynchronously?

Quick Check Answers

1. The only way to generate a proxy if you want to use the *XmlSerializer* is to use the svcutil command-line tool with the */serializer:XmlSerializer* option. Adding a service reference in Visual Studio does not support this option. As long as the contract specifies usage of the *XmlSerializer*, dynamically creating a proxy object by using the *ChannelFactory* class would also ensure that the right serializer is used, but in that case, you are generating an object dynamically rather than a class. Similarly, if you hand-code a proxy class, you are not technically *generating* a class and, again, the right serializer depends on whether the contract is declared to use the *XmlSerializer*.

2. Yes. If there is a situation in which a message being sent to a service in a OneWay operation was very large and therefore time-consuming, it can still make sense to invoke the operation asynchronously. Keep in mind that, as was discussed in Chapter 1, OneWay calls on the proxy complete only when the dispatcher on the service end has successfully dispatched the incoming message to a call on a service type instance. If the message is large, this can take longer to happen than you would like to wait in a synchronous invocation setting, thereby making asynchronous invocation an attractive alternative.

Lab: Creating and Using WCF Service Proxies

In this lab, you will use the techniques that have been covered to create WCF proxies to WCF services. The lab focuses on the different ways in which the proxy classes or objects can be created and on some of the key points for each way that you should consider in using the proxies effectively. In the first three exercises, you create proxies to communicate with the Task Manager service that was first built in Chapter 1. In the fourth exercise, you create and use a proxy that interacts with the service by using a Duplex, or callback, channel. This lab requires that you start a WCF service, so you must have the appropriate permissions to do so. You might want to run Visual Studio as an Administrator.

▶ **Exercise 1   Create a Proxy Dynamically**

In this exercise, you will use the *ChannelFactory* class to create a proxy object dynamically to communicate with the Task Manager service.

1. Navigate to the *<InstallHome>*/Chapter4/Lesson1/Exercise1/*<language>*/Before directory and double-click the Exercise1.sln file to open the solution in Visual Studio.

    The solution consists of four projects:

2. Because the solution still contains the Windows Forms client that you used in Chapter 1 to consume the Task Manger service, first explore the code there to see how that proxy code is used. After you have explored the code in this sample application, you can start creating your own proxies.

3. Add a new Console project called **DynGenProxy** to the solution.

4. To this new Console project, add references to both *System.ServiceModel* and *System .Runtime.Serialization*.

5. Add project references to both *Tasks.Services* and *Tasks.Entities*.

6. In the main code file (Program.cs or Module1.vb as appropriate), add the following imports:

```vb
' VB
Imports System.ServiceModel
Imports System.ServiceModel.Channels
Imports Tasks.Entities
Imports Tasks.Services
```

```csharp
// C#
using System.ServiceModel;
using System.ServiceModel.Channels;
using Tasks.Entities;
using Tasks.Services;
```

7. Define the *Main* method (*Program.Main* or *Module1.Main* as appropriate) so that it matches the following code, which uses the *ChannelFactory* class to create a proxy dynamically to the task service:

```vb
' VB
Sub Main()
    Dim binding As Binding
    binding = New BasicHttpBinding

    Dim factory As ChannelFactory(Of ITaskManagerService)
    factory = New ChannelFactory(Of ITaskManagerService)( _
        binding, "http://localhost:8080/Tasks/TaskManager")

    Dim proxy As ITaskManagerService
    proxy = factory.CreateChannel()

    Try
        Dim task As New Task()
        task.CreatedBy = "Vicki"
        task.AssignedTo = "Ian"
        task.DateCreated = DateTime.Now
        task.DateLastModified = task.DateCreated
        task.Description = "Clean your room"
        task.DueDate = DateTime.Now.AddDays(3)

        Dim ack As TaskAcknowledgement
```

```
                ack = proxy.AddTask(task)

                Console.WriteLine( _
                    "Task number {0} added to service", _
                    ack.TaskNumber)
            Catch ex As Exception
                Console.WriteLine("Error: {0}", ex.Message)
            End Try
        End Sub
```

```csharp
// C#
static void Main(string[] args)
{
    Binding binding = new BasicHttpBinding();

    ChannelFactory<ITaskManagerService> factory;
    factory = new ChannelFactory<ITaskManagerService>(
            binding, "http://localhost:8080/Tasks/TaskManager");

    try
    {
        ITaskManagerService proxy = factory.CreateChannel();

        Task task = new Task();
        task.CreatedBy = "Vicki";
        task.AssignedTo = "Ian";
        task.DateCreated = DateTime.Now;
        task.DateLastModified = task.DateCreated;
        task.Description = "Clean your room";
        task.DueDate = DateTime.Now.AddDays(3);

        TaskAcknowledgement ack = proxy.AddTask(task);

        Console.WriteLine(
            "Task number {0} added to service",
            ack.TaskNumber);
    }

    catch (Exception ex)
    {
        Console.WriteLine("Error: {0}",ex.Message);
    }
}
```

8. Build the solution.

9. Making sure the ServiceConsoleHost project is the startup project, start the service.

10. Make DynGenProxy the startup project and run this Console project.

    You should see that the Console application successfully submits a task to the service.

11. Leave the task service running; you will need it to be running for the next two exercises.

▶ **Exercise 2   Generate a Proxy Class, Using svcutil**

In this exercise, you will use the svcutil command-line utility to generate a proxy class that you then use to communicate with the Task Manager service. You also asynchronously invoke one of the operations on this service, using an instance of the autogenerated proxy class.

1. Navigate to the *<InstallHome>*/Chapter4/Lesson1/Exercise2/*<language>*/Before directory and double-click the Exercise2.sln file to open the solution in Visual Studio.

   The solution consists of the four projects you started with in Exercise 1, "Create a Proxy Dynamically."

2. Add a new Console project called **SvcUtilProxy** to the solution.

3. To this new Console project, add a new application configuration file item called **app.config**.

4. Open a Visual Studio command prompt to the directory in which this project resides, in this case, *<InstallHome>*/Chapter4/Lesson1/Exercise2/*<language>*/Before/SvcUtilProxy.

5. With the service still running from step 9 in Exercise 1, execute the following command to generate a proxy class. (Enter it as a single command; it is formatted here on multiple lines to fit on the printed page.)

   During this step, you might be informed that the configuration file must be reloaded; if so, just click Yes.

   ```
   ' VB
   svcutil /l:VB /async /config:app.config
       /namespace:*,SvcUtilProxy /out:TaskServiceProxy.vb
       http://localhost:8080/Tasks
   ```

   ```
   // C#
   svcutil /async /config:app.config
       /namespace:*,SvcUtilProxy /out:TaskServiceProxy.cs
       http://localhost:8080/Tasks
   ```

6. Add the TaskServiceProxy (.cs or .vb as appropriate) file, which was just generated by the svcutil command, to the SvcUtilProxy project.

7. To the SvcUtilProxy project, add references to both *System.ServiceModel* and *System.Runtime.Serialization*. If you are working in C#, also add a project reference to *Tasks.Entities*.

8. In the main code file (Program.cs or Module1.vb as appropriate), add the following imports, noting that there is an intentional difference between the Visual Basic and C# versions, stemming from the different ways project references are handled in Visual Basic.NET compared to C#:

   ```
   ' VB
   Imports System.ServiceModel
   Imports System.ServiceModel.Channels
   Imports SvcUtilProxy.SvcUtilProxy
   ```

```
// C#
using System.ServiceModel;
using System.ServiceModel.Channels;
using Tasks.Entities;
```

To experiment with the mechanics of asynchronously invoking a service operation by using a proxy, you first need to define a function that will be called back when the asynchronously invoked operation completes.

9. Define the following function directly below the *Main* method in the main code file (Program.cs or Module1.vb as appropriate):

```
' VB
Sub HandleTaskAdded(ByVal ar As IAsyncResult)
    Dim proxy As TaskManagerServiceClient
    proxy = CType(ar.AsyncState, TaskManagerServiceClient)

    Dim ack As TaskAcknowledgement
    ack = proxy.EndAddTask(ar)

    Console.WriteLine( _
        "Task number {0} was added to service", _
        ack.TaskNumber)

End Sub
```

```
// C#
static void HandleTaskAdded(IAsyncResult ar)
{
    TaskManagerServiceClient proxy = ar.AsyncState
        as TaskManagerServiceClient;

    TaskAcknowledgement ack = proxy.EndAddTask(ar);

    Console.WriteLine(
        "Task number {0} was added to service",
        ack.TaskNumber);
}
```

10. Define the *Main* method (*Program.Main* or *Module1.Main* as appropriate) so that it matches the following code, which instantiates the proxy class generated by the svcutil command and invokes the *AddTask* operation asynchronously:

```
' VB
Sub Main()
    Dim proxy As TaskManagerServiceClient
    proxy = New TaskManagerServiceClient()

    Try
        Dim task As New Task()
        task.CreatedBy = "Eric"
```

```vbnet
        task.AssignedTo = "Ian"
        task.DateCreated = DateTime.Now
        task.DateLastModified = task.DateCreated
        task.Description = "Practice your saxophone"
        task.DueDate = DateTime.Now.AddDays(3)

        Dim cb As AsyncCallback
        cb = New AsyncCallback(AddressOf HandleTaskAdded)
        proxy.BeginAddTask(task, cb, proxy)

        Console.WriteLine( _
            "Asynchronously adding a task to the service; " + _
            "Press Enter to exit")
        Console.ReadLine()
    Catch ex As Exception
        Console.WriteLine("Error: {0}", ex.Message)
    End Try
End Sub
```

```csharp
// C#
static void Main(string[] args)
{
    try
    {
        TaskManagerServiceClient proxy =
            new TaskManagerServiceClient();

        Task task = new Task();
        task.CreatedBy = "Eric";
        task.AssignedTo = "Ian";
        task.DateCreated = DateTime.Now;
        task.DateLastModified = task.DateCreated;
        task.Description = "Practice your saxophone";
        task.DueDate = DateTime.Now.AddDays(3);

        AsyncCallback cb = new AsyncCallback(HandleTaskAdded);
        proxy.BeginAddTask(task,cb,proxy);

        Console.WriteLine(
            "Asynchronously adding a task to the service; " +
            "Press Enter to exit");

        Console.ReadLine();
    }

    catch (Exception ex)
    {
        Console.WriteLine("Error: {0}", ex.Message);
    }
}
```

NOTE Usage of /async

This exercise uses the */async* option on the svcutil command to generate operations on the proxy that support asynchronous invocation. Specifically, the *BeginAddTask* and *EndAddTask* operations are generated. They are used in tandem by this exercise's version of the consumer to handle the asynchronous invocation of the *AddTask* operation.

---

11. Build the solution.

12. Making sure the service is still running and that SvcUtilProxy is the startup project, run this Console project.

    You should see that the Console application successfully submits a task to the service asynchronously and that the *HandleTaskAdded* callback method is called when the operation completes.

13. Again, leave the Task Manager service running for the next exercise.

▶ **Exercise 3   Generating a Proxy Class by Adding a Service Reference in Visual Studio**

In this exercise, you will use Visual Studio to generate a proxy class by adding a service reference. You instantiate the resulting proxy class and use the instance to communicate with the Task Manager service, this time adding a *FaultException* handler that shows how you access the *FaultInfo* class, which the service contract has declared it might issue. (Chapter 9, "When Simple Is Not Sufficient," discusses in detail handling faults and exceptions on clients.)

1. Navigate to the *<InstallHome>*/Chapter4/Lesson1/Exercise3/*<language>*/Before directory and double-click the Exercise3.sln file to open the solution in Visual Studio.

    The solution consists of the four projects you started with in Exercise 1.

2. Add a new Console project called **VSProxy** to the solution.

3. To this new Console project, add a service reference, making sure the Task Manager service is running, by right-clicking the project node in Solution Explorer and choosing Add Service Reference.

4. In the Add Service Reference dialog box, enter the **http://localhost:8080/Tasks** URL at which the service is hosted and click the Go button to list the services at that URL. After you enter **Tasks** for the namespace, click OK.

    Note that this step takes care of adding the app.config file and any needed references to the project.

5. In the main code file (Program.cs or Module1.vb as appropriate), add the following import statements:

```
' VB
Imports VSProxy.Tasks
Imports System.ServiceModel
```

```
// C#
using VSProxy.Tasks;
using System.ServiceModel;
```

6. Define the *Main* method (*Program.Main* or *Module1.Main* as appropriate) so that it matches the following code, which instantiates the proxy class generated by Visual Studio when you added the service reference:

```vb
' VB
Sub Main()
    Dim proxy As TaskManagerServiceClient
    proxy = New TaskManagerServiceClient()

    Try
        Dim task As New Task()
        task.CreatedBy = "Eric"
        task.AssignedTo = "Vicki"
        task.DateCreated = DateTime.Now
        task.DateLastModified = task.DateCreated
        task.Description = "Do the laundry"
        task.DueDate = DateTime.Now.AddDays(3)

        Dim ack As TaskAcknowledgement
        ack = proxy.AddTask(task)

        Dim taskNum As Integer
        taskNum = ack.TaskNumber
        Console.WriteLine( _
            "Task number {0} added to service", _
            taskNum)

        ' Now try to mark that same task
        ' as completed:
        proxy.MarkTaskCompleted(taskNum)

    Catch fault As FaultException(Of FaultInfo)
        Console.WriteLine("Error: {0}", fault.Detail.Reason)
    End Try
End Sub
```

```csharp
// C#
static void Main(string[] args)
{
    try
    {
        TaskManagerServiceClient proxy = new TaskManagerServiceClient();

        Task task = new Task();
        task.CreatedBy = "Eric";
        task.AssignedTo = "Vicki";
        task.DateCreated = DateTime.Now;
```

```
    task.DateLastModified = task.DateCreated;
    task.Description = "Do the laundry";
    task.DueDate = DateTime.Now.AddDays(3);

    TaskAcknowledgement ack = proxy.AddTask(task);

    int taskNum = ack.TaskNumber;
    Console.WriteLine(
        "Task number {0} added to service",
        taskNum);

    // Now try to mark that same task
    // as completed:
    proxy.MarkTaskCompleted(taskNum);
}

catch (FaultException<FaultInfo> fault)
{
    Console.WriteLine("Fault: {0}",fault.Detail.Reason);
}
}
```

NOTE   Usage of faults as part of the Service contract

This exercise's version of a consumer uses a *FaultException<FaultInfo>* exception, based on the Service contract's specification that the *MarkTaskCompleted* operation could issue a fault of type *FaultInfo*. This code shows how to access the *FaultInfo* object and its *Reason* property.

---

7. Build the solution.

8. Making sure the service is still running and that VSProxy is the startup project, run this Console project.

    You should see that it successfully submits a task to the service. You might also try modifying the code in step 6 to force an exception. This can be done easily by changing the call to *MarkTaskCompleted* to take a number for which you know there isn't a valid task, for instance, 111. Finally, you can shut down the Task Manager service.

▶ **Exercise 4   Consume a Service Using a Duplex, or Callback, Channel**

1. Chapter 1, in the section titled "Duplex," discussed a simple Hello World Service contract and service type that used a Duplex MEP by setting up a callback contract. In this exercise, you will take that as a starting point and build on it to practice going through the steps required to create a proxy that can consume the Greeting service by communicating with it using a two-way duplex (or callback) channel. Following is the code that defines the Service contract, the Callback contract, and the service type in which the Callback contract is accessed and called. You can find this code in the Services (.cs or .vb as appropriate) file when you open the solution for this lab.

```vb
' VB
Imports System.ServiceModel
Imports System.ServiceModel.Channels

<ServiceContract()> _
Public Interface IGreetingHandler
    <OperationContract(IsOneWay:=True)> _
    Sub GreetingProduced(ByVal greeting As String)
End Interface

<ServiceContract(CallbackContract:= _
                GetType(IGreetingHandler))> _
Public Interface IGreetingService
    <OperationContract(IsOneWay:=True)> _
    Sub RequestGreeting(ByVal name As String)
End Interface

<ServiceBehavior(InstanceContextMode := _
        InstanceContextMode.PerSession)> _
Public Class GreetingService
    Implements IGreetingService

    Public Sub RequestGreeting(ByVal name As String) _
            Implements IGreetingService.RequestGreeting
        Console.WriteLine("In GreetingService.RequestGreeting")
        Dim callbackHandler As IGreetingHandler
        callbackHandler = _
            OperationContext.Current.GetCallbackChannel( _
                Of IGreetingHandler)()
        callbackHandler.GreetingProduced("Hello " + name)
    End Sub
End Class
```

```csharp
// C#
using System.ServiceModel;
using System.ServiceModel.Channels;

[ServiceContract]
interface IGreetingHandler
{
    [OperationContract(IsOneWay = true)]
    void GreetingProduced(string greeting);
}

[ServiceContract(CallbackContract =
    typeof(IGreetingHandler))]
interface IGreetingService
{
    [OperationContract(IsOneWay = true)]
    void RequestGreeting(string name);
}
```

```
[ServiceBehavior(InstanceContextMode =
        InstanceContextMode.PerSession)]
class GreetingService : IGreetingService
{
    public void RequestGreeting(string name)
    {
        Console.WriteLine("In GreetingService.RequestGreeting");
        IGreetingHandler callbackHandler =
            OperationContext.Current.GetCallbackChannel<IGreetingHandler>();
        callbackHandler.GreetingProduced("Hello " + name);
    }
}
```

In this exercise, you not only create a proxy, but you also use the concept of an agent discussed in this lesson to create a simple agent that wraps the proxy and takes care of the details required both to set up the callback channel and implement the Callback contract. Finally, this lab also uses the technique of manually defining a proxy class to a service.

2. Navigate to the *<InstallHome>*/Chapter4/Lesson1/Exercise4/*<language>*/Before directory and double-click the Exercise4.sln file to open the solution in Visual Studio.

   The solution consists of only one project, a Console project in which you define both the client and the service, and you configure the endpoints in code rather than in a configuration file. You wouldn't do this in a production setting, but it is good to see how it's done to simplify code you might use to experiment with WCF. In this case, the focus is on the mechanics of creating a callback proxy, and everything else is simplified.

3. In the Program (.cs or .vb as appropriate) file, manually define a *GreetingServiceProxy* class (above the *Program* class) that you'll use to act as the proxy to the service. The class should be as follows:

```vb
' VB
Public Class GreetingServiceProxy
    Inherits DuplexClientBase(Of IGreetingService)
    Implements IGreetingService

    Public Sub New(ByVal inputInstance As InstanceContext)
        MyBase.New(inputInstance, New NetTcpBinding(), _
            New EndpointAddress("net.tcp://localhost:6789/service"))
    End Sub

    Public Sub RequestGreeting(ByVal name As String) _
            Implements IGreetingService.RequestGreeting
        Me.Channel.RequestGreeting(name)
    End Sub
End Class
```

```csharp
// C#
class GreetingServiceProxy : DuplexClientBase<IGreetingService>,
                             IGreetingService
{
```

```
public GreetingServiceProxy(InstanceContext inputInstance)
    : base(inputInstance, new NetTcpBinding(),
        new EndpointAddress("net.tcp://localhost:6789/service"))
{
}

public void RequestGreeting(string name)
{
    this.Channel.RequestGreeting(name);
}
}
```

4. In the same file, below the proxy class, define a *GreetingServiceAgent* class that wraps an instance of the proxy class you just defined. This agent class also sets up the instancing context for the proxy in its constructor, and it implements the Callback contract.

The class should be as follows:

```
' VB
Public Class GreetingServiceAgent
    Implements IGreetingService, IGreetingHandler, IDisposable

    Public Sub New()
        Try
            ' Set up instance context and pass it to proxy:
            Dim context As New InstanceContext(Me)
            _proxy = New GreetingServiceProxy(context)
            _proxy.Open()
        Catch ex As Exception
            _proxy = Nothing
        End Try
    End Sub

    Public Sub RequestGreeting(ByVal name As String) _
            Implements IGreetingService.RequestGreeting
        If Not _proxy Is Nothing Then
            _proxy.RequestGreeting(name)
        End If
    End Sub

    Public Sub GreetingProduced(ByVal greeting As String) _
            Implements IGreetingHandler.GreetingProduced
        Console.WriteLine( _
            "Called back with greeting: {0}", greeting)
    End Sub

    Public Sub Dispose() Implements IDisposable.Dispose
        If Not _proxy Is Nothing Then
            _proxy.Close()
        End If
    End Sub

    Private _proxy As GreetingServiceProxy
```

```
End Class

// C#
class GreetingServiceAgent : IGreetingService,
                             IGreetingHandler, IDisposable
{
    public GreetingServiceAgent()
    {
        try
        {
            // Set up instance context and pass it to proxy:
            InstanceContext context = new InstanceContext(this);
            _proxy = new GreetingServiceProxy(context);
            _proxy.Open();
        }

        catch
        {
            _proxy = null;
        }
    }

    public void Dispose()
    {
        if (_proxy != null)
            _proxy.Close();
    }

    public void RequestGreeting(string name)
    {
        if (_proxy != null)
            _proxy.RequestGreeting(name);
    }

    public void GreetingProduced(string greeting)
    {
        Console.WriteLine(
                "Called back with greeting: {0}", greeting);
    }

    private GreetingServiceProxy _proxy;
}
```

5. In the same file, in the *try* block of the *Main* method of the *Program* class, write the following code to call the agent:

```
' VB
Dim agent As New GreetingServiceAgent
agent.RequestGreeting("Sally")
```

```
// C#
GreetingServiceAgent agent = new GreetingServiceAgent();
agent.RequestGreeting("Sally");
```

For the sake of completeness, here is the Program class listing in its entirety:

```vb
' VB
Public Class Program

    Public Shared Sub Main()
        Dim t As Thread
        t = New Thread(New ThreadStart( _
                AddressOf Program.RunService))
        t.Start()
        autoEvent.WaitOne()

        Try
            Dim agent As New GreetingServiceAgent
            agent.RequestGreeting("Sally")
        Catch ex As Exception
            Console.WriteLine("Error: {0}", ex.Message)
        End Try

    End Sub

    Public Shared Sub RunService()
        Dim host As ServiceHost
        host = New ServiceHost(GetType(GreetingService))

        host.AddServiceEndpoint(GetType(IGreetingService), _
                New NetTcpBinding(), "net.tcp://localhost:6789/service")

        host.Open()
        autoEvent.Set()

        Console.WriteLine("Press Enter to exit")
        Console.ReadLine()
    End Sub

    Public Shared autoEvent As AutoResetEvent = New AutoResetEvent(False)
End Class
```

```csharp
// C#
class Program
{
    static void Main(string[] args)
    {
        new Thread(new ThreadStart(RunService)).Start();
        autoEvent.WaitOne();

        try
        {
            GreetingServiceAgent agent = new GreetingServiceAgent();
            agent.RequestGreeting("Sally");
        }

        catch (Exception ex)
```

```
        {
            Console.WriteLine("Error: {0}", ex.Message);
        }
    }

    static void RunService()
    {
        ServiceHost host = new ServiceHost(typeof(GreetingService));
        host.AddServiceEndpoint(typeof(IGreetingService),
            new NetTcpBinding(), "net.tcp://localhost:6789/service");
        host.Open();
        autoEvent.Set();
        Console.WriteLine("Press Enter to exit");
        Console.ReadLine();
    }

    static AutoResetEvent autoEvent = new AutoResetEvent(false);
}
```

6. Build and run the application.

   You should see that both the service and the callback object, which in this case is your agent instance, are successfully called.

Lesson Summary

- Both the command-line utility svcutil and Visual Studio can be used to generate proxy classes from a service's metadata, whose instances can be used as proxies to a service.
- Proxy classes can be manually defined by inheriting from the *ClientBase* class or from the *DuplexClientBase* class for proxies that need a callback channel.
- Proxy objects can be generated dynamically using the *ChannelFactory* class based only on the Service contract.
- Method calls on proxy objects are translated into messages sent to a remote service by the WCF client-side plumbing either synchronously or asynchronously. Asynchronous method calls use the *Begin-* and *End-* method pairs in tandem.

Lesson Review

You can use the following questions to test your knowledge of the information in Lesson 1, "Consuming WCF Services." The questions are also available on the companion CD if you prefer to review them in electronic form.

NOTE Answers

Answers to these questions and explanations of why each answer choice is correct or incorrect are located in the "Answers" section at the end of the book.

---

1. Suppose you have the following Service contract and associated Callback contract:

```vb
' VB
<ServiceContract()> _
Public Interface IRetrieveHandler
    <OperationContract(IsOneWay:=True)> _
    Sub HandleFileRetrieved( _
            ByVal fileName As String, ByVal data As Stream)
End Interface

<ServiceContract( _
    CallbackContract:=GetType(IRetrieveHandler))> _
Public Interface IStorageArchive
    <OperationContract(IsOneWay:=True)> _
    Sub RequestFileRetrieve(ByVal fileName As String)
End Interface
```

```csharp
// C#
[ServiceContract()]
public interface IRetrieveHandler
{
    [OperationContract(IsOneWay=true)]
    void HandleFileRetrieved(
            string fileName, Stream data);
}

[ServiceContract(
    CallbackContract=typeof(IRetrieveHandler))]
public interface IStorageArchive
{
    [OperationContract(IsOneWay = true)]
    void RequestFileRetrieve(string fileName);
}
```

Suppose further that you want to define a proxy class manually that can be instantiated and used to communicate with this service. Which of the following is the correct definition for the proxy class?

A.
```vb
' VB
Public Class StorageArchiveProxy
    Inherits ClientBase(Of IStorageArchive)
    Implements IStorageArchive

    Public Sub New(ByVal instanceContext As InstanceContext, _
                ByVal binding As Binding, _
                ByVal epAddr As EndpointAddress)
        MyBase.New(instanceContext, binding, epAddr)
    End Sub

    Public Sub New(ByVal instanceContext As InstanceContext, _
                ByVal endpointConfigurationName As String)
        MyBase.New(instanceContext, endpointConfigurationName)
    End Sub
```

```vb
    Public Sub RequestFileRetrieve( _
            ByVal fileName As String) _
            Implements IStorageArchive.RequestFileRetrieve
        Me.Channel.RequestFileRetrieve(fileName)
    End Sub
End Class
```

```csharp
// C#
public class StorageArchiveProxy :
        ClientBase<IStorageArchive>, IStorageArchive
{
    public StorageArchiveProxy(
            InstanceContext instanceContext,
            Binding binding, EndpointAddress epAddr)
        : base(instanceContext, binding, epAddr)
    {
    }

    public StorageArchiveProxy(
            InstanceContext instanceContext,
            string endpointConfigurationName)
        : base(instanceContext, endpointConfigurationName)
    {
    }

    public void RequestFileRetrieve(string fileName)
    {
        this.Channel.RequestFileRetrieve(fileName);
    }
}
```

B.
```vb
' VB
Public Class StorageArchiveProxy
    Inherits DuplexClientBase(Of IStorageArchive)
    Implements IStorageArchive

    Public Sub New(ByVal instanceContext As InstanceContext, _
                ByVal binding As Binding, _
                ByVal epAddr As EndpointAddress)
        MyBase.New(instanceContext, binding, epAddr)
    End Sub

    Public Sub New(ByVal instanceContext As InstanceContext, _
                ByVal endpointConfigurationName As String)
        MyBase.New(instanceContext, endpointConfigurationName)
    End Sub

    Public Sub RequestFileRetrieve( _
            ByVal fileName As String) _
            Implements IStorageArchive.RequestFileRetrieve
        Me.Channel.RequestFileRetrieve(fileName)
    End Sub
End Class
```

```csharp
// C#
public class StorageArchiveProxy :
        DuplexClientBase<IStorageArchive>, IStorageArchive
{
    public StorageArchiveProxy(
            InstanceContext instanceContext,
                Binding binding, EndpointAddress epAddr)
        : base(instanceContext,binding, epAddr)
    {
    }

    public StorageArchiveProxy(
            InstanceContext instanceContext,
                string endpointConfigurationName)
        : base(instanceContext,endpointConfigurationName)
    {
    }

    public void RequestFileRetrieve(string fileName)
    {
        this.Channel.RequestFileRetrieve(fileName);
    }
}
```

C. ' VB
```vbnet
Public Class StorageArchiveProxy
    Inherits DuplexClientBase(Of IStorageArchive)
    Implements IStorageArchive

    Public Sub New(ByVal binding As Binding, _
                ByVal epAddr As EndpointAddress)
        MyBase.New(binding, epAddr)
    End Sub

    Public Sub New(ByVal endpointConfigurationName As String)
        MyBase.New(endpointConfigurationName)
    End Sub

    Public Sub RequestFileRetrieve( _
            ByVal fileName As String) _
            Implements IStorageArchive.RequestFileRetrieve
        Me.Channel.RequestFileRetrieve(fileName)
    End Sub
End Class
```

```csharp
// C#
public class StorageArchiveProxy :
        DuplexClientBase<IStorageArchive>, IStorageArchive
{
    public StorageArchiveProxy(
            Binding binding, EndpointAddress epAddr)
        : base(binding, epAddr)
    {
```

```
        }

        public StorageArchiveProxy(
                string endpointConfigurationName)
            : base(endpointConfigurationName)
        {
        }

        public void RequestFileRetrieve(string fileName)
        {
            this.Channel.RequestFileRetrieve(fileName);
        }
    }
```

D. `' VB`
```
    Public Class StorageArchiveProxy
        Inherits ClientBase(Of IStorageArchive)
        Implements IStorageArchive

        Public Sub New(ByVal binding As Binding, _
                    ByVal epAddr As EndpointAddress)
            MyBase.New(binding, epAddr)
        End Sub

        Public Sub New(ByVal endpointConfigurationName As String)
            MyBase.New(endpointConfigurationName)
        End Sub

        Public Sub RequestFileRetrieve( _
                ByVal fileName As String) _
                Implements IStorageArchive.RequestFileRetrieve
            Me.Channel.RequestFileRetrieve(fileName)
        End Sub
    End Class
```

```
    // C#
    public class StorageArchiveProxy :
            ClientBase<IStorageArchive>, IStorageArchive
    {
        public StorageArchiveProxy(
                Binding binding, EndpointAddress epAddr)
            : base(binding, epAddr)
        {
        }

        public StorageArchiveProxy(
                string endpointConfigurationName)
            : base(endpointConfigurationName)
        {
        }

        public void RequestFileRetrieve(string fileName)
        {
```

```
        this.Channel.RequestFileRetrieve(fileName);
    }
}
```

2. Suppose you have the following Service contract:

```vb
' VB
<ServiceContract()> _
Public Interface IOrderEntryService
    <OperationContract()> _
    Function SubmitOrder(ByVal order As Order) _
            As OrderAcknowledgement

    ' Etc...
End Interface
```

```csharp
// C#
[ServiceContract()]
public interface IOrderEntryService
{
    [OperationContract()]
    OrderAcknowledgement SumbitOrder(Order order);

    // Etc...
}
```

Suppose further that you have generated a proxy class for this service that is equipped with the asynchronous *Begin-* and *End-* method pair needed to invoke the *SubmitOrder* operation asynchronously. Several steps need to be taken to successfully invoke this operation asynchronously and be called back when the operation completes. Which of the following steps to achieve this goal is incorrectly implemented?

A. Define a handler method that will be called back when the asynchronously invoked operation completes, such as:

```vb
' VB
Public Shared Sub HandleOrderSubmitted( _
        ByVal cb As AsyncCallback)
    ' Etc...
End Sub
```

```csharp
// C#
static void HandleOrderSubmitted(AsyncCallback cb)
{
    // Etc...
}
```

B. Asynchronously invoke the operation by calling the *Begin-* method as shown here:

```vb
' VB
Dim proxy As OrderEntryServiceClient
proxy = New OrderEntryServiceClient()

Dim cb As AsyncCallback
cb = New AsyncCallback(AddressOf HandleOrderSubmitted)
```

```
proxy.BeginSubmitOrder(order, cb, proxy)
```

```
// C#
OrderEntryServiceClient proxy = new OrderEntryServiceClient();
AsyncCallback cb = new AsyncCallback(HandleOrderSubmitted);
proxy.BeginSumbitOrder(order, cb, proxy);
```

C. Access the proxy object from the *AsyncState* property when the callback handler has been called:

```
' VB
Dim proxy As OrderEntryServiceClient
proxy = CType(result.AsyncState, OrderEntryServiceClient)
```

```
// C#
OrderEntryServiceClient proxy =
    result.AsyncState as OrderEntryServiceClient;
```

D. Having already accessed the proxy object in the callback handler, use it to end the call:

```
' VB
Dim ack As OrderAcknowledgement
ack = proxy.EndSubmitOrder(result)
```

```
// C#
OrderAcknowledgement ack = proxy.EndSumbitOrder(result);
```

Lesson 2: Consuming Non-WCF Services

In this lesson, the focus is still on the consumption of services but shifts away from the consumption of WCF services to look at what you need to know to use WCF effectively to consume non-WCF services, those built on other technology platforms. You'll begin by looking at what the Web services industry has defined as the minimal base of interoperability that all platforms should support and how WCF supports that. From there, you'll look into the three most common WS-* specifications that come into play when you are trying to achieve interoperability in a scenario in which the services involved go beyond that minimal base of interoperability.

After this lesson, you will be able to:

- Use the svcutil command-line tool or Visual Studio to generate proxies from the WSDL of a non-WCF service.
- Use the proxy to a non-WCF service to call operations on a non-WCF service.
- Use *BasicHttpBinding* to ensure that your WCF service is WS-I Basic Profile–compliant when exchanging messages with a non-WCF service.

Estimated lesson time: 40 minutes

Creating Proxies for Non-WCF Services

The only means available for accessing the metadata for a non-WCF service is through the standard WSDL. The two mechanisms to create WCF proxies you explored in Lesson 1 of this chapter that depend on access to an existing WCF Service contract (dynamically creating proxies using the *ChannelFactory* class and manually coding proxy classes) do not apply here. Instead, you must either use the svcutil command-line tool or add a service reference in Visual Studio to point at the WSDL of the non-WCF service you want to consume using WCF. In the lab following this lesson, you use the svcutil approach once again, this time to consume a non-WCF service.

Interoperability Through WS-I Basic Profile Support

What the software industry calls Web services is organic in the sense that the standards that comprise all the parts of XML-based Web services (XML, Hypertext Transfer Protocol [HTTP], SOAP, WSDL, XML schema definitions [XSD], WS-Addressing, to name a few) are constantly evolving. Not only are they evolving, but there is enough room for interpretation among the various standards that two Web services platform vendors could technically support all the standards but have trouble interoperating because the two vendors interpret the standards differently in important ways.

The classic example of this sort of differing interpretations comes from SOAP and the choices around *Rpc/Encoded* vs. *Document/Literal* mechanisms for structuring SOAP envelopes. (See Chapter 1 for more on these differences.) In the early days of SOAP usage, some vendors chose to use the *Rpc/Encoded* rules for formulating their SOAP messages whereas others used the SOAP *Document/Literal* rules to formulate their SOAP messages. Both were SOAP-compliant, but they could not interoperate because they were expecting their SOAP messages to be constructed differently. Enter the Web Services Interoperability Organization (WS-I).

WS-I

On its Web site at *http://www.ws-i.org/Default.aspx*, WS-I is defined as "an open industry organization chartered to establish Best Practices for Web services interoperability, for selected groups of Web services standards, across platforms, operating systems and programming languages." The approach WS-I takes is to help the Web services community by providing guidance, recommended practices, and supportive resources around the usage of existing Web services standards to promote interoperability. WS-I does not itself define any new standards; rather, its mandate is to guide the Web services community in using the existing standards to achieve interoperability.

WS-I Basic Profile

WS-I defines its Basic Profile as "...a set of non-proprietary Web services specifications, along with clarifications, refinements, interpretations and amplifications of those specifications which promote interoperability." (See *http://www.ws-i.org/deliverables/workinggroup.aspx?wg=basicprofile*.) The Basic Profile acts as a guide to the consistent usage of the foundational specifications that, taken together, form the core of Web services, namely:

- SOAP 1.1
- WSDL 1.1
- Universal Description, Discovery, and Integration (UDDI) 2.0
- XML 1.0 (Second Edition)
- XML Schema Part 1: Structures
- XML Schema Part 2: Data Types
- RFC 2246: The TLS (Transport Layer Security) Protocol Version 1.0
- RFC 2459: Internet X.509 Public Key Infrastructure Certificate and CRL Profile
- RFC 2616: Hypertext Transfer Protocol—HTTP/1.1
- RFC 2818: HTTP over TLS
- RFC 2965: HTTP State Management Mechanism
- The Secure Sockets Layer (SSL) Protocol Version 3.0

MORE INFO   The WS-I Basic Profile

You can find the latest version of the full profile at *http://www.ws-i.org/Profiles/BasicProfile-1_2(WGAD).html*. Another version that is targeted at version 1.2 of SOAP is in the works; you can find that at *http://www.ws-i.org/Profiles/BasicProfile-2_0(WGD).html*.

WCF Basic Profile Support

WCF provides support for WS-I Basic Profile 1.1 through the *BasicHttpBinding* class. Writing interoperable WCF services that are WS-I Basic Profile–compliant is as easy as using this binding, either programmatically or through a configuration file setting. Use the *BasicHttpBinding* class programmatically as shown here:

```vb
' VB
Dim host As ServiceHost
host = New ServiceHost(GetType(OrderEntryService))
host.AddServiceEndpoint(GetType(IOrderEntryService), _
    New BasicHttpBinding(), "http://localhost:8080/orders/")
host.Open()
```

```csharp
// C#
ServiceHost host = new ServiceHost(typeof(OrderEntryService));
host.AddServiceEndpoint(typeof(IOrderEntryService),
    new BasicHttpBinding(), "http://localhost:8080/orders/");
host.Open();
```

Use the *BasicHttpBinding* class through a configuration file setting as shown here:

```xml
<service name="Orders.OrderEntryService">
    <host>
        <baseAddresses>
            <add baseAddress="http://localhost:8080/orders/"/>
        </baseAddresses>
    </host>

    <endpoint address="OrderEntryService"
            binding="basicHttpBinding"
            contract="Orders.IOrderEntryService"
            name="OrderEntryServiceHttpEndpoint" />
</service>
```

One scenario in particular that comes up frequently is when WCF services need to consume existing Web services built on ASP.NET, the Microsoft Web services platform prior to WCF. In the lab following this lesson, you step through an example that uses WCF to consume the Map-Point Web service, an ASP.NET Web service Microsoft hosts that provides mapping services.

The Importance of Documentation

In theory, the WSDL that a service emits should contain enough service metadata for a Web services platform to generate proxies that are fully equipped to communicate with the service. In practice, however, there are gaps that, typically, some level of documentation is required to fill. Someday, these gaps might close, but today, they usually exist because there is a gap in the standards supported by one of the technology platforms, either on the service-provider side or on the consumer side.

As an example, look at authentication in the context of the MapPoint service you consume in the lab following this lesson. This service uses HTTP digest authentication, but the WSDL itself does not contain any policy stating this. Therefore, when you generate a WCF proxy class and configuration file to consume the service, it will fail unless you modify the configuration file to use this form of authentication.

The lab for this lesson details how to update your application to match the documentation but, for now, it's sufficient just to understand that this situation arises simply because the Map-Point service is built on the ASP.NET ASMX Web services technology (referred to as ASMX because of the .asmx extension to distinguish it from ASP.NET Web applications) and does not have any support for WS-Policy, something that is fully supported in WCF. Thus, although a WCF service would be able to emit policy information in its metadata exchange to specify its usage of this authentication mechanism, the ASMX-based MapPoint service could not. WCF consumers can still interoperate with this service, using WCF *BasicHttpBinding* (to specify Basic Profile support), and the MapPoint service documentation tells consumers how the service handles authentication.

Interoperability by Extended WS-* Support

The WS-I Basic Profile covers only the bare minimum of interoperability support, but what happens when you go beyond that and enter the realm of WS-* (WS-Security, WS-Reliable-Messaging, and so on)? WCF has strong support for many of these specifications, but what are your chances for interoperability after you start using these extended Web services standards?

Unfortunately, the answer is that, at this point in time, each case has to be looked at individually. WS-I has defined additional profiles that will help, such as the Basic Security Profile (*http://www.ws-i.org/Profiles/BasicSecurityProfile-1.0.html*) and the Reliable Secure Profile (*http://www.ws-i.org/profiles/rsp-scenarios-1.0.pdf*), but in reality, the support for many of the WS-* specifications is mixed across the various Web services platforms.

Later chapters discuss WCF support for the broader WS-* specifications (the specifications that extend beyond what the Basic Profile offers and move into the realm of the qualities of service under which a service is capable of executing). For now, understand that WCF has very strong standards-based support for interoperability in the face of the following quality-of-service challenges:

- **The efficient transfer of large binary data**   WCF supports the Message Transmission Optimization Mechanism (MTOM). MTOM allows messages that might contain large binary data to be sent across the wire as multi-part MIME (Multipurpose Internet Mail Extensions) messages in which the first part is the XML SOAP envelope that contains references to the binary parts that follow it and the binary data that is conceptually part of the message. This approach avoids the space and processing overhead inherent in having to encode the binary data in Base64, which is necessary if the binary chunk is simply placed inside the XML InfoSet.

- **Secure transmission of messages**   WCF has very strong support for WS-Security and the various other specifications related to WS-Security (for instance, WS-SecureConversation, WS-Trust, and so on). Chapter 7, "Infrastructure Security," and Chapter 8, "User-Level Security," cover WCF security.

- **The reliable exchange of messages**   WS-ReliableMessaging (WS-RM) is a standard that defines the means through which Web services platforms can provide interoperable delivery assurances at the message level. Beyond the packet-level assurances of delivery that the given transport might make available, WS-RM provides assurances that messages sent will be delivered. WCF currently supports the Exactly Once assurance—that a message sent will be delivered exactly once—with the optional feature that a given sequence of messages can be guaranteed to be delivered in order.

MORE INFO   **Key WS-* specifications**

For more about MTOM, visit *http://www.w3.org/TR/soap12-mtom/*.

For more about WS-Reliable Messaging, visit *http://specs.xmlsoap.org/ws/2005/02/rm /ws-reliablemessaging.pdf*.

Finally, for more about WS-Security, visit *http://www.oasis-open.org/committees /tc_home.php?wg_abbrev=wss*.

So if the service uses quality-of-service mechanisms outside the scope of the WS-I Basic Profile, WCF can consume the service as long as the service provider platform implements the mechanism in compliance with the relevant standard.

Quick Check

- You need to consume an ASP.NET Web service that uses HTTP NTLM authentication. However, its WSDL has no indication that HTTP NTLM authentication is its authentication policy. Does this mean that the WCF proxy that is generated will be unable to consume this service?

Quick Check Answer

■ No. As long as this policy is well documented and, therefore, known to the developers, the WCF proxy will still be able to consume the service if the developer appropriately changes the *clientCredentialType* attribute on the *transport* element in the *security* section of the configuration file. You would need to change the attribute, which would have defaulted to *clientCredentialType="None"*, to *clientCredentialType="Ntlm"* and ensure that the right credentials are created and assigned to the proxy.

Lab: Consuming a Non-WCF Mapping Service

In this lab, you will work through the details of consuming a very powerful Internet-facing mapping service, namely, the MapPoint service. It is built on the previous Microsoft Web services technology framework, ASP.NET ASMX, so it qualifies as a non-WCF service. It is also a good example of when the lack of support for WS-Policy requires the consumer to delve a little deeper into the service documentation to know how it handles authentication. This is in contrast to a WCF service which, with its full support for WS-Policy, would be able to notify consumers of its authentication policy through the service metadata it emits. In the first exercise, you focus on using the MapPoint service and then, in the second exercise, you improve the way you use it by retrieving the map images asynchronously because that retrieval can be time-consuming and, therefore, might take longer than you want to wait in a synchronous invocation setting.

▶ **Exercise 1   Consume the MapPoint Service**

In this exercise, you will go through the steps to consume the MapPoint service, owned and operated by Microsoft, a service that provides rich mapping capabilities to its consumers. It is the service behind the Microsoft Virtual Earth platform.

Virtual Earth resources

See *http://www.microsoft.com/virtualearth/* for more about the Virtual Earth platform in general. Note that if you are consuming this service in .NET, the most likely scenario would be that you would use the full Virtual Earth software development kit (SDK) or even the reusable MapControl. For more information about Virtual Earth resources for developers, see *http://dev.live.com/virtualearth/*.

For the purposes of this lab, because the focus is on consuming non-WCF services, you consume the MapPoint service (which is an ASP.NET ASMX service) directly by creating a WCF proxy to communicate with it. In addition to creating the proxy, you also use the technique, described in Lesson 1, of defining an agent that wraps the proxy to make using the service easier for application developers.

Before you can begin going through the required steps, you must have a developer account to access this service. The first steps of Exercise 1 walk you through getting an account if you don't already have one.

1. To access the MapPoint Web service, you must have a Windows Live ID. If you don't already have one, you can get one at *http://get.live.com/getlive/overview?wa=wsignin1.0*.

   When you have a Live ID and are signed in with it, you must ensure that you have a developer's ID and password that is specific to MapPoint. If you don't already have that, you can request it at *https://mappoint-css.live.com/mwssignup/*.

   After you go through this process, which includes receiving some confirmation e-mail messages, you should have an ID and password that provides you with developer access to the MapPoint Web service.

   MORE INFO   **MapPoint Web service documentation**

   The detailed developer documentation for the MapPoint Web service can be found at *http://msdn.microsoft.com/en-us/library/bb507684.aspx*.

   ---

2. Navigate to the *<InstallHome>*/Chapter4/Lesson2/Exercise1/*<language>*/Before directory and double-click the Exercise1.sln file to open the solution in Visual Studio.

   The solution consists of two projects:

3. Open a Visual Studio command prompt to the directory containing the MapPoint-ServiceAgent project, which in this case is the *<InstallHome>*/Chapter4/Lesson2/Exercise1/*<language>*/Before/Microsoft.MapPoint.ServiceAgent directory.

4. Execute the following command at the command prompt to generate a proxy to the MapPoint service whose WSDL is available at *http://staging.mappoint.net/standard-30/mappoint.wsdl*. (Enter the following as a single command; it is formatted here on multiple lines to fit on the printed page.)

   ```
   ' VB
   svcutil /l:VB /async /config:app.config
   /namespace:*,Proxy /out:MapPointProxy.vb
   http://staging.mappoint.net/standard-30/mappoint.wsdl

   // C#
   svcutil /async /config:app.config
   /namespace:*,Microsoft.MapPoint.Proxy /out:MapPointProxy.cs
   http://staging.mappoint.net/standard-30/mappoint.wsdl
   ```

5. Add the MapPointProxy (.cs or .vb as appropriate) file that was just created in the previous step by the svcutil tool to the Microsoft.MapPoint.ServiceAgent project.

6. From the app.config file (in the Microsoft.MapPoint.ServiceAgent project) that was just populated by the svcutil tool, copy the *system.serviceModel* element and its children

(everything within the *configuration* element) to the app.config file in the MapPointTest-Client project, placing it directly below the *appSettings* element that already exists there.

7. Next, modify the values in the *appSettings* section of this same configuration file so that the *MapPointWebServiceID* and *MapPointWebServicePassword* key-value pairs appropriately reflect your Virtual Earth Platform developer account ID and password (which you acquired to access the MapPoint service in step 2).

8. As discussed in the lesson, from the documentation (as opposed to a WS-Policy element in the service's metadata) you learn that this service authenticates using HTTP digest authentication, so you must alter the app.config file to reflect this. To do so, in each of the four binding elements in the configuration file, change the security from:

```
<security mode="None">
    <transport clientCredentialType="None"
        proxyCredentialType="None"
        realm="" />
    <message clientCredentialType="UserName"
        algorithmSuite="Default" />
</security>
```

to the following:

```
<security mode="TransportCredentialOnly">
    <transport clientCredentialType="Digest"
        proxyCredentialType="None"
        realm="" />
    <message clientCredentialType="UserName"
        algorithmSuite="Default" />
</security>
```

9. To the Microsoft.MapPoint.ServiceAgent project, add a new class file named **MapPoint-ServiceAgent** (.cs or .vb as appropriate), which you'll now use to define an agent that wraps some logic around the autogenerated proxy and, therefore, makes it a little easier to work with the service.

Normally, there would be more methods than this, but for the purposes here, you'll keep it simple and add only a few methods that facilitate retrieving map images by addresses. The resulting file should be as follows:

```
' VB
Imports System.Configuration
Imports System.Security.Principal
Imports System.Net

Imports Microsoft.MapPoint.ServiceAgent.Proxy

Public Delegate Sub MapRetrievedHandler( _
        ByVal mapImage As MapImage, ByVal address As Address)

Public Delegate Function GetMapDelegate( _
```

```vbnet
                        ByVal address As Address, ByVal mapHeight As Double, _
                        ByVal mapWidth As Double, ByVal dataSourceName As String) _
                            As MapImage

        Public Class MapPointServiceAgent

            Public Function GetLocationByAddress( _
                    ByVal address As Address, ByVal dataSourceName As String) _
                        As Location
                Dim findSvcProxy As FindServiceSoapClient
                findSvcProxy = InitFindServiceProxy()

                Dim addrSpec As FindAddressSpecification
                addrSpec = New FindAddressSpecification()
                addrSpec.InputAddress = address
                addrSpec.DataSourceName = dataSourceName

                ' Note: CustomerInfoFindHeader & UserInfoFindHeader
                ' can be null here since we are happy with defaults
                Dim results As FindResults = Nothing
                Try
                    results = findSvcProxy.FindAddress(Nothing, Nothing, addrSpec)
                Catch
                    results = Nothing
                End Try

                Dim res As Location = Nothing
                If Not results Is Nothing Then
                    If results.NumberFound > 0 Then
                        If Not results.Results(0).FoundLocation Is Nothing Then
                            res = results.Results(0).FoundLocation
                        End If
                    End If
                End If
                Return res
            End Function

            Public Function GetMapByLocation( _
                    ByVal location As Location) As MapImage

                If location Is Nothing Then
                    Return Nothing
                End If

                Dim renderSvcProxy As RenderServiceSoapClient
                renderSvcProxy = InitRenderServiceProxy()

                Dim mapSpec As New MapSpecification()
                mapSpec.DataSourceName = location.DataSourceName

                Dim views(0) As MapView
                views(0) = location.BestMapView.ByBoundingRectangle
                mapSpec.Views = views
```

```vb
    Dim mapImages() As MapImage
    Try
        mapImages = renderSvcProxy.GetMap(Nothing, Nothing, mapSpec)
    Catch
        mapImages = Nothing
    End Try

    Dim res As MapImage = Nothing
    If Not mapImages Is Nothing Then
        If mapImages.Length > 0 Then
            res = mapImages(0)
        End If
    End If

    Return res
End Function


Public Function GetMapByLocation( _
        ByVal location As Location, ByVal mapHeight As Double, _
        ByVal mapWidth As Double) As MapImage

    If location Is Nothing Then
        Return Nothing
    End If

    Dim renderSvcProxy As RenderServiceSoapClient
    renderSvcProxy = InitRenderServiceProxy()

    Dim mapSpec As New MapSpecification
    mapSpec.DataSourceName = location.DataSourceName

    ' Init view:
    Dim vbh As New ViewByHeightWidth()
    vbh.Height = mapHeight
    vbh.Width = mapWidth
    vbh.CenterPoint = location.LatLong

    Dim views(0) As MapView
    views(0) = vbh
    mapSpec.Views = views

    ' Init options:
    mapSpec.Options = New MapOptions()
    mapSpec.Options.Format = New ImageFormat()
    mapSpec.Options.Format.Height = Convert.ToInt32(mapHeight)
    mapSpec.Options.Format.Width = Convert.ToInt32(mapWidth)

    mapSpec.Options.Zoom = 0.001

    ' Init pushpin:
    Dim pin As New Pushpin()
```

```vbnet
                pin.IconDataSource = "MapPoint.Icons"
                pin.IconName = "1"
                pin.Label = location.Address.AddressLine
                pin.LatLong = location.LatLong

                Dim pins(0) As Pushpin
                pins(0) = pin
                mapSpec.Pushpins = pins

                Dim mapImages() As MapImage
                Try
                    mapImages = renderSvcProxy.GetMap(Nothing, Nothing, mapSpec)
                Catch ex As Exception
                    mapImages = Nothing
                End Try

                Dim res As MapImage = Nothing
                If Not mapImages Is Nothing Then
                    If mapImages.Length > 0 Then
                        res = mapImages(0)
                    End If
                End If

                Return res
            End Function


        Public Function GetSizedMapByAddress( _
                ByVal address As Address, ByVal mapHeight As Double, _
                ByVal mapWidth As Double, ByVal dataSourceName As String) _
                    As MapImage
            Dim location As Location
            location = GetLocationByAddress(address, dataSourceName)
            Return GetMapByLocation(location, mapHeight, mapWidth)
        End Function

        Public Function GetMapByAddress( _
            ByVal address As Address, ByVal dataSourceName As String) _
                As MapImage
            Dim location As Location
            location = GetLocationByAddress(address, dataSourceName)
            Return GetMapByLocation(location)
        End Function

        Public Shared Function AddressToString( _
                        ByVal address As Address) As String
            Return String.Format("{0}, {1}, {2}, {3}, {4}", _
                                address.AddressLine, _
                                address.PrimaryCity, _
                                address.Subdivision, _
                                address.PostalCode, _
                                address.CountryRegion)
```

```vb
    End Function

    Private Function InitFindServiceProxy() As FindServiceSoapClient
        Dim findSvcProxy As FindServiceSoapClient
        findSvcProxy = New FindServiceSoapClient()

        findSvcProxy.ClientCredentials.HttpDigest.ClientCredential= _
            New NetworkCredential( _
                ConfigurationManager.AppSettings(MapPointWebServiceIDKey), _
                ConfigurationManager.AppSettings(MapPointWebServicePasswordKey))

        findSvcProxy.ClientCredentials.HttpDigest.AllowedImpersonationLevel= _
            TokenImpersonationLevel.Impersonation

        Return findSvcProxy
    End Function

    Private Function InitRenderServiceProxy() As RenderServiceSoapClient
        Dim renderSvcProxy As RenderServiceSoapClient
        renderSvcProxy = New RenderServiceSoapClient()

        renderSvcProxy.ClientCredentials.HttpDigest.ClientCredential = _
            New NetworkCredential( _
                ConfigurationManager.AppSettings(MapPointWebServiceIDKey), _
                ConfigurationManager.AppSettings(MapPointWebServicePasswordKey))
        renderSvcProxy.ClientCredentials.HttpDigest.AllowedImpersonationLevel _
            = TokenImpersonationLevel.Impersonation

        Return renderSvcProxy
    End Function

    Private Const MapPointWebServiceIDKey As String = _
                    "MapPointWebServiceID"
    Private Const MapPointWebServicePasswordKey As String = _
                    "MapPointWebServicePassword"
End Class

Class MapRequestInfo
    Public invokedDelegate As GetMapDelegate
    Public mapRetrievedHandler As MapRetrievedHandler
    Public address As Address
End Class

// C#
using System.Configuration;
using System.Security.Principal;
using System.Net;

using Microsoft.MapPoint.Proxy;

namespace Microsoft.MapPoint.ServiceAgent
{
```

```csharp
public delegate void MapRetrievedHandler(
    MapImage mapImage, Address address);

public delegate MapImage GetMapDelegate(Address address,
    double mapHeight, double mapWidth, string dataSourceName);

public class MapPointServiceAgent
{
    public Location GetLocationByAddress(
                    Address address, string dataSourceName)
    {
        FindServiceSoapClient findSvcProxy = InitFindServiceProxy();
        FindAddressSpecification addrSpec =
            new FindAddressSpecification();

        addrSpec.InputAddress = address;
        addrSpec.DataSourceName = dataSourceName;

        // Note: CustomerInfoFindHeader & UserInfoFindHeader can be null
        // here since we are happy with defaults
        FindResults results;
        try
        {
            results = findSvcProxy.FindAddress(null, null, addrSpec);
        }
        catch
        {
            results = null;
        }

        Location res = null;
        if (results != null && results.NumberFound > 0 &&
            results.Results[0].FoundLocation != null)
        {
            res = results.Results[0].FoundLocation;
        }

        return res;
    }

    public MapImage GetMapByLocation(Location location)
    {
        if (location == null)
            return null;

        RenderServiceSoapClient renderSvcProxy = InitRenderServiceProxy();

        MapSpecification mapSpec = new MapSpecification();
        mapSpec.DataSourceName = location.DataSourceName;
        mapSpec.Views = new MapView[]
            { location.BestMapView.ByBoundingRectangle };

        MapImage[] mapImages;
```

```
        try
        {
            mapImages = renderSvcProxy.GetMap(null, null, mapSpec);
        }
        catch
        {
            mapImages = null;
        }

        MapImage res = null;
        if (mapImages != null && mapImages.Length > 0)
            res = mapImages[0];

        return res;
}

public MapImage GetMapByLocation(
        Location location, double mapHeight, double mapWidth)
{
    if (location == null)
        return null;

    RenderServiceSoapClient renderSvcProxy = InitRenderServiceProxy();

    MapSpecification mapSpec = new MapSpecification();
    mapSpec.DataSourceName = location.DataSourceName;

    // Init view:
    ViewByHeightWidth vbh = new ViewByHeightWidth();
    vbh.Height = mapHeight;
    vbh.Width = mapWidth;
    vbh.CenterPoint = location.LatLong;

    mapSpec.Views = new MapView[] { vbh };

    // Init options:
    mapSpec.Options = new MapOptions();

    mapSpec.Options.Format = new ImageFormat();
    mapSpec.Options.Format.Height = (int) mapHeight;
    mapSpec.Options.Format.Width = (int) mapWidth;

    mapSpec.Options.Zoom = 0.001;

    // Init pushpin:
    Pushpin pin = new Pushpin();
    pin.IconDataSource = "MapPoint.Icons";
    pin.IconName = "1";
    pin.Label = location.Address.AddressLine;
    pin.LatLong = location.LatLong;
    mapSpec.Pushpins = new Pushpin[] { pin };

    MapImage[] mapImages;
```

```
       try
       {
           mapImages = renderSvcProxy.GetMap(null, null, mapSpec);
       }
       catch
       {
           mapImages = null;
       }

       MapImage res = null;
       if (mapImages != null && mapImages.Length > 0)
           res = mapImages[0];

       return res;
   }

   public MapImage GetSizedMapByAddress(Address address,
           double mapHeight, double mapWidth, string dataSourceName)
   {
       Location location = GetLocationByAddress(
           address, dataSourceName);
       return GetMapByLocation(location,mapHeight,mapWidth);
   }

   public MapImage GetMapByAddress(
       Address address, string dataSourceName)
   {
       Location location = GetLocationByAddress(
           address, dataSourceName);
       return GetMapByLocation(location);
   }

   public static string AddressToString(Address address)
   {
       return string.Format(
               "{0}, {1}, {2}, {3}, {4}",
                           address.AddressLine,
                           address.PrimaryCity,
                           address.Subdivision,
                           address.PostalCode,
                           address.CountryRegion);
   }

   private FindServiceSoapClient InitFindServiceProxy()
   {
       FindServiceSoapClient findSvcProxy = new FindServiceSoapClient();

       findSvcProxy.ClientCredentials.HttpDigest.ClientCredential =
           new NetworkCredential(
               ConfigurationManager.AppSettings[MapPointWebServiceIDKey],
               ConfigurationManager.AppSettings[
                   MapPointWebServicePasswordKey]);
```

```
    findSvcProxy.ClientCredentials.HttpDigest.AllowedImpersonationLevel =
        TokenImpersonationLevel.Impersonation;

    return findSvcProxy;
}

private RenderServiceSoapClient InitRenderServiceProxy()
{
    RenderServiceSoapClient renderSvcProxy =
                new RenderServiceSoapClient();

    renderSvcProxy.ClientCredentials.HttpDigest.ClientCredential =
        new NetworkCredential(
            ConfigurationManager.AppSettings[MapPointWebServiceIDKey],
            ConfigurationManager.AppSettings[
                MapPointWebServicePasswordKey]);

    renderSvcProxy.ClientCredentials.HttpDigest.AllowedImpersonationLevel =
        TokenImpersonationLevel.Impersonation;

    return renderSvcProxy;
}

private const string MapPointWebServiceIDKey =
                "MapPointWebServiceID";
private const string MapPointWebServicePasswordKey =
                "MapPointWebServicePassword";
    }
}
```

NOTE   More on the usage of HTTP digest authentication

To use the required HTTP digest authentication, in addition to the modifications you have already made to the configuration file, note that in both the *InitRenderServiceProxy* and the *InitFinderServiceProxy* methods, the *NetworkCredential* objects (created with the required Map-Point service credentials) must be assigned to the proxy's *ClientCredentials.HttpDigest.Client-Credential* property.

This completes the agent library, and it should now build. Next, you finish off the Windows Forms client that consumes the service.

10. Switching to the MapPointTestClient project, open the MainForm (.cs or .vb as appropriate) code file and add the following imports, noting that they are slightly different between the Visual Basic and C# versions because of the way the two languages handle default naming of proxy namespaces:

```
' VB
Imports Microsoft.MapPoint.ServiceAgent
Imports Microsoft.MapPoint.ServiceAgent.Proxy
```

```
// C#
using Microsoft.MapPoint.Proxy;
using Microsoft.MapPoint.ServiceAgent;
```

11. In the same MainForm file, add a private field to the *MainForm* class that is a reference to one of the *MapPointServiceAgent* objects whose class you just finished defining.

```
' VB
Private _svcAgent As MapPointServiceAgent = New MapPointServiceAgent()
```

```
// C#
private MapPointServiceAgent _svcAgent = new MapPointServiceAgent();
```

12. Implement the event handler *_btnViewMap_Click* that is invoked when the user clicks the View Map button. It should be as follows:

```
' VB
Private Sub _btnViewMap_Click(ByVal sender As System.Object, _
        ByVal e As System.EventArgs) Handles _btnViewMap.Click
    Dim address As Address = New Address()

    address.AddressLine = _tboxAddressLine.Text
    address.PrimaryCity = _tboxCity.Text
    address.Subdivision = _tboxProvinceOrState.Text
    address.PostalCode = _tboxZipOrPostalCode.Text
    address.CountryRegion = CType( _
        _countriesComboBox.SelectedItem, String)

    Dim img As MapImage
    img = _svcAgent.GetSizedMapByAddress(address, _
        _mainPicBox.Height, _mainPicBox.Width, _
        DefaultDataSourceName)

    If Not img Is Nothing Then
        ' Display the map:
        Dim bmapImg As Bitmap
        bmapImg = New Bitmap( _
            New MemoryStream(img.MimeData.Bits))
        _mainPicBox.Image = bmapImg

        ' Cache the image:
        _cachedMaps.Add(address, bmapImg)

        ' And update combo box:
        _recentlyViewedComboBox.Items.Add(address)
        _recentlyViewedComboBox.SelectedIndex = _
            _recentlyViewedComboBox.Items.Count - 1
    Else
        MessageBox.Show("No map found for address:" + vbCrLf + _
            MapPointServiceAgent.AddressToString(address), _
            "Error")
    End If
```

```
      InitAddressInputFields()
End Sub

// C#
private void _btnViewMap_Click(object sender, EventArgs e)
{
    Address address = new Address();

    address.AddressLine = _tboxAddressLine.Text;
    address.PrimaryCity = _tboxCity.Text;
    address.Subdivision = _tboxProvinceOrState.Text;
    address.PostalCode = _tboxZipOrPostalCode.Text;
    address.CountryRegion = _countriesComboBox.SelectedItem as string;

    MapImage img = _svcAgent.GetSizedMapByAddress(
        address, _mainPicBox.Height,
        _mainPicBox.Width, DefaultDataSourceName);

    if (img != null)
    {
        // Display the map:
        Bitmap bmapImg = new Bitmap(
            new MemoryStream(img.MimeData.Bits));
        _mainPicBox.Image = bmapImg;

        // Cache the image:
        _cachedMaps.Add(address, bmapImg);

        // And update combo box:
        _recentlyViewedComboBox.Items.Add(address);
        _recentlyViewedComboBox.SelectedIndex =
            _recentlyViewedComboBox.Items.Count - 1;
    }
    else
    {
        MessageBox.Show(
            "No map found for address:\n" +
            MapPointServiceAgent.AddressToString(address),
            "Error");
    }

    InitAddressInputFields();
}
```

You can now build and run the application, making sure that the MapPointTestClient is the startup project and that you have an Internet connection so that the service is accessible. After it is running, you should be able to enter any valid address in the United States and Canada and display a map for that address. For example, try **1 Microsoft Way, Redmond, WA 98052, US**. You might even see the building in which WCF was built!

▶ **Exercise 2   Consume the MapPoint Service Asynchronously**

In this exercise, you will build on the result of Exercise 1 by improving the design so that the MapPoint service can be invoked asynchronously. This enhances the usability experience because the UI will now be responsive while the application retrieves map images asynchronously in the background.

To implement this, you must make two changes to the solution. In the UI code, you must add a status bar that provides a visual cue that some work is being done in the background. In the agent code, you'll add a method for invoking map retrieval asynchronously, with the method accepting a .NET delegate that can be used to call back the consumer when the retrieval is done. Note that to provide asynchronous invocation on your agent, you cannot simply map asynchronous calls on the agent to underlying asynchronous calls on the proxy. Why not? Because in defining your agent's interface, the choice made here was to wrap calls on the agent to two successive calls on the underlying proxy, so instead of trying to handle the coordination around two successive asynchronous calls on the proxy, you need to add the asynchronous invocation capability manually at the agent level and, in the separate thread that results, the two methods on the proxy can be called in a synchronous fashion.

1. Navigate to the *<InstallHome>*/Chapter4/Lesson2/Exercise2/*<language>*/Before directory and double-click the Exercise2.sln file to open the solution in Visual Studio.

   The solution consists of the two projects as they were completed in Exercise 1.

   Add two delegate declarations that will be used in this implementation. Add the following to the MapPointServiceAgent (.cs or .vb as appropriate) file, above the definition of the *MapPointServiceAgent* class:

   ```vb
   ' VB
   Public Delegate Sub MapRetrievedHandler( _
       ByVal mapImage As MapImage, ByVal address As Address)

   Public Delegate Function GetMapDelegate( _
       ByVal address As Address, ByVal mapHeight As Double, _
       ByVal mapWidth As Double, ByVal dataSourceName As String) _
           As MapImage
   ```

   ```csharp
   // C#
   public delegate void MapRetrievedHandler(
       MapImage mapImage, Address address);

   public delegate MapImage GetMapDelegate(Address address,
       double mapHeight, double mapWidth, string dataSourceName);
   ```

   Add a basic info class to store the state object you will pass when invoking a delegate asynchronously. To do so, define the following class below the *MapPointServiceAgent* class:

   ```vb
   ' VB
   Class MapRequestInfo
       Public invokedDelegate As GetMapDelegate
   ```

```
    Public mapRetrievedHandler As MapRetrievedHandler
    Public address As Address
End Class
```

```
// C#
class MapRequestInfo
{
    public GetMapDelegate invokedDelegate;
    public MapRetrievedHandler mapRetrievedHandler;
    public Address address;
}
```

Add the following method to the *MapPointServiceAgent* class, which will be the internal callback method that is called when the asynchronously invoked operation completes.

```
' VB
Private Sub ProcessGetMapResult(ByVal ar As IAsyncResult)
    ' Access the state...
    Dim reqInfo As MapRequestInfo
    reqInfo = CType(ar.AsyncState, MapRequestInfo)
    Dim gmd As GetMapDelegate = reqInfo.invokedDelegate
    Dim mapRetrievedHandler As MapRetrievedHandler = _
        reqInfo.mapRetrievedHandler
    Dim addr As Address = reqInfo.address

    ' End the async call to get the returned image:
    Dim img As MapImage
    img = gmd.EndInvoke(ar)

    ' And use the address & the returned image to call back
    ' the handler interested in processing the retrieved map:
    If Not mapRetrievedHandler Is Nothing Then
        mapRetrievedHandler(img, addr)
    End If
End Sub
```

```
// C#
private void ProcessGetMapResult(IAsyncResult ar)
{
    // Access the state...
    MapRequestInfo reqInfo = ar.AsyncState as MapRequestInfo;
    GetMapDelegate gmd = reqInfo.invokedDelegate;
    MapRetrievedHandler mapRetrievedHandler =
                        reqInfo.mapRetrievedHandler;
    Address addr = reqInfo.address;

    // End the async call to get the returned image:
    MapImage img = gmd.EndInvoke(ar);

    // And use the address & the returned image to call back
    // the handler interested in processing the retrieved map:
    if (mapRetrievedHandler != null)
        mapRetrievedHandler(img,addr);
}
```

2. Provide clients of this *MapPointServiceAgent* class with a method to invoke a map retrieval request asynchronously, one that provides them with a means to provide a delegate that the implementation can use to call back the client when the map retrieval is complete. To do so, add the following publicly available method to the *MapPointService-Agent* class:

```vb
' VB
Public Sub BeginGetSizedMapByAddress( _
        ByVal address As Address, ByVal mapHeight As Double, _
        ByVal mapWidth As Double, ByVal dataSourceName As String, _
        ByVal mapRetrievedHandler As MapRetrievedHandler)
    ' Define the delegate to be invoked asynchronously:
    Dim gmd As GetMapDelegate
    gmd = New GetMapDelegate(AddressOf Me.GetSizedMapByAddress)

    ' Define the AsyncCallback delegate to be called when
    ' the asynchronous operation is completed:
    Dim cb As AsyncCallback
    cb = New AsyncCallback(AddressOf Me.ProcessGetMapResult)

    ' Create a "state" object:
    Dim reqInfo As MapRequestInfo = New MapRequestInfo()
    reqInfo.invokedDelegate = gmd
    reqInfo.mapRetrievedHandler = mapRetrievedHandler
    reqInfo.address = address

    ' Do asnyc invoke, passing our callback & state:
    gmd.BeginInvoke(address, mapHeight, mapWidth, _
                    dataSourceName, cb, reqInfo)
End Sub
```

```csharp
// C#
public void BeginGetSizedMapByAddress(Address address,
        double mapHeight, double mapWidth,
        string dataSourceName,
        MapRetrievedHandler mapRetrievedHandler)
{
    // define the delegate to be invoked asynchronously:
    GetMapDelegate gmd = new GetMapDelegate(this.GetSizedMapByAddress);

    // Define the AsyncCallback delegate to be called when
    // the asynchronous operation is completed:
    AsyncCallback cb = new AsyncCallback(this.ProcessGetMapResult);

    // Create a "state" object:
    MapRequestInfo reqInfo = new MapRequestInfo();
    reqInfo.invokedDelegate = gmd;
    reqInfo.mapRetrievedHandler = mapRetrievedHandler;
    reqInfo.address = address;

    // Do asnyc invoke, passing our callback & state:
```

```
gmd.BeginInvoke(address,mapHeight,mapWidth,
                dataSourceName,cb,reqInfo);
}
```

This completes the improvements needed for the *MapPointServiceAgent*, and that project should now build. Next, you return to the UI and take advantage of these changes to make the UI more responsive as maps are asynchronously retrieved.

3. Open the design view of the *MainForm* and add a Status Strip control. Do this by simply dragging a Status Strip control from the toolbox onto the form. Rename it to **_statusStrip** and clear the Text property.

4. To this status strip, add a label control, renaming it to **_mainStatusLabel** and, again, clear the Text property.

5. Next, switch to code view for this form, which opens the MainForm (.cs or .vb as appropriate) file. To the *MainForm* class, add the following method that will be the callback handler, the method called when an asynchronously invoked map retrieval request has completed.

```
' VB
Private Sub HandleMapImageAvailableForDisplay( _
        ByVal img As MapImage, ByVal address As Address)
    If Not img Is Nothing Then
        _mainStatusLabel.Text = String.Format( _
            "Map for address {0} was retrieved", _
            MapPointServiceAgent.AddressToString(address))

        ' Display the map:
        Dim bmapImg As Bitmap
        bmapImg = New Bitmap( _
            New MemoryStream(img.MimeData.Bits))
        _mainPicBox.Image = bmapImg

        ' Cache the image:
        _cachedMaps.Add(address, bmapImg)

        ' And update combo box:
        _recentlyViewedComboBox.Items.Add(address)
        _recentlyViewedComboBox.SelectedIndex = _
            _recentlyViewedComboBox.Items.Count - 1
    Else
        _mainStatusLabel.Text = String.Format( _
            "There was an error retrieving map for address {0}", _
            MapPointServiceAgent.AddressToString(address))

        MessageBox.Show("No map found for address:" + vbCrLf + _
            MapPointServiceAgent.AddressToString(address), _
            "Error")
    End If
End Sub
```

```csharp
// C#
private void HandleMapImageAvailableForDisplay(
        MapImage img, Address address)
{
    if (img != null)
    {
        _mainStatusLabel.Text = string.Format(
                "Map for address {0} was retrieved",
                MapPointServiceAgent.AddressToString(address));

        // Display the map:
        Bitmap bmapImg = new Bitmap(
                new MemoryStream(img.MimeData.Bits));
        _mainPicBox.Image = bmapImg;

        // Cache the image:
        _cachedMaps.Add(address, bmapImg);

        // And update combo box:
        _recentlyViewedComboBox.Items.Add(address);
        _recentlyViewedComboBox.SelectedIndex =
                        _recentlyViewedComboBox.Items.Count - 1;
    }
    else
    {
        _mainStatusLabel.Text = string.Format(
            "There was an error retrieving map for address {0}",
            MapPointServiceAgent.AddressToString(address));

        MessageBox.Show(
            "No map found for address:\n" +
            MapPointServiceAgent.AddressToString(address),
            "Error");
    }
}
```

6. Finally, update the event handler that is called when the user clicks the View Map button so that now the map retrieval is invoked asynchronously, and a delegate reference to the handler you just defined is passed when the asynchronous operation is called. The button click handler now becomes:

```vb
' VB
Private Sub _btnViewMap_Click(ByVal sender As System.Object, _
        ByVal e As System.EventArgs) Handles _btnViewMap.Click
    Dim address As Address = New Address()

    address.AddressLine = _tboxAddressLine.Text
    address.PrimaryCity = _tboxCity.Text
    address.Subdivision = _tboxProvinceOrState.Text
    address.PostalCode = _tboxZipOrPostalCode.Text
    address.CountryRegion = CType( _
        _countriesComboBox.SelectedItem, String)
```

```
    _svcAgent.BeginGetSizedMapByAddress(address, _
        _mainPicBox.Height, _mainPicBox.Width, _
        DefaultDataSourceName, _
        AddressOf Me.HandleMapImageAvailableForDisplay)

    InitAddressInputFields()

    _mainStatusLabel.Text = String.Format( _
        "Retrieving map for address {0}", _
        MapPointServiceAgent.AddressToString(address))
End Sub

// C#
private void _btnViewMap_Click(object sender, EventArgs e)
{
    Address address = new Address();

    address.AddressLine = _tboxAddressLine.Text;
    address.PrimaryCity = _tboxCity.Text;
    address.Subdivision = _tboxProvinceOrState.Text;
    address.PostalCode = _tboxZipOrPostalCode.Text;
    address.CountryRegion = _countriesComboBox.SelectedItem as string;

    _svcAgent.BeginGetSizedMapByAddress(address,
        _mainPicBox.Height, _mainPicBox.Width,
        DefaultDataSourceName,
        this.HandleMapImageAvailableForDisplay);

    InitAddressInputFields();

    _mainStatusLabel.Text = string.Format(
        "Retrieving map for address {0}",
        MapPointServiceAgent.AddressToString(address));
}
```

Now the solution should build and run. At this point, you must also make sure that your ID and password are correct in this application's configuration file. When you run the application this time, you will notice that the application UI remains usable even when the map retrieval requests are being processed.

Lesson Summary

- You can use the svcutil command-line tool or Visual Studio to generate proxies from the WSDL of a non-WCF service.

- In some situations, when there is a lack of WS-Policy support, some of the service's policies can be found only in the documentation for the service, policies that might otherwise be found in the WSDL.

- Just as with WCF services, you can use proxy objects to call service operations either synchronously or asynchronously.

■   You can use *BasicHttpBinding*, either in code or in a configuration file, to ensure that your WCF service is WS-I Basic Profile–compliant when exchanging messages with a non-WCF service.

Lesson Review

You can use the following questions to test your knowledge of the information in Lesson 2, "Consuming Non-WCF Services." The questions are also available on the companion CD if you prefer to review them in electronic form.

NOTE   Answers

Answers to these questions and explanations of why each answer choice is correct or incorrect are located in the "Answers" section at the end of the book.

---

1. ˉ You need to consume a service built in Java. Which of the following are valid methods you can use to create a WCF proxy class to consume this service? Choose all that apply.

   A.   Use the *ChannelFactory* class to create a proxy object dynamically.

   B.   Use the svcutil command-line tool to generate a proxy class by referencing the WSDL for the service.

   C.   Manually define a proxy class that inherits from *ClientBase*.

   D.   Add a service reference in Visual Studio by referencing the WSDL for the service.

Chapter Review

To further practice and reinforce the skills you learned in this chapter, you can:

- Review the chapter summary.
- Review the list of key terms introduced in this chapter.
- Complete the case scenarios. These scenarios set up real-world situations involving the topics of this chapter and ask you to create solutions.
- Complete the suggested practices.
- Take a practice test.

Chapter Summary

- You can generate a proxy class from a service's metadata, using svcutil or Visual Studio, or define a proxy class manually. For non-WCF services, the service metadata must be expressed in the standard WSDL format.
- You can create proxies to WCF services, either dynamically by using the *ChannelFactory* class or by instantiating a proxy class.
- You can use proxies to either WCF or non-WCF services to invoke operations on remote services.

Key Terms

Do you know what these key terms mean? You can check your answers by looking up the terms in the glossary at the end of the book.

- *ChannelFactory*
- proxy
- proxy class
- service agent
- service reference
- svcutil
- WS-I
- WS-I Basic Profile

Case Scenarios

In the following case scenarios, you will apply what you've learned in this chapter. You can find answers to these questions in the "Answers" section at the end of this book.

Case Scenario 1: Building an e-Commerce Solution

You work for a consulting company that has just acquired a new customer that wants to enable its Web site for e-commerce. The Web site is composed mostly of static text and images to display the product line. The site will need, at the very least, shopping-cart capability as well as the ability to handle credit-card payment transactions and delivery of the product to the buyer. The company wants to do this on an extremely low budget. Your manager seeks your advice on how to handle this customer.

1. Your manager wants to know whether you can deliver a reasonably priced solution to the customer, one with the lowest possible upfront costs.

2. If so, what might the solution look like?

Case Scenario 2: Medical Imaging Application

You work on a team that is developing a medical imaging solution. For years now, you have provided a very powerful, rich-client application (a Windows Forms application) that radiologists inside the hospital use to view medical images and make diagnoses. However, you are being asked to provide medical image viewing to a Web application that referring physicians and partner insitutions can use outside of the hospital. Your team has decided that the Web application will be based on ASP.NET and that you will provide a set of common WCF services that both the Web application and the rich-client application can use. Your manager asks you the following questions:

1. Both the Web application and the rich-client application must deal with slow or lost connectivity, service operation retries, asynchronous submission, and retrieval of possibly large amounts of image data. What can you can do to avoid duplicating solutions to those challenges in both applications?

2. Can you maximize performance when retrieving large sets of image data for the rich-client application inside the enterprise?

Suggested Practices

To help you successfully master the exam objectives presented in this chapter, complete the following tasks.

Expand Your Knowledge of Service Agents

Improve your knowledge about service agents, and then build a more robust service agent by performing the following practices.

- **Practice 1**   Read the following articles about agents and how they can be used to solve some of the problems a consumer can have when interacting with a service.
  - ❑ The ServiceConsoleHost project, a simple console application that hosts the service
  - ❑ The TaskClient project, a Windows Forms application used to consume the service
  - ❑ The Tasks.Entities project, a class library project that defines the Data contracts used by the service
  - ❑ The Tasks.Services project, a class library project that defines the Service contract and service type
  - ❑ The MapPointTestClient project, which is a Windows Forms application you use to consume the MapPoint service.
  - ❑ The Microsoft.MapPoint.ServiceAgent project, which is a class library project that initially contains only an almost empty app.config file and a text file that contains the svcutil command you'll need in a moment to generate a proxy. The project does, however, already have the appropriate references set up.
  - ❑ *Dealing with Concurrency: Designing Interaction Between Services and Their Agents*, by Maarten Mullender, which is available at *http://msdn2.microsoft.com/en-us/library /ms978508.aspx*
  - ❑ *Transparent Connectivity: A Solution Proposal for Service Agents*, by Maarten Mullender and Jon Tobey, which is available at *http://msdn2.microsoft.com/en-us/library /aa479367.aspx*
- **Practice 2**   For the Task Manager service you worked with in Lesson 1, build a more capable TaskServiceAgent that can work in a completely offline mode. You can likely do this in several ways, but one feasible approach is to store any tasks that need to be submitted to the service in a local SQL server database until the agent is able to re-establish connectivity with the service.

Consume a Non-WCF Service

Consume another third-party service by performing the following practice.

- **Practice**   Any of the various live.com services from Microsoft would afford good practice for consuming non-WCF services.

  Failing something that interests you among the live.com services, pick any third-party service that supports developer trial access and try to write a WCF proxy to consume it.

Take a Practice Test

The practice tests on this book's companion CD offer many options. For example, you can test yourself on just one exam objective, or you can test yourself on all the 70-503 certification exam content. You can set up the test so that it closely simulates the experience of taking a certification exam, or you can set it up in study mode so that you can look at the correct answers and explanations after you answer each question.

MORE INFO **Practice tests**

For details about all the practice test options available, see the "How to Use the Practice Tests" section in this book's introduction.

Chapter 5

Configuring WCF

For some developers, the mere word *administration* has been known to cause boredom and indifference However, for systems that use Windows Communication Foundation (WCF), *administration* means more than just working to keep an application running well. One of the real strengths of WCF is the ability to postpone certain types of technical decisions until very late in the development cycle. In particular, you can decide on the transportation protocol (Web services, Transmission Control Protocol [TCP], Microsoft Message Queuing [MSMQ]) and channel requirements (security, reliability, and so on) toward the end of the process. To some, this might not seem like much of an advantage, but in many cases, architectural decisions that are made early in the development cycle limit the options that are available throughout the rest of the coding process. Although some choices must be made at the beginning of a project, some questions are better delayed until as late in the project as possible to provide the maximum flexibility when the application is deployed. When choosing the underlying communications mechanism, WCF greatly assists in postponing this decision until, in some cases, the run-time characteristics of the application are configured.

To achieve this goal, certain concessions have to be made. For example, in the case of WCF, the definition of the channel requirements must be moved outside of the application's code. In the world of .NET, "outside of the application's code" means "configuration files." This is not to say that WCF cannot be configured through code, but many of the choices can be indicated declaratively in the configuration file as well as imperatively through code. This chapter covers the basics of configuring WCF, using both techniques.

Exam objectives in this chapter:
- Configure the client endpoint.
- Dynamically configure the service by using the service model.

Lessons in this chapter:

Before You Begin

To complete the lessons in this chapter, you must have:

- A computer that meets or exceeds the minimum hardware requirements listed in the "Introduction" section at the beginning of the book.
- Any edition of Microsoft Visual Studio 2008 (including Microsoft Visual C# 2008 Express Edition or Microsoft Visual Basic 2008 Express Edition) installed on the computer.

Real World

Bruce Johnson

The first time I had a chance to use WCF in a real application was in 2005. Prior to working with WCF, I had spent time working with Web services, .NET remoting, and COM+, so I was well aware of the "fun" associated with getting two applications to talk to one another in a meaningful manner—that is, using methods that would stand up to the scrutiny of people whose goal in life was to point out problems with the security and reliability of my applications. (That would be auditors, for those of you unfamiliar with the process.)

The application I was working on was required to be able to change the protocol used to send messages between different processes, on the fly. At the time, the choice was to write multiple channels manually or to try WCF, which was then a very new technology. My surprise at the result still lingers with me. It was easy to call remote methods through a proxy. This was quite familiar from the Web services and .NET remoting technologies. What was very different was that to switch from one protocol to another required nothing more than changing a couple of characters in the configuration file. This was stunning to me, all the more so because it just worked.

Now, this is not to say that you have complete freedom to use any transport channel in any situation, but the ability to use configuration elements to make significant changes to the underlying technology was quite new. And very, very powerful. Keep a sense of just how magical the results are as you go through the details of how to configure your client in this chapter.

Lesson 1: Configuring the Client Endpoint

One of the main concepts of configuring a WCF service is that the service contains a set of endpoints. Each endpoint can reference a set of endpoint behaviors. Each endpoint can reference a predefined binding configuration. Also, the service can reference a set of service behaviors. All this functionality can be expressed using XML.

The configuration of a client endpoint is not that different from configuring a service endpoint. The client has a set of endpoints with which it can communicate. Each endpoint is associated with a binding, and each endpoint can have one or more behaviors. The difference, naturally, is that the client won't support service behaviors. Instead, the client has the ability to define callback behaviors. However, this last piece is not configurable through a configuration file and so is not within the scope of this chapter.

After this lesson, you will be able to:

- Create the client endpoint either declaratively or imperatively.
- Modify the details of the binding through behaviors.
- Change how the client behaves, with respect to both requests and callbacks.

Estimated lesson time: 50 minutes

Declarative Configuration

By now, the fundamental concepts of endpoints (address, binding, and contract) should be very familiar to you, so it stands to reason that when configuring endpoints, whether on the client or the service, you use these same fundamental concepts.

Starting with the basics, the endpoint configuration for a client takes place in the endpoint element within the *client* element in the *ServiceModel* element. What follows is a segment from a configuration file showing the most commonly used attributes.

```
<system.serviceModel>
  <client>
    <endpoint address="http://localhost:8080/UpdateService"
      binding="wsHttpBinding"
      contract="IUpdateService"
      name="WSHttpBinding_IUpdateService">
    </endpoint>
  </client>
</system.serviceModel>
```

Not surprisingly, the basic configuration element for an endpoint specifies the three fundamental components of a WCF endpoint (address, binding, and contract). The other attribute in this configuration file, *name*, provides a mechanism for programmatic reference.

Specifying the Address

Ultimately, the address needs to evaluate to the address associated with the endpoint of the service. The *address* attribute specifies that value. The value is a string that represents the absolute Uniform Resource Identifier (URI) for the service's endpoint because the client's configuration does not allow for base addresses and relative addressing. This is different from the service endpoint capabilities, which are discussed in Lesson 2. Instead, the absolute URI for the service's endpoint must be specified.

Specifying the Binding

The binding is specified by name. The value of the *binding* attribute is a string that contains the name of the binding, which must be one of the standard binding names (shown in Table 5-1) or the name of a custom binding. In the latter case, you must also define a binding extension section to link the binding to the class that implements the binding.

Table 5-1   Bindings Supported by .NET Out of the Box

Binding Name	Description
basicHttpBinding	Used to communicate with earlier (that is, pre-WCF) ASMX Web services.
basicHttpContextBinding	The same as *basicHttpBinding* except that context is provided to the requests through cookies.
msmqIntegrationBinding	Uses MSMQ as part of the transportation channel for requests. It is expected that the service on the receiving end of the request will be a non-WCF application such as a COM+ service.
netMsmqBinding	Uses MSMQ as part of the channel for requests. This binding is used when both ends of the channel are WCF applications.
netNamedPipeBinding	Provides a reliable, secure channel that is optimized for same-machine, cross-process communication, using named pipes.
netPeerTcpBinding	Allows for multiparty communication, using peer networking over TCP.
netTcpBinding	Provides a channel optimized for cross-machine message passing, using TCP as the underlying communications protocol.
netTcpContextBinding	Uses the same TCP mechanism as *netTcpBinding* to transport messages, but context is provided through information added to the message, typically in the SOAP header.
webHttpBinding	For use with endpoints that accept HTTP formatted requests (as opposed to SOAP-formatted messages).
wsDualHttpBinding	Defines a duplex channel to a service that uses SOAP formatted messages.

Table 5-1 Bindings Supported by .NET Out of the Box

Binding Name	Description
wsFederationHttpBinding	Configures the requests for communications with a service that supports WS-Federation.
wsHttpBinding	Uses HTTP for transport along with providing support for WS-Security and WS-Reliable Messaging.
wsHttpContextBinding	Uses the same channel as *wsHttpBinding*, but context is provided through cookies.
ws2007FederationHttpBinding	Provides the same functionality as *ws2007HttpBinding* along with the support for WS-Federation.
ws2007HttpBinding	Defines a binding that provides support for the correct versions of security, reliable session, and transaction flow binding elements.

Although the name of the binding is part of the basic elements of endpoint configuration, it is not the only piece that can be configured. Along with the binding attribute, there is a *binding-Configuration* attribute. This attribute, a string value, is the name of the binding configuration section that is instantiated when the client side of the endpoint is created. A more detailed discussion of the contents of *bindingConfiguration* can be found in the "Configure Bindings" section later in this lesson.

Specifying the Contract

The third piece of the address, binding, and contract puzzle is the contract, for which the *endpoint* element includes a *contract* attribute. The value given to this attribute is the name of the interface that the service is expected to implement.

The client must be aware of the methods and properties exposed by the interface. You can find this information in a number of ways. One of the most common techniques is to use the svcutil utility to generate the proxy based on the metadata exposed by the service. The svcutil utility is also used by Visual Studio 2008 when the Add Service Reference option is selected. The program queries the service to determine the methods and properties that are exposed and then generates an interface class for use by the client application. (The svcutil utility is discussed in depth in Chapter 4, "Consuming Services.")

NOTE The contract defines an interface, not binary compatibility

It is important to remember that although the contract describes the expected interface, the service and client do not have to implement the same interface; there is no binary compatibility regarding interfaces. All that the interface truly provides is the list of methods (along with the parameter and return types) that must be implemented.

Additional Information

Up to this point, the discussion has concentrated on the main attributes in the *endpoint* element in the *client* section, but some other elements can be used in the endpoint elements. They are the *identity* section, the *headers* section, and the *metadata* section. The *identity* section relates to the security WCF uses and will be covered in Chapter 8, "User-Level Security."

Defining Endpoint Headers   The *headers* element provides additional information to the endpoint. When defined in the configuration file, the specified elements will be sent along with every request made to the endpoint. The contents of the *headers* element must be well-formed XML because they are copied into the header section of the request.

Consider the following endpoint configuration:

```
<system.serviceModel>
   <client>
      <endpoint address="http://localhost:8080/UpdateOrder"
         binding="wsHttpBinding"
         contract="IUpdateService"
         name="WSHttpBinding_UpdateOrder">
         <headers>
            <Priority xmlns="http://tempuri.org/">Expedite</Priority>
         </headers>
      </endpoint>
      <endpoint address="http://localhost:8080/CancelOrder"
         binding="wsHttpBinding"
         contract="IUpdateService"
         name="WSHttpBinding_CancelOrder">
         <headers>
            <Priority xmlns="http://tempuri.org/">Standard</Priority>
         </headers>
      </endpoint>
   </client>
</system.serviceModel>
```

In the preceding example, two client endpoints are created. Associated with each Web service request is a header that indicates the type of reply, the possible values being either *Standard* or *Expedite*. Two separate endpoints are configured, either of which can be called by the client. However, the contextual information provided with the request (in the form of the headers) could help the service determine the priority for the request. As will be covered in Chapter 12, "Concurrency," it is possible to prioritize incoming requests based on contextual data such as the information in the *headers* section, which could be used to provide the necessary context.

NOTE   Client and service need to agree on headers

Headers are one of the instances (of many that exist in WCF) in which the client and service need to be in agreement. If the client configures a set of headers, the service must be configured to receive the same headers. The configuration takes place in the *headers* element for the service's endpoint definition.

Defining Endpoint Metadata   The *metadata* element associated with a client endpoint defines how metadata provided by the service will be processed. Table 5-2 shows the list of metadata processing that can be performed.

Table 5-2   Metadata Processing Elements in the Client Endpoint

Name	Description
policyImporters	Defines the types that process the policy information provided by the service's metadata.
wsdlImporters	Defines the types that process the policy information found in the Web Services Description Language (WSDL) associated with a service.

The first step in learning how these elements operate is to understand when they are invoked. The *wsdlImporter* attribute is used when the proxy class is generated. The type specified in *wsdlImporter* must implement the *IWsdlImportExtension* interface. This interface exposes *BeforeImport*, *AfterImport*, and *ImportContract* methods. The WSDL document for the service is available in each of the methods, and the *wsdlImporter* object can add to or remove from the list of ports, methods, types, and so on that the WSDL exposes. After the *ImportContract* method is complete, the resulting WSDL is used to create the proxy class.

The *policyImporter* type is similar in structure. The type must implement the *IPolicyImportExtension* interface. The importer type is responsible for three actions:

1. Locating the custom policy assertion the extension is interested in. This is accomplished by calling one of these methods: *GetBindingAssertions*, *GetMessageBindingAssertions*, or *GetOperationBindingAssertions*.
2. Removing the found policy assertion from the collection of assertions.
3. Modifying the protocol used by the binding or the contract by adding a custom binding element or by changing the contract property of the *PolicyConversionContext* class.

Of these three items, the most important to remember is the second. After all the policy importers have been given a chance to perform their functions, WCF checks to see whether any policy assertions are left in the collection. If there are, the policy import is considered a failure, so if you find and process the policy, make sure it is not left in the collection when you are finished.

Configure Bindings

The primary purpose of a binding is to express intent. Specifically, it defines how each component in the messaging application interacts with the other components. In its implementation, bindings create a pipeline of channel factory or channel listener objects, meaning that the binding is a factory.

To understand where bindings fit into the pipeline, consider the illustration in Figure 5-1.

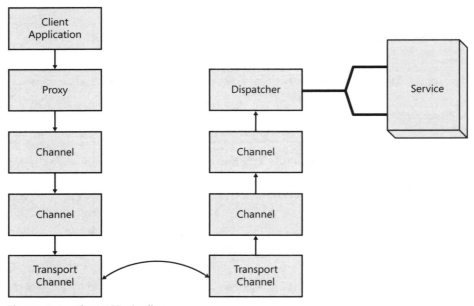

Figure 5-1   The WCF pipeline

Figure 5-1 shows the different pieces that make up the pipeline of communications from the client to the service. For bindings, the area of impact is the channel. From a configuration perspective, the bindings are exposed through the service model layer. However, the objects that are created either affect or are injected directly into the pipeline of channels. In Lesson 2, "Dynamic Service Configuration," later in this chapter, the different bindings are separated into the various *BindingElement* classes that make up the bindings. Instances of these binding elements provide the means through which WCF clients implement a particular set of messaging functionality. Ultimately, a binding is the developer-friendly mechanism for encapsulating the WCF run-time messaging functionality.

Out of the box, WCF supports a large number of transports, message encodings, protocols, and security, transaction, and concurrency options. The total number of combinations is quite large—so large, in fact, that the WCF development team worked hard to make it easier for developers to use. They bundled common combinations into a set of predefined bindings. Table 5-1 lists these bindings and their basic functionality. When specifying the endpoint, use the name of the binding in the *binding* attribute. Then the corresponding default values for the various properties will be used.

As was mentioned earlier, it is possible to provide custom configuration information for a particular binding. The starting point is to specify the name of the binding configuration in the *bindingConfiguration* attribute of the endpoint. However, to use the custom configuration, there must be a correspondingly named binding. Figure 5-2 illustrates this.

```
<system.serviceModel>
  <client>
    <endpoint address="http://localhost:8080/UpdateService"
        binding="basicHttpBinding"
        bindingConfiguration="NameOfBinding"
        contract="IUpdateService" />
  </client>
  <bindings>
    <basicHttpBinding>
      <binding name="NameOfBinding"
          receiveTimeout="00:10:00"
          sendTimeout="00:10:00"
          openTimeout="00:10:00"
          closeTimeout="00:10:00" />
    </basicHttpBinding>
  </bindings>
</system.serviceModel>
```

Figure 5-2   Specifying the binding configuration

Configure Behaviors

You use the same style of referencing system to configure client behaviors. The client behaviors are related to the endpoints defined elsewhere in the configuration file. It is expected that the *behaviorConfiguration* attribute in the endpoint will refer to the name of one of the behavior elements in the *endpointBehaviors* section. The segment from a configuration file shown in Figure 5-3 illustrates the relationship between these elements.

```
<system.serviceModel>
  <client>
    <endpoint address="http://localhost:8080/UpdateService"
        binding="basicHttpBinding"
        behaviorConfiguration="UpdateClient"
        contract="IUpdateService" />
  </client>
  <behaviors>
    <endpointBehaviors>
      <behavior name="UpdateClient">
        <clientCredentials>
          <windows allowedImpersonationLevel="Identification" />
        </clientCredentials>
      </behavior>
    </endpointBehaviors>
  </behaviors>
</system.serviceModel>
```

Figure 5-3   Specifying the behavior configuration

clientCredentials **Element**   Many services require authentication and authorization functionality. To accommodate that, the client must be able to send credential information to the
service. The *clientCredentials* element enables this.

The following is the basic structure of the element.

```
<clientCredentials type="String"
     supportInteractive="<Boolean>" >
  <clientCertificate />
  <httpDigest />
  <issuedToken />
  <peer />
  <serviceCertificate />
  <windows />
</clientCredentials>
```

Table 5-3 describes each segment.

Table 5-3   Child Elements for the *clientCredentials* Element

Element	Description

clientCertificate	Indicates the client certificate used to authenticate the client to the service. This element must be of type *X509ClientCertificateElement*. The attributes for this element are broken into two groups. The first group (*storeLocation* and *storeName*) specifies the store and location in which the X.509 certificate is found. The second group (*findValue* and *X509FindType*) identifies the certificate within the store to be used. Here is an example:
	
	```<clientCertificate findValue="Microsoft"```
	 ``` storeLocation="LocalMachine"```
	 ``` storeName="AuthRoot"```
	 ``` x509FindType="FindByIssuerName" />```

httpDigest	Specifies the digest type of credential to be used when authenticating a service. An *impersonationLevel* attribute specifies the value. Possible values are: *Identification*, *Impersonation*, *Delegation*, *Anonymous*, and *None*. Here is an example: ```<httpDigest impersonationLevel="Delegation" />```

issuedToken	Specifies the custom token passed to the service for authentication. The attributes on this element are used to specify caching parameters, the channel behaviors to use when communicating with the token issuer, and the entropy mode used when handshaking with the token issuer. Here is an example:
	
	```<issuedToken```
	 ``` cacheIssuedTokens="True"```
	 ``` defaultKeyEntropyMode="CombinedEntropy"```
	 ``` issuedTokenRenewalThresholdPercentage = "50"```
	 ``` localIssuerChannelBehaviors="String"```
	 ``` maxIssuedTokenCachingTime="01:00:00"```
	 ```</issuedToken>```

Table 5-3   Child Elements for the *clientCredentials* Element

Element	Description

peer	Specifies the credentials used to authenticate with a service when communicating in a peer-to-peer environment. Within the peer element, you can specify the certificate to use, the credentials to use for the peer-to-peer connection, and the credentials related to the message itself. Here is an example:
	
	`<peer>`
	  `<certificate/>`
	  `<peerAuthentication/>`
	  `<messageSenderAuthentication/>`
	`</peer>`

serviceCertificate	Identifies the certificate the service uses to authenticate the service to the client. The certificates accepted from the service, and sent to the service to authenticate the client are defined within this element. Here is an example:
	
	`<serviceCertificate>`
	  `<defaultCertificate />`
	  `<scopedCertificates />`
	  `<authentication />`
	`</serviceCertificate>`

windows	Indicates that the current Windows user's credentials should be used to authenticate with the service. The impersonation level is specified using the *impersonationLevel* attribute along with whether NT LAN Manager (NTLM) should be used to process the authentication. Here is an example:
	
	`<windows`
	    `allowedImpersonationLevel="Anonymous"`
	    `allowNtlm="False" />`

callbackDebug Element   The *callbackDebug* element is similar to the *serviceDebug* element used when configuring the service behaviors. The element itself is useful only if you are implementing client callbacks within your application. The element contains a single attribute called *includeExceptionDetailsInFaults*. If the attribute is set to *True*, the details of any exception raised in the callback method are sent back to the service. This enables debugging ongoing issues. As you might imagine, this element is used only when an exception is thrown from within the method called back from the service.

CAUTION   Protect your exception details

It is important to realize the dangers associated with sending exception information to an unknown client. The exception details can include not only information about how you are using a service but also a stack trace indicating details of your application. This is considered a security risk, so the *includeExceptionDetailsInFaults* attribute value should be set to *False* unless you have a specific reason to propagate the exception information back to the service.

***callbackTimeouts* Element**   The *callbackTimeouts* element also relates only to those scenarios in which the client application implements a method by which the service calls back into the client. This element has a single attribute, named *transactionTimeout*. This is a *TimeSpan* value that indicates how long any transaction will be allowed to run without completing or aborting. It is intended to override the transaction timeout value currently set on the service.

***clientVia* Element**   The *clientVia* element facilitates the debugging of messages sent between the client and the service, using a third-party tool. Under normal circumstances, the client sends the message directly to the service. To ensure that the message stream is not being attacked by a malicious user, the service validates the requesting address and port within the message with the actual address and port from which the request was sent.

However, many third-party debugging tools work by placing themselves as an intermediary between the client and the service. The client, instead of sending the request to the service, sends it to the third-party tool. The third-party tool logs it, displays it, and performs any other desired tasks on the message and then sends it to the final destination.

However, (depending on the third-party tool), the service could perceive that the request has come from a different sender. As a result, the service would reject the incoming message. To avoid this, it would use the *viaUri* attribute in the *clientVia* element. The *viaUri* attribute is set to the third-party tool's destination URI. The address for the service is left the same. Now WCF sends the message to the destination specified in the *viaUri* attribute but leaves the original destination address as being the service's address. This enables the service to accept the message while still giving the third-party tool the chance to process the request.

***dataContractSerializer* Element**   The *dataContractSerializer* element controls some of the serialization that constructs the request (or deconstructs the response). This element supports two attributes. The *MaxItemsInObjectGraph* parameter is relatively straightforward. When an object is serialized, the properties in the object are included in that serialization. If those properties are complex objects, they themselves need to be serialized. For a complex object tree, the number of items that are serialized could become quite large. The purpose of this attribute is to specify the maximum number of objects that will be serialized.

The second attribute is called *IgnoreExtensionDataObject*. This is a Boolean value that is applied when the class to which the *DataContract* attribute has been applied also implements the *IExtensibleDataObject* interface. The *IExtensibleDataObject* interface enables newer versions of the class to be deserialized by older versions of the class. More specifically, it provides a place for the new data to be stored in the old versions. If the *IgnoreExtensionDataObject* attribute is set to *True*, data added in new versions of the class are just ignored and not deserialized into the object.

***synchronousReceive* Element**   The default for when WCF receives a request is to process it asynchronously. When a message is received, the main WCF thread will accept the request and then make an asynchronous call to the service, enabling the thread to continue to accept requests.

When the *synchronousReceive* element is present, WCF creates a thread for each request. That thread is then dedicated to processing the request. Although the throughput for that request might be good, there could be a scalability problem. The number of threads available on the system is limited and, although it can be easily increased, that might not always solve the problem. Systems have a finite number of threads, so there is always the possibility of running out of threads. Note also that the only time this element is used (on the client side) is if the client application implements a callback method.

***transactedBatching* Element**   The *transactedBatching* element is yet one more element that applies to client applications that support callback methods. Just as transactions can be propagated from the client into the service, so too can transactions be propagated back from the service to the client. In fact, if you consider the possibilities, the same service (or multiple services) could call back to the client multiple times, all within the same transactions.

The *transactedBatching* element supports a single attribute, named *maxBatchSize*. This is an integer value that contains the maximum number of requests received within a single transaction.

Quick Check

Consider the following XML.

```
<system.serviceModel>
  <client>
    <endpoint address="http://localhost:8080/UpdateService"
        binding="basicHttpBinding"
        bindingConfiguration="NameOfBinding"
        contract="IUpdateService" />
  </client>
  <bindings>
    <netTcpBinding>
      <binding name="NameOfBinding"
          receiveTimeout="00:10:00"/>
    </netTcpBinding>
  </bindings>
</system.serviceModel>
```

■ Will this configuration file change the receive timeout on the *UpdateService* endpoint to be 10 minutes?

Quick Check Answer

■ No. Although the name of the binding configuration matches the name in the *bindings* collection, the type of binding is different (*basicHttpBinding* vs. *netTcpBinding*).

Imperative Configuration

Although being able to configure the client side of a WCF messaging application through a configuration file is powerful, it is not always feasible. Suppose the transport that should be used cannot be determined until run time or needs to be modified based on the capabilities of the run-time environment. In these scenarios, modifying the configuration file is not possible, so the configuration needs to take place in code. Fortunately, the names of the classes involved closely mirror the elements used to configure the service declaratively.

Building an Address

The process of building or changing the endpoint address of a service proxy is not a complicated one. The basic class involved is called *EndpointAddress*, and an instance of that class can be passed into the constructor of the proxy class. The following code demonstrates this fundamental scenario.

```
' VB
Dim endpoint As New EndpointAddress("http://localhost:8080/UpdateService")
Dim proxy As New UpdateServiceProxy(New WSHttpBinding(), endpoint)

// C#
EndpointAddress endpoint = new
    EndpointAddress("http://localhost:8080/UpdateService");
UpdateServiceProxy proxy = new UpdateServiceProxy(new WSHttpBinding(), endpoint);
```

Notice that the specification of the endpoint, at a minimum, consists of nothing more than identifying the URI that indicates the location of the service.

A second form of the constructor for the proxy takes the name of an endpoint configuration element as a parameter. This is not quite the same as dynamic configuration, but it does provide for redirecting the same proxy to different endpoints at run time.

For example, consider the following element from the configuration file.

```
<system.serviceModel>
  <client>
    <endpoint address="http://localhost:8080/UpdateService"
      binding="wsHttpBinding"
      contract="IUpdateService"
      name="WSHttpBinding_IUpdateService">
    </endpoint>
  </client>
</system.serviceModel>
```

The following code would tell the proxy to use the address and binding specified in this endpoint. Assume, for this example, that the *UpdateServiceProxy* class is the class generated when a service reference is added through Visual Studio 2008 or by using the svcutil command-line utility.

```
' VB
Dim proxy As New UpdateServiceProxy("WSHttpBinding_IUpdateService")
```

```
// C#
UpdateServiceProxy proxy = new UpdateServiceProxy("WSHttpBinding_IUpdateService");
```

Address Headers

WCF provides a mechanism, compatible with WS-Addressing, to accommodate sophisticated routing and dispatching logic. The underlying idea is to supply additional information with each request. This information can then be used either by intermediate devices or by the endpoint service itself to determine routing or processing logic.

One of the obvious questions about address headers is why you should bother. Wouldn't it be easier to just include the information that is used to determine routing or processing in the message body? That way, the client proxy would be aware of it and simply include whatever additional details are needed.

However, including this information in the contract doesn't allow for a number of common scenarios. Suppose, for example, the client doesn't have the necessary information. If the goal is to determine whether a premium or standard level of service should respond, why should the client be trusted to provide the answer? Also, suppose the routing information is attached to the message by an intermediate process. Suppose further that an intermediary receives the request, adds the routing information, and then passes the request along. In both of these cases, including the message in the contract is not appropriate.

The *AddressHeader* class (and the *Headers* property on the endpoint) are the exposed entry points to the WCF mechanism that was just described. An address header is created using the static *CreateAddressHeader* method on the *AddressHeader* class. This method takes two string parameters: the name of the header and the information to include in the header.

```
' VB
Dim header as AddressHeader = _
    AddressHeader.CreateAddressHeader("premium", _
    "http://tempuri.org/ServiceLevel", Nothing)
```

```
// C#
AddressHeader header =
    AddressHeader.CreateAddressHeader("premium",
    "http://tempuri.org/ServiceLevel", null);
```

After the *AddressHeader* object has been created, it can be associated with the *Endpoint* object, either as part of the constructor or by adding it to the Headers property.

```
' VB
Dim header as AddressHeader = _
    AddressHeader.CreateAddressHeader("premium", _
    "http://tempuri.org/ServiceLevel", Nothing)
```

```
Dim endpoint As New EndpointAddress(New _
    Uri("http://localhost:8080/UpdateService"), header)
Dim proxy As New UpdateServiceProxy(New WSHttpBinding(), endpoint)

// C#
AddressHeader header =
    AddressHeader.CreateAddressHeader("premium",
    "http://tempuri.org/ServiceLevel", null);
EndpointAddress endpoint = new
    EndpointAddress(new Uri("http://localhost:8080/UpdateService"), header);
UpdateServiceProxy proxy = new UpdateServiceProxy(new WSHttpBinding(),
    endpoint);
```

Building a Binding

The code to instantiate a proxy to a WCF service includes both an *EndpointAddress* object and a binding object. It is through this binding object that the binding information required to determine how to communicate with a WCF service is specified. Just as a reminder, the code to build and use a binding is as follows.

```
' VB
Dim endpoint As New EndpointAddress("http://localhost:8080/UpdateService")
Dim binding as New WSHttpBinding()
Dim proxy As New UpdateServiceProxy(binding, endpoint)

// C#
EndpointAddress endpoint = new
    EndpointAddress("http://localhost:8080/UpdateService");
WSHttpBinding binding = new WSHttpBinding();
UpdateServiceProxy proxy = new UpdateServiceProxy(binding, endpoint);
```

In this simple case, defining a binding for use with a WCF service is straightforward. Simply create an instance of the desired binding type and pass it into the constructor for the proxy class. In the not-so-simple case, a number of variations on this theme enable a great deal of flexibility in using WCF.

All the WCF binding classes included with .NET Framework 3.5 derive from a common abstract type, the *Binding* class in the *System.ServiceModel.Channels* namespace. Because of this, all bindings share a set of common characteristics. The good news is that the inheritance hierarchy for the *Binding* class is very shallow. It derives directly from *System.Object* and implements only the *IDefaultCommunicationTimeout* interface.

The base *Binding* object has a constructor that takes two string parameters: *name* and *namespace*. These parameters represent the XML name and namespace of the binding that is being created. The values for these parameters are distinct from the name of the binding itself. For the standard operation of the bindings, the values are not important. Instead, they are used when the capabilities of the binding need to be represented as XML metadata, such as with WSDL.

Because the *Binding* class is an abstract one, this one constructor is not the only one implemented in the bindings that are provided with WCF. In fact, each of the specialized binding classes has at least one constructor that takes additional parameters. The following sections discuss the constructors for each binding class.

Common Binding Constructors

In the first (and simplest) case, the constructor takes a string parameter that is the name of a binding in the configuration file. The following demonstrates this usage.

First, the XML from the configuration file includes a *name* attribute (shown in bold):

```
<system.serviceModel>
  <bindings>
    <basicHttpBinding>
      <binding name="NameOfBinding"
        receiveTimeout="00:10:00"
        sendTimeout="00:10:00"
        openTimeout="00:10:00"
        closeTimeout="00:10:00" />
    </basicHttpBinding>
  </bindings>
</system.serviceModel>
```

The code that calls the constructor uses the *name* attribute, as shown in bold:

```
' VB
Dim binding As New BasicHttpBinding("NameOfBinding")
```

```
// C#
BasicHttpBinding binding = new BasicHttpBinding("NameOfBinding");
```

Every one of the out-of-the-box bindings uses this style of constructor.

The second common constructor for a binding involves passing an enumeration. The actual parameter type depends on the constructor, but the purpose of the parameter is the same—it defines the level of security that is to be provided to the request.

The supported security depends greatly on the protocol. Some protocols include both message-level security (such as encryption) and transport-level security (such as is provided by Secure Sockets Layer [SSL]). Table 5-4 describes (in general) the types of values that can be provided as the parameter. The details of exactly which values can be used for each binding are covered in Chapter 7, "Infrastructure Security."

Table 5-4   Security Mode Enumeration Values

Security Mode	Description
None	No security is provided for any messages.
Transport	Security is provided at the network transport level.

Table 5-4   Security Mode Enumeration Values

Security Mode	Description
Message	The message contents are secured using SOAP message standards. This mode requires that a certificate be provided to the client system from the server running the service.
TransportWithMessageCredential	The transport layer determines the credentials to be included with the request.
TransportCredentialOnly	The message includes a set of credentials along with the message. The content is not secured, and it is up to the service to authenticate the requestor.

Building a Behavior

The idea that you're building a behavior is a bit of a misnomer. A behavior, in the context of a WCF client, is simply setting the properties on the binding to support a desired level of functionality, so when you instantiate the desired binding object (and before you associate it with an endpoint), you simply set the properties on the binding object to the necessary values. The biggest challenge in building a behavior is ensuring that the binding used by the service also supports the desired properties. The next lesson discusses the details of the properties used on each of the out-of-the-box bindings.

Lab: Configuring the Client Endpoints

In this lab, the focus is on configuring the client endpoints. The exercises discuss how to specify the binding to be used and how the binding can easily be changed through the configuration file. The exercises also demonstrate how to add custom header information to the request.

▶ **Exercise 1   Define and Change the Binding**

In this first exercise, you will define and change the binding for the Web service.

1. Navigate to the *<InstallHome>*/Chapter5/Lesson1/Exercise1/*<language>*/Before directory and double-click the Exercise1.sln file to open the solution in Visual Studio.

    The solution consists of two projects:

    ❑ The DemoService project, which is a simple WCF service library that implements the *IGetHeaders* interface. This interface consists of a single method (*GetHeaders*) that retrieves some information about the headers in the message sent to the service. For this exercise, it returns the *Action* header.

    ❑ The TestClient project, which is a console application that enables you to consume the DemoService service. A proxy to the DemoService has already been created.

2. In Solution Explorer, double-click the app.config file for the TestClient project.

    You will notice that, at the moment, the file is almost empty.

3. Add an XML element to define a *wsHttpBinding* binding. The following XML segment should be added to the existing *bindings* element.

```
<wsHttpBinding>
    <binding name="WsIGetHeaders" />
</wsHttpBinding>
```

For the binding to work correctly, you must also define an endpoint. The endpoint needs to specify the address, the binding, and the contract. The following XML segment provides this information.

4. Add it to the existing *client* element.

```
<endpoint
    address=

"http://localhost:8731/Design_Time_Addresses/DemoService/HeaderService/"
    binding="wsHttpBinding" bindingConfiguration="WsIGetHeaders"
    contract="DemoService.IGetHeaders" name="WsIGetHeaders">
</endpoint>
```

MORE INFO   Endpoint addresses and port numbers

You might notice that the URI for the endpoint address includes a port number. In this step, it is 8731. In other steps, in this or in other chapters, you might find ports 8080, 8732, or 6789 being used. These are arbitrary values that specify the port through which communication between the client and service will take place. In most cases, the reason for being explicit is to avoid a conflict between the lab exercise and a Web server that you might have installed on your computer. Because the default port for HTTP traffic is 80, port 8731 should be open on your computer. If it is not, you can change it to any other available port as long as the same change is made to both the client and the service.

To use this binding explicitly, the constructor for the proxy object can take the name of the binding. You will notice from the first segment that was added that the binding name is *wsHttpBinding*.

5. To add this, in Solution Explorer, double-click the Program.cs or Module1.vb file.

The first line of executable code declares and instantiates the *GetHeadersClient* object.

6. In the constructor for the object, pass the name of the binding to use as the sole parameter.

The first line in the *Main* method will look like the following.

```
' VB
Dim proxy As DemoService.GetHeadersClient = _
    New DemoService.GetHeadersClient("WsIGetHeaders")
```

```
//C#
DemoService.GetHeadersClient proxy =
    new DemoService.GetHeadersClient("WsIGetHeaders");
```

7. At this point, ensure that TestClient is set as the startup project and run the application by pressing F5.

    The result in the output window will indicate that the *Action* for the request is *http://tempuri.org/IGetHeaders/GetHeaders as illustrated in Figure 5-4.*

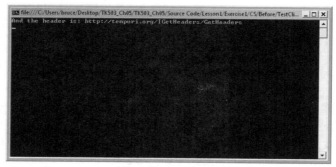

Figure 5-4   TestClient output

8. Press Enter to terminate the application.

MORE INFO   **WcfSvcHost and Visual Studio 2008**

If you run the application without debugging, you will see an exception raised as the Test-Client attempts to invoke the service. The reason for this is related to how services are run from within Visual Studio 2008. When TestClient is launched in debug mode (by pressing F5, for example), Visual Studio also starts the WCF service project by using the WcfSvcHost utility as the hosting application. This allows the interactions between the client and service to be tested. However, if the TestClient project is started in non-debugging mode (by pressing Ctrl+F5, for instance), the WCF service project is not launched using WcfSvcHost. This means that, unless the WCF service is running separately, any communication attempt between the client and the service will fail.

The binding can easily be changed by defining a different binding.

9. Start to add a TCP-based binding by adding the following XML segment to the *bindings* section in the app.config file that is already open.

```
<netTcpBinding>
    <binding name="TcpIGetHeaders" />
</netTcpBinding>
```

The binding also must have a corresponding endpoint. You might notice that this endpoint is almost identical to the previously added one. The main functional differences are in the address and binding attributes.

10. Add the following *endpoint* element to the *client* section.

```
<endpoint
    address=
"net.tcp://localhost:8731/Design_Time_Addresses/DemoService/HeaderService/"
```

```
binding="netTcpBinding" bindingConfiguration="TcpIGetHeaders"
   contract="DemoService.IGetHeaders" name="TcpIGetHeaders">
</endpoint>
```

To communicate successfully with the service, the service also must expect to receive a message through the same channel. The current setting for the service is to use the *wsHttpBinding* binding (which is expected, given that it worked the first time the application was executed).

11. To change the binding, double-click the app.config file associated with the DemoService project in Solution Explorer.

12. Locate the *baseAddresses* section in the file. Change the *add* element so that the *baseAddress* element is now in a *net.tcp* format.

The following XML segment illustrates what the element should look like after the change.

```
<add baseAddress = "net.tcp://localhost:8731/Design_Time_Addresses/DemoService/
HeaderService/"
/>
```

A few lines below, the *wsHttpBinding* associated with the endpoint should be modified to use *netTcpBinding*. The following is what the *<endpoint>* element will look like after the change.

```
<endpoint address ="" binding="netTcpBinding"
   contract="DemoService.IGetHeaders">
```

Finally, you must modify the client to use the TCP binding. In the Program.cs or Module1.vb file, the constructor for the proxy object should use the name of the TCP binding.

```
' VB
Dim proxy As DemoService.GetHeadersClient = _
   New DemoService.GetHeadersClient("TcpIGetHeaders")
```

```
//C#
   DemoService.GetHeadersClient proxy =
      new DemoService.GetHeadersClient("TcpIGetHeaders");
```

13. Run the application by pressing F5. Notice that the URI associated with the *GetHeaders* action is returned, indicating that the call to the service was executed successfully.

▶ **Exercise 2 Add Headers to the Message**

Headers are a constant part of WCF. Whether they specify actions, provide credentials, or provide information for routing, headers are integral to the workings of WCF, but they can also provide information for use by the service alone (that is, not a part of WCF). This exercise describes the technique you use to accomplish this.

1. Navigate to the *<InstallHome>*/Chapter5/Lesson1/Exercise2/*<language>*/Before directory and double-click the Exercise2.sln file to open the solution in Visual Studio.

The solution consists of two projects:

❑ The DemoService project, which is a simple WCF service library that implements the *IGetHeaders* interface. This interface consists of a single method (*GetHeaders*) that retrieves some information about the headers in the message sent to the service. Although currently the method returns the *Action* header, it won't by the time the exercise is complete.

❑ The TestClient project, which is a Console application that enables you to consume the DemoService service. A proxy to the DemoService has already been created.

2. In Solution Explorer, double-click the app.config file for the TestClient project.

You will notice the standard binding and client endpoint has already been configured. First, you must add the custom header that will be sent. A *headers* element can be added to the client's *endpoint* section. The custom headers can be added within the new *headers* element.

3. Add the following XML to the existing *endpoint* element.

```
<headers>
    <MyHeader xmlns="http://tempuri.org" name="Sample">
        <Data>This is my header data</Data>
    </MyHeader>
</headers>
```

4. Notice the namespace used (*http://tempuri.org*) and the element name (*MyHeader*). You will use this information shortly.

5. In Solution Explorer, double-click the HeaderService file in the DemoService project.

The current implementation for *GetHeaders* simply returns the *Action* header. You can access the headers that are available (including both the standard headers and any custom values) through the *RequestMessage.Headers* property. Although this looks like it might be a collection of headers, it's not. To retrieve a header, the *FindHeader* method must be used. The following code replaces the current implementation of the *GetHeaders* method.

```
' VB
Dim result As String = String.Empty
Dim myHeaderIndex As Integer
MyHeaderIndex = OperationContext.Current.RequestContext. _
    RequestMessage.Headers.FindHeader("MyHeader", "http://tempuri.org")

If MyHeaderIndex <> -1 Then
    result = OperationContext.Current.RequestContext.RequestMessage. _
        Headers.GetHeader(Of String)(myHeaderIndex)
Else
    result = OperationContext.Current.RequestContext.RequestMessage. _
        Headers.Action
End If
```

```
Return result.ToString()

// C#
string result = String.Empty;
int myHeaderIndex =
OperationContext.Current.RequestContext.RequestMessage.Headers.FindHeader
   ("MyHeader", "http://tempuri.org");
if (myHeaderIndex != -1)
   result = OperationContext.Current.RequestContext.RequestMessage.
      Headers.GetHeader<String>(myHeaderIndex);
else
   result = OperationContext.Current.RequestContext.RequestMessage.
      Headers.Action;

return result.ToString();
```

6. To launch the application, ensure that TestClient is set as the startup project, and then press F5.

   After a few seconds, you will have a *SerializationException* thrown because the contents of the header (the portion that includes the *Data* tags) cannot be deserialized. Figure 5-5 illustrates the exception.

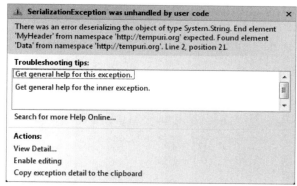

Figure 5-5   SerializationException output

The purpose of running the application with the exception is to illustrate what is actually happening when the custom header is processed: the header contents are deserialized.

7. To correct this, change the app.config for the TestClient project so that the *headers* section looks like the following:

```
<headers>
   <MyHeader xmlns="http://tempuri.org" name="Sample">
      This is my header data
   </MyHeader>
</headers>
```

8. Launch the application (by pressing F5) one more time.

This time, the header value is returned, albeit with carriage return (or line feed). Within the header, white space is not ignored. Figure 5-6 illustrates the result.

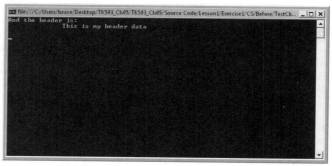

Figure 5-6   TestClient output

9. To stop running the application, press Enter.

Lesson Summary

- Client endpoint configuration starts from the same address, binding, and contract basis as services do.
- If one of the standard bindings is specified, the default values for that binding are used.
- You can define additional binding behaviors through a *behaviorConfiguration* section.
- If the client supports callbacks, you can define a number of client behaviors through the *endpointBehaviors* section.
- All the configuration that can be performed declaratively can also be performed imperatively.
- All the bindings can be instantiated using the name of a configuration section. Alternatively, the binding can be instantiated separately, assigned the desired properties, and then set to be used by the proxy.

Lesson Review

You can use the following questions to test your knowledge of the information in Lesson 1, "Configuring the Client Endpoint." The questions are also available on the companion CD if you prefer to review them in electronic form.

NOTE   Answers

Answers to these questions and explanations of why each answer choice is correct or incorrect are located in the "Answers" section at the end of the book.

1. Consider the following segment from a configuration file.

```
<system.serviceModel>
  <client>
    <endpoint address="http://localhost:8080/UpdateService"
      binding="basicHttpBinding"
      bindingConfiguration="NameOfBinding"
      contract="IUpdateService" />
  </client>
  <bindings>
    <basicHttpBinding>
      <binding name="NameOfBinding"
        receiveTimeout="00:01:00"
        sendTimeout="00:00:10"
        openTimeout="00:05:00"
        closeTimeout="00:20:00" />
    </basicHttpBinding>
  </bindings>
</system.serviceModel>
```

(handwritten: how long client keeps conn - w/ the service open in case of callback)

Which of the following statements are true? (Choose all that apply.)

A. The service found at *http://localhost:8080/UpdateService* could be an ASMX Web service. *(handwritten: basic Http binding)*

B. The service found at *http://localhost:8080/UpdateService* could be a WCF service that uses only named pipes. *(handwritten: ≠ basic HTTPBinding)*

C. The service found at *http://localhost:8080/UpdateService* supports only the methods found in the *IUpdateService* interface. *(handwritten: other Interfaces may be imple.)*

D. If the service found at *http://localhost:8080/UpdateService* doesn't return a response within one minute, an exception is raised. *(handwritten: receive Timeout)*

E. If the service found at *http://localhost:8080/UpdateService* doesn't return a response within ten seconds, an exception is raised. *(handwritten: send Timeout - length of time client will wait for response from service before excep. is raised)*

2. Consider the following segment from a configuration file.

```
<system.serviceModel>
  <client>
    <endpoint address="net.tcp://localhost:8888/UpdateService"
      binding="netTcpBinding"
      contract="IUpdateService"
      name="UpdateEndpoint"
      behaviorConfiguration="DefaultBehavior"/>
  </client>
  <bindings>
    <basicHttpBinding>
      <binding name="BasicTimeout" openTimeout="00:10:00" />
    </basicHttpBinding>
    <netTcpBinding>
      <binding name="DefaultBinding"
        openTimeout="00:05:00" />
      <binding name="TcpTimeout" openTimeout="00:20:00" />
```

```
        </netTcpBinding>
      </bindings>
      <behaviors>
        <endpointBehaviors>
          <behavior name="UpdateClient">
            <clientCredentials>
              <windows allowedImpersonationLevel="Identification" />
            </clientCredentials>
          </behavior>
        </endpointBehaviors>
      </behaviors>
    </system.serviceModel>
```

[handwritten: no name is specified in binding config. attr. so default settings are used]

[handwritten: defaults are used]

[handwritten: default Timeout for operation is 1 min.]

[handwritten: this is for basic HttpBinding]

Which of the following statements are true? (Choose all that apply.)

A. When a call is made to the service, the connection will remain open for five minutes.

B. When a call is made to the service, the connection will remain open for one minute.

C. When a call is made to the service, the connection will remain open for 10 minutes.

D. When a call is made to the service, the service will process the request as the default user for that service. *[handwritten: because impersonationLevel = Identification]*

E. When a call is made to the service, the service will process the request, using the credentials of the user who is running the client. *[handwritten: ImpersonationLevel = Impersonation or Delegation]*

3. Consider the following segment from a configuration file for a WCF service.

```
<system.serviceModel>
  <services>
    <service name="UpdateService" >
      <endpoint address="net.pipe://localhost/UpdateService"
          contract="IUpdateService"
          binding="netNamedPipeBinding" />
    </service>
  </services>
</system.serviceModel>
```

Which of the following code segments would be used to configure the client-side proxy?

A. ' VB
```vb
Dim binding As New NetNamedPipeBinding()
Dim ep As New EndpointAddress("net.pipe://localhost/UpdateService")
Dim proxy As New UpdateServiceProxy(binding, ep)
```

```csharp
// C#
NetNamedPipeBinding binding = new NetNamedPipeBinding();
EndpointAddress ep = new
    EndpointAddress("net.pipe://localhost/UpdateService");
UpdateServiceProxy proxy = new UpdateServiceProxy(binding, ep);
```

B.
```vb
' VB
Dim binding As New WsHttpBinding()
Dim ep As New EndpointAddress("http://localhost/UpdateService")
Dim proxy As New UpdateServiceProxy(binding, ep)
```

```csharp
// C#
WsHttpBinding binding = new WsHttpBinding();    incorr.
EndpointAddress ep = new
    EndpointAddress("http://localhost/UpdateService");
UpdateServiceProxy proxy = new UpdateServiceProxy(binding, ep);
```

C.
```vb
' VB
Dim binding As New NetNamedPipeBinding()
Dim ep As New EndpointAddress("http://localhost/UpdateService")
Dim proxy As New UpdateServiceProxy(binding, ep)
```

```csharp
// C#
NetNamedPipeBinding binding = new NetNamedPipeBinding();
EndpointAddress ep = new    incorrect
    EndpointAddress("http//localhost/UpdateService");
UpdateServiceProxy proxy = new UpdateServiceProxy(binding, ep);
```

D.
```vb
' VB
Dim binding As New BasicHttpBinding()
Dim ep As New EndpointAddress("net.pipe://localhost/UpdateService")
Dim proxy As New UpdateServiceProxy(binding, ep)
```

```csharp
// C#
BasicHttpBinding binding = new BasicHttpBinding();    not appr.
EndpointAddress ep = new
    EndpointAddress("net.pipe://localhost/UpdateService");
UpdateServiceProxy proxy = new UpdateServiceProxy(binding, ep);
```

Lesson 2: Dynamic Service Configuration

As you saw in Chapter 2, "Exposing the Services," it is possible to expose a service by using declarative techniques (by adding elements to the configuration file). From earlier in this chapter, you learned that both declarative and imperative methods work for configuring the client. What remains is the mechanism used to configure the service imperatively. Fortunately, the classes involved are quite similar.

> **After this lesson, you will be able to:**
> - Imperatively configure the endpoints for a service.
> - Customize the information provided by the service for consumption by a proxy generator.
> - Identify the binding elements used to create the out-of-the-box bindings.
>
> **Estimated lesson time: 50 minutes**

Imperative Configuration

To get started, consider a simple service and the process of building the endpoint program-matically. The *ServiceHost* class exposes a method called *AddServiceEndpoint*, which takes an interface indicating the contract the endpoint is supporting, a binding used to support com-munications with the client, and the address the endpoint is listening on. The following code is the first example showing how to add an endpoint for a TCP binding.

```
' VB
Dim host As New ServiceHost(GetType(UpdateService))
host.AddServiceEndpoint(GetType(IUpdateService), _
    New NetTcpBinding(), "net.tcp://localhost:8000/UpdateService")
```

```
// C#
ServiceHost host = new ServiceHost(typeof(UpdateService));
host.AddServiceEndpoint(typeof(IUpdateService),
    new NetTcpBinding(), "net.tcp://localhost:8000/UpdateService");
```

It should not be surprising that three elements are associated with the service endpoint. The contract supported by the service is indicated through the first parameter. The binding to be used is specified through the second parameter, and, finally, the address supported by the endpoint is indicated through the third parameter. All the letters are there, just in the reverse order, but they will be covered in the ABC order that makes the mnemonic so useful. Because the contract component has already been covered in Chapter 2, the focus in this chapter is on addresses and bindings.

Building an Address

Keep in mind when dynamically configuring the address of a service endpoint that the fundamental goal is to define the address on which the service will listen for incoming requests. There are two ways to go about defining the address. The first, and most straightforward, is just to provide the complete address. The valid format of the address depends on the binding used, but many of them look very similar to the format for a URL with which you're familiar. That layout is:

```
protocol://servername[:portNumber]/pathToEndpoint
```

So, for example, the following strings are valid addresses.

1. *http://localhost/SubDirectory/UpdateService*
2. *net.tcp://localhost:8080/UpdateService*
3. *net.pipe://localhost/Directory/UpdateService*

However, for some protocols, such as the MSMQ-based bindings, the address will be completely different: *msmq.formatname:DIRECT=OS:.\private$\updateQueue.*

When the address is fully specified, such as in the preceding examples, the process of creating the endpoint programmatically is simple. The first example (in the "imperative Configuration" section) showed one way, with the address specified as a string in the third parameter. It is also possible to create a *Uri* object and use that instance instead of a string, as shown here:

```vb
' VB
Dim host As New ServiceHost(GetType(UpdateService))
Dim address As New Uri("net.tcp://localhost:8000/UpdateService")
host.AddServiceEndpoint(GetType(IUpdateService), _
   New NetTcpBinding(), address)
```

```csharp
// C#
ServiceHost host = new ServiceHost(typeof(UpdateService));
Uri address = new Uri("net.tcp://localhost:8000/UpdateService");
host.AddServiceEndpoint(typeof(IUpdateService),
   new NetTcpBinding(), address);
```

The second technique you can use to build the address is called *relative addressing*. In this case, a base address is specified when the host is created. Then, when the service endpoint is added to the host, the relative address for the endpoint is specified. The complete address is constructed by concatenating the base address and the relative address. The following example would create exactly the same endpoint as the previous example, the only difference being that relative addressing is used.

```vb
' VB
Dim host As New ServiceHost(GetType(UpdateService), _
   New Uri() { New Uri("net.tcp://localhost:8000") } )
host.AddServiceEndpoint(GetType(IUpdateService), _
   New NetTcpBinding(), "UpdateService")
```

```csharp
// C#
ServiceHost host = new ServiceHost(typeof(UpdateService),
   new Uri[] { new Uri("net.tcp://localhost:8000") } );
host.AddServiceEndpoint(typeof(IUpdateService),
   new NetTcpBinding(), "UpdateService");
```

Although this completes the basics of addressing, there are a number of areas in which additional capabilities are required. You probably would not need them under normal conditions, but in situations that require more complex solutions, they can easily become critical. Some of these situations are described in the next few sections.

Multiple Service Endpoints

The examples shown to this point have covered the idea that a *ServiceHost* object will support a single endpoint, but there is no such restriction in *ServiceHost*. It is quite possible to add multiple endpoints for a single host. That host will then listen on the defined endpoints and process the incoming requests in the expected fashion. The following example demonstrates how the same endpoint can support two separate contracts (*IUpdateService* and *IRetrieveService*).

```vb
' VB
Dim host As New ServiceHost(GetType(UpdateService))
Dim binding As New NetTcpBinding()
host.AddServiceEndpoint(GetType(IUpdateService), _
   binding, "net.tcp://localhost:8000/UpdateService")
host.AddServiceEndpoint(GetType(IRetrieveService), _
   binding, "net.tcp://localhost:8000/UpdateService")
```

```csharp
// C#
ServiceHost host = new ServiceHost(typeof(UpdateService));
NetTcpBinding binding = new NetTcpBinding();
host.AddServiceEndpoint(typeof(IUpdateService),
   binding, "net.tcp://localhost:8000/UpdateService");
host.AddServiceEndpoint(typeof(IRetrieveService),
   binding, "net.tcp://localhost:8000/UpdateService");
```

Notice that the same *NetTcpBinding* object is passed into both *AddServiceEndpoint* methods. If you had created two different *NetTcpBinding* objects and passed each one into an *AddServiceEndpoint* call, the second call to *AddServiceEndpoint* would have caused a run-time exception with the message indicating that a binding instance had already been associated with the endpoint address. There must be a one-to-one correlation between bindings and endpoint addresses.

It is also possible for a single *ServiceHost* object to expose the same contract on different bindings. For example, the following code defines a service host that allows requests to arrive either through TCP or HTTP.

```vb
' VB
Dim host As New ServiceHost(GetType(UpdateService))
host.AddServiceEndpoint(GetType(IUpdateService), _
    New NetTcpBinding(), "net.tcp://localhost:8000/UpdateService")
host.AddServiceEndpoint(GetType(IUpdateService), _
    New WsHttpBinding(), "http://localhost/UpdateService")
```

```csharp
// C#
ServiceHost host = new ServiceHost(typeof(UpdateService));
host.AddServiceEndpoint(typeof(IUpdateService),
    new NetTcpBinding(), "net.tcp://localhost:8000/UpdateService");
host.AddServiceEndpoint(typeof(IRetrieveService),
    new WsHttpBinding("http://localhost/UpdateService"));
```

Sharing a Listener URI

One of the formats of *AddServiceEndpoint* allows for the definition of a listener URI. This parameter is used as the fourth parameter in the *AddServiceEndpoint* call. The listener provides an intermediate point for the client to send a request. The client can provide a *viaUri* attribute so that that the correct endpoint is eventually used to process the request. Here is an example:

```vb
' VB
Dim host As New ServiceHost(GetType(UpdateService))
Dim commonUri As New Uri("net.tcp://localhost:8888/common")
Dim binding As New NetTcpBinding()
host.AddServiceEndpoint(GetType(IUpdateService), _
    binding, "/UpdateService1", commonUri)
host.AddServiceEndpoint(GetType(IUpdateService), _
    binding, "/UpdateService2", commonUri)
```

```csharp
// C#
ServiceHost host = new ServiceHost(typeof(UpdateService));
Uri commonUri = new Uri("net.tcp://localhost:8888/common");
NetTcpBinding binding = new NetTcpBinding();
host.AddServiceEndpoint(typeof(IUpdateService),
    binding, "/UpdateService1", commonUri);
host.AddServiceEndpoint(typeof(IUpdateService),
    binding, "/UpdateService2", commonUri);
```

For a service defined in this manner, the client code to connect to it would look like the following.

```vb
' VB
Dim endpoint As New EndpointAddress("net.tcp://localhost:8000/UpdateService1")
Dim binding As New NetTcpBinding()
Dim commonUri As Uri = new Uri("net.tcp://localhost:8888/common")
```

```
Dim proxy As New UpdateServiceProxy(binding, endpoint)
proxy.Endpoint.Behaviors.Add(newViaUriBehavior(commonUri))

// C#
EndpointAddress endpoint = new
    EndpointAddress("net.tcp://localhost:8000/UpdateService2");
NetTcpBinding binding = new NetTcpBinding();
Uri commonUri = new Uri("net.tcp://localhost:8888/common");
UpdateServiceProxy proxy = new UpdateServiceProxy(binding, endpoint);
proxy.Endpoint.Behaviors.Add(newViaUriBehavior(commonUri));
```

Building a Binding

The second building block in creating the WCF endpoint is the binding. You have already seen the basic example of using bindings with service endpoints, that being to instantiate the desired binding and include it in the call to *AddServiceEndpoint*. However, each of the bindings that can be used has properties that add to the binding's functionality, properties that tend to be directly related to the binding itself. Therefore, this section offers a detailed look at the bindings available with .NET Framework 3.5.

The challenge when looking at the bindings is to find an easy way to collect all the information. One option is just to present a list of all the bindings and then describe the properties of each, but that would result in a lot of repetition. Instead, consider what a binding actually consists of: *BindingElement* classes. In fact, that is all a binding is: a set of binding elements that have been predefined as a group so that they can be used as a single unit. Therefore, as you go through the bindings described in the following sections, the focus is on the *BindingElement* classes that are used because after a binding element is understood, it doesn't matter in which binding it is used–the purpose, functionality, and properties remain the same. Because binding elements are reused in other bindings, you can simply refer to the initial place where the other bindings' elements are defined in this section.

basicHttpBinding Binding

The starting point is the default binding for WCF, the one used for basic HTTP messaging. This binding has four security modes, defined through the *Security.Mode* property on the binding. The security mode affects the binding elements used. To start with, consider the simplest case in which no security is provided at all.

The *basicHttpBinding* with no security uses two binding elements, *TextMessageEncodingBindingElement* and *HttpTransportBindingElement*. The *TextMessageEncodingBindingElement* encodes the message in a format suitable for text-based SOAP messages. Table 5-5 contains the properties exposed by this binding element. To be clear, when a property is exposed by the element, that means the binding class (*basicHttpBinding*, in this case) has a corresponding property.

Table 5-5 *TextMessageEncodingBindingElement* **Properties**

Property	Description
MaxReadPoolSize	Determines the number of readers allocated to the pool. These readers will be used to process incoming requests.
MaxWritePoolSize	Determines the number of writers allocated to the pool. These writers will be used to process outgoing requests.
MessageVersion	Contains the SOAP and WS-Addressing versions used to determine the details of the message encoding.
ReaderQuotas	Defines the constraints on the complexity of SOAP messages processed. The constraints include the maximum length, the longest string content, the number of bytes processed per read, the maximum depth of the message hierarchy, and the number of characters in the name table.
WriteEncoding	The encoding used to format the characters in the text message.

The *HttpTransportBindingElement* class supports the transmission of the message over the HTTP protocol. This particular protocol is the standard one used by WCF to achieve maximum interoperability. Table 5-6 provides a list of the properties included in this binding element.

Table 5-6 *HttpTransportBindingElement* **Properties**

Property	Description
AllowCookies	A Boolean value that indicates whether cookies are accepted by the client and then presented to the service on subsequent requests.
AuthenticationScheme	The authentication scheme used by the client to authenticate with the HTTP listener on the service.
BypassProxyOnLocal	A Boolean value that indicates whether any configured proxy server should be bypassed if the address for the service is a local address.
HostNameComparison-Mode	Indicates how the host name will be matched in the URI. The possible values include an exact match (which would preclude interchanging localhost and the machine name, for example) or a strong and weak wildcard match.
KeepAliveEnabled	A Boolean value indicating whether a persistent connection to the service should be established.
ProxyAddress	The URI for the proxy that will be used as part of the transport chain.
ProxyAuthentication-Scheme	The scheme that will be used to authenticate the client with the proxy prior to sending the request.
Realm	The realm used by basic and digest authentication to segregate different sets of protected resources.

Table 5-6   *HttpTransportBindingElement* **Properties**

Property	Description
TransferMode	The mode by which the request will be transferred over the transport layer. The possible choices include buffered or streamed. With the streamed option, the response, the request, or both can be streamed.
UnsafeConnectionNtlm-Authentication	This value indicates whether connection sharing is occurring on the server. If connection sharing is enabled, NTLM authentication will be performed once for each TCP connection. This is necessary because those connections could be shared, and the security context might be different for each connection.
UseDefaultWebProxy	A Boolean value that indicates whether the machine-wide proxy will be used instead of the custom one defined elsewhere in the binding element.

Now that you understand the basic non-secure mode, look at how the binding elements change when security is added. First, if the security mode is set to *Transport*, HTTPS transmits the message. This means that *HttpTransportBindingElement* will be replaced by *HttpsTransport-BindingElement* and, because *HttpsTransportBindingElement* derives from *HttpTransportBinding-Element*, you need to consider only the extra members added to support HTTPS, as shown in Table 5-7.

Table 5-7   Properties Added to *HttpsTransportBindingElement* **Class**

Property	Description
RequreClientCertificate	A Boolean value that indicates whether SSL client authentication is required.
Scheme	Although this property actually comes from the *TransportBindingElement* class, the value of the property will be *https* for this class.

When the security mode is set to *Message* or *TransportWithMessageCredentials*, the *Asymmetric-SecurityBindingElement* and *TransportSecurityBindingElement* classes are added (respectively) to the stack. Chapter 8 discusses the properties associated with these elements.

The last change you can make to *basicHttpBinding* is to set MessageEncoding to Message Transmission Optimization Mechanism (MTOM). This causes *TextMessageEncodingBindingElement* to be replaced with *MtomMessageEncodingBindingElement*. This class doesn't have any additional properties beyond the standard *TransportBindingElement* class.

netTcpBinding Binding

The *netTcpBinding* attribute uses, not surprisingly, TCP as the underlying basis. As a result, the *BindingElement* classes that are involved reflect this. In this case, three binding elements are involved. The *BinaryMessageEncodingBindingElement* class is responsible for converting the message into a binary format for transmission. This class has no properties beyond the properties found on the *TransportBindingElement* class.

The second binding element in the stack is the *TransactionFlowBindingElement* class. The only property of interest in this class is *TransactionProtocol*. This property specifies how transactions are flowed from the client to the service. The default value is *OleTransaction*, but WCF also supports WS-Atomic Transactions.

The final binding element is the *TcpTransportBindingElement*. Table 5-8 contains the properties and descriptions found on the class.

Table 5-8 *TcpTransportBindingElement* **Properties**

Property	Description
ChannelInitializationTimout	The time limit for a channel initialization request to be accepted.
ConnectionBufferSize	The size of the buffer used to transmit the serialized message.
ConnectionPoolSettings	The collection of settings used to control the connection pool.
ListenBacklog	The maximum number of queued connection requests that can be pending.
PortSharingEnabled	A Boolean value indicating whether the sharing of the TCP port is enabled for the connection.
TeredoEnabled	Teredo is a technology used to access clients who are behind a firewall. This Boolean value indicates whether the technology should be employed for this connection.
TransferMode	The mode by which the request will be transferred over the transport layer. The possible choices include buffered or streamed. With the streamed option, the response, the request, or both can be streamed.

netNamedPipeBinding Binding

Now you start to see some commonality as you build your stack of binding elements. There are three binding elements in the standard stack. The first, *TransactionFlowBindingElement*, was discussed in the "*netTcpBinding* Binding" section. The second, *BinaryMessageEncodingBindingElement*, was also covered in the "*netTcpBinding* Binding" section. The third element is *NamedPipeTransportBindingElement*. Table 5-9 contains the properties found in that class.

Table 5-9 *NamedPipeTransportBindingElement* **Properties**

Property	Description
ChannelInitializationTimeout	The time limit for a channel initialization request to be accepted.
ConnectionBufferSize	The size of the buffer used to transmit the serialized message.
ConnectionPoolSettings	The collection of settings used to control the connection pool.

Table 5-9 *NamedPipeTransportBindingElement* **Properties**

Property	Description
TransferMode	The mode by which the request will be transferred over the transport layer. The possible choices include buffered or streamed. With the streamed option, the response, the request, or both can be streamed.

netMsmqBinding Binding

Continuing through the different binding types, you arrive at *netMsmqBinding*. Here the transport layer depends on MSMQ as the underlying mechanism, and the stacking of binding elements illustrates that. This binding has only two elements because MSMQ does not support transaction flow. One of the binding elements, *BinaryMessageEncodingBindingElement*, was discussed in the "*netTcpBinding* Binding" section. The second binding element is *MsmqTransportBindingElement*. Table 5-10 contains a list of the properties and descriptions.

Table 5-10 *NetMsmqTransportBindingElement* **Properties**

Property	Description
CustomDeadLetterQueue	The URI for a custom dead-letter queue that requests that cannot be delivered will be sent to.
DeadLetterQueue	The collection of properties associated with the dead-letter queue.
Durable	Determines whether the messages sent using the binding are durable or volatile.
ExactlyOnce	Indicates whether messages sent through this binding will have exactly-once delivery assurances.
MaxRetryCycles	Value indicating the maximum number of attempts to deliver the message to the receiving application.
MsmqTransportSecurty	Used to set the transport-level security that will be used by messages sent through the binding.
QueueTransferProtocol	Specifies the mechanism used to send messages between queue managers. The choices are to use the native MSMQ protocol, SOAP reliable message protocol (SRMP), and SRMP secure. If the *UseActiveDirectory* property is set to *True*, only the native protocol can be used without throwing an exception.
ReceiveErrorHandling	Enumerated value that determines how errors that occur during the receive process are to be handled. The choices are to generate a fault back to the client, drop the message, reject the message by sending a negative acknowledgement, or move the message to the poison-message queue.

Table 5-10 *NetMsmqTransportBindingElement* **Properties**

Property	Description
ReceiveRetryCount	Indicates the number of attempts made to send a message before it is moved into the retry queue.
RetryCycleDelay	Value specifying the number of seconds to wait before attempting another retry cycle.
TimeToLive	A numeric value specifying how long a message will be allowed to exist in the various retry cycles before it is moved to the dead-letter queue.
TransactedReceiveEnabled	Boolean value indicating whether the receive operation for a message should be part of a transaction.
UseActiveDirectory	Boolean value indicating whether the queue address should be converted using Active Directory Domain Services (AD DS).
UseMsmqTracing	Boolean value that enables or disables the tracing functions built into MSMQ.
UseSourceJournal	A Boolean flag that indicates whether copies of the message processed through the binding should be stored in the source journal queue.

netPeerTcpBinding Binding

The last of the main transport types is *netPeerTcpBinding*. This is a peer-to-peer transport type. This binding has three binding elements in the stack. *BinaryMessageEncodingBindingElement* has already been discussed in the "*netTcpBinding* Binding" section. Two elements, however, still need discussion.

The *PnrpPeerResolverBindingElement* class is a key part of the peer-to-peer mechanism. It provides the implementation of the Peer Name Resolution Protocol (PNRP), which is required to establish a peer-to-peer connection. There is only one property, called *ReferralPolicy*, that is distinctive to this class. *ReferralPolicy* determines whether the resolver process will share referrals with others. The valid choices include *Share* and *DoNotShare*. The *ReferralPolicy* value can also be determined by querying the resolver service.

The third binding element is called *PeerTransportBindingElement*. Table 5-11 contains the properties and their descriptions, which are distinctive.

Table 5-11 *PeerTransportBindingElement* **Properties**

Property	Description
ListenIPAddress	Specifies the IP address on which the peer node will listen for incoming requests
Port	Specifies the port number on which requests will be listened for
Security	The collection of settings used to control the security this binding uses

wsDualHttpBinding

The *wsDualHttpBinding* attribute adds a twist to the binding elements used in the HTTP-based bindings, yet it implements *TransactionFlowBindingElement, TextMessageEncodingBinding-Element,* and *HttpTransportBindingElement.* These have been described in the "*basicHttpBinding* Binding" section. There are, however, two additions.

CompositeDuplexBindingElement enables callbacks to occur. The element defines a single property, *ClientBaseAddress.* This is the address to which callback messages will be sent.

The idea of a callback message is worth a few additional words. The *wsDualHttpBinding* is a duplex binding, which means that it allows not only for the client to send messages to the service but also for the service to send messages back to the client. This pattern facilitates event-like behavior, so the service can notify the client while the session is maintained.

For this to occur, the binding must enable creation of a duplex channel. One channel is used (as it is with other bindings) to send messages from the client to the service. A second channel has the client acting as the listener. The service can send messages along this channel, knowing that they will be received by the client. Chapter 12 discusses duplex bindings and services in more detail.

The other binding element that has been added is the *ReliableSessionBindingElement.* This element, which can actually be added to many of the different transports, ensures an ordered arrival of messages at the service (or by the client through a callback). Table 5-12 contains the properties and their descriptions, which are distinctive.

Table 5-12   *ReliableSessionBindingElement* Properties

Property	Description
AcknowledgementInterval	Specifies the amount of time that the service will wait before sending an acknowledgement to the client
EnableFlowControl	A Boolean value that indicates whether flow control is enabled within the binding
InactivityTimeout	Determines how long the service will remain active when there is no processing of requests
MaxPendingChannels	The largest number of messages that can be waiting before an exception is raised
MaxRetryCount	The maximum number of attempts to be made before an exception is raised
MaxTransferWindowSize	The largest number of messages that can be buffered, either on the sending or receiving side
Ordered	Boolean value indicating whether the binding should ensure that messages are received in exactly the same order as the order in which they are sent

---

Quick Check

1. What is the difference between a duplex binding and a nonduplex binding?
2. Are there limitations regarding the type of shared listeners that can be configured on a single endpoint?

Quick Check Answers

1. Duplex bindings allow the service to send a callback to the client. The underlying assumption is that the client is capable of receiving WCF messages as well as sending them.
2. The only limitation is found in the physical capabilities of the binding. It would not be possible to have two HTTP-based bindings at the same endpoint because the listener would not be able to distinguish between the incoming messages.

The Rest of the Bindings

Now that you have gone over all the basic bindings, look at the result. Table 5-13 displays the bindings that were not covered explicitly, along with the binding elements that they use.

Table 5-13   Binding Elements Used in Other Out-of-the-Box Bindings

Binding	Binding Elements
basicHttpContextBinding	*TextMessageEncodingBindingElement*, *HttpTransportBindingElement*. Both of these are described in the "*basicHttpBinding* Binding" section. The main difference is that *allowCookies* is set to *True*.
msmqIntegrationBinding	*BinaryMessageEncodingBindingElement*, *MsmqTransportBindingElement*. These elements are described in the "*netMsmqBinding* Binding" section.
netTcpContextBinding	*BinaryMessageEncodingBindingElement*, *TransactionFlowBindingElement*, *TcpTransportBindingElement*. These elements are described in the "*netTcpBinding* Binding" section.
webHttpBinding	*TextMessageEncodingBindingElement*, *HttpTransportBindingElement*. Both of these are described in the "*basicHttpBinding* Binding" section. The main difference in this binding is the formatting of the message.

Table 5-13   Binding Elements Used in Other Out-of-the-Box Bindings

Binding	Binding Elements
wsFederationHttpBinding	*TransactionFlowBindingElement,* *TextMessageEncodingBindingElement,* *HttpTransportBindingElement.* These elements are described in the "*basicHttpBinding* Binding" section.
wsHttpContextBinding	*TransactionFlowBindingElement,* *TextMessageEncodingBindingElement,* *HttpTransportBindingElement.* These elements are described in the "*basicHttpBinding* Binding" section.
ws2007FederationhttpBinding	*TransactionFlowBindingElement,* *TextMessageEncodingBindingElement,* *HttpTransportBindingElement.* These elements are described in the "*basicHttpBinding* Binding" section.
ws2007HttpBinding	*TransactionFlowBindingElement,* *TextMessageEncodingBindingElement,* *HttpTransportBindingElement.* These elements are described in the "*basicHttpBinding* Binding" section.

Exam Tip   It is likely that the different types of bindings and the capabilities they provide will form the basis for exam questions. The type of question that arises might include the difference between duplex and nonduplex, the support for different authentication types, and the ability to provide reliable message delivery.

Lab: Dynamically Building a Service Endpoint

In this lab, the focus is on creating a service endpoint through code. You create a simple, self-hosted service and then create shared endpoints and multibinding shared endpoints.

▶ **Exercise 1   Create a Self-Hosted Service Through Code**

In this first exercise, you will create a self-hosted service. Functionally, the service will be similar to the one constructed in the lab for the first lesson in this chapter in that it will implement the *IGetHeaders* interface.

1. Navigate to the <*InstallHome*>/Chapter5/Lesson2/Exercise1/<*language*>/Before directory and double-click the Exercise1.sln file to open the solution in Visual Studio.

   The solution consists of two projects:

❑ The DemoService project, a WCF service library that implements the *IGetHeaders* interface. This interface consists of a single method (*GetHeaders*) that retrieves some information about the headers in the message sent to the service. For this exercise, it returns the *Action* header.

❑ The TestClient project, a Console application that enables you to consume the DemoService service. A proxy to the DemoService has already been created.

2. In Solution Explorer, double-click the Program.cs or Module1.vb file in the DemoService project.

Because you are creating a self-hosted service, the code to instantiate the *ServiceHost* object and define the endpoints will be added to the *Main* method.

3. To start, create the basic structure for this process. Add the following code to the *Main* method.

```
' VB
Dim host As ServiceHost
host.Open()
Console.WriteLine("Host is running...hit Enter to terminate")
Console.ReadLine()
host.Close()
```

```
// C#
ServiceHost host;
host.Open();
Console.WriteLine("Host is running...hit Enter to terminate");
Console.ReadLine();
host.Close();
```

4. One overload for the constructor for *ServiceHost* takes a type (the implementation class for the service) and a URI (that defines the endpoint address). For this exercise, a *netTcpBinding* binding will be used. Add the following code immediately below the declaration for the *ServiceHost* object.

```
' VB
host = New ServiceHost(GetType(HeaderService), _
    New Uri() { New Uri("net.tcp://localhost:8240/DemoService") } )
```

```
// C#
host = new ServiceHost(typeof(HeaderService),
    new Uri[] { new Uri("net.tcp://localhost:8240/DemoService") } );
```

5. After *ServiceHost* has been instantiated, the service's endpoint needs to be added to it. Do this through the *AddServiceEndpoint* method. Add the following code below the just added lines.

```
' VB
Dim binding As New NetTcpBinding()
host.AddServiceEndpoint(GetType(IGetHeaders), binding, _
    "net.tcp://localhost:8240/DemoService")
```

```
// C#
NetTcpBinding binding = new NetTcpBinding();
host.AddServiceEndpoint(typeof(IGetHeaders), binding,
    "net.tcp://localhost:8240/DemoService");
```

6. Build the project by choosing the Build DemoService item from the Build menu.

7. Using Windows Explorer, navigate to the just created executable at *<InstallHome>*/Chapter5/Lesson2/Exercise1/*<language>*/Before/bin/debug.

8. Double-click DemoService.exe. (It's possible, if you are running antivirus software, that you might be prompted to allow the executable to run. If so, take whatever action is required to allow the application to run.) A command window will appear, indicating that the host is running.

9. In Visual Studio 2008, ensure that the TestClient project is set as the startup project, then launch the client application by pressing F5.

   Because TestClient has been marked as the startup project, the client will execute. A message will appear in the command window, indicating that the header is called *GetHeaders*. This indicates that the service host has been successfully defined and executed imperatively.

10. Press Enter in the Test Client command window.

11. Press Enter in the Demo Service command window.

▶ **Exercise 2   Add Multiple Endpoints**

Creating a single service that supports multiple endpoints and bindings simultaneously is only slightly more challenging than creating a service that exposes a single endpoint.

1. Navigate to the *<InstallHome>*/Chapter5/Lesson2/Exercise2/*<language>*/Before directory and double-click the Exercise2.sln file to open the solution in Visual Studio.

   The solution consists of two projects:

   ❑ The DemoService project, a WCF service library that implements the *IGetHeaders* interface. This interface consists of a single method (*GetHeaders*) that retrieves some information about the headers in the message sent to the service. For this exercise, it returns the *Action* header. You implement a second interface, *ICalculate*, as part of this exercise.

   ❑ The TestClient project, a console application that enables you to consume the DemoService service. A proxy to the DemoService has already been created.

2. In Solution Explorer, double-click the HeaderService file.

   The project already has an *ICalculate* interface defined. (It consists of a single method called *Sum*.) This method will be implemented in the *HeaderService* class.

3. In the class declaration for *HeaderService*, indicate that the class implements the *ICalculate* interface. Change the class declaration to look like the following.

```vb
' VB
Public Class HeaderService
    Implements IGetHeaders, ICalculate
```

```csharp
// C#
public class HeaderService : IGetHeaders, ICalculate
```

4. Implement the *ICalculate* interface. This requires that a *Sum* method be added. The method takes an array of doubles and returns a double. Add the following code to the *HeaderService* class.

```vb
' VB
Public Function Sum(values As Double()) As Double _
    Implements ICalculate.Sum
    Dim result As double
    Dim value As double
    For Each value in values
        result += value
    Next
    Return result
End Function
```

```csharp
// C#
public double Sum(double[] values)
{
    double result = 0.0;
    foreach (double value in values)
        result += value;
    return result;
}
```

Now that *ICalculate* has been implemented, you must add to the service the endpoint through which it can be accessed.

5. In Solution Explorer, double-click the Program.cs or Module1.vb file in the DemoService project.

6. Below the existing code that adds a service endpoint, add another call to the *AddService-Endpoint* method. This call adds the endpoint for the *ICalculate* methods, as shown here:

```vb
' VB
host.AddServiceEndpoint(GetType(ICalculate), binding, _
    "net.tcp://localhost:8240/DemoService")
```

```csharp
// C#
host.AddServiceEndpoint(typeof(ICalculate), binding,
    "net.tcp://localhost:8240/DemoService");
```

7. To demonstrate this new endpoint, you must make some changes to the TestClient project. Start by double-clicking the app.config file in the TestClient project within Solution Explorer.

8. In the *bindings* section, you must add a new binding for *wsHttpBinding*. Add the following XML segment to the *netTcpBinding* section.

   ```
   <binding name="TcpICalculate" />
   ```

   The binding that you just added includes a reference to an endpoint with a name of *TcpICalculate*. You must add this endpoint to the *client* element within the app.config file.

9. Add the following element to the *client* element.

   ```
   <endpoint address="net.tcp://localhost:8240/DemoService"
       binding="netTcpBinding" bindingConfiguration="TcpICalculate"
       contract="DemoService.ICalculate" name="TcpICalculate" />
   ```

   Finally (at least for TestClient), you must modify the console application to make the call to the *Sum* method found in *ICalculate*.

10. In Solution Explorer, double-click the Program.cs or Module1.vb file. In the *Main* method, add the following code below the current call to *Console.WriteLine*.

   ```
   ' VB
   Dim calcProxy As DemoService.CalculateClient = _
       New DemoService.CalculateClient("TcpICalculate")
   Console.WriteLine("And the sum is: " + _
       calcProxy.Sum(New double() { 1.4, 3.5, 7.8 }).ToString())
   ```

   ```
   // C#
   DemoService.CalculateClient calcProxy =
       new DemoService.CalculateClient("TcpICalculate");
   Console.WriteLine("And the sum is: " +
       calcProxy.Sum(new double[] { 1.4, 3.5, 7.8 }));
   ```

11. Build the project by right-clicking the DemoService project in Solution Explorer and selecting Build.

12. Using Windows Explorer, navigate to the newly created executable. It can be found at *<InstallHome>*/Chapter5/Lesson2/Exercise2/*<language>*/Before/bin/debug.

13. Double-click DemoService.exe.

   As mentioned in Exercise 1, it's possible, if you are running antivirus software, that you might be prompted to allow the executable to run. If so, take whatever action is required.)

   A command window will appear indicating that the host is running.

14. In Visual Studio 2008, ensure that TestClient is set as the startup project, then launch the client application by pressing F5.

   A message will appear in the Console window, indicating that the header is called *GetHeaders*, and the sum of array of doubles passed to the *Sum* method displays. This indicates that the service host has been successfully defined and executed imperatively. Figure 5-7 shows the expected results in the Console window.

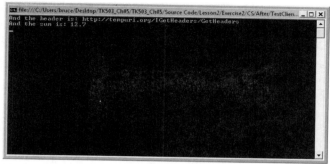

Figure 5-7 TestClient output

15. Press Enter in the Test Client Console window.

16. Press Enter in the Demo Service Console window.

17. To add a second endpoint for the same interface (*ICalculate*), go back to the Program.cs or Module1.vb file for the DemoService project.

    The *AddServiceEndpoint* method will be used again, except that this time, a *wsHttpBinding* binding will be specified.

18. Add the following code below the existing calls to *AddServiceEndpoint*.

    Notice that not only is the binding different but so is the port number on which the service will listen for requests.

```vb
' VB
host.AddServiceEndpoint(GetType(ICalculate), _
    New WSHttpBinding(), "http://localhost:8241/DemoService")
```

```csharp
// C#
host.AddServiceEndpoint(typeof(ICalculate), new WSHttpBinding(),
    "http://localhost:8241/DemoService");
```

    Again, you must modify the client to use the new binding.

19. In the app.config file for TestClient, add the following XML segment to the *<bindings>* section.

```xml
<wsHttpBinding>
    <binding name="WsICalculate" />
</wsHttpBinding>
```

    The binding that was just added includes a reference to an endpoint with a name of *WsICalculate*. You must add this endpoint to the client element within the app.config file.

20. Add the following element to the client element.

```xml
<endpoint address="http://localhost:8241/DemoService"
    binding="wsHttpBinding" bindingConfiguration="WsICalculate"
    contract="DemoService.ICalculate" name="WsICalculate" />
```

Now you must modify the TestClient application to use the *wsHttpBinding* binding.

21. In the Program.cs or Module1.vb file of the TestClient project, modify the constructor for the *CalculateClient* object as follows:

```vb
' VB
Dim calcProxy As DemoService.CalculateClient = _
    New DemoService.CalculateClient("WsICalculate")
```

```csharp
// C#
DemoService.CalculateClient calcProxy =
    new DemoService.CalculateClient("WsICalculate");
```

22. Build the project by right-clicking the DemoService project in Solution Explorer and selecting Build.

23. Using Windows Explorer, navigate to the newly created executable at *<InstallHome>*/ Chapter5/Lesson2/Exercise2/*<language>*/Before/bin/debug.

24. Double-click DemoService.exe.

    Again, it's possible, if you are running antivirus software, that you might be prompted to allow the executable to run. If so, take whatever action is required to allow the application to run. You must also start the service with appropriate permissions.

    A Console window will appear indicating that the host is running.

25. In Visual Studio 2008, launch the client application by pressing F5.

    A message will appear in the command window, indicating that the header is called *GetHeaders*, and the result of the *Sum* method displays.

26. Press Enter in the Test Client command window. If you are prompted to press a key to continue, do so.

27. Press Enter in the Demo Service command window. If you are prompted to press a key to continue, do so.

Lesson Summary

- A single service can support multiple endpoints on either the same binding or different bindings.
- Bindings are made up of different combinations of different binding elements. Each binding element provides a set of functionality that is customized (through properties) for a particular binding.

Lesson Review

You can use the following questions to test your knowledge of the information in Lesson 2, "Dynamic Service Configuration." The questions are also available on the companion CD if you prefer to review them in electronic form.

NOTE Answers

Answers to these questions and explanations of why each answer choice is correct or incorrect are located in the "Answers" section at the end of the book.

1. You have created a client application that needs the WCF service to invoke a callback method. Which of the following bindings supports this requirement?

    A. *basicHttpBinding*

    B. *wsHttpBinding*

    C. *wsHttpContextBinding*

    D. *wsDualHttpBinding*

2. You have created a client application that needs the WCF service to invoke a callback method. Which of the following bindings does not support this requirement?

    A. *netTcpBinding*

    B. *netNamedPipeBinding*

    C. *netMsmqBinding*

    D. *netTcpContextBinding*

Chapter Review

To further practice and reinforce the skills you learned in this chapter, you can:

- Review the chapter summary.
- Review the list of key terms introduced in this chapter.
- Complete the case scenario. This scenario sets up a real-world situation involving the topics of this chapter and asks you to create a solution.
- Complete the suggested practices.
- Take a practice test.

Chapter Summary

- WCF offers great flexibility in configuring client or service endpoints. Either a declarative or imperative technique can work in most situations.
- Bindings consist of a collection of binding elements, each of which provides a building block of functionality. The blocks can be combined either in the standard bindings or through custom-built bindings.

Key Terms

Do you know what these key terms mean? You can check your answers by looking up the terms in the glossary at the end of the book.

- absolute URI
- base address
- relative addressing
- svcutil
- WS-Addressing

Case Scenario

In the following case scenario, you will apply what you've learned in this chapter. You can find answers to these questions in the "Answers" section at the end of this book.

Case Scenario: Defining Multiple Endpoints

Your company has developed a WCF service that will be exposed to external clients through the Internet. You would like to support as many protocols as possible for connecting to the service.

Answer the following questions for your manager:

1. Are there any protocols that cannot be supported in this environment?
2. Is it possible for the same service to support multiple protocols on the same endpoint?
3. Is it possible for the same service to support multiple endpoints?
4. Can one service expose multiple contracts on the same endpoint?

Suggested Practices

To help you successfully master the exam objectives presented in this chapter, complete the following tasks.

Connecting with Services

Communicate by using ASMX and message queues.

- **Practice 1**   Create a client application that sends a message to an ASMX Web service. For an additional challenge, pass along your Windows user credentials to the Web service.
- **Practice 2**   Create a service that sends requests to Windows services that receive messages through MSMQ.

Watch a Webcast

Watch a webcast about configuring WCF.

- **Practice**   Watch the MSDN webcast, "Bindings" by Michele Leroux Bustamante, available on the companion CD in the Webcasts folder.

Take a Practice Test

The practice tests on this book's companion CD offer many options. For example, you can test yourself on just one exam objective, or you can test yourself on all the 70-503 certification exam content. You can set up the test so that it closely simulates the experience of taking a certification exam, or you can set it up in study mode so that you can look at the correct answers and explanations after you answer each question.

MORE INFO   Practice tests

For details about all the practice test options available, see the "How to Use the Practice Tests" section in this book's introduction.

Chapter 6

Instrumentation

Effort is involved in instrumenting an application. Many developers agree with the need for instrumentation, but the number that enthusiastically embraces it is much smaller. Typically, the main beneficiaries of instrumentation are administration and operations personnel who need to view and monitor the state of many applications, both Windows Communication Foundation (WCF) applications and non-WCF applications. Developers don't get much benefit for the effort in most applications.

However, instrumenting a WCF application can help you develop as well as monitor and maintain your application. In the distributed world, instrumentation is much more important than in your typical ASP.NET or Windows Forms application. As you have already seen, one of the more useful features of WCF is that it hides many of the tedious details of how to communicate between different processes and across different transport channels. To do this, WCF is pretty much a black box: requests go in one end (the client) and pop out the other, ready to be processed by services. Responses go back into the black box and appear as if by magic at the client. If you are interested—and what developer isn't—in where these messages go and what happens to them, then instrumentation is the key to understanding.

Exam objectives in this chapter:

- Implement end-to-end service tracing.
- Monitor service health.
- Log messages.
- Implement inspectors.

Lessons in this chapter:

Before You Begin

To complete the lessons in this chapter, you must have:

- A computer that meets or exceeds the minimum hardware requirements listed in the "Introduction" section at the beginning of the book.
- Any edition of Microsoft Visual Studio 2008 (including Microsoft Visual C# 2008 Express Edition or Microsoft Visual Basic 2008 Express Edition) installed on the computer.
- Microsoft Windows software development kit (SDK) 6.1A installed on the computer.

Real World

Bruce Johnson

As a developer who prides himself on going deep into technology, I find black boxes difficult to deal with. To be clear, I use the term *black box* to mean a piece of software whose internal details I can't see. Many of the more advanced applications fall into this category. Microsoft BizTalk, Office SharePoint Server, ASP.NET, and Windows Workflow Foundation are the technologies that spring immediately to mind, but there are others, to be sure. There is no question that WCF is included on this list.

I should be clear that it's not that these tools are black boxes that, in and of itself, causes me grief. It is that, when something goes wrong, a lack of transparency into the inner workings of the black box just makes the job of debugging more challenging and potentially frustrating. The key to getting past this challenge (and to being a true expert in the technology) is to have ways to dig into exactly what is happening. In the case of WCF, a main tool in the toolbox to accomplish this is in the tracing mechanism and the extensibility points, so pay close attention to this chapter. Although the content might not provide answers to the how of WCF, it will show you what you need to do to discover that on your own.

Lesson 1: Basic WCF Tracing

The tracing mechanism used in WCF is based on classes found in the *System.Diagnostics* namespace. For this reason, the starting point will be a review of these classes and the concepts involved. After the basics, the lesson will quickly move to the specifics of tracing as it applies to WCF. This includes the trace sources that are provided and how tracing can be configured both declaratively and imperatively.

After this lesson, you will be able to:
- Enable tracing in a WCF application.
- Identify the appropriate tracing level for messages.
- Define the listeners that will receive tracing messages.

Estimated lesson time: 25 minutes

Tracing Basics

The fundamental concepts behind tracing are not that difficult to grasp, especially if you consider for a moment the problem that tracing is intended to solve. The first half of this equation is that you have an application (a WCF application or otherwise) that desires to provide information about itself. It could be the value of the parameters that are being used in method calls. It could be the internal state of an object. It could even be the fact that the application has started or finished a particular task. Regardless of the content of the information, the premise is the same: the application has information of interest to provide.

The second half of the equation consists of a listener that is interested in "hearing" about your application. This listener keeps its electronic ear to the ground, receiving the information that comes to it and redirecting it to an appropriate location. The appropriate location could be a Console window, a Windows Forms control, a log file, the Windows Event Log, a database, or literally any other place that .NET is capable of reaching.

It's fortunate that .NET provides a number of classes to achieve both sides of this functionality. First, to produce the trace information, .NET includes a *Trace* class that includes a number of static methods (such as *Write*, *WriteLine*, *WriteIf*, and *WriteLineIf*). These methods publish information without knowing at the start where the information might be used. Consider the following sample code, demonstrating the generation of tracing information:

```
' VB
Trace.WriteLine("CategoryName", "The trace information")
```

```
// C#
Trace.WriteLine("CategoryName", "The trace information");
```

The result from the execution of these statements is that tracing information (in the form of the two strings) is sent out for anybody to receive and process. However, this simple statement is not the only way to accomplish this task. It is also possible to produce tracing information by using the *TraceSource* class. In this case, the *TraceSource* object is instantiated using a string value that represents the name of the source. After it's created, the *TraceSource* object can send trace information in the same manner as the *Trace* class:

```vb
' VB
Dim ts As New TraceSource("DemoSource")
ts.TraceEvent(TraceEventType.Error, 1, "The trace information")
```

```csharp
// C#
TraceSource ts = new TraceSource("DemoSource");
ts.TraceEvent(TraceEventType.Error, 1, "The trace information");
```

On the receiving end of the trace data is a *TraceListener* class (or, more precisely, a class that is derived from the *TraceListener* class). This class routes the tracing information to a specific data sink. The active trace listeners are typically defined through the configuration file, although, as is detailed shortly, it is possible to build a collection of listeners imperatively.

Turning Tracing On

By default, WCF is configured to have tracing disabled. This means that to start getting tracing information, you need to turn tracing on. Four steps accomplish this: configuring WCF to emit trace information, setting the tracing level to something other than *Off*, configuring a trace listener, and enabling message logging.

Emitting Trace Information

Although a WCF application can produce tracing information by invoking the *TraceEvent* method on a *TraceSource* object, WCF can also produce some data automatically. To start with, WCF defines a separate trace source for each assembly in the .NET Framework that takes part in WCF functionality. Table 6-1 contains a list of the assemblies that have been configured as a trace source and a description of the types of tracing information they produce.

Table 6-1 WCF Assembly-Level Trace Sources

Assembly Name	Description
System.ServiceModel	The most active (from a tracing perspective) of the assemblies. All the stages in the WCF message process are logged, including reading configuration information, performing transport-level actions, and processing security requests.
System.ServiceModel .MessageLogging	Generates tracing information for all the messages that flow through the system.

Table 6-1 WCF Assembly-Level Trace Sources

Assembly Name	Description
System.ServiceModel .IdentityModel	Generates trace data related to the authentication and authorization mechanism used within WCF.
System.ServiceModel .Activation	Creates traces related to the activation of the service portion of a WCF communication channel.
System.Runtime .Serialization	Provides tracing information when objects are serialized or deserialized. Because this activity occurs quite often in WCF, this set of tracing information is useful for seeing some of the raw content associated with messages.
System.IO.Log	Generates trace messages associated with accessing the interface to the Common Log File System (CLFS).
CardSpace	Generates trace messages related to any CardSpace identity processing that occurs within the context of a WCF application.

MORE INFO **CardSpace**

CardSpace is a piece of software that runs as a client application. It enables users to provide a digital identity securely to online services. When a user needs to be identified to a Web site or Web service, CardSpace displays a list of information cards from which the user can select. The chosen identity is then transmitted to the Web site or service. You can find more details about CardSpace at *http://netfx3.com/content/WindowsCardspaceHome.aspx*.

Setting the Trace Level

One piece of functionality provided by tracing in .NET is the ability to define levels of messages. Each trace message that is produced can be associated with a specific level. Listeners can be configured to process only messages that are at or above a certain level.

A number of tracing levels, described in Table 6-2, are included in the .NET Framework.

Table 6-2 Supported Tracing Levels

Trace Level	Description
Off	All trace messages are ignored.
Critical	Unexpected processing events or unhandled exceptions have occurred. The expectation is that the application will terminate immediately or shortly thereafter.
Error	An unexpected processing event or exception has occurred. However, unlike the critical level, the application is still capable of continuing its processing.

Table 6-2 Supported Tracing Levels

Trace Level	Description
Warning	This type of trace message indicates that a possible problem has occurred. The application is functioning correctly, but that state (the state of "correctness") might not continue.
Information	This is the first tracing level that is positive in nature. It indicates the passing of successful milestones within the application.
Verbose	This is similar to the *Information* level in that the messages are supposed to indicate milestones within the application. However, the *Verbose* level is expected to provide more of these types of messages than the *Information* level, specifically at a more granular level of milestone.
ActivityTracing	Messages generated for this level of source tracing are related to the flow of messages between components and the activities related to these messages. Included in messages at this level is sufficient information to enable correlation across various service boundaries.
All	All messages are captured, regardless of the tracing level.

Because the listeners use the concept of "above," the levels in Table 6-2 are listed in order from highest to lowest in terms of importance. For the levels between *Critical* and *Verbose*, inclusive, messages from the "higher" levels are also included when the "lower" levels are indicated. For example, if you specify a tracing level of *Information*, all *Critical*, *Error*, *Warning*, and *Information* messages are included.

Exam Tip   It is expected that the lower the level of tracing you specify, the more messages are generated. For a level such as *Verbose*, the number of messages created could be quite significant. If you include *ActivityTracing*, remember that the number of messages has the potential to affect the performance of the application negatively.

You indicate the trace level by setting the *switchValue* attribute for the trace source. The following sample from a configuration file shows how the messages generated by the *System.Service-Model* trace source will be filtered so that all *Information*-level (and higher) messages, as well as the *ActivityTracing* messages, are processed:

```
<system.diagnostics>
    <sources>
        <source name="System.ServiceModel"
            switchValue="Information, ActivityTracing">
            <listeners>
                <add name="xml" />
            </listeners>
        </source>
    </sources>
</system.diagnostics>
```

Configuring the Listeners

As was mentioned earlier, at least one listener is necessary for trace messages to be persisted into any useful location. As part of the run-time processing, WCF sends the trace messages, using the listeners configured as shown at the end of the previous section. Filtering is performed by using the *switchValue* attribute, and the defined listeners (of which there can be more than one) process the trace information according to the format and destination of the output.

There are two ways to configure listeners. The most direct is simply to provide the details in the *listeners* section within the *sources* element of the configuration. The following segment from a configuration file would send the traces generated from the *System.ServiceModel* namespace, with a level of *Information* (or more severe) or *ActivityTracing* to the Traces.svclog file in the C:\log directory:

```
<system.diagnostics>
   <sources>
      <source name="System.ServiceModel"
         switchValue="Information, ActivityTracing">
         <listeners>
            <add name="log"
               type="System.Diagnostics.XmlWriterTraceListener"
               initializeData="c:\log\Traces.svclog" />
         </listeners>
      </source>
   </source>
</system.diagnostics>
```

The *add* element contains a number of attributes. The *name* attribute, in this instance, doesn't have any purpose. It can be used to access the listener programmatically, but this functionality is not required for this discussion. The *type* attribute indicates the class that implements the listener. In this example, the trace information will be formatted into an XML document. The *initializeData* attribute, in this instance, contains the path to the file the listener will generate. In general, however, the contents and use of the *initializeData* value depend on the listener.

The second way to configure listeners is to define a shared listener. The components are similar, but they are placed into different sections, as illustrated in the following segment from a configuration file:

```
<system.diagnostics>
   <sources>
      <source name="System.ServiceModel"
         switchValue="Information, ActivityTracing">
         <listeners>
            <add name="log" />
         </listeners>
      </source>
      <source name="System.ServiceModel.MessageLoging"
         switchValue="Critical">
         <listeners>
```

```
            <add name="log" />
         </listeners>
      </source>
   </sources>
   <sharedListeners>
      <add name="log" type="System.Diagnostics.XmlWriterTraceListener"
         initializeData="c:\log\Traces.svclog" />
   </sharedListeners>
   <trace autoflush="true" />
</system.diagnostics>
```

In the *source* section, two sources are created, each of which will send trace information to a listener with the name of "log". In the *sharedListeners* section, an *XmlWriterTraceListener* is defined with a name of "log". As a result, the *XmlWriterTraceListener* processes the trace information of the two sources.

NOTE **Listeners, multithreading, and performance**

Not all trace listeners are thread-safe. The *XmlWriterTraceListener* is not, for example. As part of its processing, the listener may lock resources to ensure integrity. The result, when many threads are accessing the same listener, is the possibility of performance issues stemming from the need to respect exclusive locks.

The second technique for configuring listeners is through code. This requires a couple of steps, albeit fairly simple ones. To start with, an instance of the listener class is created. Each of the listeners that can be defined through the configuration file also has a corresponding class. The difference between these classes is the parameters used in the constructor. Depending on the listener's requirements, different parameters are used. The parameters roughly correspond to the information that would have been included in the *initializeData* attribute in the configuration file. The following code demonstrates how to instantiate a *TextWriterTraceListener*:

```
' VB
Dim traceLog As New FileStream("C:\log\Traces.svclog", _
   FileMode.OpenOrCreate)
Dim myListener As New TextWriterTraceListener(traceLog)
```

```
// C#
FileStream traceLog = new FileStream("C:\\log\\Traces.svclog",
   FileMode.OpenOrCreate);
TextWriterTraceListener myListener = new TextWriterTraceListener(traceLog);
```

After the instance of the listener object has been created, it should be added to the *Listeners* collection associated with the *Trace* class. This is shown in the following code:

```
' VB
Trace.Listeners.Add(myListener)
```

```
// C#
Trace.Listeners.Add(myListener);
```

After the listener is created, you actually have two methods you can use to send messages to it. Naturally, the write methods associated with the *Trace* class (*Write*, *WriteLine*, *WriteIf*, *WriteLineIf*, and so on) will work (assuming that the listener is associated with the source specified in the parameter list). However, you can also call the *Write*, *WriteIndent*, and *WriteLine* methods that are exposed on the listener, as shown here:

```
' VB
myListener.WriteLine("Sending trace information")
```

```
// C#
myListener.WriteLine("Sending trace information");
```

Unlike the *Trace* write methods, when you use the write methods on the listener, the output will be directed to that listener only. Also, it might be necessary to manually flush the output sent directly to the listener. If you call the *Flush* static/shared method on the *Trace* class, all the trace messages in all the listeners are flushed to their respective persistence mechanism. However, if you use the listener *Write* methods and that listener is not included in the *Trace.Listeners* collection, calling *Trace.Flush* will have no effect. Instead, you must flush the listener explicitly, as shown here:

```
' VB
Trace.Flush()
myListener.Flush()
```

```
// C#
Trace.Flush();
myListener.Flush();
```

Enabling Message Logging

The last of the four steps involves the configuration file. To enable WCF message logging, the *messageLogging* element must be added to the *diagnostics* section of the configuration file. The following is an example of such an element:

```
<system.serviceModel>
  <diagnostics>
    <messageLogging
        logEntireMessage="true"
        logMalformedMessages="false"
        logMessagesAtServiceLevel="true"
        logMessagesAtTransportLevel="false"
        maxMessagesToLog="3000"
        maxSizeOfMessageToLog="2000"/>
  </diagnostics>
</system.serviceModel>
```

WCF logs messages at two levels:

- **Service level** Messages are logged as they are entering user code (in the receive side) or as they leave user code (in the send side). At the service level, all messages, including most infrastructure messages, are logged. The exception in the infrastructure messages are that *ReliableMessaging* messages are not logged.
- **Transport level** Messages are logged as they are ready to be encoded or decoded; at the transport level, all infrastructure messages are logged, even those related to reliable messaging.

Beyond these two levels, WCF also logs malformed messages. A malformed message is one that is rejected by any part of the WCF stack. Every malformed message is logged as is. If the message is encrypted, the encrypted version is logged. If the XML that forms the message is invalid, that invalid XML is logged.

As you can see from the configuration segment shown previously, there are a number of attributes that can be defined for the *messageLogging* element. Table 6-3 lists the *messageLogging* attributes and descriptions of their functions.

Table 6-3 *MessageLogging* **Attributes**

Attribute	Description
logEntireMessage	A Boolean value that indicates whether the entire message should be logged. If set to the default value, which is *false*, only the header will be logged.
logMalformedMessages	A Boolean value that indicates whether malformed messages should be logged.
logMessagesAtServiceLevel	A Boolean value that indicates whether service-level messages should be logged.
logMessagesAtTransportLevel	A Boolean value that indicates whether transport-level messages should be logged.
maxMessageToLog	An integer value that sets a quota on the number of messages that will be logged. Every message that is logged applies to the quota. As soon as the quota is reached, an additional message is posted indicating that the quota has been reached and no further messages are logged.
maxSizeOfMessageToLog	Specifies the maximum size (in bytes) of the messages that will be logged. If a message is larger than the specified value, it will not be placed into the log. The default value is 256Kb.

NOTE   When max is not the max

The *maxSizeOfMessageToLog* attribute specifies the limit on the size of logged message *prior* to serialization. It is quite likely that, when serialized, the message will be larger. So when calculating the impact of the messages on storage space, it is a good idea to expect a serialization inflation of approximately 10 percent.

Part of the message-logging infrastructure for WCF is the ability to filter the messages that are logged. This is configured through a *filters* element that is associated with the *messageLogging* element, as shown here:

```
<messageLogging logEntireMessage="false"
    logMalformedMessages="true"
    logMessagesAtServiceLevel="true"
    logMessagesAtTransportLevel="false"
    maxMessagesToLog="100">
    <filters>
        <add nodeQuota="10"
            xmlns:soap="http://www.w3.org/2003/05/soap-envelope">
                /soap:Envelope/soap:Header
        </add>
    </filters>
</messageLogging>
```

The *add* element adds a filter to message logging. The basic idea is to specify an XPath query in the body of the *add* element. If at least one match is found when this XPath is applied to the headers of a message, the message is logged. The *nodeQuota* attribute limits the number of nodes that are searched to find the match. The *xmlns* attribute, along with the contents of the *add* element, define the matching criteria.

Lab: Capturing a Basic Trace

In this lab, the focus is on basic tracing functionality. In particular, the exercise describes how to configure WCF to generate some basic trace information. One thing to keep in mind is that, although the trace information is being generated in this exercise, the detailed evaluation of the trace log is deferred until Lesson 2, "End-to-End Tracing."

▶ **Exercise 1   Set Up the Trace**

In this exercise, you will configure a basic trace. The data goes into a log file placed in the root directory.

1. Navigate to the *<InstallHome>*/Chapter6/Lesson1/Exercise1/*<language>*/Before directory and double-click the Exercise1.sln file to open the solution in Visual Studio.

   The solution consists of two projects. You might recognize the projects as the same ones used in Chapter 5, "Configuring WCF." They are as follows:

❏ The DemoService project, a simple WCF service library that implements the *IGetHeaders* interface. This interface consists of a single method (*GetHeaders*) that retrieves some information about the headers in the message sent to the service. For this exercise, it returns the *Action* header.

❏ The TestClient project, a Console application that enables you to consume the DemoService service. This client is the target for your tracing.

2. In Solution Explorer, double-click the app.config file for the TestClient project.

Notice that initially the file contains some basic binding configuration information.

To start, you must define the source for the trace by adding a *sources* element to the app.config file. The *sources* element is a part of the *system.diagnostics* element.

3. Add the following segment above the existing *system.serviceModel* element:

```
<system.diagnostics>
    <sources>
        <source name="System.ServiceModel.MessageLogging"
            switchValue="Information, ActivityTracing">
        </source>
    </sources>
</system.diagnostics>
```

Along with defining the source, you must create a listener. One of the ways to do this is to add a *listener* tag within the *source* tag.

4. Add the following XML segment to the body of the just-added *source* tag:

```
<listeners>
    <add name="log" type="System.Diagnostics.XmlWriterTraceListener"
        initializeData="Traces.svclog" />
</listeners>
```

At this point, the source is set up and ready to go. It includes the switch values, indicating the level of information to be traced, along with a listener that directs the output, in an XML format, to a file. However, the information published into the trace is not automatically pushed into the file immediately. Instead, the trace information is buffered, which, in the case of this exercise, means that it might not be visible.

5. To address this problem, set the *autoflush* property on the trace to *true* by adding the following XML element below the closing tag for the *sources* element in the app.config file:

```
<trace autoflush="true" />
```

You have completed three of the four steps. The final step is to turn message logging on for WCF through the *messageLogging* element.

6. Add the following element to the *system.serviceModel* element within the app.config file:

```
<diagnostics>
    <messageLogging
        logEntireMessage="true"
        logMalformedMessages="false"
        logMessagesAtServiceLevel="false"
```

```
    logMessagesAtTransportLevel="true"
    maxMessagesToLog="3000"
    maxSizeOfMessageToLog="2000"/>
</diagnostics>
```

Now you can run the application and view the tracing information.

7. Ensure that TestClient is set as the startup project, and then launch the application by pressing F5.

   A Console window appears, indicating that the client has successfully communicated with the service.

8. Press Enter to exit the application.

9. To see the trace that was created, use Windows Explorer to navigate to the directory where the TestClient application ran, which is at *<InstallHome>*/Chapter6/Lesson1   /Exercise1/*<language>*/Before/TestClient/bin/Debug.

   You will see a newly added file called Traces.svclog. If you open the file, using any text editor, a large and fairly convoluted XML document is visible.

10. While you are in Windows Explorer, delete the file.

    Next, you define a filter on the data captured in the trace file by adding a *filters* element to the *messageLogging* element.

11. Replace the current *messageLogging* element with the following XML segment to include only messages that have an action that starts with "http://schemas.xmlsoap.com" in the trace log file:

```
<messageLogging
    logEntireMessage="true"
    logMalformedMessages="false"
    logMessagesAtServiceLevel="false"
    logMessagesAtTransportLevel="true"
    maxMessagesToLog="3000"
    maxSizeOfMessageToLog="2000">
    <filters>
       <add xmlns:soap="http://www.w3.org/2003/05/soap-envelope"
            xmlns:a="http://www.w3.org/2005/08/addressing">
            /soap:Envelope/soap:Header/a:Action[
            starts-with(text(),'http://schemas.xmlsoap.org')]
       </add>
    </filters>
    </filters>
</messageLogging>
```

12. Launch the application by pressing F5.

    A Console window appears, indicating that the client has successfully communicated with the service.

13. Press Enter to exit the application.

14. Use Windows Explorer to navigate to the *<InstallHome>*/Chapter6/Lesson1/Exercise1 /*<language>*/Before/TestClient/bin/Debug directory.

15. You will see a newly created file called Traces.svclog. As before, use Windows Explorer to delete the file. To see the impact of the filter, go back to the app.config file in Visual Studio 2008.

16. Modify the XPath query, which is used to filter the message. This was originally added in step 11. Change the action so that it looks for "tempuri.org". The filters section in app.config file should be changed to look like the following:

```
<filters>
    <add xmlns:soap="http://www.w3.org/2003/05/soap-envelope"
        xmlns:a="http://www.w3.org/2005/08/addressing">
        /soap:Envelope/soap:Header/a:Action[
        starts-with(text(),'http://tempuri.org')]
    </add>
</filters>
```

In the messages for this application, none of the actions include "http://tempuri.org". So when the application is run, the Traces.svclog file will not be created.

17. Launch the application by pressing F5.

18. When the Console window displays the header information, press Enter to terminate the application.

19. Use Windows Explorer to navigate to the *<InstallHome>*/Chapter6/Lesson1/Exercise1 /*<language>*/Before/TestClient/bin/Debug directory. You will see that no "traces.svclog" has been created.

Lesson Summary

- Tracing requires a source for the information and a listener that processes the information.
- The default in WCF is to have tracing disabled. It must be enabled for the built-in trace information to be generated.
- Four steps are associated with using tracing with WCF: configuring WCF to generate trace data, setting the appropriate trace level, configuring trace listeners, and enabling message logging.

Lesson Review

You can use the following questions to test your knowledge of the information in Lesson 1, "Basic WCF Tracing." The questions are also available on the companion CD if you prefer to review them in electronic form.

NOTE Answers

Answers to these questions and explanations of why each answer choice is correct or incorrect are located in the "Answers" section at the end of the book.

1. Consider the following element from a configuration file:

```
<system.serviceModel>
  <diagnostics>
    <messageLogging
        logEntireMessage="true"
        logMalformedMessages="false"
        logMessagesAtServiceLevel="true"
        logMessagesAtTransportLevel="false"
        maxMessagesToLog="1000"
        maxSizeOfMessageToLog="2000"/>
  </diagnostics>
</system.serviceModel>
```

What is the maximum number of WCF messages that will appear in the trace log?

- A. 1,000
- **B. 1,001**
- C. 2,000
- D. No limit.

2. One of your developers has created a WCF application. She believes that she has configured the client portion of the application to capture tracing information. However, when the application runs, only some of the expected information appears in the log file. It appears that the last few log entries are missing. Which of the following is likely to be the cause of the problem?

- A. A listener has not been defined for the source of the tracing information.
- B. A source has not been defined for the tracing information.
- C. The *logEntireMessage* attribute of the *messageLogging* element is set to *false.*
- D. The *autoflush* property of the *trace* element has not been set to *true.*

only headers will be logged

Lesson 2: End-to-End Tracing

In a distributed application, being able to generate tracing information is just the first part of the battle. Although creating traces can be quite useful, in a distributed environment, the data will likely exist in separate and distinct data stores. Even if you went so far as to create a trace listener that persisted the trace data into a database, the messages are still sent in isolation. Each message will appear to be just a record of data. There is no way to relate one message to any other message.

Now, if you're in a scenario in which only one application is making requests, you would (with some effort) be able to stitch together the sequence of trace messages that occur. However, if you have multiple client applications running on multiple computers each client will have some trace records. The service will have some trace records. The timing of the records is such that unraveling them without some additional help would be almost impossible. The additional help comes in the form of end-to-end (E2E) tracing.

> **After this lesson, you will be able to:**
> - Configure a WCF application for end-to-end tracing.
> - Programmatically start and stop activities.
> - Propagate activities between client and service.
>
> **Estimated lesson time: 35 minutes**

Activities

For end-to-end tracing in WCF, the basic unit of information is called an *activity*. Although the definition of activity is relatively vague, this fluidity actually makes it more useful in the real world. An activity contains any trace information that is correlated from the perspective of an application. So, for example, a request made to a service and the corresponding response can be part of a single activity, as can a request, a callback, a callback response, and a response to the original request. Even multiple request/response pairs to the same (or different) services can be included in the scope of a single activity.

As you might expect with a definition this amorphous, identifying when an activity starts and stops can be left up to the developer. WCF includes a number of predefined activities for the most common scenarios. Indeed, the out-of-the-box activities cover the scenarios that will make up most of your WCF development experience. This flexibility means that you can make an activity be whatever you require for the tracing information to be correlated in a meaningful way.

Use the same simple process as has already been mentioned to turn on the capability for WCF to generate activity-level tracing. The following XML segment from a configuration file demonstrates the technique. The key setting is the *switchValue* attribute of the *source* tag, as shown in bold here:

```
<system.diagnostics>
   <sources>
      <source name="System.ServiceModel"
         switchValue="ActivityTracing">
         <listeners>
            <add name="log"
               type="System.Diagnostics.XmlWriterTraceListener"
               initializeData="c:\log\Traces.svclog" />
         </listeners>
      </source>
   </sources>
</system.diagnostics>
```

If *switchValue* contains the *ActivityTracing* keyword, the activity tracing for that source is turned on. The example turns on activity tracing only for traces generated by the *System.ServiceModel* source. The same setting can be used for any of the sources as well as by any custom tracing source.

Activity Scoping

The actual boundaries of the activity are defined by the developer at design time. To flow activities across the various boundaries found in WCF, all trace information must be tagged with an *activity identifier*. The identifier for an activity correlates tracing messages. If two traces have the same activity identifier, they are considered to be part of the same activity.

The activity identifier is also scoped. The scoping level affects whether the identifier is moved along with the request or response. WCF provides for two levels of scoping activities.

- **Global (per application)**   The identifier in this scope is a 128-bit *globally unique activity identifier* (gAId). When a request or response moves across the boundaries, the gAId is propagated.
- **Local (per endpoint)**   The identifier in this scope still includes a gAId. However, the name of the trace source and the process ID that initiated the trace are also included in this *local activity identifier* (lAId).

An activity is defined at design time and denotes a logical unit of work. Emitted traces with the same activity identifier are directly related; they are part of the same activity. Because an activity can cross endpoint boundaries (for instance, a request), two scopes for an activity are defined.

- **Global scope, per application**   In this scope, the activity is identified by its 128-bit gAId. The gAId is what is propagated across endpoints.

- **Local scope, per endpoint**   In this scope, the activity is identified by its gAId along with the trace source name emitting the activity traces and the process ID. This triplet constitutes the local activity identifier, lAId. The lAId defines the (local) boundaries of an activity.

The question about how to define whether an activity is global or local in scope is next. This is actually less explicit than one might expect. The starting point for understanding is found in the *CorrelationManager* class.

The .NET tracing mechanism uses the *CorrelationManager* class to provide the ability to group different aspects of a trace. *CorrelationManager* is actually a static property on the *Trace* class. The *CorrelationManager* class has a property called *ActivityId*. This property is generally assigned a globally unique identifier (GUID). The following code demonstrates how this is done:

```
' VB
Trace.CorrelationManager.ActivityId = Guid.NewGuid()
```

```
// C#
Trace.CorrelationManager.ActivityId = Guid.NewGuid();
```

The key to the *ActivityId* property is where the data is persisted. Specifically, it is kept in *thread local storage* (TLS). What makes TLS special is that it is storage associated with a particular thread. It follows the thread regardless of the method, class, or *AppDomain* in which the thread is running. As a result, it is a good place to store information that needs to flow along with the current execution context.

Knowing about *ActivityId* and TLS still doesn't answer the question of how to set the scope of an activity. As it turns out, WCF determines the scope automatically. Although the *ActivityId* will always have a GUID, as long as the activity stays within the same process it is considered to be local. Only when the activity crosses a boundary does the GUID stored in the *ActivityId* property become the gAId.

But wait, there's more. Because the *ActivityId* is stored in TLS, it will automatically flow along the execution chain, but requests will cross over process and machine boundaries. To correlate the traces, the activity ID will need to cross the boundary, too.

Activity Propagation

Whether activities can be propagated is defined in the source. Consider the following configuration file, which uses the *propagateActivity* attribute (shown in bold) to allow activities to be transferred across service boundaries:

```
<system.diagnostics>
    <sources>
        <source name="System.ServiceModel"
            switchValue="ActivityTracing" propagateActivity="true">
            <listeners>
```

```
        <add name="log"
           type="System.Diagnostics.XmlWriterTraceListener"
           initializeData="c:\log\Traces.svclog" />
      </listeners>
    </source>
  </sources>
</system.diagnostics>
```

Notice first (very important), that *propagateActivity* is set on the *System.ServiceModel* source. This is necessary for activities to propagate across endpoints. Also, as it turns out, propagation of activities requires more than just setting the *propagateActivity* attribute to *true*.

A number of specific conditions need to exist for activity propagation to take place. For Activity A to be propagated to Activity B, all the following must be true.

- Activity B must be created because of some request or action by Activity A.
- The gAId for Activity A must be known to Activity B.
- The gAId for Activity B must be the same as Activity A.

If these conditions are met, the gAId will be passed through the *ActivityId* message header.

Activity Tracing Enabled   When the *ServiceModel* activity tracing is enabled (*ActivityTracing* is set to *true*), there are two parts of the requests where activity functionality occurs, and both of them revolve around the *ProcessAction* information that is included with a message.

On the client, every operation call is processed within the context of a *ProcessAction* activity. This is just a built-in identifier that can be used to correlate tracing activity within a single operation. When the client builds the request that is to be sent to the service, it determines, based on whether the current activity should be propagated, what value should be provided. If no activity is to be propagated, no value is provided for the *ProcessAction*. Regardless of the value to be sent, it is included within the SOAP header portion of the request.

On the receiving end, WCF looks at the SOAP header for a *ProcessAction* value. If the message contains *ProcessAction* with an ID, the *ActivityId* within the service is set to the same value. This allows the activity to be transferred across the boundary.

If, however, there is no *ProcessAction* ID (which occurs if the client has *propagateActivity* set to *false*), the service will generate a new GUID and assign that value to the service-side *ActivityId*. This has the effect of creating a new activity.

How the client side of the WCF connection deals with the *ActivityId* is a little more complicated. Remember that the activity does not have to start in the client for it to be propagated back to the client. In other words, the activity could be created in the service and sent back to the client, where any additional traces would need to be correlated.

If the client is running as a synchronous, single-threaded application, any activity identifier included in the response is ignored. Instead, the activity that is associated with the request is used. If the client is either asynchronous or multithreaded, the *propagateActivity* value is set to *true*, and the response from the service includes an *ActivityId*, the service's value indicates the activity associated with any further trace messages.

Activity Tracing Disabled   The second part of the propagation puzzle is when the *Service-Model* activity tracing is disabled (*ActivityTracing=false*). Again, the value of the *propagateActivity* flag in the service model must be considered as well.

When *propagateActivity* is set to *true*, the behavior on the client and the service are the same. However, the behavior applies to user-generated traces only. Traces that come out of the *Service-Model* class will not be part of the same activity. As the request is being formed (or the response is being built), the *ActivityId* in TLS will be used for any traces. As soon as the request passes into the *ServiceModel* classes, the *ActivityId* will not appear in any traces. However, the user-generated *ActivityId* will be included in the headers for the message.

On the receiving end, the *ActivityId* is pulled from the message as soon as the message object is created. That *ActivityId* will be used for any user-generated traces. However, it will not appear in any traces that are created in the *ServiceModel* classes unless the traces are executed in the same thread as the user-generated code.

The purpose for these gyrations is to allow user-created activities to be propagated in the same manner as *ServiceModel* activities. It does not guarantee that the *ServiceModel* traces will be in the same activity as the user-generated traces, although it might be in some cases.

NOTE   **Activity propagation and faults**

Traces that occur while in the middle of processing a fault follow the same rules for activity propagation as was just described for regular processing. There is no special change in how and when the activity identifier is passed across boundaries if the message indicates an error condition instead of a normal condition.

Transferring Activities

In WCF, activity propagation is not sufficient. There are times when an activity will perform an action that causes a new activity to be created. If the trace simply displayed the new *ActivityId*, how would one be able to follow the flow of traces emitted? In WCF, the answer is an *activity transfer*. A transfer between two activities is a representation of a causal relationship between events within an endpoint. Typically, there is a flow of control between the activities, such as a method call that crosses the activity boundaries or when bytes are inbound to a service. A Listen At activity is part of the listening function for a service. When the bytes arrive, a message object is created, but this object creation is part of the Receive Bytes activity. A transfer is set up between the Listen At and Receive Bytes activities.

Although it might appear to be a requirement, there does not have to be a nested relationship between the activities that are on either side of a transfer. Consider a situation in which there are two activities, named A and B. As part of its processing, A creates a transfer to B. At the time, B might already exist. B could perform some work for A and then return, with B continuing on to do work for other activities. In this scenario, although there is a transfer relationship between A and B, there is no nesting.

Further, there is no requirement that a transfer from A to B necessarily be followed by a transfer back from B to A. A could certainly spawn B, but if the method is *OneWay*, A will not expect to hear back from B. In such a scenario, the activities will continue on, even though the transfer will be left in the trace log for viewing in the future.

Just to complete the discussion of transfers, following are the steps that occur when a transfer is made between A and B (and B doesn't already exist).

1. A new activity is created. This includes the generation of a new gAId.
2. A *Transfer* trace is emitted. The source is the original gAId. The destination is the new gAId.
3. The new *ActivityId* is stored in TLS.
4. A *Start* trace for the new activity is generated.

After the B activity is finished, the following steps occur:

1. A *Transfer* trace is emitted. The source is Activity B's gAId, and the destination is Activity A's gAId.
2. A *Stop* trace is emitted to indicate that Activity B is complete.
3. The TLS is updated with Activity A's gAId.

The following code demonstrates these steps:

```vb
' VB
Dim ts As New TraceSource("DemoTraceSource")
Dim firstActivityId As Guid = Guid.NewGuid()
Trace.CorrelationManager.ActivityId = firstActivityId
ts.TraceEvent(TraceEventType.Start, 0, "Start Activity")
    ' processing code
Dim newActivityId As Guid = Guid.NewGuid()
ts.TraceTransfer(0, "Transferring…", newActivityId)
Trace.CorrelationManager.ActivityId = newActivityId
ts.TraceEvent(TraceEventType.Start, 0, "Get Header")
    ' more processing code
ts.TraceEvent(TraceEventType.Information, 0, "Stuff happened")
    ' more processing code
ts.TraceTransfer(666, "Transferring...",  firstActivityId)
ts.TraceEvent(TraceEventType.Stop, 0, "Get Header")
Trace.CorrelationManager.ActivityId = firstActivityId
```

```csharp
// C#
TraceSource ts = new TraceSource("ClientCalculatorTraceSource");
Guid firstActivityId = Guid.NewGuid();
Trace.CorrelationManager.ActivityId = firstActivityId;
```

```
ts.TraceEvent(TraceEventType.Start, 0, "Start Activity");
  // processing code
Guid newActivityId = Guid.NewGuid();
ts.TraceTransfer(0, "Transferring...", newActivityId);
Trace.CorrelationManager.ActivityId = newActivityId;
ts.TraceEvent(TraceEventType.Start, 0, "Get Header");
  // more processing code
ts.TraceEvent(TraceEventType.Information, 0, "Stuff happened");
  // more processing code
ts.TraceTransfer(666, "Transferring…",  firstActivityId);
ts.TraceEvent(TraceEventType.Stop, 0, "Get Header");
Trace.CorrelationManager.ActivityId = firstActivityId;
```

Viewing Activities

Now that the traces from the various sources on either one or more systems have been generated, the next task is to bring them together into a single view. This can be easily accomplished through the Service Trace Viewer utility. The Service Trace Viewer tool is actually part of the .NET 3.5 SDK.

MORE INFO   Downloading the .NET 5 SDK

You can download the SDK from *http://www.microsoft.com/downloads/details.aspx?FamilyId=E6E1C3DF-A74F-4207-8586-711EBE331CDC&displaylang=en*. As a word of warning, the label on this download indicates that it is the Windows SDK for Windows Server 2008 and .NET Framework 3.5. Even though it might seem to be solely for Windows Server 2008, the SDK portion of the download (the part that includes the Service Trace Viewer) will run on both Windows Vista and Windows XP.

Start with the fundamental operation of the Service Trace Viewer. To launch the Service Trace Viewer, use the All Programs option from the Start menu. Navigate to the Tools menu under the Microsoft Windows SDK item and click Service Trace Viewer. After the utility has been started, you can choose Open from the File menu to open a .svclog file created by the *XmlWriterTraceListener* listener class. At this point, all the traces found in the log file are displayed. For each trace, the following information is available:

- The name of the activity (if it was included in the trace generation)
- The time when the trace was emitted
- The tracing level
- The name of the trace's source
- The name of the process that emitted the trace
- The identifier of the thread from which the trace was emitted
- Optionally, a URL that points to an online MSDN library entry that contains more information about the trace

This is the basic information about the trace, and if these were all that the utility could do, it wouldn't be worth the time taken in the writing. Where the Service Trace Viewer shines is in its ability to correlate traces based on the *ActivityId*. Figure 6-1 displays the initial screen for Service Trace Viewer (that is, after a trace log has been loaded).

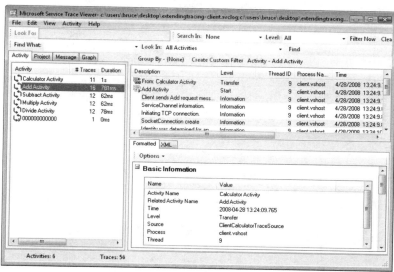

Figure 6-1   Service Trace Viewer screen

The left panel contains a list of the activities present in the trace. When any activity is selected, the upper right panel contains the traces that are associated with that activity. When any trace is selected, the lower right panel shows the detailed information for that trace.

However, this is just the starting point. You can expand the activities on the left side to see more detail. For example, if you double-click the Add Activity activity, a graphical representation of the client-side WCF traces is displayed. Figure 6-2 shows what the Service Trace Viewer looks like in this view.

Within this same view, you can see additional details about certain traces. For example, if you click Sent A Message Over A Channel, the panel in the lower right includes more details about the message, as shown in Figure 6-3.

Up to this point, only the client messages have been covered. However, you can use the Service Trace Viewer to correlate messages between the client and service also. When you add the .svclog file from the service (assuming that *propagateActivity* has been set to *true*), the service-side traces are rolled into the client-side traces. The appearance of the screens is the same. All that happens is that the trace information for each trace file is interlaced based on activity IDs and a time stamp.

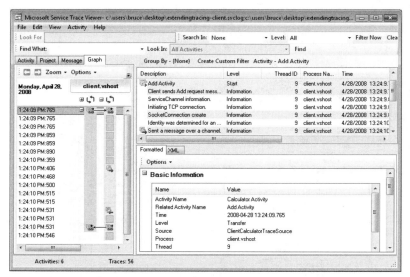

Figure 6-2   Graphical representation of an activity

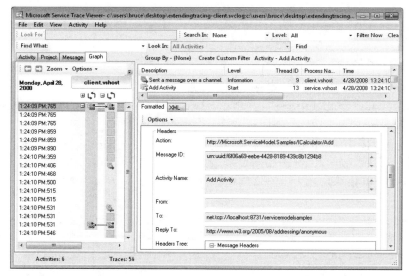

Figure 6-3   Message details

Activity Lifetime

The starting and ending points for an activity are fairly evident, occurring with the first and last time the activity is used with an emitted trace. However, there is a predefined set of trace types that are used to mark the boundaries of the activity lifetime explicitly.

- **Start**   Indicates the beginning of the activity. Consider this to be the initial milestone in the process, the first time the *ActivityId* will be found in any of the traces for a particular endpoint. Thus, there could be multiple *Start* traces for a single activity, with each *Start* trace indicating a new boundary crossing. In the typical WCF model, a *Start* trace is generated by the creation of a new processing thread or the entry of a method that uses tracing to mark the milestone.

- **Stop**   Indicates the end of an activity. As with *Start*, there is one *Stop* trace per endpoint per activity, and the same basic events generate the *Stop* trace, one being created with the termination of a thread or the exit of a method that had be marked with a *Start* trace on entry.

- **Suspend**   Generated when the processing of an activity is suspended. The Suspend trace differs from the Stop trace in that there is an expectation that processing will continue at some point. While the activity is suspended, no traces for the corresponding *ActivityId* will be emitted. The sort of situations in which an activity might be paused would be when calling an external library function or while waiting for a resource to free up.

- **Resume**   This trace occurs upon the resumption of a previously suspended trace. An activity would resume at times that correspond to the *Suspend* trace, such as when an external library function call is complete or when a resource that had previously blocked the application becomes available.

- **Transfer**   In the world of WCF, it is possible for one activity to cause a second activity to start or two activities to be related to one another. The *Transfer* trace records the directed relationship (that is, the creation) of one activity by another.

Knowing that these trace types exist and how they are related can help as you are navigating through the graphical representation found in the Service Trace Viewer. The following guidelines indicate ways the viewer can be used effectively to profile or debug a WCF application.

- **Output is not a tree**   The output from the trace is not a tree. It is a directed cyclic graph. This means that control for any activity will always be returned to the spawning activity.

- **New method = new activity**   Each WCF method, on both the client and the server, results in the creation of a new activity. This enables profiling and debugging to get down to the method level quickly. After the method or activity is finished, the calling activity is brought back into scope.

- **Long-running activities**   The *Start* and *Stop* trace types can be used to determine the boundary for a long-running activity. Included in this list would be activities associated with listening for connections or incoming requests.

- **Interpretation**   Activities are not objects. They are not even business objects. Instead, they are milestones on actions that take place within the WCF processing. When examining the application code, think of the activity as "when X was happening, this trace was emitted."

Lab: Creating an End-to-End Trace

In this lab, you will take tracing to the next level. Through activities, you will capture and correlate the tracing for both sides of a WCF session. To ensure that this is happening correctly, you will use the Service Trace Viewer application.

▶ **Exercise 1   Instrument a WCF Application for End-to-End Tracing**

In this first exercise, you will use the *TraceSource* object and the *Trace* class to instrument both the client and service for end-to-end tracing. You create and propagate an activity across the service boundary into the service implementation code.

1. Navigate to the *<InstallHome>*/Chapter6/Lesson2/Exercise1/*<language>*/Before directory and double-click the Exercise1.sln file to open the solution in Visual Studio.

   The solution consists of two projects. You might recognize the projects as the same ones used in Chapter 5 as well as in Lesson 1 of this chapter. They are as follows:

   ❑ The DemoService project, a simple WCF service library that implements the *IGetHeaders* interface. This interface consists of a single method (*GetHeaders*) that retrieves some information about the headers in the message sent to the service. For this exercise, it returns the *Action* header.

   ❑ The TestClient project, a Console application that enables you to consume the DemoService service. This client is the target for your tracing.

2. In Solution Explorer, double-click the Program.cs or Module1.vb file in the TestClient project.

   To correlate activities, *ActiviyId* in *CorrelationManager* on the *Trace* class must be assigned a value. Typically, as a new activity is created, a new activity ID is generated by creating a new GUID. Also, because there is a need to revert back to the original activity after the new activity is finished, the current activity ID should be saved.

3. Add the following code to the beginning of the *using* block:

   ```
   ' VB
   Dim originalActivityId As Guid = Trace.CorrelationManager.ActivityId
   Dim newActivityId As Guid = Guid.NewGuid()
   Trace.CorrelationManager.ActivityId = newActivityId
   Console.WriteLine(newActivityId)
   ```

   ```
   // C#
   Guid originalActivityId = Trace.CorrelationManager.ActivityId;
   Guid newActivityId = Guid.NewGuid();
   Trace.CorrelationManager.ActivityId = newActivityId;
   Console.WriteLine(newActivityId);
   ```

4. After the call to the service has been created, the activity should be set back to the original value. Add the following code below *Console.WriteLine* where the *GetHeaders* method is called:

```
' VB
Trace.CorrelationManager.ActivityId = originalActivityId
```

```
// C#
Trace.CorrelationManager.ActivityId = originalActivityId;
```

5. In Solution Explorer, double-click the HeaderService file in the DemoService project.

6. At the beginning of the *GetHeaders* method, add the following line of code:

```
' VB
Trace.WriteLine(Trace.CorrelationManager.ActivityId)
```

```
// C#
Trace.WriteLine(Trace.CorrelationManager.ActivityId);
```

    The purpose of this just-added line of code isn't to display the activity ID in the service. (There is no user interface to the service, so the *WriteLine* output would not be visible.) Instead, set a breakpoint on this line. Then when the application is running, the value of *ActivityId* can be compared to the value on the client to ensure that propagation took place.

7. To propagate the activity, the trace source must be configured appropriately. In Solution Explorer, double-click the App.config file in the DemoService project.

8. Find the *source* element for *System.ServiceModel*. In the *source* tag, add a *propagateActivity* attribute. The value of the attribute should be set to *"true"*.

    When you are finished, the value of the *source* element will appear as follows:

```
<source name="System.ServiceModel"
    switchValue="Warning" propagateActivity="true">
```

9. The same change is required for the configuration file on the client side. In Solution Explorer, double-click the app.config file in the TestClient project.

10. Find the *source* element for *System.ServiceModel*. In the *source* tag, add a *propagateActivity* attribute. The value of the attribute should be set to *"true"*.

    When you are finished, the value of the *source* element will appear as follows:

```
<source name="System.ServiceModel"
    switchValue="Warning" propagateActivity="true">
```

11. Ensure that TestClient is set as the startup project, and then launch the application by pressing F5.

    After a few seconds, you will see a command window appear. At the top, a GUID will be displayed.

12. Note the value (or at least move the window so that it remains visible behind Visual Studio). In another few seconds, the breakpoint that was set in the service will be reached.

13. While at the breakpoint, check the value of the *Trace.CorrelationManager.ActivityId* property. Notice that it is the same as the GUID that was displayed on the client side.

14. To finish running the application, stop debugging by choosing Stop Debugging from the Debug menu in Visual Studio 2008.

▶ **Exercise 2   Visualize Activities by Using the Service Trace Viewer**

Along with being able to propagate activities, it can be useful to raise events specifically and publish information about a service and client within that client. In this exercise, you create a new activity and label it with an informative value. Then you use the Service Trace Viewer to display the activity details.

1. Navigate to the *<InstallHome>*/Chapter6/Lesson2/Exercise2/*<language>*/Before directory and double-click the Exercise2.sln file to open the solution in Visual Studio.

2. In Solution Explorer, double-click the Program.cs or Module1.vb file in the TestClient project.

   As a starting point for this exercise, you must create a new activity named Demo Activity, which will be the containing activity for any other activities you create. There are two steps to creating an activity. The first is to generate a GUID and assign it to the *ActivityId* property on *CorrelationManager*.

3. Add the following code to the beginning of the *Main* method in Program.cs or Module1.vb:

   ```
   ' VB
   Dim newActivityId As Guid = Guid.NewGuid()
   Trace.CorrelationManager.ActivityId = newActivityId
   ```

   ```
   // C#
   Guid newActivityId = Guid.NewGuid();
   Trace.CorrelationManager.ActivityId = newActivityId;
   ```

4. The second step in the process is to emit a *TraceEvent*, indicating that an activity has started. To do this, add the following the code below the code added in the previous step:

   ```
   ' VB
   Dim ts As New TraceSource("DemoServiceTraceSource")
   ts.TraceEvent(TraceEventType.Start, 0, "DemoService Actvitity")
   ```

   ```
   // C#
   TraceSource ts = new TraceSource("DemoServiceTraceSource");
   ts.TraceEvent(TraceEventType.Start, 0, "DemoService Actvitity");
   ```

   Now that that containing activity has been established, the activity context needs to be switched. Do this by creating a new activity ID (that is, a new GUID) and invoking the *TraceTransfer* method.

5. Add the following code at the beginning of the *using* block:

   ```
   ' VB
   Dim originalActivityId As Guid = Trace.CorrelationManager.ActivityId
   newActivityId = Guid.NewGuid()
   ts.TraceTransfer(0, "Transfer", newActivityId)
   ```

   ```
   // C#
   Guid originalActivityId = Trace.CorrelationManager.ActivityId;
   newActivityId = Guid.NewGuid();
   ts.TraceTransfer(0, "Transfer", newActivityId);
   ```

After the transfer has occurred, the *ActivityId* should be updated with the new GUID and the activity started.

6. Add the following code below the just-added lines:

```
' VB
Trace.CorrelationManager.ActivityId = newActivityId
ts.TraceEvent(TraceEventType.Start, 0, "GetHeader Activity")
```

```
// C#
Trace.CorrelationManager.ActivityId = newActivityId;
ts.TraceEvent(TraceEventType.Start, 0, "GetHeader Activity");
```

To include some informational messages in the trace log, surround the call to the service with a couple of statements that generate informational data, using the *TraceEvent* method.

7. At the current bottom of the *using* block, a *Console.WriteLine* statement invokes the service. Replace that line with the following lines:

```
' VB
ts.TraceEvent(TraceEventType.Information, 0, _
    "Client sending message to DemoService")
Console.WriteLine("And the headers are: " & proxy.GetHeaders())
ts.TraceEvent(TraceEventType.Information, 0, _
    "Client received response from DemoService")
```

```
// C#
ts.TraceEvent(TraceEventType.Information, 0,
    "Client sending message to DemoService");
Console.WriteLine("And the headers are: " + proxy.GetHeaders());
ts.TraceEvent(TraceEventType.Information, 0,
    "Client received response from DemoService");
```

Now that the *GetHeaders* activity is complete, the activity needs to be transferred back to the original activity and a *Stop* event generated.

8. Add the following code to the end of the *using* block:

```
' VB
ts.TraceTransfer(667, "Transfer to DemoService Actitity", _
    originalActivityId)
ts.TraceEvent(TraceEventType.Stop, 0, "GetHeader Activity")
Trace.CorrelationManager.ActivityId = originalActivityId
```

```
// C#
ts.TraceTransfer(667, "Transfer to DemoService Actitity",
    originalActivityId);
ts.TraceEvent(TraceEventType.Stop, 0, "GetHeader Activity");
Trace.CorrelationManager.ActivityId = originalActivityId;
```

Finally, the containing activity (the one called DemoService Activity) needs to be stopped.

9.   Add the following line of code outside the *using* block but above the *Console.ReadLine* statement:

```vb
' VB
ts.TraceEvent(TraceEventType.Stop, 0, "DemoService Activity")
```

```csharp
// C#
ts.TraceEvent(TraceEventType.Stop, 0, "DemoService Activity");
```

At this point, the client portion of the application has been instrumented. Now it's time to instrument the service.

10.   In Solution Explorer, double-click the HeaderService file.

If the service is going to work with the activity, it shouldn't start by assuming that one has been provided by the client. As you saw in Exercise 1, "Instrument a WCF Application for End-to-End Tracing," some configuration needs to be done to propagate the *ActivityId* between the client and the service.

11.   The following code should be added to the beginning of the *GetHeaders* method to ensure that an activity ID is available for use:

```vb
' VB
If Trace.CorrelationManager.ActivityId = Guid.Empty Then
   Trace.CorrelationManager.ActivityId = Guid.NewGuid()
End If
```

```csharp
// C#
if (Trace.CorrelationManager.ActivityId == Guid.Empty)
   Trace.CorrelationManager.ActivityId = Guid.NewGuid();
```

12.   Within the method, you need to start an activity by using the *TraceEvent* method. Add the following code below the just-added lines:

```vb
' VB
Dim ts As New TraceSource("DemoServiceTraceSource")
ts.TraceEvent(TraceEventType.Start, 0, "GetHeader Activity")
```

```csharp
// C#
TraceSource ts = new TraceSource("DemoServiceTraceSource");
ts.TraceEvent(TraceEventType.Start, 0, "GetHeader Activity");
```

As you did with the client, an information message will be emitted into the trace log before and after the actual processing done by the method.

13.   To start, add the following line of code below the just-added lines:

```vb
' VB
ts.TraceEvent(TraceEventType.Information, 0, _
   "Service receives GetHeader request message.")
```

```csharp
// C#
ts.TraceEvent(TraceEventType.Information, 0,
   "Service receives GetHeader request message.");
```

14. Also add the following code just prior to the *return* statement at the bottom of the method. It provides the second piece of informational data to the trace log:

```
' VB
ts.TraceEvent(TraceEventType.Information, 0, _
    "Service sends GetHeaders response message.")
```

```
// C#
ts.TraceEvent(TraceEventType.Information, 0,
    "Service sends GetHeaders response message.");
```

Finally, for the service code, you must stop the activity that was started at the beginning of the method.

15. Add the following code after the just-added lines and before the *return* statement:

```
' VB
ts.TraceEvent(TraceEventType.Stop, 0, "GetHeader Activity")
```

```
// C#
ts.TraceEvent(TraceEventType.Stop, 0, "GetHeader Activity");
```

Even though you have instrumented the service and client, you still need to make a couple of configuration changes. Specifically, you need to configure the trace source that was created in both client and server (named *DemoServiceTraceSource*) to capture both *Information* and *ActivityTracing* traces.

16. In Solution Explorer, double-click the App.config file for the DemoService project.

17. Add the following configuration information for the DemoServiceTraceSource to the *sources* element:

```
<source name="DemoServiceTraceSource"
    switchValue="Information,ActivityTracing">
    <listeners>
        <add name="log"/>
    </listeners>
</source>
```

18. The same block of configuration XML needs to be defined on the client side as well. In Solution Explorer, double-click the app.config file for the TestClient project.

19. Insert the following configuration XML into the *sources* element of the file:

```
<source name="DemoServiceTraceSource"
    switchValue="Information,ActivityTracing">
    <listeners>
        <add name="log"/>
    </listeners>
</source>
```

20. Ensure that the TestClient project is set as the startup project and launch the application by pressing F5.

In a couple of seconds, the Console window will display a message, indicating that the header has been received.

21. Press Enter to terminate the application.

Although the application has finished, the trace information is still available.

22. To view it, launch the Service Trace Viewer tool by clicking Start. From the All Programs menu, choose Microsoft Windows SDK V6.1. Select Tools, and then click Service Trace Viewer.

23. In Service Trace Viewer, choose Open from the File menu. Navigate to the <*InstallHome*>/Chapter6/Lesson2/Exercise2/<*language*>/Before/TestClient/bin/Debug directory and open the Traces.svclog file.

24. After the log file has been opened, ensure that the Activity tab on the left side is selected. You will see that there are two activities, named DemoService Activity and GetHeader Activity. Select the DemoService Activity node.

25. On the top right, a list of the details for DemoService Activity appears, as shown in Figure 6-4. You should be able to see the start for DemoService and that a transfer to GetHeader Activity occurred.

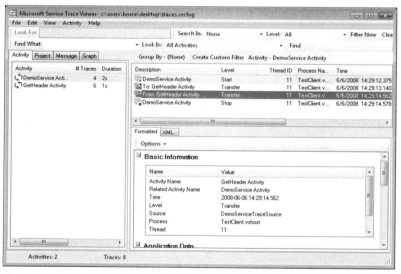

Figure 6-4   Main view for the Service Trace Viewer

26. Double-click the *To: GetHeader Activity* node.

The contents of the top right pane change to display the details for GetHeader Activity. The incoming transfer is noted, along with the start, the informational messages, the outgoing transfer, and the stop.

27. Choose Add from the File menu. Navigate to the <*InstallHome*>/Chapter6/Lesson2/Exercise2/<*language*>/Before/DemoService/bin/Debug directory.

There you will find a file that starts with a GUID and ends with Traces.svclog. This is the service side of the log file.

28. Select that file and click Open.

The pane on the left hasn't changed. However, the pane in the top right has had a few lines added. These are the trace messages from the service side that were correlated to GetHeader Activity. Figure 6-5 illustrates the combined log files.

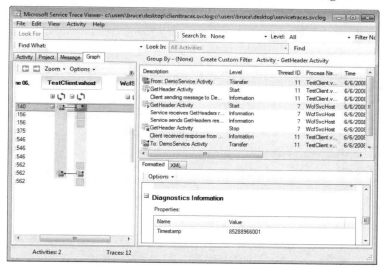

Figure 6-5   Service and client trace log files combined

These include the start and stop events along with the informational messages emitted by the service. For example, in the top right pane, you see two GetHeader Activitiy entries marked as having a Start level. These are the client and service activity boundaries. You can use Process Name or Thread Id to distinguish between the two sides.

Lesson Summary

- You can use activities to correlate traces across service boundaries.
- The propagation of activities across service boundaries depends on both the proper instrumentation of the application code and the appropriate configuration of WCF.
- Although activities must be created by hand, the resulting traces can be viewed through the Service Trace Viewer.

Lesson Review

You can use the following questions to test your knowledge of the information in Lesson 2. The questions are also available on the companion CD if you prefer to review them in electronic form.

NOTE Answers

Answers to these questions and explanations of why each answer choice is correct or incorrect are located in the "Answers" section at the end of the book.

---

1. You have created a WCF application. You would like to implement end-to-end tracing. You believe you have done so, but when you look at the Service Trace Viewer, the client and service traces do not appear to be correlated. Moreover, when you check the *Trace.CorrelationManager.ActivityId* property in the service, it is not the same as in the client. Which of the following is NOT a potential solution to this problem?

    A. The *switchValue* attribute for the *System.ServiceModel* source is not set to *Activity-Tracing*.

    B. In the client side, the *Trace.CorrelationManager.ActivityId* has not been assigned a new GUID value.

    C. The *propagateActivity* attribute in the *System.ServiceModel* source has not been set to *true*.

    D. A *Transfer* trace has not been emitted on the client.

2. You are designing an activity to correlate functionality across multiple clients and services. Specifically, a client sends a request to a service, which then sends a request to a different service. This last service is not in your control, so you don't want the trace information generated by the service to be included in your activity. Which of the following methods should be called immediately prior to invoking the third-party service?

    A. *Trace.TraceEvent(TraceEvent.Start, 0, "My Activity")*

    B. *Trace.TraceEvent(TraceEvent.Stop, 0, "My Activity")*

    C. *Trace.TraceEvent(TraceEvent.Suspend, 0, "My Activity")*

    D. *Trace.TraceEvent(TraceEvent.Transfer, 0, "My Activity")*

Lesson 3: WCF Extensibility

Up to this point, the focus has been on how to provide information about the steps involved in processing a WCF message. Whether the tracing is explicit or done as part of the underlying infrastructure, the output tends to be driven by milestones, and to get specific information, the tracing code would need to be in place already. What do you do if you are working with third-party code? Or the developer (not you, but those other developers) haven't had the foresight to instrument the code with tracing statements. You can find the answer in the details of the WCF pipeline.

> **After this lesson, you will be able to:**
> - Identify the extensibility points in the WCF pipeline.
> - Programmatically inspect messages and parameters.
> - Inject logic into the dispatching of operations.
>
> **Estimated lesson time: 45 minutes**

WCF Extensibility

There is no question that WCF has been designed and implemented to be extensible in a number of different areas. In fact, if you need to change the format of the message, add or remove parameters, or send the various messages to a log file, the question is not whether this can be done but where you should inject the functionality. To answer that question, a quick tour of the path a message takes is imperative. Figure 6-6 provides a wire diagram illustrating this path.

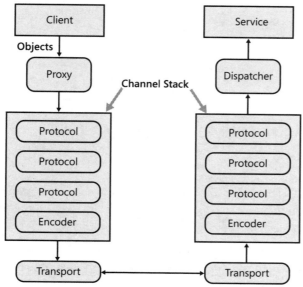

Figure 6-6   WCF message pipeline

Starting in the top left of Figure 6-6, there is the client application. From within the client application, methods on a proxy class are called with zero or more objects being sent as parameters. The purpose of the proxy is to create a WCF *Message* object, which contains all the information related to the method being called, the parameters being passed, and the requirements of the transport. This *Message* object is then passed to the *channel stack* for transmission on the wire to the service.

On the service side, a transport stream is received. The service's channel stack takes the stream and converts it back into a *Message* object. The *Message* object is given to a dispatcher, which examines the properties and makes the call to the appropriate method on the service's implementation object.

This pipeline provides many extensibility points into which custom classes can plug additional functionality. Included in these options are validating parameters, logging messages, and transforming message formats, implementing special serializing and deserializing mechanisms, object caching, and pooling and performing authorization.

Extensibility Points

Take a deeper look at the two sides of this pipeline, starting with the proxy layer. Figure 6-7 illustrates the proxy pipeline and the points at which extensibility can occur.

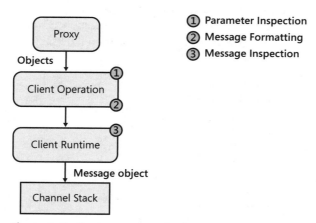

Figure 6-7 Proxy message pipeline

The first point of extensibility occurs when the parameters being sent to the service can be inspected. Part of this extension includes the ability to perform validation on the parameters and either modify them or reject the message before it is sent to the service.

The second point of extension occurs when the message information is serialized. The default serialization for the parameters depends on the binding, with the most common formats being binary or XML. However, you can write a message formatter and inject it into the pipeline so that you can use any type of serialization that you require. (If you are going to customize the parameter serialization on the client, you need to ensure that the service is expecting the same serialization format.)

NOTE Method-by-method configuration

Although it might not be readily apparent, the extensibility functionality at the first two points can be configured on a method-by-method basis or, more accurately, you can use information about the method that was called to change the functionality that is provided.

The final point of extension on the proxy pipeline occurs after the *Message* object has been created. It is known as *Message Inspection*, and it is typically used to perform functions that are not specific to one operation or service but instead can apply to many different methods. Message logging is an example of such a function in that it has the potential to be used by many differ- *clie* ent operations.

These extension points can be configured through *ClientOperation* objects (for parameter inspection and message formatting) and through *ClientRuntime* objects (for message inspection). One *ClientOperation* object is created for each service operation (that is, for each method exposed by the service) and one *ClientRuntime* object is created for the entire proxy.

As you would expect, the service side of the pipeline also has a number of extension points. Basically, there are the same extension points as on the client (albeit executed in reverse order), plus some additional points. Figure 6-8 illustrates the service-side pipeline.

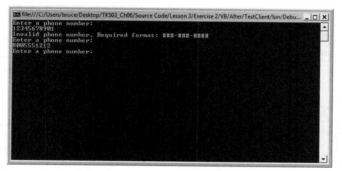 *Service*

Figure 6-8   Service-side message pipeline

When the channel stack delivers a message to the service side, the first extension point is a message inspector. After the message has been inspected, an operation selector extension is available, which enables you to customize which operation should be invoked. By default, the invoked operation matches the name of the method, but you can examine the properties of the method and determine that a different operation should be used.

After the operation has been identified, the dispatch deserializes the message into the objects to be used as parameters. At this point, the service side provides extensibility points for message formatting (the counterpart of the message formatting on the proxy side) and parameter inspection. Finally, the target method is invoked, with the parameters passed in. However, this last step is also an extensibility point in that you can provide a custom invoker that dynamically determines how the target method will be called.

These extension points are configured through the *DispatchRuntime* and *DispatchOperation* objects. In the next few sections, you will see not only how to implement some of these extension points but also how to configure these objects to inject the functionality into the pipeline.

Parameter Inspectors

One of the main purposes for implementing a parameter inspector is to validate parameters prior to sending the message to the service. Although it would be quite possible to perform validation inside the service's method (and you probably should), the downside is that messages containing invalid parameters still have to make the trip from the client to the service. The service's throughput is reduced because it has to deal with the deserialization of the message and the construction of the response. It would be better to avoid this overhead and just reject the message on the client side.

The key to implementing a parameter inspector is to implement the *IParameterInspector* interface. This interface contains two methods: *BeforeCall* and *AfterCall*. The signature for these methods follows:

```vb
' VB
Sub AfterCall (operationName As String, outputs As Object(), _
    returnValue As Object, correlationState As Object)
Function BeforeCall(operationName As String, inputs As Object()) _
    As Object
```

```csharp
// C#
void AfterCall(string operationName, object[] outputs, object returnValue,
    object correlationState);
object BeforeCall(string operationName, object[] inputs);
```

In both cases, the parameters sent to the method are presented to these methods as an array of objects. However, their position in the pipeline depends on whether the inspector is inserted on the client side or the service side.

On the Client Side

When injected on the client side, the *BeforeCall* method is invoked just prior to the parameters being serialized into the request *Message* object. If you are implementing client-side parameter validation, this is the place to put the logic to minimize network and service traffic. The *After-Call* method is invoked just after the parameters from the response *Message* object have been deserialized. This means that the *BeforeCall* method happens prior to the call, and the *AfterCall* method is applied to the response to that call.

Injecting the parameter inspector class (the one that hasn't yet been created) on the client side must be done through code. Specifically, it needs to be added to the *OperationDescription* object found on the proxy. The following code demonstrates how this can be done:

```vb
' VB
Dim proxy As New UpdateServiceClient()
Proxy.Endpoint.Contract.Operations(0).Behaviors.Add(New _
   EmailAddressInspector())
```

```csharp
// C#
UpdateServiceClient proxy = new UpdateServiceClient();
Proxy.Endpoint.Contract.Operations[0].Behaviors.Add(new
   EmailAddressInspector());
```

On the Server Side

On the server side, the processing for the parameter inspector is similar. The *BeforeCall* method is invoked just after the parameters to be passed into the operation have been deserialized into .NET objects, and the *AfterCall* method is invoked immediately after the service operation has completed its processing, prior to any serialization of the return value or parameters. As for injecting the inspection class, the server side provides an alternative mechanism. Specifically, you can create a custom attribute to perform the injection.

In the following code, a custom attribute is created. The attribute class implements the *IOperationBehavior* interface. This allows it to be applied to an operation on the Service contract. Within the class, the *ApplyDispatchBehavior* method is overridden. In that method, the instance of the parameter inspector class is then added to the operation behavior:

```vb
' VB
Public Class EmailAddressInspectorAttribute
   Inherits Attribute
   Implements IOperationBehavior

   Public Sub ApplyDispatchBehavior( _
      operationDescription As OperationDescription, _
      dispatchOperation As DispatchOperation) _
      Implements IOperationBehavior.ApplyDispatchBehavior

      dispatchOperation.ParameterInspectors.Add( _
         New EmailAddressInspector())

   End Sub

   Public Sub AddBindingParameters(ByVal operationDescription As _
      OperationDescription, ByVal bindingParameters As _
      BindingParameterCollection) Implements _
```

```
        IOperationBehavior.AddBindingParameters

    End Sub

    Public Sub ApplyClientBehavior(ByVal operationDescription As _
        OperationDescription, ByVal clientOperation As _
        ClientOperation) Implements IOperationBehavior.ApplyClientBehavior

    End Sub

    Public Sub Validate(ByVal operationDescription As _
        OperationDescription) Implements _
        IOperationBehavior.Validate

    End Sub
End Class
```

```
// C#
public class EmailAddressInspectorAttribute
    : Attribute, IOperationBehavior
{
    public void ApplyDispatchBehavior(
        OperationDescription operationDescription,
        DispatchOperation dispatchOperation
        )
    {
        dispatchOperation.ParameterInspectors.Add(
            new EmailAddressInspector());
    }

    public void AddBindingParameters(OperationDescription
        operationDescription, BindingParameterCollection bindingParameters)
    { }

    public void ApplyClientBehavior(OperationDescription
        operationDescription, ClientOperation clientOperation)
    { }

    public void Validate(OperationDescription operationDescription)
    { }
}
```

Along with the *ApplyDispatchBehavior* method, three other methods need to be implemented to fulfill the contract required by the *IOperationBehavior* interface.

- **AddBindingParameters** This method is used to pass information into the behavior at run time. The parameters to this method are a description of the operation being performed and a collection of binding parameters. Any information that needs to be given to the behavior is added to the binding parameter collection.

- **ApplyClientBehavior** This method is similar to *ApplyDispatchBehavior*. The difference is that it modifies the behavior associated with the client side of the request. It takes an

OperationDescription object and a *ClientOperation* object as parameters. Modification of the client operation behavior is achieved through properties exposed by the *ClientOperation* object.

- **Validate** This method is used to determine whether the operation meets some criteria required for the behavior to be successful. An *OperationDescription* object is passed into the method. Perhaps unexpectedly, there is no return value from the method. If the operation doesn't meet the criteria, an exception is thrown. Otherwise, the method completes normally.

Implementing the Inspector

Now to the implementation of the inspector that was promised. The purpose of the following class is to validate that an e-mail parameter is in the correct format. You define the correct format by using a regular expression pattern. Also, because the validation is taking place prior to the call, you need to implement only the *BeforeCall* method. Note that if the parameter is invalid, a *FaultException* is thrown. The following code block illustrates an inspector that validates the e-mail parameter:

```vb
' VB
Public Class EMailAddressInspector
   Implements IParameterInspector

   Public Function BeforeCall(operationName As String, _
      inputs as Object()) As Object _
      Implements IParameterInspector.BeforeCall

      Dim emailAddress As String = TryCast(inputs(0), String)
      If Not Regex.IsMatch(emailAddress, _
         "^[A-Z0-9._%+-]+@[A-Z0-9.-]+\.[A-Z]{2,4}$", _
         RegexOptions.None) Then
           throw new FaultException("Invalid email address format.")
      End If
       Return Nothing
   End Function

   Public Sub AfterCall (operationName As String, outputs As Object(), _
     returnValue As Object, correlationState As Object)

   End Sub
End Class
```

```csharp
// C#
public class EMailAddressInspector : IParameterInspector
{
    public object BeforeCall(string operationName, object[] inputs)
    {
        string emailAddress = inputs[0] as string;
        if (!Regex.IsMatch(emailAddress,
           "^[A-Z0-9._%+-]+@[A-Z0-9.-]+\.[A-Z]{2,4}$", RegexOptions.None))
```

```
            throw new FaultException(
                "Invalid email address format.");
        return null;
    }

    public void AfterCall(string operationName,
        object[] outputs, object returnValue, object correlationState)
    { }
}
```

Two elements are worth further discussion. The first argument to *BeforeCall* is *operationName*. The purpose of the parameter is to provide information about which operation is being called. Although this might seem like an easy thing to understand, there is something important to keep in mind. The *operationName* parameter is the name of the operation as exposed in the contract. This might or might not be the name of the method called on the proxy object, and it might or might not be the same as the method name on the service's implementation class. So the *operationName* parameter contains whatever has been assigned to the *Name* property in the *OperationContract* attribute.

The second aspect worth discussing is the return value from *BeforeCall*. Its purpose is to allow *BeforeCall* methods to be correlated with *AfterCall* methods. The value returned from a *BeforeCall* will be passed into the corresponding *AfterCall*. Specifically, it's in the *correlationState* parameter.

Message Inspectors

The second extension point to be discussed is the message inspector. As already mentioned, this function is performed after the parameters have been inspected and serialized into the *Message* object. To create a message inspector, interfaces must be involved. The difference between message inspection and parameter inspection is that each side (client and service) has its own interface: *IClientMessageInspector* and *IDispatchMessageInspector*. The signatures for the methods can be found in this code sample:

```
' VB
Public Interface IClientMessageInspector
    Sub AfterReceiveReply(ByRef reply As Message, _
        correlationState As Object)
    Function BeforeSendRequest(ByRef request As Message, _
        Channel As IClientChannel) As Object
End Interface

Public Interface IDispatchMessageInspector
    Function AfterReceiveRequest(ByRef request As Message, _
        Channel As IClientChannel, instanceContext As InstanceContext) _
        As Object
    Sub BeforeSendReply(ByRef reply As Message, _
        correlationState As Object)
End Interface
```

```csharp
// C#
public interface IClientMessageInspector
{
    void AfterReceiveReply(ref Message reply, object correlationState);
    object BeforeSendRequest(ref Message request, IClientChannel channel);
}
public interface IDispatchMessageInspector
{
    object AfterReceiveRequest(ref Message request,
        IClientChannel channel, InstanceContext instanceContext);
    void BeforeSendReply(ref Message reply, object correlationState);
}
```

As you can see, all four of the methods in these two interfaces accept a *Message* object as a parameter—not surprising, given the purpose of the interfaces. The *Message* object contains the serialized parameters, operation name, and other information about the message being inspected. However, there is more to the *Message* object than to act as a container for information, at least for message inspection.

The *Message* Class and Its Lifetime

One of the design choices for the *Message* class is that it supports streaming. The body of the message—that actual thing that will get sent across the wire—is implemented as a streamed object. Although the capability to handle streaming is good for performance, it does have one consequence. The body of a message can be processed only once during the lifetime of the *Message* object. The implication is that you can retrieve the body only once. A second (or subsequent) attempt to process the body of a message will result in an *InvalidOperationException*.

For an external program to determine the state of the stream, the *Message* class exposes a *MessageState* property. There are five possible values for this property.

- **Created**   The message has been created, but no additional processing has been performed.
- **Written**   The message body has been written to.
- **Read**   The message body has been read.
- **Copied**   The message body has been copied.
- **Closed**   The message has been closed and can no longer be accessed.

The *Created* state is the only state within which the message body can be processed. The next three states (*Written*, *Read*, and *Copied*) are all set after the message body has been processed.

Processing the message body is relatively easy. The *ToString* method does this, as does the *GetBody<T>* method. After you have retrieved the message body, you are free to do with it what you please. However, you can't pass the *Message* object on to be used by the rest of the channel because as the *Message* object flows down the channel, other pieces will attempt to access the body, and exceptions will be raised.

The solution is to use the *CreateBufferedCopy* method. This method returns a *MessageBuffer* object that contains the body of the method. As with the previously mentioned methods, you can manipulate the body of the message that has been copied. Further, by using the *CreateMessage* method on the *MessageBuffer* object, you can re-create a *Message* object that can be processed by the downstream channel components. The following code illustrates this process:

```vb
' VB
Public Function BeforeSendRequest(ByRef request As Message, _
    ByVal Channel As IClientChannel) As Object _
    Implements IClientMessageInspector.BeforeSendRequest
    Dim buffer As MessageBuffer = request.CreateBufferedCopy(Int32.MaxValue)
    Dim body As T = buffer.CreateMessage.GetBody(Of T)()
    request = buffer.CreateMessage()
    Return Nothing

End Function
```

```csharp
// C#
public object BeforeSendRequest(ref Message request,
    IClientChannel channel)
{
    MessageBuffer buffer = request.CreateBufferedCopy(Int32.MaxValue);
    T body = buffer.CreateMessage().GetBody<T>();
    request = buffer.CreateMessage();
    return null;
}
```

On the Client Side

The interface used to inspect messages on the client side (*IClientMessageInspector*) exposes two methods. The *BeforeSendRequest* method is invoked prior to the message being sent to the service. The *AfterReceiveReply* method is invoked prior to the response from the service being processed.

In the *BeforeSendRequest* method, the second parameter is an *IClientChannel* object. This object provides information about the channel into which the message will be sent and, unlike the *Message* object, it can be used with impunity. As for the *Message* parameter, notice that it is passed by reference. This allows a new *Message* object to be created and returned—convenient, given that you need to do exactly that to work with the body of the *Message* object in this method.

The value returned by *BeforeSendRequest* is a correlation object. It performs the same task as the correlation object in the parameter inspectors. It is an opaque object in that none of the elements in the WCF pipeline will care about the type or contents of the object. However, it is presented as one of the parameters in the *AfterReceiveReply* method.

In the *AfterReceiveReply* method, two parameters are present. The *Message* object faces the same issues as with the *BeforeSendRequest* method: the body can't be processed directly. The second parameter is the correlation object. This is the same object that was returned from the *BeforeSendRequest* method and can be used to match up the pre-call and post-call processing in these methods.

On the Server Side

Again, the interface used to implement message inspection on the server side has two methods, and the positioning of those methods within the pipeline is quite similar. The *AfterReceiveRequest* method is fired after the message has been received but prior to invoking the service operation, and the *BeforeSendReply* is called after the response has been constructed by the service operation.

In terms of parameters, the *AfterReceiveRequest* method has the ever-present *Message* object as well as an *IClientChannel* object to provide information about the channel. The third parameter is the instance context for the current service object. The instance context exposes some details about the service that is processing this request.

The value returned from the *AfterReceiveRequest* is the correlation object used on the dispatch side of the processing. This value will be returned into the *correlationState* parameter that is passed into the *BeforeSendReply*. The *correlationState* parameter is the second of two for this method, the other being the *Message* object.

Adding Message Inspectors to the Pipeline

You can choose from three ways to add a message inspector to either the client or the service side of the WCF pipeline. In general, you must do some coding to accomplish it.

First, you must create a behavior. You add message inspectors to the pipeline by modifying the behavior of the service model at run time, so to add such an inspector, you must create a custom behavior. Further, because a behavior implements the *IEndpointBehavior* interface, what remains is, at a minimum, a class that implements the four methods that are part of *IEndpointBehavior*. The four methods, along with their purposes, are as follows:

- **AddBindingParameters**   Adds the parameters required by this behavior to the binding at run time
- **ApplyClientBehavior**   Provides the customization to the endpoint on the client side of the request
- **ApplyDispatchBehavior**   Provides the customization to the endpoint on the service side of the request
- **Validate**   Performs whatever validation is required to ensure that the endpoint is capable of supporting the applied behavior

If a message inspector is added, then the two methods that are mostly likely to be of interest are *ApplyClientBehavior* (to add inspection to the client side) and *ApplyDispatchBehavior* (to add inspection to the service side). The other methods will be implemented only if the particular inspector requires more information or needs some resource to be present to function.

In terms of how to inject the inspector, the key is to find the appropriate run-time object. For the client side, the *ClientRuntime* object is passed into the *ApplyClientBehavior* as a parameter. On the service side, the *DispatchRuntime* object is available, but it's a little more hidden. The *ApplyDispatchBehavior* takes an *EndpointDispatcher* object as a parameter. On that object is a *ServiceRuntime* object.

After you have found these run-time objects, the process of adding the message inspector is the same. It involves adding an instance of the inspector class (the class that implements the *IClientInspector* or the *IDispatchInspector* interfaces) to the *MessageInspectors* collection.

For the following code, assume that a message inspector is implemented in a class called *MessageLogInspector*. More specifically, the *MessageLogInspector* class implements both the *IClientInspector* and the *IDispatchInspector* interfaces. The following code creates a behavior that injects the inspector into the WCF pipeline:

```vb
' VB
Public Class LoggingEndpointBehavior
   Implements IEndpointBehavior

   Public Sub AddBindingParameters(endpoint As ServiceEndpoint, _
      bindingParameters as BindingParameterCollection) _
      Implements IEndpointBehavior.AddBindingParameters
   End Sub

   Public Sub ApplyClientBehavior(endpoint As ServiceEndpoint, _
      clientRuntime As ClientRuntime) _
      Implements IEndpointBehavior.ApplyClientBehavior
      Dim inspector As New MessageLogInspector()
      clientRuntime.MessageInspectors.Add(inspector)
   End Sub

   Public Sub ApplyDispatchBehavior(endpoint As ServiceEndpoint, _
      dispatcher As EndpointDispatcher) _
      Implements IEndpointBehavior.ApplyDispatchBehavior
   End Sub

   Public Sub Validate(endpoint As ServiceEndpoint) _
      Implements IEndpointBehavior.Validate
   End Sub
End Class

// C#
public class LoggingEndpointBehavior : IEndpointBehavior
{
   public void AddBindingParameters(ServiceEndpoint endpoint,
      BindingParameterCollection bindingParameters)
   { }
```

```
    public void ApplyClientBehavior(ServiceEndpoint endpoint,
        ClientRuntime clientRuntime)
    {
        MessageLogInspector inspector = new MessageLogInspector();
        clientRuntime.MessageInspectors.Add(inspector);
    }

    public void ApplyDispatchBehavior(ServiceEndpoint endpoint,
        EndpointDispatcher endpointDispatcher)
    {
        MessageLogInspector inspector = new MessageLogInspector();
        endpointDispatcher.DispatchRuntime.MessageInspectors.Add(inspector);
    }

    public void Validate(ServiceEndpoint endpoint)
    { }
}
```

Now that you have a behavior, it needs to be added to a behavior extension. After the behavior is added to such an extension, it can be added to the WCF pipeline through the configuration file. The behavior extension is actually a class that derives from the *BehaviorExtensionElement* class, and the minimum functionality for the class is to override the *CreateBehavior* method so that it returns an instance of the desired behavior. The following code demonstrates this, using the *LoggingEndpointBehavior*.

```
' VB
Public Class LoggingBehaviourExtensionElement
    Inherits BehaviorExtensionElement

    Public Overrides ReadOnly Property BehaviorType() As Type
        Get
            Return GetType(LoggingEndpointBehavior)
        End Get
    End Property

    Protected Overrides Function CreateBehavior() As Object
        Return New LoggingEndpointBehavior ();
    End Function
End Class
```

```
// C#
public class LoggingBehaviorExtensionElement : BehaviorExtensionElement
{
    public override Type BehaviorType
    {
        get
        {
            return typeof(LoggingEndpointBehavior);
        }
    }
```

```
    protected override object CreateBehavior()
    {
        return new LoggingEndpointBehavior();
    }
}
```

After the behavior extension is implemented, you can add the behavior (which is a message inspector) by adding a *behaviorExtension* element in the extensions section of the *serviceModel* element. After the extension has been referenced, you can add it to an *endpointBehavior* element as shown in bold in the following code:

```
<system.serviceModel>
  <behaviors>
    <endpointBehaviors>
      <behavior name="LoggingEndpointBehavior">
        <messageLogger />
      </behavior>
    </endpointBehaviors>
  </behaviors>
  <extensions>
    <behaviorExtensions>
      <add name="messageLogger"
           type="assembly.LoggingBehaviorExtensionElement, assembly,
               Version=1.0.0.0, Culture=neutral, PublicKeyToken=null"/>
    </behaviorExtensions>
  </extensions>
</system.serviceModel>
```

You might notice the fully qualified assembly name in the *behaviorExtensions* tag. This is a requirement, at least at the moment. If the type name is not fully qualified, a *Configuration-ErrorsException* exception is thrown. In fact, in what some consider to be a bug, the type name is actually white space–sensitive. If you removed any of the spaces from the type name, the same *ConfigurationErrorsException* is thrown.

Exam Tip You'll notice from the example that the name of the behavior extension matches the name of the node within the behavior. This is required for the extension to function properly.

Alternatively, the behavior can be added imperatively by accessing the endpoint behaviors through the proxy object. Making the assumption that the proxy class is called *UpdateService-Client*, the following code will added to the just created logging message inspector:

```
' VB
Dim client As New UpdateServiceClient()
client.Endpoint.Behaviors.Add(New LoggingEndpointBehavior())

// C#
UdpateServiceClient client = new UpdateServiceClient();
client.Endpoint.Behaviors.Add(new LoggingEndpointBehavior());
```

Lab: Using Extensibility Points

In this lab, you will explore some of the extensibility points exposed by WCF. In particular, you will use the parameter inspection technique to validate that a particular parameter matches a regular expression pattern. You will also use message inspection to send the contents of the request and response message to an output window.

▶ **Exercise 1   Use Message Inspection**

In this first exercise, you will use message inspection to direct a copy of the request and response messages to an output window. The purpose of the exercise is to demonstrate how you can use inspection to access the message. When accessed, you can modify the message prior to sending it, including adding information or changing the format.

1. Navigate to the <*InstallHome*>/Chapter6/Lesson3/Exercise1/<*language*>/Before directory and double-click the Exercise1.sln file to open the solution in Visual Studio.

   The solution consists of two projects. They are as follows:

   ❑ The DemoService project, a simple WCF service library that implements the *IContact* interface. This interface consists of a single method (*UpdatePhone*) that retrieves some information about the headers in the message sent to the service. For this exercise, the method displays the phone number that has been passed into the method in the trace output.

   ❑ The TestClient project, a Console application that enables you to consume the DemoService service. This client is the target of the message inspector injection.

2. In Solution Explorer, right-click the TestClient project. Select Add and then Class from the context menu.

3. In the Add New Item dialog box, change the name to **MessageTracer** and click Add.

4. Add the following statements to the top of the file:

   ```
   ' VB
   Imports System.ServiceModel.Dispatcher
   Imports System.ServiceModel.Channels
   Imports System.ServiceModel
   ```

   ```
   // C#
   using System.ServiceModel.Dispatcher;
   using System.ServiceModel.Channels;
   using System.ServiceModel;
   ```

   The *MessageTracer* class is the implementation of the inspection. As such, it needs to implement the *IClientMessageInspector* interface.

5. Change the class declaration to be the following:

   ```
   ' VB
   Public Class MessageTracer
       Implements IClientMessageInspector
   ```

```
// C#
public class MessageTracer : IClientMessageInspector
```

The purpose of the class is to direct a copy of the message to the *Trace* output device (which defaults, in Visual Studio, to a debug window).

6. Create a method called *TraceMessage* that creates a copy of the *Message* object and uses it in a *WriteLine* method by adding the following code to the beginning of the *MessageTracer* class:

```
' VB
Private Function TraceMessage(buffer As MessageBuffer) As Message
    Dim msg as Message = buffer.CreateMessage()
    System.Diagnostics.Trace.WriteLine("Message contents" & _
        msg.ToString())
    Return buffer.CreateMessage()
End Function
```

```
// C#
private Message TraceMessage(MessageBuffer buffer)
{
    Message msg = buffer.CreateMessage();
    System.Diagnostics.Trace.WriteLine("Message contents" +
        msg.ToString());
    return buffer.CreateMessage();
}
```

The *IClientMessageInspector* interface requires implementation of two methods. The first is called *BeforeSendRequest*. It will be invoked immediately before the message is sent to the client. In this exercise, the *TraceMessage* method will be called, passing a copy of the message.

7. Add the following code below the *TraceMessage* method:

```
' VB
Public Function BeforeSendRequest(ByRef request As Message, _
    Channel As IClientChannel) As Object _
    Implements IClientMessageInspector.BeforeSendRequest

    request = TraceMessage(request.CreateBufferedCopy(Integer.MaxValue))
    Return Nothing
End Function
```

```
// C#
public object BeforeSendRequest(ref Message request,
    IClientChannel channel)
{
    request = TraceMessage(request.CreateBufferedCopy(int.MaxValue));
    return null;
}
```

The second method the *IClientMessageInspector* interface includes is named *AfterReceive-Reply*. It is invoked after the response comes back from the service.

8. Add the following code below the *BeforeSendRequest* method:

```vb
' VB
Public Sub AfterReceiveReply(ByRef reply As Message, _
   correlationState As object) _
   Implements IClientMessageInspector.AfterReceiveReply
      reply = TraceMessage(reply.CreateBufferedCopy(Integer.MaxValue))
End Sub
```

```csharp
// C#
public void AfterReceiveReply(ref Message reply,
   object correlationState)
{
   reply = TraceMessage(reply.CreateBufferedCopy(int.MaxValue));
}
```

Now that the message inspector has been created, it needs to be associated with an endpoint behavior. To do this, you must create a class that implements the *IEndpointBehavior* interface.

9. In Solution Explorer, right-click the TestClient project, choose Add, and then select Class from the context menu.

10. In the Add New Item dialog box, change the name of the class file to **TraceMessage-Behavior** and click Add.

11. Add the following statements to the top of the file:

```vb
' VB
Imports System.ServiceModel.Channels
Imports System.ServiceModel.Dispatcher
Imports System.ServiceModel.Description
Imports System.ServiceModel
```

```csharp
// C#
using System.ServiceModel.Channels;
using System.ServiceModel.Dispatcher;
using System.ServiceModel.Description;
using System.ServiceModel;
```

12. Change the declaration of the *TraceMessageBehavior* class so that it indicates that the *IEndpointBehavior* interface will be implemented. Modify the declaration to look like the following:

```vb
' VB
Public Class TraceMessageBehavior
   Implements IEndpointBehavior
```

```csharp
// C#
public class TraceMessageBehavior : IEndpointBehavior
```

The *IEndpointBehavior* interface requires the implementation of four methods. Three (*AddBindingParameters*, *Validate*, and *ApplyDispatchBehavior*) are not part of this exercise, so they can be left stubbed.

13. Add the following methods to the *TraceMessageBehavior* class:

```vb
' VB
Public Sub AddBindingParameters(endpoint As ServiceEndpoint, _
    bindingParameters As BindingParameterCollection) _
    Implements IEndpointBehavior.AddBindingParameters
End Sub

Public Sub Validate(endpoint As ServiceEndpoint) _
    Implements IEndpointBehavior.Validate
End Sub

Public Sub ApplyDispatchBehavior(endpoint As ServiceEndpoint, _
        endpointDispatcher As EndpointDispatcher) _
    Implements IEndpointBehavior.ApplyDispatchBehavior
End Sub
```

```csharp
// C#
public void AddBindingParameters(ServiceEndpoint endpoint,
    BindingParameterCollection bindingParameters)
{ }

public void Validate(ServiceEndpoint endpoint)
{ }

public void ApplyDispatchBehavior(ServiceEndpoint endpoint,
    EndpointDispatcher endpointDispatcher)
{  }
```

Now that the unused methods have been dealt with, look at the one that actually has some code in it. To add a message inspector to the client, you use the *ClientRuntime* object. This object maintains a collection of the inspectors to be used on the client side.

14. Add the following method to the *TraceMessageBehavior* class:

```vb
' VB
Public Sub ApplyClientBehavior(endpoint As ServiceEndpoint, _
    clientRuntime As ClientRuntime) _
    Implements IEndpointBehavior.ApplyClientBehavior
    Dim inspector As New MessageTracer()
    clientRuntime.MessageInspectors.Add(inspector)
End Sub
```

```csharp
// C#
public void ApplyClientBehavior(ServiceEndpoint endpoint,
    ClientRuntime clientRuntime)
{
    MessageTracer inspector = new MessageTracer();
    clientRuntime.MessageInspectors.Add(inspector);
}
```

The third element in adding the inspector is to create an extension to house the behavior. This requires you to create another class.

15. In Solution Explorer, right-click the TestClient project, choose Add, and then select Class from the context menu.

16. In the Add New Item dialog box, change the name to **TraceMessageBehaviorExtension** and click the Add button.

17. Add the following statements to the top of the file:

```
' VB
Imports System.ServiceModel.Configuration
```

```
// C#
using System. ServiceModel.Configuration;
```

You must derive the just-added class from the *BehaviorExtension* class.

18. Change the class declaration to read as follows:

```
' VB
Public Class TraceMessageBehaviorExtension
    Inherits BehaviorExtensionElement
```

```
// C#
public class TraceMessageBehaviorExtension : BehaviorExtensionElement
```

For a class to inherit the *BehaviorExtension* class, it must override two elements. The first is the *BehaviorType* property. This property returns the type associated with this extension. For this exercise, that is the *TraceMessageBehavior* type.

19. Add the following code to the *TraceMessageBehaviorExtension* class:

```
' VB
Public Overrides ReadOnly Property BehaviorType() As Type
    Get
        Return GetType(TraceMessageBehavior)
    End Get
End Property
```

```
// C#
public override Type BehaviorType
{
    get { return typeof(TraceMessageBehavior); }
}
```

The second required element is the *CreateBehavior* method. This method returns an instance of the behavior.

20. Add the following method to the *TraceMessageBehaviorExtension* class:

```
' VB
Protected Overrides Function CreateBehavior() As Object
    Return New TraceMessageBehavior()
End Function
```

```
// C#
protected override object CreateBehavior()
```

```
{
    return new TraceMessageBehavior();
}
```

Now that you've created the classes, you must add them to the WCF pipeline. Do this through changes to the application configuration file.

21. In Solution Explorer, double-click the app.config file for the TestClient project.

22. To start, add a definition for the extension. Add the following XML segment to the *system.serviceModel* element.

CAUTION   Type value must be on a single line

One warning about this XML segment: the *type* attribute has been split across two lines to fit on the printed page. When you add this XML to the app.config file, the value of the *type* attribute must be on a single line:

```
<extensions>
    <behaviorExtensions>
        <add name="messageTracer"
            type="TestClient.TraceMessageBehaviorExtension, TestClient,
                Version=1.0.0.0, Culture=neutral, PublicKeyToken=null"/>
    </behaviorExtensions>
</extensions>
```

23. After you define the extension, the behavior is associated with an endpoint behavior. Add the following XML segment to the *system.serviceModel* element:

```
<behaviors>
    <endpointBehaviors>
        <behavior name="MessageTracingBehavior">
            <messageTracer />
        </behavior>
    </endpointBehaviors>
</behaviors>
```

Finally, the endpoint behavior needs to be associated with the binding. Do this by adding a *behaviorConfiguration* attribute to the *endpoint* element. The value of the attribute will match the name attribute in the *behavior* element. The *endpoint* element will look like this:

```
<endpoint address=
    "http://localhost:8731/Design_Time_Addresses/DemoService/UpdateService/"
    binding="wsHttpBinding" bindingConfiguration="IContact"
    contract="DemoService.IContact" name="IContact"
    behaviorConfiguration="MessageTracingBehavior">
```

24. Although the application is ready to be executed, the Output window must be visible to see the messages. If it is not already visible, from the Debug menu in Visual Studio 2008 choose Window and then Output.

25. Ensure that the TestClient is set as the startup project, and then launch the application by pressing F5.

After a few seconds, the Console window will show the results of the call, and the messages that complete the application will be visible in the Output window.

▶ **Exercise 2   Validate Parameters by Using Inspectors**

Inspectors are not just for messages. It's possible to inject inspectors into the WCF pipeline so that they are invoked when parameters are being built for passing to the operation. In this way, it becomes possible to examine the password values and abort the processing before the operation is called. In this exercise, you evaluate an incoming parameter, using a regular expression that defines what a valid phone number should look like.

1. Navigate to the *<InstallHome>*/Chapter6/Lesson3/Exercise2/*<language>*/Before directory and double-click the Exercise1.sln file to open the solution in Visual Studio.

The solution consists of two projects. They are as follows:

❑ The DemoService project, a simple WCF service library that implements the *IContact* interface. This interface consists of a single method (*UpdatePhone*) that would (theoretically) update a data store with a new phone number. For this exercise, it simply emits the new number into the *Trace* subsystem.

❑ The TestClient project, a Console application that enables you to consume the DemoService service. It prompts for user input (ostensibly a phone number) and sends it to the *UpdatePhone* operation on the service.

The starting point is the creation of the inspector class that will perform the validation.

2. In Solution Explorer, right-click the DemoService project. Choose Add, and then select Class from the context menu.

3. In the Add New Item dialog box, change the name of the class to **PhoneNumberParameter-Validator** and click the Add button.

4. In the newly created class, a number of using/Imports statements need to be added. Insert the following code at the top of the just added class file:

```VB
' VB
Imports System.ServiceModel.Dispatcher
Imports System.ServiceModel
Imports System.Text.RegularExpressions
```

```C#
// C#
using System.ServiceModel.Dispatcher;
using System.ServiceModel;
using System.Text.RegularExpressions;
```

To operate within the WCF pipeline, the newly added class must implement the *IParameter-Inspector* interface.

5. Change the class declaration of the newly created class to be the following:

```vb
' VB
Public Class PhoneNumberParameterValidator
    Implements IParameterInspector
```

```csharp
// C#
public class PhoneNumberParameterValidator : IParameterInspector
```

The implementation of an interface requires the addition of a couple of methods, specifically *AfterCall* and *BeforeCall*. In this instance, the *AfterCall* method is not used, but you must still define it.

6. Add the following method to the *PhoneNumberParameterValidator* class:

```vb
' VB
Public Sub AfterCall(operationName As String, outputs As Object(), _
    returnValue As Object, correlationState As Object) _
    Implements IParameterInspector.AfterCall

End Sub
```

```csharp
// C#
public void AfterCall(string operationName, object[] outputs,
    object returnValue, object correlationState)
{ }
```

The second method in the interface, *BeforeCall*, actually has some code in it. This method, which is invoked prior to the operation being called, will validate the incoming parameter against a regular expression.

7. Add the following method to the *PhoneNumberParameterValidator* class:

```vb
' VB
Public Function BeforeCall(operationName As String, _
    inputs As Object()) As Object _
    Implements IParameterInspector.BeforeCall

    Dim phoneNumberParam As String = _
        TryCast(inputs(phoneNumberParamIndex), String)

    If Not Regex.IsMatch(phoneNumberParam, phoneNumberFormat, _
        RegexOptions.None) Then
            Throw new FaultException("Invalid phone number. " & _
                "Required format: ###-###-####")
    End If

    Return Nothing
End Sub
```

```csharp
// C#
public object BeforeCall(string operationName, object[] inputs)
{
    string phoneNumberParam = inputs[phoneNumberParamIndex] as string;
```

```
    if (!Regex.IsMatch(phoneNumberParam, phoneNumberFormat,
        RegexOptions.None))
        throw new FaultException("Invalid phone number. " +
            "Required format: ###-###-####");

    return null;
}
```

If you look closely at that last method, there are a couple of values that are not yet defined. First, you must define the *phoneNumberParamIndex* value. This is an integer that represents the position of the phone number parameter within the method's parameter list. As such, it needs to be defined not only as a class-level variable but also by providing a value. This value is included in the constructor for the class.

8. Add the following field and constructors to the *PhoneNumberParameterValidator* class:

```
' VB
Dim phoneNumberParamIndex As Integer

Public Sub New()
    Me.New(0)
End Sub

Public Sub New(phoneNumberParamIndex As Integer)
    Me.phoneNumberParamIndex = phoneNumberParamIndex
End Sub
```

```
// C#
int phoneNumberParamIndex;
public PhoneNumberParameterValidator() : this(0) { }

public PhoneNumberParameterValidator(int phoneNumberParamIndex)
{
    this.phoneNumberParamIndex = phoneNumberParamIndex;
}
```

The second variable that must be defined for the *BeforeCall* method is the *phoneNumber-Format* value. This is a string that contains the regular expression to match against the incoming parameter value. In this class, it has been defined as a string variable to separate its definition from the functionality being provided.

9. To define it, add the following code to the *PhoneNumberParameterValidator* class:

```
' VB
Dim phoneNumberFormat As String = _
    "^(?:\([2-9]\d{2}\)\ ?|[2-9]\d{2}(?:\-?|\ ?))[2-9]\d{2}[- ]?\d{4}$"
```

```
// C#
String phoneNumberFormat =
    @"^(?:\([2-9]\d{2}\)\ ?|[2-9]\d{2}(?:\-?|\ ?))[2-9]\d{2}[- ]?\d{4}$";
```

At this point, the inspector is complete, but it does need to be injected into the WCF pipeline. You do this declaratively by adding an attribute to the contract. However, before that can take place, you must create an attribute class for this inspector.

10. In Solution Explorer, right-click the DemoService project, choose Add and then select Class from the context menu.

11. Change the name of the class to PhoneNumberValidationAttribute and click Add.

12. In the newly created class, a number of using/Imports statements need to be added. Insert the following code at the top of the just-added class file:

```
' VB
Imports System.ServiceModel.Description
Imports System.ServiceModel.Dispatcher
```

```
// C#
using System.ServiceModel.Description;
using System.ServiceModel.Dispatcher;
```

The *PhoneNumberValidationAttribute* class needs to have two relations with other classes and interfaces. Because it will be used as an attribute, it needs to derive from the *Attribute* class. Also, because it will affect the WCF pipeline, it needs to implement the *IOperation-Behavior* interface.

13. Change the class declaration to the following:

```
' VB
Public Class PhoneNumberValidationAttribute
    Inherits Attribute
    Implements IOperationBehavior
```

```
// C#
public class PhoneNumberValidationAttribute : Attribute,
    IOperationBehavior
```

Having the class inherit from *Attribute* requires no additional work on your part. However, implementing *IOperationBehavior* does mean that you must create some methods. Three methods, *AddBindingParameters*, *Validate*, and *ApplyClientBehavior*, don't need any functionality for this exercise.

14. Add the following code to the PhoneNumberValidationAttribute class:

```
' VB
Public Sub AddBindingParameters(operationDescription As _
    OperationDescription, bindingParameters As _
    BindingParameterCollection) _
    Implements IOperationBehavior.AddBindingParameters
End Sub

Public Sub Validate(operationDescription As OperationDescription) _
    Implements IOperationBehavior.Validate
End Sub
```

```vb
Public Sub ApplyClientBehavior(operationDescription As _
    OperationDescription, clientOperation As ClientOperation) _
    Implements IOperationBehavior.ApplyClientBehavior
End Sub
```

```csharp
// C#
public void AddBindingParameters(OperationDescription operationDescription,
    System.ServiceModel.Channels.BindingParameterCollection
    bindingParameters)
{ }

public void Validate(OperationDescription operationDescription)
{ }

public void ApplyClientBehavior(OperationDescription operationDescription,
    ClientOperation clientOperation)
{ }
```

The last method required by *IOperationBehavior*, *ApplyDispatchBehavior*, is integral to the correct functioning of the parameter inspection. It creates an instance of the parameter inspector and adds it to the list of inspectors maintained by the dispatch operation.

15. Add the following code to the *PhoneNumberValidationAttribute* class:

```vb
' VB
Public Sub ApplyDispatchBehavior(operationDescription As _
    OperationDescription, dispatchOperation As DispatchOperation) _
    Implements IOperationBehavior.ApplyDispatchBehavior
    Dim inspector As New PhoneNumberParameterValidator()
    dispatchOperation.ParameterInspectors.Add(inspector)
End Sub
```

```csharp
// C#
public void ApplyDispatchBehavior(
    OperationDescription operationDescription,
    DispatchOperation dispatchOperation)
{
    PhoneNumberParameterValidator inspector = new
        PhoneNumberParameterValidator();
    dispatchOperation.ParameterInspectors.Add(inspector);
}
```

Now that you've created the attribute, the final step is to decorate the appropriate method in the contract.

16. In Solution Explorer, double-click the IContact file.

17. Locate the *UpdatePhone* method and add the *PhoneNumberValidation* attribute. When you are finished, the *UpdatePhone* method should look like the following:

```vb
' VB
<PhoneNumberValidation> _
<OperationContract> _
Sub UpdatePhone(ByVal newPhone As String)
```

```csharp
// C#
[PhoneNumberValidation]
[OperationContract]
void UpdatePhone(string newPhone);
```

18. Ensure that TestClient is set as the startup project and launch the application by pressing F5.

    You will be presented with a prompt asking for a phone number.

19. Enter 11 digits (an invalid phone number, according to the regular expression) and press Enter.

    An exception is raised on the service side. If you continue executing (by pressing F5 again), a message appears in the Console window, indicating that the phone number is invalid.

20. At the same prompt, enter a 10-digit number in the required format (a valid phone number as long as the first digit is not 0 or 1).

    The invalid format message doesn't appear, and you are prompted for the next phone number. Figure 6-9 illustrates the results from these last three steps.

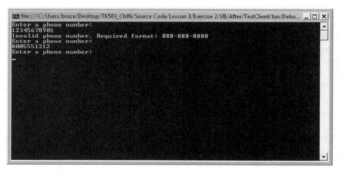

Figure 6-9   Results from Exercise 2

21. To finish running the application, press Enter without typing in a phone number.

Lesson Summary

- The WCF message pipeline has numerous extensibility points.
- Parameters and messages can be inspected on both the client and service sides.
- On the service side, the operations that are executed can be affected through code injected into the pipeline.

Lesson Review

You can use the following questions to test your knowledge of the information in Lesson 3, "WCF Extensibility." The questions are also available on the companion CD if you prefer to review them in electronic form.

NOTE   Answers

Answers to these questions and explanations of why each answer choice is correct or incorrect are located in the "Answers" section at the end of the book.

---

1. On the service side for a WCF application, which of the following extension points must have some extension functionality implemented also on the client side?

    A. Message Inspection

    B. Message Formatting — *enables direct control over deserialization*

    C. Parameter Inspection

    D. Operation Invoker

    not required

2. In a *Message* object, the *MessageState* property is set to *Written*. Which of the following must have already occurred?

    A. The *GetReaderAtBodyContents* method has been called. — *sets to Read*

    B. The *WriteBodyContents* method has been called. — *written*   *sets to Read*

    C. The *CreateBufferedCopy* method has been called. — *sets to Read*

    D. The *CreateMessage* method has been called. — *sets to created*

Lesson 4: Monitoring WCF

Part of the instrumentation of any application (not just a WCF one) is health monitoring. Are all the necessary services running? Is the data store reachable? Is performance at an acceptable level? These (and others) are questions an operations group considers critical to be able to answer. Ideally, there are ways to be notified when any of these states change. In this lesson, the focus is on the various ways information about the status of a WCF application can be communicated to an operations team.

After this lesson, you will be able to:
- Enable the performance counters supported by WCF.
- Log event information into the Windows Event Log and Windows Management Instrumentation

Estimated lesson time: 20 minutes

Performance Counters

One of the most obvious choices for exposing status information is through performance counters. It should not be surprising that WCF includes a large number of built-in performance counters. Although using the Performance Monitor application to view the counters or using the *PerformanceCounter* object to modify counter values is beyond the scope of this book, a number of WCF-specific performance counters must be given consideration.

MORE INFO Modifying performance counters

If you are interested in finding out how to modify existing performance counters, read the article entitled "Walkthrough: Changing and Retrieving Performance Counter Values," which can be found at *http://msdn.microsoft.com/en-us/library/s155t6ta(VS.71).aspx*.

Enabling the Counters

By default, the WCF performance counters are turned off because the counters have the potential to increase the memory footprint of the WCF application significantly. To enable the performance counters, the following section should be added to the configuration file, on either the client or the service side:

```
<system.serviceModel>
    <diagnostics performanceCounters="All" />
</system.serviceModel>
```

The *performanceCounters* attribute is one of a set of values that determine which group or groups of performance counters are displayed. Table 6-4 displays the list of valid values.

Table 6-4 Values for *performanceCounters* Attribute

Value	Description
All	All the categories of counters (*ServiceModelService*, *ServiceModelEndpoint*, and *ServiceModelOperation*) are enabled.
ServiceOnly	Only the *ServiceModelService* counters are enabled.
Off	No counters, regardless of category, are enabled.

It is also possible to enable performance counters imperatively. The following code sample demonstrates how to do this. For the code to be executed, the *System.Configuration*, *System.Service-Model.Configuration*, and *System.ServiceModel.Diagnostics* namespaces need to be referenced by the containing project:

```
' VB
Dim config As Configuration = ConfigurationManager.OpenExeConfiguration( _
    ConfigurationUserLevel.None)
Dim sg As ServiceModelSectionGroup = _
    ServiceModelSectionGroup.GetSectionGroup(config)
sg.Diagnostic.PerformanceCounters = PerformanceCounterScope.All
config.Save()
```

```
// C#
Configuration config = ConfigurationManager.OpenExeConfiguration(
    ConfigurationUserLevel.None);
ServiceModelSectionGroup sg =
    ServiceModelSectionGroup.GetSectionGroup(config);
sg.Diagnostic.PerformanceCounters = PerformanceCounterScope.All;
config.Save();
```

As you can readily deduce from Table 6-4, WCF contains three categories of performance counters: service, endpoint, and operation.

Service Performance Counters The group of counters called *ServiceModelService* is responsible for tracking information about a WCF service as a whole. In Performance Monitor, you see these counters under the ServiceModelService 3.0.0.0 label. Each instance for these counters has a name with a pattern of *ServiceName@ServiceEndpointAddress*.

The types of counters in this group fall into a number of basic categories, as displayed in Table 6-5.

Table 6-5 Performance Counters in the *ServiceModelService*

Counter Type	Description
Call	This type includes the number and duration of the call; the number of failed calls; the number of faulted and outstanding calls; and the rates for calls per second, failed calls per second, and faulted calls per second.

Table 6-5 Performance Counters in the *ServiceModelService*

Counter Type	Description
Instance	This type shows the number of instances created and the rate at which they are created. This is an interesting category in that the creation of an instance is not always what people expect. A new instance can be created when a message is received by an existing service or when a single instance might be transferred from one session to another. Don't assume this counter is the number of times a service becomes active.
Queued Messages	This type shows the number and rate for dropped, rejected, and poisoned messages in a queue. A poisoned message is one that is permanently unable to be successfully processed by the receiving application.
Reliable Messaging	This type shows the number of messages dropped (including a per-second rate) and the number of sessions faulted (with a per-second rate).
Security	This type displays the number of calls that were not authorized and the number of validation and authorization failures. These counters include a per-second rate.
Transacted Operations	This type shows the number of aborted and commit-transacted requests. It also includes the number of transactions that have not yet been resolved and how many transactions were propagated from a client to the service. For each of these, a per-second rate is included.

Endpoint Performance Counters The group of counters called *ServiceModelEndpoint* is responsible for tracking information about the endpoints for a WCF service. In Performance Monitor, you see these counters under the ServiceModelEndPoint 3.0.0.0 label. Each instance for these counters has a name with a pattern of *ServiceName.ContractName@(endpointListenerAddress)*.

NOTE Duplicate endpoints accumulate into a single counter

If two endpoints have identical contract names and addresses, the counter values will be accumulated in a single counter instance.

The types of counters in this group fall into a number of basic categories, shown in Table 6-6.

Table 6-6 Performance Counters in the *ServiceModelEndpoint*

Counter Type	Description
Call	This type includes the number and duration of the call; the number of failed calls; the number of faulted outstanding calls; and the rates for calls per second, failed calls per second, and faulted calls per second.
Reliable Messaging	This type shows the number of messages dropped (including a per-second rate) and the number of sessions faulted (with a per-second rate).

Table 6-6 Performance Counters in the *ServiceModelEndpoint*

Counter Type	Description
Security	This type shows the number of calls that were not authorized and the number of validation and authorization failures. These counters include a per-second rate.
Transacted Operations	This type shows the number of aborted and commit-transacted requests. It also includes the number of transactions that have not yet been resolved and how many transactions were propagated. For each of these, a per-second rate is included.

Operation Performance Counters The group of counters called *ServiceModelOperation* is responsible for tracking information about the operations within a WCF service. In Performance Monitor, you will see these counters under the ServiceModelOperation 3.0.0.0 label. There can be many instances of these counters. Consider that if a particular contract exposed by an endpoint exposes t10 operations, 10 instances of these counters will be available through Performance Monitor. Each instance has a name with a pattern of *ServiceName.ContractName.OperationName@(first endpoint listener address)*.

NOTE Duplicate operations into a single counter

If there are duplicate operations on a contract, the counter values will be aggregated into a single counter instance.

The types of counters in this group fall into a number of basic categories, as the list in Table 6-7 shows.

Table 6-7 Performance counters in the *ServiceModelOperation*

Counter Type	Description
Call	This type includes the number and duration of the call; the number of failed calls; the number of faulted outstanding calls; and the rates for calls per second, failed calls per second, and faulted calls per second.
Security	This type displays the number of calls that were not authorized and the number of validation and authorization failures. These counters include a per-second rate.
Transacted Operations	This type shows the number of aborted and commit-transacted requests. It also includes the number of transactions that have not yet been resolved and how many transactions were propagated. For each of these, a per-second rate is included.

It has already been mentioned that, due to the potential generation of a large number of performance counters, setting the performanceCounters attribute to All (or doing the equivalent through code) can affect memory. The specifics of this situation relate to the fact that WCF uses separate shared memory for these categories.

By default, the separate shared memory allocated to these counters is set to a quarter of the entire memory allocated to performance counters globally. The global default value is 524,288 bytes. This means that each of the three WCF categories would have a default size of roughly 128KB. Depending on the run-time details of the WCF application, it is quite possible that the memory allocated for performance counters can become full. From the application's perspective, this causes an InvalidOperationException with a message indicating that the custom counters file view is out of memory.

You can change the amount of memory allocated to support the WCF performance counters. It does require a change to the registry. There is a DWORD value named FileMappingSize. The value of this entry is the number of bytes allocated to the performance counters for the various WCF categories. A separate registry entry is required for each category. The locations of the registry entries are as follows:

- HKLM\System\CurrentControlSet\Services\ServiceModelEndpoint3.0.0.0
  \Performance
- HKLM\System\CurrentControlSet\Services\ServiceModelOperation3.0.0.0
  \Performance
- HKLM\System\CurrentControlSet\Services\ServiceModelService3.0.0.0
  \Performance

Event Logging

WCF deposits logging information for internal events in a number of places. One of the locations is the Windows Event Log. However, you can configure a WCF application also to publish events into Windows Management Instrumentation (WMI). In WMI, the events can be detected and acted upon by the tools frequently used by the operations staff. This kind of monitoring fits best in companies that care deeply about monitoring their WCF services.

Logging of events is enabled by default. WCF does not expose a mechanism for disabling logging, so your WCF applications can always create event log entries.

For the most part, the events generated by WCF will appear in the Application Event Log. The types of events that appear include the following:

- Failures on message logging and tracing.
- Failure of the WCF TCP Port Sharing Service to start.
- Failure when the CardSpace service does not start.
- Critical events within WCF, including startup failure or unexpected service crashes.

- Each time message logging is turned on. The reason for this event is that sensitive information might be logged as part of the message-logging process. Administrators (generally) like to know when the possibility for a security hole has occurred.

- When the *enableLoggingKnownPII* attribute in the machine.confg file is set to *true*. This element determines whether Personally Identifiable Information (PII) should be logged by any application running on the computer. Because it represents a potential security hole, administrators like to be informed.

- When the *logKnownPii* attribute in the applications configuration file (app.config or web.config) is set to *true*, but the *enableLoggingKnownPII* is set to *false*, that is, when an attempt is made to override the ability to log known PII.

NOTE Protection from logging failures

When a failure occurs while logging or tracing a message, WCF implements a 10-minute blackout period. This means that after the first failure occurs and WCF logs that to the event log, it will not write a second entry (for the same type of failure) for 10 minutes. This prevents the event log from becoming completely filled with trace or logging failures.

WCF will also place entries related to the auditing of security events into the Security Event Log. WCF does not log anything into the System Event Log.

Logging in WMI

WCF provides inspection data regarding its services at run time through a WCF WMI provider. Unlike the event log, WMI is not enabled by default. To enable the built-in provider, you can set an attribute on the diagnostic element. The following segment from a configuration file contains an example:

```
<system.serviceModel>
    <diagnostics wmiProviderEnabled="true" />
</system.serviceModel>
```

After you have enabled the WMI provider, management applications can connect to this interface and access the instrumentation for the WCF service.

The WCF WMI provider enables management applications to discover the services running in an environment. For this reason, be careful about granting access to it. The default rights are that you need to be an administrator to access the provider. If this criterion is relaxed, sensitive data could be exposed, and flooding attacks could occur, especially if remote WMI access is enabled.

By default, the WCF WMI provider grants Execute Method, Provider Write, and Enable Account permissions for administrators and Enable Account permission for ASP.NET, Local Service, and Network Service. If the system is not running Windows Vista, the ASP.NET account has read access to the WMI ServiceModel namespace.

NOTE WMI and privileges

If WMI is enabled through the configuration file, but the security context in which the service is running does not have sufficient privileges, WMI will not be enabled. However, this failure is not logged.

If these permissions need to be modified, either to include additional users or groups or to restrict permission, perform the following steps.

1. Click Start, type **compmgmt.msc**, and then press Enter.

2. Expand the *Services And Applications* node, and then select the WMI Controls node. Figure 6-10 illustrates the Computer Management application at this point.

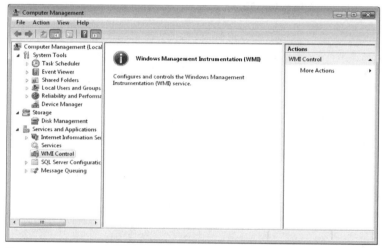

Figure 6-10 Computer Management application

3. Now right-click the WMI Controls node and select Properties from the context menu.

4. Click the Security tab.

5. Expand the Root folder, select the ServiceModel namespace as shown in Figure 6-11, and click the Security button.

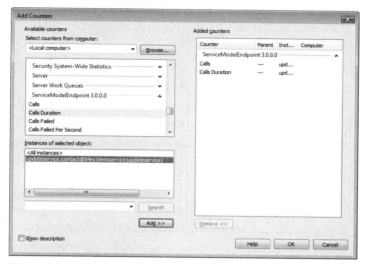

Figure 6-11   Security tab for the ServiceModel namespace

6. Select the desired group or user. Configure permissions by using the Allow or Deny check boxes.

Lab: Monitoring a WCF Application

In this lab, you will explore the performance counters and event logging capabilities of WCF.

▶ **Exercise   Enable and View Performance Counters**

In this exercise, you will configure one of the applications created earlier in the chapter (specifically, from Lesson 2) to update performance counters.

1. Navigate to the *<InstallHome>*/Chapter6/Lesson4/Exercise1/*<language>*/Before directory and double-click the Exercise1.sln file to open the solution in Visual Studio.

   The solution consists of two projects. They are as follows:

   ❑ The DemoService project, a simple WCF service library that implements the *ICon-tact* interface. This interface consists of a single method (*UpdatePhone*) that would (theoretically) update a data store with a new phone number. For this exercise, it simply emits the new number into the *Trace* subsystem.

   ❑ The TestClient project, a Console application that enables you to consume the DemoService service. It prompts for user input.

   Before the performance counters can be viewed, they must be enabled through the configuration file.

2. In Solution Explorer, double-click the app.config file in the DemoService project.

   The *diagnostics* element is where you enable the counters. This element includes a *performanceCounters* attribute that can be set to limit the performance counter values that are updated.

3. For this exercise, enable all of them by adding the following XML to the *system.service-Model* element in the configuration file:

   ```
   <diagnostics performanceCounters="All" />
   ```

   Prior to running the application, none of the performance counters associated with this instance will be visible. However, after the application is running, you can view them through the Performance Monitor application.

4. To launch the performance monitor application, click the Start button, enter **Perfmon** in the Start Search text box, and then click the Perfmon.exe item that appears in the search list. In the left pane, expand Monitoring Tools and click Performance Monitor.

   In Performance Monitor, you might want to delete the existing counters just to clear up the display. Regardless, you can add a couple of counters associated with the service.

5. Click the Add button or press Ctrl + I to add a counter.

6. In the Add Counters dialog box, (shown in Figure 6-12), find and select ServiceMode-lEndpoint 3.0.0.0 from the list of available counters on the local computer.

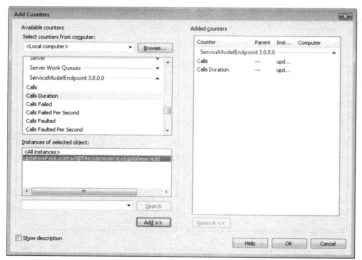

Figure 6-12   The Add Counters dialog box

7. If the WCF service is running, one or more instances will appear in the instance list on the right of the form. Only one instance should be visible. The name starts with update-service. Click it.

8. In the available counter list, click the down-arrow to the right of the ServiceModelEndpoint 3.0.0.0 counter. This displays a list of the counters that belong to this group.

9. Click the Calls counter, and then click the Add button. Click the Calls Duration counter and again click the Add button. This adds the two counters to the monitor display.

10. Click Close.

11. In Visual Studio, make sure TestClient is set as the startup project, and then launch the application by pressing F5.

12. In the Console window for the application, type a 10-digit number that doesn't start with 0 or 1, and then press Enter.

     In Performance Monitor, the number of calls should increase by one, and the Calls Duration value should increase slightly. This latter might not happen, however, because the lowest granularity for the counter is one thousandth of a second.

13. Stop running the application.

14. In Solution Explorer, double-click the UpdateService file.

     To see the impact on the Calls Duration counter, a slight delay will be added to the service's operation.

15. In the *UpdatePhone* method, add the following line of code:

     ```
     ' VB
     System.Threading.Thread.Sleep(2000)
     ```

     ```
     // C#
     System.Threading.Thread.Sleep(2000);
     ```

16. Launch the application by pressing F5.

17. In the console window for the application, enter a 10-digit number that doesn't start with 0 or 1.

18. In Performance Monitor, select the Calls Duration counter.

     Notice that the last value is slightly greater than two seconds, which is the delay just introduced into the operation.

Lesson Summary

■ WCF uses a number of performance counters, which must be explicitly enabled within the application before any WCF data is logged.

■ Although the logs WCF publishes to the Windows Event Log cannot be turned off, WCF can be configured not to publish PII.

Lesson Review

You can use the following questions to test your knowledge of the information in Lesson 4, "Monitoring WCF." The questions are also available on the companion CD if you prefer to review them in electronic form.

NOTE Answers

Answers to these questions and explanations of why each answer choice is correct or incorrect are located in the "Answers" section at the end of the book.

---

1. Which of the following statements is true when discussing the use of Performance Counters in a WCF application?

   A. The default setting for WCF performance counters is to not update any performance counters.

   B. The performance counters can be captured even when the WCF service is not running.

   C. If the service exposes the same endpoint address and contract across multiple bindings, the performance counter information is maintained separately.

   D. The performance counters associated with the client side of a WCF application can be captured only while the client application is running.

2. You have created a WCF service. You would like to integrate health monitoring of this service with WMI. You think you have configured the service appropriately, but messages from your service do not appear to be posted into WMI. Which of the following could NOT be a potential cause of the problem?

   A. You are running the WCF service in the Local Service security context.

   B. You have not added a registry entry named wmiProviderEnabled to the HKLM\System\CurrentControlSet\Services\ServiceModelService 3.0.0.0\Performance registry key.

   C. The wmiProviderEnabled attribute in the diagnostics element in system.serviceModel is set to true.

   D. The application processing the WMI events is running on a remote computer.

Chapter Review

To further practice and reinforce the skills you learned in this chapter, you can:

- Review the chapter summary.
- Review the list of key terms introduced in this chapter.
- Complete the case scenario. This scenario sets up a real-world situation involving the topics of this chapter and asks you to create a solution.
- Complete the suggested practices.
- Take a practice test.

Chapter Summary

- WCF provides a great deal of built-in tracing information as well as the ability to correlate trace information across service boundaries.
- Through its extensibility points, WCF applications can be instrumented to validate and display parameters and entire messages.
- Custom dispatching logic can be injected into the pipeline to control the methods that a service invokes while processing a request.
- WCF supports a number of performance counters that can be used to monitor the health and efficiency of the application.

Key Terms

Do you know what these key terms mean? You can check your answers by looking up the terms in the glossary at the end of the book.

- activity identifier
- activity transfer
- channel stack
- Common Log File System
- globally unique activity identifier (gAId)
- local activity identifier (lAId)
- Message Inspection
- ReliableMessaging
- thread local storage

Case Scenario

In the following case scenario, you will apply what you've learned in this chapter. You can find answers to these questions in the "Answers" section at the end of this book.

Case Scenario: Using Activity Tracing

Your company has developed an application that will be distributed to your clients. It enables your clients to build an order, submit it to your customer service application programming interface (API), and view the status up to the point at which the order is shipped. The technology used to implement the communication between the client portion and the service is WCF. Answer the following questions for your manager.

1. Does it make sense to configure the application to use activity tracing?
2. At which points in the application should a new activity be created?

Suggested Practices

To help you successfully master the exam objectives presented in this chapter, complete the following tasks.

End-to-End Tracing

Practice multi-service tracing and extending WCF.

- **Practice 1**   WCF can maintain an activity between multiple clients and services. Create a client application that sends requests to two separate services within the same activity.

  Create an application that chains activities in a series of two (or more) requests. That is, have the client application invoke a method on Service A that in turn invokes a method on Service B.

- **Practice 2**   Create a message inspector that adds a header containing timing information to the SOAP message. When the request is sent from the client, the starting time is recorded in the header. When the request is received back from the service, the starting time is retrieved and used to calculate the elapsed time for the request.

Watch a Webcast

Watch a webcast about configuring WCF.

- **Practice**   Watch the MSDN "Bindings" webcast by Michele Leroux Bustamante, available on the companion CD in the Webcasts folder or by visiting *http://msevents.microsoft.com /CUI/WebCastEventDetails.aspx?culture=en-US&EventID=1032344331&CountryCode=US*.

Take a Practice Test

The practice tests on this book's companion CD offer many options. For example, you can test yourself on just one exam objective, or you can test yourself on all the 70-503 certification exam content. You can set up the test so that it closely simulates the experience of taking a certification exam, or you can set it up in study mode so that you can look at the correct answers and explanations after you answer each question.

MORE INFO   **Practice tests**

For details about all the practice test options available, see the "How to Use the Practice Tests" section in this book's introduction.

Chapter 7
Infrastructure Security

After years of stories of viruses, stolen personal information, and denial-of-service attacks, it's clear that security is important for every application. Although security matters to any application, distributed applications are even more exposed. Distributed applications contain at least two pieces, client and service, and messages between the two must be sent and received. The surface area for security issues is much larger than in a typical monolithic application, and because a Windows Communication Foundation (WCF) application is a platform for building distributed applications, it shouldn't be a surprise that security is embedded in the plumbing.

This chapter and the next discuss WCF security. In this chapter, the focus is on security related to the infrastructure—how security at the transport and message layer can prevent unauthorized viewing and tampering with the message while en route. The next chapter deals with user-level security: authentication and authorization.

Exam objectives in this chapter:
- Implement transport-level security.
- Implement message-level security.

Lessons in this chapter:

Before You Begin

To complete the lessons in this chapter, you must have:

- A computer that meets or exceeds the minimum hardware requirements listed in the introduction at the beginning of the book.
- Any edition of Microsoft Visual Studio 2008 (including Microsoft Visual C# 2008 Express Edition or Microsoft Visual Basic 2008 Express Edition) installed on the computer.

Real World

Bruce Johnson

I firmly believe that security should be deeply integrated into the development of an application. It's not a milestone that can be scheduled at some point (typically toward the end of a project). Instead, it should be included right from the design of the application, considered during the implementation, and tested frequently along the way.

In WCF, the security infrastructure is embedded in the various bindings. If you are using one of the built-in bindings, you need to be aware of the configuration settings that affect security, but you don't need to test it to ensure that the message is encrypted or the transport is running over Secure Sockets Layer (SSL) because details at the transport layer are handled by WCF. However, when you create a custom binding, you become responsible for security at the transport layer, so be aware of the ramifications. And be ready to test for it.

Lesson 1: Transport-Level Security

This first lesson talks about the security options at the transport layer. For most bindings, the capabilities are built into the binding. Some bindings will be able to use SSL. Others will use IPsec. Still others might not provide any capabilities for transport-level security.

In general, when discussing security at the transport layer, the main concern is with the integrity, privacy, and (to a certain extent) authentication of the message as it travels along the wire. Exactly how WCF provides this functionality depends on the binding. This lesson discusses the basic transport security capabilities WCF provides and the bindings that support them.

> **After this lesson, you will be able to:**
> - Identify the different types of transport security provided by WCF.
> - Determine which bindings are capable of supporting transport security.
> - Modify configuration details on the implemented transport security.
>
> **Estimated lesson time: 50 minutes**

Transport Security Basics

The first thing to be aware of is that WCF security is not unlike other security platforms. If you are aware of the existing security technologies, much of this topic will be familiar. Some of the coverage in this chapter discusses the details of the security mechanisms, but previous familiarity with Hypertext Transfer Protocol over SSL (HTTPS) or IPsec helps. WCF uses the security infrastructure provided by .NET, so any existing knowledge is still quite applicable.

In WCF, the secure transports available for use are HTTP, Transmission Control Protocol (TCP), Internet Protocol (IP), and Microsoft Message Queuing (MSMQ). For a transport to be secure, all the communications that take place across the channel must be encrypted. Contrast this with message-level security, which would encrypt only the message component of the communications. The goals of transport-level security are to provide integrity, privacy, and authentication. Integrity is provided by ensuring that the encryption key is shared between only the two parties involved in the communications. Privacy is guaranteed through the encryption process—the contents are not readable by anyone other than the parties involved. Mutual authentication of sender and receiver is provided because the credentials of the sender are encrypted as part of the message. The recipient can be certain of the party who sent the message with the credentials, and the sender can be sure that only the intended recipient can read it.

For transport security to be effective, the sender and receiver must negotiate the details at the outset. Fortunately, from a development perspective, this step is handled automatically by the secure protocol. In fact, much about the transport security layer is automatically handled. This means that, in terms of simplicity, transport-layer security is the easiest to implement, and because it covers the entirety of the communications, nothing in the message is left exposed. Finally, the protocols used are well understood and accepted by the community. They are not individually developed but rather are standards based on years of effort and scrutiny, so you can be confident of their ability to secure the communications.

A number of benefits accrue by using transport security. The following list enumerates some of the common threats that can be mitigated by security at the transport layer.

- Sniffing network traffic to obtain sensitive information
- Phishing attacks in which rogue services impersonate a service to intercept messages
- Message alteration while in transit
- Replay attacks in which the same message is sent multiple times to the same service

In general, the transport-layer security found in WCF, regardless of the type of binding, provides the following guarantees.

- Authentication of the sender
- Authentication of the service
- Message integrity
- Message confidentiality
- Replay detection

The security offered at the transport layer in WCF takes advantage of any existing security solutions. This would include SSL or *Kerberos*, for example. Also, some security solutions use information within the Microsoft Windows infrastructure such as Active Directory Domain Services (AD DS), for example. The security offered by WCF at the transport (and the message) layer is capable of integrating with these technologies.

Although the protocols that are built into some of the bindings are more than capable of providing security guarantees, not every binding can use them. To enable those bindings to benefit from these guarantees, WCF implements a Message Security mode. In this mode, WCF uses specifications such as WS-Security to implement the capabilities of transfer security without relying on the transport-layer protocols.

Message security does have some benefits, including transport protocol independence. The details of message security are covered in Lesson 2, "Message-Level Security," later in this chapter. There is also a third mode that combines the two techniques called Transport with Message Credential. It too is covered in Lesson 2.

Bindings and Security

As has already been mentioned, transport-layer security is directly related to the bindings. The types of transport security that are available depend on the binding used. With one exception (*basicHttpBinding*), all the bindings available out of the box for WCF include a default security mode. However, the real question is which security modes are available for each binding and how one determines that. In this section, each of the bindings that support transport security is covered along with the supported modes.

basicHttpBinding

The purpose of *basicHttpBinding* is to support a range of existing technologies. These include the following.

- ASP.NET Web Services (ASMX) version 1
- Web Service Enhancement (WSE) applications
- Sites that support *Basic Profile*. Basic Profile is an implementation of the Web Service Interoperability (WS-I) standard
- Sites that support the basic security profile that is also defined in WS-I

The *basicHttpBinding* binding is the only built-in binding that is not secure when configured using its default values. The rationale for this choice has to do with its intended target, which is interoperability with ASMX services. However, it is possible to enable security on this binding. Then the binding will interoperate seamlessly with the Microsoft Internet Information Server (IIS) security mechanism. It is also capable of supporting HTTPS transport security.

You can configure *basicHttpBinding* for transport security either in code or through a configuration file. In the configuration file, add a *security* element to the *basicHttpBinding* element. The following sample configures the binding to use Transport security:

```
<basicHttpBinding>
    <binding name="TransportBinding">
        <security mode="Transport">
            <transport clientCredentialType="Basic"
                proxyCredentialType="Basic"
                realm="contoso" />
        </security>
    </binding>
</basicHttpBinding>
```

Notice the mode attribute on the *security* element has been set to *Transport*. This indicates that transport-layer security is to be used. Because the binding uses HTTP as the underlying protocol, the request will occur over an SSL-secured connection.

You will also notice that a *transport* element is part of the segment. This element defines the credentials used to provide the authentication required for the transport-layer guarantee. Three attributes can be defined on the *transport* element. Table 7-1 lists the attributes and their purposes.

Table 7-1 Attributes for the *transport* Element

Attribute	Description
clientCredentialType	This attribute defines the type of credentials that will be included in the transport-layer authentication. The possible values for this attribute are *Basic*, *Certificate*, *Digest*, *None*, *Ntlm*, and *Windows*.
proxyCredentialType	This attribute defines the type of credentials that will be used to authorize the request with any proxy server to be used. The possible values for this attribute are: *Basic*, *Digest*, *None*, *Ntlm*, and *Windows*.
realm	This attribute defines the realm to be used by the authentication if the credentials are *Basic* or *Digest*.

NOTE Credential types

You might have recognized the *clientCredentialType* values as being the credential types from IIS. If you think about it, it makes sense because IIS is part of the underlying protocol support. However, for completeness, a description of the credential type values is as follows:

- **Basic**   Basic authentication is used where the credentials are passed with the message.
- **Certificate**   A certificate is provided by the client to the service to authenticate the requester.
- **Digest**   Credentials are hashed prior to being passed with the message.
- **None**   No credentials are provided. Requests are treated as anonymous.
- **Ntlm**   Authentication are performed using the NT LAN Manager (NTLM) protocol.
- **Windows**   Windows credentials of the current user are provided for authentication.

You can set security declaratively as well as through code. The following code defines a *BasicHttpBinding* object and configures it to use transport security:

```vb
' VB
Dim binding As BasicHttpBinding = New BasicHttpBinding()
binding.Name = "TransportBinding"
binding.Security.Mode = BasicHttpSecurityMode.Transport
```

```csharp
// C#
BasicHttpBinding binding = new BasicHttpBinding();
binding.Name = "TransportBinding";
binding.Security.Mode = BasicHttpSecurityMode.Transport;
```

wsHttpBinding

As indicated by the name of the binding, *wsHttpBinding* also uses the HTTP protocol for the underlying communications. Unlike *basicHttpBinding*, the target service for *wsHttpBinding* is one that supports SOAP v1.2 and *WS-Addressing*. From a transport security perspective, the protocol of choice is HTTPS.

You can configure *wsHttpBinding* for transport security either in code or through a configuration file. In the configuration file, add a *security* element to the *wsHttpBinding* element. The following code sample configures the binding to use Transport security:

```
<wsHttpBinding>
    <binding name="TransportBinding">
        <security mode="Transport">
            <transport clientCredentialType="Basic"
                proxyCredentialType="Basic"
                realm="contoso" />
        </security>
    </binding>
</wsHttpBinding>
```

At this point, you should be noticing a similarity between *WSHttpBinding* and *basicHttpBinding*. The structure of the code sample is the same, even in the attributes of the *transport* element. The *basicHttpBinding* section of Table 7-1 describes these attributes. The following sample illustrates how to configure *WSHttpBinding* through code:

```
' VB
Dim binding As WSHttpBinding = New WSHttpBinding()
binding.Name = "TransportBinding"
binding.Security.Mode = SecurityMode.Transport
```

```
// C#
WSHttpBinding binding = new WSHttpBinding();
binding.Name = "TransportBinding";
binding.Security.Mode = SecurityMode.Transport;
```

wsDualHttpBinding

Although this binding does have HTTP in the name, it's an example of a binding that does not support transport security, which makes sense. This is a duplex binding that enables the service to make calls back into the client. This means, at an HTTP level, there must be the equivalent of a service listening for the inbound requests. This includes calls that are going from the service to the client, but a generic port listener (that is, one that is not a Web service) will not understand the details that are required to make SSL work. Although it is true that some clients might be able to do so, bindings are not supposed to depend on the client or service host implementation. For this reason, transport security cannot be configured using this binding.

netTcpBinding

This binding moves the discussion out of the realm of HTTP protocols and into TCP, again as evidenced by the name. The use of TCP means that it is possible to use transport-level security. Although it is not based on IIS, many of the same credential choices are available to perform authentication as part of the transport security.

It should not be a surprise that the *netTcpBinding* can be configured for transport security through either code or a configuration file. In the configuration file, it is accomplished by adding a *security* element to the *netTcpBinding* element. The following code sample configures the binding to use Transport security:

```
<netTcpBinding>
   <binding name="TransportBinding">
      <security mode="Transport">
         <transport clientCredentialType="Windows"
            protectionLevel="EncryptAndSign" />
      </security>
   </binding>
</netTcpBinding>
```

Two attributes in the transport binding need mention. The *clientCredentialType* attribute specifies the mechanism used to perform client authentication for the transport security. Table 7-2 shows the valid choices for the attribute.

Table 7-2   Values for the *netTcpBinding clientCredentialType* attribute

clientCredentialType	Description
Certificate	A certificate is provided to authenticate the requester.
None	No credentials are provided. Requests are treated as anonymous.
Windows	The Windows credentials of the current user are provided for authentication.

The other attribute in *netTcpBinding* is *protectionLevel*. Because TCP doesn't support encryption in the same manner that HTTP does, WCF has to provide a different implementation. The *protectionLevel* attribute provides access to the mechanism. Table 7-3 displays a list and descriptions of the three possible values for this attribute.

Table 7-3   Values for the *protectionLevel* Attribute

protectionLevel	Description
None	No protection is provided on the message. It is sent unencrypted across the wire.
Sign	The message is digitally signed to ensure that the contents cannot be tampered with during transmission. The message is still sent unencrypted, but unauthorized modifications will be noticed.
EncryptAndSign	The message is encrypted prior to being signed. The encryption ensures that the message will not be visible while being transmitted.

You can also configure the *netTcpBinding* through code, as illustrated in the following code sample:

```vb
' VB
Dim binding As New NetTcpBinding
binding.Name = "TransportBinding"
binding.Security.Mode = SecurityMode.Transport
binding.Security.Transport.ClientCredentialType = _
    TcpClientCredentialType.Windows
```

```csharp
// C#
NetTcpBinding binding = new NetTcpBinding();
binding.Name = "TransportBinding";
binding.Security.Mode = SecurityMode.Transport;
binding.Security.Transport.ClientCredentialType =
    TcpClientCredentialType.Windows;
```

netNamedPipeBinding

As you might have guessed, named pipes transport the messages. Named pipes are optimized for on-machine, cross-process communications. Because it's much more difficult to sniff traffic crossing a named pipe connection than through an HTTP connection, named pipes don't have the same built-in consideration for security that HTTP does, for example.

Yet named pipes as a WCF binding type support transport security. In fact, the provided implementation is basically the same as the security in TCP binding. The main difference between named pipes and TCP is that TCP implements a few additional features. The following configuration element demonstrates the differences:

```xml
<netNamedPipeBinding>
    <binding name="TransportBinding">
        <security mode="Transport">
            <transport protectionLevel="EncryptAndSign" />
        </security>
    </binding>
</netNamedPipeBinding>
```

Notice that there is no specification for the client credentials within the *transport* element. With named pipes, the only type of credential allowed is Windows. That is the only difference, however. Named pipes provide the same choices for protection level. Table 7-3 displays a list of choices for the *protectionLevel*.

You can configure the *netNamedPipeBinding* through code, also, as illustrated in the following code sample:

```vb
' VB
Dim binding As NetNamedPipeBinding = New NetNamedPipeBinding()
binding.Name = "TransportBinding"
binding.Security.Mode = NetNamedPipeSecurityMode.Transport
```

```
// C#
NetNamedPipeBinding binding = new NetNamedPipeBinding();
binding.Name = "TransportBinding";
binding.Security.Mode = NetNamedPipeSecurityMode.Transport;
```

msmqIntegrationBinding

The *msmqIntegrationBinding* binding is optimized for creating WCF clients and services that interoperate with non-WCF MSMQ endpoints. This binding supports transport security with Windows security used for authentication (including AD DS as the certificate authority). These requirements mean that using transport security with this binding is valid only if both client and service are in the same domain.

With message signing, MSMQ provides the ability to attach an arbitrary certificate to the message (not just one that is registered with AD DS). The certificate, in this instance, is not used for authentication but to ensure that the message was signed using the certificate. The following code sample shows an example:

```
<msmqIntegrationBinding>
    <binding name="TransportBinding">
        <security mode="Transport">
            <transport msmqAuthenticationMode="WindowsDomain "
                msmqEncryptionAlgorithm="AES"
                msmqProtectionLevel="EncryptAndSign"
                msmqSecureHashAlgorithm="SHA1" />
        </security>
    </binding>
</msmqIntegrationBinding>
```

You might have noticed that the *transport* element has become much more complicated than the previous bindings or, at least, more options are available to configure. The attributes can be divided into two categories. The *msmqAuthenticationMode* attribute controls how the user who is requesting that a message be sent is to be authenticated. The other three attributes (*msmqEncryptionAlgorithm*, *msmqProtectionLevel*, and *msmqSecureHashAlgorithm*) deal with securing the message itself.

For the *msmqAuthenticationMode* attribute, there are three possible values. If this attribute is set to *None*, no authentication is performed as part of the transport security. By setting the attribute to *WindowsDomain*, you are telling WCF to use AD DS to retrieve the security identifier (SID) for the sender. This SID will be included in the message and will be used to authenticate the sender.

If the attribute is set to *Certificate*, the message will use a certificate taken from the certificate store to enable authentication. This means that AD DS integration is not required (by MSMQ, that is). In some instances, this is the only value that will enable transport security. For example, if MSMQ is installed in workgroup mode, it is not part of AD DS. In that situation, Windows

Domain authentication would fail and *Certificate* authentication is the only way to implement transport security across an MSMQ-based binding.

When a message is sent using *Certificate* authentication, no Windows SID is associated with the message. As a result, the permissions on the target queue must allow anonymous users to post a message to the queue. This might seem a little odd, especially given that a certificate credential has been provided with the message. However, when WCF receives a message, the incoming message is checked to see whether it was signed with a certificate, and there is no guaranteed connection between the certificate that was used to sign the message and the identity of the user who sent the message to the queue. Again, there *might* be a connection, but the relationship can't be guaranteed. As a result, WCF won't use the signing certificate to perform authentication of the requester. With no authentication mechanism available, the request must be made anonymously to be posted.

The *msmqProtectionLevel* attribute has the same values as the *protectionLevel* attribute in some of the earlier bindings. Table 7-3 displays a detailed list of the values and their meanings. The one caveat is that to encrypt a message, WCF must have access to AD DS because the key used to encrypt the message is the public key from the receiving queue, and that information (the key) will be retrieved from AD DS as part of the encryption process. If the message is sent in an environment in which no AD DS is available, there would be no way to encrypt the message so that only the recipient could decrypt it. This also implies that encrypting the message is not possible unless MSMQ has been installed using AD DS integration (that is, not in workgroup mode).

The *msmqEncryptionAlgorithm* attribute determines the algorithm used to encrypt the message. Valid values for the attribute are *RC4Stream* and *AES*. Both algorithms are available natively within .NET. The AES algorithm is valid only if the sender has MSMQ 4.0 installed and the target queue is hosted on MSMQ 4.0.

The *msmqSecureHashAlgorithm* attribute specifies how the digest of any signatures will be hashed. As with the *msmqEncryptionAlgorithm*, there is only a short list of possible choices: MD5, SHA1, SHA256, and SHA512.

You can configure the *MsmqIntegrationBinding* also through code, as illustrated in the following code sample:

```vb
' VB
Dim binding As MsmqIntegrationBinding = New MsmqIntegrationBinding()
binding.Name = "TransportBinding"
binding.Security.Mode = MsmqIntegrationSecurityMode.Transport
binding.Security.Transport.MsmqAuthenticationMode = _
   MsmqAuthenticationMode.WindowsDomain
```

```csharp
// C#
MsmqIntegrationBinding binding = new MsmqIntegrationBinding();
binding.Name = "TransportBinding";
```

```
binding.Security.Mode = MsmqIntegrationSecurityMode.Transport;
binding.Security.Transport.MsmqAuthenticationMode =
    MsmqAuthenticationMode.WindowsDomain;
```

netMsmqBinding

Although this binding uses the same transport protocol (MSMQ) as the *msmqIntegrationBinding*, the target service is different. With this binding, it is expected that a WCF service that requires queued message support will be on one end of the channel.

By default, the binding uses transport security. The configuration of the binding is quite similar to the *msmqIntegrationBinding*. In fact, when using the configuration mode, it is practically identical, as the following sample illustrates:

```
<netMsmqBinding>
   <binding name="TransportBinding">
     <security mode="Transport">
       <transport msmqAuthenticationMode="WindowsDomain "
          msmqEncryptionAlgorithm="AES"
          msmqProtectionLevel="EncryptAndSign"
          msmqSecureHashAlgorithm="SHA1" />
     </security>
   </binding>
</netMsmqBinding>
```

For the *transport* element, the attributes and the options available on those attributes are identical to the *transport* element in the *msmqIntegrationBinding* and have already been covered (in the previous section). From a coding perspective, there is also no difference other than the name of the class involved. Here is an example:

```
' VB
Dim binding As NetMsmqBinding = New NetMsmqBinding()
binding.Name = "TransportBinding"
binding.Security.Mode = NetMsmqSecurityMode.Transport
binding.Security.Transport.MsmqAuthenticationMode = _
   MsmqAuthenticationMode.WindowsDomain
```

```
// C#
NetMsmqBinding binding = new NetMsmqBinding();
binding.Name = "TransportBinding";
binding.Security.Mode = NetMsmqSecurityMode.Transport;
binding.Security.Transport.MsmqAuthenticationMode =
   MsmqAuthenticationMode.WindowsDomain;
```

Lab: Observing Transport Security

In this lab, you will implement transport security in a WCF application. Because the security involved is at the transport level, there is no simple way to view the secured message. Instead, you look at the effects that occur when only part of the channel is configured for security.

▶ **Exercise 1   Transport Security in TCP-Based Bindings**

In this first exercise, you will configure transport security over a TCP-based binding. To do this, you will use a simple WCF application. The service side of the application exposes a method (*GetHeaders*) that returns a string. The client application sends a request to the service and emits the result to the Console window.

1. Navigate to the <InstallHome>/Chapter7/Lesson1/Exercise1/<language>/Before directory and double-click the Exercise1.sln file to open the solution in Visual Studio.

   The solution consists of two projects. They are as follows:

   ❑ The DemoService project, a simple WCF service library that implements the *IGetHeaders* interface. This interface consists of a single method (*GetHeaders*) that strips a custom header out of the request and returns it to the client.

   ❑ The TestClient project, a Console application. The application generates a request for the service and displays the result in the Console window.

2. In Solution Explorer, double-click the app.config file for the TestClient project.

3. Start by configuring the client to use the *netTcpBinding* binding. To do so, locate the *endpoint* element in the app.config file. The *address* attribute has a value that starts with "http". Change it so that a TCP binding can be used by modifying it to the following value.

   ```
   address=
       "net.tcp://localhost:8731/Design_Time_Addresses/DemoService/HeaderService/"
   ```

   Also in the *endpoint* element, you find a *binding* attribute. Currently, the value is *wsHttpBinding*, but it needs to be *netTcpBinding* to support the protocol.

4. Change the attribute to read as follows:

   ```
   binding="netTcpBinding"
   ```

   You'll continue with changes to the client configuration in a few steps.

5. Next, in Solution Explorer, double-click the App.config file in the DemoService project.

6. The service also needs to be modified to use the *netTcpBinding* binding. As with the client, locate the *endpoint* element and modify the *address* attribute to represent a TCP address by modifying it to the following value:

   ```
   address=
       "net.tcp://localhost:8731/Design_Time_Addresses/DemoService/HeaderService/"
   ```

7. Locate the *binding* attribute in the *endpoint* element and change the value so that it reads as follows:

   ```
   binding="netTcpBinding"
   ```

   To set up the transport security, you must create a binding configuration.

8. Although it hasn't been added yet, set up a reference to the about-to-be-added element in the *endpoint* element by adding a *bindingConfiguration* attribute. Add the following inside the *endpoint* element.

```
bindingConfiguration="SecurityDemo"
```

You must now create a binding configuration.

9. To start this, add a *binding* element to the service's configuration file by adding the following segment within the *system.serviceModel* element:

```
<bindings>
    <netTcpBinding>
        <binding name="SecurityDemo">
        </binding>
    </netTcpBinding>
</bindings>
```

10. Within the *binding* element, add a *security* element. This element indicates the security mode. Add the following segment between the opening and closing *binding* tags.

```
<security mode="Transport">
</security>
```

11. Finally, specify the properties associated with transport security in the *transport* element by adding the following segment to the *security* element:

```
<transport protectionLevel="Sign" clientCredentialType="Windows" />
```

12. Now that the service has been configured, ensure that TestClient is set as the startup project, and then launch the application by pressing F5.

NOTE   WCF debugging disabled

In some cases, when the application launches, you might receive an error message indicating that you are "Unable to automatically debug 'DemoService'. The Remote Procedure could not be debugged". This is frequently caused by having debugging disabled in WCF, a state that has been the default in past versions. For the purpose of this exercise, it is safe to ignore the message by clicking OK. However, you can usually eliminate the error message by performing the following steps.

---

13. Open a command prompt and navigate to the location where the Orcas executable is located, typically %ProgramFiles%\Microsoft Visual Studio 9.0\Common7\IDE.

14. Run vsdiag_regwcf.exe –i.

15. The command will output "Command completed successfully" if WCF debugging was successfully enabled.

You might be surprised to see that the application works as expected, even though the security mode has been defined. The reason is because the settings you have just changed indicate the *minimum* security considered acceptable by the service. In the environment you're running in (from within Visual Studio on the same computer), the actual transport security will include a signed and encrypted message, using Windows credentials. Because this is more than the minimum, the message is allowed

▶ **Exercise 2   Transport Security in HTTP-Based Binding**

In this exercise, you will learn how to configure WCF to use transport security, and you explore how WCF applications behave when the defined transport doesn't support the required minimum capabilities.

1. Navigate to the *<InstallHome>*/Chapter7/Lesson1/Exercise2/*<language>*/Before directory and double-click the Exercise2.sln file to open the solution in Visual Studio.

   The solution consists of 2 projects. They are as follows.

   ❑ The DemoService project, a simple WCF service library that implements the *IGet-Headers* interface. This interface consists of a single method (*GetHeaders*) that strips a custom header out of the request and returns it to the client.

   ❑ The TestClient project, a Console application that generates a request for the service and displays the result on the Console window.

2. In Solution Explorer, double-click the App.config file for the DemoService project.

3. Start by configuring the service to require transport security. Add the following *security* element to the *system.serviceModel* element.

   ```
   <bindings>
     <wsHttpBinding>
       <binding name="SecurityDemo">
         <security mode="Transport">
           <transport clientCredentialType="Windows" />
         </security>
       </binding>
     </wsHttpBinding>
   </bindings>
   ```

4. Still in the app.config file, the newly created binding needs to be associated with an endpoint. Locate the *<endpoint>* element. Add a *bindingConfiguration* attribute to the endpoint, setting the value to the name of the *wsHttpBinding*, specifically "SecurityDemo". When you're finished the *<endpoint>* element will look like the following.

   ```
   <endpoint address=
   "http://localhost:8731/Design_Time_Addresses/DemoService/HeaderService/"
   binding="wsHttpBinding" contract="DemoService.IGetHeaders"
   bindingConfiguration="SecurityDemo">
   ```

5. Ensure that TestClient is set as the startup project, and then launch the application by pressing F5.

   After a few seconds, the service host application will indicate that an error has occurred. Specifically, an *InvalidOperationException* is thrown with a detailed message approximating "Could Not Find A Base Address That Matches Scheme Https For The Endpoint."

This message indicates that an address specified in the service endpoint isn't sufficient for the minimum level of transport security as you just configured it. As well, the client application will have an exception raised because of its inability to connect to the service.

6. Stop running the application and go back to the configuration process.

Because the problem was with the base address, that seems like an appropriate place to go next.

7. In the DemoService configuration file, locate the *baseAddresses* element.

It contains an element that addresses an HTTP-based address.

8. Change the http to https. Also, change the port number to 8732 (so that it can be distinguished from the non-SSL port of 8731 that has been used to this point).

```
<baseAddresses>
  <add baseAddress=
    "https://localhost:8732/Design_Time_Addresses/DemoService/HeaderService/" />
</baseAddresses>
```

9. In Solution Explorer, double-click the app.config file in the TestClient project.

10. For the client to communicate with the service, both need to agree on the binding. Start with the endpoint address and locate the *endpoint* element.

The *endpoint* element contains an *address* attribute you must modify to match the address listened to by the service.

11. Change the attribute value to the following:

```
address=
    "https://localhost:8732/Design_Time_Addresses/DemoService/HeaderService/"
```

For the connection to be made, you must specify the transport security as well. To prepare for this, add a *bindingConfiguration* attribute to the *endpoint*.

12. Add the following attribute to the *endpoint* element:

```
bindingConfiguration="SecurityDemo"
```

You must define the corresponding binding. This is the same *bindings* element that was already added to the service's configuration file. Even the *security* and *transport* elements are the same.

13. Add the following XML segment to the *system.serviceModel* element in the configuration file.

```
<bindings>
  <wsHttpBinding>
    <binding name="SecurityDemo">
      <security mode="Transport">
        <transport clientCredentialType="Windows" />
      </security>
    </binding>
  </wsHttpBinding>
</bindings>
```

At this point, the application is ready to be executed. However, you might have a problem running the application on your computer if you haven't previously installed an SSL certificate or associated the SSL certificate with port 8732. Over the next few steps, you walk through the process of creating a self-signed SSL certificate for development use. If you already have an SSL available, skip to step 20.

14. Launch the Visual Studio 2008 command prompt in elevated mode by clicking Start and choosing All Programs. Select Microsoft Visual Studio 2008, and then choose Visual Studio Tools.

15. Right-click Visual Studio 2008 Command Prompt and choose Run As Administrator. If you are prompted to allow the application to run, give it permission.

16. Use the makecert utility to create a self-signed certificate for the root authority. Enter the following command at the command prompt.

    The commands in this step and the steps that follow should be entered as a single command; they have been formatted here on multiple lines to fit on the printed page.

    ```
    makecert -n "CN=MyLocalCA" -r -sv MyLocalCA.pvk MyLocalCA.cer
        -sky exchange
    ```

17. You will be prompted to provide a private key password for the certificate file. Provide a password and make a note for later in the exercise. Immediately after providing the first password (and confirming it), you might be prompted for a second password. If so, again provide a password. There is no problem with using the same password in both instances.

18. Add the newly created certificate to the Trusted Root Certificate Authority Store, using the certmgr utility. Enter the following command at the command prompt:

    ```
    certmgr -add MyLocalCA.pvk -s -r localmachine root
    ```

    The makecert utility generates the SSL certificate against the root certificate. It also opens up the Certmgr application. It can be closed because it is not required to add the certificate. (That was done with the command line.)

19. Enter the following command at the command prompt.

    ```
    makecert -sky exchange -sk localhost -iv MyLocalCA.pvk -n "CN=localhost"
        -ic MyLocalCA.cer localhost.cer -sr localmachine -ss My
    ```

    When prompted, enter the same password as you used earlier. At this point, you've created the certificate and installed it in your personal store. However, even if you had previously created an SSL certificate, you must associate it with the port and computer combination by using the *netsh http add* command (or the *httpsys* command if you are in Windows XP.). Before the command can be executed, the thumbprint value for the certificate is required.

20. In the command prompt window, type the command **mmc**.

21. Add the Certificates snap-in by choosing Add/Remove Snap-in from the File menu.

22. In the Add/Remove Snap-in dialog box, select Certificates, and then click the Add button.

23. When prompted, indicate that you want to manage certificates for the Computer account and click Next.

24. Click Finish.

25. Click OK.

26. In the tree on the left of the screen, navigate to Console Root/Certificates (Local Computer)/Personal/Certificates.

27. On the right, a certificate with the first column of localhost is visible. Double-click the certificate.

28. Select the Details tab.

29. In the properties that appear at the top, scroll down to the Thumbprint value. Select Thumbprint.

    The value appears in the text box in the lower portion of the form.

30. Select the value in the textbox and use Ctrl+C to copy it to your clipboard.

31. In the Visual Studio 2008 command prompt window, enter the following command:

    ```
    netsh http add sslcert ipport=0.0.0.0:8732 certhash=<thumbprint>
        appid=<guid>
    ```

    The <thumbprint> value should be replaced with the thumbprint value on your clipboard.

32. Be sure to remove the spaces in the thumbprint after they have been pasted into the command prompt window.

NOTE Registering the certificate in Windows XP

If you are using Windows XP, the command that is used to register the certificate is different. Instead of using the *netsh* command, you enter the following into the command line:

```
httpsys add ssl -I 0.0.0.0:8732 -h <thumbprint> -Personal
```

The <guid> referenced in the preceding command is intended to indicate which application owns the SSL reservation that is being created. For this exercise, any GUID will be sufficient.

33. To create a GUID in Visual Studio 2008, select Create GUID from the Tools menu.

34. In the Create GUID dialog box, set the GUID format to Registry format and click Copy.

    This places the GUID on your clipboard, and it can now be pasted into the command. The correct format for the <guid> value in the command does include the brackets (for instance, *appid={DC002...1C6}*).

    At this point, you have now installed the SSL certificate, and the application is ready to use.

35. Launch the application by pressing F5.

    You will notice that the Console window indicates a successful execution.

Lesson Summary

- Transport security secures the entire message, not just the payload. The only information left unsecured is that which is necessary to deliver the message.
- WCF transport security uses the security that is built into the underlying protocol as much as possible. The binding that is used has the potential to limit the available number of transport security options.
- All of the configuration that can be performed declaratively can also be performed imperatively.

Lesson Review

You can use the following questions to test your knowledge of the information in Lesson 1, "Transport-Level Security." The questions are also available on the companion CD if you prefer to review them in electronic form.

NOTE Answers

Answers to these questions and explanations of why each answer choice is correct or incorrect are located in the "Answers" section at the end of the book.

1. Which of the following statements about transport-level security are NOT true?
   A. Transport-level security encrypts the entire message, even the header information.
   B. Transport-level security supports only the security mechanisms that the underlying binding is capable of using.
   C. Every WCF binding can be configured to use or not use transport-level security as required.
   D. Transport-level security ensures that the message cannot be modified while in transit between the client and the service.

2. Which of the following bindings does NOT provide any support for transport-level security?
   A. *basicHttpBinding*
   B. *netTcpBinding*
   C. *wsDualHttpBinding*
   D. *netNamedPipeBinding*

3. Which of the following bindings requires the presence of AD DS to provide transport-level security for a WCF application when the client and service are on different computers?

    A. *wsHttpBinding*

    B. *netNamedPipeBinding*

    C. *netTcpBinding*

    D. *msmqIntegrationBinding*

Lesson 2: Message-Level Security

Lesson 1 covered the details associated with securing WCF communications. As was discussed, security at the transport layer uses the protocols associated with the specifics of the wire standard. When securing messages, some standards also come into play. WS-Security is one of the most commonly used, but there are other standards as well as the easy approach of simply encrypting the message in a manner that client and service expect. This lesson examines the options available for securing messages and the imperative and declarative techniques that enable you to do so.

After this lesson, you will be able to:
- Configure a WCF application to use message-level security.
- Combine both message- and transport-level security within a single binding.
- Identify the appropriate authentication mechanism to support message security.

Estimated lesson time: 50 minutes

Message Security Basics

WCF actually provides three modes for security. They are *Transport*, *Message*, and *TransportWithMessageCredential*. The third mode is actually a combination of the first two. This lesson discusses the second and third modes.

The main difference between transport and message security is that message security includes any necessary credentials and claims along with the message. Contrast this with transport security, which uses handshaking or external resources (such as AD DS) to verify the credentials associated with a message.

A number of benefits are associated with using message security. The biggest is that the message is self-contained because it allows a number of scenarios that are not possible using transport security. For example, transport security secures messages from endpoint to endpoint only. After the message has been received, it is unencrypted. Message security provides end-to-end encryption. Even after a message has been received, it is still encrypted.

A second reason for considering message security over transport security is the ability to provide multiple levels of security; different parts of the message can be secured by using different encryption mechanisms. You can even apply different sets of credentials to encrypt different parts of the message. This enables a single message to have different audiences based on the credentials, or, for example, you can send unencrypted the information used by a router to deliver a message to the correct destination without compromising the security of other parts of the body.

The underlying protocol that message security uses in WCF is WS-Security. This means that all the protocols WCF uses support message security out of the box and, unlike transport security, there is no dependence on any of the protocols for providing message security. Every WCF message is secured regardless of the protocol.

Client Credential Types

A common setting in message security involves the *clientCredentialType* value, which determines the set of credentials sent from the client to the service. Table 7-4 displays a list of eight possible values for the client credential type, all the possible values, and a description of each one.

Table 7-4   Client Credential Types for Message Security

Credential Type	Description
Certificate	A certificate is provided by the client for use by the service to authenticate. The *ClientCredentials* property on the proxy exposes a *clientCertificate* object. By calling the *SetCertificate* method, the certificate can be retrieved from a particular certificate store.
IssuedToken	Authentication is provided by a central token-issuing service. Prior to making a request to a service, the client requests a security token from the central service. That token is then provided to the service, which will validate it against the same service to authenticate the requester.
None	No authentication information is provided by the client. This is the equivalent of anonymous access to the service.

UserName	The client is authenticated by providing a username and password. There is no way to configure the values used in this credential type. They must be provided through code by assigning the *UserName* and *Password* properties of the *UserName* property on the proxy's *ClientCredentials* property, as shown here:
	
	```proxy.ClientCredentials.UserName.UserName=```
	``` "user"```
	```proxy.ClientCredentials.UserName.Password=```
	``` "password"```

Windows	The credentials for the currently logged-on Windows users are provided to the service for authentication.

The values that appear in Table 7-4 are valid for specifying message-level security for every binding type with the sole exception of *basicHttpBinding*, which supports only *UserName* and *Certificate*.

You can specify which credential type to use either imperatively or declaratively. The declarative technique is illustrated in the configuration element that follows:

```
<binding name="myBinding">
  <security mode="Message"/>
  <message clientCredentialType="Certificate"/>
</binding>
```

Note that the security mode has been set to be message level. It's important to be aware that additional message security elements can be applied to different binding types. In some instances, merely setting the client credential type is not sufficient.

Exam Tip   The default value for the *clientCredentialType* is *Windows*. An important aspect of taking the Microsoft certification exam is to be aware of some of the criteria for the answers. It is not possible for a correct answer to a certification exam question to be "Don't do anything." This means that you should never have "set *clientCredentialType* for message security to *Windows*" as part of the correct answer to any question.

These are the basics of providing client credentials to the service for message-level security. Chapter 8, "User-Level Security," describes the details surrounding the client credentials. The remainder of this lesson discusses other configurable elements in message security.

algorithmSuite Attribute

The *algorithmSuite* attribute is used in a number of different bindings. It specifies the type of algorithm used to encode the message. A surprising number of values are considered acceptable for this attribute. However, you need to understand the situations in which it might be necessary to change the default values. An algorithm suite is a set of properties associated with a particular type of encryption technique. The properties that comprise the suite include:

- Encryption type
- Symmetric and asymmetric key signatures
- Symmetric and asymmetric key wrap
- The computed key
- Maximum and minimum key lengths for both symmetric and asymmetric keys

The details and specifics of what goes into an algorithm suite are actually defined as part of the WS-SecurityPolicy specification. All the algorithms share some of the values for these attributes. For each of the suites, the following is true:

- The symmetric key signature is *HmacSha1*.
- The asymmetric key signature is *RsaSha1*.
- The computed key is *PSha1*.
- The maximum symmetric key length is 256 bits.
- The minimum asymmetric key length is 1024 bits.
- The maximum asymmetric key length is 4096 bits.

It is in the rest of the values that the algorithm suites differ. Table 7-5 lists some of the other differences.

Table 7-5   Algorithm Suites and Distinguishing Values

Value	Digest	Encryption Type	Minimum Symmetric Key Length
Basic128	Sha1	Aes128	128
Basic256	Sha1	Aes256	256
Basic192	Sha1	Aes192	192
TripleDes	Sha1	TripleDes	192
Basic256Rsa15	Sha1	Aes256	256
Basic192Rsa15	Sha1	Aes192	192
Basic128Rsa15	Sha1	Aes128	128
TripleDesRsa15	Sha1	TripleDes	192
Basic256Sha256	Sha256	Aes256	256
Basic192Sha256	Sha256	Aes192	192
Basic128Sha256	Sha256	Aes128	128
TripleDesSha256	Sha256	TripleDes	192
Basic256Sha256Rsa15	Sha256	Aes256	256
Basic192Sha256Rsa15	Sha256	Aes192	192
Basic128Sha256Rsa15	Sha256	Aes128	128
TripleDesSha256Rsa15	Sha256	TripleDes	192

The purpose for specifying a specific type of algorithm suite is typically for interoperability purposes. The default value of *Basic256* is generally sufficient for communications between most WCF endpoints. However, a different algorithm suite is used when sending messages to external clients who, for whatever reason, require a different set of properties.

To reinforce this fact, the *algorithmSuite* attribute is valid for the following bindings only:

- *basicHttpBinding*
- *basicHttpContextBinding*
- *netMsmqBinding*
- *netTcpBinding*
- *netTcpContextBinding*
- *wsDualHttpBinding*
- *wsFederationHttpBinding*
- *wsHttpBinding*

- *ws2007FederationHttpBinding*
- *ws2007HttpBinding*

The named pipe bindings are missing from this list. That is because named pipes are an on-machine protocol. Because you won't use named pipes to send messages to a remote machine, there is no reason to vary from the default algorithm suite.

establishSecurityContext Attribute

The underlying purpose of the *establishSecurityContext* attribute is to determine whether a secure conversation is established between the client and the service before any application messages are exchanged. The secure conversation used in WCF is WS-SecureConversation.

WS-SecureConversation is a Web service standard aimed at building a mechanism through which messages can be exchanged in a secure manner. It is based on the WS-Security standard to provide authentication of the message, and the underlying premise is that, although message-level authentication is fine for single or one-way messages, if the client and service wish to exchange multiple messages, a more efficient approach is required. Specifically, a security context could be established between the two parties. This context (called a Security Context Token, or SCT) could then be used to authenticate the messages.

By default, the *establishSecurityContext* attribute is set to *true*. The basic assumption is that multiple messages will be sent along the WCF communications channel. The only reason to change the value is if you are sure the channel will be used only a single time, such as in the case of a one-time or one-way message.

The *establishSecurityContext* attribute is valid only in the following bindings:

- *wsHttpBinding*
- *wsHttpContextBinding*
- *ws2007HttpBinding*

negotiateServiceCredential Attribute

For message security to occur, a form of mutual authentication must take place. Although this is a Boolean value, more than two scenarios are possible.

First, if the attribute value is set to *true*, the service credentials are handled automatically through a negotiation process. The protocol used for this negotiation is called Windows Services SP Negotiation (SPNEGO). The details of the protocol are actually tunneled through a series of SOAP messages for maximum interoperability. The result of this negotiation is that the certificate associated with the service is given to the client as part of this negotiation and initialization process.

If the attribute is set to *false*, there are a couple of possibilities. If the *clientCredentialType* is set to *None*, *UserName*, or *Certificate*, the expectation is that the service's certificate will be available in a certificate store that is accessible from the client. In a case such as this, the service behavior must define the location of the service certification. The following configuration segment shows an example of how this can be accomplished:

```
<behavior name="MyBehavior">
   <serviceCredentials>
      <serviceCertificate
         x509FindType="FindBySubjectName"
         findValue="ServiceCertificateSubject"
         storeLocation="LocalMachine"
         storeName="My"/>
   </serviceCredentials>
</behavior>
```

Chapter 8 covers the details of the *serviceCertificate* element.

The final scenario is when the *negotiateServiceCredential* attribute is set to *false* and the *client-CredentialType* is set to *Windows*. This means that Kerberos-based authentication will take place. Although this is convenient, it does have one significant impact on the deployment model. The client and service must be part of the same Kerberos domain. Regardless of the binding (the Kerberos token is compatible with SOAP-based protocols), the token must be authenticated against the same domain.

Exam Tip   This type of detail (when Kerberos can and can't be used) is the sort of tricky question frequently found in certification questions. It's not truly a trick in that the required knowledge is quite legitimate. However, it is a small detail that is easily overlooked among a number of other requirements. If faced with a question about why a client might not be able to authenticate with a service, one of the first possibilities that should come to mind is that Kerberos across different AD DS domains could be the culprit.

The *negotiateSecurityContext* attribute is valid in the following bindings only:

- *wsDualHttpBinding*
- *wsFederationHttpBinding*
- *wsHttpBinding*
- *wsHttpContextBinding*
- *ws2007FederationHttpBinding*
- *ws2007HttpBinding*

Lab: Defining the Message Security

In this lab, you will configure some of the elements associated with message-level security and view the differences that exist in the number and purpose of the messages that are sent and received.

▶ **Exercise 1   Configure Basic Message Security**

In this first exercise, you will configure a client and service to use basic message-level security. To see the format of the secured message, you use the Service Trace Viewer utility.

1. Navigate to the *InstallHome*>/Chapter7/Lesson2/Exercise1/<*language*>/Before directory and double-click the Exercise1.sln file to open the solution in Visual Studio.

   The solution consists of two projects. They are as follows:

   ❑ The DemoService project, a simple WCF service library that implements the *IGet-Headers* interface. This interface consists of a single method (*GetHeaders*) that strips a custom header out of the request and returns it to the client.

   ❑ The TestClient project, a Console application that generates a request for the service and displays the result in the Console window.

   To get a sense of how message security changes the message, start by creating a baseline trace.

2. In Windows Explorer, navigate to the *InstallHome*>/Chapter7/Lesson2/Exercise1/<*language*>/Before/DemoService/bin/Debug directory and delete any .svclog files you find there.

3. In Visual Studio 2008, ensure that TestClient is set as the startup project, and then launch the application by pressing F5.

   In a few seconds, the Console window appears, and the text indicates that the call was successful.

4. Press Enter to terminate the application.

5. In Solution Explorer, double-click the app.config file for the DemoService project.

6. Locate the *bindings* element.

   In this element there is a *wsHttpBinding* element for the SecurityDemo binding configuration. You must add the XML elements necessary to implement message-level security by giving the mode attribute in the *security* element a value of *Message*.

7. To do so, locate the security element in the *wsHttpBinding* element. Replace the existing element with the following:

   ```
   <security mode="Message">
   </security>
   ```

   For message security to function, you must provide client credentials.

8. For this example, specify the Windows credentials by adding the following XML element between the starting and ending *security* tags that you just added.

   ```
   <message clientCredentialType="Windows" />
   ```

   The same configuration must be performed in the client application.

9. In Solution Explorer, double-click the app.config file for the TestClient project.

10. Locate the *bindings* element. In the *wsHttpBinding* element, replace the existing security element with the following XML:

```
<security mode="Message">
</security>
```

11. For message security to function, you must provide client credentials. As with the service, specify the Windows credentials by adding the following XML element between the starting and ending *security* tags that were just added:

```
<message clientCredentialType="Windows" />
```

12. Launch the application by pressing F5.

In a few moments, the Console window indicates that the call is complete.

13. Press Enter to terminate the application.

Now look at the two request chains.

14. Launch the Service Trace Viewer by clicking the Start button. Choose All Programs, and then select Microsoft Windows SDK v6.1. Choose Tools, and then select Service Trace Viewer.

15. In the Service Trace Viewer, choose Open from the File menu, and then browse to *Install-Home>*/Chapter7/Lesson2/Exercise1/*<language>*/Before/DemoService/bin/Debug and open the Traces.svclog file.

Notice that roughly 120 message log traces were recorded in the log. The two runs are likely to be distinguishable by the Thread Id column.

The first message in each group will show the unencrypted message (through the XML tab). Figure 7-1 shows the Service Trace Viewer view of this message.

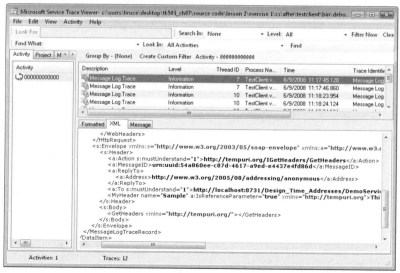

Figure 7-1 An unencrypted message as seen in the Service Trace Viewer

16. Compare this to the corresponding message in the second group (about the fourth or fifth from the bottom, and illustrated in Figure 7-2).

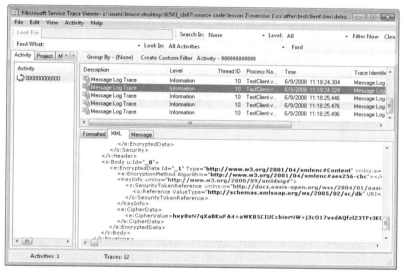

Figure 7-2   An encrypted message as seen in the Service Trace Viewer

In the first message, the *Body* element of the message is in clear text. However, in the second message, the *Body* element has been converted to an encrypted version.

▶ **Exercise 2   Use a Security Context**

If you are making more than one call to a service, and message security is being used, it is more efficient to establish a secure conversation. In this exercise, you will configure a secure conversation.

1. Navigate to the *<InstallHome>*/Chapter7/Lesson2/Exercise2/*<language>*/Before directory and double-click the Exercise2.sln file to open the solution in Visual Studio.

   The solution consists of two projects. They are as follows:

   ❑ The DemoService project, a simple WCF service library that implements the *IGet-Headers* interface. This interface consists of a single method (*GetHeaders*) that strips a custom header out of the request and returns it to the client.

   ❑ The TestClient project is a Console application that generates a request for the service and displays the result in the Console window.

   The configuration portion of establishing a secure conversation is quite simple.

2. In Solution Explorer, double-click the app.config file for the TestClient project.

3. Locate the *message* element that is part of the *wsHttpBinding* security node. Add the following attribute to the *message* element:

```
establishSecurityContext="true"
```

4. Make the same change for the service-side configuration. In Solution Explorer, double-click the app.config file in the DemoService project.

5. Locate the *message* element that is part of the *wsHttpBinding* security node. Add the following attribute to this element:

   ```
   establishSecurityContext="true"
   ```

   Notice that the values for the attributes are set to *true*. This indicates that the security context will be established. To see the extra messages generated between the client and service, compare the traces that you are about to generate to the traces from Exercise 1, "Configure Basic Message Security," in this lesson.

6. Ensure that the TestClient project is set as the startup project and launch the application by pressing F5.

   In a few seconds, the Console window will display a message.

7. Press Enter to terminate the application.

   Use the Service Trace Viewer application to view the different traces.

8. Launch the Service Trace Viewer by clicking the Start button and choosing All Programs. Select Microsoft Windows SDK v6.1, click Tools, and then choose Service Trace Viewer.

9. In the Service Trace Viewer, choose Open from the File menu, browse to <*InstallHome*>/ Chapter7/Lesson2/Exercise1/<*language*>/Before/DemoService/bin/Debug, and open the Traces.svclog file.

   About three messages down, you will see a TransportSend message with a method of *RequestSecurityToken*. This is followed by a number of messages related to receiving the secure token. In the scenario for this exercise, the difference is minimal. However, when the service host is IIS and the number of requests made through the same proxy is greater than two, the difference can be significant.

Lesson Summary

■ Message security is implemented so as not to be dependent on the capabilities of the underlying transport.

■ Message security allows different parts of the message to be secured using different algorithms.

■ The *clientCredentialType* attribute determines the mechanism used to secure the message.

■ It is possible to configure WCF to provide a secure token. This token can then be used to secure subsequent messages.

Lesson Review

You can use the following questions to test your knowledge of the information in Lesson 2, "Message-Level Security." The questions are also available on the companion CD if you prefer to review them in electronic form.

NOTE   Answers

Answers to these questions and explanations of why each answer choice is correct or incorrect are located in the "Answers" section at the end of the book.

---

1. Which of the following statements about WCF message-level security is NOT true?
   A. Message-level security does not depend on the capabilities of the underlying protocol.
   B. Message-level security allows for the ability to secure only a portion of the message.
   C. All the built-in bindings support *Windows* authentication as a means for securing messages.
   D. The authentication method used to secure messages can be specified through the configuration file.

2. You have a WCF application. When deployed, the client and service will be installed on different computers. The *<binding>* element for the application looks like the following:

```
<binding name="myBinding">
    <security mode="Message"/>
    <message clientCredentialType="Windows"
        negotiateServiceCredentials="true"/>
</binding>
```

   When the application is executed, an exception is thrown, indicating that the client cannot be authenticated. Which of the following is a potential cause for the problem?
   A. The client computer and the service computer are not in the same domain.
   B. The client computer and the service computer are in the same domain.
   C. The *establishSecurityContext* attribute should be added and given a value of *true*.
   D. A client-side certificate needs to be created and associated with the service's credentials.

Chapter Review

To further practice and reinforce the skills you learned in this chapter, you can:

- Review the chapter summary.
- Review the list of key terms introduced in this chapter.
- Complete the case scenario. This scenario sets up a real-world situation involving the topics of this chapter and asks you to create a solution.
- Complete the suggested practices.
- Take a practice test.

Chapter Summary

- The type of transport security available depends on the underlying protocol.
- Message security is not dependent on the protocol but is implemented in the channel stack.

Key Terms

Do you know what these key terms mean? You can check your answers by looking up the terms in the glossary at the end of the book.

- Basic Profile
- Kerberos
- security identifier (SID)
- WS-Addressing
- WS-SecureConversation
- WS-SecurityPolicy

Case Scenario

In the following case scenario, you apply what you've learned in this chapter. You can find answers to these questions in the "Answers" section at the end of this book.

Case Scenario: Choosing the Security Mechanism

Your company has developed an application that will be distributed to your clients. It enables them to build an order, submit it to your customer service application programming interface (API), and view the status up to the point at which the order is shipped. The technology used to implement the communication between the client portion and the service is WCF. Answer the following questions for your manager:

1. Is transport security an important consideration for your application?
2. Based solely on the importance of transport-level security, which bindings are the most likely choices?

Suggested Practices

To help you successfully master the exam objectives presented in this chapter, complete the following tasks.

Connecting with Services

Practice configuring transport security with non-WCF MSMQ and using certificates to provide message security.

- **Practice 1**   Create a client application that sends a message to a message queue with the expectation that the receiving application is not WCF. Write an application to remove the incoming requests from the message queue to verify the contents.
- **Practice 2**   Create a WCF application that uses a client-side certificate to provide message-level security.

Take a Practice Test

The practice tests on this book's companion CD offer many options. For example, you can test yourself on just one exam objective, or you can test yourself on all the 70-503 certification exam content. You can set up the test so that it closely simulates the experience of taking a certification exam, or you can set it up in study mode so that you can look at the correct answers and explanations after you answer each question.

MORE INFO   Practice tests

For details about all the practice test options available, see the "How to Use the Practice Tests" section in this book's introduction.

Chapter 8

User-Level Security

The previous chapter discussed the security embedded in Windows Communication Foundation (WCF). This included transport-level security, as offered by the protocol used to transmit the messages, and message-level security, provided through a number of standards. The second part of the security story in WCF deals with authentication and authorization.

This chapter starts by covering the different mechanisms that exist to enable the client and the service to support mutual authentication. Also covered in this chapter are the details of how to integrate your own custom authentication into WCF. The second lesson discusses WCF authorization. The topic of authorization also includes impersonation because what is impersonation if not changing the access typically allowed through the authorization process?

Exam objectives in this chapter:
- Authenticate clients.
- Authorize clients.
- Impersonate clients.

Lessons in this chapter:

Before You Begin

To complete the lessons in this chapter, you must have:

- A computer that meets or exceeds the minimum hardware requirements listed in the introduction at the beginning of the book.
- Any edition of Microsoft Visual Studio 2008 (including Microsoft Visual C# 2008 Express edition or Microsoft Visual Basic 2008 Express edition) installed on the computer.

Real World

Bruce Johnson

User-level security crops up in many applications throughout the .NET world. A large part of where I have used it in the past relates to ASP.NET applications, which, as it turns out, is a good lead-in for WCF.

WCF user-level security has many of the same issues as ASP.NET, and it addresses them in a similar manner. The difference is that the knobs that need to be turned to implement WCF security are in a different place and, in some cases, are harder to find.

When you use WCF in a typical environment, user-level security will be an issue. Figuring out how to get a remote user authenticated by the service; ensuring that operations are properly restricted; enabling the service to act on behalf of the requester with respect to accessing resources—these are real problems, and the solutions can be challenging or frustrating to discover, depending on your perspective. This chapter covers the details associated with all these topics, and they are concepts that are not only a big part of the certification exam but also will be useful when you apply your WCF knowledge to real applications.

Lesson 1: Authentication

Although it might seem like it should be a simple process to determine who someone is, the reality is that it's not. The problems are well understood. Who confirms the credentials? Which encryption is used? Should a federation process be used? Describing how WCF provides answers to these questions and others is the purpose of this lesson.

> **After this lesson, you will be able to:**
> - Specify the mechanism that passes client credentials across service boundaries.
> - Define the credentials the service presents to the client.
> - Create a custom authentication mechanism.
>
> **Estimated lesson time: 50 minutes**

Authentication Basics

Fundamentally, authentication is the process of one party verifying that the claims regarding the identity of a second party are correct. In distributed applications, this would typically be perceived as the client needing to be verified by the service. However, it is possible (indeed, preferable) for the service to also authenticate itself with the client. After all, without the service authentication, there is no way for the client to be certain that the service's endpoint isn't being maliciously impersonated.

WCF offers a variety of authentication mechanisms.

- **No authentication**   This might also be considered anonymous authentication. Even if the client provides a set of credentials, no attempt is made to validate that the credentials are correct.

- **Windows authentication**   The service uses one of two built-in mechanisms for Windows authentication. If the service is deployed in an environment in which a Windows domain server is available, Kerberos is used. If the deployment environment is in a workgroup or on a standalone system, WCF uses Microsoft Windows NT LAN Manager (NTLM) for authentication.

- **Username and password**   The client provides the service with a set of credentials, typically a username and password. The service then authenticates the credentials against some data store.

- **X.509 certificate**   The client identifies itself by using a certificate. Generally, the certificate must be known by the service in advance so that it can properly correlate it with a set of user information. Alternatively, the service could trust the issuer of the certificate and accept any client that presents the certificate as being legitimate.

- **Issued tokens**   The client passes a token to the service to identify the sender. The source of the token is known to both the client and the service. The client provides the credentials to a secure token service (STS). After validation, the STS returns a token to the client. This token is provided to the service. After it's received, the service sends the token to the STS to retrieve access to any necessary client identifying information.

- **Custom**   Within WCF, the authentication process can be replaced by any desired custom mechanism, so it is possible, for example, to use biometrics or a secure card to authenticate the client.

Security Policy

In authentication, the client and the service must agree on many aspects related to security. For example, WCF won't work if the client encrypts the message by using SHA-1, but the service expects the message in plaintext. A mechanism is required that enables the client and the service to agree on the standards to be used or, more accurately, a mechanism that enables a service to publish the capabilities that are supported and that any client wishing to use the service must meet.

This requirement is filled by a combination of WS-* protocols that WCF implements. Information about the security (and other) requirements is provided through WS-Policy. The capabilities supported by a particular service are represented as a collection of *policy assertions*. Each assertion is a single capability, property, or behavior. These assertions are pulled together into a collection called a *policy alternative*. The collection of policy alternatives defined for a service is known as the service's policy. Through the WS-Policy standard, a policy framework exists to share the policy information, typically through the Web Services Description Language (WSDL) used to describe the service.

Within the area of policy, a number of standards exist to assist in the coordination process. *WS-PolicyAssertions* and *WS-SecurityPolicy* help define a set of standard policy assertions that client and service can agree on. It would seem that now and in future versions, one of the expectations is to enable code generators to read the policy exposed by a service and generate a proxy class that can send requests, using the appropriate behaviors.

Client Credentials

With authentication, it should be no surprise that the client providing credentials to the service is a common scenario. Two questions must be addressed: which credentials should be used and how they should be provided.

Table 8-1 shows a list of eight possible values, and a description of each one, for the client credential type.

Table 8-1   Client Credential Types for Message Security

Credential Type	Description
Certificate	The client provides a certificate for the service to authenticate. The *Client-Credentials* property on the proxy exposes a *ClientCertificate* object. By calling the *SetCertificate* method, the certificate can be retrieved from a particular certificate store.
IssuedToken	Authentication is provided by a central token-issuing service. Prior to making a request to a service, the client requests a security token from the central service. That token is then provided to the service, which will validate it against the same service to authenticate the requester.
None	No authentication information is provided by the client. This is the equivalent of anonymous access to the service.

UserName	The client is authenticated by providing a username and password. There is no way to configure the values used in this credential type. They must be provided through code by assigning the *UserName* and *Password* properties of the *UserName* property on the proxy's *ClientCredentials* property.
	
	`proxy.ClientCredentials.UserName.UserName =`
	`    "user"`
	`proxy.ClientCredentials.UserName.Password =`
	`    "password"`

Windows	The credentials for the currently logged-on Windows users are provided to the service for authentication.

Although this is a list of the possible sources for the client credentials, not all types are valid for all bindings. The client credential type used depends on the security mode required by the service. If the binding is using transport security, the client credentials must use Windows credentials or certificates. If the binding supports message security, the list of possible client credentials increases. The values that appear in Table 8-1 are valid for specifying message-level security for every binding type with the sole exception of the *basicHttpBinding* binding, which supports *UserName* and *Certificate* only.

You can specify which credential type to use, either imperatively or declaratively. The declarative technique is illustrated in the configuration element that follows:

```
<binding name="myBinding">
   <security mode="Message">
      <message clientCredentialType="Certificate"/>
   </security>
</binding>
```

Note that the security mode has been set to message level. It's important to be aware that additional message security elements can be applied to different binding types. In other words, in some instances, merely setting the client credential type is not sufficient.

Exam Tip   The default value for the *clientCredentialType* is *Windows*. An important aspect in the Microsoft certification exam is to be aware of some of the criteria for the answers. It is not possible for a correct answer to a certification exam question to be "don't do anything." This means that you should never have "set *clientCredentialType* for message security to *Windows*" as part of the correct answer to any question.

Now that the fundamentals of message-level security have been addressed, the next sections detail one credential type at a time.

Certificate Credentials

When the certificate credential type is specified, the client provides a certificate to the service for authentication. Because the service must perform the authentication, start by looking at the configuration for the service:

```
<behaviors>
    <serviceBehaviors>
        <behavior name="ServiceCredentialsBehavior">
            <serviceCredentials>
                <serviceCertificate findValue="Contoso.com"
                    x509FindType="FindBySubjectName" />
            </serviceCredentials>
        </behavior>
    </serviceBehaviors>
</behaviors>
```

The *serviceCredentials* element contains information about how the client is to be authenticated to the service. Within the *serviceCredentials* element, different elements are used, with each one related to a different credential type.

Issued Token Credentials

The main idea behind the issued token credentials is to allow a third-party token granting authority to perform the authentication process. The client requests a token and then includes that token in the request to the WCF service. The WCF service then hands that token to the token-granting authority to retrieve information about the requester.

In the .NET world, one of the main users of this type of credential is *CardSpace*. *CardSpace* provides a number of capabilities above and beyond token issuing, and there are other services that can provide similar functionality. However, *CardSpace* does provide a nice foundation for talking about an example. Figure 8-1 illustrates the flow between the WCF client and service and the token provider.

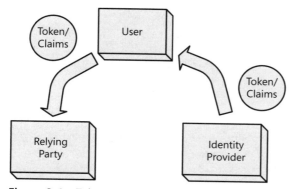

Figure 8-1   Token passing with issued token credentials

Because the WCF service is part of the equation, look at what needs to occur on the service side to handle issued tokens. The configuration takes place in the behaviors for the service. Consider the following code sample from the service's configuration file:

```
<services>
    <service name="UpdateService"
        behaviorConfiguration="ServiceCredentials">
        <endpoint address="" binding="wsHttpBinding"
            bindingConfiguration="requireInfoCard"
            contract="IUpdateService" >
            <identity>
                <certificateReference
                    findValue="545c3b8e97d99fd75c75eb52c6908320088b4f50"
                    x509FindType="FindByThumbprint"
                    storeLocation="LocalMachine"
                    storeName="My" />
            </identity>
        </endpoint>
    </service>
</services>
<bindings>
    <wsHttpBinding>
        <binding name="requireInfoCard">
            <security mode="Message">
                <message clientCredentialType="IssuedToken" />
            </security>
        </binding>
    </wsHttpBinding>
</bindings>
<behaviors>
  <serviceBehaviors>
    <behavior name="ServiceCredentials">
      <serviceCredentials>
        <serviceCertificate
```

```
            findValue="545c3b8e97d99fd75c75eb52c6908320088b4f50"
            x509FindType="FindByThumbprint"
            storeLocation="LocalMachine"
            storeName="My" />
          <issuedTokenAuthentication allowUntrustedRsaIssuers="true" />
        </serviceCredentials>
      </behavior>
    </serviceBehaviors>
</behaviors>
```

The first thing to note is the *identity* element (shown in bold) in the *endpoint* section. This element allows a different endpoint to provide authentication functionality to the service. In this particular case, the enclosed *certificateReference* element provides the details of which authentication facility to use.

certificateReference Element

This particular element indicates the certificate that should be provided to the client to verify the service's identity. Its placement within the *identity* element of the endpoint should help clarify its purpose. However, the real reason to concentrate on this element is because other elements use the same attributes when referencing a certificate.

Referencing a certificate is really a two-step process. The first step is to define the store to be searched. The *storeName* attribute identifies the particular store that contains the certificate. Table 8-2 contains a list of the valid values, and their meanings, for this attribute.

Table 8-2   Values for the *storeName* Attribute

Value	Description
AddressBook	Store for use by other users
AuthRoot	Store containing third-party certificate authorities (CAs)
CertificateAuthority	Store for intermediate CAs
Disallowed	Store for certificates that have been revoked
My	Store for personal certificates
Root	Store for trusted root CA certificates
TrustedPeople	Store for certificates related to directly trusted people and resources
TrustedPublisher	Store for certificates related to directly trusted publishers

Two attributes are involved with actually performing the search. The *X509FindType* attribute specifies the type of search. Then the *findValue* attribute defines the value that is searched for. Table 8-3 lists the different types of searches that can be performed.

Table 8-3 Certificate Find Types

Value	Description
FindByThumbprint	Searches for the certificate that matches the thumbprint specified in the *findValue* attribute.
FindBySubjectName	Searches for the certificate that matches the subject name specified in the *findValue* attribute. It is possible that using this type of search will return more than one certificate. The search is case-insensitive and looks for any subject that contains the indicated value.
FindBySubjectDistinguishedName	Searches for the certificate that matches the subject name specified in the *findValue* attribute. The difference between this search type and *FindBySubjectName* is that the specified value must match the distinguished name precisely.
FindByIssuerName	Searches for the certificate that matches the issuer name specified in the *findValue* attribute. It is possible that using this type of search will return more than one certificate. The search is case-insensitive and looks for any issuer name that contains the indicated value.
FindByIssuerDistinguishedName	Searches for the certificate that matches the issuer name specified in the *findValue* attribute. The difference between this search type and *FindByIssuerName* is that the specified value must match the distinguished name precisely.
FindBySerialNumber	Searches for the certificate that matches the serial number specified in the *findValue* attribute. The serial number must be in reverse order because it is an integer. The reason for needing to reverse the value is because the serial number is stored with the least significant byte first. However, if the serial number is specified as an integer, the least significant byte is last, so to find the desired serial number by using an integer, you need to reverse the bytes that appear in the serial number.
FindByTimeValid	Searches for certificates that are valid as of the *DateTime* value specified in the *findValue* attribute.
FindByTimeNotYetValid	Searches for certificates that are not yet valid as of the *DateTime* value specified in the *findValue* attribute.
FindByTimeExpired	Searches for certificates that have expired as of the *DateTime* value specified in the *findValue* attribute.
FindByTemplateName	Searches for certificates in which the template name matches the name provided in the *findValue* attribute. A template name is an X509 v3 extension that specifies the uses of the certificate.

Table 8-3 **Certificate Find Types**

Value	Description
FindByApplicationPolicy	Searches for the certificate in which the *findValue* attribute matches either the application policy friendly name or the object identifier of the certificate.
FindByCertificatePolicy	Searches for the certificate in which the *findValue* attribute matches either the friendly name or the object identifier of the certificate policy.
FindByExtension	Searches for the certificate in which the *findValue* attribute matches a string describing the certificate's extension.
FindByKeyUsage	Searches for the certificate in which the *findValue* attribute matches either a string representing the key usage or an integer representing a bit mask containing all the requested key usages.
FindBySubjectKeyIdentifier	Searches for the certificate in which the *findValue* attribute matches the string representing the subject key identifier in hexadecimal.

NOTE   Getting all the certificates

As a result of the way the search types are defined, the *FindByTimeValue*, *FindByTimeNotYetValid*, and *FindByTimeExpired* types should each contain a unique set of certificates. When these sets are merged, the combination should include all the certificates in the store being searched.

In the specific example from the "Issued Token Credentials" section, the identity element is configured to request a SAMLToken from *CardSpace*. This fact is not immediately obvious from merely examining the configuration file. However, notice that the binding is set to use an issued token to secure the message, and the certificate that is referenced by the *certificateReference* element was provided by *CardSpace*. The fact that *CardSpace* was the source of the certificate is not visibly apparent.

In addition, the same certificate information is provided in the *serviceCredentials* element in the service behavior. As you will see shortly, the same certificate information is used in the client configuration.

Windows Credentials

As has already been mentioned, Windows credentials are the default value for client credentials with message security. On the client side, configuration for using Windows credentials is straightforward. As always, you can do it either declaratively or imperatively. Look at the declarative version in the following configuration section:

```
<bindings>
    <wsHttpBinding>
        <binding name="messageSecurity">
            <security mode="Message">
                <message clientCredentialType="Windows"/>
            </security>
        </binding>
    </wsHttpBinding>
</bindings>
```

The imperative version is not much more complex. An example of how to set the client credential type to Windows through code follows.

```
' VB
Dim proxy As New UpdateServiceClient()
proxy.ClientCredentials.Windows.ClientCredential = _
    CredentialCache.DefaultCredentials
Proxy.ClientCredentials.Windows.AllowedImpersonationLevel = _
    TokenImpersonationLevel.Impersonation
Proxy.ClientCredentials.Windows.AllowNtlm = False
```

```
// C#
UpdateServiceClient proxy = new UpdateServiceClient();
proxy.ClientCredentials.Windows.ClientCredential =
    CredentialCache.DefaultCredentials;
proxy.ClientCredentials.Windows.AllowedImpersonationLevel =
    TokenImpersonationLevel.Impersonation;
proxy.ClientCredentials.Windows.AllowNtlm = false;
```

As you can see, a number of other properties can be set with the Windows credentials.

AllowedImpersonationLevel

The *allowedImpersonationLevel* attribute determines the types of impersonation the service can perform on behalf of the client. This is a standard setting when Windows credentials are passed between different processes or computers. The concept of impersonation has to do with the security context under which requests for certain resources are made. Lesson 2, "Authorization and Impersonation," discusses more details about impersonation levels and the implications of them.

AllowNtlm

The Windows NT LAN Manager (NTLM) is an authentication protocol used on networks that include earlier systems running Windows NT or standalone and workgroup systems. The purpose of the *AllowNtlm* attribute is to determine the type of authentication used to validate the credentials. If *AllowNtlm* is set to *false*, the WCF service is forced to use Kerberos when it performs any Windows SSPI Negotiate authentication. When set to *true*, NTLM authentication is used if appropriate.

If the WCF service is deployed in certain environments, where local accounts or the work-group in which the service is running require NTLM authentication, setting this value to *false* can result in authentication failures. Alternatively, if the WCF service is deployed in a manner that requires mutual authentication, the flag must be set to *false* because NTLM does not support this scenario (and Kerberos does support it).

NOTE   NTLM vs. Kerberos

Although Kerberos is the preferred choice because of the greater security it provides (as compared to NTLM), NTLM is still supported by WCF. If the network includes systems running versions of Windows NT 4.0 and earlier, or if the service is running on a standalone system, NTLM must be allowed.

On the service side, the identity of the request is available through the *OperationContext* object. Specifically, the following code will retrieve the name of the Windows user who made the request:

```
' VB
Dim currentUser As String = _
   OperationContext.Current.ServiceSecurityContext.WindowsIdentity.Name
```

```
// C#
String currentUser =
   OperationContext.Current.ServiceSecurityContext.WindowsIdentity.Name;
```

Quick Check

■ Which credential types do not require a certificate to authenticate the client to the WCF service?

Quick Check Answer

■ Only the *Certificate* credentials mechanism requires that a certificate be provided. The issued token credentials can use a certificate to authenticate with the token issuing service, but it is not a requirement for use.

Service Credentials

There is also a way for the service to present a set of credentials to the client. This is required to support mutual authentication and message protection. Also, when transport security is specified, the service's credentials might be needed to provide the required functionality.

In the absence of any information to indicate differently, the Windows credentials for the service are used, assuming that the binding requires mutual authentication because of transport security or message security. If you desire a different set of credentials for the service, you must specify them in the *serviceCredentials* element within the *behaviors* section. For example, the following segment from a configuration file tells the service to use the certificate with a subject name of UpdateKey in the local certificate store:

```
<behaviors>
  <serviceBehaviors>
    <behavior name="serviceBehavior" >
      <serviceCredentials>
        <serviceCertificate findValue="RPKey"
          storeLocation="LocalMachine" storeName="My"
          x509FindType="FindBySubjectName" />
      </serviceCredentials>
    </behavior>
  </serviceBehaviors>
</behaviors>
```

If you plan on using an alternative set of credentials, it is important to be aware of some of the potential ramifications. For example, in the preceding segment, a certificate is specified for the service's credentials. If the client needs to encrypt the message sent to the service, the public key portion of this certificate must be available to the client. This can be provided either out of band (by providing the public key information to install on the client) or it can be negotiated with an initial handshake. The choice you make is specified in the *negotiateServiceCredential* attribute in the *message* element of the binding, as shown in bold in the following example:

```
<wsHttpBinding>
  <binding name="wsHttp">
    <security mode="Message">
      <message clientCredentialType="Certificate"
        negotiateServiceCredential="true" />
    </security>
  </binding>
</wsHttpBinding>
```

Again, as a caveat, the protocols used to negotiate are not interoperable in all situations. For Windows credentials, the SPNEGO protocol is used. For *UserName*, *Certificate*, or anonymous credentials, the TLSNEGO protocol is used. These protocols request the correct encryption token dynamically before any messages are exchanged.

Alternatively, when the automatic negotiation of service credentials is disabled, there are also some limitations. If Windows client credentials are to be used, a Kerberos domain must be available. This domain retrieves the encryption token. For other client credential types, the service credentials can be hard-coded, as shown in bold in the following segment:

```
<behavior name="Client">
  <clientCredentials supportInteractive="false">
    <clientCertificate storeLocation="CurrentUser"
      storeName="TrustedPeople" x509FindType="FindBySubjectName"
      findValue="UpdateKey"/>
    <serviceCertificate>
```

```
     <defaultCertificate storeLocation="CurrentUser"
        storeName="TrustedPeople x509FindType="FindBySubjectName"
        findValue="localhost"/>
   </serviceCertificate>
  </clientCredentials>
</behavior>
```

Alternatively, an encoded version of the public portion of the service's certificate can be supplied in the definition of the endpoint. For example, the following segment from a configuration file is generated by the svcutil utility:

```
<client>
  <endpoint address="http://localhost:8000/UpdateService"
     binding="wsHttpBinding" contract="UpdateService"
     name="WSHttpBinding_UpdateService">
     <identity>
       <certificate encodedValue="AwAAAAEAAAAUAAAA...oVbTtOA=="/>
     </identity>
  </endpoint>
</client>
```

Custom Authentication

Although the options that WCF offers for authentication are helpful, there are always gaps through which specific requirements will fall. It is not possible to guarantee that all the available choices will cover every possible scenario, so in the typical WCF manner, you can extend the authentication process with your own custom mechanism. This section describes the process for doing this, along with some of the ramifications.

First, to use custom authentication, the client credential type must be set to *UserName*. This enables the username and password to be submitted to the service to perform the authentication. A side effect is that with a *UserName* client credential type, WCF requires the service to reference a certificate that contains a public/private key pair. The public key portion of the certificate then encrypts the credentials before they are transmitted to the service.

The default, when the client credential type is *UserName*, is for the service to use Windows to perform the authentication. To intercept this process, the starting point is to create a class that derives from the *UserNamePasswordValidator* class, which is in the *System.IdentityModel.Selectors* namespace. Within this class, the authentication mechanism is introduced into the process by overriding the *Validate* method, which is involved when WCF is in the middle of authentication.

Probably the most interesting aspect of the *Validate* method is that it doesn't return a Boolean value. In fact, this method call doesn't return any value at all. If the method completes, WCF assumes that the credentials were valid. To invalidate the credentials, a *SecurityTokenValidation-Exception* exception must be raised. An example of such a class can be seen in the following code:

```vb
' VB
Public Class CustomAuthenticator
   Inherits UserNamePasswordValidator

   Public Overrides Sub Validate(userName As String, password As String)
      If (userName <> "anyuser" OR password <> "good") Then
         Throw New SecurityTokenValidationException("Invalid credentials")
      End If
   End Sub

End Class
```

```csharp
// C#
public class CustomAuthenticator : UserNamePasswordValidator
{
   public override void Validate(string userName, string password)
   {
      if (userName != "anyuser" || password != "good")
         throw new SecurityTokenValidationException("Invalid credentials");
   }
}
```

After the *Validator* class has been created, the next step is to configure the service to use its functionality. You do this by specifying the validator type as part of the service's behavior configuration. The following segment from a configuration file defines a service behavior that does just this:

```xml
<serviceBehaviors>
   <behavior name="CustomValidator">
      <serviceCredentials>
         <userNameAuthentication
            userNamePasswordValidationMode="Custom"
            customUserNamePasswordValidatorType=
               "ThisAssembly.CustomAuthenticator, ThisAssembly"/>
         <serviceCertificate
            findValue="localhost" x509FindType="FindBySubjectName"
            storeLocation="CurrentUser" storeName="My" />
      </serviceCredentials>
   </behavior>
</serviceBehaviors>
```

The *userNameAuthentication* element contains the details that specify the custom authentication module. Although the *serviceCertificate* element doesn't have anything to do directly with the custom authentication, it is one of the techniques you can use to provide the certificate information to encode the credentials for transmission.

Note also that the behavior just defined is not a part of any service by default. The service must specify this behavior by setting the *behaviorConfiguration* attribute to the name of the behavior (*CustomValidator* in this example). Also, the client must ensure that the client credential type is set to *UserName*.

To actually provide the credentials requires just a small piece of coding on the client side. If you are using the *ChannelFactory* class to create a proxy, the following code will submit a set of credentials with the request, and it will use the configuration information associated with the endpoint that has a name attribute of *DemoEndpoint*:

```VB
' VB
Dim factory As New _
    ChannelFactory(Of IUpdateService)("DemoEndpoint")
factory.Credentials.UserName.UserName = "anyuser"
factory.Credentials.UserName.Password = "good"
```

```C#
// C#
ChannelFactory<IUpdateService> factory =
    new ChannelFactory<IUpdateService>("DemoEndpoint");
factory.Credentials.UserName.UserName = "anyuser";
factory.Credentials.UserName.Password = "good";
```

NOTE Custom authentication

When using custom authentication, you cannot specify the username and password automatically through configuration. The credentials must be assigned explicitly.

It is possible that you might have to specify a Domain Name System (DNS) identity to use the certificate. This might be necessary if the client authenticates the service's certificate prior to sending a request. This type of problem is indicated through a message similar to the following:

```
Identity check failed for outgoing message. The expected DNS identity of the remote endpoint
was 'X' but the remote endpoint provided DNS claim 'Y'. If this is a legitimate remote
endpoint, you can fix the problem by explicitly specifying DNS identity 'Y' as the Identity
property of EndpointAddress when creating channel proxy.
```

The solution, as the message quite nicely suggests, is to set the identity explicitly for the DNS. You can do this by adding an *identity* element to the endpoint definition within the client's configuration file, as shown here:

```
<identity>
    <dns value="Y"/>
</identity>
```

Lab: Working with Authentication

This lab illustrates some of the less frequently used mechanisms for authenticating users. This includes a certificate to authenticate the user along with a demonstration of the custom validation of credentials.

▶ **Exercise 1 Use Certificates for Authentication**

In this first exercise, you will use a certificate to provide authentication to the service. You might use such a scenario if the client is supposed to be authenticated with the service but without providing a user ID and password. Instead, you can issue the client a certificate attached to the request from the proxy.

1. You must run Visual Studio 2008 as an administrator in this exercise. In Visual Studio 2008, navigate to the *<InstallHome>*/Chapter8/Lesson1/Exercise1/*<language>*/Before directory and double-click the Exercise1.sln file to open the solution in Visual Studio.

   The solution consists of two projects. They are as follows:

   ❑ The DemoService project, a simple WCF service library that implements the *IGet-Headers* interface. This interface consists of a single method (*GetHeaders*) that strips a custom header out of the request and returns it to the client.

   ❑ The TestClient project, a Console application. The application generates a request for the service and displays the result in the Console window.

   To configure the client certificate, a number of settings are external to Visual Studio. Specifically, you must create a certificate for Secure Sockets Layer (SSL) and associate it with a client-side certificate. These are the same steps that were performed in Exercise 2 of Lesson 1 in Chapter 7, "Infrastructure Security," so if you have already performed these steps, there is no need to do them again. However, they are required to run the application successfully.

2. Launch the Visual Studio 2008 command prompt in elevated mode. Click Start, choose All Programs, select Microsoft Visual Studio 2008, and then choose Visual Studio Tools.

3. Right-click Visual Studio 2008 Command Prompt and select Run As Administrator. If you are prompted to allow the application to run, give it permission.

   You use the makecert utility to create a self-signed certificate for the root authority.

4. Enter the following command at the command prompt:

   ```
   makecert -n "CN=MyLocalCA" -r -sv MyLocalCA.pvk MyLocalCA.cer
     -sky exchange
   ```

   The commands in this step and the steps that follow should be entered as a single command. They have been formatted here on multiple lines to fit on the printed page.

   You will be prompted to provide a private key password for the certificate file.

5. Provide a password and make a note for later in the exercise.

   Immediately after providing the first password (and confirming it), you might be prompted for a second password. If so, provide a password again. There is no problem with using the same password in both instances.

6. Add the newly created certificate to the Trusted Root Certificate Authority Store, using the certmgr utility by typing the following command at the command prompt:

   ```
   certmgr -add MyLocalCA.pvk -s -r localmachine root
   ```

   The makecert utility generates the SSL certificate against the root certificate. It also opens up the Certmgr application.

7. In the pane on the left side of the form, expand the Trusted Root Certificate Authorities node and right-click the Certificates folder.

8. In the context menu that appears, select All Tasks, and then select Import.

9. On the Certificate Import Wizard welcome screen, click Next.

10. On the File to Import page, click Browse.

11. Browse to the location of the signed Root Certificate Authority MyLocalCA.cer file created in Step 4, select the file, and then click Open.

12. On the File To Import page, click Next.

13. On the Certificate Store page, accept the default choice, and then click Next.

14. On the Completing The Certificate Import Wizard page, click Finish. If you are prompted with a Security Warning, click Yes.

15. In the command prompt, enter the following command:

```
makecert -sky exchange -sk localhost -iv MyLocalCA.pvk -n "CN=localhost"
    -ic MyLocalCA.cer localhost.cer -sr localmachine -ss My
```

16. Enter the same password you chose earlier and click OK.

    At this point, you've created the certificate and installed it in your personal store. However, even if you had previously created an SSL certificate, you must associate it with the port and computer combination by using the *httpsys* command. Before the command can be executed, the thumbprint value for the certificate is required.

17. In the command prompt window, type **mmc**.

18. Add the Certificates snap-in by choosing Add/Remove Snap-in from the File menu. In the Add/Remove Snap-in dialog box, select Certificates, and then click the Add button.

19. When prompted, indicate that you want to manage certificates for the Computer account and click Next.

20. Click Finish.

21. Click OK.

22. In the tree on the left of the screen, navigate to Console Root/Certificates (Local Computer)/Personal/Certificates.

23. On the right, a certificate with the first column of Localhost is visible. Double-click the certificate.

24. Select the Details tab.

25. In the properties that appear at the top, scroll down to the thumbprint value. Select Thumbprint, and the value appears in the text box in the lower portion of the form. Select the value in the textbox and press Ctrl+C to copy it to your clipboard.

26. In the Visual Studio 2008 command prompt window, enter the following command:

```
netsh http add sslcert ipport=0.0.0.0:8732 certhash=<thumbprint>
    appid=<guid>
```

The *<thumbprint>* value should be replaced with the thumbprint value on your clipboard. Be sure to remove the spaces in the thumbprint after they have been pasted into the command prompt window.

The *<guid>* referenced in this command is intended to indicate which application "owns" the SSL reservation that is being created. For this exercise, any GUID will be sufficient.

27. To create a GUID, in Visual Studio 2008, choose Create GUID from the Tools menu.

28. In the Create GUID dialog box, set the GUID format to Registry Format and click Copy.

    This places the GUID on your clipboard, and it can now be pasted into the command. The correct format for the *<guid>* value in the command does include the curly braces (for example, *appid={DC002...1C6}*).

    At this point, you have now installed the SSL certificate, and you are ready to modify the application.

    The starting point will be to configure the service to accept the certificate.

29. In Solution Explorer, double-click the app.config file in the DemoService project.

30. Locate the *security* element.

    The mode is currently set to *Transport*. When certificates are being used to provide authentication, this is an acceptable value. However, the *transport* element within the *security* element currently has the client credential type set to *Windows*. For certificates to work as authentication, it needs to be set to *Certificate*. When you make this change, the *security* element will look like the following:

```
<security mode="Transport">
  <transport clientCredentialType="Certificate"/>
</security>
```

31. In the same app.config file, modify the base address to a protocol that supports certificate authentication.

    With an HTTP-based binding, this means HTTPS will be used instead of HTTP.

32. To do so, first locate the *baseAddresses* element.

    Contained in this element is an *add* element that defines the base address for the WCF service host.

33. Modify this address to support HTTPS, which involves changing the protocol in the URL. Also, just for the purposes of this exercise, modify the port number to 8732.

    When you are finished, the *<baseAddresses>* element should look like the following:

```
<baseAddresses>
  <add baseAddress=
  "https://localhost:8732/Design_Time_Addresses/DemoService/HeaderService/"
    />
</baseAddresses>
```

Now that the service has been configured to use certificates, you must modify the client to communicate using the same address as well as using the same transport security.

34. In Solution Explorer, double-click the app.config file in the TestClient project.

35. Locate the *security* element. The mode is already *Transport*, but you must set the *credential* type to *Certificate*. When you make this *change*, the *security* element should look like the following:

```
<security mode="Transport">
   <transport clientCredentialType="Certificate"/>
</security>
```

The other change to the client's configuration is in the endpoint's address. It must use the same protocol (HTTPS) and port (8732) as the service is configured to use.

36. Locate the *endpoint* element. Change the *address* attribute to the following:

```
address=
  "https://localhost:8732/Design_Time_Addresses/DemoService/HeaderService/"
```

At the moment, the client and service have been configured to communicate with one another. However, the client is not providing a certificate to the service for authentication. There are two ways to accomplish this: declaratively and imperatively.

37. To start the imperative process, in Solution Explorer, double-click the Program.cs or Module1.vb file in the TestClient project.

The *proxy* object exposes a *ClientCertificate* property. This object has a *SetCertificate* method, which provides the information necessary to identify the certificate to use. In this usage, the distinguished name (*CN=localhost*) is provided along with information necessary to locate the certificate in the store.

38. Add the following code as the first line in the *using* statement block:

```
' VB
proxy.ClientCredentials.ClientCertificate.SetCertificate("CN=localhost", _
   System.Security.Cryptography.X509Certificates. _
   StoreLocation.LocalMachine, _
   System.Security.Cryptography.X509Certificates.StoreName.My)
```

```
// C#
proxy.ClientCredentials.ClientCertificate.SetCertificate("CN=localhost",
   System.Security.Cryptography.X509Certificates.StoreLocation.LocalMachine,
   System.Security.Cryptography.X509Certificates.StoreName.My);
```

The application is ready to run.

39. Ensure that TestClient is set as the startup project, and then launch the application by pressing F5.

You will see that the application runs correctly and, if you look in the Console window, the user ID as recorded on the service side is set to *null* (your user ID when the application was run at the beginning of the exercise) because, even though the client has been authenticated, it has not been mapped to any Windows user.

40. In the Console window, press Enter to stop running the application.

41. To define the certificate usage declaratively, start by commenting out the call to *SetCertificate* that you just added.

42. Open the app.config file for the TestClient project.

    You must add an endpoint behavior to the configuration to specify the client certificate that should be used for the client credentials. The client certificate is specified in a manner similar to the *SetCertificate* method. The attributes for the *clientCertificate* element in the behavior are used to specify the type of search to be performed as well as the location of the certificate store.

43. Add the following element to the *system.serviceModel* element in the configuration file:

```
<behaviors>
  <endpointBehaviors>
    <behavior name="CertificateDemo">
      <clientCredentials>
        <clientCertificate findValue="localhost"
          storeLocation="LocalMachine"
          storeName="My" x509FindType="FindBySubjectName" />
      </clientCredentials>
    </behavior>
  </endpointBehaviors>
</behaviors>
```

    To be associated with an endpoint, the *behaviorConfiguration* attribute in the *endpoint* element must be set to the name of the behavior.

44. Locate the *endpoint* element in the configuration file and add the following attribute to it:

```
behaviorConfiguration="CertificateDemo"
```

45. Launch the application by pressing F5.

    You will notice (in a few seconds) that the application is working as it did when the certificate was specified imperatively.

46. Press Enter to terminate the application.

▶ **Exercise 2 Create a Custom Authenticator**

The purpose of this exercise is to demonstrate how to create a custom authentication component. As you will see in the code itself, the validation of the credentials is not complex. If you create a real custom authentication component for WCF, you naturally use a different technique than is demonstrated here. Specifically, you would probably use a data store to persist user information instead of hard coding it as this exercise does. However, the process of creating the authentication component and how the WCF pipeline can be configured to use it would still be the same. This exercise demonstrates this process.

1. Navigate to the <*InstallHome*>/Chapter8/Lesson1/Exercise2/<*language*>/Before directory and double-click the Exercise2.sln file to open the solution in Visual Studio.

    The solution consists of two projects. They are as follows:

❑ The DemoService project, a simple WCF service library that implements the *IGet-Headers* interface. This interface consists of a single method (*GetHeaders*) that strips a custom header out of the request and returns it to the client.

❑ The TestClient project, a Console application that generates a request for the service and displays the result in the Console window.

The first step in your process is to create the implementation for the authentication component. This is a class that inherits from *UserNamePasswordValidator*.

2. Right-click the DemoService project in Solution Explorer and select Add Class from the context menu.

3. Change the name of the class in the Add New Item dialog box to **CustomCredentials-Validator** and click Add.

4. Add the following lines to the top of the file to make class references cleaner and add any appropriate references to the DemoService project.

```
' VB
Imports System.IdentityModel.Selectors
Imports System.IdentityModel.Tokens
```

```
// C#
using System.IdentityModel.Selectors;
using System.IdentityModel.Tokens;
```

As has been mentioned, the class must be derived from the *UserNamePasswordValidator* class.

5. Change the class declaration to look like the following:

```
' VB
Public Class CustomCredentialsValidator
    Inherits UserNamePasswordValidator
```

```
// C#
public class CustomCredentialsValidator : UserNamePasswordValidator
```

To provide validation functionality, the class must override the *Validate* method. This method takes the credentials as parameters and throws an exception if the validation fails. Typically, the credentials would be compared to some stored data value, but in this case, hard-coded values will do.

6. Add the following method to the *CustomCredentialsValidator* class.

```
' VB
Public Overrides Sub Validate(username As String, password As String)

    If userName <> "demo" Or password <> "tk503" Then
        Throw New SecurityTokenValidationException("Invalid credentials")
    End If

End Sub
```

```csharp
// C#
public override void Validate(string userName, string password)
{
    if (userName != "demo" || password != "tk503")
        throw new SecurityTokenValidationException("Invalid credentials");
}
```

Now that the class has been created, inject it into the WCF pipeline.

7. In Solution Explorer, double-click the app.config file in the DemoService application.

8. Locate the *serviceBehaviors* element.

   Two changes must be made in this element, both of which are added to a *serviceCredentials* element associated with this behavior. The first change is to add a *userNameAuthentication* element, which will contain a reference to the *CustomCredentialsValidator* class. It links the *Validator* class to the process.

9. Locate the behavior element with the name *DemoService.HeaderServiceBehavior*. In this element, add the following XML element:

```xml
<serviceCredentials>
   <userNameAuthentication
      userNamePasswordValidationMode="Custom"
      customUserNamePasswordValidatorType=
        "DemoService.CustomCredentialsValidator, DemoService"/>
</serviceCredentials>
```

   The second change is to define a certificate to be used by the service. The reason for requiring the certificate is because custom authentication is being defined. It would not be safe to transmit the credentials in plaintext, so WCF requires the credentials to be encrypted. However, to encrypt the credentials, the service must present some of the information in a certificate to the client, which, in turn, means that a certificate must be made available to the service.

10. Add the following *serviceCertificate* element to the just added *serviceCredentials* element:

```xml
<serviceCertificate
    findValue="localhost" x509FindType="FindBySubjectName"
    storeLocation="LocalMachine" storeName="My" />
```

   The last change in the service configuration is to indicate that the credentials will be transmitted within the SOAP headers. Do this by setting the *clientCredentialType* for the *message* element to *UserName*.

11. Add the following element to the *security* element.

```xml
<message clientCredentialType="UserName"/>
```

   You must also set the security mode to *TransportWithMessageCredential* because this enables the use of both HTTPS and the custom authentication validation.

12. Change the *security* element to look like the following:

```xml
<security mode="TransportWithMessageCredential">
```

13. Change the *transport* element within the *security* element to look like the following:

```
<transport clientCredentialType="Certificate"/>
```

Now that the service is ready to go, you must modify the client to pass the credentials.

14. In Solution Explorer, double-click the app.config file in the TestClient project.

15. Locate the *security* element and add the following element, which indicates that the credentials will be sent in the SOAP headers:

```
<message clientCredentialType="UserName"/>
```

As with the service, in the client you must also set the security mode to *TransportWithMessage-Credential* to enable the use of both HTTPS and the custom authentication validation.

16. Change the *security* element to look like the following:

```
<security mode="TransportWithMessageCredential">
```

17. Change the *transport* element within the *security* element to look like the following:

```
<transport clientCredentialType="Certificate"/>
```

To send the credentials, they need to be collected from the user and attached to the request.

18. In Solution Explorer, double-click the Program.cs or Module1.vb file.

In this file, you will see a couple of *Console.Write* statements that request a username and password to be entered. Immediately after each prompt, you must collect input and assign it to a property in the proxy.

19. Add the following line of code immediately after the prompt for the user name:

```
' VB
proxy.ClientCredentials.UserName.UserName = Console.ReadLine()
```

```
// C#
proxy.ClientCredentials.UserName.UserName = Console.ReadLine();
```

20. Use the same basic step to assign the password to the proxy. Add the following line below the prompt for the password:

```
' VB
proxy.ClientCredentials.UserName.Password = Console.ReadLine()
```

```
// C#
proxy.ClientCredentials.UserName.Password = Console.ReadLine();
```

Now the application is ready to run.

21. Ensure that TestClient is set as the startup application, and then press F5 to launch the application. When prompted, type **demo** and **tk503** as the username and password, respectively.

The application will display the expected results.

22. Press Enter to stop the current run, and then restart the application. When prompted, enter a different set of credentials.

   After you have provided a password, an exception will be raised on the server and displayed in the client's window.

Lesson Summary

- Authentication involves any method for confirming the identity of the requester to the service.
- WS-* standards provide the expectations and capabilities of the service to the client.
- All bindings support all client credential types with the exception of *basicHttpBinding* (which supports *UserName* and *Certificate* only).
- Windows credentials are the default authentication mechanism.
- For certain authentication schemes, such as any custom mechanism, the service must be able to present information to the client such as a public key that would be used to encrypt the credentials.

Lesson Review

You can use the following questions to test your knowledge of the information in Lesson 1, "Authentication." The questions are also available on the companion CD if you prefer to review them in electronic form.

NOTE Answers

Answers to these questions and explanations of why each answer choice is correct or incorrect are located in the "Answers" section at the end of the book.

---

1. You have created a WCF application that is using *basicHttpBinding*. You would like to enable the client to log on to the service without needing to provide a user ID and password every time. Which of the following authentication mechanisms should you choose?
    - **A.** *Certificate*
    - **B.** *UserName*
    - **C.** *Windows*
    - **D.** *IssuedToken*

2. You have created a WCF application that is intended to use custom authentication. The configuration file contains the following relevant sections.

```
<bindings>
  <wsHttpBinding>
    <binding name="QuestionBinding" >
```

```
      <security mode="TransportWithMessageCredential">
        <transport clientCredentialType="Certificate"/>
        <message clientCredentialType="Certificate" />
      </security>
    </binding>
  </wsHttpBinding>
</bindings>
<behaviors>
  <endpointBehaviors>
    <behavior name="QuestionBehavior">
      <clientCredentials>
        <clientCertificate findValue="localhost"
          storeLocation="LocalMachine"
          storeName="My" x509FindType="FindBySubjectName" />
      </clientCredentials>
    </behavior>
  </endpointBehaviors>
</behaviors>
```

The endpoint used by the WCF application references both the *QuestionBinding* binding and the *QuestionBehavor* behavior. When the application is executed, a *MessageSecurity-Exception* is raised, with the inner exception indicating that an error occurred while verifying security for the message. Which of the following changes will correct the problem?

A.   Change the *x509FindType* attribute in the *clientCertificate* element to *FindByDistinguishedSubjectName*.

B.   Change the *clientCertificateType* attribute in the *transport* element to *UserName*.

C.   Change the *clientCertificateType* attribute in the *message* element to *UserName*.

D.   Change the *findValue* attribute in the *clientCertificate* element to *CN=localhost*.

Lesson 2: Authorization and Impersonation

The first lesson covered the details associated with securing WCF communications. As was discussed, security at the transport layer uses the protocols associated with the specifics of the wire standard. When securing messages, some standards come into play. WS-Security is one of the most commonly used ones, but there are others, not to mention the easy approach of simply encrypting the message in a manner that client and service expect. In this lesson, the focus is on the options available for securing messages and the imperative and declarative techniques that enable you to do so.

After this lesson, you will be able to:
- Restrict or allow access to operations based on the requester's identity or roles.
- Access the set of security claims through the *ServiceSecurityContext* object.
- Configure impersonation of the requester by the service.

Estimated lesson time: 40 minutes

Authorization

Being able to identify the client is just half the process. Included in the security story for WCF is authorization, which determines the access that is allowed to various resources. This is related to granting access on the service side. Three main elements affect the ability of a service to access resources.

Process Identity

As you know by now, WCF services run in a service host. This host runs in a process, either on its own or combined with other hosts, and the process in which the host is running has a security context, or process identity, that controls the access rights accorded to the process.

You are probably familiar with this concept when applied to ASP.NET. The host for ASP.NET typically runs as a local user called ASP.NET. It is possible for an administrator to change this user ID, but that's a rare occurrence, so when a Web page is executed (or, as it turns out, a WCF service is hosted within Microsoft Internet Information Server [IIS]), its access is restricted to whatever rights have been granted to the ASP.NET user (normally, not very many rights, for security reasons).

Security Principal

Along with the process identity, a security principal is attached to each executing thread. The principal is a container for the caller's identity and the roles that are associated with it. The main difference between the process identity and the security principal is the level of control that is possible. A developer cannot change the process identity for a running process. An element of impersonation is possible (and is discussed later in this lesson), but the underlying process identity is immutable.

In many cases, the principal might be related to a Windows account, but this is not a requirement. Developers can create a new security principal object, complete with its own identity and set of roles. The principal object can then be associated with a running thread. Because the principal contains not just identity information but also the roles to which the user belongs, this provides a mechanism for role-based authentication to be implemented.

The mechanism through which the roles associated with a principal can be used to control access to a method uses the *PrincipalPermissionAttribute*. If you are familiar with .NET permission coding (either imperative or declarative), the pattern will not be new to you. In the declarative form, the *PrincipalPermissionAttribute* is applied to the method in the class that implements the service's contract:

```vb
' VB
<PrincipalPermission(SecurityAction.Demand, Role := "Updaters")> _
Public Function Update() As Boolean
    Return True
End Function
```

```csharp
// C#
[PrincipalPermission(SecurityAction.Demand, Role = "Updaters")]
public bool Update()
{
    return true;
}
```

In this example, the current principal is checked to see whether it belongs to a role called Updaters. In the actual implementation of the attribute, the *IsInRole* method on the principal is called.

NOTE *PrincipalPermissionAttribute* **and Service contracts**

If the *PrincipalPermissionAttribute* is applied to the Service contract (as opposed to the method), an exception is thrown. This attribute can be associated only with a method.

For imperative determination of the *PrincipalPermissionAttribute*, an instance of the *PrincipalPermission* class is created. The constructor for *PrincipalPermission* takes the username and role as a parameter. When instantiated, the *Demand* method can be called to determine whether the current principal has the necessary permissions. The following code provides an example:

```vb
' VB
Dim p As New PrincipalPermission(Nothing, "Updaters")
```

```
p.Demand()

// C#
PrincipalPermission p = new PrincipalPermission(null, "Updaters");
p.Demand();
```

Exam Tip   The source for the principal used by the *PrincipalPermission* class (or the attribute) is not important. It doesn't matter whether the principal is associated with a Windows user or was created by a custom membership provider. All that matters is the result from the *IsInRole* call made while evaluating the permission.

ServiceSecurityContext

The *ServiceSecurityContext* class provides run-time access to information about the security context for a request. It might seem that this is basically the same function as is performed by the security principal. However, this class includes not just identity information but also a set of claims and authorization policies. This additional information enables a much more finely grained level of authorization. The next section discusses the details of how this is accomplished.

Claims-Based Authorization

Along with being able to be integrated into Windows authentication, WCF also supports a claims-based technique for authorization. Before going into the mechanics of claims-based authorization, a couple of moments defining the terminology are helpful.

A *claim* describes an individual right or action that is applicable to a specific resource. It is defined by a combination of three pieces of information: the type of claim, the right that is being claimed, and the resource to which the claim applies. As an example, an *identity claim* might consist of an *identity* claim type, a *possess property* right, and a *username* resource. This claim might be used to represent the identity associated with the requester (as indicated by the username resource) in a WCF communication. It is not difficult to imagine that the client could make claims of other types to represent concepts such as public keys, e-mail addresses, roles, and so on.

A *claim set* (or *ClaimSet*) is an ordered list of the claims that come from a common issuer. For example, a number of claims can be made based on the use of an X.509 certificate. This includes the common name, the DNS name, the public key, and the e-mail address. Although each of these items is an individual claim, the fact that there is a common issuer for the claims means that the claims can be considered as a single group. This abstraction allows a group of claims to be applied or rejected en masse.

An *authorization policy* is an extensibility point by which new claim sets can be added to the current WCF calling context. There are two sources (in WCF) for authorization policies. First, these policies are created based on the security tokens supplied by the requester. The idea with these policies is to provide a common representation for tokens that are generated by heterogeneous sources. The tokens can come from X.509, Kerberos, or username/password combinations. The authorization policy permits a representation that is independent of the source for the data.

The second type of authorization policy comes from configuration details set by an administrator. The goal here is to add claims to the calling context for use with authorization by the service. The types of claims that fit into this category are ones related to local security policy and information. For example, perhaps a service-side database maps requesters to roles. This list of roles is a claim set that is not known to the client but is instead added to the request when it reaches the service.

As part of the authorization process, the *service authorization manager* is the final authority for deciding whether a particular requester should be granted or denied access to a service. The manager is called for each request that arrives at the service. It examines the operation that is being called, along with any available evidence about the caller (found in the *Authorization-Context* object). The *AuthorizationContext* contains all the claim sets that are created based on the various authorization policies, so at the point at which the manager makes its decision, it has access to any claims regarding identity, public keys, e-mail addresses, and so on. After this information has been digested, the service authorization manager makes a go/no go decision for the incoming request.

NOTE   Claims-based authorization

Although the claims-based authorization system is quite powerful, it is not a replacement for the common language runtime (CLR) authorization model that is built into the .NET Framework. Indeed, in many instances, the claims-based authorization mechanism will make changes to the principal that is available to the current thread by adding or removing roles to which the current user belongs.

Accessing the Claims

Now that you know the fundamental terminology, turn your focus to how the claims are used. One of the classes at the heart of claims-based authorization is the *ServiceSecurityContext*. Through this class, it is possible to gain access to the *AuthorizationContext* (which contains the claim sets), the authorization policies, and the identity claim.

Exam Tip   If no security is being applied by WCF, the *ServiceSecurityContext* object will be null. Even if the caller's identity is anonymous, this does not guarantee that the *ServiceSecurityContext* will be instantiated and populated. However, an *IsAnonymous* property on the *ServiceSecurityContext* object can be used to determine whether an anonymous identity was used to build the security context object.

The *ServiceSecurityContext* is exposed through a static property on the *OperationContext*. You can retrieve the *ServiceSecurityContext* as shown here:

```vb
' VB
Dim securityContext As ServiceSecurityContext = _
    OperationContext.Current.ServiceSecurityContext
```

```csharp
// C#
ServiceSecurityContext securityContext =
    OperationContext.Current.ServiceSecurityContext;
```

After the *ServiceSecurityContext* object is retrieved, you can examine it to find out the go/no go decision based on the claim sets. For example, the following code would check to see whether an e-mail address has been included in any of the claims.

```vb
' VB
Dim email As String = String.Empty

Dim claims as IEnumerable(Of Claim) = _
    securityContext.AuthorizationContext.ClaimSets(0).FindClaims _
        (ClaimTypes.Email, Rights.PossessProperty)

Dim c As Claim
For Each c in claims
  email = TryCast(c.Resource, String)
Next

If String.IsNullOrEmpty(email) Then
  Throw New SecurityException("Email address claim not found.")
End If
```

```csharp
// C#
string email = String.Empty;

IEnumerable<Claim> claims =
    securityContext.AuthorizationContext.ClaimSets[0].FindClaims
        (ClaimTypes.Email,Rights.PossessProperty);

foreach (Claim c in claims)
{
  email = c.Resource as string;
}

if (String.IsNullOrEmpty(email))
  throw new SecurityException("Email address claim not found.");
```

The preceding code uses a couple of concepts that are worth consideration. First, notice that the claim sets associated with the request are exposed through the *ClaimSets* property in the *AuthorizationContext* object. This collection (the *ClaimSets* property) contains all the claims associated with the request. You can find the details about any of the claims generated either by the processing of the incoming security tokens or through administrator-configured settings in this collection.

The *ClaimSet* class has a method called *FindClaims*. This method retrieves an *IEnumerable* list of *Claim* objects that meet a specific set of criteria. The specified criteria include the type of claim and the rights of the claim. After the *Claim* objects have been retrieved, it becomes a simple matter to iterate over them to perform any authorization logic required.

Although you might get the impression from looking at the call to *FindClaims* that the type and rights are enumerated values, this is incorrect. Instead, these values are strings that represent a uniform resource indicator (URI) for the claim type and right. There is a *ClaimTypes* class and a *Rights* class that have a number of static properties containing URIs for common types and rights. Table 8-4 and Table 8-5 list the types and rights in these classes.

Table 8-4   Properties on the *ClaimTypes* Class Representing *Claim* URIs

Name	Description
Anonymous	The anonymous user claim.
Authentication	Indicates whether an identity is authenticated.
AuthorizationDecision	Specifies the authorization decision on an entity.
Country	Indicates the country region in which an entity resides.
DateOfBirth	Specifies the entity's date of birth.
DenyOnlySid	Indicates a deny-only security identifier (SID) for an entity.
Dns	Specifies the DNS name associated with the computer name or with the alternative name of either the subject or issuer of an X.509 certificate.
Email	Indicates the e-mail address of an entity.
Gender	Specifies the gender of an entity.
GivenName	Represents the given name of an entity. This is typically the first name of the person represented by the entity.
Hash	Specifies a hash value for the entity.
HomePhone	Indicates the home phone number of an entity.
Locality	Specifies the locale in which an entity resides.
MobilePhone	Indicates the mobile phone number of an entity.
Name	Specifies the name of an entity.
NameIdentifier	Specifies an alternative name for an entity.
OtherPhone	Indicates the alternative phone number of an entity.
PostalCode	Gets the URI for a claim that specifies the postal code of an entity.
PPID	Gets the URI for a claim that specifies the private personal identifier (PPI) of an entity.

Table 8-4   Properties on the *ClaimTypes* Class Representing *Claim* URIs

Name	Description
Rsa	Gets the URI for a claim that specifies an RSA key.
Sid	Gets the URI for a claim that specifies an SID.
Spn	Gets the URI for a claim that specifies a service principal name (SPN) claim.
StateOrProvince	Gets the URI for a claim that specifies the state or province in which an entity resides.
StreetAddress	Gets the URI for a claim that specifies the street address of an entity.
Surname	Gets the URI for a claim that specifies the surname of an entity. This would typically be the last name of a person represented by the entity.
System	Gets the URI for a claim that identifies the system entity.
Thumbprint	Gets the URI for a claim that specifies a thumbprint.
Upn	Gets the URI for a claim that specifies a user principal name (UPN).
Uri	Gets the URI for a claim that specifies a URI.
Webpage	Gets the URI for a claim that specifies the Web page of an entity.
X509DistinguishedName	Gets the string that contains the URI for a distinguished name claim of an X.509 certificate.

Table 8-5   Properties on the *Rights* Class Representing Right URIs

Name	Description
Identity	Gets a string that specifies that the right represents an identity
PossessProperty	Gets a string that specifies that the right represents a property that the entity associated with a claim possesses

The code from the previous example (which determined whether any claim represented an e-mail address) is intended to be included in the logic for a service operation. However, that is not necessarily the best place to be performing this type of logic. In many cases, the desire to reuse authorization logic or to decouple the logic from the operations would lead to a more independent solution. In this case, the logic would be a custom authorization policy.

To implement a custom authorization policy, start by creating a class that implements the *IAuthorizationPolicy* interface. The interface itself is fairly straightforward. There are two properties: *Id* and *Issuer*. The *Id* property is a unique identifier for the authorization component (which, in this case, is the instance of the custom policy class). The *Issuer* property is a *ClaimSet* that represents the entity that issued this policy. In both cases, these are read-only properties. From an implementation perspective, this means that the backing values for these properties should be set in the constructor and returned in the property *Get* function. This is demonstrated in the following code. Please be aware that this example is not, by itself, a full implementation of the *CustomPolicy* class. Specifically, the *Evaluate* method that is part of the *IAuthorizationPolicy* interface is covered later in this section.

```vb
' VB
Public Class CustomPolicy
   Implements IAuthorizationPolicy

   Private _id As String
   Private _issuer As ClaimSet

   Public Sub New()
      _id = Guid.NewGuid().ToString()
      _issuer = ClaimSet.System
   End Sub

   Public ReadOnly Property Id() As String _
      Implements IAuthorizationPolicy.Id
      Get
          Return _id
      End Get
   End Property

   Public ReadOnly Property Issuer() As ClaimSet _
      Implements IAuthorizationPolicy.Issuer
      Get
          Return _issuer
      End Get
   End Property

End Class
```

```csharp
// C#
public class CustomPolicy : IAuthorizationPolicy
{
   private string id;
   private ClaimSet issuer;

   public CustomPolicy()
   {
      id = Guid.NewGuid().ToString();
      issuer = ClaimSet.System;
   }

   public string Id
   {
      get { return id; }
   }

   public ClaimSet Issuer
   {
      get { return issuer; }
```

```
    }
}
```

In the constructor, the value of the *Issuer* property is set to the *ClaimSet.System* value. This value is used if the current application is the issuer of the claim. Technically, it indicates an application-trusted issuer without needing to provide additional details about the issuer. However, conventionally, it is used when the current application (or something that has been configured within the current application's configuration file) is issuing the claim.

The only method that appears in the *IAuthorizationPolicy* interface is called *Evaluate*. This is where the majority of the work associated with the custom authorization policy takes place. The signature of the method includes an *EvaluationContext* and a *state* object.

```
' VB
Public Function Evaluate(ByVal context As EvaluationContext, _
    ByRef state As Object) As Boolean _
    Implements IAuthorizationPolicy.Evaluate
```

```
// C#
public bool Evaluate(EvaluationContext context, ref object state)
```

The *EvaluationContext* object represents the results of an authorization policy doing its work. If claims are generated as part of an authorization policy, these claims are added to the evaluation context. The *state* object is simply an object that is passed into every invocation of the *Evaluate* method for a particular authorization policy. The actual method signature marks the *state* object as being passed by reference. This means that that method can create a new object and assign it to the *state* parameter. In practice, this parameter is frequently used as a cache for previously created claims or to ensure that claims are added only once.

After the authorization policy has been created, it must be associated with the WCF authorization process. You can do this either imperatively or declaratively. When you do so imperatively, there is a little more work than normal. Start by creating a *List* of *IAuthorizationPolicy* objects. After all the policies have been added to the list, a read-only version of the list is assigned to the *ExternalAuthorizationPolicies* property on the *Authorization* property for the service host. The following code demonstrates this technique:

```
' VB
Dim policies As List(Of IAuthorizationPolicy) = _
    New List(Of IAuthorizationPolicy)()
policies.Add(New CustomPolicy())
Dim host As New ServiceHost(GetType(TestService))
host.Authorization.ExternalAuthorizationPolicies = _
    policies.AsReadOnly()
```

```
// C#
List<IAuthorizationPolicy> policies = new List<IAuthorizationPolicy>();
policies.Add(new CustomPolicy());
ServiceHost host = new ServiceHost(typeof(TestService));
```

```
host.Authorization.ExternalAuthorizationPolicies =
    policies.AsReadOnly();
```

The declarative technique is a little easier. You can place an *authorizationPolicies* element within the *serviceAuthorization* element for a service's behavior. The following segment from a configuration file demonstrates adding the *CustomPolicy* authorization policy to the service.

```
<behavior name="DemoBehavior">
  <serviceAuthorization>
    <authorizationPolicies>
      <add policyType="DemoLibrary.CustomPolicy" />
    </authorizationPolicies>
  </serviceAuthorization>
</behavior>
```

Security Token Authentication

The custom authorization policy (or any authorization policy) is built to add claims to the security context for the request. However, this is not the only place where claims are added. When a request first arrives at the service, the security tokens included with the request are evaluated. These claims are also added to the security context.

The process of actually interpreting the token and adding the claims is left to a set of classes known as *Token Authenticators*. There is a separate authenticator for each type of token. Table 8-6 contains a list of the most commonly used token authenticators.

Table 8-6   Commonly Used Security Token Authenticators

SecurityTokenAuthenticator Type	Description
WindowsSecurityTokenAuthenticator	Ensures that the token is a valid Windows token. A *WindowsClaimSet* is generated.
KerberosSecurityTokenAuthenticator	Ensures that the token is a valid Kerberos token. A *WindowsClaimsSet* is generated.
X509SecurityTokenAuthenticator	Validates the certificate. If possible, the certificate is mapped to a Windows identity. An *X509ClaimSet* is generated. A *WindowsClaimSet* is generated if the identity mapping was successful.
WindowsUserNameSecurityToken-Authenticator	Creates a Windows token for the username and password provided. A *WindowsClaimSet* is generated.
CustomUserNameSecurityToken-Authenticator	Validates the username and password against the configured membership provider or password validator. A *UserNameClaimSet* is generated.
SamlSecurityTokenAuthenticator	Ensures that the SAML token is valid. Includes the claims that are part of the token in the security context.

Because a single request can contain more than one token, it is possible that more than one authenticator will be used for the same request. Also, the data store used for authentication depends on the type of token. Windows tokens are authenticated against the Windows domain, as are username tokens, unless another provider has been specified. To change the provider for username tokens, change the *userNamePasswordValidationMode* attribute from *Windows* to *MembershipProvider*. This causes the ASP.NET membership provider to be used. Alternate membership providers can be specified in a single *userNameAuthentication* element. The following segment illustrates the attributes available to this element:

```
<userNameAuthentication
    cacheLogonTokenLifetime="<TimeSpan>"
    cacheLogonTokens="<Boolean>"
    customUserNamePasswordValidatorType="<String>"
    includeWindowsGroups="<Boolean>"
    maxCacheLogonTokens="<Integer>"
    membershipProviderName="<String>"
    userNamePasswordValidationMode="<Windows|MembershipProvider|Custom>" />
```

A number of attributes are directly related to caching the tokens. The *cacheLogonTokenLifetime* attribute specifies how long any individual token should be cached. The *maxCacheLogonTokens* attribute indicates how many tokens should be kept in the cache at one time. Caching tokens is controlled through the *cacheLogonTokens* attribute. If tokens are cached, the claim set generated by the token is stored so that if the token is presented again, the cache claims can be added without having to go back to the security data store.

The *includeWindowsGroups* attribute determines whether the Windows groups to which a user belongs should be included in the generated claim set. If this attribute is set to *true*, there is a potential performance implication because all the Windows groups will be expanded to ensure that all the appropriate groups are included in the claims.

The last three attributes are related to how the username token is authenticated. If the *userNamePasswordValidationMode* is set to *MembershipProvider*, the membership provider specified in the *membershipProviderName* attribute validates the credentials. If the *userNamePasswordValidationMode* is set to *Custom*, the password validator identified by the *customUserNamePasswordValidatorType* attribute authenticates the credentials.

Certificates are authenticated using the rules specified in the *clientCertificate* section of the service behavior. There are two components in the *clientCertificate* configuration. The *certificate* element specifies which certificate to use when secure communication with the client must be arranged. This would normally be required when a secure duplex channel is used and is not part of the authorization process.

The second component is the *authentication* element. This element specifies how the certificate should be authenticated. The following segment illustrates the options that are available:

```
<authentication
    customCertificateValidatorType="<typeName>"
    certificateValidationMode="<validationMode>"
    includeWindowsGroups="<Boolean>"
    mapClientCertificateToWindowsAccount="<Boolean>"
    revocationMode="<NoCheck|Online|Offline>"
    trustedStoreLocation="<CurrentUser|LocalMachine>" />
```

Notice the *includeWindowsGroups* attribute. The value of this attribute determines whether groups are included in the generated claim set. This is the same function as is found in the *userNameAuthentication* element.

There are three types of validation modes. If *certificateValidationMode* is set to *Custom*, the type indicated by the *customerCertificateValidatorType* attribute validates the certificate. If the validation mode is set to *ChainTrust*, the client certificate is validated against the root certificate on the service's computer. A validation mode of *PeerTrust* ensures that the public key portion of the certificate is in the Trusted People certificate store on the service's computer. It is also possible to set the validation mode to *ChainOrPeerTrust*, which simply applies an OR to the previous two descriptions.

As part of the certificate validation, it is possible to use the *trustedStoreLocation* attribute to indicate where peer trust looks for the public keys. The options for this attribute are either *CurrentUser* or *LocalMachine*.

The last attribute associated with the *authentication* element is the *revocationMode*. There is a certificate revocation list, which is a list of certificates that are no longer considered to be valid. The *revocationMode* attribute indicates whether and when the incoming certificates should be checked against this list. If the value is set to *NoCheck*, no check is performed. If the value is set to *Online*, the certificate will be checked with every request. When set to *Offline*, the certificate will be verified against a cached list of revoked certificates.

Impersonation

Impersonation is a commonly used technique, especially within a distributed application. The basic idea is that a service is actually performing an action at the request of a client. However, due to some of the restrictions that were discussed at the beginning of this lesson (such as process identity), it is possible that the service doesn't have access to all the resources required to fulfill the request. However, suppose the client does have the appropriate rights. Wouldn't it be useful for the service to assume the rights of the client? After all, if the client were accessing the resources directly, it would have the necessary rights.

The purpose of impersonation is to extend the access of a service to resources that might be off-limits. It does this by taking the rights of the requester into consideration. Impersonation enables the service to assume the security context of the requester when it must determine whether access to a particular resource is to be allowed.

Impersonation Level

Given that impersonation involves the temporary transfer of rights, the question becomes how far those rights extend. Does impersonation allow the service to use all the rights of the client across the entire network, or is it restricted to accessing local resources? The answer is specified by the impersonation level. This value is provided at the point at which impersonation is defined, and it describes the scope of the impersonation process. Table 8-7 contains a list of the valid impersonation levels and their meanings.

Table 8-7 *AllowedImpersonationLevel* **Values**

Impersonation Level	Description
None	No impersonation level is provided.
Anonymous	No impersonation is allowed. In fact, the service will not be able to obtain any identification information about the client.
Identification	The service is able to obtain identification information about the client, including username and privileges, but the service is not able to make any resource requests on behalf of the client. The service will be restricted to those resources it is allowed access to.
Impersonation	The service is able to make requests for resources, using the client's credentials on the local system. This means that the service might be able to access resources it would not be able to access on its own. However, this capability is restricted to local resources.
Delegation	The service is able to make requests for resources both locally and on remote systems.

Exam Tip For impersonation to take place, the request must have a Windows identity. Without a Windows identity, it is not possible to extend the rights of the service. This makes sense because if the client doesn't have a Windows identity, there are no additional rights that could be conveyed to the service.

Transport-Level Impersonation

Impersonation within WCF can take place at two different levels. Transport impersonation means that the credentials used to secure the transport layer are provided to the service to control access. The most common types of impersonation at the transport layer are *Identify* and *Impersonate*. The *None* and *Anonymous* levels are not recommended for use and are not supported by many transport protocols. The *Delegate* level is a very powerful option and should be used only when the client and the service are both trusted applications.

For the service to use *Impersonate* or *Delegate* levels, it needs to have the *SetImpersonatePrivilege* privilege set. Although any user can be configured to have this privilege, by default, it is available only to members of the Administrators group or accounts that have the Service SID (Local System, Local Service, or Network Service).

As was already mentioned, the transport choice affects the ability to perform impersonation. For example, if named pipes are used as the transport, impersonation and delegation are not supported. If HTTP is used as the transport, the limitations on impersonation become related to the authentication scheme. Table 8-8 shows the authentication schemes and the different levels of impersonation that are allowed.

Table 8-8 Relationship Between HTTP Authentication and SOAP-Based Impersonation

Authentication Scheme	Supported Impersonation Levels
Anonymous	None.
Basic	*Delegate* only. All lower levels are upgraded to *Delegate*.
Digest	*Impersonate* and *Delegate*.
NTLM	*Delegate*.
Kerberos	All.

The second technique used to implement impersonation involves the use of SOAP. Keep in mind the requirement that a Windows identity must be available to the service, so any request needs to have information about the identity included in the metadata associated with the request. SOAP accomplishes this by using one of two methods, cached token impersonation and Service-for-User (S4U) impersonation.

Cached Token Impersonation   When an incoming call is processed, a token is requested from the Security Support Provider Interface (SSPI) or Kerberos authenticator. This is a token associated with a Windows identity and is then cached at the service so that future requests from the same user can be processed more efficiently.

Cached token impersonation is available to some types of bindings.

- *wsHttpBinding*, *wsDualHttpBinding*, and *netTcpBinding* when the client presents a Windows credential.

- *basicHttpBinding* and *basicHttpSecurityBinding* when the security mode is set to *TransportWithMessageCredentials*. In this case, the credentials provided must map to a Windows identity.

- Any custom binding when a Windows client credential is presented and *requireCancellation* is set to *true*. The *requireCancellation* attribute ensures that the validation of the identity is performed with every request, enabling the caller's information to be populated into the Windows *identity* element.

- Any custom binding when a *UserName* client credential is presented and can be mapped to a Windows user. Again, the *requireCancellation* attribute must be set to *true*, and the credentials must use a provider that validates against a Windows domain.

Service-for-User (S4U) Impersonation   The idea behind S4U impersonation is that the token retrieved from Kerberos contains information about the type of impersonation that can be performed—the token that arrives at the service is used directly to provide the required level of impersonation. The types of bindings that can use this impersonation are:

- *wsHttpBinding*, *wsDualHttpBinding*, and *netTcpBinding* when the client presents a certificate credential that can be mapped to a Windows identity.

- A custom binding when a Windows client credential is presented and *requireCancellation* is set to *false*. This last requirement enables the token information to be flowed from the client to the service.

- A custom binding requiring a secure conversation and providing *UserName* credentials. Again, *requireCancellation* must be set to *false*.

Implementing Impersonation

In most cases, impersonation is driven by the need for the service to apply client credentials. For this reason, the configuration options for impersonation take place within the service. The simplest way to implement impersonation is declaratively on the service's methods. The *OperationBehavior* attribute includes a property called *Impersonation*. This property can be set to *Required* or *Allowed*. The following code demonstrates this.

```VB
' VB
<OperationBehavior(Impersonation := ImpersonationOption.Allowed)> _
Public Function Update() As Boolean
    Return True
End Function
```

```C#
// C#
[OperationBehavior(Impersonation = ImpersonationOption.Allowed)]
public bool Update()
{
    return true;
}
```

If the *Impersonation* property is set to *Allowed*, the client credentials can flow to the service. If *Impersonation* is set to *Required*, the service must assume the client's credentials.

Exam Tip   If *Impersonation* is set to *Required*, the service will assume the rights associated with the client even if the service actually has a higher set of privileges. If *Impersonation* is set to *Allowed*, the service will use the client rights only if the service rights don't allow access.

There are times when not all of a method might require impersonation. Perhaps impersonation is required only when a file is being accessed, for example. To allow for this, it is possible to implement impersonation imperatively by using the *WindowsImpersonationContext* class.

To start, you must retrieve the Windows identity associated with the current request. This is available through the *ServiceSecurityContext.Current* object. If the *WindowsIdentity* property is not null (remembering that a Windows identity is required for impersonation), you can invoke the *Impersonate* method on the identity. The following code demonstrates this technique:

```vb
' VB
Dim callerIdentity As WindowsIdentity = _
   ServiceSecurityContext.Current.WindowsIdentity
If (callerIdentity Is Nothing) Then
   Throw New InvalidOperationException( _
      "The caller cannot be mapped to a WindowsIdentity")
End If
Dim context As WindowsImpersonationContext = _
   callerIdentity.Impersonate()
Using (context)
   ' Access a file as the caller.
End Using
```

```csharp
// C#
WindowsIdentity callerIdentity =
   ServiceSecurityContext.Current.WindowsIdentity;
if (callerIdentity == null)
   throw new InvalidOperationException(
      "The caller cannot be mapped to a WindowsIdentity");

using (WindowsImpersonationContext context = callerIdentity.Impersonate())
{
    // Access a file as the caller.
}
```

Although not required, it is a good idea to use a *using* statement when performing impersonation. This enables the statements that use impersonation to be clearly bounded. If you choose not to use the *using* construct, you increase the chance for subtle security bugs to creep into your application.

The two impersonation techniques demonstrated so far operate on a method-by-method basis. It is also possible to enable impersonation for all methods in a service. You do this by setting the *ImpersonateCallerForAllOperations* property on the *ServiceAuthorization* behavior to *true*. You can do this as shown in the following code sample:

```vb
' VB
Dim _serviceHost As New ServiceHost(GetType(TestService))
Dim behavior As ServiceAuthorizationBehavior = _
   _serviceHost.Description.Behaviors.Find _
   (Of ServiceAuthorizationBehavior)()
behavior.ImpersonateCallerForAllOperations = True
```

```
// C#
ServiceHost serviceHost = new ServiceHost(typeof(TestService));
ServiceAuthorizationBehavior behavior =
    serviceHost.Description.Behaviors.Find<ServiceAuthorizationBehavior>();
behavior.ImpersonateCallerForAllOperations = true;
```

If you use this technique, whether impersonation is done depends on a combination of the *ImpersonateCallerForAllOperations* property and the *ImpersonationOption* in the *Operation-Behavior* element. The matrix shown in Table 8-9 illustrates the combinations of values and the impersonation outcome.

Table 8-9 Outcome of Combined Impersonation Option Settings

Impersonation-Option	ImpersonateCallerFor AllOperations	Outcome
Required	true or false	Caller is impersonated.
Allowed	false	Caller is not impersonated.
Allowed	true	Caller is impersonated.
NotAllowed	false	Caller is not impersonated.
NotAllowed	true	An *InvalidOperationException* is thrown.

Quick Check

- Which impersonation type should be used to allow a service to access a local resource (local to the computer on which the service is running), using the client's credentials?

Quick Check Answer

- Setting *ImpersonationLevel* to *Impersonation* is the correct choice. Although setting the level to *Delegate* would work as well, that option provides more access than the *Impersonation* option (the service would be able to impersonate the client on non-local resources as well as local resources). It is always better to allow only the minimum level of security required to perform a function.

Lab: Authorization in WCF

In this lab, the focus is on the process of authorization within WCF in two distinct areas. In the first exercise, the focus is on providing or restricting access to an operation based on the credentials and group membership of the requester. The second exercise will involve the creation of a custom authentication policy.

▶ **Exercise 1   Role-Based Authentication**

In this exercise, you will restrict access to an operation based on the role membership of the requester. The *GetHeaders* operation, which starts off as being accessible, will be restricted to only those people who belong to the HeaderPeople group. Before stepping through this procedure, you must have created a certificate as in Lesson 1, Exercise 1, "Use Certificates for Authentication."

1. Navigate to the *<InstallHome>*/Chapter8/Lesson2/Exercise1/*<language>*/Before directory and double-click the Exercise1.sln file to open the solution in Visual Studio.

   The solution consists of two projects. They are as follows:

   ❑ The DemoService project, a simple WCF service library that implements the *IGet-Headers* interface, which consists of a single method (*GetHeaders*) that strips a custom header out of the request and returns it to the client.

   ❑ The TestClient project, a Console application that generates a request for the service and displays the result in the Console window.

   Initially, the application is configured to work properly. You will notice in the configuration files that the binding has been configured to use Windows authentication within transport security. This has the side effect of providing authentication of the requester's Windows credentials by the service.

   To restrict a particular operation declaratively, the method must be decorated with an attribute.

2. In Solution Explorer, double-click the HeaderService file.

3. Find the *GetHeaders* method. This method will be restricted as to which requester can access it. Add the following attribute to the method declaration.

   ```
   ' VB
   <PrincipalPermission(SecurityAction.Demand, Role := "HeaderPeople")> _
   ```

   ```
   // C#
   [PrincipalPermission(SecurityAction.Demand, Role="HeaderPeople")]
   ```

4. Assuming that you are not currently in a role called HeaderPeople, make sure that the TestClient is the startup project, and then launch the application by pressing F5. (If you are in a HeaderPeople role, change all references to HeaderPeople in this exercise to **HeaderPeoples**, and everything should work as expected.)

   Initially, you will see an exception thrown in the service's method. If you continue executing the application, the service-side exception will be converted to a *SecurityAccess-DeniedException* that is raised in the client.

5. Press Shift+F5 to terminate the application.

   You will now implement the same security restriction imperatively.

6. Start by removing the attribute that was added in step 2.

You must create a new permission object. The constructor for this object, an instance of the *PrincipalPermission* class, includes the user ID and role as parameters.

7. Add the following line to the beginning of the *GetHeaders* method:

```
' VB
Dim p As New PrincipalPermission(Nothing, "HeaderPeople")
```

```
// C#
PrincipalPermission p = new PrincipalPermission(null, "HeaderPeople");
```

After the permission object has been created, the *Demand* method determines whether the appropriate permissions exist in the current security context.

8. Add the following lines of code below the declaration of the *PrincipalPermission* object:

```
' VB
p.Demand()
```

```
// C#
p.Demand();
```

9. Launch the application by pressing F5.

You will see the same series of exceptions being thrown, first on the service and then (if you continue running the application) a *SecurityAccessDeniedException* on the client. When you are finished, terminate the application by pressing Shift+F5.

▶ **Exercise 2   Use Custom Authorization Policies**

By creating a class that implements the *IAuthorizationPolicy* interface, it is possible to inject custom functionality into the authorization process. In this exercise, the customer policy will determine whether WCF has authenticated the requester and, if so, will create a principal object in the HeaderPeople role.

1. Navigate to the *<InstallHome>*/Chapter8/Lesson2/Exercise2/*<language>*/Before directory and double-click the Exercise2.sln file to open the solution in Visual Studio.

The solution consists of two projects. They are as follows:

   ❑ The DemoService project, a simple WCF service library that implements the *IGetHeaders* interface. This interface consists of a single method (*GetHeaders*) that strips a custom header out of the request and returns it to the client.

   ❑ The TestClient project, a Console application. The application generates a request for the service and displays the result in the Console window.

   You must create the class that contains the authorization policy code.

2. In Solution Explorer, right-click the DemoService project, select Add, and then choose Class.

3. In the Add New Item dialog box, change the name to **SpecificRoleAuthorizationPolicy** and click Add.

The class must implement *IAuthorizationPolicy*.

4. Change the class declaration to the following:

```vb
' VB
Public Class SpecificRoleAuthorizationPolicy
    Implements IAuthorizationPolicy
```

```csharp
// C#
public class SpecificRoleAuthorizationPolicy : IAuthorizationPolicy
```

Before implementing the *IAuthorizationPolicy* interface, create a couple of local variables. The *id* class-level variable provides a globally unique identifier (GUID) that uniquely identifies the instance of the policy. Although not used in this exercise, it could be used to help cache values associated with this instance in the *state* parameter passed into the *Validate* method. The *issuer* class-level variable stores the *ClaimSet* that represents the issuer of the policy. Set these values in the constructor.

5. Add the following code to the *SpecificRoleAuthorizationPolicy* class:

```vb
' VB
Dim _id As String
Dim _issuer As ClaimSet

Public Sub New()
    _id = Guid.NewGuid().ToString()
    _issuer = ClaimSet.System
End Sub
```

```csharp
// C#
private string id;
private ClaimSet issuer;

public SpecificRoleAuthorizationPolicy()
{
    id = Guid.NewGuid().ToString();
    issuer = ClaimSet.System;
}
```

The private variables need to have a public property. Both of these are read-only, and they happen to be two of the methods that are part of the *IAuthorizationPolicy* interface.

6. Add the following code to the class:

```vb
' VB
Public ReadOnly Property Id() As String _
    Implements IAuthorizationPolicy.Id
    Get
        Return _id
    End Get
End Property

Public ReadOnly Property Issuer() As ClaimSet _
Implements IAuthorizationPolicy.Issuer
    Get
        Return _issuer
```

```
    End Get
End Property
```

```
// C#
public string Id
{
    get { return id; }
}
```

```
public ClaimSet Issuer
{
    get { return issuer; }
}
```

The second method the *IAuthorizationPolicy* interface requires is named *Evaluate*. This method is invoked in the authorization part of WCF.

7. Start by adding the following method definition to the class.

```
' VB
Public Function Evaluate(context As EvaluationContext, _
    ByRef state As Object) As Boolean _
    Implements IAuthorizationPolicy.Evaluate

End Function
```

```
// C#
public bool Evaluate(EvaluationContext context, ref object state)
{
}
```

Within this method, you add a principal that contains the HeaderPeople role to the evaluation context. To do this, you must get an object that implements *IIdentity*. Such an object is available if WCF has authenticated the request. This information is available in the *Properties* collection of the *EvaluationContext* object.

8. Add the following code to the *Evaluate* method:

```
' VB
Dim prop As Object = Nothing
If Not context.Properties.TryGetValue("Identities", prop) Then
    Return False
End If
```

```
// C#
object prop;
if (!context.Properties.TryGetValue("Identities", out prop))
    return false;
```

When the *Identities* property has been retrieved, the result (found in the *prop* variable) should be a list of *IIdentity* objects. If so, an instance of a *GenericPrincipal* object is created and assigned to the *Principal* property within the *EvaluationContext*.

9. Add the following code below the just-added lines in the *Evaluate* method.

```
' VB
Dim identities As List(Of IIdentity) = TryCast(prop, List(Of IIdentity))
If identities Is Nothing OrElse identities.Count = 0 Then
    Return False
End If

context.Properties("Principal") = new GenericPrincipal(identities(0), _
    New String() { "HeaderPeople" })
Return True
```

```
// C#
List<IIdentity> identities = prop as List<IIdentity>;
if (identities == null || identities.Count == 0)
    return false;

context.Properties["Principal"] = new GenericPrincipal(identities[0],
    new string[] { "HeaderPeople" });

return true;
```

Now that the policy has been created, you must add it into the WCF pipeline.

10. In Solution Explorer, double-click the app.config file in the DemoService project.

11. Locate the *behaviors* section.

You will see that a behavior is already defined with a name of *DemoService.HeaderService-Behavior*.

Because you are dealing with the authorization process, using the *serviceAuthorization* element makes sense. Within that element, *authorizationPolicies* includes a list of the classes that implement *IAuthorizationPolicy*. Inclusion in this list indicates to WCF that the policy should be processed.

12. Add the following XML within the *behavior* element.

```
<serviceAuthorization>
    <authorizationPolicies>
        <add policyType=
            "DemoService.SpecificRoleAuthorizationPolicy,DemoService" />
    </authorizationPolicies>
</serviceAuthorization>
```

Although it might appear that this should be sufficient, it isn't. Specifically, the *Principal* property that was added to the *EvaluationContext* is not processed by the WCF pipeline unless the service is explicitly directed to process it. To tell WCF to process the *Principal* property, the *principalPermissionMode* attribute must be set to *Custom*.

13. Change the *serviceAuthorization* element to look like the following:

```
<serviceAuthorization principalPermissionMode="Custom">
```

14. Ensure that TestClient is set as the startup project, and then launch the application by pressing F5.

    You will see that the application works, even though you are running it as a user who does not belong to the HeaderPeople role (as required by the attribute decorating the *GetHeaders* method).

Lesson Summary

- You can restrict access to methods based on the role membership of the requester.
- You can define method restrictions either declaratively or through direct access to permission objects.
- The set of claims that WCF creates can be used to evaluate the authorization requests.
- Token authenticators are responsible for validating tokens included with the request.
- Custom authenticators can be used when the token being passed doesn't fall within the mechanisms that WCF provides out of the box.
- Impersonation enables the service to access resources on behalf of the requester by temporarily using the requester's security context.

Lesson Review

You can use the following questions to test your knowledge of the information in Lesson 2, "Authorization and Impersonation." The questions are also available on the companion CD if you prefer to review them in electronic form.

NOTE Answers

Answers to these questions and explanations of why each answer choice is correct or incorrect are located in the "Answers" section at the end of the book.

---

1. Regarding the WCF authorization process, which of the following statements is true?
    A. Access to methods cannot be restricted based on the username of the requester, using declarative techniques.
    B. For WCF authorization to occur, the client's configuration file must be modified specifically to support it.
    C. Additional claims on which authorization is based cannot be injected into the WCF pipeline while a request is being processed.
    D. A WCF application can use a custom token to maintain a security context over multiple requests between the same client and service.

2. You have created a WCF application that uses Windows authentication to verify the identity of the requester. The service is being hosted in a Windows service that needs to access a file that is local to the computer on which the service is running. The identity under which the service is running does not have access to the file, but the requester does. Which is the minimum impersonation level that should be used?

   A. *Anonymous*

   B. *Identification*

   C. *Impersonation*

   D. *Delegation*

3. You have created a WCF application that uses Windows authentication to verify the identity of the requester. The service is being hosted in a Windows service that needs to access a file through a Universal Naming Convention (UNC) path. The identity under which the service is running does not have access to the file, but the requester does. Which is the minimum impersonation level that should be used?

   A. *Anonymous*

   B. *Identification*

   C. *Impersonation*

   D. *Delegation*

Chapter Review

To further practice and reinforce the skills you learned in this chapter, you can:

- Review the chapter summary.
- Review the list of key terms introduced in this chapter.
- Complete the case scenario. This scenario sets up a real-world situation involving the topics of this chapter and asks you to create a solution.
- Complete the suggested practices.
- Take a practice test.

Chapter Summary

- The built-in WCF authentication mechanisms cover most of the commonly found security scenarios. Authentication can be performed using either transport or message security, depending on the mechanism.
- In some cases, the service might need the ability to identify itself to the client. In these cases, a reference to a certificate is defined for the service, and the information from that certificate is provided to the client as requested.
- WCF provides for a combination of integrated and custom authorization functionality.
- Authorization within WCF can be customized to look at the set of claims that are produced by WCF as part of its authentication process.
- WCF provides a similar type of impersonation to what is offered through ASP.NET. The service can use various levels of impersonation from having no access to the client credentials to having the ability to act on behalf of the client anywhere within the network.

Key Terms

Do you know what these key terms mean? You can check your answers by looking up the terms in the glossary at the end of the book.

- authorization policy
- claim
- claim set
- policy alternative
- policy assertion
- service authorization manager
- token authenticator
- WS-PolicyAssertions
- WS-SecurityPolicy

Case Scenario

In the following case scenario, you will apply what you've learned in this chapter. You can find answers to these questions in the "Answers" section at the end of this book.

Case Scenario: Choosing the Appropriate Authentication Type

Your company has developed an application that will be distributed to your clients. It enables them to build an order, submit it to your customer service application programming interface (API), and view the status up to the point at which the order is shipped. The technology used to implement the communication between the client portion and the service is WCF. Answer the following questions for your manager:

1. Which type of authentication should be used in the application?
2. Which type of authorization should be used in the application?
3. Which level of impersonation should be used in the application?

Suggested Practices

To help you successfully master the exam objectives presented in this chapter, complete the following tasks.

Authentication

Practice implementing authentication by using the ASP.NET membership provider and custom token authentication.

- **Practice 1**   Create a service that is hosted in IIS. Configure the service to use the ASP.NET membership provider.
- **Practice 2**   Create a custom token authenticator. Configure a Transmission Control Protocol (TCP)-based service to use the token to maintain security information between calls to the service.

Authorization and Impersonation

Practice using custom authorization and impersonation.

- **Practice 1**   Create a custom authorization policy that uses the credentials of the authenticated user to retrieve a list of valid roles from Active Directory Domain Services (AD DS).
- **Practice 2**   Create a service that is hosted in IIS. From within a method, access a file that has been created on the local system. Restrict access to the file so that the IIS user doesn't have access to it. Configure impersonation so that the service can open the file.

Watch a Webcast

Watch a webcast about authentication and authorization.

- **Practice**   Watch the MSDN webcast, "Choosing the Right Authentication and Authorization in Windows Communication Foundation: Part One and Part Two," available on the companion CD in the Webcasts folder.

Take a Practice Test

The practice tests on this book's companion CD offer many options. For example, you can test yourself on just one exam objective, or you can test yourself on all the 70-503 certification exam content. You can set up the test so that it closely simulates the experience of taking a certification exam, or you can set it up in study mode so that you can look at the correct answers and explanations after you answer each question.

MORE INFO   **Practice tests**

For details about all the practice test options available, see the "How to Use the Practice Tests" section in this book's introduction.

Chapter 9

When Simple Isn't Sufficient

For a large number of scenarios, the functionality offered by Windows Communication Foundation (WCF) is stunning in its combination of capability and ease of use. Bindings can be changed at run time, as can encryption or transaction requirements. Developers (within some reasonable bounds) don't need to know which transport is being used. With its goal of providing a single application programming interface (API) for distributed application development, WCF is definitely a success.

Where WCF truly shines, however, is in the nooks and crannies, the places where WCF can be extended to meet whatever needs you might have—and many you don't even know you have. That is the purpose of this chapter: to uncover some of these hidden nuggets and provide enough exposure to them that you realize that if you think WCF can do it, it probably can.

Exam objectives in this chapter:
■ Process generic messages.

    ❑ Handle exceptions on clients.

Lessons in this chapter:

Before You Begin

To complete the lessons in this chapter, you must have:

■ A computer that meets or exceeds the minimum hardware requirements listed in the introduction at the beginning of the book.

■ Any edition of Microsoft Visual Studio 2008 (including Microsoft Visual C# 2008 Express edition or Microsoft Visual Basic 2008 Express edition) installed on the computer.

Real World

Bruce Johnson

In the real world, I find the majority of my time is spent trying to solve challenging problems. I am asked about obscure parts of the .NET Framework, such as how to invoke the parameterless constructor on a generic collection. I have clients who want to find ways to make a .NET application communicate with an ActiveX control when the .NET application is multithreaded and the ActiveX control must be hosted on a form. In other words, I spend an inordinate amount of time trying to make .NET do things that, I suspect, the designers never expected to be done.

While working in this mode, I find WCF to be incredibly useful. If you want to communicate between *AppDomain* instances or processes or even across computers, WCF is the way to go. Test communications locally and then deploy across distributed computers and know that it will work. Need to process incoming messages in which the format cannot be guaranteed up front? WCF has a way to make it happen. If the problem involves communications, odds are pretty good that WCF can help. I don't expect that the information provided in this chapter will be immediately useful for everyone, but if you read this chapter with an eye to how the information might help in the future, you will find that, someday, your recall of one of these topics will save you a great deal of time and energy.

Lesson 1: Dealing with POX

Plain old XML (POX) is not going away anytime in the near future. There is, and will continue to be, the need to create services that receive an arbitrary message in the form of an XML document. Based on some information in the XML, the service will route the XML to another destination, which could be a method within the service. The XML could be sent on to another service or back-end server. Regardless of the details, the service needs to be able to examine the message without knowing at the outset exactly how it is structured. This lesson explains how to handle POX requests in a WCF application.

After this lesson, you will be able to:
- Identify the different types of transport security provided by WCF.
- Determine which bindings are capable of supporting transport security.
- Modify configuration details on the implemented transport security.

Estimated lesson time: 25 minutes

Untyped Messages

Many clients cannot create a SOAP-formatted message. Web browsers, for example, do not have native support for SOAP-based protocols. They are incapable (outside of using some Java-Script functions) of performing anything other than an HTTP-GET request. In situations like this, the request appears as a formatted string or as XML. POX is also useful when the requests arrive over Hypertext Transfer Protocol (HTTP) and there are no requirements for any WS-* functionality. Requests based on the Representational State Transfer (REST) architecture can provide the information required in the Uniform Resource Locator (URL) that is passed to the service.

In both cases, the service must be able to accept the message, regardless of the format, and process it manually. Processing might involve parsing the contents into local objects, determining which operation should be called, and invoking the appropriate method. This lesson discusses the details of how to handle generic, or untyped, messages in WCF.

Wildcarded Actions

To handle untyped messages, you must understand two concepts. The first involves using the *Action* or *SoapAction* value. An *action* is an optional value included with a request. The purpose of the value is to provide a Uniform Resource Identifier (URI) that identifies the intent of the message. If the message is in SOAP format, this is also known as the *SoapAction* value. In SOAP, the intent of the message is expressed as the name of the method on the exposed service that is to be executed. Most interesting of all is that the *Action* value is not required. Although the action might be used as a hint to optimize processing, it should not be required.

In the WCF world, this means that most (but not necessarily all) of the messages that arrive at a service will have an *Action* value. If the request is coming from an unmodified proxy as generated by svcutil, the *Action* value will definitely exist. The scenario being dealt with, however, is when requests are sent by a different client, one that will not necessarily have an *Action* value. Because the *Action* value describes the method to be invoked, there must be a mechanism to handle requests that don't have an *Action* value.

This is accomplished through the *OperationContract* attribute. This attribute includes an *Action* property. To be completely accurate, the value of this property is the URI to be used to map any incoming request with an action to the decorated method. For example, consider the following code:

```vb
' VB
<ServiceContract> _
Public Interface IMessageHandler
    <OperationContract(Action:="uri://service/description")> _
    Function HandleThisMessage(request As Message) As Message
End Interface
```

```csharp
// C#
[ServiceContract]
public interface IMessageHandler
{
    [OperationContract(Action="uri://service/description")]
    Message HandleThisMessage(Message request);
}
```

This interface definition tells WCF to route any message that contains an action of "uri://service/description" to the *HandleThisMessage* method. If no action is specified, then by default, the *OperationContract* attribute uses the name of the method combined with the namespace for the service as the action. This provides the behavior that you have come to expect.

The goal is not, however, to specify a different action. It is to find a way to map unrecognized or nonexistent actions onto a method by setting the *Action* property to an asterisk. The following code illustrates the technique (in bold), although you're not at a working example yet:

```vb
' VB
<ServiceContract> _
Public Interface IMessageHandler
    <OperationContract(Action:="*")> _
    Function HandleAllMessages(request As Message) As Message
End Interface
```

```csharp
// C#
[ServiceContract]
public interface IMessageHandler
{
    [OperationContract(Action="*")]
    Message HandleAllMessages(Message request);
}
```

NOTE   Only one wildcard action

For what should be obvious reasons, no more than one method can be defined within a single interface that has the *Action* property set to "*".

Now when a request arrives and there is no action (or the action is not recognized), the *Handle-AllMessages* method will be invoked. You might also have noticed that the *HandleAllMessages* method actually returns an object of type *Message*. This is the response the client expects to see. If you just want to process the request and not deliver a response to the client, the operation should be marked as being one-way, such as is shown in bold here:

```vb
' VB
<ServiceContract> _
Public Interface IMessageHandler
   <OperationContract(Action:="*", IsOneWay:=True)> _
   Sub HandleAllMessages(request As Message)
End Interface
```

```csharp
// C#
[ServiceContract]
public interface IMessageHandler
{
   [OperationContract(Action="*", IsOneWay=true)]
   void HandleAllMessages(Message request);
}
```

When the *IsOneWay* attribute in the *OperationContract* attribute is set to *true*, the client will not expect a message to be returned from a call to the service. This is different from the behavior expected if the *IsOneWay* attribute were set to *false* in the preceding example. In that case, the client would wait for an empty response to be returned.

Setting *IsOneWay* to *true* is typically done when the call of the service is basically a notification message. The client simply is telling the service that something happened; it has no reason to get a response.

For the scenario involving wildcard actions, however, you expect to send a response back from the service. The format of the response is not known. (It could be based on information provided in the request, for example.) At the same time, the mechanism WCF uses to send information expects a namespace to be included with the response. The default value for the response namespace is the request namespace with the literal "Response" appended. For example, if the *Action* value were "uri://tempuri.org/Update", the default response namespace would be "uri://tempuri.org/UpdateResponse".

If you don't know the action of the request, how could you know the namespace for the response? You can't. Instead, the *ReplyAction* property on the *OperationContract* attribute defines (or suppresses) the action included in the response. The following code specifies that the incoming action should be "Update" and the response should be "UpdateResponse":

```vb
' VB
<ServiceContract> _
Public Interface IMessageHandler
    <OperationContract(Action:="uri://tempuri.org/Update", _
        ReplyAction:="uri://tempuri.org/UpdateResponse")> _
    Function HandleAllMessages(request As Message) As Message
End Interface
```

```csharp
// C#
[ServiceContract]
public interface IMessageHandler
{
    [OperationContract(Action="uri://tempuri.org/Update",
        ReplyAction="uri://tempuri.org/UpdateResponse")]
    Message HandleAllMessages(Message request);
}
```

Although you can specify a URI directly, you can also use wildcarding. This actually causes WCF not to place an Action (or SoapAction) header into the message.

Message Parameters

You might have noticed the *Message* class as the parameter and return value for *HandleAll-Messages*. When performing untyped message processing, such as is demonstrated in the example, the request and response information is communicated through instances of the *Message* class. As it turns out, most message handling is done against a *Message* object. However, in most cases, the *Message* class is hidden beneath layers of functionality.

Still, it is possible to work with the *Message* objects directly. Normally, the scenarios in which the *Message* object is accessed directly include:

- Processing incoming requests without creating .NET objects.
- Generating a response that does not consist of serialized .NET objects.
- Manipulating incoming messages in a generic manner (that is, not one directly related to calling an operation). This includes routing, forwarding, or load balancing applications.

The scenario under discussion falls into the first category. A method receives a *Message* object as a parameter and returns a different *Message* object. When an operation uses a *Message* object, whether it is a parameter or a return value, a number of criteria must be met:

- The operation cannot have any *out* or *ref* parameters.
- The operation can have only zero or one parameters. If there is a parameter, it must either be of type *Message* or a Message contract type.

- If the operation returns a value (a *void* operation is quite acceptable), the return type must either be a *Message* object or a Message contract type.

Four parts of the message can be accessed programmatically. They are the headers, the properties, the version, and the body. The body contains the bulk of what most people think of as the message. It is also the most complex to use, so it's a good place to start.

Accessing the Message Body   The *message body* is retrieved using the *GetReaderAtBody-Contents* method. This method returns an *XmlReader* that can then be used to read the body of the message. A detailed description of the *XmlReader* class is beyond the scope of this book. Suffice it to say that the message body can be traversed from node to node, up and down the hierarchy of the XML document. The implication (which is actually a requirement) is that the request must arrive in an XML format. This is true regardless of the underlying binding.

The *Message* class exposes a *State* property that indicates the state of the message. When a message first arrives at the service, the state is *Created*. After the *GetReaderAtBodyContents* method is called, the state is transitioned to *Read*. The following code demonstrates the use of *GetReaderAtBodyContents*. The message variable used in the code is of type *Message*:

```vb
' VB
Function HandleMessage(msg As Message) As Message
    Dim body As XmlReader = _
        msg.GetReaderAtBodyContents()
    While body.Read()
        Dim bodyText As String = body.ReadString()
        ' Process the body
    End While
    body.Close()
    ' Rest of processing
End Function
```

```csharp
// C#
Message HandleMessage(msg As Message)
{
    XmlReader body = msg.GetReaderAtBodyContents();
    while (body.Read())
    {
        string bodyText = body.ReadString();
        // Process the body
    }
    body.Close();
    // Rest of processing
}
```

Exam Tip   The state of the *Message* object is set to *Read* when *GetReaderAtBodyContents* is called, not when the returned *XmlDictionaryReader* is used.

As well as using *State* to see whether the message has been processed, it is also a good practice to use the *IsEmpty* property to determine whether the message even has a body. When set to *true*, *IsEmpty* means that the body associated with the current message contains no data. This is different than having a message object that is set to *null* or *Nothing*. An empty message can still contain headers and properties.

NOTE   Use *IsEmpty* first

If you call *GetReaderAtBodyContents* on a message in which *IsEmpty* has been set to *true*, an *Invalid-OperationException* is raised.

As an alternative to *GetReaderAtBodyContents*, the *GetBody* method can be used. *GetBody* is a generic method. The type provided with the method is the .NET class that was originally used when the message was created on the client side. The most common usage for *GetBody* is the generic version that takes a *DataContractSerializer* object with the *MaxItemsInObjectGraph* quota disabled. This form of the method emulates the standard deserialization that occurs within WCF in the absence of additional settings. An example of *GetBody* used in this manner follows:

```
' VB
Public Sub HandleAllMessages(request As Message)
    Dim c As Customer = request.GetBody(Of Customer)()
    ' Process the incoming customer object
End Sub
```

```
// C#
public void HandleAllMessage(Message request)
{
    Customer c = request.GetBody<Customer>();
    // Process the incoming customer object
}
```

The message body can be processed only once. This might not be obvious, although the presence of the *State* property and the fact that it is set to *Read* might be a signal. An attempt to access the message body (including a call to *GetBody*) after *State* has been set to *Read* results in an *InvalidOperationException*.

It is possible, however, to access a copy of the message body after it has been processed. To developers, that is good enough. The key is a method named *CreateBufferedCopy* on the *Message* object. The *CreateBufferedCopy* method takes an integer as a parameter and returns a *Message-Buffer* object. The *MessageBuffer* object accesses information about the copied message, including about the body of the message. Because the original message body is processed only once (to make the copy), that restriction is circumvented.

The integer provided as a parameter to *CreateBufferedCopy* defines the maximum number of characters passed into the *MessageBuffer* object. The *MessageBuffer* class includes a number of methods that can be used to work with the message. The *CreateMessage* method returns a copy of the original message. This newly created message has a newly created body with the *State* set to *Created*. The body of this new message can then be processed without impacting the *State* property on the original message.

If your preference is to work with just a portion of the message's body, the *MessageBuffer* class exposes a *CreateNavigator* method. This method returns an *XPathNavigator* object that can then be used to manipulate those sections of the message body in which you are interested.

Regardless of the method used to work with the message body, it is important to finish up by calling the *Close* method. This method releases the resources associated with the *MessageBuffer* object as well as with the *Message* that is passed into the constructor for the object. The following example demonstrates both the *CreateMessage* and *Close* methods:

```vb
' VB
Public Sub HandleAllMessages(request As Message)
    Dim mb As MessageBuffer = request.CreateBufferedCopy(32767)
    Dim c As Customer = mb.CreateMessage().GetBody(Of Customer)()
    ' Process the incoming customer object
    mb.Close()
End Sub
```

```csharp
// C#
public void HandleAllMessage(Message request)
{
    MessageBuffer mb = request.CreateBufferedCopy(32767);
    Customer c = mb.CreateMessage().GetBody<Customer>();
    // Process the incoming customer object
    mb.Close();
}
```

Other Parts of the Message   The body, although important, is not the only part of a message in which a developer might have interest. The *IsEmpty* property has already been discussed. There is also an *IsFault* property that indicates whether the message is actually a SOAP fault message and a *Version* property that indicates the SOAP version used by the SOAP and WS-Addressing structures. Beyond these, a couple of additional properties also require more detailed consideration.

The *Headers* property contains the list of headers associated with the message. The property has a type of *MessageHeaders*, which is an *IEnumerable* collection of *MessageHeaderInfo* objects. Each message header corresponds roughly to a SOAP header, although this is not a requirement. Individual headers can be accessed through the index on *MessageHeaders* or by iterating across the collection. The result from this is the aforementioned *MessageHeaderInfo* object. The properties on this object, shown in Table 9-1, contain the information used to process the header.

Table 9-1   Properties of the *MessageHeaderInfo* Class

Property Name	Description
Actor	This property indicates the intended target of the header.
IsReferenceParameter	This is a Boolean value that indicates whether the message header is associated with a *ReferenceParameters* element in the WS-Addressing specification.
MustUnderstand	This is a Boolean value that indicates whether the service that processes this message must understand the header. If *true* and the service does not understand the header (the actor or the format is not recognizable), a SOAP fault message should be returned.
Name	This is the name of the message header.
Namespace	This is the namespace for the message header.
Relay	This is a Boolean value indicating whether the message header can be relayed.

The *Properties* property is a *Dictionary* of arbitrary objects associated with the *Message* object. There is no correspondence between the values in the *Properties* property and the information sent to the recipient of the message. In general, the values in the *Properties* collection are used by various parts of the *WCF channel stack* to provide hints about the optimal processing to perform.

Creating the Message   Up to this point, the focus has been on processing untyped messages in the service. However, another side to this process is the creation of the original request.

The main method used to build a message is called *CreateMessage*. It is a static method on the *Message* class. The most commonly used overloads for *CreateMessage* take a *version* parameter (to specify the SOAP and WS-Addressing version), a *string* parameter that indicates the name of the SOAP action, and an optional *object*. If the *object* is provided, it is serialized and included as the body of the request. If no *object* is passed to *CreateMessage*, the body of the request is left empty. The following code illustrates how a message can be created:

```vb
' VB
Dim c As New Customer()
c.Name = "Contoso"
c.City = "Redmond"
Dim version As MessageVersion = MessageVersion.Soap12
Dim m As Message = Message.CreateMessage(version, "HandleAllMessages", c)
```

```csharp
// C#
Customer c = new Customer();
c.Name = "Contoso";
c.City = "Redmond";
MessageVersion version = MessageVersion.Soap12;
Message m = Message.CreateMessage(version, "HandleAllMessage", c);
```

After the *Message* object is created, it is sent to the service by passing it to the appropriate method on the proxy in the same manner as any other parameter.

The *CreateMessage* method has two other overloads, which provide alternative mechanisms for specifying the body of the resulting *Message* object. One overload takes an *XmlReader* object or an *XmlDictionaryReader* object. In this case, the XML document that results from processing the reader is passed as the message.

In another overload, the *CreateMessage* method takes a *BodyWriter* object as a parameter. The *BodyWriter* class is an abstract class that generates the XML for the message body. The idea is to create a custom class that is derived from the *BodyWriter* class. In the custom class, the *OnWriteBodyContents* method is overridden. The parameter to *OnWriteBodyContents* is an *XmlDictionaryWriter*. In the method, you construct whatever XML should be placed into the body and inject it into the XML writer.

The last group of *CreateMessage* overloads to consider is one that's typically used in the service rather than in the client. The purpose of these overloads is to create a SOAP fault message. The most basic version takes a *MessageFault* object. There is a separate overload that takes a *FaultCode* and a *string* that contains the reason for the fault. In both cases, when the message is returned to the client, it is processed as a service-side exception.

Lab: Working with Messages

There are times when working with the raw message is a necessary challenge. In this lab, you will create a WCF service that can accept any message. The lab also displays the technique used to examine the body and the headers.

▶ Exercise 1   **Process an Arbitrary Message**

In this first exercise, you will create a service that can accept an arbitrary message. In this case, the message is one that is actually intended for a different Web service.

1. Navigate to the *<InstallHome>*/Chapter9/Lesson1/Exercise1/*<language>*/Before directory and double-click the *Exercise1.sln* file to open the solution in Visual Studio.

   The solution consists of two projects. They are as follows:

   ❑ The DemoService project, a library application. The artifacts in the library include the *IRouter* interface and the *RouterService* class. The *IRouter* interface consists of a single method (*RouteMessage*) that accepts a *Message* object as a parameter. The implementation of this method iterates through the headers in the message and sends the *Name* to the *Trace* output.

   ❑ The TestClient project, a Console application using a proxy to a Web service used in previous chapters, specifically the Header service. It makes a call to the *GetHeaders* method in the proxy.

2. In Solution Explorer, double-click the app.config file in the TestClient project.

3. Locate the endpoint in the configuration file. Notice that the contract is the *IGetHeaders* interface and that the target address is port 8731.

4. In Solution Explorer, double-click the IRouter file in the DemoService project.

    For an untyped message to be processed, the *Action* attribute in the *OperationContract* must be set to a wildcard. For this exercise, the *IsOneWay* attribute is set to *true*.

5. Change the declaration for the *RouteMessage* method in the interface to the following:

    ```
    ' VB
    <OperationContract(Action:="*", IsOneWay:=true)> _
    Sub RouteMessage(requestMessage As Message)
    ```

    ```
    // C#
    [OperationContract(Action="*", IsOneWay=true)]
    void RouteMessage(Message requestMessage);
    ```

6. In Solution Explorer, double-click the RouterService file.

    The service class must be configured to avoid filtering on the address, and the *MustUnderstand* attribute in any headers should be ignored. Otherwise, the service, which just passes the message along anyway, will reject headers marked as *MustUnderstand*.

7. Change the declaration for the service class to the following:

    ```
    ' VB
    <ServiceBehavior(InstanceContextMode:=InstanceContextMode.Single, _
        AddressFilterMode:=AddressFilterMode.Any, _
        ValidateMustUnderstand:=False)> _
    Public class RouterService
        Implements IRouter
    ```

    ```
    // C#
    [ServiceBehavior(InstanceContextMode=InstanceContextMode.Single,
        AddressFilterMode=AddressFilterMode.Any, ValidateMustUnderstand=false)]
    public class RouterService : IRouter
    ```

    In the *RouteMessage* method, the names of the headers are sent to the *Trace* output. The *Headers* property in the *Message* object is a collection of *MessageHeaderInfo* objects.

8. Add the following code to the *RouteMessage* method:

    ```
    ' VB
    Dim h As MessageHeaderInfo
    For Each h in incomingMessage.Headers
        Trace.WriteLine(h.Name)
    Next
    ```

    ```
    // C#
    foreach (MessageHeaderInfo h in incomingMessage.Headers)
        Trace.WriteLine(h.Name);
    ```

9. Ensure that the TestClient project is set to be the startup project, and then launch the application by pressing F5.

In a few moments, you will see a message appear in the Console window, indicating that the message was sent.

10. Open the Output window by choosing Windows from the Debug menu and then selecting Output.

    You will see that a list of the headers, including one named MyHeader, appears in the output.

11. Press Enter in the Console window to terminate the application.

▶ **Exercise 2   Create and Process *Message* Objects**

This exercise explores the *Message* class in more detail and demonstrates the technique to create *Message* objects that can then be passed to WCF services. The exercise also illustrates a mechanism that retrieves the body of a *Message* object.

1. Navigate to the <InstallHome>/Chapter9/Lesson1/Exercise2/<language>/Before directory and double-click the Exercise2.sln file to open the solution in Visual Studio.

   The solution consists of two projects. They are as follows:

   ❑ The DemoService project, a library application. The artifacts in the library include the *IRouter* interface and the *RouterService* class. *The IRouter* interface consists of a single method (*RouteMessage*) that accepts a *Message* object as a parameter. The implementation of this method sends several pieces of information to the *Trace* output, specifically, the state of the object both before and after the body has been retrieved.

   ❑ The TestClient project, a Console application. The application creates a *Message* object manually and then sends it to the WCF service.

   To start with, you create a *Message* object by using the *CreateMessage* method in the *Message* class. The overload you use takes the action for the message as part of the parameter list.

2. First, in Solution Explorer, select the TestClient project.

3. Still in Solution Explorer, click the Show All Files toolbar button.

4. In the TestClient project, navigate to the Reference file under the Service References node (Service References/DemoService/Reference.svcmap/Reference). Double-click the Reference file.

5. Locate the *RouteMessage* method in the *IRouter* interface.

   You will notice that the *OperationContract* attribute has an *Action* property. The value of this property ("http://tempuri.org/IRouter/RouteMessage") will be used when the *Message* object is created.

6. In Solution Explorer, double-click the Program.cs or Module1.vb file in the TestClient project.

   The *Message* object is created in the *using* block for the *proxy* object.

7. Add the following code to the *using* block in the *Main* method:

```vb
' VB
Dim m As Message = _
    Message.CreateMessage(MessageVersion.Soap12WSAddressing10, _
    "http://tempuri.org/IRouter/RouteMessage", _
    "Testing message processing")
```

```csharp
// C#
Message m = Message.CreateMessage(MessageVersion.Soap12WSAddressing10,
    "http://tempuri.org/IRouter/RouteMessage",
    "Testing message processing");
```

After the *Message* object is created, it must be sent to the WCF service.

8. Add the following line immediately after the creation of the message:

```vb
' VB
Dim response As Message = proxy.RouteMessage(m)
```

```csharp
// C#
Message response = proxy.RouteMessage(m);
```

9. When the response comes back from the proxy, display the contents of the message or, if the response is a fault message, display the body of the response. Add the following code after the call to the WCF service:

```vb
' VB
If Not response.IsFault Then
    Console.WriteLine(response.GetBody(Of String)())
Else
    Console.WriteLine(response.ToString())
End If
```

```csharp
// C#
if (!response.IsFault)
    Console.WriteLine(response.GetBody<string>());
else
    Console.WriteLine(response.ToString());
```

10. In Solution Explorer, double-click the RouterService file in the DemoService project.

    The processing of the incoming message involves sending the state to the Trace output and retrieving the body of the request.

11. Add the following code to the *RouteMessage* method:

```vb
' VB
Trace.WriteLine("Initial state is " & incomingMessage.State)
Dim body As String = incomingMessage.GetBody(Of String)()
Trace.WriteLine(body)
Trace.WriteLine("Final state is " & incomingMessage.State)
```

```csharp
// C#
Trace.WriteLine("Initial state is " + incomingMessage.State);
string body = incomingMessage.GetBody<string>();
```

```
Trace.WriteLine(body);
Trace.WriteLine("Final state is " + incomingMessage.State);
```

After the message has been processed, the response must be constructed. If you go back to the Reference file and find the *RouteMessage* method again, there is a *ReplyAction* property on the *OperationContract* attribute. This action creates the *Message* object.

12. Add the following code after the just-added lines:

```vb
' VB
Dim returnMessage As Message = _
   Message.CreateMessage(MessageVersion.Soap12WSAddressing10, _
   "http://tempuri.org/IRouter/RouteMessageResponse", "Done " + body)

Return returnMessage
```

```csharp
// C#
Message returnMessage =
   Message.CreateMessage(MessageVersion.Soap12WSAddressing10,
   "http://tempuri.org/IRouter/RouteMessageResponse", "Done " + body);

return returnMessage;
```

13. Ensure that the TestClient project is set to be the startup project, and then launch the application by pressing F5.

    After a few moments, the "Done Testing Message Processing" message appears in the Console window. This indicates that the WCF service was successful.

14. Open the Output window by choosing Windows from the Debug menu, and then selecting Output.

    You will see, along with the body of the message, that the state of the message changes from *Created* (a value of 0) to *Read* (a value of 1).

15. Press Enter in the Console window to terminate the application.

Lesson Summary

- You can create a WCF service that accepts an arbitrary message as opposed to the typical strongly typed message.
- The *Message* class plays a critical part in this process by providing access to the raw information.
- The *Message* class cannot be combined as a parameter or a return value with other data types.
- Operations that process untyped messages should not be required to understand all headers, and a wildcarded action (and possibly a wildcarded reply) are necessary.
- The body of the *Message* object can be processed only once. After it has been processed, the status is set to *Read*, and any further attempts to use it result in an exception being thrown.

Lesson Review

You can use the following questions to test your knowledge of the information in Lesson 1, "Dealing with POX." The questions are also available on the companion CD if you prefer to review them in electronic form.

NOTE **Answers**

Answers to these questions and explanations of why each answer choice is correct or incorrect are located in the "Answers" section at the end of the book.

---

1. You would like to create a WCF service that is capable of processing any message that arrives at an endpoint. Which one of the following statements is true?

    A. The *Action* property of the *OperationContract* attribute that decorates the method must be set to '*'.

    B. The *Action* property of the *OperationContract* attribute that decorates the method must be set to the namespace for the WCF service's exposed interface.

    C. The *ReplyAction* property of the *OperationContract* attribute that decorates the method must be set to '*'.

    D. The *ReplyAction* property of the *OperationContract* attribute that decorates the method must be set to the namespace for the WCF service's exposed interface.

2. The *State* property of a *Message* object indicates the status of the message body. To retrieve the contents of the message, the generic *GetBody* function is used. What state must the *Message* object be in so that *GetBody* does not throw an exception?

    A. Created

    B. Read

    C. Copied

    D. Written

    E. Closed

Lesson 2: Handling Exceptions in the Client

Chapter 1, "Contracts," began this discussion about faults and WCF. Specifically, Chapter 1 contains a description of how to define the types of exceptions that are raised by the service. Although there was a brief mention of how to deal with exceptions within the client in Chapter 4, "Consuming Services," now is the time to deal with it in earnest.

WCF uses SOAP faults to transmit exception information between the client and the service. Two types of faults can be used, declared and undeclared, and these faults can be transmitted over both one-way and duplex channels. This lesson covers all these combinations of faults.

> **After this lesson, you will be able to:**
> - Create a typed and untyped fault in a WCF service.
> - Determine the type of class that can be used in a typed fault.
> - Handle the faults raised in the service from within the client application.
>
> **Estimated lesson time: 20 minutes**

Receiving Faults

It is certainly possible for many different exceptions to arise as a result of using WCF. However, in the vast majority of cases, there really are only two exceptions that most clients will deal with explicitly. The *TimeoutException* is raised when one of the timeout periods associated with a request or a service is exceeded. The other type of common exception is the *CommunicationException*. This exception is thrown when a recoverable communication error is detected on either the service or the client.

Within the *CommunicationException*, two exceptions are of special note. There is both a generic and a nongeneric *FaultException*. The difference between these two has to do with the client's expectation. The nongeneric version appears when the client has no expectation regarding the exception. The generic version is used when the client has been given advance notice (through the Service contract). This is basically the difference between declared and nondeclared SOAP faults.

Declared SOAP Faults

A *declared SOAP fault* is one in which the operation is decorated with a *FaultContract* attribute. As part of the definition of a *FaultContract* attribute, a custom class that contains information about the fault is included. These two elements make up the declaration of the SOAP fault and, because the elements are part of the Service contract, the client knows, prior to any operation being invoked, that this fault could be thrown. The following code provides a sample of how this could be done:

```vb
' VB
<ServiceContract()> _
Public Interface IFaultService
    <OperationContract()> _
    <FaultContract(GetType(DemoFault))> _
    Function Hello(name As String) As String
End Interface

<DataContract()> _
Public Class DemoFault
    <DataMember()> _
    Public ErrorText As String

    Public Sub New(errorMessage As String)
        ErrorText = errorMessage
    End Sub
End Class
```

```csharp
// C#
[ServiceContract()]
public interface IFaultService
{
    [OperationContract()]
    [FaultContract(typeof(DemoFault))]
    string Hello(string name);
}

[DataContract()]
public class DemoFault
{
    [DataMember()]
    public string ErrorText;

    public DemoFault(string errorMessage)
    {
        ErrorText = errorMessage;
    }
}
```

On the client side, a *FaultException* is caught just like any other exception, which is to say that a *try/catch* block is used, as shown here:

```vb
' VB
Try
    Dim proxy As New FaultServiceClient()
    Console.WriteLine(proxy.Hello("World"))
Catch helloFault As FaultException(Of DemoFault)
    Console.WriteLine(hellofault.Detail.ErrorText)
End Try
```

```csharp
// C#
try
```

```
    {
        FaultServiceClient proxy = new FaultServiceClient();
        Console.WriteLine(proxy.Hello("World"));
    }
    catch (FaultException<DemoFault> helloFault)
    {
        Console.WriteLine(hellofault.Detail.ErrorText);
    }
```

You'll notice that the exception defined in the *catch* statement is the generic version of the *FaultException* class. You might also notice the use of the *Detail* property of the *FaultException* object. In the generic version, the *Detail* property exposes the instance of the fault type returned by the service, which in this example is the *DemoFault* type.

One minor caveat should be noted, and it's the kind of situation that either has no impact on you or is something you need to watch closely for, depending on how you work with exceptions. Specifically, it arises when the type associated with the *FaultException* is a *System.String*.

Typically, the easy way to extract information about an *Exception* object is to use the *ToString()* method. Code such as the following would be considered normal:

```
' VB
Try
    ' Processing
Catch ex As Exception
    Console.WriteLine(ex.ToString())
End Try

// C#
try
{
    // Processing
}
catch (Exception ex)
{
    Console.WriteLine(ex.ToString());
}
```

This is fine for the typical exception, but it will not work as expected for the generic version of the *FaultException*. More precisely, it won't display the string value that appears in the *Detail* property. The solution is to use the *Detail* property directly, as in *Console.WriteLine(ex.Detail)*.

Undeclared SOAP Faults

As you might expect, an undeclared SOAP fault occurs when the nongeneric version of the *FaultException* is thrown. The main difference is that there is no expectation of the type of information included with the exception. In fact, it is just like any other exception in that a

Message property contains information regarding the defaults of the exception. Like any other exception, a *try/catch* block handles it:

```vb
' VB
Try
   Dim proxy As New FaultServiceClient()
   Console.WriteLine(proxy.Hello("World"))
Catch fe As FaultException
   Console.WriteLine(fe.Message)
End Try
```

```csharp
// C#
try
{
   FaultServiceClient proxy = new FaultServiceClient();
   Console.WriteLine(proxy.Hello("World"));
}
catch (FaultException fe)
{
   Console.WriteLine(fe.Message);
}
```

None of this should be exceptionally surprising to an experienced developer because this is the standard pattern for processing exceptions. Indeed, in processing undeclared SOAP faults, the biggest problem is ensuring that the *catch* statements are placed in the correct order if multiple exceptions are caught.

In terms of the inheritance hierarchy, the *CommunicationException* is at the top. The nongeneric version of *FaultException* inherits from *CommunicationException*, and the generic version of *FaultException* derives from the nongeneric version, so any generic *FaultException* objects should occur before the nongeneric version. The *CommunicationException* should be placed after all of them. This is demonstrated in the following example:

```vb
' VB
Try
   Dim proxy As New FaultServiceClient()
   Console.WriteLine(proxy.Hello("World"))
Catch de As FaultException(Of DemoFault)
   Console.WriteLine(de.Detail.ErrorText)
Catch fe As FaultException
   Console.WriteLine(fe.Message)
Catch ce As CommunicationException
   Console.WriteLine(ce.Message)
End Try
```

```csharp
// C#
try
{
   FaultServiceClient proxy = new FaultServiceClient();
   Console.WriteLine(proxy.Hello("World"));
}
```

```
catch (FaultException<DemoFault> de)
{
    Console.WriteLine(de.Detail.ErrorText);
}
catch (FaultException fe)
{
    Console.WriteLine(fe.Message);
}
catch (CommunicationException ce)
{
    Console.WriteLine(ce.Message);
}
```

It should also be pointed out that SOAP faults, both declared and undeclared, can also be used in duplex scenarios. When the service performs a callback into the client, it is possible for the client to throw a *FaultException* (both generic and nongeneric). The key is to have the *Fault-Contract* attribute decorating the operation in the callback interface.

Lab: Exceptions in WCF Services

In this lab, you will examine the two mechanisms for returning exceptions from WCF services. In the first exercise, a typed fault is created and returned from a WCF service operation. In the second exercise, an untyped fault serves the same purpose.

▶ **Exercise 1   Return Typed Faults**

In this exercise, you will create and return a typed fault from a method call. The *RouteMessage* method will look for a particular header in the request. If the request does not contain the header, a fault type will be returned.

1. Navigate to the *<InstallHome>*/Chapter9/Lesson2/Exercise1/*<language>*/Before directory and double-click the Exercise1.sln file to open the solution in Visual Studio.

   The solution consists of two projects. They are as follows:

   ❑ The DemoService project, a library application. The artifacts in the library include the *IRouter* interface and the *RouterService* class. The *IRouter* interface consists of a single method (*RouteMessage*) that accepts a *Message* object as a parameter. The implementation of this method sends a number of pieces of information to the *Trace* output, specifically, the state of the object both before and after the body has been retrieved.

   ❑ The TestClient project, a Console application. The application creates a *Message* object manually and then sends it to the WCF service.

   In Solution Explorer, right-click the DemoService project, select Add, and then choose Class from the context menu.

2. Change the name to RouterFault and click Add.

   To be returned in a fault, the class declaration must be marked with the *DataContract* attribute.

3. Change the class declaration to the following:

```vb
' VB
<DataContract()> _
Public Class RouterFault
```

```csharp
// C#
[DataContract()]
public class RouterFault
```

This class must have two properties. *ErrorText* contains a description of the fault, and *MissingHeader* contains the name of the header that was not present in the request.

4. Change the implementation of the *RouterFault* class to the following:

```vb
' VB
<DataMember()> _
Public ErrorText As String

<DataMember()> _
Public MissingHeader As String

Public Sub New(_error As String, _missingHeader As String)
    ErrorText = _error
    MissingHeader = _missingHeader
End Sub
```

```csharp
// C#
[DataMember()]
public string ErrorText;

[DataMember()]
public string MissingHeader;

public RouterFault(string error, string missingHeader)
{
    ErrorText = error;
    MissingHeader = missingHeader;
}
```

To indicate to the client that the fault could be returned, the *RouteMessage* method on the interface must be decorated with the *FaultContract* attribute.

5. In Solution Explorer, double-click the IRouter file.

6. Change the declaration of the *RouteMessage* method in the interface to the following:

```vb
' VB
<OperationContract()> _
<FaultContract(GetType(RouterFault))> _
Sub RouteMessage(requestMessage As Message)
```

```csharp
// C#
[OperationContract]
[FaultContract(typeof(RouterFault))]
void RouteMessage(Message requestMessage);
```

The last piece is to throw the *RouterFault* when appropriate. You do this in the *Route-Message* method.

7. In Solution Explorer, double-click the RouterService file in the DemoService project. The *RouterFault* will be thrown when a header named MyHeader is not found.

8. Add the following code to the *RouteMessage* method:

```vb
' VB
Dim customHeaderFound As Boolean = False
Dim h As MessageHeaderInfo

For Each h In incomingMessage.Headers
    If h.Name = "MyHeader" Then
        customHeaderFound = True
    End If
Next

If Not customHeaderFound Then
    Throw New FaultException(Of RouterFault)( _
        New RouterFault("Missing a required header", "MyHeader"), _
        New FaultReason("A header is missing"))
End If
```

```csharp
// C#
bool customHeaderFound = false;
foreach (MessageHeaderInfo h in incomingMessage.Headers)
    if (h.Name == "MyHeader")
        customHeaderFound = true;

if (!customHeaderFound)
    throw new FaultException<RouterFault>(
        new RouterFault("Missing a required header", "MyHeader"),
        new FaultReason("A header is missing"));
```

To catch the exception, the client must include it in the *try/catch* block.

9. In Solution Explorer, double-click the Program.cs or Module1.vb file in the TestClient project.

10. Replace the call to the WCF service with the following code (in C# you must delete the *if* statement that checks *response*):

```vb
' VB
Try
    proxy.RouteMessage(m)
Catch ex As FaultException(Of DemoService.RouterFault)
    Console.WriteLine(ex.Message)
End Try
```

```csharp
// C#
try
{
    proxy.RouteMessage(m);
```

```
}
catch (FaultException<RouterFault> ex)
{
    Console.WriteLine(ex.Message);
}
```

Because the *RouterFault* class was added to the DemoService project (as well as included in the contract information), the proxy to DemoService must be updated.

11. In Solution Explorer, expand the Service References node. Right-click DemoService and select Update Service Reference from the context menu.

In a few moments, the DemoService proxy will be updated. You might need to build the DemoService application before updating the service reference. At this point in C#, in the TestClient project, you must add a reference to DemoService as well as add a *using* statement to the top of the file.

12. Also, updating the service reference for DemoService caused the app.config file in the TestClient project to have duplicate endpoints created. One of them needs to be removed for the project to work correctly. In Solution Explorer, double-click on the app.config file in the TestClient project.

13. Locate the two *endpoint* elements in the file. You will notice that one of them contains an *identity* element while the other one does not. Delete the *endpoint* that does contain the *identity* element.

14. Ensure that the TestClient project is set as the startup project, and then launch the application by pressing F5.

In a few moments, you might see an exception thrown from within the WCF service. This is the exception raised in the service when the necessary header is missing.

15. If you receive the exception, continue running the application by pressing F5 again.

Now the *RouterFault* is passed back to the client application, where the exception is caught and the appropriate message is displayed in the Console window.

16. Press Enter to stop running the application.

17. In Solution Explorer, double-click the app.config file in the TestClient project.

To correct the exception, a header must be added to the endpoint.

18. Add the following XML element to the *endpoint* element in the configuration file:

```
<headers>
    <MyHeader name="Sample"
        xmlns="http://tempuri.org">This is my header data</MyHeader>
</headers>
```

19. Launch the application by pressing F5.

Now the application runs without an exception being raised.

20. Press Enter to terminate the application.

▶ **Exercise 2 Return Untyped Faults**

The first exercise explored how a strongly typed fault can be returned from a WCF service. This exercise looks at the alternative, an untyped fault generated while a service processes a request.

1. Navigate to the *<InstallHome>*/Chapter9/Lesson2/Exercise2/*<language>*/Before directory and double-click the Exercise2.sln file to open the solution in Visual Studio.

   The solution consists of two projects. They are as follows:

   ❑ The DemoService project, a library application. The artifacts in the library include the *IRouter* interface and the *RouterService* class. The *IRouter* interface consists of a single method (*RouteMessage*) that accepts a *Message* object as a parameter. The implementation of this method sends several pieces of information to the *Trace* output, specifically, the state of the object both before and after the body has been retrieved.

   ❑ The *TestClient* project, a Console application. The application creates a *Message* object manually and then sends it to the WCF service.

2. In Solution Explorer, double-click the RouterService file in the DemoService project.

   Near the end of the *RouteMessage* method, there is a call to the *GetBody* method on the *Message* object. This is a generic call and is currently set up to require the body to be a *string* object.

3. In Solution Explorer, double-click the Program.cs or Module1.vb file in the TestClient project.

4. In the *CreateMessage* call, change the last parameter so that, instead of a string, it is an integer. Modify the statement that declares the *Message* object to read as follows:

```vb
' VB
Dim m As Message = _
    Message.CreateMessage(MessageVersion.Soap12WSAddressing10, _
    "http://tempuri.org/IRouter/RouteMessage", 5)
```

```csharp
// C#
Message m = Message.CreateMessage(MessageVersion.Soap12WSAddressing10,
    "http://tempuri.org/IRouter/RouteMessage", 5);
```

At the moment, the *try/catch* block is looking for a specific *FaultException*.

5. To capture a general fault that is generated in the WCF service, add the following *catch* block to the end of the *try/catch* statement:

```vb
' VB
Catch fex As FaultException
    Console.WriteLine(fex.Message)
```

```csharp
// C#
catch (FaultException fex)
{
```

```
        Console.WriteLine(fex.Message);
    }
```

6. Ensure that the TestClient is set to be the startup project, and then launch the application by pressing F5.

   In a few moments, you see an exception thrown in the client. The exception indicates that an invalid type was used as a parameter.

7. Stop running the application.

   To provide more information about the exception, the service will need to raise a *FaultException* instead of allowing the default exception to pass through.

8. Go to the *RouteMessage* method in the RouterService file.

   You must wrap the call to the *GetBody* (and the *WriteLine*) method with a *try/catch* block. Then, in the *catch* portion, you create a *FaultException* manually. This exception can then be raised to the client.

9. Replace the *GetBody* and *WriteLine* statements with the following:

```
' VB
Try
    Dim body As String = incomingMessage.GetBody(Of String)()
    Trace.WriteLine(body)
Catch ex As Exception
    Throw New FaultException( _
        New FaultReason("The body is the wrong type"))
End Try
```

```
// C#
try
{
    string body = incomingMessage.GetBody<string>();
    Trace.WriteLine(body);
}
catch (Exception ex)
{
    throw new FaultException(new
        FaultReason("The body is the wrong type"));
}
```

10. Launch the application by pressing F5.

    In a few moments, an exception is raised in the service object.

11. Continue running the application by pressing F5.

    A message from the *FaultException* (The Body Is The Wrong Type) appears on the console because the *FaultException* was successfully caught and processed by the client.

Lesson Summary

- A WCF service can raise both declared and undeclared faults.
- Declared faults have the advantage of providing more detailed contextual information about the exception being raised than what is available through the built-in *Exception* classes.
- It is important to ensure that the exceptions that can be thrown by the service are caught in the correct order.

Lesson Review

You can use the following questions to test your knowledge of the information in Lesson 2, "Handling Exceptions in the Client." The questions are also available on the companion CD if you prefer to review them in electronic form.

NOTE Answers

Answers to these questions and explanations of why each answer choice is correct or incorrect are located in the "Answers" section at the end of the book.

1. Consider a class that is expected to be used as a typed fault for a WCF operation. Which one of the following statements is true?

   A. The class must derive from the *System.Exception* class.

   B. The class must be serializable.

   C. The class must be implemented in a dynamic-link library (DLL) library that is shared by both the client and the service.

   D. All the properties in the class must be initialized as part of the constructor.

2. Consider the following code from a WCF client application.

```vb
' VB
Try
    Dim proxy As New FaultServiceClient()
    Console.WriteLine(proxy.Hello("World"))
Catch de As FaultException(Of DemoFault)
    Console.WriteLine("DemoFault returned")
Catch fe As FaultException
    Console.WriteLine("FaultException returned")
Catch ce As CommunicationException
    Console.WriteLine("CommunicationException returned")
End Try
```

```csharp
// C#
try
{
    FaultServiceClient proxy = new FaultServiceClient();
    Console.WriteLine(proxy.Hello("World"));
}
catch (FaultException<DemoFault> de)
{
    Console.WriteLine("DemoFault returned");
}
catch (FaultException fe)
{
    Console.WriteLine("FaultException returned");
}
catch (CommunicationException ce)
{
    Console.WriteLine("CommunicationsException returned");
}
```

In the service class, the following code is executed:

```vb
' VB
Throw New ApplicationException("Bad stuff happened")
```

```csharp
// C#
throw new ApplicationException("Bad stuff happened");
```

Which of the following would appear in the Console window?

   A. Hello World

   B. DemoFault returned

   C. FaultException returned

   D. CommunicationException returned

Chapter Review

To further practice and reinforce the skills you learned in this chapter, you can:

- Review the chapter summary.
- Review the list of key terms introduced in this chapter.
- Complete the case scenario. This scenario sets up a real-world situation involving the topics of this chapter and asks you to create a solution.
- Complete the suggested practices.
- Take a practice test.

Chapter Summary

- WCF provides a mechanism that allows a service to receive and send the raw *Message* object instead of the strongly typed method calls that are more typically used.
- Exceptions thrown in the service are converted to a *FaultException* prior to being passed to the client.

Key Terms

Do you know what these key terms mean? You can check your answers by looking up the terms in the glossary at the end of the book.

- action
- declared SOAP fault
- message body
- Plain old XML (POX)
- WCF channel stack

Case Scenario

In the following case scenario, you apply what you've learned about POX and handling exceptions on the client. You can find answers to these questions in the "Answers" section at the end of this book.

Case Scenario: Working with Raw Messages

Your company has developed a WCF service that will be exposed to external clients through the Internet. Unfortunately, the latest version of the service includes a signficant breaking change to the interface being used. However, you cannot force your clients to upgrade simultaneously, meaning that you must continue to support both the old and the new versions of the interface for the foreseeable future.

Answer the following questions for your manager:

1. What is the best way to deal with this situation?
2. If a generic message handling service is used, should that service also perform logging functionality?

Suggested Practices

To help you successfully master the exam objectives presented in this chapter, complete the following tasks.

Working with POX

Version a WCF service.

- **Practice**   Create a WCF service that can handle different versions of an interface. Examine the incoming message to determine which version of the service should receive and process the request.

Watch a Webcast

Watch a webcast about configuring WCF.

- **Practice**   Watch the MSDN webcast, "Exceptions and Faults," by Michele Leroux Bustamante, available on the companion CD in the Webcasts folder.

Take a Practice Test

The practice tests on this book's companion CD offer many options. For example, you can test yourself on just one exam objective, or you can test yourself on all the 70-503 certification exam content. You can set up the test so that it closely simulates the experience of taking a certification exam, or you can set it up in study mode so that you can look at the correct answers and explanations after you answer each question.

MORE INFO   **Practice tests**

For details about all the practice test options available, see the "How to Use the Practice Tests" section in this book's introduction.

Chapter 10

Sessions and Instancing

When a discussion of Windows Communication Foundation (WCF) turns to the concepts and details of sessions and instancing, it seems as though you're starting to tread on common ground with Web developers. ASP.NET developers are likely to be familiar with the concepts associated with sessions. Although less directly, ASP.NET developers also deal with some of the aspects associated with instancing in relation to having a Web site hosted on a Web farm. However, the instancing issues will be more familiar to developers who have used .NET remoting in the past.

This chapter finds common ground for all developers, regardless of their background, and answers the question of how sessions function within the WCF world. It also describes the various instancing options and the implications each choice has on the available functionality. This content is definitely part of the certification exam; however, pay close attention because it is also frequently at the heart of real-world design choices.

Exam objectives in this chapter:
- Manage instances.
- Manage sessions.

Lessons in this chapter:

Before You Begin

To complete the lessons in this chapter, you must have:

- A computer that meets or exceeds the minimum hardware requirements listed in the introduction at the beginning of the book.
- Any edition of Microsoft Visual Studio 2008 (including Microsoft Visual C# 2008 Express edition or Microsoft Visual Basic 2008 Express edition) installed on the computer.

Real World

Bruce Johnson

The session side of this chapter is, again, probably familiar to those of you who have worked with ASP.NET. The idea is a simple one: By allowing the service to identify the client that made a request, it becomes possible to save state information with that client. This information can facilitate sophisticated interactions between the client and the service. What is nice about the session model that WCF provides is that the binding is, for the most part, irrelevant. Like so much else in WCF, the details are hidden from view, and it just works.

The instancing side of this chapter is a little different. It's more in the category of "what you need to know to be an expert." In most cases, you will not need to know the details of instancing beyond the need to set the mode to per call, per session, or singleton, but within that world, some strange things have been known to happen. You are moving into an area in which subtle bugs can arise, and if you have the detailed knowledge provided in this chapter, you will be able to identify the source of the problem more quickly and give off the heroic aura that experts are expected to have.

Lesson 1: Instancing Modes

Instancing should, for the most part, be a service-side implementation detail that has no effect on the client, and this is generally the case. However, the demands of the client frequently do influence the instancing that should be used. Instancing can affect scalability, throughput, transactions, and queued calls, so although the client might be oblivious to the instancing mode, the service can't reciprocate. This lesson considers the different types of possible instancing, along with how they are set up and the ramifications of the choices.

After this lesson, you will be able to:
- Identify the different instancing modes supported by WCF.
- Configure the service to preserve state information for calls from a single client.
- Share an instance of a proxy class between two or more clients.

Estimated lesson time: 50 minutes

Instancing

WCF is responsible for binding an incoming message to a particular service instance. When a request comes in, WCF determines whether an existing instance of the service class (the *service instance*) can process the request. The decision matrix for this choice is basically the instancing management that WCF provides.

When it comes to the question of which instancing mode to use, there is no correct answer. A variety of factors must be balanced to determine the most appropriate mode for the given situation. For this reason, this lesson covers all the modes in great detail and provides scenarios in which they might be the most appropriate choice. However, even with the given scenarios, the choice is seldom clear, and a small change in the importance of one factor can tip the scale to another choice. Your benefit from this discussion should be a general sense of when a particular mode is more or less likely to be chosen.

The determination of the instancing mode is done on the service side. This is to be expected because it is an implementation detail that should be hidden from the caller. The mode is defined within the service behavior. This means that the instancing mode is used across all the endpoints of a service. It can also be applied directly in the service's implementation class.

Three choices are available for the *InstanceContextMode*. They are per call mode, per session mode, and singleton mode. The meanings of these modes are described in the next few sections, but those are not the only available choices. In the original version of WCF, there was also an option in the *InstanceContextMode* enumeration called *Shareable*. Although the functionality still exists, the enumerated value does not. Instead, to share the same service instance across multiple requests, the service must intercept the request, determine which instance the requestor wants, and then provide that instance to the run time. The upcoming sections describe how this is done.

Per Call Mode

In per call mode, every single request gets its own copy of a service implementation object. Figure 10-1 illustrates the basic flow for the request

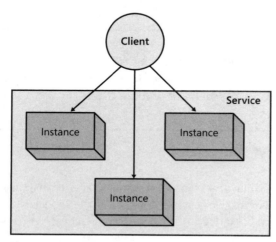

Figure 10-1   Per call instantiation

The client makes a request to the service through a proxy. When the request arrives at the service host, the host creates an instance of the service's implementation class. This class is then called to process the request. After the request is complete and the response returned to the client, the implementation object is disposed of.

NOTE   IDisposable **and** Dispose

Each implementation object implements the *IDisposable* interface. When the object is finished (defined by the instancing mode), the *Dispose* method is called. Although the object has not necessarily been garbage collected immediately, it is in a state in which no further calls can be made to any method.

Per call instancing is the default mode for WCF. There are a number of reasons for making this particular choice. For the developer, per call mode requires the least amount of consideration given to concurrency. If each request has its own copy of the object, there is no need to worry about a shared value being updated in a non-atomic manner.

Historically, the instancing mode many client/server applications used was one implementation object per client. This is a simple approach, but a number of problems affect performance.

For example, consider the issue associated with a scarce resource. If the service object opens a connection to a database and keeps that connection open for its lifetime, the resource is unavailable for use by other instances, yet the period of time the resource might actually be required is quite small.

It is well understood by designers of distributed applications that this model has scalability weaknesses. One of the solutions is to reduce the time the implementation object exists. This is the genesis for the per call mode. In per call, the implementation object is instantiated as soon as it is needed, and it is disposed of as soon as the request is completed. If the object holds on to a scarce resource, the lifetime of the object has been reduced to minimize the impact holding that resource has on overall performance.

However, "simple to use" is not the same as "best." And that per call instancing hides many of the challenges associated with distributed applications doesn't mean that it should be the mode you always use. Consider some of the drawbacks associated with this approach.

A **scarce resource** is one that is expensive to allocate or is limited in the number available for use. A canonical example is a file that resides on the service system's hard drive. If the file is opened for update, only one service implementation instance can have it open at a time, so in a per call instancing mode, only the first request in can be processed through to completion. The second (and subsequent) requests will block, waiting for the physical file to become available. Although a physical file is an extreme scenario, there are many other scenarios. Database connections, network connections (used to make Web service calls), or communications ports all qualify as scarce resources.

One of the keys to making this model work is the existence of a proxy object for the service. The typical programming model that has already been discussed has the client instantiating an object and maintaining a reference to it for the life of the application. However, in per call mode, the object that is referred to *should* be disposed of. This would typically invalidate the reference, a generally undesirable outcome. However, in the world of WCF, the client is actually holding a reference to the proxy. The proxy is not disposed of with every call. Instead, it becomes part of the proxy's job to re-create the service implementation object as necessary.

An ancillary benefit to this model is how it works with transactional applications. The need to re-create the object and reconnect to scarce resources works well in an environment in which the instance state must be deterministic.

As has already been mentioned, the instancing mode is set at the service level. The following code demonstrates (in bold) how to set the mode to per call.

```vb
' VB
<ServiceBehavior(InstanceContextMode:=InstanceContextMode.PerCall)> _
Public Class UpdateService
    Implements IUpdateService
```

```
    ...
End Class

// C#
[ServiceBehavior(InstanceContextMode = InstanceContextMode.PerCall)]
class UpdateService : IUpdateService {...}
```

Although, theoretically, the client doesn't need to be aware of whether the service is running in per call mode, the reality is that per call means that no state can exist between calls. It becomes a design issue, but the client cannot expect that the results from one call will be preserved or used in the second call to the service. If this is a requirement, regardless of the reason, it becomes part of the service's task to ensure that state is saved across calls. This would typically be done by persisting the state into a service-local store (such as a database). Then, when subsequent requests come in, the previously saved state can be restored and used.

If the service's design calls for this pattern, there is an impact on the design of the Service contract. Specifically, each operation must include a parameter that identifies the client making the request. This allows the service method to retrieve the state associated with the client. The actual parameter that is used could be a business-level value (customer number, order number, account number) or a meaningless value (such as *guid*).

From a general design perspective, per call mode is best used when individual operations are short and the operation does not spawn any background threads that continue processing after the request is complete. The reason for this second stipulation has to do with the disposal of the implementation object. If an operation were to spin up something that isn't completed prior to the response being returned to the client, the object will not be around to receive the result. It will have been destroyed as soon as the request is finished.

Per Session Mode

Given the idea that a parameter would be passed into a service's method to retrieve state, it seems a short jump to this next mode. WCF can maintain a private session between a client and a particular instance of the service's implementation object.

The key to understanding the intricacies of per session mode is understanding what is happening internally. Each client, upon the first request to the service, gets an instance of the service's implementation object. This instance is dedicated to processing the requests that come from that client. Any subsequent calls are considered to be part of the same session (with some exceptions that will be described shortly), and the calls are processed by the same instance of the implementation object. Figure 10-2 illustrates this relationship.

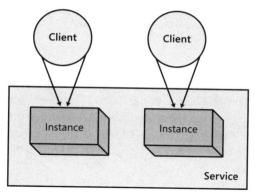

Figure 10-2   Per session mode interactions

There are two components to per session mode. The contractual piece involves letting the client know that a session is required. This is necessary because to maintain the session, the client must include an identifier to locate the appropriate implementation object in the service. To indicate to the contract that a session is to be maintained, the *ServiceContract* attribute includes a *SessionMode* property. For per session mode to be used, this Boolean value must be set to *SessionMode.Required*, as demonstrated in bold in the following code.

```vb
' VB
<ServiceContract(SessionMode:=SessionMode.Required)> _
Public Interface IUpdateService
    ' Interface definition code goes here
End Interface
```

```csharp
// C#
[ServiceContract(SessionMode = SessionMode.Required)]
public interface IUpdateService
{
    // Interface definition code goes here
}
```

The second component of the configuration is behavioral in nature. WCF needs to be told that you would like to use per session mode and that the service instance should be kept alive throughout the session. You do this by setting the *InstanceContextMode* in the service behavior as illustrated in bold in the following code.

```vb
' VB
<ServiceBehavior(InstanceContextMode:=InstanceContextMode.PerSession)> _
Public Class UpdateService
    Implements IUpdateService

    ' Implementation code goes here

End Class
```

```csharp
// C#
[ServiceBehavior(InstanceContextMode = InstanceContextMode.PerSession)]
public class UpdateService : IUpdateService
{
    // Implementation code goes here
}
```

Now it's time to talk about some of the details. The relationship isn't quite between the client and the service. It is actually between a specific instance of the proxy class used by the client and the service. When you create a proxy for a WCF service, an identifier for that proxy is generated. This identifier is used by the service host to direct any requests to the appropriate instance. However, the identifier is associated with the instance of the proxy class, so if a single client creates more than one instance of the proxy class, those instances will not combine sessions. Each proxy will get its own instance of the service implementation class.

After an instance is created for a proxy, the instance remains in memory for the length of the session. For this reason, it is possible to maintain state in memory. This makes the programming model quite similar to the traditional client–server approach, but this also means that per session mode suffers from the same issues that the client server model has. It has issues with scalability, needs to be aware of state, and can have problems with transactions. The practical limit for a service is no more than a few hundred clients.

As mentioned earlier, the service instance lasts until the client no longer requires it. Again, there are caveats to that generalization. The most efficient path for session termination involves the client closing the proxy. This causes a notification to be sent to the service that the session has ended, but what happens if the client doesn't close the proxy? What happens if the client doesn't terminate gracefully or a communications issue between the client and service prevents the notification from being received? In these cases, the session will automatically terminate after ten minutes of inactivity. After the session has been terminated in such a manner, the client will receive a *CommunicationObjectFaultedException* if it attempts to use the proxy.

This ten-minute timeout is just the default value. Whether the default can be changed depends on the binding. If the binding supports a reliable session, you can set the *InactivityTimeout* property associated with the reliable session. The following code demonstrates how to do this with a *netTcpBinding* binding.

```vb
' VB
Dim binding As New NetTcpBinding()
binding.ReliableSession.Enabled = True
binding.ReliableSession.InactivityTimeout = TimeSpan.FromMinutes(60)
```

```csharp
// C#
NetTcpBinding binding = new NetTcpBinding();
binding.ReliableSession.Enabled = true;
binding.ReliableSession.InactivityTimeout = TimeSpan.FromMinutes(60);
```

You can make the same setting through configuration files, as illustrated in the following segment:

```
<netTcpBinding>
    <binding name="timeoutSession">
        <reliableSession enabled="true" inactivityTimeout="01:00:00"/>
    </binding>
</netTcpBinding>
```

Exam Tip As you might surmise, it is possible for the inactivity timeout to be configured at both the client and the service. If the times are different, the shortest configured timeout prevails.

Speaking of reliable sessions, support for reliable sessions is required for a binding to support sessions. All the endpoints that expose the Service contract must use bindings that support reliable transport sessions, and the session must be enabled as shown in the earlier code example. This constraint is validated when the service is loaded; an *InvalidOperationException* is thrown if there is a mismatch.

One binding that is unable to support sessions is *basicHttpBinding*. Within the protocol that underlies this binding, there is no way to pass the information necessary to maintain the session. You can overcome the problem with the transport protocol within the format of the messages. The *wsHttpBinding* binding is capable of providing the necessary data to support sessions, for example.

There is one exception to the reliable session rule. The named pipe binding supports reliability by definition, so there is no need for the reliable messaging protocol to be implemented—and the *netNamedPipeBinding* binding does support sessions.

Singleton Mode

In this mode, only one instance of the service's implementation class is created. This instance is enlisted to handle every request that arrives at the service. The instance lives forever (or close to forever) and is disposed of only when the host process shuts down.

Singleton mode does not require any session information to be transmitted with the message. As a result, there is no restriction on the ability of the binding to support transport-level sessions. Nor is there a need for the protocol or binding to provide a mechanism that appears to emulate session behavior. If the contract exposed by the service has a session, the client must provide the session, but there is no requirement for sessions for singleton mode to work. Further, if a session is associated with the request, that session will never expire. The session identifier is maintained within the client proxy until the proxy is destroyed.

Alternatively, if no session information is exposed by the contract, the communications don't fall back to per call mode (unlike other modes). Instead, the request continues to be handled by the single instance of the singleton service.

Configure a singleton service in a manner similar to the other modes. The *InstanceContextMode* property of the *ServiceBehavior* attribute is set to *Single*. The following code demonstrates this, as shown in bold:

```vb
' VB
<ServiceBehavior(InstanceContextMode:=InstanceContextMode.Single)> _
Public Class UpdateService
    Implements IUpdateService
' Implementation code goes here
End Class
```

```csharp
// C#
[ServiceBehavior(InstanceContextMode = InstanceContextMode.Single)]
public class UpdateService : IUpdateService
{
    // Implementation code goes here
}
```

One of the features the singleton behavior offers is the ability to initialize the implementation instance through the constructor. For the other behaviors, the instance object is created behind the scenes at a time determined by the host process, but for singletons, you have the option to create the singleton instance and pass it into the host process.

Naturally, this begs the question of why you would want to do this. Typically, the rationale involves performing initialization processing outside the scope of the first request. If the service instance needs to allocate some resources (such as connecting to a database), the default behavior is to have the first request pay that performance price. It might be that logic should be injected into the service instance that is not available to the client (and, therefore, couldn't be included in the request). In both of these cases (and there are other reasons as well), having the service host create the singleton instance is not the best alternative.

However, in singleton mode, you can create the service instance before the host is even started. This instance can then be passed into the host as the host is getting started. One of the constructors for the *ServiceHost* class takes a singleton instance as a parameter. When constructed in this manner, the host will direct all incoming requests to the provided instance. The following code demonstrates how this is accomplished.

```vb
' VB
Dim singletonInstance As New SingletonUpdateService()
Dim host As New ServiceHost(singletonInstance)
host.Open()
```

```csharp
// C#
SingletonUpdateService singletonInstance = new SingletonUpdateService();
ServiceHost host = new ServiceHost(singletonInstance);
host.Open();
```

For the preceding code to work, the service (*SingletonUpdateService* in this example) must be defined with the *InstanceContextMode* property in the *ServiceBehavior* attribute set to *Single*.

When the service host is using a singleton instance, it is also possible for other objects to reach into the instance to call methods or set parameters. The *ServiceHost* class exposes a *Singleton-Instance* property that references the instance processing the incoming requests. The following code demonstrates how to update a member of the instance:

```vb
' VB
Dim instance As SingletonUpdateService = _
    TryCast(host.SingletonInstance, SingletonUpdateService)
instance.Counter += 50
```

```csharp
// C#
SingletonUpdateService instance = host.SingletonInstance as
    SingletonUpdateService;
instance.Counter += 50;
```

Even if the local host object variable is not available, you can still gain access to the instance. The *OperationContext* class exposes a read-only *Host* property, so from within an operation, the singleton instance can be accessed.

```vb
' VB
Dim host As ServiceHost = TryCast(OperationContext.Current.Host, _
    ServiceHost)
If host IsNot Nothing Then
    Dim instance as SingletonUpdateService = _
        TryCast(host.SingletonInstance, SingletonUpdateService)
    If instance IsNot Nothing Then
        Instance.Counter += 1
    End If
End If
```

```csharp
// C#
ServiceHost host = OperationContext.Current.Host as ServiceHost;
if (host != null)
{
    SingletonUpdateService instance = host.SingletonInstance
        as SingletonUpdateService;
    if (instance != null)
        instance.Counter += 1;
}
```

That every request is handled by a single instance of the implementation class has potential implications for contention issues. If multiple requests arrive at the service, they will be processed, in many cases, by the same instance but in a different worker thread. This means that any variable scoped outside of the current method (that is a class-level variable) can be corrupted if the value is updated by two worker threads at once. You must ensure that updates are performed using concurrency techniques such as locking.

The side effect of dealing with concurrency is that, at least in areas that are synchronized, only one request can be processed at a time. If the singleton service has a number of areas that require synchronization, or even if there is only one but it is in a frequently used method, performance can be negatively affected.

From a design perspective, singleton services are best used when they are modeling a singleton resource—a log file, perhaps, that allows a single writer only or, as has recently happened in the real-world job mentioned earlier, communicating with a single robot. If there is a possibility that, in the future, the service might no longer be a singleton, think hard before using this model. Subtle dependencies can be introduced while using the singleton model. The client might come to expect that state will be shared across multiple requests. Although the change to reconfigure the service to be something other than a singleton is simple, the challenge of tracking down dependency bugs can be much worse.

Sharing Instances

As has been mentioned, the mechanism for sharing a service instance between multiple clients has changed from the original approach. By creating a class that implements the *IInstance-ContextProvider* interface and then injecting the class into the dispatch pipeline, you can have a great deal of control over which instance of the service class will be used to service each request.

The starting point must come from the client. For the service to distinguish between the different clients, it examines each incoming request. Based on information that exists within the request, an existing instance is provided (or a new one is created). This generally means that the client needs to place something in the request, such as a message header. The easiest way to accomplish this is to use the *MessageHeader* class factory to create an instance of a *Message-Header* object. That object can then be added to the message headers that are sent with the request. The following code demonstrates how to do this.

NOTE Import the *System.ServiceModel.Channels* namespace

The *MessageHeader* class used in this code exists in the *System.ServiceModel.Channels* namespace. Unless this namespace is imported into the code file, you might receive an error message indicating that *MessageHeader* is a generic type that expects a parameter.

```vb
' VB
Dim header As MessageHeader = _
   MessageHeader.CreateHeader("headerName", "headerNamespace", _
   "instanceId")

Using SessionClient proxy As NewSessionClient()
   Using (New OperationContextScope(proxy.InnerChannel))
      OperationContext.Current.OutgoingMessageHeaders.Add(header)
      ' use the proxy object
```

```
    End Using
End Using

// C#
MessageHeader header = MessageHeader.CreateHeader("headerName",
    "headerNamespace", "instanceId");

using (SessionClient proxy = new SessionClient())
{
    using (new OperationContextScope(proxy.InnerChannel))
    {
        OperationContext.Current.OutgoingMessageHeaders.Add(header);
        // Use the proxy object
    }
}
```

The idea is that any client making a request to the service will use this pattern of code. If two clients must share an instance, the instance ID from one client will be sent to the second client, which would then include that in the message header it sends to the service.

Sending the header information is just the starting point. On the service side, the presence of the instance ID must be recognized and extracted from the request. This ID is then used as the key to a collection of previously created instances. If the corresponding instance already exists in the collection, it must be used to process the request. If the instance ID does not exist, a new instance must be created and then added to the collection to handle future requests.

The mechanism to implement the preceding scenario might not be obvious. Fortunately, Microsoft uses a provider model for the creation of instances to process requests. The interface for this is named *IInstanceContextProvider*. This interface exposes four methods: *GetExisting-InstanceContext*, *InitializeInstanceContext*, *IsIdle*, and *NotifyIdle*. These four methods actually work in two groups.

GetExistingInstanceContext and *InitializeInstanceContext* work in concert to determine which instance of the service's implementation object will be used to create the response. The *Get-ExistingInstanceContext* method is invoked as part of the process of handling an incoming request. The result from this method is either an existing instance context or a value of *null/Nothing*. In the latter case, WCF recognizes that no instance has been previously created, so it creates a new instance and then invokes the *InitializeInstanceContext* method. The idea is that any setup that must be performed on the new instance will be done in the *InitializeInstance-Context* method. In the case of the instance-sharing mode, this would normally include saving the new instance so that it can be retrieved in a future call to *GetExistingInstanceContext*.

WCF uses the *IsIdle* and *NotifyIdle* methods when it believes that all the activities associated with an instance have been completed. At this point, the *IsIdle* method is invoked. It is up to this method to determine whether the client (or clients) no longer needs the instance. The method returns a Boolean value, and if it returns *true*, then WCF will close the context.

Alternatively, if *IsIdle* returns *False*, that is a signal to WCF that the client might still need the particular instance. At this point, WCF invokes the *NotifyIdle* method. This method includes as one of the parameters a callback method. The idea is that, after the instance is no longer required (as determined by the provider), the method reference by the callback parameter will be invoked. This notifies WCF that the instance is no longer required. It will then start the instance deactivation process (including a call to the *IsIdle* method) once again.

Lab: Instance Modes

In this lab, you will focus on experimenting with the different instancing modes available in WCF. The first exercise looks at the *InstanceContextMode* enumeration, illustrating the different possible behaviors. The second exercise walks you through the creation of an instance context provider and illustrates how it can be used to share instances between clients.

▶ **Exercise 1 Per Session, Per Call, and Singleton Modes**

In this first exercise, you will use the *InstanceContextMode* value to determine the instancing WCF uses as well as to demonstrate the behavior of each mode by using a variable that is private to the implementation class.

1. Navigate to the *<InstallHome>*/Chapter10/Lesson1/Exercise1/*<language>*/Before directory and double-click the Exercise1.sln file to open the solution in Visual Studio.

   The solution consists of two projects. They are as follows:

   ❑ The DemoService project, a simple WCF service library that implements the *ISession* interface. This interface consists of a single method (*GetSessionStatus*) that returns a string indicating the number of times the method has been called within the current service instance.

   ❑ The TestClient project, a Console application that generates a request for the service and displays the result in the Console window.

2. In Solution Explorer, double-click the Program.cs or Mobile1.vb file in the TestClient project.

   In this file, you can see the lines of code that send requests to the service. Initially, there are two calls, back to back. First, set up the service to use the *PerCall* instance method. This is actually redundant because that is the default mode, but it does set up for the other modes.

3. To start, in Solution Explorer, double-click the SessionService file.

   The declaration for the *SessionService* class includes the *ServiceBehavior* attribute. One of the properties for that class is named *InstanceContextMode*. You can assign this value through the attribute by using a named parameter format.

   Change the class declaration to be the following:

   ```
   ' VB
   <ServiceBehavior(InstanceContextMode:=InstanceContextMode.PerCall)> _
   ```

```
Public Class SessionService
    Implements ISession
```

```
// C#
[ServiceBehavior(InstanceContextMode=InstanceContextMode.PerCall)]
public class SessionService : ISession
```

4. Ensure that TestClient is set as the startup project and launch the application by pressing F5.

   After a few moments, you will see that two messages appear. Each message indicates that the instance has been called only one time, even though the same proxy object is being used. This is to be expected when the instance is created once per call.

5. Press Enter to stop running the application.

6. In the SessionService file, change the instance context mode from *PerCall* to *PerSession*. When you are finished, the class declaration will look like the following (changes shown in bold):

   ```
   ' VB
   <ServiceBehavior(InstanceContextMode:=InstanceContextMode.PerSession)> _
   Public Class SessionService
       Implements ISession
   ```

   ```
   // C#
   [ServiceBehavior(InstanceContextMode=InstanceContextMode.PerSession)]
   public class SessionService : ISession
   ```

   For session mode to work, the service interface must be marked as requiring an interface.

7. In Solution Explorer, double-click the ISession file.

   The declaration for the *ISession* interface includes a *ServiceContract* attribute. The attribute includes a *SessionMode* property, which you must set to *Required*.

8. Modify the interface's declaration as shown in bold to look like the following:

   ```
   ' VB
   <ServiceContract(SessionMode:=SessionMode.Required)> _
   Public Interface ISession
   ```

   ```
   // C#
   [ServiceContract(SessionMode=SessionMode.Required)]
   public interface ISession
   ```

9. Launch the application by pressing F5.

   After a few moments, you will see that two messages appear. The messages indicate that a single instance of the service class has been called twice. Again, this is the expectation when the instance is created once per session.

10. Press Enter to terminate the application.

    To simulate two clients, the client application can create two separate *using* blocks.

11.   In the Program.cs or Module1.vb file, add a second *using* block that creates a new proxy object and invokes the service. Change the *Main* method so that the body looks like the following:

```vb
' VB
Using proxy As New DemoService.GetSessionStatusClient()
   Console.WriteLine("First call: " + proxy.GetSessionStatus())
End Using

Using proxy As New DemoService.GetSessionStatusClient()
   Console.WriteLine("Second call: " + proxy.GetSessionStatus())
End Using
Console.ReadLine()
```

```csharp
// C#
using (DemoService.GetSessionStatusClient proxy = new
   DemoService.GetSessionStatusClient())
{
    Console.WriteLine("First call: " + proxy.GetSessionStatus());
}

using (DemoService.GetSessionStatusClient proxy = new
   DemoService.GetSessionStatusClient())
{
    Console.WriteLine("Second call: " + proxy.GetSessionStatus());
}
Console.ReadLine();
```

12.   Launch the application by pressing F5.

In a few moments, the messages will appear on the console. The messages indicate that even though the instance context mode is set to *PerSession*, the different *using* blocks result in two different sessions.

13.   Press Enter to terminate the application.

14.   In the SessionService file, change the instance mode to Single.

The declaration for the *SessionService* class should read as follows (changes shown in bold):

```vb
' VB
<ServiceBehavior(InstanceContextMode:=InstanceContextMode.Single)> _
Public Class SessionService
   Implements ISession
```

```csharp
// C#
[ServiceBehavior(InstanceContextMode=InstanceContextMode.Single)]
public class SessionService : ISession
```

15.   Launch the application one last time by pressing F5.

In a few moments, the console messages appear. In this case, they indicate that even though two different sessions have been created (there are still two *using* blocks), they both use the same session instance.

16.   Press Enter to terminate the application

▶ **Exercise 2   Share Service Instances**

The fourth instancing mode for WCF services used to be known as *Shareable*. WCF uses a provider model to determine which instance of a service implementation class should be used. In this exercise, you will create a custom provider for instances and inject it into the WCF pipeline. The instance ID will be a number typed into the client to emulate the sharing process.

1.   Navigate to the *<InstallHome>*/Chapter10/Lesson1/Exercise2/*<language>*/Before directory and double-click the Exercise2.sln file to open the solution in Visual Studio.

The solution consists of two projects. They are as follows:

❑   The DemoService project, a simple WCF service library that implements the *ISession* interface. This interface consists of a single method (*GetSessionStatus*) that returns a string indicating the number of times the method has been called within the current service instance.

❑   The TestClient project, a Console application that generates a request for the service and displays the result in the Console window.

2.   In Solution Explorer, double-click the DemoContextInfo file.

This file will store information about an individual instance context. The provider will maintain a dictionary of DemoContextInfo files. This class implements the *IExtension* interface. The interface facilitates the aggregation of classes into the WCF pipeline, although in this particular case, the methods associated with this interface (*Attach* and *Detach*) are not needed for the implementation.

3.   In Solution Explorer, double-click the DemoContextProvider file.

This file will provide the implementation for the provider. This class must implement the *IInstanceContextProvider* interface.

4.   Change the class declaration to be as follows:

```vb
' VB
Public Class DemoContextProvider
    Implements IInstanceContextProvider
```

```csharp
// C#
public class DemoContextProvider : IInstanceContextProvider
```

The interface requires four methods to be added.

5.   Add the following method blocks to fulfill this requirement:

```vb
' VB
Public Function GetExistingInstanceContext(message As Message, _
    channel As IContextChannel) As InstanceContext _
```

```
    Implements IInstanceContextProvider.GetExistingInstanceContext
End Function

Public Sub InitializeInstanceContext(instanceContext As InstanceContext, _
    message As Message, channel As IContextChannel) _
    Implements IInstanceContextProvider.InitializeInstanceContext
End Sub

Public Function IsIdle(instanceContext As InstanceContext) As Boolean _
    Implements IInstanceContextProvider.IsIdle
End Function

Public Sub NotifyIdle(callback As InstanceContextIdleCallback, _
    instanceContext As InstanceContext) _
  Implements IInstanceContextProvider.NotifyIdle
End Sub

// C#
public InstanceContext GetExistingInstanceContext(Message message,
    IContextChannel channel) { }

public void InitializeInstanceContext(InstanceContext instanceContext,
    Message message, IContextChannel channel) { }

public bool IsIdle(InstanceContext instanceContext)
{
    return false;
}

public void NotifyIdle(InstanceContextIdleCallback callback,
    InstanceContext instanceContext) { }
```

In the *GetExistingInstanceContext* method, the first step is to retrieve the instance ID from the request.

6. Add the following code to the *GetExistingInstanceContext* method.

```
' VB
Dim headerIndex As Integer = message.Headers.FindHeader(headerName, _
    headerNamespace)

Dim _instanceId As String = String.Empty
If headerIndex <> -1 Then
    _instanceId = message.Headers.GetHeader(Of String)(headerIndex)
End If

// C#
int headerIndex = message.Headers.FindHeader(headerName, headerNamespace);

string instanceId = String.Empty;
if (headerIndex != -1)
    instanceId = message.Headers.GetHeader<string>(headerIndex);
```

7. If the request is associated with a session, the information about the instance will have been added as one of the extensions in the channel. If so, retrieve it. Add the following code below the newly added lines.

```vb
' VB
Dim info As DemoContextInfo = Nothing
Dim hasSession As Boolean = (channel.SessionId IsNot Nothing)
If hasSession Then
    info = channel.Extensions.Find(Of DemoContextInfo)()
End If
```

```csharp
// C#
DemoContextInfo info = null;
bool hasSession = (channel.SessionId != null);
if (hasSession)
    info = channel.Extensions.Find<DemoContextInfo>();
```

8. If the request has an instance ID associated with it, there might already be a context to use. If so, retrieve it from the dictionary. Otherwise, instantiate a new *DemoContextInfo* object and add it to the dictionary. Add the following code to the *GetExistingInstance-Context* method below the lines added in the previous step.

```vb
' VB
Dim isNew As Boolean = False
If String.IsNullOrEmpty(_instanceId) OrElse Not _
    contextMap.TryGetValue(_instanceId, info) Then
    info = New DemoContextInfo(_instanceId)
    isNew = True
    contextMap.Add(_instanceId, info)
    If hasSession Then
        channel.Extensions.Add(info)
    End If
End If
```

```csharp
// C#
bool isNew = false;
if (String.IsNullOrEmpty(instanceId) ||
    ! contextMap.TryGetValue(instanceId, out info))
{
    info = new DemoContextInfo(instanceId);
    isNew = true;
    contextMap.Add(instanceId, info);
    if (hasSession)
        channel.Extensions.Add(info);
}
```

At the end of the *GetExistingInstanceContext* method, the choice is to return a *null/Nothing* value (if there was no existing instance context) or return the instance context the provider found. In the latter case, information about the channel is added to the channels associated with the instance. This enables the instance to track the different channels with which it is operating.

9. Add the following code at the bottom of the *GetExistingInstanceContext* method:

```vb
' VB
If isNew Then
    Return Nothing
Else
    Dim _instance As InstanceContext = info.Instance
    If hasSession Then
        _instance.IncomingChannels.Add(channel)
    End If
    Return _instance
End If
```

```csharp
// C#
if (isNew)
{
    return null;
}
else
{
    InstanceContext instanceContext = info.Instance;
    if (hasSession)
        instanceContext.IncomingChannels.Add(channel);

    return instanceContext;
}
```

In this interface, the other method of importance is *InitializeInstanceContext*. This method is called when the *GetExistingInstanceContext* returns *null/Nothing* and a new instance context has to be created. For this exercise, the code in this method will add the new instance to the dictionary of instances.

10. To start, check whether there is an existing session because, if so, the instance is already associated with the channel through the *Extensions* collection. Add the following code to the beginning of the *InitializeInstanceContext* method:

```vb
' VB
Dim info As DemoContextInfo = Nothing
Dim hasSession As Boolean = (channel.SessionId IsNot Nothing)

If hasSession Then
    instanceContext.IncomingChannels.Add(channel)
    info = channel.Extensions.Find(Of DemoContextInfo)()
End If
```

```csharp
// C#
DemoContextInfo info = null;
bool hasSession = (channel.SessionId != null);

if (hasSession)
{
    instanceContext.IncomingChannels.Add(channel);
```

```
    info = channel.Extensions.Find<DemoContextInfo>();
}
```

11. If there is no existing session, get the instance ID from the headers in the request and see whether the ID can be found in the dictionary of previously used instances. Add the following *else* clause to the just-added *if* statement.

```vb
' VB
Else
    Dim headerIndex As Integer = message.Headers.FindHeader(headerName, _
        headerNamespace)
    If headerIndex <> -1 Then
        Dim instanceId As String = _
            message.Headers.GetHeader(Of string)(headerIndex)
        If instanceId IsNot Nothing Then
            contextMap.TryGetValue(instanceId, info)
        End If
    End If
```

```csharp
// C#
else
{
    int headerIndex = message.Headers.FindHeader(headerName,
        headerNamespace);
    if (headerIndex != -1)
    {
        string instanceId = message.Headers.GetHeader<string>(headerIndex);
        if (instanceId != null)
            this.contextMap.TryGetValue(instanceId, out info);
    }
}
```

If, for any reason, the instance context was found, it must be added to the *DemoContextInfo* object that will be used to process the request.

12. Add the following lines to the bottom of the *InitializeInstanceContext* method:

```vb
' VB
If info IsNot Nothing Then
    Info.Instance = instanceContext
End If
```

```csharp
// C#
if (info != null)
    info.Instance = instanceContext;
```

There are a number of ways to inject this functionality into the WCF pipeline. They are described in Chapter 9, "When Simple Is Not Sufficient," in the discussion of the details surrounding the *DispatchRuntime* object. For this exercise, you create an attribute to decorate the implementation class. The file for the attribute already exists.

13. In Solution Explorer, double-click the ShareableAttribute file.

The class is already decorated with the *IServiceBehavior* interface. This requires the three methods in the class to be defined. To add the *InstanceContextProvider*, the only method that must have code is *ApplyDispatchBehavior*. In this method, every endpoint dispatcher on every channel will set the *InstanceContextProvider* property to a new instance of the *DemoContextProvider* class.

14. Add the following code to the *ApplyDispatchBehavior* method:

```
' VB
Dim extension As New DemoContextProvider()
Dim dispatcherBase As ChannelDispatcherBase
For Each dispatcherBase In serviceHostBase.ChannelDispatchers
    Dim dispatcher As ChannelDispatcher = TryCast(dispatcherBase, _
        ChannelDispatcher)
    Dim _endpointDispatcher As EndpointDispatcher
    For Each _endpointDispatcher in dispatcher.Endpoints
        _endpointDispatcher.DispatchRuntime.InstanceContextProvider = _
            extension
    Next
Next
```

```
// C#
DemoContextProvider extension = new DemoContextProvider();
foreach (ChannelDispatcherBase dispatcherBase in
    serviceHostBase.ChannelDispatchers)
{
    ChannelDispatcher dispatcher = dispatcherBase as ChannelDispatcher;
    foreach (EndpointDispatcher endpointDispatcher in dispatcher.Endpoints)
    {
        endpointDispatcher.DispatchRuntime.InstanceContextProvider =
            extension;
    }
}
```

Now that the attribute has been created, the service's implementation class must be decorated with it.

15. First, in Solution Explorer, double-click *SessionService*.

16. In the class declaration, add the *Shareable* attribute. When you're finished, the class *declaration* should look like the following:

```
' VB
<ServiceBehavior(InstanceContextMode:=InstanceContextMode.Single)> _
<Shareable> _
Public Class SessionService
    Implements ISession
```

```
// C#
[ServiceBehavior(InstanceContextMode=InstanceContextMode.Single)]
[Shareable]
public class SessionService : ISession
```

17. Before starting the demo, in Solution Explorer, double-click the Program.cs or Module1.vb file in TestClient.

    Notice that there is a loop that prompts for an instance ID. Within that loop, there is a *using* block for the proxy to the service. This means that the same session will not be used for each call and that the only way for the instances to be maintained is through the provider that you have just written.

18. Ensure that TestClient is set to be the startup project, and then launch the application by pressing F5.

    You will prompted for an instance ID.

19. Enter the instance ID of your choice (say, 123, to keep it simple).

    The returned message indicates that this method has been called once.

20. Enter the same instance ID, and the instance has been called twice. Enter a different instance ID, and the counter restarts; if you later duplicate an earlier instance ID, you will see the previous counter incremented in the output on the console. When you have finished exercising the application, press Enter to terminate.

Lesson Summary

- The instance mode determines the relationship between the client and the instance of the service's implementation class.
- Along with the standard modes, WCF also provides a provider model to determine the instance context that should be used to process a request.
- *PerCall* is the default mode, and it maintains a one-to-one association between method calls and instances.
- *PerSession* creates an instance for each client proxy whereas an instance mode of *Single* results in one instance handling every request.

Lesson Review

You can use the following questions to test your knowledge of the information in Lesson 1, "Instancing Modes." The questions are also available on the companion CD if you prefer to review them in electronic form.

NOTE Answers

Answers to these questions and explanations of why each answer choice is correct or incorrect are located in the "Answers" section at the end of the book.

1. You have created a WCF application by which the client communicates with the service, using the *netTcpBinding*. You would like to minimize any possible threading and synchronization issues in the service. Which instance mode should you use?

   A. Per call
   B. Per session
   C. Singleton
   D. Instance context provider

2. You have created a WCF application by which the client communicates with the service, using the *wsTcpBinding*. A number of methods in the service retrieve a large quantity of relatively static data. You would like to minimize the processing time spent retrieving the data (and keep the data in a cache within the service object). Which instance mode should you use?

   A. Per call
   B. Per session
   C. Singleton
   D. Instance context provider

Lesson 2: Working with Instances

The instance mode WCF uses is just the start of working with instances. You can manipulate a number of details to improve the performance and scalability of a WCF service. WCF provides throttling and quota capabilities that can help prevent denial of service (DoS) attacks as well as ensure that the servers aren't overloaded by handling requests. Along the same lines, you can control the activation and deactivation of the instances used to process requests to a degree that is finer than the default functionality.

Not only does WCF allow for performance to be protected, some attributes can be set to demarcate operations. The demarcation ensures that, where necessary, some operations cannot be completed before or after other operations. This is not a complete workflow management function, but it does allow a service to ensure that a particular operation is called first and that no operations can be called after a finalize operation has been performed.

> **After this lesson, you will be able to:**
> - Protect a WCF service by setting the throttling and quota parameters.
> - Demarcate service operations.
> - Manage instance activation and deactivation at a very granular level.
>
> **Estimated lesson time: 50 minutes**

Protecting the Service

When WCF is deployed in the real world (where *real* is defined as a distributed environment in which requests arrive at a pace that is outside of your control), a number of potential problems can arise. Some of the performance differences associated with the different instancing modes have already been covered. However, beyond pure performance problems, WCF services have to contend with some of the same problems that a Web site has to contend with. This includes the potential for being flooded with client requests, similar to a denial of service attack.

Denial of service attacks are attempts to deplete the resources required by the service to process incoming requests to the point that no additional resources are available. The type of depleted resources can include any scarce resource the service uses. WCF provides a number of ways to mitigate the problem through either throttling requests or applying quotas to the resource.

Throttling

The goal of throttling is twofold. First, it prevents the service host from being overrun by a flood of requests. Second, it enables the load on the WCF service (and the server on which the service is running) to be smoothed out. In both cases, the intent is to place a limit on the number of incoming requests so that the service will be able to handle them in a timely manner.

The default WCF setting for throttling is to have none at all. When throttling is engaged, WCF will check the current counters for each request that arrives. If the configured settings are exceeded, WCF automatically places the request in a queue. As the counters come down below the threshold, the requests are then retrieved from the queue in the same order and presented to the service for processing. The result of this is that, in many cases, the observed behavior for a service that has reached its maximum is to have the client request time out.

Three settings in the service behavior control the number of requests the service host will be allowed to process simultaneously. Each of these is defined in the *ServiceThrottlingBehavior* section of the configuration file. The following paragraphs describe the three settings and are followed by an example of how you can configure them.

MaxConcurrentCalls   The *MaxConcurrentCalls* value specifies the number of simultaneous calls the service will accept. The default value is 16 calls. Of the three settings, this is the only one that covers all the types of requests that arrive.

MaxConcurrentSessions   The *MaxConcurrentSessions* value determines the maximum number of channels requiring sessions that the service will support. The default value for this setting is 10 session-aware channels. Any attempt to create a channel beyond this maximum will throw a *TimeoutException*. Because this setting is concerned with session-aware channels only, if the binding is not session-aware (such as the *basicHttpBinding*), this setting has no impact on the number of requests that can be processed.

MaxConcurrentInstances   The *MaxConcurrentInstances* setting sets the maximum number of instances of the service implementation object that will be created. The default value for this setting is *Int32.MaxValue*, and the impact this value has on the service depends on the mode. If the mode is per call, this is the same as *MaxConcurrentCalls* because each call gets its own instance. If the mode is per session, the setting works the same as *MaxConcurrentSessions*. For singleton mode, the value of the number of instances is always 1, so the setting is really only useful when the *IInstanceContextProvider* is being used.

The following segment from a configuration file demonstrates how you can configure these settings:

```
<behaviors>
   <serviceBehaviors>
      <behavior name="throttlingBehaviort">
         <serviceThrottling maxConcurrentCalls="10"
            maxConcurrentInstances="10"
            maxConcurrentSessions="5"/>
      </behavior>
   </serviceBehaviors>
</behaviors>
```

You can set the same configuration through code. The following segments demonstrate the technique:

```vb
' VB
Dim host As New ServiceHost(GetType(UpdateService), _
    New Uri("http://localhost:8080/UpdateService"))
host.AddServiceEndpoint("IUpdateService", _
    New WSHttpBinding(), String.Empty)
Dim throttlingBehavior As New ServiceThrottlingBehavior()
throttlingBehavior.MaxConcurrentCalls = 10
throttlingBehavior.MaxConcurrentInstances = 10
throttlingBehavior.MaxConcurrentSessions = 5
host.Description.Behaviors.Add(throttlingBehavior)
host.Open()
```

```csharp
// C#
ServiceHost host = new ServiceHost( typeof(UpdateService),
    new Uri("http://localhost:8080/UpdateService"));
host.AddServiceEndpoint( "IUpdateService",
    new WSHttpBinding(), String.Empty);
ServiceThrottlingBehavior throttlingBehavior = new ServiceThrottlingBehavior();
throttlingBehavior.MaxConcurrentCalls = 10;
throttlingBehavior.MaxConcurrentInstances = 10;
throttlingBehavior.MaxConcurrentSessions = 5;
host.Description.Behaviors.Add(throttlingBehavior);
host.Open();
```

As has been mentioned, when the throttling limits are reached, the client will throw an exception. Specifically, the exception the client receives is the previously mentioned *TimeoutException*. Because this one exception fits all scenarios (that is, the same exception is raised regardless of which of the throttling settings caused the problem), it is left up to you to discover the cause. A couple of hints can help. If the problem is caused by the concurrent sessions limit, you will most likely see the exception raised within the *SendPreamble* method. If it turns out that the *Send* method is the source of the time out, it is more likely to be caused by the maximum concurrent calls limit.

NOTE   No need to use code

There is little reason to configure the throttling behavior in code. By keeping it in the configuration file, you enable administrators to adjust the service's performance on an as-needed basis.

Reading Throttling Settings

It is possible to read (but not update) the current throttling settings after the service host has been opened. Applications do this, typically to provide diagnostic information about the service. You do this by accessing the dispatcher for the service, which is responsible for implementing the throttling, so it makes sense that the dispatcher would have all the information close at hand.

The *ServiceHost* class exposes a collection of dispatchers in the *ChannelDispatchers* property. This is a strongly typed collection of *ChannelDispatched* objects. The *ChannelDispatcher* object has a property called *ServiceThrottle*. Through the *ServiceThrottle* object, you have access to all the throttling properties, including *MaxConcurrentCalls*, *MaxConcurrentInstances*, and *MaxConcurrentSessions*. The following code demonstrates this technique:

```
' VB
Dim dispatcher As ChannelDispatcher = _
    TryCast(OperationContext.Current.Host.ChannelDispatchers(0), _
    ChannelDispatcher)

Dim throttle as ServiceThrottle = dispatcher.ServiceThrottle

Trace.WriteLine(String.Format("MaxConcurrentCalls = {0}", _
    throttle.MaxConcurrentCalls))
Trace.WriteLine(String.Format("MaxConcurrentSessions = {0}", _
    throttle.MaxConcurrentSessions))
Trace.WriteLine(String.Format("MaxConcurrentInstances = {0}", _
    throttle.MaxConcurrentInstances))
```

```
// C#
ChannelDispatcher dispatcher =
    OperationContext.Current.Host.ChannelDispatchers[0] as ChannelDispatcher;

ServiceThrottle throttle = dispatcher.ServiceThrottle;

Trace.WriteLine(String.Format("MaxConcurrentCalls = {0}",
    throttle.MaxConcurrentCalls));
Trace.WriteLine(String.Format("MaxConcurrentSessions = {0}",
    throttle.MaxConcurrentSessions));
Trace.WriteLine(String.Format("MaxConcurrentInstances = {0}",
    throttle.MaxConcurrentInstances));
```

Quotas

The quota mechanism available through WCF involves controlling the amount of memory used by the service host and the various service implementation objects. The premise behind a DoS attack that is aimed at memory is to find a way to make the processing of the request(s) allocate an inordinately large amount of memory. As additional requests arrive (whether good ones or malicious ones), an *OutOfMemoryException* or a *StackOverflowException* might be raised.

When you apply a quota to a WCF service, the *QuotaExceededException* is raised. However, instead of this exception causing the service to terminate (as the out of memory or stack overflow condition might), the message being processed is simply discarded. The service then processes the next request and carries on.

A number of settings affect the level of quota.

MaxReceivedMessageSize The *MaxReceivedMessageSize* value (along with the other settings associated with quotas) is set on the binding directly. It controls how large a message size can be. The default value is 65,536 bytes, which should be sufficient for most messages. You can set this value through either code or configuration. The following demonstrates a configuration element that will set the value of the maximum message size to 128,000 bytes:

```
<bindings>
    <netTcpBinding>
        <binding name="netTcp"
            maxReceivedMessageSize="128000" />
    </netTcpBinding>
</bindings>
```

CAUTION Setting the *MaxReceivedMessageSize* value

Setting this value (or leaving it to the default) can have a number of unintended consequences. Specifically, if you legitimately have an occasional large message, ensure that you configure the *maxReceivedMessageSize* to accommodate such large messages. Otherwise, the message will be rejected.

You can set this value imperatively also, as demonstrated in the following code sample:

```
' VB
Dim binding As New NetTcpBinding()
binding.MaxReceivedMessageSize = 128000
Dim host As New ServiceHost(GetType(UpdateService), _
    New Uri("net.tcp://localhost:1234/UpdateService"))
host.AddServiceEndpoint("IUpdateService", _
    binding, String.Empty)
host.Open()
```

```
// C#
NetTcpBinding binding = new NetTcpBinding();
binding.MaxReceivedMessageSize = 128000;
ServiceHost host = new ServiceHost( typeof(UpdateService),
    new Uri("net.tcp://localhost:1234/UpdateService"));
host.AddServiceEndpoint( "IUpdateService",
    binding, String.Empty);
host.Open();
```

ReaderQuotas The *ReaderQuotas* property of the binding sets limits on the complexity of the messages received by the service. They protect that service from memory-based denial of service by specifying a set of criteria within which all messages must fall. Table 10-1 contains a list of the properties that can be set on the *ReaderQuotas* object and their meanings.

Table 10-1 *ReaderQuotas* **Properties**

Property	Default	Description
MaxDepth	32	The maximum depth to which the nodes in the message can go. This is like saying that the XML that represents the message can have no more than 32 generations (where a parent node and a child node make up a generation) at the deepest point in the schema.
MaxStringContentLength	8192	The longest that any string value in the message can be. A string value would be the value of an attribute or the value of the inner text for any node.
MaxArrayLength	16384	The maximum number of elements that can appear in a single array.
MaxBytesPerRead	4096	The maximum number of bytes returned by each call to *Read* while the message is processed.
MaxNameTableCharCount	16384	The maximum number of characters that can appear in a table name.

NOTE DoS protection

It might seem a little odd to restrict the number of bytes returned by a *Read* method. However, for an XML file to be processed, the entire starting tag must be loaded into memory. It is a common attack to provide an XML document with an extraordinarily long starting tag. Because this tag would need to be loaded, limiting it is an obvious way to prevent DoS attacks.

Demarcating Operations

Conceptually, a session simply means that the service can determine which client a request is coming from. This enables the service to maintain state between the individual requests. However, there are times when the order in which the operations are executed actually matters, and this requirement calls for an extension to the sessioning mechanism.

The idea of needing to maintain the order in which methods are called might seem a little bizarre. After all, in the vast majority of business applications, the client is quite capable of ensuring this, but in many cases, the ability of the client to dictate the order of operations is not as solid as you might think.

Consider, for example, any HTTP-based binding. Although it would seem that if *MethodA* is invoked before *MethodB*, then in every case, *MethodA* will be executed on the service before *MethodB*. However, suppose *MethodA* and *MethodB* are executed on different threads. Still, isn't it possible to ensure that the two threads are synchronized to the point that the client can guarantee execution order?

The answer is no. When using an HTTP-based binding, there is no guarantee of the order of arrival. Even though the client executes *MethodA* before *MethodB* (on different threads; this doesn't apply to synchronous calls), HTTP will not guarantee that the request associated with *MethodA* will arrive at the service prior to *MethodB*. Unless the service is enlisted in the mechanism to guarantee operation order, no such guarantee can be made.

Consider the following Service contract:

```vb
' VB
<ServiceContract(SessionMode:=SessionMode.Required)> _
Public Interface IProcessOrders
    <OperationContract> _
    Sub InitializeOrder(customerId As Integer)
    <OperationContract> _
    Sub AddOrderLine(productId As String, _
        Quantity As Integer)
    <OperationContract> _
    Function GetOrderTotal() As Double
    <OperationContract> _
    Function SubmitOrder() As Boolean
End Interface
```

```csharp
//C#
[ServiceContract(SessionMode = SessionMode.Required)]
public interface IProcessOrders
{
    [OperationContract]
    void InitializeOrder(int customerId);
    [OperationContract]
    void AddOrderLine(string productId, int quantity);
    [OperationContract]
    double GetOrderTotal();
    [OperationContract]
    bool SubmitOrder();
}
```

The business rules associated with this interface are that the first method to be called has to be *InitializeOrder*. This instantiates an *Order* object and populates the fields with default values. Then the *AddOrderLine* method must be called at least once (although it can be called multiple times). Next, *GetOrderTotal* is called to calculate the order totals. Finally, the *Submit-Order* method is called. This last method also closes the session.

WCF provides a mechanism that enables contract designers to indicate operations, which cannot be the first or last method, by setting the *IsInitiating* and *IsTerminating* properties on the *OperationContract* attribute. If *IsInitiating* is set to *true* for a method and no session has been established when that method is called, a session is created. If a session already exists, the method is called within that session.

If *IsTerminating* is set to *true* for a method, when the method completes, the session is closed. This is not the same as disposing of the service instance, however. The client still needs to execute the *Close* method on the proxy to close the connection. However, any subsequent methods on this proxy will be rejected with an *InvalidOperationException*.

By using these properties, it is possible to mark the start and end of an operation. The default value for *IsInitiating* is *true*, and the default value for *IsTerminating* is *false*. Because of this, the settings that are required in the sample interface should be set as follows (changes shown in bold):

```vb
' VB
<ServiceContract(SessionMode:=SessionMode.Required)> _
Public Interface IProcessOrders
    <OperationContract> _
    Sub InitializeOrder(customerId As Integer)
    <OperationContract(IsInitiating:=False)> _
    Sub AddOrderLine(productId As String, _
        Quantity As Integer)
    <OperationContract(IsInitiating:=False)> _
    Function GetOrderTotal() As Double
    <OperationContract(IsInitiating:=False, IsTerminating:=True)> _
    Function SubmitOrder() As Boolean
End Interface
```

```csharp
//C#
[ServiceContract(SessionMode = SessionMode.Required)]
public interface IProcessOrders
{
    [OperationContract]
    void InitializeOrder(int customerId);
    [OperationContract(IsInitiating=false)]
    void AddOrderLine(string productId, int quantity);
    [OperationContract(IsInitiating=false)]
    double GetOrderTotal();
    [OperationContract(IsInitiating=false, IsTerminating=true)]
    bool SubmitOrder();
}
```

Consider how these settings will work. Of the four methods, only *InitializeOrder* can start a session. So, if one of the other methods is called prior to *InitializeOrder*, it throws an *InvalidOperationException*. The remaining methods can then be called in any order required, with one exception. If *SubmitOrder* is called because of the *IsTerminating* property, the session is closed.

NOTE   Demarcated services must be session aware

To use this demarcating technique, either the service must be session aware (such as having a *Per-Session* instancing mode) or the service must be a singleton.

Instance Deactivation

The details of the issues associated with sessions and service instances are, not surprisingly, more complicated. Consider Figure 10-3, which represents a view closer to reality of a service.

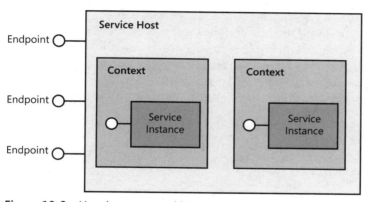

Figure 10-3   How instances and hosts are related

As you can see in Figure 10-3, the service instance is actually loaded into a *Context* object, and the session information routes client messages not to the specific instance but to the context.

When a session is created, the service host creates a new context. This context is terminated when the session ends. This means that the lifetime of the context matches the instance hosted within it by default. WCF enables the developer of the service to separate the two lifetimes.

WCF goes a step further in that you can create a context that has no instance at all. The way to control context deactivation is through the *ReleaseInstanceMode* property of the *Operation-Behavior* attribute.

You can set various values in that *ReleaseInstanceMode* to identify when the service instance should be released in relation to a particular method control. The choices are *BeforeCall*, *After-Call*, *BeforeAndAfterCall*, or *None*.

The default release mode is *None*. This means that the service instance continues to exist as method requests arrive and processes are returned. This is the mode that you have come to expect from a service instance.

If the release mode is set to *BeforeCall*, a new instance is created with the beginning of the call. If a service instance already exists, it is deactivated and the *Dispose* method called on it. The client is blocked while this is going on because it is assumed to be important to have the new service instance available to process the request. This style is normally used when the method allocates a scarce resource, and it must to be certain that any previous use has been cleaned up.

If the release mode is set to *AfterCall*, the current service instance is deactivated and disposed of when the method is completed. This would normally be set when the method is deallocating a scarce resource. The idea is that, after the method is finished, the service instance is disposed of immediately, ensuring that the resource will be available for the next caller.

The last release mode is *BeforeAndAfterCall*. This mode disposes of any existing service instance prior to executing the method and then disposes of the just created service instance after the method is finished. You might recognize this as the same as the per call instance mode. The difference, however, is that this mode can be set on an individual method, so you can configure one method to be (basically) per call instancing, whereas the other methods in the service can use a different instancing model.

You can define the release mode declaratively, using code that looks like the following:

```vb
' VB
Public Class UpdateService
   Implements IUpdateService

   <OperationBehavior( _
      ReleaseInstanceMode:=ReleaseInstanceMode.BeforeAndAfterCall)> _
   Public Sub Update()
      ' Implementation code goes here
   End Sub

End Class
```

```csharp
// C#
public class UpdateService : IUpdateService
{
   [OperationBehavior(ReleaseInstanceMode=ReleaseInstanceMode.BeforeAndAfterCall)]
   public void Update()
   {
      // Implementation code goes here
   }
}
```

You also have the option of making a run-time decision to deactivate the current service instance (when the method is complete). The instance context exposes a *ReleaseServiceInstance* method. When called, the current instance is marked to be deactivated and disposed of after the method is finished. The instance context is part of the operation context, so the way to call this method looks like the following:

```
' VB
OperationContext.Current.InstanceContext.ReleaseServiceInstance()
```

```
// C#
OperationContext.Current.InstanceContext.ReleaseServiceInstance();
```

This technique is intended to provide a high level of granularity to optimize the service. However, as is true with many such techniques, the normal course of events doesn't require this level of effort. It is better to design and develop your application using more standard techniques, falling back on these only if performance and scalability goals are not being met.

Lab: Throttling and Demarcation

In this lab, you will work with two separate functions. The first exercise will illustrate some of the throttle configuration you can perform. The effect that some of the settings (such as large request limits, maximum levels in deserialization, and so on) have on incoming requests can be a little challenging to illustrate. As a result, the exercise shows the ones that can be easily demonstrated.

The second exercise will create a service with demarcated operations and demonstrate the exceptions raised when the specified order is violated.

▶ **Exercise 1   Throttle WCF Requests**

In this first exercise, you will restrict the number of simultaneous instances a service can create. You will use a service similar to the one constructed in the lab for Lesson 1 in this chapter.

1. Navigate to the *<InstallHome>*/Chapter10/Lesson2/Exercise1/*<language>*/Before directory and double-click the Exercise1.sln file to open the solution in Visual Studio.

   The solution consists of two projects. They are as follows:

   ❑ The DemoService project, a simple WCF service library that implements the *ISession* interface. This interface consists of a single method (*GetSessionStatus*) that returns a string indicating the number of times the method has been called within the current service instance.

   ❑ The TestClient project, a Console application that generates a request for the service and displays the result in the Console window.

   You can find the settings for throttling a service in the configuration file for the service.

2. In Solution Explorer, double-click the App.config file in the DemoService project.

3. Locate the behavior named *ThrottleBehavior* in the *serviceBehaviors* element.

   The throttle is set in the *serviceThrottling* element.

4. Set the maximum number of concurrent instances to 2 by adding the following XML to the *behavior* element within the *serviceBehaviors* element:

   ```
   <serviceThrottling maxConcurrentInstances="2" />
   ```

5. Ensure that TestClient is set as the startup project, and then launch the application by pressing F5.

6. When prompted for an instance ID, enter a value of 123 and press Enter.

    This creates the first instance.

7. When prompted for the instance ID again, enter a value of 456 and press Enter.

    This creates the second instance.

8. Finally, when prompted for the instance ID again, enter a value of 789.

    This is the third instance and, rather than displaying a string on the console, it will wait. In fact, it will wait until the timeout value has been exceeded and an exception is thrown.

9. Choose Stop Debugging from the Debug menu to end the application.

▶ **Exercise 2   Demarcate Operations**

As mentioned, WCF provides some functionality aimed at regulating the order in which operations can be executed. In this exercise, you will configure the service to use this capability. Then you will modify the client to test not only the successful path but also an execution order that would violate the configured order.

1. Navigate to the *<InstallHome>*/Chapter10/Lesson2/Exercise2/*<language>*/Before directory and double-click the Exercise2.sln file to open the solution in Visual Studio.

    The solution consists of two projects. They are as follows:

    ❑ The DemoService project, a simple WCF service library that implements the *ISession* interface. This interface consists of three methods (*FirstMethod*, *GetSessionStatus*, and *LastMethod*), each of which returns a string indicating which method has been called.

    ❑ The TestClient project, a Console application. The application generates a request for the service and displays the result in the Console window.

2. In Solution Explorer, double-click the ISession file.

    You will notice that three methods are defined within the contract.

3. To start, configure *FirstMethod* to be the first operation called, by setting the *IsInitiating* property on the *OperationContract* attribute to *true*.

    The *IsInitiating* property for the other methods in the interface also must be set to *false*, but you do that shortly.

4. Change the declaration of *FirstMethod* (as shown in bold) to look like the following:

```
' VB
<OperationContract(IsInitiating:=True)> _
Function FirstMethod() As String
```

```
// C#
[OperationContract(IsInitiating = true)]
string FirstMethod();
```

Now the *IsInitiating* property for the *GetSessionStatus* method must be set to *false*.

5. Change the method declaration (as shown in bold) to the following:

```vb
' VB
<OperationContract(IsInitiating:=False)> _
Function GetSessionStatus() As String
```

```csharp
// C#
[OperationContract(IsInitiating = false)]
string GetSessionStatus();
```

The third method also must have *IsInitiating* set to *false*. However, the intent is for this method to be the last method called. For this reason, the *IsTerminating* property must be set to *true*.

Change the method declaration (as shown in bold) to the following:

```vb
' VB
<OperationContract(IsInitiating:=False, IsTerminating:=True)> _
Function LastMethod() As String
```

```csharp
// C#
[OperationContract(IsInitiating = false, IsTerminating = true)]
string LastMethod();
```

6. In Solution Explorer, double-click Program.cs or Module1.vb.

Notice the order in which the methods are called. This is what is expected by the configuration in the service.

7. Ensure that TestClient is set as the startup project, and then launch the application by pressing F5.

Note that the messages appear as expected.

8. End the application.

9. To modify the order of the method calls, move the call to *GetSessionStatus* so that it occurs before the call to *FirstMethod*.

The body of the *using* block in the *Main* method should look like the following:

```vb
' VB
Console.WriteLine(proxy.GetSessionStatus())
Console.WriteLine(proxy.FirstMethod())
Console.WriteLine(proxy.LastMethod())
```

```csharp
// C#
Console.WriteLine(proxy.GetSessionStatus());
Console.WriteLine(proxy.FirstMethod());
Console.WriteLine(proxy.LastMethod());
```

10. Launch the application by pressing F5.

You will find that an *InvalidOperationException* or an *ActionNotSupportedException* is raised with the *GetSessionStatus* call. The message in the exception indicates that *Get-SessionStatus* was invoked before a method in which *IsInitiating* has been set to *true*.

11. Choose Stop Debugging from the Debug menu to end the application.

12. Finally, move the call to *GetSessionStatus* so that it occurs after the call to *LastMethod*. The body of the *using* block in the *Main* method should look like the following:

```
' VB
Console.WriteLine(proxy.FirstMethod())
Console.WriteLine(proxy.LastMethod())
Console.WriteLine(proxy.GetSessionStatus())
```

```
// C#
Console.WriteLine(proxy.FirstMethod());
Console.WriteLine(proxy.LastMethod());
Console.WriteLine(proxy.GetSessionStatus());
```

13. Launch the application by pressing F5.

    Again, you will find that an *InvalidOperationException* is raised with the *GetSessionStatus* call. This time, the message in the exception indicates that *GetSessionStatus* was invoked after a method in which *IsTerminating* has been set to *true* was called.

14. Choose Stop Debugging from the Debug menu to end the application.

Lesson Summary

- Client endpoint configuration starts from the same address, binding, and contract bases as services do.
- If one of the standard bindings is specified, the default values for that binding are used.
- You define additional binding behaviors through a *behaviorConfiguration* section.
- If the client supports callbacks, you can define a number of client behaviors through the *endpointBehavior* section.
- All of the configuration that can be performed declaratively can also be performed imperatively.
- You can instantiate all the bindings by using the name of a configuration section. Alternatively, you can instantiate the binding separately, assign the desired properties, and then associate it with the proxy.

Lesson Review

You can use the following questions to test your knowledge of the information in Lesson 2, "Working with Instances." The questions are also available on the companion CD if you prefer to review them in electronic form.

1. Consider the following segment from a configuration file.

```
<behaviors>
    <serviceBehaviors>
        <behavior name="throttlingBehaviort">
            <serviceThrottling maxConcurrentCalls="15"
                maxConcurrentInstances="10"
                maxConcurrentSessions="5"/>
        </behavior>
    </serviceBehaviors>
</behaviors>
```

   Which of the following statements is true?

   A. The service can accept no more than fifteen simultaneous requests.

   B. The service can accept no more than ten simultaneous requests.

   C. The service can accept no more than five simultaneous requests.

   D. There is no limit to the number of simultaneous requests the service can accept.

2. Consider the properties of the OperationContract that demarcate an operation. Which of the following statements is false?

   A. You can specify which method must be the first one called within the service.

   B. You can ensure that no methods in the service can be called after a specific method is called.

   C. You cannot ensure the order of all the methods in a service unless two or fewer methods are exposed.

   D. You can ensure that a particular method will always be called when the service is finished.

Chapter Review

To further practice and reinforce the skills you learned in this chapter, you can:

- Review the chapter summary.
- Review the list of key terms introduced in this chapter.
- Complete the case scenarios. These scenarios set up real-world situations involving the topics of this chapter and ask you to create a solution.
- Complete the suggested practices.
- Take a practice test.

Chapter Summary

- The available instance modes offer a wide range of options. The decision regarding which mode to use should consider both performance and threading issues.
- By using throttling settings and quotas, WCF can help prevent denial of service attacks or simply ensure that servers do not become overloaded with requests.
- The developer can control when service instances are created and destroyed even within the instance modes.

Key Terms

Do you know what these key terms mean? You can check your answers by looking up the terms in the glossary at the end of the book.

- scarce resource
- service instance

Case Scenarios

In the following case scenarios, you will apply what you've learned about instancing modes and working with instances. You can find answers to these questions in the "Answers" section at the end of this book.

Case Scenario 1: Choosing the Appropriate Instancing Mode

Your company has developed a WCF application that will be distributed to your clients. You would like to arrange for a single instance of the service implementation class to be active for each client. The service, therefore, should act as a singleton for each client.

Answer the following question for your manager:

- Which type of instancing should be used in the application?

Case Scenario 2: Protecting Your WCF Application

Your company has developed a WCF application that will be distributed to a large number of clients. Because the service portion of the application is being exposed on a publicly accessible server, you are concerned about the possibility of denial of service attacks. You want to ensure also that, in the case of heavy usage, the client experience is acceptable.

Answer the following questions for your manager.

1. Which type of instancing should be used in the application?
2. Which changes should be made to the throttling settings?
3. Which changes should be made to the quota settings?

Suggested Practices

To help you successfully master the exam objectives presented in this chapter, complete the following tasks.

Working with Service Instances

Create an application to practice instance sharing.

- **Practice**   Create a WCF application that uses the IP address from which the request originated to determine which instance context should be used.

WCF Protection

Create an application to practice setting quotas.

- **Practice**   Create a WCF application that is configured to reject messages that are over 4 KB in size. Test the application by sending both large and small requests to the service.

Watch a Webcast

Watch a webcast about configuring WCF.

- **Practice**   Watch the MSDN webcast, "Instancing Modes," by Michele Leroux Bustamante, available on the companion CD in the Webcasts folder.

Take a Practice Test

The practice tests on this book's companion CD offer many options. For example, you can test yourself on just one exam objective, or you can test yourself on all the 70-503 certification exam content. You can set up the test so that it closely simulates the experience of taking a certification exam, or you can set it up in study mode so that you can look at the correct answers and explanations after you answer each question.

MORE INFO   **Practice tests**

For details about all the practice test options available, see the "How to Use the Practice Tests" section in this book's introduction.

Chapter 11

Transactional Services

In the world of distributed applications, transactions have always posed a difficult challenge. When updates are spread across multiple computers and multiple data stores, coordinating the updates in a manner that preserves the fundamental properties of a transaction is not an easy proposition. Windows Communications Foundation (WCF) has implemented an approach that minimizes the amount of technical knowledge developers require. This doesn't mean that a developer can remain unenlightened about transactions, but WCF does take care of the details, enabling the developer to focus on the bigger picture. This chapter covers the features of WCF that coordinate one service's updates with other services and applications.

Exam objectives in this chapter:

- Manage transactions

Lessons in this chapter:

Before You Begin

To complete the lessons in this chapter, you must have:

- A computer that meets or exceeds the minimum hardware requirements listed in the introduction at the beginning of the book.
- Any edition of Microsoft Visual Studio 2008 (including Microsoft Visual C# 2008 Express edition or Microsoft Visual Basic 2008 Express edition) installed on the computer.
- Microsoft Distributed Transaction Controller (MSDTC) configured to allow WS-AT Transactions.

Real World

Bruce Johnson

In the opening paragraph for this chapter, notice that WCF is described as providing a solution to the technical side of the transaction equation only. If all you are doing is updating a single database, the technical details are where all the work occurs. You, as the developer, simply wrap the related updates into a single transaction, and the database handles the rest (committing or rolling back the transaction).

However, when services get involved, it becomes more challenging. At a minimum, a little more effort is required from the developer. Putting aside the possibility of business issues, ensuring that the desired changes are made across different systems requires careful coding. As much as possible, WCF strives to hide the technical issues from the developer. Your job is to be aware of how transactions interact with the incoming and outgoing messages. Read this chapter to solidify your understanding of how propagation and nested transactions work within the WCF model.

Lesson 1: Transaction Basics

At the simplest level, a transaction is a group of operations that must be executed as a single, atomic unit. If one operation in the group fails, none of them must be allowed to succeed. Consider, as an example, the movement of money from one bank account to another. Although conceptually this is a single function, it requires two operations to complete: debiting the account the money is being taken from and crediting the account into which the money is being deposited. If either of these operations fails, you don't want the other to succeed. This is a canonical example of a transaction.

To begin the journey through the landscape of WCF transactions, quickly review the basic concepts of transactional processing in this lesson.

After this lesson, you will be able to:
- Identify the fundamental properties of a transaction.
- Create both a client and a service capable of participating in a transaction.
- Define the bindings (both client and service) that are able to flow transaction information between the client and the service.

Estimated lesson time: 45 minutes

Transaction Properties

For a transaction to be considered successful, it must exhibit the following four attributes. In the nomenclature of transactions, these attributes are known as ACID—atomic, consistent, isolated, and durable.

Atomic

The root of the word is a good indication of its meaning. In Greek, *atamos* means "indivisible." In transactions, atomic means that all the operations must either succeed as a group or fail (that is, be rolled back) as a group. In the example of the bank account, the indivisible nature of the transaction is that both the credit and the debit must take place.

Consistent

Of the four attributes that make up ACID, consistency is the one that cannot be addressed by a transaction manager. A consistent transaction is one that, when it is complete, has left the data store in a legal state. In this usage, *legal* means that no integrity constraints (for instance, referential, uniqueness, and so on) are violated. Transaction managers don't have much impact on this property because a rogue developer could easily create a series of operations that is not consistent upon completion.

Isolated

For a transaction to be isolated, the changes that are part of the transaction should not be available until the transaction is complete. For the bank account example, you wouldn't want a credit check to view your bank account totals when only the withdrawal had occurred.

In the real world, different levels of transaction isolation are available because the computational cost of creating completely isolated transactions can become very expensive. However, even in these situations, it is incumbent on the development team to be aware of the possibility that the information being requested might be in a state of transition.

Durable

A transaction that is durable must survive failure: After the transaction has been committed, any kind of failure that might affect the data store (power outage, hardware failure, and so on) must not impact the data that was updated as part of the transaction. When the transaction is run against a single data store, ensuring durability is relatively straightforward. However, when there are multiple data stores on multiple computers, the complexity of ensuring durability is more challenging. This chapter addresses those challenges.

Quick Check

■ Of the four fundamental properties of a transaction, which one cannot be directly addressed by a resource manager such as a database?

Quick Check Answer

■ The integrity of the transaction is, to a certain extent, up to the developer to ensure. Although databases are capable of evaluating certain types of integrity constraints (referential, for example), they cannot evaluate a transaction's integrity from the perspective of business logic. Consider a transaction that involves transferring money from one account to another. The inclusion of both a debit and a credit update within the transaction, as well as ensuring that the amounts match, is something that only the developer can guarantee.

Implementing ACID

For a transaction to meet the ACID test successfully, a number of techniques can be used. Even against a single data store, a transaction can require many small operations to be performed, including updating indices, reorganizing rows, or executing triggers. When the transaction is distributed across different data stores running on difference physical machines, the problems increase greatly.

In a single data store, there are two common approaches to implementing ACID. Record locking ensures that multiple simultaneous attempts to read or update information cannot occur. Durability is ensured through write-ahead logging (writing updates to a log file prior to updating the data) or shadow paging so that pages are copied when they are written to, and the original page is updated only when the transaction is committed.

In a distributed environment, the most common approach is to use a *two-phase commit* approach that allows all the nodes in the transaction to vote on success or failure before the commit occurs. As its name suggests, the two-phase commit has two distinct phases.

Prepare Phase

The *transaction coordinator* coordinates the phases. The transaction coordinator is typically located on the computer that initiates the transaction. After all the updates have been performed, a request is made to the transaction coordinator to commit the transaction. The transaction coordinator sends a Prepare request to a *transaction manager* on each participating computer.

Each transaction manager is responsible for determining whether the updates within the scope of the resources that it manages are valid. If the transaction is valid, the transaction manager returns a Success message to the transaction coordinator. If there is a problem with the updates, the transaction manager returns a Failure message to the transaction coordinator. After all the transaction managers return either a Success or a Failure message, the Prepare phase is complete.

Commit Phase

The second phase in the process has two possible paths. If all the transaction managers return a Success message, the transaction coordinator sends out a Commit request to all the transaction managers. Upon receipt of this message, the transaction manager performs a commit on the updates and returns an acknowledgement to the coordinator. When the coordinator has received all the acknowledgements, the transaction is considered complete.

The second possible path occurs if any of the transaction managers returned a Failure message in the Prepare phase. A single failure means that all the updates should be rolled back, so the transaction coordinator sends out an Abort request to the transaction managers. The managers perform a rollback of the updates under their control and send an acknowledgement to the coordinator.

This is the basic flow through the two-phase commit process. Naturally, there are a number of other options. For example, the Prepare phase will have a timeout so that if no response is received from one of the transaction managers after a period of time, the transaction will be aborted. The same would happen if a transaction manager didn't receive a commit or abort message within a reasonable time frame. Also, from a responsiveness perspective, the entire two-phase commit process is a blocking event because locks must be maintained by each of the transaction managers from the start of the Prepare phase until the commit or abort request is received. This time span can range from fractions of a second to a minute or more, depending on the networking and timeout parameters.

Transaction Protocols

Although WCF supports the two-phase commit process, the transaction manager that is used depends on the situation. WCF supports three types of transaction managers: lightweight, OLE Transactions, and WS-Atomic Transactions (WS-AT). Although the word is slightly misused here, these types are called *transaction protocols*. Although all the protocols use two-phase processing, there are differences that relate to whether remote calls are required and the type of communication protocols that are used.

Underlying every transaction is one or more resources. It is updates to these resources that transactions are actually protecting from failure and integrity violations. Each resource in a transaction is managed by a *resource manager*. The resource manager works in conjunction with the transaction manager to provide the atomicity and isolation required by the transaction.

A resource manager manages either volatile or durable data. A resource manager that manages durable data is capable of supporting failure recovery. If the resource manager fails anytime after the Prepare phase, a new instance of the manager is created. The new instance would then receive and act on notifications from the transaction manager as if it were the original resource manager. In this way, the transaction does not have to be aborted due to failure of the resource manager.

A resource manager that manages volatile data, however, is unable to recover from some types of failure. Say you have an in-memory representation of some data stored in a transacted hash table. Although the resource manager is able to deal with transaction commits and rollbacks, it is unable to continue with the transactions if there is a system failure. All the data will be lost because there is no persistence. That data changes are saved to a more permanent store (such as a file system or a database) is the main distinguishing characteristic between durable and volatile data.

Lightweight Protocol

The traditional transaction manager has always involved high processing overhead. The ability to manage transactions in a distributed environment means that a variety of scenarios must be addressed. Scenarios, such as how to handle a network failure, are unnecessary if the transaction doesn't span multiple computers. The Lightweight Transaction Manager (LTM) was introduced in .NET Framework 2.0. Through the *System.Transaction* namespace, the LTM provides transaction management capability within a limited number of scenarios. Specifically, the scenario must have the following characteristics:

- It must be within a single AppDomain.
- It must use any number of volatile resources (enlisted by using the EnlistVolatile method on the Transaction class).
- It can have no more than one durable resource (enlisted by using the EnlistDurable method on the Transaction class).
- It must support single-phase notifications if a durable resource is present. (It must implement the ISinglePhaseNotification interface.)
- None of the resources can write the transaction outcome to the file system as part of the transaction.

NOTE   Not as restrictive as it sounds

Satisfying these restrictions is not that rare within the real world of application development. A large percentage of business applications' database changes fall into this category, so although the conditions might seem onerous, many transactions do fall into the realm of the LTM.

One of the benefits of using the LTM is its awareness of these criteria. If a situation arises that violates one of these criteria, the LTM will transfer ownership of the transaction to the MSDTC.

The LTM is enlisted as the transaction manager through the *TransactionScope* class. The *TransactionScope* class is implemented in the *System.Transactions* assembly. A reference to this assembly must be added (along with a *using* or *Imports* statement) before the class can be used. The following code creates a lightweight transaction and updates a database within the transaction:

```vb
' VB
Using ts As New TransactionScope()
   Using cn1 As New SqlConnection(connectionString)
      insertRecord(cn1, "User1")
      Using cn2 As New SqlConnection(connectionString)
         insertRecord(cn2, "User2")
   End Using
   End Using
   ts.Complete()
End Using

Private Sub insertRecord(cn As SqlConnection, userName As String)
   Dim cmd As New SqlCommand(String.Format("Insert INTO [Users]" & _
      " VALUES('{0}')", username), cn)
   cn.Open()
   cmd.ExecuteNonQuery()
End Sub
```

```csharp
// C#
using (TransactionScope ts = new TransactionScope())
{
   using (SqlConnection cn1 = new SqlConnection(connectionString))
```

```
    {
        insertRecord(cn1, "User1");
        using(SqlConnection cn2 = new SqlConnection(connectionString))
        {
            insertRecord(cn2, "User2");
        }
    }
    ts.Complete();
}

private void insertRecord(SqlConnection cn, string userName)
{
    SqlCommand cmd = new SqlCommand(String.Format("Insert INTO [Users]" +
        " VALUES('{0}')", userName), cn);
    cn.Open();
    cmd.ExecuteNonQuery();
}
```

To commit the transaction, the *Complete* method is invoked. This indicates that all the updates within the transaction have been performed successfully. When the *TransactionScope* object is disposed of (in the preceding example, that would happen when it leaves the *using* block), the updates are committed if and only if the *Complete* method has been called. If *Complete* has not been called, the updates are rolled back.

A close look at the sample code might cause you to wonder why the *using* blocks are nested within one another and not placed one after the other. For example, it might seem that the following would be more natural:

```
' VB
Using ts As New TransactionScope()
    Using cn1 As New SqlConnection(connectionString)
        insertRecord(cn1, "User1")
    End Using
    Using cn2 As New SqlConnection(connectionString)
        insertRecord(cn2, "User2")
    End Using
    ts.Complete()
End Using
```

```
// C#
using (TransactionScope ts = new TransactionScope())
{
    using (SqlConnection cn1 = new SqlConnection(connectionString))
    {
        insertRecord(cn1, "User1");
    }
    using (SqlConnection cn2 = new SqlConnection(connectionString))
    {
        insertRecord(cn2, "User2");
    }
    ts.Complete();
}
```

The problem is that, in this scenario, the LTM believes that a second durable resource manager is being enlisted. A human can see that the same connection will be used, but the LTM currently does not. As a result, the use of the second connection causes the transaction to be promoted from the LTM to MSDTC.

OLE Transaction Protocol

The OLE Transaction (OleTx) protocol is the standard for use with distributed transactions in a homogeneous environment. Although MSDTC can support other types of transactions, the default is to use OleTx when working with transactions that don't fit the criteria required by the LTM. Due to some of the details related to how OleTx works (including the use of remote procedure calls [RPCs] and a precise binary format for the calls), this protocol is feasible in a local Microsoft Windows networking environment only. It cannot be marshaled across firewalls, nor does it interoperate with non-Windows systems.

WS-Atomic Transaction Protocol

Conceptually, the WS-Atomic (WS-AT) protocol is not that different from OleTx in terms of its capabilities. It is a two-phase protocol that can propagate transactions across process, AppDomain, and computer boundaries. The main difference is that although OleTx is limited to computers running Windows behind a firewall, WS-AT is an industry standard that can be used over Hypertext Transfer Protocol (HTTP) (including through a firewall). Although it is technically feasible to use WS-AT in any scenario in which MSDTC could be used, it is primarily used when transactions include non-Windows environments or are crossing the Internet.

MORE INFO   Enabling WS-AT for MSDTC

MSDTC does provide support for the WS-AT protocol. The details can be configured through the same Microsoft Management Console (MMC) snap-in that is used for MSDTC. Instructions for installing (if necessary) and configuring WS-AT support for MSDTC can be found in the Configuring WS-Atomic Transaction Support topic, found at *http://msdn.microsoft.com/en-us/library /ms733943.aspx*. After installation, a WS-AT tab appears in the component services properties for the current computer. At a minimum, a check box is provided that enables or disables WS-AT protocol support. However, as the article describes, it is also possible to configure WS-AT over Secure Sockets Layer (SSL), using both self-signed and third-party certificates.

Propagating Transactions

Because WCF is targeted for distributed applications, it should not be surprising that there is support for propagating transactions across the boundaries of a service. By doing so, a service can participate in a transaction initiated by a client. In fact, the client can enlist multiple WCF services in a single transaction. The choice to propagate the transaction is not, however, the default WCF configuration setting. Both the client and the service(s) must indicate their willingness to be included in any transactions, and only certain bindings are capable of participating in distributed transactions. In general, these are the Transmission Control Protocol (TCP), interprocess communication (IPC), and WS-related bindings, but the complete list is *netTcpBinding*, *netNamedPipedBinding*, *wsHttpBinding*, *wsDualHttpBinding*, and *wsFederationHttpBinding*.

As has been mentioned, participation in a transaction is an opt-in setting. Both the client and the service need to be configured to transmit and accept transactions explicitly. Each of the binding classes listed at the end of the previous paragraph has a Boolean property called *TransactionFlow*. When set to *true* (the default is *false*), transaction details will be propagated across the connection. The value of this property can be set either programmatically or through the configuration file.

```vb
' VB
Dim binding As New WSHttpBinding()
binding.TransactionFlow = True
```

```csharp
// C#
WSHttpBinding binding = new WSHttpBinding();
binding.TransactionFlow = true;
```

```xml
<!--XML-->
<bindings>
   <wsHttpBinding>
      <binding name="Transactional" transactionFlow="true" />
   </wsHttpBinding>
</bindings>
```

CAUTION   *TransactionFlow* **value in the binding is not part of WCF metadata**

The value of the *TransactionFlow* property as defined in the configuration file is not published as part of the service's metadata, so the client proxy generation tools such as Visual Studio 2008 or svcutil will not set the *TransactionFlow* property on the client side. It must be set manually (either through code or configuration) to enable transaction propagation.

Configuring the binding to support transaction propagation is only half the battle. The client must have a transaction to propagate; more is discussed about that later. In addition, the operations in the service must indicate a desire to participate in the transaction. This latter piece is a service-level choice and is included as part of the contractual agreement between the client and the service. WCF defines a *TransactionFlow* attribute that is used to decorate methods. This attribute takes a *TransactionFlowOption* as value and uses this information to determine what, if anything, should be done with transactions during the operation. The choices for the *TransactionFlowOption* are described in the following sections.

TransactionFlowOption.NotAllowed

This option is the default value for the *TransactionFlow*. When set to *NotAllowed*, no transaction will be propagated across the binding, regardless of whether the binding enables transaction flow. Any existing client transaction will be silently ignored (the transaction does not result in an exception being raised), and the service will not have access to the client's transaction.

TransactionFlowOption.Allowed

Using this option allows a client transaction to be propagated to the service. However, the fact that a transaction is allowed to flow across the service boundary does not mean that a transaction must be created on the client side or that the service must use any provided transaction. As a result of this flexibility, setting *TransactionFlow* to *Allowed* does not restrict the binding options to just those that require transactions. A transaction-unaware binding can still be used.

Even with this relaxed restriction, both the client and the service must agree on the transaction awareness of the binding. If the operation allows transactions to be flowed but the binding on the service does not have transactions enabled, the client must ensure that transactions are disallowed on its binding. If it does not, an exception will be raised if the client attempts to flow a transaction. The exception occurs because the message received from the client will have transaction information that the service does not understand.

NOTE Unexpected information

The important part of the agreement between the client and the service is that the service does not receive data in the message that it does not expect. If the service's binding is configured to allow transaction flow but the client binding has transaction flow disabled, no exception will be raised because no unexpected information is received by the service.

If, for example, the *TransactedMethod* on the *IDemoContract* interface allowed an existing transaction to be propagated to the service, the definition would be as follows:

```vb
' VB
<ServiceContract> _
Public Interface IDemoContract
    <OperationContract> _
    <TransactionFlow(TransactionFlowOption.Allowed)> _
    Sub TransactedMethod(...)
End Interface
```

```csharp
// C#
[ServiceContract]
public interface IDemoContract
{
    [OperationContract]
    [TransactionFlow(TransactionFlowOption.Allowed)]
```

```
    void TransactedMethod(...);
}
```

On the client side of this equation, the *TransactionFlow* attribute is used to decorate the method in the proxy class. The code would look like the following:

```
' VB
Public Class DemoService
    Implements IDemoContract

    <TransactionFlow(TransactionFlowOption.Allowed)> _
    Public Sub TransactedMethod(...)
        ...
    End Sub
End Class

//C#
public class DemoService : IDemoContract
{
    [TransactionFlow(TransactionFlowOption.Allowed)]
    public void TransactedMethod(...)
    {...}
}
```

TransactionFlowOption.Mandatory

When an operation is configured so that transaction flow is mandatory, both the service and the client must use a transaction-aware binding with the *TransactionFlow* property set to *true*. This configuration will be checked by WCF when the service is loaded, and an *InvalidOperationException* is thrown if any of the service endpoints is not compatible with this requirement.

Also, from the client's perspective, the Mandatory option means that the client must propagate a transaction to the service. If the service is called without an active transaction, a *FaultException* is raised by the client.

Transactions and One-Way Calls

As you might expect after reading about the communication necessary for two-phase commits, the typical model for working with distributed transactions involves communications between the transaction coordinator and the services. But how does this communication work when a *one-way call* is involved?

The answer is that it doesn't. There is no way it could. By definition, a one-way call does not have a reply message, and it is through the reply message that the results of both of the two phases are sent from the service to the transaction coordinator. Without that reply message, no distributed transaction is possible.

WCF is smart enough to detect this scenario. If, when the service is loaded, an Operation contract is marked as being one way and the transaction flow is set to anything other than *Not-Allowed*, an exception is raised.

Lab: Using Transactions in Services

In this lab, you will create a transaction-aware client and service. Even if you create a distributed transaction of staggering complexity, you must still understand what is happening at this fundamental level.

▶ **Exercise 1   Create a Transaction-Aware Service**

In this first exercise, you will build a transaction-aware service. This includes defining the Operation contract and the binding to support the flow of transaction from the client into this service.

1. Navigate to the Chapter 11/Lesson 1/Exercise 1/<*language*>/Before directory. Select the Exercise1 solution and click Open.

2. In Solution Explorer, double-click the IUpdateService file.

   This opens the code window for the *IUpdateService* interface.

   You will add two methods (called *UpdateNoTransaction* and *UpdateWithTransaction*) to this interface, which is the Service contract for the service that you are creating. Each of these methods takes a single string parameter and returns an integer.

3. Add the following code immediately below the declaration for the *IUpdateService* interface:

   ```
   ' VB
   <OperationContract> _
   Function UpdateNoTransaction(SqlStmt As String) As Integer

   <OperationContract> _
   Function UpdateWithTransaction(SqlStmt As String) As Integer

   // C#
   [OperationContract]
   int UpdateNoTransaction(string sqlStmt);

   [OperationContract]
   int UpdateWithTransaction(string sqlStmt);
   ```

4. In Solution Explorer, double-click the UpdateService file.

   Because the *UpdateService* class is the implementation for the WCF contract, it must implement the *IUpdateService* interface.

5. Change the declaration for the *UpdateService* class to the following:

   ```
   ' VB
   Public Class UpdateService
       Implements IUpdateService
   ```

```
// C#
public class UpdateService : IUpdateService
```

The UpdateService class must include definitions for the two methods in *IUpdateService*. In both cases, the methods call the already defined private method named *update*.

6. Add the following code to the region called *IUpdateService Members*:

```
' VB
Public Function UpdateNoTransaction(SqlStmt as String) As Integer _
    Implements IUpdateService.UpdateNoTransaction
    Return update(SqlStmt)
End Function

Public Function UpdateWithTransaction(SqlStmt as String) As Integer _
    Implements IUpdateService.UpdateWithTransaction
    Return update(SqlStmt)
End Function
```

```
// C#
public int UpdateNoTransaction(string sqlStmt)
{
    return update(sqlStmt);
}

public int UpdateWithTransaction(string sqlStmt)
{
    return update(sqlStmt);
}
```

At this point, you can test the service.

7. In Solution Explorer, right-click the TransactionalService project, click Debug, and then select Start New Instance.

This causes the WcfsvcHost application to run the service, and the WCF Test Client starts.

In a few seconds, in the WCF Test Client, you see a list of the methods in the service that you're creating.

8. Double-click the UpdateNoTransaction method in the left pane.

9. On the right side, set the value for the SqlStmt parameter to **INSERT INTO DemoTable VALUES (1, 'Sample Data')**, and then click Invoke. If a Security Warning dialog box appears, click OK.

In a few seconds, you will see that the response value is *1*, indicating that the update on the service side was successful. The WCF Test Client can be closed to stop the debugging session.

Based on the names of the methods, you would expect one of the methods (the one named *UpdateWithTransaction*) to have an active transaction. To ensure this, the method must be marked as such in the *OperationContract* attribute.

10. In Solution Explorer, double-click the IUpdateService file.

11. Decorate the *UpdateWithTransaction* method with the following attribute:

    ```
    ' VB
    <TransactionFlow(TransactionFlowOption.Mandatory)> _

    // C#
    [TransactionFlow(TransactionFlowOption.Mandatory)]
    ```

    If you attempt to run the service now, you will receive an error indicating that the binding being used doesn't support transactions. You must modify the binding definition in the app.config file to support transactions.

12. In Solution Explorer, double-click the App.config file.

13. Find the first *endpoint* tag. Add a *bindingConfiguration* attribute that sets the name of the binding configuration to *TransactionalBinding*, as shown here:

    ```
    <endpoint address ="" binding="wsHttpBinding"
        bindingConfiguration="TransactionalBinding"
        contract="TransactionalService.IUpdateService">
    ```

    Because you just indicated that the current binding has a particular configuration, you must now add it.

14. Below the closing tag for the *services* element, add the following XML elements to configure the *wsHttpBinding* to allow transactions to flow across the service boundary, as shown here:

    ```
    <bindings>
      <wsHttpBinding>
        <binding name="TransactionalBinding" transactionFlow="true" />
      </wsHttpBinding>
    </bindings>
    ```

15. Launch the service application one more time to ensure that the binding has been configured correctly. In Solution Explorer, right-click the TransactionalService project, select Debug, and then choose Start New Instance.

    If everything is working, the WCF Test Client will appear with a list of the methods in the UpdateService service.

▶ **Exercise 2   Create a Transaction-Aware Client**

Create the client side for the transaction-aware service that was created in Exercise 1, "Create a Transaction-Aware Service."

1. Navigate to the Chapter 11/Lesson 1/Exercise 2/<language>/Before directory. Select the TransactionalService solution and click Open.

2. In Solution Explorer, double-click the Program file in the TransactionalClient project.

    Notice that the first line of the *Main* method is a call to the *SetData* method for the current *AppDomain*. The purpose of this call is to allow a relative path to be defined for the connection string to the database. It has nothing to do with WCF transactions and everything to do with ensuring that the lab will work on your system.

3. Create the proxy object that communicates with the WCF service. Add the following code after the first call to *Console.WriteLine*:

```vb
' VB
Using client As New TransactionalServiceProxy.UpdateServiceClient()
End Using
```

```csharp
// C#
using (TransactionalServiceProxy.UpdateServiceClient client =
    new TransactionalClient.TransactionalServiceProxy.UpdateServiceClient())
{
}
```

Next, you create the *TransactionScope* object. As with the proxy client, a *using* block is called for.

4. Add the following code to the just-added *using* block:

```vb
' VB
Using ts As New TransactionScope(TransactionScopeOption.Required)
End Using
```

```csharp
// C#
using (TransactionScope ts = new TransactionScope(TransactionScopeOption.Required))
{
}
```

Now it's time to add the calls to the WCF service. In this call, a SQL statement is passed to the service that inserts a record to the DemoTable table.

5. Add the following code to the *using* block for the *TransactionScope* object:

```vb
' VB
Dim updatedRecords As Integer = 0
updatedRecords += client.UpdateWithTransaction( _
    "INSERT INTO DemoTable VALUES (1, 'Demo Data')")
```

```csharp
// C#
int updatedRecords = 0;
updatedRecords += client.UpdateWithTransaction(
    "INSERT INTO DemoTable VALUES (1, 'Demo Data')");
```

6. To create a second database update within the same transaction, make another call to the *UpdateWithTransaction* method. Add the following line of code below the just-added code:

```vb
' VB
updatedRecords += client.UpdateWithTransaction( _
    "INSERT INTO DemoTable VALUES (2, 'More Data')")
```

```csharp
// C#
updatedRecords += client.UpdateWithTransaction(
    "INSERT INTO DemoTable VALUES (2, 'More Data')");
```

7. To see how many records have been added to the database, add the following line of code below the second call to UpdateWithTransaction.

    ```
    ' VB
    Console.WriteLine(String.Format("The record count is {0}", updatedRecords))
    ```

    ```
    // C#
    Console.WriteLine(String.Format("The record count is {0}",
        updatedRecords));
    ```

    Now you roll back the changes by aborting the transaction.

8. Add the following line of code immediately after the just-added statement:

    ```
    ' VB
    ts.Dispose()
    ```

    ```
    // C#
    ts.Dispose();
    ```

9. To allow the application to pause before displaying the record count after the rollback, add the following code just after the using block for the inner TransactionScope object:

    ```
    ' VB
    Console.ReadLine()
    ```

    ```
    // C#
    Console.ReadLine();
    ```

10. Ensure that TransactionalClient is set as the startup project, and then launch the application by pressing F5.

    After a few moments, you receive an *InvalidOperationException*. The message associated with the exception indicates that the client-side binding is not configured to flow transaction information as the service requires.

11. Terminate the application by pressing Shift+F5.

12. To correct this problem, in Solution Explorer, double-click the app.config file in the TransactionalClient project.

13. Locate the bindings element in the file. You must add a binding for *wsHttpBinding* that supports transactions. Modify the bindings element to look like the following:

    ```
    <bindings>
       <wsHttpBinding>
          <binding name="TransactionBinding" transactionFlow="True" />
       </wsHttpBinding>
    </bindings>
    ```

    For the binding to be associated with the endpoint, the binding configuration for the endpoint must be directed to the just created *TransactionBinding*.

14. Add the following attribute to the endpoint configuration that already exists in the app.config file:

    ```
    bindingConfiguration="TransactionBinding"
    ```

15. Now that the problem with transaction flow has been corrected, launch the application by pressing F5.

    After a few moments, you see that the two records have been updated.

16. Press Enter to continue running the application and roll back the transaction.

    After you press Enter, the transaction is aborted by the call to the *Dispose* method. Then the number of records left in the table is displayed. If the transaction is successfully aborted, this value will be *0*.

17. Press Enter to terminate the application.

Lesson Summary

- The fundamental purpose of transactions is to guarantee ACID behavior across updates to one or more resource managers.

- A number of transaction managers can become involved in coordinating a transaction. If System.Transaction is used as a starting point, the minimal service will be used. Promotion occurs automatically on an as-needed basis.

- Transactions can be allowed to flow across service boundaries, or they can be blocked. Both the client and the service make the decision, although if the service requires a transaction, blocking them on the client will cause the application to fail.

Lesson Review

You can use the following questions to test your knowledge of the information in Lesson 1, "Transaction Basics." The questions are also available on the companion CD if you prefer to review them in electronic form.

NOTE Answers

Answers to these questions and explanations of why each answer choice is correct or incorrect are located in the "Answers" section at the end of the book.

1. You have a standalone Windows Forms application. Within a single transaction, your application must update two Microsoft SQL Server databases. Which transaction coordinator manages the transactions?

    A. Lightweight Transaction Manager

    B. Microsoft Distributed Transaction Controller

    C. Kernel Transaction Manager

    D. Web Services Transaction Manager

2. You have an ASP.NET application. As part of processing a page request, a call is made to a WCF service, and an UPDATE statement is issued against a SQL Server database. Both the WCF call and the UPDATE command are made within a single *TransactionScope* block. Which transaction coordinator is used to manage the transactions?

   A. Lightweight Transaction Manager
   B. Microsoft Distributed Transaction Controller
   C. Kernel Transaction Manager
   D. Web Services Transaction Manager

Lesson 2: Programming Transactions

Although it is possible to declaratively configure most of the settings associated with WCF transactional processing, there are instances in which you must use the imperative model. In this lesson, the focus is on the imperative techniques used to build transactional clients and services.

After this lesson, you will be able to:
- Create a transaction that can be used by WCF.
- Allow a WCF service to vote to complete or abort a transaction.
- Determine the appropriate isolation level for a transaction.

Estimated lesson time: 35 minutes

Ambient Transactions

The .NET Framework 2.0 and the *System.Transaction* namespace introduced the idea of an *ambient transaction*. By definition, an ambient transaction exists in the current thread or object context. Its existence can be queried by any interested parties (within the thread or context). If the ambient transaction exists, any resource manager can (if desired) enlist all its updates in that transaction, allowing the actions to be performed according to the principles of ACID.

In general, developers don't pay much attention to the ambient transaction. That is mostly left up to database proxies (such as System.Data, OLEDB, and ODBC). However, if necessary, you can obtain a reference to the ambient transaction by using the static *Current* property as shown here:

```
' VB
Dim ambientTransaction As Transaction = Transaction.Current
```

```
// C#
Transaction ambientTransaction = Transaction.Current;
```

If there is no ambient transaction, *Transaction.Current* is null.

The ambient transaction is stored in thread local storage. As a result, it is available to any piece of code and, as the thread moves between different objects, methods, and properties, the ambient transaction is available to all who need access to it. With respect to WCF, the ambient transaction is critical to flowing transactions. Any WCF-compatible resource manager (SQL Server or a volatile resource manager) will automatically enlist in the ambient transaction. When a service is called through a binding that has transaction flow enabled, the ambient transaction is propagated to the service.

You can use the same transaction for both local and distributed transactions. The promotion from local to distributed occurs automatically, based on criteria that have already been discussed.

However, through a couple of properties, it is possible to determine whether the ambient transaction is local or distributed.

The *Transaction* class (and, specifically, the *Transaction.Current* object) exposes a property called *TransactionInformation*. This is actually an object (of type *TransactionInformation*), which itself has two properties. The *LocalIdentifier* property is a string that contains a unique identifier for the current transaction. The *DistributedIdentifier* property is a globally unique identifier (GUID) that represents the distributed transaction. If the transaction has not been promoted, *DistributedIdentifier* will be *Guid.Empty*.

TransactionScope Class

In working with WCF transactions programmatically, the *TransactionScope* class is at the heart of the process. As the name suggests, *TransactionScope* objects define the scope of a transaction:

```
' VB
Using ts As New TransactionScope()
   ' updates go here
   ts.Complete()
End Using

// C#
using (TransactionScope ts = new TransactionScope())
{
   // updates go here
   ts.Complete();
}
```

Depending on the existence of an ambient transaction, the construction of the *Transaction-Scope* object causes either a new LTM transaction to be created (if there is no ambient transaction) or enlists in the existing ambient transaction.

The key to the *TransactionScope* is how the transaction is finished. The scope of the transaction lasts until the instance is disposed. When the *using* statement is used, that would be at the end of the block. Alternatively, you can call the *Dispose* method on the *TransactionScope* explicitly. What should not happen is to allow the *TransactionScope* object to go out of scope. Although it is true that, eventually, the object would be disposed, the garbage collection process means this won't happen in a deterministic manner. It is possible that the transaction times out (and thus is aborted) prior to garbage collection. This might or might not be the desired behavior.

Voting on Transactions

As has been discussed, LTM transactions participate in a two-phase commit process. To do so, any resource manager (and, subsequently, your code) must be able to vote on the success or failure of the transaction in the first phase.

The *TransactionScope* class has, internally, a consistency bit. When first instantiated, this bit is set to *false*. If the *TransactionScope* object is disposed while this bit is false, the transaction is aborted or, more accurately, the transaction will inform the transaction coordinator that it is voting to abort the transaction.

There should be some way to set the consistency bit to *true*. This is done by calling the *Complete* method on the *TransactionScope* object. This method has to be invoked before the object is disposed, and it can be invoked only once. If there is a second call for the same transaction, an *InvalidOperationException* will be raised. In general, it is a good idea for the call to *Complete* to be the last statement in the *using* block so that if an exception is thrown within the block, the call to *Complete* will be skipped.

Keep in mind that calling *Complete* does not guarantee that the transaction will be committed. Although it is true that all attempts are made to complete the transaction, in a two-phase commit, any of the participating resource managers can vote to abort. As a result, it is possible that when the *TransactionScope* is being disposed, a transaction that you think will be committed is actually aborted. In such a situation, a *TransactionAbortedException* is raised from the *Complete* method. To address this, the following is an example of how *TransactionScope* should be used:

```vb
' VB
Try
    Using ts As New TransactionScope( )
        ' Perform updates here
        ts.Complete( )
    End Using
Catch e As TransactionAbortedException
    ' Rollback updates, if necessary
End Try
```

```csharp
// C#
try
{
    using(TransactionScope ts = new TransactionScope( ))
    {
        /* Perform updates here */
        ts.Complete( );
    }
}
catch(TransactionAbortedException e)
{
    /* Rollback updates, if necessary */
}
```

> ## Quick Check
> - Within an existing transaction, you have a method that wants to vote to abort a transaction. Is there a difference between explicitly voting to abort and simply allowing the method to exit without invoking the Complete method?
>
> ## Quick Check Answer
> - Yes, there is a difference. Specifically, if the method exits without explicitly voting to abort, then its vote won't be cast until a garbage collection has occurred. Although, in many applications, there won't be a long passage of time between garbage collections, it is still technically nondeterministic. Theoretically, seconds could pass before the collection occurs, and until the vote is cast, other applications waiting for the outcome are blocked from continuing execution.

Nesting Transactions

If the instantiation of a new *TransactionScope* object creates a new transaction, that scope is called the *root scope*. The configuration of transaction scoping in the app.config file and the presence of an ambient transaction affect whether a root scope is created. The name "root scope" implies the ability to nest scopes within one another, and that is possible. In fact, not only is it possible, but the developer can ensure that there is an existing scope through one of the overloaded constructors for the *TransactionScope* class.

One of the constructors for the *TransactionScope* class accepts a parameter of type *TransactionScopeOption*. This enumeration has three values, as seen in Table 11-1.

Table 11-1   Values for the *TransactionScopeOption* Enumeration

Value	Description
Required	Either the ambient transaction is used or a new transaction is created. This is the default value because the assumption is that if you're trying to create a *TransactionScope* object, it's likely that you want it to be part of a transaction, whether it exists or it has to be created for you.
RequiresNew	A new transaction is created, regardless of whether an ambient transaction exists. This transaction becomes the root transaction for any upcoming transactions. More important, it segregates the updates from any existing transaction. This type of scenario might be useful in a logging application. In such a situation, it is useful to log the attempt to update the data even if the transaction is ultimately rolled back.

Table 11-1   Values for the *TransactionScopeOption* Enumeration

Value	Description
Suppress	Even if an ambient transaction exists, any changes within the scope will not be enlisted. This is a rarely used option, with the most likely scenario being a block of code that is using a transaction-aware resource but must include its own compensating transaction logic. Do not call a service that requires a transaction from within a transaction scope that has been suppressed. The *Suppress* option means that the transaction will not be propagated to the service call, so the call is guaranteed to fail.

Now that this basic definition has been established, take a look at nested transactions and answer some of the tough questions. Consider the following code, showing a pair of nested transactions:

```vb
' VB
Using ts1 As New TransactionScope()
   Using ts2 As New TransactionScope()
      ts2.Complete()
   End Using
   ts1.Complete()
End Using
```

```csharp
// C#
using(TransactionScope ts1 = new TransactionScope())
{
   using(TransactionScope ts2 = new TransactionScope())
   {
      ts2.Complete();
   }
   ts1.Complete();
}
```

Notice that, for the consistency bit for both *TransactionScope* objects to be set to *true*, the *Complete* method must be called twice. Contrast this example with the following code:

```vb
' VB
Using ts1 As New TransactionScope()
   Using ts2 As New TransactionScope()
      ts2.Complete( )
   End Using
End Using
```

```csharp
// C#
using(TransactionScope ts1 = new TransactionScope())
{
   using(TransactionScope ts2 = new TransactionScope())
   {
      ts2.Complete();
   }
}
```

Although the *ts2 TransactionScope* has been marked as complete, the *ts1 TransactionScope* has not been. Therefore, all the updates from both scopes will be rolled back.

The other question that arises, regarding nested transactions, deals with isolation: Are any changes made within the transaction created by *ts1* visible from within the code block for *ts2*? Some of the overloaded constructors for *TransactionScope* accept a *TransactionOptions* structure as a parameter. This structure includes a property called *IsolationLevel*, which is a value from the *IsolationLevel* enumeration. Table 11-2 shows the possible isolation levels.

Table 11-2   Isolation Levels for a *TransactionScope*

Member Name	Description
Serializable	This is the highest level of isolation. Other users cannot view or change data that has been updated as part of the transaction. Other processes will be unable to update or add conflicting data during the transaction.
RepeatableRead	Other processes are able to view the updated data, but that data cannot be modified as data is viewed. This means, as the name indicates, that the data can be read repeatedly without any other process being able to make a change. However, it is possible for additional data from a different process to be added, and, therefore, to become visible within this transaction scope.
ReadCommitted	The resource manager holds a shared lock on the data, which prevents other processes from being able to read uncommitted data.
ReadUncommitted	Other processes are able to read and modify updated data prior to it being committed.
Snapshot	Volatile data can be read. Before a transaction modifies data, it verifies whether another transaction has changed the data after it was initially read. If the data has been updated, an error is raised. This enables a transaction to get to the previously committed value of the data.
Chaos	The pending changes from more highly isolated transactions cannot be overwritten.
Unspecified	A different isolation level than the one specified is being used, but the level cannot be determined. An exception is thrown if this value is set.

The valid isolation level for a given transaction scope depends on the resource manager. Not every resource manager supports the complete range of isolation levels. If the resource manager doesn't support the requested level, it will change the isolation level to a supported value based on an algorithm specific to that manager.

In the .NET world, the answer to the original question (regarding the visibility of updates in nested transactions) changes, based on the resource manager. For the LTM, the answer is, "Yes, they are visible." The LTM does not provide any isolation for nested transactions. If the resource manager is SQL Server, the listed isolation levels are supported.

CAUTION   Identical isolation levels required

When using nested *TransactionScope* objects, all the scopes must use the same isolation level if they want to join the ambient transaction. If the specified level is different, an *ArgumentException* is thrown.

Transaction Timeouts

For completeness, there is one other constructor overload of interest:

```
' VB
Dim ts As New TransactionScope(TransactionScopeOption.Required, _
    New TimeSpan(0, 10, 0))
```

```
// C#
TransactionScope ts = new TransactionScope(TransactionScopeOption.Required,
    new TimeSpan(0, 10, 0));
```

With the use of such a constructor, the transaction is required to complete within the specified timeout. If it doesn't, the transaction will be aborted (as the only active transaction) or the transaction will vote to abort the transaction (if it is part of a larger transaction).

It is possible to create a transaction that has an infinite timeout by using a timeout of zero.

```
' VB
Dim ts As New TransactionScope(TransactionScopeOption.Required, _
    TimeSpan.Zero)
```

```
// C#
TransactionScope ts = new TransactionScope(TransactionScopeOption.Required,
    TimeSpan.Zero);
```

This means that the ongoing updates will not be interrupted, regardless of how long they take to complete. The vote to commit or abort the transaction (the entire transaction) must wait until the updates have finished. As you might imagine, setting a transaction to have an infinite timeout is potentially risky because, in some instances, it can cause a deadlock to occur in the transaction.

When a transaction scope joins an existing transaction, the timeout value on the scope is compared to the value in the ambient transaction. If the *TransactionScope* timeout is smaller, the created transaction will respect the smaller timeout. This means that if the timeout expires (in that smaller period of time), it will cause the transaction to abort, which in turn aborts the earlier transaction. Consider the following code:

```
' VB
Using ts1 As New _
    TransactionScope(TransactionScopeOption.Required, _
    new TimeSpan(0, 2, 0) )
    ' A transaction with a timespan of 2 minutes is created
```

```
    Using ts2 As New _
       TransactionScope(TransactionScopeOption.Required, _
       new TimeSpan(0, 1, 0) )
       ' A transaction with a timespan of 1 minute is created
       Thread.Sleep(90000)
    End Using
End Using
```

```
// C#
using(TransactionScope ts1 = new
    TransactionScope(TransactionScopeOption.Required,
    new TimeSpan(0, 2, 0) ))
{
    // A transaction with a timespan of 2 minutes is created
    using(TransactionScope ts2 = new
    TransactionScope(TransactionScopeOption.Required,
    new TimeSpan(0, 1, 0) ))
    {
      // A transaction with a timespan of 1 minute is created
       Thread.Sleep(90000);
    }
}
```

In this example, transaction A with a timeout value of two minutes is created with the first *TransactionScope* object. Transaction B has a timeout of one minute. With the Sleep statement taking longer than a minute, transaction B times out, causing it to roll back. Because transaction B votes to abort, it also rolls back transaction A.

NOTE What if inner has a longer timeout than outer?

If the inner transaction (Transaction B in the example) has a longer time span than the outer transaction (Transaction A), the difference has no effect on the behavior of the code. The outer transaction would be rolled back on the shorter, which would immediately abort and roll back the inner transaction.

From a practical perspective, there are generally two reasons to set the timeout to something other than the default. To test the behavior of an application when a transaction fails, the timeout value can be set to a millisecond. Alternatively, it is used when the transaction might be involved in resource contention. So, rather than waiting for the default timeout to expire, you might choose to set the timeout value to something shorter, enabling the detection to be handled more quickly.

The default timeout value can be modified through the configuration file. Specifically, it is set in the *system.transactions* tag in the appropriate configuration file. The following XML sample sets the default timeout for the *TransactionScope* to ten seconds.

```
<system.transactions>
   <defaultSettings timeout="00:00:10" />
</system.transactions>
```

Lab: Programming Transactions

In this lab, you will use the *TransactionScope* class to create transactions that can be propagated to a WCF service. The exercises will look at committing and rolling back transactions in both a simple and a nested environment.

▶ **Exercise 1   Commit and Roll Back a Transaction**

In this first exercise, you will use the *TransactionScope* object to both commit and abort changes made through both a WCF service and the execution of a local SQL command. The service you use is similar to the one constructed in the lab for the first lesson in this chapter.

1. Navigate to the Chapter 11/Lesson 2/Exercise 1/<language>/Before directory. Select the Exercise1 solution and click Open.

2. In Solution Explorer, double-click the Program file in the TransactionalClient project.

3. Create the proxy object that will be used to communicate with the WCF service. Add the following code after the first call to *Console.WriteLine*:

```
' VB
Using client As New TransactionalServiceProxy.UpdateServiceClient()
End Using
```

```
// C#
using (TransactionalServiceProxy.UpdateServiceClient client =
    new TransactionalClient.TransactionalServiceProxy.UpdateServiceClient())
{
}
```

Next, you create the *TransactionScope* object. As with the proxy client, you use a *using* block.

4. Add the following code to the just-added *using* block:

```
' VB
Using ts As New TransactionScope(TransactionScopeOption.Required)
End Using
```

```
// C#
using (TransactionScope ts = new TransactionScope(TransactionScopeOption.Required))
{
}
```

Now you add the call to the WCF service. In this call, you pass to the service a SQL statement that inserts a record to the DemoTable table.

5. Add the following code to the *using* block for the *TransactionScope* object:

```
' VB
client.UpdateWithTransaction( _
    "INSERT INTO DemoTable VALUES (1, 'Demo Data')")
```

```
// C#
client.UpdateWithTransaction(
    "INSERT INTO DemoTable VALUES (1, 'Demo Data')");
```

The call to the WCF service adds a record within the transaction. Now, add one locally. In the file, there is a static method called *addRecord*. This record performs the same INSERT into the database as found in the WCF service.

6. Add a call to this method by inserting the following line of code below the call to the WCF service:

```
' VB
addRecord()
```

```
// C#
addRecord();
```

7. To see what the record count is after the two updates, add the following line of code below the just-added statement:

```
' VB
Console.WriteLine(String.Format( _
    "Before the abort, the record count is {0}", getRecordCount()))
```

```
// C#
Console.WriteLine(String.Format(
    "Before the abort, the record count is {0}", getRecordCount()));
```

8. Finally, abort the transaction by adding the following line of code at the bottom of the transaction scope's *using* block:

```
' VB
ts.Dispose()
```

```
// C#
ts.Dispose();
```

9. Ensure that TransactionalClient is set as the startup project, and then launch the application by pressing F5.

After a few moments, you will see that the number of records in the table before the abort is two. After the abort has been performed, the value is back to zero.

10. Press Enter to terminate the application.

11. In the Program file, change the code so that the transaction completes. Locate the call to the Dispose method and replace it with the following:

```
' VB
ts.Complete()
```

```
// C#
ts.Complete();
```

12. Launch the application by pressing F5.

    After a few moments, you see that the number of records in the table before the records are committed is two and, after the commit has been performed, the number of records is still two.

13. Press Enter to terminate the application.

▶ Exercise 2   Nested Transactions with Timeouts

A nesting transaction is not a complicated process. In this exercise, you will create a nested transaction and then observe the behavior when different scenarios occur. First, the inner transaction is aborted, and then the outer transaction is aborted using a timeout.

1. Navigate to the Chapter 11/Lesson 2/Exercise 2/<language>/Before directory. Select the Exercise2 solution and click Open.

2. In Solution Explorer, double-click the Program file found in the TransactionalClient project.

3. Create the proxy object that will communicate with the WCF service. Add the following code after the first call to *Console.WriteLine*:

```
' VB
Using client As New TransactionalServiceProxy.UpdateServiceClient()
End Using
```

```
// C#
using (TransactionalServiceProxy.UpdateServiceClient client =
    new TransactionalClient.TransactionalServiceProxy.UpdateServiceClient())
{
}
```

4. Create the *TransactionScope* object. As with the proxy client, you use a *using* block. Add the following code to the just-added *using* block:

```
' VB
Try
    Using ts1 As New TransactionScope()
    End Using
Catch ex As Exception
    Console.WriteLine(ex.Message)
End Try
```

```
// C#
try
{
    using (TransactionScope ts1 = new
        TransactionScope(TransactionScopeOption.Required))
    {
    }
}
catch (Exception ex)
{
```

```
    Console.WriteLine(ex.Message);
}
```

5. Add the first call to the WCF service by inserting the following line of code in the *using* block for the *TransactionScope* that was just added.

```
' VB
client.UpdateWithTransaction( _
    "INSERT INTO DemoTable VALUES (1, 'Demo Data')")
```

```
// C#
client.UpdateWithTransaction(
    "INSERT INTO DemoTable VALUES (1, 'Demo Data')");
```

Next, start the second transaction scope inside the *using* block for the *TransactionScope* object added in Step 4.

6. Add the following lines below the call to the WCF service:

```
' VB
Using ts2 As New TransactionScope()
End Using
```

```
// C#
using (TransactionScope ts2 = new TransactionScope())
{
}
```

7. Inside this second *using* block, add a call to the WCF service by placing the following code inside the just-added transaction scope block:

```
' VB
client.UpdateWithTransaction( _
    "INSERT INTO DemoTable VALUES (2, 'Demo Data')")
```

```
// C#
client.UpdateWithTransaction(
    "INSERT INTO DemoTable VALUES (2, 'Demo Data')");
```

8. After the second call to the WCF service, check to see how many records are in the table by adding the following line of code after the call:

```
' VB
Console.WriteLine(String.Format( _
    "Before the abort, the record count is {0}", getRecordCount()))
```

```
// C#
Console.WriteLine(String.Format(
    "Before the abort, the record count is {0}", getRecordCount()));
```

9. Finally, abort the inner transaction by adding the following line of code to the bottom of the second transaction scope's *using* block:

```
' VB
ts2.Dispose()
```

```
// C#
ts2.Dispose();
```

10. To confirm that it's the inner transaction that is aborting the entire transaction, add the following line of code outside of the inner *TransactionScope* block but within the outer *TransactionScope* block:

```
' VB
ts1.Complete()
```

```
// C#
ts1.Complete();
```

11. Ensure that the TransactionalClient project is set to be the startup project, and then launch the application by pressing F5.

    After a few moments, you will see that two records were created by the call to the WCF service. The transaction is aborted, and the record count returns to 0.

12. Press Enter to terminate the application.

    Next, you use the transaction timeout to abort the transaction.

13. Locate the line at which the inner transaction is aborted (*ts2.Dispose*) and delete it.

14. Then, in the constructor for the inner *TransactionScope* object, use the overload to set the timeout value. For this exercise, set it to 1 millisecond by changing the *using* statement to the following:

```
' VB
Using ts2 As New TransactionScope(TransactionScopeOption.Required, _
    New TimeSpan(1))
```

```
// C#
using (TransactionScope ts2 = new TransactionScope(
    TransactionScopeOption.Required, new TimeSpan(1)))
```

15. Launch the application by pressing F5.

    You'll notice that the transaction will abort (probably) even before the line that displays the number of records in the database table will execute.

Lesson Summary

■ The ambient transaction refers to the active transaction that is available to the current process. If there is an active transaction that is not propagated across the service boundary, the ambient transaction will be null.

■ The TransactionScope class is a critical component of working with transactions in WCF. It provides the fundamental functionality as well as the automatic ability to promote the transaction to the appropriate coordinator.

■ The TransactionScope class does not, by default, support all the different isolation levels. It is dependent on the resource manager to implement isolation.

Lesson Review

You can use the following questions to test your knowledge of the information in Lesson 2, "Programming Transactions." The questions are also available on the companion CD if you prefer to review them in electronic form.

NOTE Answers

Answers to these questions and explanations of why each answer choice is correct or incorrect are located in the "Answers" section at the end of the book.

---

1. You have created a WCF service and a client application that calls the service. Which steps must to be performed to ensure that an ambient transaction is available in the method on the service? (Choose all that apply.)

   A. The client calls the WCF service from within a *using* block that defines a *TransactionScope* object.

   B. The binding configuration for the client includes a *TransactionFlow='true'* attribute.

   C. The binding configuration for the client includes a SendTimeout='00:01:00' attribute.

   D. The binding configuration for the service includes a *TransactionFlow='true'* attribute.

   E. The binding configuration for the service includes a *ReceiveTimeout='00:01:00'* attribute.

   F. Decorate the method in the service's class with the *OperationBehavior(TransactionScopeRequired = true)* attribute.

   G. Decorate the method in the service's class with the *OperationBehavior(TransactionAutoComplete = true)* attribute.

   H. Decorate the method in the service's Service contract (the interface) with the *TransactionFlow(TransactionFlowOption.Allowed)* attribute.

2. In the following code sample, what is the expected outcome?

```vb
' VB
Using ts1 As New TransactionScope(TransactionScopeOption.Required, _
    New Timespan(0, 0, 30))
    Using ts2 As New TransactionScope(TransactionScopeOption.Required, _
        New Timespan(0, 0, 40))
        ' Update database
        ' Sleep for 35 seconds
        ts2.Complete()
    End Using
    ts1.Complete()
End Using
```

```csharp
// C#
using(TransactionScope ts1 = new
    TransactionScope(TransactionScopeOption.Required,
    new Timespan(0, 0, 30)))
{
    using(TransactionScope ts2 = new
        TransactionScope(TransactionScopeOption.Required,
        new Timespan(0, 0, 40)))
    {
        // Update database
        // Sleep for 35 seconds
        ts2.Complete( );
    }
    ts1.Complete();
}
```

A. Both transactions are committed.

B. Both transactions are rolled back.

C. Transaction *ts2* is committed, but *ts1* is rolled back.

D. Transaction *ts1* is committed, but *ts2* is rolled back.

Chapter Review

To further practice and reinforce the skills you learned in this chapter, you can:

- Review the chapter summary.
- Review the list of key terms introduced in this chapter.
- Complete the case scenario. This scenario sets up a real-world situation involving the topics of this chapter and asks you to create a solution.
- Complete the suggested practices.
- Take a practice test.

Chapter Summary

- Both the client and the service need to agree on whether transactions will flow from client to service.
- The introduction of the Lightweight Transaction Manager (LTM) means that developers can worry less about the overhead of distributed transactions.
- A TransactionScope object is capable of participating in a two-phase commit process, regardless of whether the transaction coordinator is the LTM or the MSDTC.

Key Terms

Do you know what these key terms mean? You can check your answers by looking up the terms in the glossary at the end of the book.

- ambient transaction
- one-way call
- resource manager
- root scope
- transaction coordinator
- transaction manager
- transaction protocol
- two-phase commit

Case Scenario

In the following case scenario, you will apply what you've learned about transactional services. You can find answers to these questions in the "Answers" section at the end of this book.

Case Scenario: Transactional Services

Your company has developed a WCF application that will be used by employees within your company. In one of the methods in your service, a separate call is made to a WCF service hosted by another company. In that same method, updates to your corporate database occur. You would like to arrange for all these updates to be performed within a single transaction.

Answer the following questions for your manager:

1. What needs to be installed or configured on the client portion of the application to fulfill these requirements?
2. What needs to be installed or configured on the service portion of the application to fulfill these requirements?
3. Are there any technical barriers that might prevent this application from executing successfully?

Suggested Practices

To help you successfully master the exam objectives presented in this chapter, complete the following tasks.

Build WCF Services

Create a pair of transaction-aware services.

■ **Practice**   Create two WCF services, using different bindings (say, *wsHttpBinding* and *netTcpBinding*). Build a client application that creates a TransactionScope and calls methods on the services that update a database. Check the results of the updates in scenarios in which the transaction is committed and aborted.

Watch a Webcast

Watch a webcast about Terminal Services in Windows Server 2008.

■ **Practice**   Watch the MSDN webcast, "Transactions in Distributed Solutions with Windows Communication Foundation," by Christian Weyer, available on the companion CD in the Webcasts folder.

Take a Practice Test

The practice tests on this book's companion CD offer many options. For example, you can test yourself on just one exam objective, or you can test yourself on all the 70-503 certification exam content. You can set up the test so that it closely simulates the experience of taking a certification exam, or you can set it up in study mode so that you can look at the correct answers and explanations after you answer each question.

MORE INFO Practice tests

For details about all the practice test options available, see the "How to Use the Practice Tests" section in this book's introduction.

Chapter 12
Concurrency

Concurrency in any application has the potential to provide a seemingly unending source of intractable problems. In the realm of Windows Communication Foundation (WCF) services, concurrency relates to the ability for a service to handle multiple incoming messages simultaneously. The ability to do this correctly can mean the difference between a robust and scalable application and one that crashes for no apparent reason or becomes unresponsive when placed under a high load. This chapter discusses not only the concepts associated with concurrent programming but also how they can be addressed in WCF services and clients.

Exam objectives in this chapter:
- Manage concurrency.

Lessons in this chapter:

Before You Begin

To complete the lessons in this chapter, you must have:

- A computer that meets or exceeds the minimum hardware requirements listed in the introduction at the beginning of the book.
- Any edition of Microsoft Visual Studio 2008 (including Microsoft Visual C# 2008 Express edition or Microsoft Visual Basic 2008 Express edition) installed on the computer.

Real World

Bruce Johnson

Concurrency is, indirectly, a passion of mine. I say indirectly because I don't go out of my way to think about or work with concurrency, but I do spend a surprising amount of time working with multithreaded applications. If you're dealing with multiple threads, it is critical to be aware of the issues associated with concurrency; otherwise, you're likely to confront the kind of situation all developers dread: a bug that shows up only sporadically and goes away when you attach a debugger and step through your application.

The easiest way to solve concurrency bugs is to avoid them in the first place. Yes, this is a truism. Yes, it applies to almost any bug you can mention. However, there is a difference with concurrency issues. Most other bugs can be addressed using the tools that are part of every developer's toolbox. Attach a debugger, set some break points, and analyze what your application is doing. Multithreading and concurrency issues generally fall outside the scope of what most debugging tools can address effectively. Although Visual Studio 2008 (and earlier versions) aid in debugging multithreaded applications, timing issues are frequently at the root of the problem, and a good tool to help visualize the various paths a multithreaded application can take (with the choice for different paths based solely on timing) isn't available. In the case of concurrency, understanding the challenges and common solutions beforehand is the best way to avoid having to deal with the problems later.

Lesson 1: Concurrency in WCF Applications

Concurrency in a WCF service occurs when more than one call is made simultaneously to a given service. You might have already dealt with concurrency in other parts of your development experience. Your familiarity with concurrency depends a great deal on your background. If you are a developer for the Microsoft Windows platform, you are probably aware that the values of controls on a form can't be modified on a background thread. This is how .NET protects you from inadvertently running into concurrency problems. Ironically, if you are an ASP.NET developer, you are less likely to be aware of concurrency problems, even though Microsoft Internet Information Server (IIS) is inherently multithreaded. Again, ASP.NET protects developers from some of the problem areas while still enabling multiple requests to be processed simultaneously.

WCF is slightly less forgiving than either of these environments. Therefore, this chapter starts by considering some of the problem areas (with an emphasis on "some"), with a particular concentration on areas in which WCF can help mitigate the risks.

After this lesson, you will be able to:

- Identify the fundamental modes that WCF uses for concurrency.
- Determine the most appropriate concurrency mode for your WCF service.
- Implement the proper protection for a reentrant WCF service.

Estimated lesson time: 45 minutes

Concurrency and WCF

The purpose of a WCF service is to process incoming requests. When a request arrives at a service, the service model dispatches the message on its own thread, which is taken from a pool of threads. If multiple requests arrive at or near the same time, additional threads are grabbed from the same pool and designated to process the requests. This is fundamental behavior for any WCF service.

Associated with each request is a *service object*, an instantiation of the class that implements the service interface. It is this code the service model will call to process the request and build the response. Within WCF, concurrency issues arise based on how these service objects are created and shared between the individual requests.

WCF provides three possible sharing modes for the service object. Table 12-1 contains the acceptable values along with a brief description of the provided functionality. Additional details about each type follow the table.

Table 12-1 *ConcurrencyMode* Enumeration Values

Value	Description
Single	Each thread that is handling a request can access the service object, but only one thread at a time can access the service object.
Reentrant	Although only one thread can access the service object at a time, it is possible for that thread to leave the object and reenter it at some point in the future. The implications to other threads is described in detail in the "Reentrant Concurrency Mode" section.
Multiple	The service object satisfies multiple requests, potentially simultaneously. From a concurrency perspective, this is the most challenging option because great care must be taken to protect shared resources.

The concurrency mode is defined using the *ServiceBehavior* attribute on the class that implements the service, as shown in bold here:

```
' VB
<ServiceBehavior(ConcurrencyMode:=ConcurrencyMode.Single)> _
Public Class ServiceImplementation
    Implements IServiceInterface
    ' Implementation code
End Class
```

```
// C#
[ServiceBehavior(ConcurrencyMode=ConcurrencyMode.Single)]
public class ServiceImplementation : IServiceInterface
{
    // Implementation code
}
```

Single Concurrency Mode

Configuring a service so that the *ConcurrencyMode* property is set to *ConcurrencyMode.Single* provides the safest environment for concurrency. Before the service begins to process a request, a lock is acquired on the service object. The lock is maintained until the request is complete. If a second (or third, fourth, or greater) request comes, that request is queued up until the service object becomes available. Requests are processed on a first-in, first-out basis.

Processing only a single request at a time eliminates any concurrency concerns. The only time you have to worry about concurrency is when the service object itself is performing multi-threaded operations. There is a tradeoff, however. In this case, the tradeoff depends on the instancing mode. If the instancing mode is set to *Singleton* (*InstanceContextMode.Singleton*), only one call is processed at a time because there is only one service object, and each request holds a lock that prevents other requests from being serviced by that object. If the instancing mode is *PerCall* or *PerSession* (*InstanceContextMode.PerCall* or *InstanceContextMode.PerSession*), an object is created for each request. In both of these scenarios, concurrency in the service object is not an issue because the *Single* concurrency mode ensures that only one request is processed at a time.

CAUTION Beware of unexpected consequences

The combination of instance context, session, and concurrency settings can lead to some unexpected consequences. If *ConcurrencyMode* is set to *Single*, WCF maintains the in-order delivery guarantee. That is, requests will arrive and be processed in the same order in which they are sent from the client. If the binding uses sessions (the default behavior for *netTcpBinding* or *netNamed-PipeBinding*), there is no difference in behavior (from a concurrency perspective) between *PerCall* and *PerSession* instancing.

Multiple Concurrency Mode

Single concurrency mode has the potential problem of low throughput because of the serialization of incoming requests through a single object. As a result, multiple threads must be created to handle incoming requests for services that require a higher level of service. When *ConcurrencyMode* is set to *Multiple*, a lock is no longer acquired on the service object before a request is processed, and the service objects can (depending on the instancing mode) process multiple requests simultaneously. All shared state and resources must be protected using the standard .NET synchronization techniques.

NOTE *Multiple* mode means no locking on service object

Although it seems logical, a large number of concurrent requests will not necessarily result in a matching number of active service requests. Setting *ConcurrencyMode* to *Multiple* means only that no locking is associated with access to the service object. Other configuration elements can still be used to set a limit on the number of concurrently processed requests.

There are further ramifications. Objects generally fall into the categories of *thread-safe* and *thread-unsafe*. A thread-safe object handles its own concurrency issues. It makes sure that if two threads are accessing the object at the same time, appropriate locking occurs to keep the object from entering an inconsistent state. A thread-unsafe object doesn't do this. Instead, it ignores threading, leaving it up to the application using the object to handle the situation.

From the service object's concurrency perspective, it needs to consider values (both internal and external variables) that are thread-unsafe. Thread-safe values are already protected against simultaneous updates. Also, the values of interest are only those created at the class level. Variables that are more locally scoped (such as at a method level) don't have to deal with concurrency. Even if two threads access the same method at the same time, the method-level variables will get their own instances, so the focus for managing concurrency in the service object is to ensure that class-level variables are manually protected from threading problems by using one of the .NET synchronization mechanisms.

IMPORTANT   No explicit deadlock detection in WCF

When you're dealing with multiple threads, deadlocks are possible. WCF doesn't detect deadlocks, but in such a situation, the client will receive a *TimeoutException*. For this reason, it is not a good idea to set the timeout to be exceptionally long. As well as receiving the exception, the channel used to communicate with the service will be set to the faulted state, meaning that to send additional messages, a new channel will have to be created. However, in some cases (such as when the service is running as a singleton), creating a new channel will not be sufficient—the service must be aborted to remove the deadlock situation.

Reentrant Concurrency Mode

Creating a service that supports reentrancy is necessary only under rare and specific situations, which is a good thing because the logic associated with working out the details can be quite convoluted.

With respect to locking the service object, setting the concurrency mode to *Reentrant* acts the same as setting it to *Single*. Before the request is processed, a lock on the service object is grabbed. The lock is maintained for as long as the service object is processing the request. The difference between *Reentrant* and *Single* mode has to do with what can happen while processing the requests.

It is possible that, as part of the process, the service object makes a call to a service outside of itself. It could be a callback request sent to the WCF client. It could be a call to an external service, whether using WCF or not. However, regardless of the destination, the request being processed must wait for a response.

So what happens to any other request to the service object? The answer is that other requests wait for the request currently being processed to complete, which in turn must wait for the call to the external service to complete. Figure 12-1 illustrates the problem.

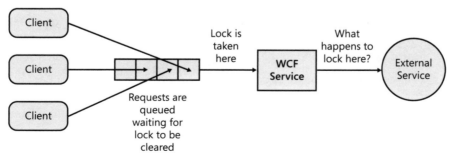

Figure 12-1   Reentrancy in WCF services

Aside from the throughput issues caused by this approach, there is one other concern. What happens if the external service calls into the WCF service? The request would be placed into the request queue. The service object won't be unlocked, and a deadlock situation will occur. This is the problem *Reentrant* mode is designed to address.

Programmatically, there are two possible outcomes. First, one of the requests could time out. Second, WCF could detect the situation and cause an *InvalidOperationException* to be raised. In both scenarios, you will be able to address the situation in code.

NOTE   One-way callback methods still a problem

Even if the callback method is one-way, there is still a problem. The callback method could still make a callback into the WCF service. That request will now attempt to grab a lock on the service object, be unable to because the original request still has it, and enter a deadlock situation.

Fortunately, WCF detects this situation and raises an *InvalidOperationException*. However, suppose the situation is not only acceptable but required? In this case, you must mark the service object as having a *ConcurrencyMode* of *Reentrant*.

As has been mentioned, a *Reentrant* service operates in the same manner as a *Single* service. The difference is that when the service object executes a callback method or makes a call to another service, the lock is released. This allows other requests to be processed. When the response from the callback or other service is received, it is queued (along with other requests) so that it can reacquire the lock and complete its work.

Reentrancy does pose a potential problem regarding the state of the service object. Because sending a request to the callback method or downstream call releases the lock on the service object, other requests can be processed. Those requests can modify the state that is maintained within the service object. Now when the callback method or downstream call has finished processing, the state is not the same as when the request to the callback method or downstream call was made. This can be alleviated by placing a manual lock on the service resource.

However, even with manual synchronization, you must ensure that a deadlock situation doesn't occur. For example, if the original request locks the state resource and then sends a request to the callback method or downstream call without unlocking, the next request would grab a lock on the service object but be unable to get the lock for the state resource.

Designing for Reentrancy

Although configuring a service for reentrancy is easy, the developer must accept a level of responsibility when doing so. Deadlocks can be a problem, but there can be issues beyond that. Specifically, the developer needs to ensure that, when the service calls out (thus allowing other calls into the service by unlocking the service object), the state of the service must be consistent. A consistent, thread-safe state means that the reentrant service should not interact with its own members, either public or private, instance or static, and the state should be such that no object is left in a logically unacceptable state. For example, if you are building a tree structure, you should not leave the tree object so that the root node is not defined. To do so leaves any incoming requests vulnerable to unexpected failure.

Along the same lines, when the reentrant service returns from its outgoing call, it should refresh all the local variables. It has no way of knowing which requests might have been processed while it was gone, and it is dangerous to assume that nothing has been changed.

Lab: Defining Concurrency Modes

This lab demonstrates the different concurrency modes. This includes both the different behaviors between *Single* and *Multiple* modes (as shown in the first exercise) and what a concurrency mode of *Reentrant* allows (in the second exercise).

▶ Exercise 1   Single and Multiple Concurrency

In this first exercise, you will use the *TransactionScope* object to commit changes made through both a WCF service and a local SQL command. The service you use is similar to the one constructed in the lab for the first lesson in the previous chapter.

1. Navigate to the *<InstallHome>*/Chapter12/Lesson1/Exercise1/*<language>*/Before directory and double-click the Exercise1.sln file to open the solution in Visual Studio.

   The solution consists of two projects. They are as follows:

   ❑ The DemoService project, a simple WCF service library that implements the *IConcurrency* interface. This interface consists of a single method (*GetCallCount*) that returns a string, indicating the number of times the method has been called within the current service instance. The parameter to *GetCallCount* determines how long to wait before returning. In this exercise, this delay makes the concurrency of the calls more apparent.

   ❑ The TestClient project, a Console application. The application generates a request for the service and displays the result on the Console window.

2. In Solution Explorer, double-click the ConcurrencyService file in the DemoService project.

   The concurrency mode for the service is defined in the *ServiceBehavior* attribute. To start, you set the concurrent mode to *Multiple*. This is actually the default value, but you're really setting up for the second part of the exercise.

3. Change the class declaration to the following, as shown in bold:

```vb
' VB
<ServiceBehavior(ConcurrencyMode:=ConcurrencyMode.Multiple, _
InstanceContextMode:=InstanceContextMode.Single)> _
Public Class ConcurrencyService
    Implements IConcurrency
```

```
// C#
[ServiceBehavior(ConcurrencyMode=ConcurrencyMode.Multiple,
    InstanceContextMode=InstanceContextMode.Single)]
public class ConcurrencyService : IConcurrency
```

On the client side, you must add some code to check when calls to the service are executed. This will enable you to check the concurrency model.

4. In Solution Explorer, double-click the Program.cs or Module1.vb file in the TestClient project.

In the *Main* method for the class defined in this file, you see some code that creates a number of background threads. Each of these threads makes a call to a method named *CallWcfService*. The ID for the thread is passed into this method, enabling the messages in the method to indicate which thread made the call. By having these threads run simultaneously, you can create concurrent service calls.

5. Locate the definition of the *CallWcfService* method. Add the following code to the method to create a proxy to the WCF service in the *CallWcfService* method:

```
' VB
Using proxy As New DemoService.ConcurrencyClient()
End Using
```

```
// C#
using (DemoService.ConcurrencyClient proxy = new
    DemoService.ConcurrencyClient())
{
}
```

6. Add the call to the *GetCallCount* WCF service to the just-added *using* block and add a couple of calls to the *WriteLine* method to indicate the starting and ending time of the proxy call, as shown here:

```
' VB
Console.WriteLine(String.Format("Call {0} Start: {1}", _
    identifier.ToString(), DateTime.Now.ToLongTimeString()))
Console.WriteLine(String.Format("Call {0} : {1}", _
    identifier.ToString(), proxy.GetCallCount(5000)))
Console.WriteLine(String.Format("Call {0} End: {1}", _
    identifier.ToString(), DateTime.Now.ToLongTimeString()))
```

```
// C#
Console.WriteLine(String.Format("Call {0} Start: {1}",
    identifier.ToString(), DateTime.Now.ToLongTimeString()));
Console.WriteLine(String.Format("Call {0} : {1}",
    identifier.ToString(), proxy.GetCallCount(5000)));
Console.WriteLine(String.Format("Call {0} End: {1}",
    identifier.ToString(), DateTime.Now.ToLongTimeString()));
```

7. Ensure that the TestClient project is set to be the startup project, and then launch the application by pressing F5.

8. At the prompt to enter the number of concurrent calls to create, type **2** and press Enter.

   After a few moments, you see a series of messages. If you look at the messages closely, you find that the two threads each make a call to the WCF service and that the service responds at approximately the same instance.

9. Press Enter to terminate the running application.

10. In the ConcurrencyService file, in the *ServiceBehavior* attribute, change the concurrency mode to *Single*. This will limit the number of incoming calls to one at a time. The class declaration should look like the following (with changes shown in bold):

    ```
    ' VB
    <ServiceBehavior(ConcurrencyMode:=ConcurrencyMode.Single, _
        InstanceContextMode:=InstanceContextMode.Single)> _
    Public Class ConcurrencyService
        Implements IConcurrency
    ```

    ```
    // C#
    [ServiceBehavior(ConcurrencyMode=ConcurrencyMode.Single,
        InstanceContextMode=InstanceContextMode.Single)]
    public class ConcurrencyService : IConcurrency
    ```

11. Launch the application by pressing F5.

12. At the prompt to enter the number of concurrent calls to run, type **2** and press Enter.

    After a few moments, similar messages to the first run appear. The difference is that the two threads no longer execute simultaneously but, instead, appear in sequence. Figure 12-2 illustrates the result.

13. Press Enter to terminate the running application.

Figure 12-2   Messages showing that two threads executed sequentially

▶ **Exercise 2   *Reentrant* Concurrency**

In this exercise, you will create a callback to the client. To have this work successfully, the concurrency for the service must be set to *Reentrant*.

1. Navigate to the *<InstallHome>*/Chapter12/Lesson1/Exercise2/*<language>*/Before directory and double-click the Exercise2.sln file to open the solution in Visual Studio.

The solution consists of three projects. They are as follows:

❑ The DemoService project, a simple WCF service library that implements the *IConcurrency* interface. This interface consists of a single method (*GetCallCount*) that returns a string indicating the number of times the method has been called within the current service instance. The parameter to *GetCallCount* determines how long to wait before returning. In this exercise, this delay makes the concurrency of the calls more apparent.

❑ The DemoClient project, a Windows Forms application. The application generates a request for the service and displays the result in a list box on the main form.

❑ The DemoLibrary project, a class library application that is shared between the DemoClient and DemoService projects. It contains the interface used for the callback from the service to the client.

2. In Solution Explorer, double-click the IConcurrencyCallback file in the DemoLibrary project.

This is the interface that will be used for the callback. It must have one method defined, named *ReceiveCallCount*. This method will take an integer parameter to be displayed in the client. To indicate that the method is part of the WCF process, it must be decorated with the *OperationContract* attribute.

3. Add the following code to the *IConcurrencyCallback* interface:

```vb
' VB
<OperationContract()> _
Sub ReceiveCallCount(callCount As Integer)
```

```csharp
// C#
[OperationContract()]
void ReceiveCallCount(int callCount);
```

4. In Solution Explorer, double-click the ConcurrencyService file in the DemoService project.

Notice that the concurrency mode is set to *Single*. This will cause a problem with the application.

5. Locate the *GetCallCount* method.

You add a callback to the client immediately preceding the *return* statement by getting the callback channel from the current operation context. After the callback channel is retrieved and cast to the callback interface, you can invoke the desired method.

6. Add the following code immediately prior to the *return* statement in the *GetCallCount* method:

```vb
' VB
Dim callback As IConcurrencyCallback = _
    OperationContext.Current.GetCallbackChannel(Of IConcurrencyCallback)()
callback.ReceiveCallCount(callCount)
```

```
// C#
IConcurrencyCallback callback =
    OperationContext.Current.GetCallbackChannel<IConcurrencyCallback>();
callback.ReceiveCallCount(callCount);
```

7. Set DemoClient as the startup project, and then launch the application by pressing F5.

    The WCFsvcHost application displays an error because the binding specified doesn't support duplex mode, which is a requirement for creating a callback.

8. In Visual Studio, press Shift+F5 to terminate the application.

9. In Solution Explorer, double-click the app.config file for the DemoService project.

10. Locate the *endpoint* element.

11. Currently, the binding is set to *wsHttpBinding*. Modify it so that the binding is *wsDualHttp-Binding* to enable the callback to function as desired. When you are finished, the endpoint element will look like the following (with the change shown in bold):

    ```
    <endpoint address="" binding="wsDualHttpBinding"
        contract="DemoService.IConcurrency" />
    ```

    The client portion of the application must be modified to support the callback.

12. In Solution Explorer, right-click the Form1 file in the DemoClient project and select View Code.

    To receive the callback, the *Form1* class must implement the *IConcurrencyCallback* interface.

13. Modify the class declaration for the form to the following, as shown in bold:

    ```
    ' VB
    Public Class Form1
        Implements IConcurrencyCallback
    ```

    ```
    // C#
    public partial class Form1 : Form, IConcurrencyCallback
    ```

    The *ReceiveCallCount* method must be implemented in the *Form1* class. This method accepts an integer as a parameter. It builds a string, using the incoming value, and displays it on the form. Use the *Invoke* method to accomplish the display because the *List-Box* control must be updated on the user interface (UI) thread.

14. Add the following method to the *Form1* class:

    ```
    ' VB
    Public Sub ReceiveCallCount(callCount As Integer) _
        Implements DemoLibrary.IConcurrencyCallback.ReceiveCallCount
        Dim updateMethod As New SendMessage(AddressOf addToLabel)
        Me.Invoke(updateMethod, String.Format("The updated callCount is {0}.", _
            callCount))
    End Sub
    ```

    ```
    // C#
    public void ReceiveCallCount(int callCount)
    {
        SendMessage updateMethod = new SendMessage(addToLabel);
    ```

```
this.Invoke(updateMethod, String.Format("The updated callCount is {0}.",
    callCount));
}
```

The binding on the service was modified (in step 11) to support a duplex binding. The client application must use the same binding.

15. In Solution Explorer, double-click the app.config file in the DemoClient project.

16. Locate the *endpoint* element. Set the binding on the *endpoint* element to use the *wsDual-HttpBinding* binding.

When you are finished, the *endpoint* element should look like the following. (Note that *address=* and the URL that follows should be typed on a single line; they are formatted here to fit on the printed page.)

```
<endpoint
    address=
    "http://localhost:8731/Design_Time_Addresses/DemoService/ConcurrencyService/"
    binding="wsDualHttpBinding" contract="DemoService.IConcurrency"
    name="IConcurrency" />
```

17. Launch the application by pressing F5.

18. In the Windows form that appears, type **1** into the Number Of Concurrent Clients text box and press the Start Demo button.

In a few seconds, an *InvalidOperationException* will appear in the *ConcurrencyService* class. The problem is that when the concurrency mode is marked as single, making a callback means that a deadlock might occur (if the client were to call back into the service).

19. Stop running the application.

20. In the ConcurrencyService file, locate the *ServiceBehavior* attribute.

To correct this problem, the concurrency mode should be changed to *Reentrant*. The class declaration should look like the following (with changes shown in bold):

```
' VB
<ServiceBehavior(ConcurrencyMode:=ConcurrencyMode.Reentrant, _
    InstanceContextMode:=InstanceContextMode.Single)> _
Public Class ConcurrencyService
    Implements IConcurrency
```

```
// C#
[ServiceBehavior(ConcurrencyMode=ConcurrencyMode.Reentrant,
    InstanceContextMode=InstanceContextMode.Single)]
public class ConcurrencyService : IConcurrency
```

21. Launch the application by pressing F5.

22. In the Windows form that appears, type **1** into the Number Of Concurrent Clients text box and press the Start Demo button.

Now the messages that appear in the list box are correct, indicating that the callback took place. Press Shift+F5 to terminate the application.

Lesson Summary

- Using a *ConcurrencyMode* of *Single* minimizes the issues associated with concurrency.
- The relationship between the *ConcurrencyMode* and the *InstanceContextMode* must be taken together to determine when concurrency must be addressed.
- When more than one request is allowed into a service object, care must be taken to avoid deadlocks or inconsistent state.
- Designing a reentrant system requires the developer not only to be aware of synchronization of state access but also to handle the possibility of state changes during the execution of an external method call.

Lesson Review

You can use the following questions to test your knowledge of the information in Lesson 1, "Concurrency in WCF Applications." The questions are also available on the companion CD if you prefer to review them in electronic form.

NOTE   Answers

Answers to these questions and explanations of why each answer choice is correct or incorrect are located in the "Answers" section at the end of the book.

---

1. Consider the following class, which contains the implementation of a WCF service.

   ```vb
   ' VB
   <ServiceBehavior()> _
   Public Class ServiceImplementation
       Implements IServiceInterface
       Private hitCounter As Integer

       Public Sub Increment()
           hitCounter += 1
       End Sub
   End Class
   ```

   ```csharp
   // C#
   [ServiceBehavior()]
   public class ServiceImplementation : IServiceInterface
   {
       private int hitCounter;

       public void Increment()
       {
           hitCounter++;
       }
   }
   ```

How should the *ServiceImplementation* class be decorated so that concurrency issues can be eliminated without needing to change any code in the class? (Choose all that apply.)

  A. Set the *ConcurrencyMode* to *Multiple* and the *InstanceContextMode* to *Single*.

  B. Set the *ConcurrencyMode* to *Single* and the *InstanceContextMode* to *PerSession*.

  C. Set the *ConcurrencyMode* to *Multiple* and the *InstanceContextMode* to *PerSession*.

  D. Set the *ConcurrencyMode* to *Single* and the *InstanceContextMode* to *Single*.

2. Consider the following class that contains the implementation of a WCF service.

```vb
' VB
<ServiceBehavior()> _
Public Class ServiceImplementation
    Implements IServiceInterface
    Private Shared hitCounter As Integer

    Public Sub Increment()
        hitCounter += 1
    End Sub
End Class
```

```csharp
// C#
[ServiceBehavior()]
public class ServiceImplementation : IServiceInterface
{
    private static int hitCounter;

    public void Increment()
    {
        hitCounter++;
    }
}
```

How should the *ServiceImplementation* class be attributed so that concurrency issues can be eliminated without needing to change any code in the class?

  A. Set the *ConcurrencyMode* to *Multiple* and the *InstanceContextMode* to *Single*.

  B. Set the *ConcurrencyMode* to *Single* and the *InstanceContextMode* to *PerSession*.

  C. Set the *ConcurrencyMode* to *Multiple* and the *InstanceContextMode* to *PerSession*.

  D. Set the *ConcurrencyMode* to *Single* and the *InstanceContextMode* to *Single*.

Lesson 2: Synchronization

For the most part, .NET applications are quite comfortable with multiple threads. For developers, this is wonderful because misunderstanding the complexities of multithreaded applications can lead to headaches. But there are times when an application must be aware of the details of the thread on which it runs. The most common instance of this is in Windows Forms applications, in which the properties and methods of a control must be accessed on the thread in which the control was originally created. Another common scenario is when thread local storage is used to save context information. If the running process were to change threads unexpectedly, the context data would disappear. This lesson examines how Microsoft .NET Framework addresses these problems and, more specifically, how WCF can participate in the solutions.

> **After this lesson, you will be able to:**
> - Describe the mechanism behind the WCF synchronization model.
> - Host a WCF service in a Windows form.
> - Create a custom synchronization context.
>
> **Estimated lesson time: 45 minutes**

Synchronization Context

A seldom-used feature known as synchronization context was introduced with .NET Framework 2.0. This feature, implemented in the *SynchronizationContext* class in the *System.Threading* namespace, helps applications determine whether they are on the correct thread (correct, depending on the application's requirements) and, if not, move information and instructions onto the desired thread.

This is a challenging concept for most developers to understand because developers, being the inquisitive lot that they are, want to know how synchronization contexts work. The answer is that a combination of thread local storage and properties built into the .NET Framework keep track of the necessary details. More important, developers don't really need to know how these contexts work. It's enough to be aware that the contexts make the lives of developers easier.

Every thread created in the .NET Framework has the potential to include a synchronization context. The context, if there is one, is maintained in thread local storage, and a static property called *Current* (accessed as *SynchronizationContext.Current*) represents the ambient context (conceptually similar to the ambient transaction). When a method is to be executed on a thread that is not the same as the current thread, the calling thread creates a delegate of type *SendOrPostCallback* that references the desired method. This delegate is then provided to either the *Send* (synchronous) or *Post* (asynchronous) method on the *SynchronizationContext* object.

To get a feel for the sort of work the synchronization context has to perform, consider the common example of updating user interface controls. Stretching from Windows Presentation Foundation (WPF) all the way back to Microsoft Foundation Classes (MFC), only the thread that creates a window is allowed to update the window. The reason for this limitation has to do with the Windows message loop and the thread messaging architecture but, ultimately, when you have a multithreaded application using Windows, you need to ensure that updates to the user interface (UI) elements take place on the main thread. To address this situation, the synchronization context object converts all the *Post* and *Send* calls into Windows messages and places them into the queue used by the Windows message loop.

WCF and Synchronization

Why should synchronization context affect WCF? The answer is found in some of the implementation details associated with WCF services. Unless configured differently, all WCF service calls and callbacks use threads from the input/output (I/O) completion thread pool. By default, there are 1,000 threads in this pool, but none of them are under the control of your application.

Consider the situation that would arise if the WCF service needed to update some user interface. Because user interface updates must take place on the creating thread, a mechanism would have to marshal the calls to the correct thread. Not surprisingly, the mechanism that accomplishes this is the synchronization context. The *ServiceBehavior* attribute exposes a property named *UseSynchronizationContext*. It can be configured using the following syntax:

```
' VB
<ServiceBehavior(UseSynchronizationContext:=True)> _
Public Class UpdateService
    Implements IUpdateService
```

```
// C#
[ServiceBehavior(UseSynchronizationContext=true)]
public class UpdateService : IUpdateService
```

When set to *true* (which is the default value for this attribute), WCF examines the thread that opened the host. If that thread has a synchronization context and *UseSynchronizationContext* is set to *true*, WCF marshals all the calls to the service into that synchronization context. The developer has to do nothing other than set the attribute to ensure that it works properly.

IMPORTANT **Synchronization and Windows Forms**

If you use a Windows Forms/WPF application as the host for a WCF service, the timing of the synchronization context creation matters. As part of its instantiation process, a form or Window ensures that a synchronization context exists for its thread. If you create the host for the WCF service prior to the construction of the form or Window, no synchronization context is available, so any attempt to update the user interface will fail. You must make sure that the host is created after the form is instantiated.

Consider an example of this functionality. Assume that you have a service called *FormHosted-Service* that implements an *IServiceInterface* interface. The definition of the service class would look like the following:

```
' VB
<ServiceBehavior(InstanceContextMode:=InstanceContextMode.PerCall, _
    UseSynchronizationContext:=True)> _
Public Class FormHostedService
    Implements IServiceInterface
    ' Implementation code goes here
End Class
```

```
// C#
[ServiceBehavior(InstanceContextMode=InstanceContextMode.PerCall,
    UseSynchronizationContext=true)]
public class FormHostedService : IServiceInterface
{
    // Implementation code goes here
}
```

There are two possible approaches to using a Windows form (or a WPF Window—the concept applies in both situations even though the code is different). The first is to create the host service in the same static or shared *Main* method that starts the Windows message pump:

```
' VB
Sub Main()
    Dim host As New ServiceHost(GetType(FormHostedService))
    host.Open()
    Application.Run(New Form1())
End Sub
```

```
// C#
static void Main()
{
    ServiceHost host = new ServiceHost(typeof(FormHostedService));
    host.Open();
    Application.Run(new Form1());
}
```

As it turns out, this technique is incorrect. At the time the service host is instantiated and opened, no synchronization context is associated with the user interface. (The *Form1* object in the preceding example has not yet been constructed.) Because the synchronization context is not yet created, the host is unaware of it and is therefore unable to update any of the user interface elements on *Form1*.

Instead, a better technique is to create the host service within the constructor of the form, as shown in the following code:

```
' VB
Partial Class HostForm
    Inherits Form
```

```
    Dim host As ServiceHost
    Public Sub New()
       InitializeComponent()
       host = New ServiceHost(Me)
       host.Open()
    End Sub
    ' Remainder of the implementation
End Class

// C#
partial class HostForm : Form
{
    ServiceHost host;
    public HostForm( )
    {
       InitializeComponent( );
       host = new ServiceHost(this);
       host.Open( );
    }
    // Rest of the implementation
}
```

Now the *ServiceHost* object is not created until after the form has been instantiated. As a result, it is aware of the synchronization context and able to use it to communicate with user interface elements on the form.

Custom Synchronization Contexts

Although it is not readily apparent, synchronization contexts provide an interesting extension point for WCF. Natively, .NET and WCF provide only one type of synchronization context. This is the context that provides the user interface thread synchronization for Windows Forms. It is possible, however, to create your own synchronization context and apply it to a WCF service.

When might you need to do this? To arrive at an answer, consider what the synchronization context is really doing. The synchronization context object is examining the requests that arrive at a WCF service and determining the thread on which each request will run. The context is also responsible for marshaling any request information onto the correct thread. To accomplish this, the synchronization context must be aware of all the requests that arrive at the service and, because the context determines which thread handles which requests, it also can adjust the order and location (that is, the process or system) in which requests are processed. This means that synchronization contexts can be used to maintain thread affinity of a particular session (if the WCF service was using thread local storage, for example) or create a prioritized WCF service in which high-priority requests are handled before lower ones, regardless of when they arrive.

There are two steps in the creation of a custom synchronization context. The first is to create a class that derives from *SynchronizationContext*. This class performs all the logic associated with processing the incoming requests. The second piece involves associating the synchronization context with a particular service. The association process can be performed either imperatively or declaratively. The declarative approach requires a custom attribute class to be created. Both methods will be demonstrated shortly.

As an example, create a custom synchronization context that uses a thread pool sized through a parameter passed to the constructor. (If you want to run this example, you need a couple of helper classes that are not described in the text. They are available in the *<InstallHome>/* Chapter12/SynchronizationContextExample directory on the accompanying CD.) These classes are the *WorkerThread* class, which is responsible for maintaining information about each thread in the pool, and the *WorkItem* class, which represents a process that is currently running on the thread.

The focus of the code described in the rest of this section is on what needs to be done within the synchronization context class. First, the class must derive from the *SynchronizationContext* class, and the constructor will contain whatever parameters are required for the custom logic— the *SynchronizationContext* constructor is parameterless.

```vb
' VB
Public Class ThreadPoolSynchronizer
   Inherits SynchronizationContext
   Implements IDisposable

   Dim workItemQueue As Queue(Of WorkItem)
   Dim workerThreads As WorkerThread()

   Public Sub New(poolSize as Integer)
      If poolSize <= 0 Then
         Throw New ArgumentOutOfRangeException("The Pool Size must be " + _
            "greater than zero", "poolSize")
      End If
      workItemQueue = New Queue(Of WorkItem)()
      workerThreads = New WorkerThread(poolSize)
      Dim index As Integer
      For index = 0 to poolSize - 1
         workerThreads(index) = New WorkerThread(index + 1, Me)
      Next index
   End Sub
End Class
```

```csharp
// C#
public class ThreadPoolSynchronizer : SynchronizationContext, IDisposable
{
   Queue<WorkItem> workItemQueue;
   WorkerThread[] workerThreads;

   public ThreadPoolSynchronizer(int poolSize)
```

```
    {
        if (poolSize <= 0)
            throw new InvalidOperationException("Pool size cannot be zero");

        workItemQueue = new Queue<WorkItem>();

        workerThreads = new WorkerThread[poolSize];
        for (int index = 0; index < poolSize; index++)
            workerThreads[index] = new WorkerThread(index + 1, this);
    }
}
```

To provide synchronization functionality, five methods must be implemented by the custom synchronization context. These methods basically fall into two categories: operational and functional. The three operational methods (*Close*, *Abort*, and *Dispose*) deal with stopping the threads that are handling requests. The two functional methods (*Post* and *Send*) are invoked by the WCF service to ensure that methods are called on the appropriate thread. The operational methods are shown here:

```
' VB
Public Sub Close()
    Dim thread As WorkerThread
    For Each thread in workerThreads
        thread.Kill()
    Next thread
End Sub

Public Sub Abort()
    Dim thread As WorkerThread
    For Each thread in workerThreads
        thread.Abort()
    Next thread
End Sub

Public Sub Dispose() Implements IDisposable.Dispose
    Me.Close()
End Sub

// C#
public void Close()
{
    foreach (WorkerThread thread in workerThreads)
        thread.Kill();
}

public void Abort()
{
    foreach (WorkerThread thread in workerThreads)
        thread.Abort();
}

public void Dispose()
```

```
{
   this.Close();
}
```

The functional methods are really where the work is initiated, but, as already mentioned, the *Post* and *Send* methods must be implemented within the custom synchronization context class. These two methods perform basically the same function with the difference that the *Send* method is an asynchronous one:

```vb
' VB
Public Overrides Sub Post(method As SendOrPostCallback, state as Object)
   Dim _workItem As New WorkItem(method, state)
   ' QueueWorkItem is a method implemented in the source code
   ' provided on the CD
   QueueWorkItem(_workItem)
End Sub

Public Overrides Sub Send(method As SendOrPostCallback, state as Object)
   If SynchronizationContext.Current.Equals(Me) Then
      method(state)
      Return
   End If

   Dim _workItem As New WorkItem(method, state)
   ' QueueWorkItem is a method implemented in the source code
   ' provided on the CD
   QueueWorkItem(_workItem)
   workItem.AsyncWaitHandle.WaitOne()
End Sub
```

```csharp
// C#
public override void Post(SendOrPostCallback method, Object state)
{
   WorkItem workItem = new WorkItem(method,state);
   // QueueWorkItem is a method implemented in the source code
   // provided on the CD
   QueueWorkItem(workItem);
}

public override void Send(SendOrPostCallback method, Object state)
{
   if (SynchronizationContext.Current == this)
   {
      method(state);
      return;
   }
   WorkItem workItem = new WorkItem(method,state);
   // QueueWorkItem is a method implemented in the source code
   // provided on the CD
   QueueWorkItem(workItem);
   workItem.AsyncWaitHandle.WaitOne();
}
```

The check for the current context in the *Send* method is necessary to avoid the possibility of a deadlock. Also, notice that the difference between the *Send* and *Post* methods is that the *Send* method calls *WaitOne* on the *WorkItem* object to wait until the *WorkItem* object has finished invoking the method.

This is the first step in creating a custom synchronization context. After it has been created, the synchronization context must be associated with the WCF service. Programmatically, this is a very straightforward process because an instance of the custom synchronization class can be assigned to the synchronization context by using the *SetSynchronizationContext* method.

```vb
' VB
Dim syncContext as New ThreadPoolSynchronizer(3)
SynchronizationContext.SetSynchronizationContext(syncContext)
Try
    Dim host as New ServiceHost(GetType(UpdateService))
    host.Open()
    ' Block until ready to quit
    host.Close()
Finally
    syncContext.Dispose()
End Try
```

```csharp
// C#
ThreadPoolSynchronizer syncContext = new ThreadPoolSynchronizer(3);
SynchronizationContext.SetSynchronizationContext(syncContext);
try
{
    ServiceHost host = new ServiceHost(typeof(UpdateService));
    host.Open();
    // Block until ready to quit
    host.Close();
}
finally
{
    syncContext.Dispose();
}
```

Although this solution does work, it is not the most robust implementation possible. Specifically, it requires the developer of the hosting application to write code to enable it. If you were implementing the host service, this wouldn't be a problem, but it's a dangerous strategy to depend on the diligence of every developer to follow through with the same steps. Instead of placing the code into the host service startup logic, it would be better (architecturally) to decorate the service with an attribute that causes the *ThreadPoolSynchronizer* to be used. For example, one solution would be to define the service as follows:

```vb
' VB
<ThreadPoolSynchronization(3, GetType(UpdateService))> _
<ServiceBehavior(typeof(IUpdateService))> _
Public Class UpdateService
    Implements IUpdateService
```

```
// C#
[ThreadPoolSynchronization(3, typeof(UpdateService))]
[ServiceBehavior(typeof(IUpdateService))]
public class UpdateService : IUpdateService
```

To add this attribute to the service class's declaration, you must create a *ThreadPoolSynchronizationAttribute* class. The creation of such a class is not, by itself, a complicated challenge. You define a class that derives from the *Attribute* class and create a constructor that takes an integer (the pool size) and a *Type* (the service's class). The key to making this work is knowing how to connect the dispatcher for the service to an instance of the synchronization context.

IContractBehavior Interface

To handle the dispatching, the attribute class must implement the *IContractBehavior* interface. This interface exposes a set of methods that enable aspects of a service to be modified at run time. For the methods to be used, objects that implement *IContractBehavior* must be added either through code or as an attribute on the service. They cannot be added through the application configuration files. Table 12-2 contains a list of the methods that *IContractBehavior* objects must implement and how they will be used.

Table 12-2   Methods in the *IContractBehavior* Interface

Method Name	Description
AddBindingParameters	Modifies the bindings to include additional properties and objects required to support the contract behavior.
ApplyClientBehavior	Modifies or extends the client runtime across some or all the messages being sent to the service. The method is called once for each endpoint that implements a particular interface, so it's possible to change the injected behavior at the endpoint level as well.
ApplyDispatchBehavior	The service-side version of *ApplyClientBehavior*. It extends or modifies the service runtime across all or some of the received messages. As with *ApplyClientBehavior*, it is invoked once per endpoint.
Validate	Confirms that the contract and endpoint can support the contract behavior implemented in the object.

Because you are trying to arrange for all the requests made to a WCF service to be processed from threads in a thread pool, it seems that the likely candidate for the method that must be implemented is *ApplyDispatchBehavior*. The method skeleton looks like the following:

```vb
' VB
Sub ApplyDispatchBehavior(description As ContractDescription, _
    Endpoint As ServiceEndpoint, dispatchRuntime As DispatchRuntime) _
    Implements IContractBehavior.ApplyDispatchBehavior

End Sub
```

```
// C#
void ApplyDispatchBehavior(ContractDescription
  description, ServiceEndpoint endpoint, DispatchRuntime dispatchRuntime)
{
}
```

This isn't an implementation. To do that, you must associate an instance of the *ThreadPoolSynchronizer* class with the dispatch runtime. The following code, when added to this *ApplyDispatchBehavior* method, accomplishes that:

```
' VB
If dispatchRuntime.SynchronizationContext Is Nothing Then
    dispatchRuntime.SynchronizationContext = New ThreadPoolSynchronizer(3)
End If
```

```
// C#
if (dispatchRuntime.SynchronizationContext == null)
    dispatchRuntime.SynchronizationContext = new ThreadPoolSynchronizer(3);
```

When the host for the service is opened (and before processing any incoming request), the *ApplyDispatchBehavior* method for the attribute is invoked. The *DispatchRuntime* parameter represents the mechanism by which WCF transforms messages into objects and then dispatches them. The result, in the present example, is that the runtime now has a synchronization context that is passed along to every incoming request.

The actual implementation of the attribute as found on the companion CD contains a couple of differences. As has been mentioned, the *ApplyDispatchBehavior* is called once for each endpoint. However, in that scenario, and using the code that you've implemented so far, a new thread pool would be created for each endpoint. The synchronization context is assigned to a new instance of the custom synchronization context. Because you really want all the endpoints for this WCF service to share the same pool, the code on the CD uses a helper class to maintain a single instance of the synchronization context object.

Synchronization and Callbacks

WCF supports the concept of client callbacks. In concurrency, callbacks bear some discussion, not just due to the possibility of multiple concurrent callbacks (although that is not outside the realm of possibility). Even in a single callback scenario, the service might launch multiple threads, each of which uses the callback reference. These duplex callbacks can enter the client on worker threads and can (unless synchronization techniques are used) corrupt the state of the client. Ultimately, if a client allows a callback scenario, the implementation must be aware of the synchronization issues that can arise. It should synchronize access to any in-memory resources and ensure that updates to shared data cannot fail due to concurrent access.

Similar to how a WCF service defines its synchronization mode, the client's concurrency mode can be defined using either declarative or imperative techniques. To use the declarative approach, WCF includes a *ConcurrencyMode* property in the *CallbackBehavior* attribute. This attribute decorates the client class:

```vb
' VB
<CallbackBehavior(ConcurrencyMode:=ConcurrencyMode.Single)> _
Public Class CallbackClient
    Implements ICallback
    ' Implementation code
End Class
```

```csharp
// C#
[CallbackBehavior(ConcurrencyMode = ConcurrencyMode.Single)]
class CallbackClient : ICallback
{
    // Implementation code
}
```

As with the *ConcurrencyMode* property in the *ServiceBehavior*, there are three possible values: *Single*, *Multiple*, and *Reentrant*.

Callbacks with *ConcurrencyMode.Single*

When the callback is configured using *Single* mode, only one callback is allowed at a time. Although, conceptually, this is the same as *Single* mode on the service level, the implications are different. In a WCF service, the instance of the service implementation class is controlled by WCF. Only processes running on the worker threads dispatched by WCF will ever access the service instance. This is not the case with a client callback. The client could be a Windows form, a Web application, or, literally, any type of .NET program. These applications are all quite capable of containing multiple threads, any of which are accessing the same data the client callback method requires.

If you set the *ConcurrencyMode* to *Single*, you are ensuring that only one WCF callback at a time will send a request. This mode will *not* ensure that all the threads within the client application respect the singleness of the request. Although only one WCF request is permitted, one or more calls into the same method can come from within the client. Synchronization on the client side must be done manually rather than relying on WCF to do it for you.

Consider the following example as one way to accomplish this. It is not necessarily the best way to implement synchronization. In an ideal world, the amount of locked code will be limited to a block that is as small as possible (following the *just-in-time-locking/as-soon-as-possible-releasing* model), but the example does demonstrate one way to provide synchronization inside of a client callback method:

```vb
' VB
<CallbackBehavior(ConcurrencyMode:=ConcurrencyMode.Single)> _
```

```
Public Class CallbackClient
    Implements ICallback
    Public Sub CallbackMethod(parameter As String)
        SyncLock Me
            ' Implementation code goes here
        End SyncLock
    End Sub
End Class
```

```
// C#
[CallbackBehavior(ConcurrencyMode = ConcurrencyMode.Single)]
public class CallbackClient : ICallback
{
    public void CallbackMethod(string paremeter)
    {
        lock (this)
        {
            // Implementation code
        }
    }
}
```

As one last point regarding the *Single* concurrency mode with a WCF callback method, it is important to realize that there is more than one queue of requests. Any callbacks from the WCF service will be queued in the endpoint processing (the client's host mechanism). Any calls from within the client application itself (that is, calls that don't go through WCF) will be blocked on the *lock* statement. The result is two basically independent queues of requests for the methods, and there is no way to ensure that the order in which the requests are processed is the same as the order in which they are initially invoked.

Callbacks with *ConcurrencyMode.Multiple*

In a callback scenario, there is not a lot of difference (from a coding perspective) between *ConcurrencyMode.Single* and *ConcurrencyMode.Multiple*. WCF no longer prevents multiple simultaneous requests to the callback method. This means that you must implement manual synchronization in the callback method, using the same set of techniques that are available in the *Single* mode.

Probably the biggest difference between *Single* and *Multiple* is that a single queue of requests can be formed. This queue is handled by the locking mechanism you use (the *lock* statement in the example shown in the preceding *Single* section). It is no longer possible for a call to be blocked by WCF and then blocked again by the *lock* statement.

Callbacks with *ConcurrencyMode.Reentrant*

Configuring a callback method by using a concurrency mode of *Reentrant* doesn't change the need for manual synchronization. The *Reentrant* mode allows for another round of callbacks, so it is possible for the method that is called back to call the WCF services again. This is allowed if the WCF service itself is marked as being reentrant (by setting the *ConcurrencyMode* of the *ServiceBehavior* attribute to *ConcurrencyMode.Reentrant*). It is also possible for that WCF service method to invoke the callback method a second time. In this scenario (which is admittedly quite roundabout), the callback method would need to be decorated with a *CallbackBehavior* attribute where the *ConcurrencyMode* is set to *Reentrant*.

Callbacks and Synchronization Contexts

It is also possible that a callback method might access a resource that has some thread affinity. The canonical example is if the client needs to access a Windows Forms user interface thread, but the rationale for requiring thread affinity is irrelevant. In both cases, you would like the callback to be marshaled onto the appropriate thread before executing.

This is accomplished by setting the *UseSynchronizationContext* property of the *CallbackBehavior* attribute to *true*.

```vb
' VB
<CallbackBehavior(UseSynchronizationContext:=True)> _
Public Class CallbackClient
    Implements ICallback
    ' Implementation code
End Class
```

```csharp
// C#
[CallbackBehavior(UseSynchronizationContext=true)]
public class CallbackClient : ICallback
{
    // Implementation code
}
```

The synchronization context the callback uses is determined when the proxy to the WCF service is first opened. Keep in mind that "open" can be either implicit, such as when a method on the WCF service is called, or explicit, with a direct call to the *Open* method on the proxy object.

After the synchronization context is identified, the same context is used for all callbacks to that endpoint. No other call to the WCF service has the opportunity to select the context. This can be important if, for example, the proxy is opened before the Windows Forms message queue is started (by using the *Application.Run* method).

IMPORTANT   UI thread affinity could block the callback

If you do establish affinity with the user interface thread in a Windows Forms application, you are causing any request to the callback method to be dispatched by the Windows message queue mechanism. This means that if you block the user interface thread, the callback method will not be executed. Also, while the callback method is being processed, no user interface event is processed, so it is important to be aware of the potential performance ramifications of using thread-affinity callbacks in a Windows Forms application.

Callbacks, Thread Affinity, and Deadlocks

One other element to be aware of when using callbacks in a thread-affinity situation is the possibility of deadlocks. Consider the scenario shown in Figure 12-3.

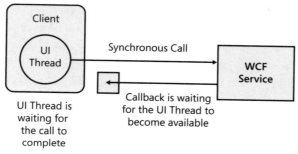

Figure 12-3   Possible deadlock in a WCF callback

Here, the initial call to the WCF service is made from a button click event. That method is invoked on the user interface thread for the form. The WCF service performs a callback to a method on the form, and *UseSynchronizationContext* is set to *true*. Now the call is marshaled to the user interface thread, where it waits for the previous operation (the call to the WCF service) to complete, which will never happen. The result is a deadlock.

Even if the callback method was defined as being one-way, the problem will not be solved. The call still must be marshaled to the user interface thread prior to the one-way call completing. The only way to correct this problem is to set *UseSynchronizationContext* to *false*.

Lab: Using Synchronization Contexts

In this lab, you will examine how a synchronization context allows WCF services to interact with a Windows Forms application. The first exercise illustrates a scenario (one not used as often as it could be) with a Windows Forms application acting as the host for a WCF service. The second exercise demonstrates the use of synchronization contexts to allow callbacks from a WCF service into a Windows Forms client application.

▶ **Exercise 1   Host a WCF Service in a Windows Forms Application**

In this exercise, you will explore how a WCF service can be hosted in a Windows Forms application. The most challenging portion of this process is if a call to the service must interact with the user interface presented by the application. If it does, either the update to the user interface must be marshaled onto the UI thread or, as is the case in this example, the WCF synchronization context must be used.

1. Navigate to the *<InstallHome>*/Chapter12/Lesson2/Exercise1/*<language>*/Before directory and double-click the Exercise1.sln file to open the solution in Visual Studio.

The solution consists of two projects. They are as follows:

- ❏ The DemoService project, a Windows Forms application. The form implements the *ISynchronization* interface. This interface consists of a single method (*Update-Status*) that accepts a string as a parameter. The value of this parameter is added to the *ListBox* control on the form hosting the WCF service.

- ❏ The TestClient project, a Console application. The application prompts the user for a string and then sends the string to the DemoService service for display on the hosting form.

2. In Solution Explorer, right-click the ServiceHostForm in the DemoService client and select View Code.

   To host the WCF service, two elements must be added to the *Form* class. First, it must implement the *ISynchronization* interface.

3. Change the class declaration to the following:

```
' VB
Public Class ServiceHostForm
    Implements ISynchronization
```

```
// C#
public partial class ServiceHostForm : Form, ISynchronization
```

   The *Form* class must be decorated with a *ServiceBehavior* attribute. Because a new *Form* object shouldn't be created with each request (think about what the user's experience would look like if it did), the instancing mode for the service should be set to *Single*.

4. Change the class declaration, as shown in bold, to the following:

```
' VB
<ServiceBehavior(InstanceContextMode:=InstanceContextMode.Single, _
    UseSynchronizationContext:=False)> _
Public Class ServiceHostForm
    Implements ISynchronization
```

```
// C#
[ServiceBehavior(InstanceContextMode=InstanceContextMode.Single,
    UseSynchronizationContext=false)]
public partial class ServiceHostForm : Form, ISynchronization
```

   To maintain the *ServiceHost* object that acts as the host for the WCF service, the object should be a variable declared at the module level. Otherwise, when the variable goes out of scope, the form will stop hosting the WCF service.

5. Add the following line of code to the top of the *ServiceHostForm* class:

```
' VB
Dim host As ServiceHost
```

```
// C#
ServiceHost host;
```

The *ServiceHost* object must be instantiated after the synchronization context for the form is established in the constructor for the *Form* object. After the *ServiceHost* object is instantiated, it should be opened to allow the form to accept requests.

6. Modify the constructor to look like the following:

```VB
' VB
Public Sub New()
    InitializeComponent()
    host = New ServiceHost(Me)
    host.Open()
End Sub
```

```C#
// C#
public ServiceHostForm()
{
    InitializeComponent();
    host = new ServiceHost(this);
    host.Open();
}
```

Because the *ServiceHostForm* class is specified to implement the *ISynchronization* interface, you must add the corresponding method. The *UpdateStatus* method takes a string as a parameter and adds that string to the items in the list box on the form.

7. Add the following method to the *ServiceHostForm* class:

```VB
' VB
Public Sub UpdateStatus(newMessage As String) _
    Implements ISynchronization.UpdateStatus

    messageListBox.Items.Add(newMessage)

End Sub
```

```C#
// C#
public void UpdateStatus(string newMessage)
{
    messageListBox.Items.Add(newMessage);
}
```

To run the application, you must define the startup project appropriately. Unlike many of the other exercises in this book, you cannot use *WcfsvcHost*, so the DemoService project must be started along with the DemoClient.

8. In Solution Explorer, right-click the Exercise1 solution and select Set Startup Projects.

9. Select the Multiple Startup Projects option button.

10. For each of the two projects in the list (DemoService and TestClient), set the Action column to Start, and then click OK.

11. Launch the application by pressing F5.

12. At the prompt to enter a status message, type **Hello world** and press Enter.

In a few seconds, an exception will be thrown in the service. Specifically, the exception indicates that an attempt was made to update a control while not on the user interface thread.

13. To correct this problem, in Solution Explorer, right-click the ServiceHostForm file and select View Code.

    In the *ServiceBehavior* attribute, the *UseSynchronizationContext* property must be set to *true*. This automatically marshals incoming requests for the WCF service onto the UI thread.

14. Change the class declaration, as shown in bold, to the following:

```
' VB
<ServiceBehavior(InstanceContextMode:=InstanceContextMode.Single, _
    UseSynchronizationContext:=True)> _
Public Class ServiceHostForm
    Implements ISynchronization
```

```
// C#
[ServiceBehavior(InstanceContextMode=InstanceContextMode.Single,
    UseSynchronizationContext=true)]
public partial class ServiceHostForm : Form, ISynchronization
```

15. Launch the application by pressing F5.

16. At the prompt to enter a status message, type **Hello world** and press Enter.

    In a few seconds, the message Hello World appears on the form.

17. In Visual Studio, press Shift+F5 to terminate the debugging session.

▶ **Exercise 2   Call Back into a Windows Forms Client**

When a Windows client calls a WCF service, there is the same need for synchronization for any callback methods back into the client. This exercise demonstrates this technique.

1. Navigate to the *<InstallHome>*/Chapter12/Lesson2/Exercise2/*<language>*/Before directory and double-click the Exercise2.sln file to open the solution in Visual Studio.

    The solution consists of three projects. They are as follows:

    ❑ The DemoService project, a simple WCF service library that implements the *IConcurrency* interface. This interface consists of a single method (*GetCallCount*) that returns a string indicating the number of times the method has been called within the current service instance. The parameter to *GetCallCount* determines how long to wait before returning. In this exercise, this delay makes the concurrency of the calls more apparent.

    ❑ The DemoClient project, a Windows Forms application. The application generates a request for the service and displays the result in a list box on the main form.

    ❑ The DemoLibrary project, a class library application shared between the DemoClient and DemoService projects. It contains the interface used for the callback from the service to the client.

The starting point for this exercise will be in the client project. You want the client (in this case, a Windows form) to accept callbacks from the WCF service. The callback method is defined in the *IConcurrencyCallback* interface. The form class must implement this interface.

2. In Solution Explorer, right-click the Form1 file and select View Code.
3. Change the declaration of the Form1 class so that it implements the desired interface. The class declaration will look like the following:

```
' VB
Public Class Form1
    Implements IConcurrencyCallback
```

```
// C#
public partial class Form1 : Form, IConcurrencyCallback
```

The *IConcurrencyCallback* interface is not recognized by IntelliSense. When you add the appropriate library reference in this case, there are two possibilities.

4. For the application to work correctly, add the following code to the top of the Form1 file:

```
' VB
Imports DemoClient.DemoService
```

```
// C#
using DemoClient.DemoService; Also, because this class is the target for a callback
method, it must be decorated with the CallbackBehavior attribute.
```

5. Change the declaration for the *Form1* class to look like the following:

```
' VB
<CallbackBehavior(ConcurrencyMode:=ConcurrencyMode.Single, _
    UseSynchronizationContext:=True)> _
Public Class Form1
    Implements IConcurrencyCallback
```

```
// C#
[CallbackBehavior(ConcurrencyMode=ConcurrencyMode.Single,
    UseSynchronizationContext=true)]
public partial class Form1 : Form, IConcurrencyCallback
```

The final piece on the client side is to provide an implementation for the *IConcurrency-Callback* interface, which requires a *ReceiveCallCount* method.

6. Add the following method to the *Form1* class:

```
' VB
Public Sub ReceiveCallCount(ByVal callCount As Integer) _
    Implements IConcurrencyCallback.ReceiveCallCount

    Thread.Sleep(2000)
    addToLabel(String.Format("The updated callCount is {0}.", _
        callCount))

End Sub
```

```
// C#
public void ReceiveCallCount(int callCount)
{
    Thread.Sleep(2000);
    addToLabel(String.Format("The updated callCount is {0}.",
        callCount));
}
```

The client side of the exchange is found in the DemoService project.

7. In Solution Explorer, double-click the ConcurrencyService file in the DemoService project.

8. Examine the *GetCallCount* method.

9. This method creates two threads, each of which invokes the *makeCallback* method. The *makeCallback* method, which you will create shortly, invokes the callback for the service, and it updates a local string variable so that the processing order can be displayed.

10. Add the following method to the *ConcurrencyService* class.

```
' VB
Private Sub makeCallback(ByVal callback As Object)
    callback.ReceiveCallCount(Thread.CurrentThread.ManagedThreadId)
    SyncLock Me
        result += Environment.NewLine & _
            String.Format("Callback from {0} at {1}", _
            Thread.CurrentThread.ManagedThreadId, _
            DateTime.Now.ToLongTimeString())
    End SyncLock
End Sub
```

```
// C#
private void makeCallback(object callback)
{
    ((IConcurrencyCallback)callback).ReceiveCallCount
        (Thread.CurrentThread.ManagedThreadId);
    lock(this)
    {
        result += Environment.NewLine +
            String.Format("Callback from {0} at {1}",
            Thread.CurrentThread.ManagedThreadId,
            DateTime.Now.ToLongTimeString());
    }
}
```

11. Ensure that the DemoClient project is set as the startup project, and then launch the application by pressing F5.

12. In the Concurrent Clients To Start text box, type a value of **1** and click the Start Demo button.

   After a few minutes, you see an exception thrown, indicating that a control was accessed from the wrong thread.

13. Press Shift+F5 to terminate the application.

14. Go back to the *Form1* class.

    The call must be modified so that the *addToLabel* method is executed on the appropriate thread.

15. Change the *ReceiveCallCount* method, as shown in bold, to the following:

```
' VB
Public Sub ReceiveCallCount(ByVal callCount As Integer) _
    Implements IConcurrencyCallback.ReceiveCallCount

    Thread.Sleep(2000)
    Dim updateMethod As New SendMessage(AddressOf addToLabel)
    Me.Invoke(updateMethod, String.Format("The updated callCount is {0}.", _
        callCount)) End Sub
```

```
// C#
public void ReceiveCallCount(int callCount)
{
    Thread.Sleep(2000);
    SendMessage updateMethod = new SendMessage(addToLabel);
    this.Invoke(updateMethod, String.Format("The updated callCount is {0}.",
        callCount));
}
```

16. Press F5 to launch the application.

17. In the Concurrent Clients To Start text box, type a value of **1** and click the Start Demo button.

    After a few minutes, you see a series of messages, indicating that the callback was successful.

18. In Visual Studio, press Shift+F5 to terminate the application.

Lesson Summary

- The synchronization context class determines which thread should be used to process a WCF request.
- Custom synchronization contexts can be used to extend the mechanism that dispatches requests.
- Synchronization contexts can also be used to support thread affinity in callback situations.

Lesson Review

You can use the following questions to test your knowledge of the information in Lesson 2, "Synchronization." The questions are also available on the companion CD if you prefer to review them in electronic form.

NOTE Answers

Answers to these questions and explanations of why each answer choice is correct or incorrect are located in the "Answers" section at the end of the book.

---

1. Under which of the following scenarios must the synchronization context of a WCF service be used?

    A. The WCF service is performing an update to a Microsoft SQL Server database.

    B. The WCF service is making a call to an external Web service.

    C. The WCF service is hosted by a Windows Forms application and must interact with the user interface.

    D. The WCF service uses a couple of threads from the thread pool to perform a number of actions in parallel.

2. Which of the following must be performed to associate a custom synchronization context object with a particular request?

    A. Derive the service class from the custom synchronization context class.

    B. Decorate the service class with the *ServiceBehavior* attribute, setting the *UseSynchronizationContext* attribute to *true*.

    C. Have the service class implement the *IContextBehavior* interface.

    D. Decorate the service class with an attribute that implements the *IContextBehavior* interface.

Chapter Review

To further practice and reinforce the skills you learned in this chapter, you can:

- Review the chapter summary.
- Review the list of key terms introduced in this chapter.
- Complete the case scenario. This scenario sets up a real-world situation involving the topics of this chapter and asks you to create a solution.
- Complete the suggested practices.
- Take a practice test.

Chapter Summary

- Concurrency becomes an issue in a WCF service or callback when more than one request can be processed simultaneously.
- Setting the concurrency mode to *Single* removes most of the issues associated with concurrency but at a cost of potential scalability issues.
- The synchronization context, a .NET Framework 2.0 addition, enables thread affinity information to be conveyed to WCF services and client callbacks.

Key Terms

Do you know what these key terms mean? You can check your answers by looking up the terms in the glossary at the end of the book.

- client callback
- just-in-time-locking/as-soon-as-possible-releasing
- service object
- thread affinity
- thread local storage
- thread-safe

Case Scenario

In the following case scenario, you apply what you've learned about concurrency in WCF. You can find answers to these questions in the "Answers" section at the end of this book.

Case Scenario: Using WCF as a Gateway

Your company has an earlier application that must be exposed through a service. The decision was made to create a WCF serivce that exposes the desired interface and marshals the incoming requests to the earlier application (as well as providing the results back to the client). There is some concern about the ability of the earlier application to support a large number of requests.

Also, some of the requests made to the earlier application can take a significant (from the application's perspective) amount of time. While the request is being processed, the earlier application provides update messages to the WCF service, which must be sent back to the client.

Answer the following question for your manager:

- What is the best concurrency model to use in this situation?

Suggested Practices

To help you successfully master the exam objectives presented in this chapter, complete the following tasks.

Address Concurrency Problems

Create a custom synchronization context.

- **Practice** Create a custom synchronization context that ensures that only one request from a user is processed at a time. Associate this context with all incoming requests for a WCF service.

Watch a Webcast

Watch a webcast about WCF concurrency.

- **Practice** Watch the MSDN webcast, "Concurrency, Throughput and Throttling," by Michele Leroux Bustamante, available on the companion CD in the Webcasts folder.

Take a Practice Test

The practice tests on this book's companion CD offer many options. For example, you can test yourself on just one exam objective, or you can test yourself on all the 70-503 certification exam content. You can set up the test so that it closely simulates the experience of taking a certification exam, or you can set it up in study mode so that you can look at the correct answers and explanations after you answer each question.

MORE INFO Practice tests

For details about all the practice test options available, see the "How to Use the Practice Tests" section in this book's introduction.

Answers

Chapter 1: Lesson Review Answers

Lesson 1

1. **Correct Answer: C**

   A. **Incorrect:** Although the *FaultContractAttribute* might be required, you will need the *OperationContractAttribute* to first declare an operation as part of the Service contract before you can declare that it might issue faults.

   B. **Incorrect:** The *OperationContractAttribute* is required, and the *FaultContractAttribute* might be required, but neither can be applied unless the *ServiceContractAttribute* has first been used to declare a Service contract.

   C. **Correct:** At a minimum, you will need the *ServiceContractAttribute* to declare the contract and the *OperationContractAttribute* to declare any operations in that Service contract. Other attributes might be needed, but you will always need at least these two.

   D. **Incorrect:** The *OperationContractAttribute* is required, and the *MessageParameterAttribute* might be needed, but neither can be applied unless the *ServiceContractAttribute* has first been used to declare a Service contract.

2. **Correct Answers: B, E, and F**

   A. **Incorrect:** Although using a well-defined namespace might be advantageous, the lesson explicitly stated that the name of the resulting service must be InventoryService, not IInventoryService, as it is if you don't explicitly use the *Name* property.

   B. **Correct:** The *RemoveItem* operation might issue faults, and those faults will be packaged inside string objects.

   C. **Incorrect:** Although the return type is *void* and, therefore, nothing comes back from the operation, you cannot use the OneWay MEP here because the *RemoveItem* operation might issue faults.

   D. **Incorrect:** Using the *FaultContract* attribute is correct, but it is missing the property indicating the type of fault detail, which, in this case, is simply the string type.

   E. **Correct:** The *OperationContract* attribute is required because the *RemoveItem* operation is part of your Service contract.

   F. **Correct:** The *ServiceContract* attribute is required to declare your interface to be a Service contract, and the service's name should be InventoryService, not IInventoryService, so you need to use the *Name* property to control this explicitly.

G. **Incorrect:** The *ServiceContract* attribute is required to declare your interface to be a Service contract; the *Name* property is used properly to control the service's name explicitly, but there was no mention of a Callback contract.

Lesson 2

1. **Correct Answer: A**

   A. **Correct:** When you apply the ordering rules, *Country* and *StateOrProvince* are ordered first because no explicit *Order* value was assigned. Then *AddressLine*, *City*, and *ZipOrPostalCode* are next, ordered according to their *Order* value, with *AddressLine* coming before *City* because they both have *Order* value 0, but *AddressLine* is first alphabetically. Finally, *ApartmentNumber* is not declared a *DataMember*, so it is not part of the contract.

   B. **Incorrect:** *ApartmentNumber* should not be included in this list because it is not declared a *DataMember*, and is not part of the contract. Everything else in the list is correct.

   C. **Incorrect:** This order has the explicitly ordered members ordered correctly within that group and the remaining alphabetically ordered members order correctly within that group, but it is incorrect because the explicitly ordered group appears before the alphabetically ordered group.

   D. **Incorrect:** This order is close to being correct; the only problem is that among the explicitly ordered members, *AddressLine* should come before *City* because they both have *Order* value 0, but *AddressLine* is first alphabetically.

2. **Correct Answer: D**

   A. **Incorrect:** The message has exactly the right structure, but the elements are incorrectly named. They are all named as they appear in the Message contract definition, which is not as they should be because the *Name* property was used to control them explicitly.

   B. **Incorrect:** Because the default for *IsWrapped* is *true*, the body members will be wrapped inside a wrapper element named after the Message contract.

   C. **Incorrect:** The *TheCustomHeader* element belongs in the SOAP header, not in the body.

   D. **Correct:** This is correct because, according to the default *IsWrapped = true*, the body members are wrapped in an element named after the Message contract, the header is included, and all elements are named as they were explicitly controlled in the contract using the *Name* property.

Chapter 1: Case Scenario Answers

Case Scenario 1: First Identifying a Service

1. The best solution would likely be to put a Lead Management service in front of the leads database so that it can be consumed by both the rich client and the Java Web application. Especially because it is not an internal application, allowing a vendor to have direct access to your database is not a good idea.

2. Yes, a Web service would lend itself well to support a future mobile device client that consumes the service.

3. The best way to support version tolerance would be to design your leads as a Data contract that uses the *IExtensibleDataObject* mechanism.

Case Scenario 2: Working with Legacy Systems

1. Yes, WCF should be able to provide support for this use of SOAP.

2. Your service will need to be declared to use the *XmlSerializer*, using the *XmlSerializerFormat* attribute with its *Style* property set to *Rpc* and its *Use* property set to *Encoded*.

3. You will need to define a Message contract that takes your Data contract as a member, annotated with the *MessageBodyMember* attribute, and that sets the *IsWrapped* property to *false*.

Chapter 2: Lesson Review Answers

Lesson 1

1. **Correct Answer: D**
   A. **Incorrect:** The basic binding exposes a service such as an earlier ASMX Web service and cannot be used for same-machine communication.
   B. **Incorrect:** The TCP binding is used for cross-machine communication across the Internet.
   C. **Incorrect:** The peer network binding is used for peer networking and cannot be used for same-machine communication.
   D. **Correct:** The named pipe binding uses named pipes as a transport for same-machine communication, using an efficient binary encoding method.

2. **Correct Answer: C**
   A. **Incorrect:** The basic binding exposes a service such as a former ASMX Web service and cannot support MSMQ.

      B. **Incorrect:** The Web service binding provides reliability, security, and transactions but does not support MSMQ.

      C. **Correct:** The *msmqIntegrationBinding* is an interoperable binding used when replacing existing MSMQ applications because it can be used for COM and native C++ APIs.

      D. **Incorrect:** The *netMsmqBinding* is used for new MSMQ applications on WCF computers.

  3. **Correct Answer: A**

      A. **Correct:** When the *HttpGetEnabled* property, which is part of the *serviceMetadata* element, is set to *true*, clients can access service metadata over HTTP-GET by using a Web browser.

      B. **Incorrect:** The *ServiceMetadataBehavior* type defines a metadata behavior element programmatically.

      C. **Incorrect:** The *AddServiceEndpoint* method specifies an endpoint for a service.

      D. **Incorrect:** The *behaviors* element contains all behaviors related to a service when using a configuration file.

Lesson 2

  1. **Correct Answer: C**

      A. **Incorrect:** The *netTcpBinding* enables the binary encoding method only and does not support MTOM.

      B. **Incorrect:** The *netNamedPipeBinding* enables the binary encoding method only and does not support MTOM.

      C. **Correct:** You would need to customize the *wsHttpBinding* and set the *messageEncoding* property to *Mtom* because the default for this binding is text.

      D. **Incorrect:** The default method for the *wsHttpBinding* is text, not MTOM.

  2. **Correct Answers: A and B**

      A. **Correct:** The transport element is required when creating a custom binding.

      B. **Correct:** The message encoding method is required when creating a custom binding.

      C. **Incorrect:** The security element is optional.

      D. **Incorrect:** The reliability element is optional.

Chapter 2: Case Scenario Answers

Case Scenario 1: Configuring an Endpoint

■ In this case, the *basicHttpBinding* would be the most suitable choice. It's intended to be used for WCF services that replace previous Web services and is an interoperable binding that supports both HTTP and HTTPS.

Case Scenario 2: Choosing a Binding

■ No, *basicHttpBinding* will not be appropriate because it does not support reliability. In this case, it would be best to use *wsDualHttpBinding* for which, by default, reliability is always enabled. This will keep the callback channel to the client alive, even over HTTP.

Chapter 3: Lesson Review Answers

Lesson 1

1. **Correct Answer: C**
   A. **Incorrect:** IIS 5.1 supports only the HTTP protocol.
   B. **Incorrect:** IIS 6.1 supports only the HTTP protocol.
   C. **Correct:** WAS is a component of IIS 7.0, and it supports non-HTTP protocols such as TCP, named pipes, and MSMQ.
   D. **Incorrect:** IIS 7.0 does support non-HTTP protocols, using the WAS component.

2. **Correct Answer: B**
   A. **Incorrect:** The Non-HTTP activation check box is not available under the Windows Activation Service node.
   B. **Correct:** You must select the check box named Windows Communication Foundation Non-HTTP Activation.
   C. **Incorrect:** The Non-HTTP activation check box is not available under the Internet Information Services node.
   D. **Incorrect:** To create a WAS application, you must create a Service.svc file, but this is not needed to support the TCP protocol.

3. **Correct Answers: A and C**
   A. **Correct:** You must create a private queue, and it should be named the same as the Service.svc file, including the Web application name.
   B. **Incorrect:** You must grant receive and peek permissions to the NETWORK SERVICE account rather than read permissions.

C. **Correct:** You must specify the private queue name when defining the endpoint in the web.config file.

D. **Incorrect:** You do not need to include an MSMQ element in the web.config file.

Lesson 2

1. **Correct Answers: A, B, C, and D**

    A. **Correct:** WCF services can be hosted in a Windows Forms application. You will be responsible for adding code to open and close the host as well as manage the availability of the service.

    B. **Correct:** WCF services can be hosted by a Windows Presentation Foundation UI application because they are also managed .NET applications.

    C. **Correct:** WCF services can easily be hosted by a Console application, which is typical during the development process.

    D. **Correct:** WCF services can be hosted with Windows services, formerly known as Windows NT services.

2. **Correct Answer: B**

    A. **Incorrect:** The machine.config file stores Web configuration settings for a server computer.

    B. **Correct:** You can run the installutil command-line utility to install the service. The service will then be available through the service control manager.

    C. **Incorrect:** Although you do need to configure the app.config file for the Windows service, this does not control loading the Windows service.

    D. **Incorrect:** You would need to install the Windows service first.

Chapter 3: Case Scenario Answer

Case Scenario: Upgrading a Series of Earlier Web Services

1. Because your customers access the Web services through HTTP using an ASP.NET application, you can host your new WCF services on IIS. The only decision involves which version of IIS you use. Because your Web server is running IIS 6.1 with Windows Server 2003, you do not have .NET Framework 3.5 installed, which you would need before you can start hosting WCF services on the Web server. You must either upgrade to .NET Framework 3.5 on the existing server and configure it for HTTP activation or upgrade the server to Windows Server 2008 in a way that involves minimal downtime for the customer.

2. Because the current solution uses more than one Web service, it would be easiest to use the existing ASP.NET application and convert the Web services to WCF services. To minimize downtime, the new WCF services could be converted in phases and not all at one time. During the conversion process, there might be times when the ASP.NET application is accessing both WCF services and Web services. This is all right because WCF services can be located in the same application domain as existing ASPX and ASMX Web services.

Chapter 4: Lesson Review Answers

Lesson 1

1. **Correct Answer: B**

   A. **Incorrect:** This version correctly offers constructors that accept an *InstanceContext* object, something that is required for callbacks to work, but incorrectly inherits from *ClientBase* when in fact it should inherit from *DuplexClientBase*.

   B. **Correct:** This version correctly inherits from the *DuplexClientBase* class, not from the *ClientBase* class, and offers constructors that accept an *InstanceContext* object, which is required for callbacks to work.

   C. **Incorrect:** This version correctly inherits from the *DuplexClientBase* class, not from the *ClientBase* class, but fails to offer constructors that accept an *InstanceContext* object, which is required for callbacks to work.

   D. **Incorrect:** This version incorrectly inherits from *ClientBase* when, in fact, it should inherit from *DuplexClientBase* and fails to offer constructors that accept an *InstanceContext* object, which is required for callbacks to work.

2. **Correct Answer: A**

   A. **Correct:** This is the one step that is incorrect because it specifies the wrong signature for the callback handler. The type of the parameter to the callback method should be *IAsyncResult* instead of *AsyncCallback*.

   B. **Incorrect:** This is exactly how the operation should be invoked asynchronously, which includes passing the proxy itself as the state object.

   C. **Incorrect:** Inside the callback handler, this would be precisely how you access the state object, which in this case is the proxy object.

   D. **Incorrect:** After you have a reference to the proxy object inside the callback handler, this would be how you would end the call.

Lesson 2

1. **Correct Answers: B and D**

    A. **Incorrect:** *ChannelFactory* creates only proxy objects, not classes. An even greater limiting factor is that this approach requires a WCF Service contract, something that wouldn't exist in the context of consuming a Java service.

    B. **Correct:** This is a perfectly viable way of creating a proxy class and definitely offers the most options for defining the resulting proxy class.

    C. **Incorrect:** This approach requires a WCF Service contract, something that wouldn't exist in the context of consuming a Java service.

    D. **Correct:** This, too, is a viable way of creating a proxy class as long as you have access to the service's WSDL.

Chapter 4: Case Scenario Answers

Case Scenario 1: Building an e-Commerce Solution

1. Yes, you can. As services become more pervasive, it is getting easier to build complex applications quickly (implying lower startup costs) by assembling composite applications that simply consume other services.

2. In this situation, many options are available to embrace services. Many providers offer shopping services, all the major credit cards now provide Web services access to enable financial transactions, and, finally, most of the major courier and logistics providers also now offer Web services access to their capabilities. Thus, a relatively low entry point to e-commerce–enable this Web site is possible with fairly low upfront costs. Some of the upfront costs will be deferred to the ongoing costs the company will pay out to the service providers for consumption of their services.

Case Scenario 2: Medical Imaging Application

1. Yes. Because both the Web application and the rich-client application will be on .NET, you can define a service agent in a common class library that wraps all the logic of retries, asynchronous invocation, and so on around a proxy to the service. Then, this common assembly can be used by both clients.

2. Yes. Because both the clients and the service are in a position to use WCF, you know there are no issues with using MTOM, which will definitely help performance when retrieving large sets of image data. Thus, both the consumers and the service can be configured to use the MTOM encoding. MTOM can help get images to the Web application faster; however, ultimately, the bandwidth between the browser and the Web tier will affect how quickly Web application users see image data.

Chapter 5: Lesson Review Answers

Lesson 1

1. **Correct Answers: A and E**

    A. **Correct:** The *basicHttpBinding* attribute is used to communicate with ASMX Web services.

    B. **Incorrect:** The *basicHttpBinding* attribute cannot be used to communicate with a WCF service that is expecting a connection through named pipes.

    C. **Incorrect:** Even though the WCF service will have to implement the *IUpdateService* interface, it is quite possible for the same service to implement other interfaces, exposed either at the same endpoint or on different endpoints.

    D. **Incorrect:** The *ReceiveTimeout* value associated with the *basicHttpBinding* attribute (which is the only one set to one minute) has to do with how long the client should keep a connection with the service open in case of a callback method. It has no impact on how long the client will wait for a response before an exception is raised.

    E. **Correct:** The *SendTimeout* value associated with the *basicHttpBinding* attribute provides the length of time that the client will wait for a response from the service before a CommunicationException or a TimeoutException is raised.

2. **Correct Answers: B and D**

    A. **Incorrect:** When no name is specified in the *bindingConfiguration* attribute, the default settings are used. The binding marked "DefaultBinding" is not really the default binding.

    B. **Correct:** When no name is specified for the binding configuration, the default values are used. The default value for the openTimeout attribute is one minute. So, in the absence of a specified binding configuration, the connection will be closed in a minute.

    C. **Incorrect:** The only binding with a receive timeout of ten minutes is the one used for *basicHttpBinding*. Because the endpoint doesn't use this type of binding, the value of *ReceiveTimeout* is irrelevant to how the client request is processed.

    D. **Correct:** Although the Windows user credentials for the current user will be available to the service, because the *impersonationLevel* attribute is set to *Identification*, the credentials are available for authentication purposes only. All the processing done in the service will run as the default user.

    E. **Incorrect:** For the WCF service to run using the current user's credentials, the *impersonationLevel* attribute would need to be set to *Impersonation* or *Delegation*.

3. **Correct Answer: A**

A. **Correct:** The address for the endpoint includes the *net.pipe* protocol, and the binding is appropriate (*netNamedPipeBinding*) for the endpoint.

B. **Incorrect:** The *wsHttpBinding* binding cannot be used to communicate with an endpoint that is expected to be a named pipe transport type, and the address's protocol ("http") is not appropriate for the endpoint.

C. **Incorrect:** The protocol specified on the address is the incorrect type for the endpoint.

D. **Incorrect:** The *basicHttpBinding* attribute is not appropriate for the endpoint's binding.

Lesson 2

1. **Correct Answer: D**

    A. **Incorrect:** The standard HTTP binding does not support callback functionality.

    B. **Incorrect:** This binding is still an HTTP-based binding that does not support callbacks. It is *basicHttpBinding* with SOAP messages formatted to interact better with WCF services.

    C. **Incorrect:** This binding is still an HTTP-based binding, with cookie support added.

    D. **Correct:** Although this binding is still an HTTP-based binding, *CompositeDuplexBindingElement* has been added to support the client's listening for a request from the service.

2. **Correct Answer: C**

    A. **Incorrect:** The standard TCP bindings include support for the duplex functionality required to support callbacks.

    B. **Incorrect:** The underlying transport layer (named pipes) supports bidirectional communication. As such, any binding that uses named pipes as the transport layer supports callbacks.

    C. **Correct:** MSMQ does not provide support for callbacks. If you contemplate the mechanism used to transport the messages, you'll understand why this is the case. This is not to say that a custom binding providing such support isn't possible, only that the out-of-the-box implementation does not have any duplex channel functionality.

    D. **Incorrect:** Any binding that has TCP as the underlying transport layer is capable of supporting callbacks.

Chapter 5: Case Scenario Answers

Case Scenario: Defining Multiple Endpoints

1. Yes, there are some protocols that cannot be supported. The limitation is not in WCF itself but in the transport mechanism used to send messages between the client and the service. For example, in an externally-facing WCF service, any protocol based on named pipes will not be possible. The reason for this is that the named pipes protocol can be used only when the client and service are on the same system. In addition, MSMQ-based bindings will probably not be appropriate. Using MSMQ-based bindings is more costly because it involves configuring certificates on both sides of the application and defining authorization based on these certificates.

2. The answer is no; it is not possible for the same service to support multiple protocols on the same endpoint, because, technically, an endpoint consists of an address, a binding, and a contract. Changing the address would mean there is a different endpoint.

3. Yes, a service can support multiple endpoints, as was demonstrated in one of the exercises in this chapter.

4. Yes, one service can expose multiple contracts on the same endpoint. However, there are a number of restrictions. First, the binding for each of the contracts must be the same. It is not possible to have the same URI support both *basicHttpBinding* and *wsHttpBinding* at the same time. Each contract would have to use the same binding type.

5. The second restriction arises from the mechanism that WCF uses to route the message to the appropriate operation. Two steps are involved: an address filter and a contract filter. The address filter examines the *To* attribute in the SOAP message to help determine the final destination. The contract filter uses the *Action* attribute in the SOAP message as the second part of the determination. The attribute values must be sufficient to identify the appropriate service object uniquely. If, for example, the *Action* attribute were the same for two different contracts, those contracts could not both be hosted within the same service host.

Chapter 6: Lesson Review Answers

Lesson 1

1. **Correct Answer: B**
   A. **Incorrect:** Although the element indicates that the quota is 1,000, WCF generates one additional message that indicates the quota has been reached.

B. **Correct:** When the quota for logging messages is reached, WCF generates one additional message to indicate that the quota has been reached, so the actual number of log entries will be the specified quota plus 1.

C. **Incorrect:** The *maxSizeOfMessageToLog* attribute constrains the size of the individual logged message. It has no impact on the number of log entries.

D. **Incorrect:** The *maxMessagesToLog* attribute places an upper limit on the number of log entries that are generated.

2. **Correct Answer: D**

A. **Incorrect:** If no listener is defined, there would be no trace message in the log at all.

B. **Incorrect:** If no source is defined, there would be no trace messages in the log at all.

C. **Incorrect:** If *logEntireMessage* is set to *false*, only the headers will be logged. Although setting it to *true* will increase the amount of information in the log file, it will not prevent all the messages from being logged in one way or another.

D. **Correct:** If only a few messages are missing, then it is probably because they are still in the trace buffer. By setting *autoflush* to *true*, you can ensure that all messages are directed to the trace output location immediately.

Lesson 2

1. **Correct Answer: D**

A. **Incorrect:** The *ActivityTracing* switch is a requirement for built-in activities to be included in the tracing logs.

B. **Incorrect:** If a GUID has not been assigned to the *ActivityId* property, WCF considers that a global activity has not been created and will not propagate it.

C. **Incorrect:** Unless the *propagateActivity* is set to *true*, WCF will not propagate an activity between the client and the service.

D. **Correct:** The trace does not need to be transferred for the activity to be propagated. The transfer is used to facilitate correlation between activities, but it is not a requirement for propagation.

2. **Correct Answer: C**

A. **Incorrect:** The *Start* event indicates the beginning of an activity, but because the activity ID hasn't been changed, it wouldn't be appropriate in this scenario.

B. **Incorrect:** The *Stop* event indicates that an activity is complete. This isn't the case in this scenario because the expectation is that the activity will continue after the third-party service has been called.

C. **Correct:** The *Suspend* event is the appropriate one to call. It keeps the current activity from being used in any traces until the *Resume* event is emitted.

D. **Incorrect:** The *Transfer* event marks the propagation of an activity across a service boundary. It doesn't prevent the activity from being used. In fact, it is intended that the same activity will be used in the traces, the opposite of what the question requires.

Lesson 3

1. **Correct Answer: B**

   A. **Incorrect:** Message Inspection involves viewing and manipulating the message as it arrives at and leaves the service. Although it is possible to have an inspector coordinate with similar functionality on the client side (such as if encryption was involved), such coordination is not a requirement.

   B. **Correct:** The Message Formatting extension point enables direct control over the deserialization of the message. However, to function, it needs to agree with the serialization process that occurred on the client.

   C. **Incorrect:** The Parameter Inspection extension point enables viewing, validation, and manipulation of the values, but this does not require any cooperation from the client.

   D. **Incorrect:** The Operation Invoker controls the operation that will be called within the service. Again, it is possible that information sent from the client could be used, but sending information from the client not required for an Operation Invoker to function.

2. **Correct Answer: B**

   A. **Incorrect:** Calling *GetReaderAtBodyContents* sets the MessageState property to *Read*.

   B. **Correct:** The *Written* state occurs after the message body has been written to.

   C. **Incorrect:** Calling *CreateBufferedCopy* sets the *MessageState* property to *Read*.

   D. **Incorrect:** Calling the *CreateMessage* method sets the *MessageState* property to *Created*.

Lesson 4

1. **Correct Answer: A**

   A. **Correct:** To help ensure that a WCF application is as efficient as possible by default, performance counters are turned off unless explicitly enabled in the configuration file.

   B. **Incorrect:** The WCF performance counters are instance based. This means that to be captured, an instance of the service must be running. If there is no service, no counters are updated.

C. **Incorrect:** WCF performance counters are instance based at the address and contract level. The name of the instance under which the counters are accumulated uses the address and contract as the distinguishing characteristics. This means that if multiple bindings share address and contract, the counters will be incremented within that single instance.

D. **Incorrect:** None of the WCF performance counters relate to the client side at all. They are all service-side counters.

2. **Correct Answer: A**

A. **Correct:** It is quite legitimate for a WCF service that is running as a Local Service to publish WMI events.

B. **Incorrect:** The specified registry key is used to update the memory allocated to the performance counter updates in WCF. The key has nothing to do with WMI.

C. **Incorrect:** To publish WMI information, the *wmiProviderEnabled* attribute must be set to *true*.

D. **Incorrect:** The WMI infrastructure is designed to allow for remotely monitoring an application. This ability is one reason care should be taken in enabling WMI event publication on an application.

Chapter 6: Case Scenario Answers

Case Scenario: Using Activity Tracing

1. The answer to this question depends on whether you want the clients to be able to submit information that might be useful in identifying the source of problems. Activity tracing is useful when trying to correlate client actions with service actions. To do this, trace logs must be generated by both the client and the service. If the client application is deployed at another site, you need to provide a mechanism that enables the trace logs from the client portion of the application to be sent in.

   As for whether allowing this tracing to be performed is a good idea, the answer is almost inevitably yes. Problems are quite likely to be associated with the communications between the two pieces. Being able to correlate the traces will frequently be beneficial to the support staff, and it could very well help the development team identify bugs that would otherwise be difficult to track down.

2. An activity can be defined from either the business or technical perspective. The choice depends on the type of correlation needed. To debug a technical problem, creating a new activity with each call is a good idea. To address business-level issues, keeping track of the multiple calls within a business transaction might be effective. Ultimately, the decision about when a new activity should be created will depend on how the information is expected to be used.

Chapter 7: Lesson Review Answers

Lesson 1

1. **Correct Answer: C**

   A. **Incorrect:** One of the differences between transport- and message-level security is that transport encrypts the entire message. The encryption and decryption of the message in transport-level security takes place below the WCF channel stack, so there is no need to leave any portion of the message unsecured.

   B. **Incorrect:** Transport security is dependent upon the capability of the underlying protocol. If the protocol doesn't support the security mechanism, WCF transport security can be configured to use it.

   C. **Correct:** If the transport security is built into the protocol, there is no way for WCF to turn it off. It's not possible to disable transport security in an SSL-based connection, for example.

   D. **Incorrect:** Message integrity is one of the guarantees offered by transport-level security.

2. **Correct Answer: C**

   A. **Incorrect:** The *basicHttpBinding* provides transport-level security using SSL.

   B. **Incorrect:** The *netTcpBinding* provides transport-level security, although the implementation is done within WCF instead of using SSL.

   C. **Correct:** The *wsDualHttpBinding* doesn't support transport-level security because there is no way to guarantee that the client is capable of receiving an SSL-encrypted message.

   D. **Incorrect:** The *netNamedPipeBinding* supports the same transport-level security options that TCP does because the implementation for the security takes place within the WCF channel.

3. **Correct Answer: D**

   A. **Incorrect:** The *wsHttpBinding* can use SSL as the transport security mechanism, a technique that does not require AD DS to function.

   B. **Incorrect:** The *netNamedPipeBinding* uses named pipes, a transport protocol that is not intended to be used in cross-machine applications.

   C. **Incorrect:** The *netTcpBinding* uses a WCF implementation of transport security that is not dependent on AD DS. In fact, *netTcpBinding* is capable of using a custom authentication mechanism as part of transport security.

   D. **Correct:** For *msmqIntegrationBinding* to implement transport security, both client and service must be in the same domain. Clients and services in the same domain in a Windows network require AD DS.

Lesson 2

1. **Correct Answer: C**
    A. **Incorrect:** WCF uses parts of the WS-Security specification to secure the message. This specification is independent of the underlying transport protocol.
    B. **Incorrect:** The encrypting of a message can be directed at all or part of the message body.
    C. **Correct:** The *basicHttpBinding* binding doesn't support *Windows* authentication.
    D. **Incorrect:** Not only can the authentication mechanism be defined through configuration but it can also be specified or modified at run time.

2. **Correct Answer: A**
    A. **Correct:** For *Windows* authentication to work across computers for the described application, the two computers must be in the same domain.
    B. **Incorrect:** Being in the same domain is a requirement for the applications to communicate. In this instance, if the computers are in the same domain, no problems would arise.
    C. **Incorrect:** The *establishSecurityContext* attribute determines whether a secure token should be requested from the service and reused in subsequent requests. However, to establish a security context, it must be possible for the client to be authenticated in the service, and that is not currently happening.
    D. **Incorrect:** Using a client-side certificate to provide authentication could work as part of a solution. However, given the configuration that was provided, a certificate would not be provided to the service and, therefore, would not solve the stated problem.

Chapter 7: Case Scenario Answers

Case Scenario: Choosing the Security Mechanism

1. The client application will send potentially sensitive information back to the service. For this reason, some form of security is required. It becomes a question of whether transport security is required or message security is sufficient. The answer depends a great deal on the client. Theoretically, message security should be sufficient. However, some clients prefer the confidence of using transport security, especially if it is a commonly used standard such as SSL.

2. If transport security is necessary, it will be because of the need to use a standard protocol. In the realm of messages sent over the Internet, the most respected standard is SSL and, to provide SSL transport security, one of the HTTP-based bindings should be used.

Chapter 8: Lesson Review Answers

Lesson 1

1. **Correct Answer: A**

    A. **Correct:** Having authentication based on a certificate that has been installed on the client keeps the user from having to provide credentials, and being able to decrypt the message indicates to the service that the requester is who he or she says he or she is.

    B. **Incorrect:** The *UserName* authentication requires a set of credentials with the request.

    C. **Incorrect:** Windows authentication is not valid when using *basicHttpBinding*.

    D. **Incorrect:** As with *Windows* authentication, *IssuedToken* authentication is not valid when using *basicHttpBinding*.

2. **Correct Answer: C**

    A. **Incorrect:** Given the *findValue* attribute set to *localhost*, changing the search type of *FindByDistinguishedSubjectName* will result in no certificate being found because the format of a distinguished subject name would be *CN=localhost*.

    B. **Incorrect:** The client credentials type for the *transport* element cannot be set to *UserName*. This is not a valid value for the attribute.

    C. **Correct:** As stated in the question, custom authentication is being used. To use custom authentication, the client credentials for the *message* element must be *User-Name*.

    D. **Incorrect:** This suggestion actually presents the same credentials to the service as the original configuration because the full subject name for the certificate would be *CN=localhost*.

Lesson 2

1. **Correct Answer: D**

    A. **Incorrect:** The *User* property in the *PrincipalPermission* attribute specifies the user-name of the requests to be required to allow access.

    B. **Incorrect:** Although the WCF client does need to be configured to enable authentication in general, no additional change must be made to enable additional authorization.

    C. **Incorrect:** Claims can be added to the WCF pipeline through the *EvaluationContext* as part of a custom authorization policy.

     D. **Correct:** It is possible to build a custom security token and use it to provide authentication and authorization functionality. You can accomplish this by creating a custom *TokenAuthenticator*.

2. **Correct Answer: C**

     A. **Incorrect:** If impersonation is set to *Anonymous*, no information about the client is sent to the service. As a result, there is no way for the service to access the file on behalf of the requester.

     B. **Incorrect:** With *Identification*, the service can discover who the requester is, and whether the requester has access to the file, but it still won't be able to access the file.

     C. **Correct:** When the *ImpersonationLevel* is set to *Impersonation*, the service is able to use the client's credentials to access local resources. The service will not, however, be able to access network resources by using the client's credentials.

     D. **Incorrect:** Although the *Delegation* level works for accessing the local resources, it provides more access than is specified in the question.

3. **Correct Answer: D**

     A. **Incorrect:** If impersonation is set to *Anonymous*, no information about the client is sent to the service. As a result, there is no way for the service to access the file on behalf of the requester.

     B. **Incorrect:** With *Identification*, the service can discover who the requester is and whether the requester has access to the file, but it still won't be able to access the file.

     C. **Incorrect:** Having the *ImpersonationLevel* set to *Impersonation* allows the service to access local resources, but not remote resources, on behalf of the client.

     D. **Correct:** The *Delegation ImpersonationLevel* works for accessing not only the local resources but also for resources that are available throughout the network.

Chapter 8: Case Scenario Answers

Case Scenario: Choosing the Appropriate Authentication Type

1. There are only two options for authentication in this scenario. Windows authentication isn't feasible unless the client and service are in the same domain. The same restriction applies to *Ntlm*. Further, in the given scenario, it seems highly unlikely that all the clients would be in the same domain as the service. It would be possible to have no authentication at all, but given the type of application, that, too is not a good choice, so the remaining choices are *UserName* and *Certificate*.

2. The difference between *UserName* and *Certificate* is how the credentials are to be collected from the user. If *Certificate* authentication is used, the client can connect to the service silently, so there is no need to provide any credentials manually. The *UserName* mode implies that the user will be asked for his or her credentials.

3. The authorization used in the application will be driven by the specific business requirements. For example, some of the methods might need to be restricted based on functional levels within the application (administrator vs. user, for example). Alternatively, the authorization method could handle licensing issues if some clients are licensed to have access to more operations than other clients are.

4. In this type of application, impersonation is not possible. To perform impersonation, WCF needs to map the incoming requester to a Windows account, which requires Windows authentication. However, as has already been pointed out, Windows authentication is not likely to be feasible.

Chapter 9: Lesson Review Answers

Lesson 1

1. **Correct Answer: A**

   A. **Correct:** Setting the *Action* property to the wildcard character indicates that any action found in a message received at the endpoint (that isn't handled by other operations) should be routed to this method.

   B. **Incorrect:** Setting the *Action* property to any value means that the WCF dispatching process will route requests only with a matching action to that method. This is not what is required in the question.

   C. **Incorrect:** Setting the *ReplyAction* property to a wildcard means that the message returned by the method can contain any action, but it doesn't have any impact on the routing of incoming messages.

   D. **Incorrect:** Setting the *ReplyAction* property to anything other than a wildcard means that the action must be part of the *Message* object that is returned from the method. It does not, however, have any impact on the routing of inbound messages.

2. **Correct Answer: A**

   A. **Correct:** This is the first state the *Message* object is in, and it is the only state in which the *GetBody* method can be used successfully.

   B. **Incorrect:** The *Message* body can be read only once. When the state is set to *Read*, the body has already been processed, and an attempt to process the body again will cause an exception to be thrown.

C. **Incorrect:** To copy the body, it must be processed. Based on the rule that the body can be processed only once, *GetBody* will fail with an exception when a *Message* object is in this state.

D. **Incorrect:** The *Written* state occurs when the *Message* object has been created initially. At this point, the message is ready to be transmitted, but *GetBody* cannot be called.

E. **Incorrect:** After the message has been closed, no further processing is possible, and this includes calling the *GetBody* method.

Lesson 2

1. **Correct Answer: B**

A. **Incorrect:** The values in the fault class will be serialized before being sent from the service to the client. However, the *Exception* class is not serializable, so if the fault class does derive from *System.Exception*, it cannot be used in the *FaultContract* attribute.

B. **Correct:** The fault class will be serialized before being sent from the service to the client. For the data to be sent successfully, the class must be serializable.

C. **Incorrect:** The fault class is actually XML serialized. For this reason, the values can be assigned to any class that implements the same set of properties. In fact, a client-side version of the fault class is generated when a service reference is added through Visual Studio 2008.

D. **Incorrect:** There is no requirement for the properties to be initialized in the constructor. As long as the values are provided before the *FaultException* object is created, they will be serialized and sent to the client.

2. **Correct Answer: C**

A. **Incorrect:** An exception is thrown in the service, so the return value for the proxy will not be the expected string.

B. **Incorrect:** The generic version of the *FaultException* is raised only if it is explicitly called on the service. Because this is not the case, the *DemoFault* is not returned.

C. **Correct:** When an exception is raised in the service, WCF converts that exception into a *FaultException* for the client. For this reason, *FaultException* is returned.

D. **Incorrect:** The *CommunicationException* is raised only when there are issues with the communications channel. That is not the case here, so that exception will not be raised.

Chapter 9: Case Scenario Answers

Case Scenario: Working with Raw Messages

1. The answer depends on how much the interface has changed. In general, a breaking interface is one in which the parameters being passed to a method have been changed (in terms of their type), reordered, or eliminated. In such a scenario, the first reaction might be to question whether such a significant change is required. It is the kind of situation that is best avoided.

   Still, there are situations when breaking changes must be made. In that case, the technical challenge is to have both the old and new versions of the WCF service available to clients. For that, a generic message handler could be a very good solution. Such a handler can accept incoming messages, regardless of the parameter format. It could then examine the request to determine which version of the service is to be called and pass the message along to the appropriate internal endpoint.

2. It is quite possible for a generic message handler to provide logging functionality. As a WCF service, it is capable of supporting logging and tracing in the same manner as any other WCF service. It becomes more of a philosophical question than a technical one. Does it make sense to put logging functions into the generic service as opposed to putting logging functions in the services that ultimately provide the request processing? Arguments can certainly be made for both alternatives, although, from a consistency perspective, it is probably better to let the individual services determine their tracing and logging requirements instead of forcing them to share a centralized setting.

Chapter 10: Lesson Review Answers

Lesson 1

1. **Correct Answer: A**
   A. **Correct:** With per call instancing, each method called gets its own instance of the implementation object. This mode minimizes the possibility of threading issues.
   B. **Incorrect:** Per session mode is slightly less thread-safe than per call mode. Each client proxy will have its own session, but threading issues are still possible within the service methods invoked by that one proxy.
   C. **Incorrect:** Having the WCF service running in single instance mode exposes even more potential threading problems because then every single request to the service will be processed by a single instance.

D. **Incorrect:** Even with the ability to control which request gets which instance, there is still a potential issue with threading. More specifically, a race condition exists if two clients are using the same as-yet uncreated instance. The race exists between the call to *GetExistingInstanceContext* and the corresponding *InitializeInstanceContext* so that some care is required to ensure that thread synchronization techniques are used.

2. **Correct Answer: C**

A. **Incorrect:** With per call mode, a new instance (complete with a new need to retrieve the data) is created for each method. This is probably the least efficient technique.

B. **Incorrect:** The per session mode will cache the information for each client proxy object, but when a new proxy object is created, a new service instance is created.

C. **Correct:** The singleton instancing mode creates a singleton instance object. This means that the data can be retrieved once and used within the instance object, regardless of the source of the request.

D. **Incorrect:** Although it is possible to use the instance context provider to cache the data, threading issues could arise. The provider could inject the data into the service instance, but each instance running in its own thread offers some potential problems with synchronization within the data.

Lesson 2

1. **Correct Answer: C**

A. **Incorrect:** If you selected this answer because the throttling configuration for *maxConcurrentCalls* is 15, this is not the limiting parameter for the throttling.

B. **Incorrect:** If you selected this answer because the throttling configuration for *maxConcurrentInstances* is 10, this is not the limiting parameter for the throttling.

C. **Correct:** Given the settings, the limiting parameter is the number of concurrent instances allowed. With the default values, operation calls are instanced on a *PerCall* basis, so with five simultaneous requests, that would mean five instances of the service class are created. This is the configured throttling value.

D. **Incorrect:** Throttling limits can apply to incoming requests.

2. **Correct Answer: D**

A. **Incorrect:** By setting the *IsInitializing* property to *true*, you can ensure that a method must be called before others in the service.

B. **Incorrect:** By setting the *IsTerminating* property to *true*, you can ensure that a method must be called after all the others in the service and that no methods can be called after it.

C. **Incorrect:** It is indeed not possible to order each of the exposed methods. Only the first and last methods can be indicated.

D. **Correct:** There is no way to ensure that the terminating method is called. All the *IsTerminating* property does is make sure that no methods can be called after the method for which the *IsTerminating* property is set to *true*.

Chapter 10: Case Scenario Answers

Case Scenario 1: Choosing the Appropriate Instancing Mode

- There are really only two available options for instancing. The correct choice will depend on how many instances of the application will be running at each client. If only one application is running at each client location, the instancing mode could be set to *Per-Session* because the one-to-one correspondence between the client and the service can be maintained with this configuration.

  However, if more than one instance of the application can be running at each client, a *PerSession* instance mode will not achieve the desired results because all the instances from one client will not be sharing a service instance. If this is the scenario, the solution would be to implement a custom *IInstanceContextProvider*. The logic in this provider would need to determine, based on the contents of the message, which client made the request and hand out the appropriate instance. Determination of the client could be based on the IP address from which the request came or the set of credentials used to access the service, or, as part of the client configuration, a token (such as an instance ID) could be sent along with each message.

Case Scenario 2: Protecting Your WCF Application

1. From a scalability perspective, the *PerCall* mode is probably the best choice for this scenario. Depending on the business requirements, it might be necessary to use *PerSession*, but depending on the number of people who might be making simultaneous requests, this might reduce the ability of the server to handle the load. A memory requirement is associated with each session. (The service instance must be kept in memory, for example.) This is an example of a choice that should be made early in the design of the application, even though it is possible to change at the last moment. It is likely that dependencies are related to the use of a *PerSession* instancing mode such that changing to a *PerCall* mode might cause the application to break. Therefore, although WCF does give you the flexibility to reconfigure an application at run time to use different behaviors, that doesn't mean making such a change will be successful from the perspective of the execution of the application.

2. It is likely that the throttling values must be set higher. How much higher depends on both the instancing mode and the number of expected simultaneous users. If per call mode is used, both the *MaxConcurrentCalls* and *MaxConcurrentInstances* need to be set to the same value. This value should be roughly the peak number of simultaneous users that you expect. Also, because the per call instance mode is being used, the *MaxConcurrentSessions* value is irrelevant.

3. The values for the quota settings can be left at their defaults. However, some of those values might be high (with respect to the actual construction of the application). As such, they can be lowered without affecting the functionality of the application. For example, the maximum message size could be lowered to be closer to the expected maximum request size for the system. The same type of change can be made to the *MaxDepth* setting. Changing the values is not a requirement, but it does slightly reduce the attack surface for the service portion of the application.

Chapter 11: Lesson Review Answers

1. **Correct Answer: B**
   A. **Incorrect:** The Lightweight Transaction Manager is not able to coordinate a transaction that includes multiple durable resources (the two databases).
   B. **Correct:** The Distributed Transaction Coordinator is automatically enlisted when multiple SQL Server databases are in the same transaction.
   C. **Incorrect:** The Kernel Transaction Manager manages transactions associated with kernel mode or user mode resources, such as the file system.
   D. **Incorrect:** The Web Services Transaction Manager currently is just an Organization for the Advancement of Structure Information Standards (OASIS) standard. At the moment, no implementation is available as part of WCF.

2. **Correct Answer: A**
   A. **Correct:** The Lightweight Transaction Manager is capable of mediating a transaction across a WCF call and a durable resource.
   B. **Incorrect:** Although the DTC is capable of handling the transaction, the LTM will not promote to the DTC based on the criteria given.
   C. **Incorrect:** The Kernel Transaction Manager manages transactions associated with kernel mode or user mode resources such as the file system.
   D. **Incorrect:** The Web Services Transaction Manager currently is just an OASIS standard. At the moment, there is no implementation available as part of WCF.

Lesson 2

1. **Correct Answers: A, B, D, and H**

   A. **Correct:** The LTM that is invoked by creating the *TransactionScope* object will instantiate the transaction that will ultimately become the ambient one.

   B. **Correct:** The client binding must specify that the transaction will be propagated to the service.

   C. **Incorrect:** The *SendTimeout* attribute determines how long the client will wait for a response before raising an exception.

   D. **Correct:** The service binding must specify that a transaction will be propagated.

   E. **Incorrect:** The *ReceiveTimeout* attribute determines how long will be given to the receive operation before an exception is raised.

   F. **Incorrect:** Although requiring a transaction in the operation behavior will not keep an ambient transaction from being visible within the methods, it is not a requirement for this attribute to exist.

   G. **Incorrect:** The auto-completion of the transaction doesn't affect whether the service has an ambient transaction.

   H. **Correct:** The Service contract on the service must have the transaction flow option set to *Allowed*. (It could also be set to *Mandatory*.)

2. **Correct Answer: B**

   A. **Incorrect:** The outer transaction will not complete prior to the 30-second timeout that is specified, so it will be rolled back.

   B. **Correct:** Because the outer transaction fails (due to the timeout), both transactions will be rolled back.

   C. **Incorrect:** Although *ts2* will complete, the timeout that occurs in *ts1* will prevent the transaction from being committed.

   D. **Incorrect:** The outer transaction (*ts1*) will fail because it is not completed prior to the timeout.

Lesson 11: Case Scenario Answers

Case Scenario: Transactional Services

1. The client is not involved in this transaction at all, other than to initiate the call to the internal WCF service. Because the transaction originates with the service and not with the client application, no configuration or deployment issues arise.

2. To propagate transaction information across the Internet, the WS-AtomicTransaction (WS-AT) protocol must be used, which requires the Microsoft Distributed Transaction

Controller (MSDTC) to be running on the computer that hosts the internal WCF service. Also, WS-AT must be enabled within the MSDTC configuration. From a configuration perspective, the endpoint associated with the external WCF service must use a binding that is capable of supporting transactions, and that particular binding should be marked as allowing transaction information to flow from the client to the service because, in this instance, the internal WCF service is actually the client to the external WCF service.

3. As it turns out, using WCF as the transaction mechanism eliminates most of the technical challenges. Within WCF, it is already possible for transaction information to move easily from client to service and for all updates to complete within that structure. The real challenge is in configuring the external WCF service properly. It too must be running MSDTC with WS-AT enabled and using a data source that can participate in an MSDTC-driven transaction. In addition, an underlying assumption is that the service will act in a properly transactional way, so no data updates will take place on the external service that cannot be part of the transaction.

Lesson 12: Lesson Review Answers

Lesson 1

1. **Correct Answers: B and D**

   A. **Incorrect:** These options would cause a single instance of the service object to be created for all requests. The concurrency mode of *Multiple* means that more than one simultaneous request is possible. With multiple requests, the possibility of concurrency issues associated with updating the *hitCounter* variable exists.

   B. **Correct:** The use of a concurrency mode of *Single* ensures that only one request at a time can be processed. Even though more than one session could be active, the fact that the *hitCounter* variable is an instance variable means that it cannot be updated by more than one thread at a time.

   C. **Incorrect:** Even though the *InstanceContextMode* is set to *PerSession*, more than one request, even from the same session, can occur. This means that two requests can be processed in the same instance, which, in the case of the class, means that concurrency problems can occur.

   D. **Correct:** The *Single* concurrency mode ensures that only one request is processed at a time, and the *Single* instance context mode means that only one instance is ever created.

2. **Correct Answer: D**

A. **Incorrect:** These options would cause a single instance of the service object to be created for all requests. The concurrency mode of *Multiple* means that more than one simultaneous request is possible and, with multiple requests, the possibility of concurrency issues associated with updating the *hitCounter* variable exists.

B. **Incorrect:** Although a concurrency mode of *Single* ensures that each service object can process only one request at a time, this is not sufficient when a shared or static variable is being used. The fact that the instance context mode is *PerSession* means that multiple service objects can be instantiated, each of which could update *hitCounter*. This introduces the possibility of concurrency problems.

C. **Incorrect:** Having a *PerSession* instance context means multiple service objects, and a concurrency mode of *Multiple* means that simultaneous requests in each object are possible. Either one of these is sufficient to open up the possibility of concurrency issues.

D. **Correct:** The concurrency mode ensures that only one request is processed at a time, and the instance context mode means that only one instance is ever created. This combination is required for static or shared variables to be safe from concurrency violations.

Lesson 2

1. **Correct Answer: C**

A. **Incorrect:** Updating a SQL Server database (or any database) does not require any thread affinity.

B. **Incorrect:** Calls to external Web services do not require thread affinity to be involved.

C. **Correct:** To interact with the user interface on the Windows form, you must process the requests on the user interface thread. This requires the synchronization context to be used.

D. **Incorrect:** Using threads in the thread pool does not innately require a synchronization context to be created.

2. **Correct Answer: D**

A. **Incorrect:** Deriving the service class from the *SynchronizationContext* class means that it could be used as a synchronization context, but it does not mean that requests processed by that service will use that context.

B. **Incorrect:** Setting *UseSynchronizationContext* to *true* means that, if the host has an active synchronization context, the incoming requests will use it. It does not cause the host to have a synchronization context.

C. **Incorrect:** Although the *IContextBehavior* interface associates a custom context with a request, having the service class implement it doesn't activate the necessary mechanism.

D. **Correct:** The attribute that implements *IContextBehavior* is required to attach the custom synchronization object to an incoming request.

Lesson 12: Case Scenario Answers

Case Scenario: Using WCF as a Gateway

■ The choice of concurrency model really comes down to selecting between *Single* and *Multiple*. Although *Reentrant* is certainly a possibility, there is nothing in the scenario to indicate that the client will need to call back to the WCF service while processing the status update events generated by the earlier application.

The decision between *Single* and *Multiple* rests on how many simultaneous requests the earlier application can support. If that system is limited to processing a single request at a time, then *Single* is really the only choice. If the concurrency is set to *Multiple*, the implication is that the earlier application must be able to support multiple simultaneous requests.

The choice of *Multiple* concurrency, however, requires caution. By default, setting concurrency to *Multiple* does not set a limit on the number of simultaneous requests, and each request will establish a connection to the earlier application, potentially straining the ability of that system to provide timely responses. If this is a limit on the system, service throttling should be used to limit the incoming requests to a number that can be supported simultaneously.

Glossary

absolute URI   A URI that is the full address for an endpoint as opposed to a relative address, which consists of a base address and a variable portion.

action   An optional attribute included in a SOAP request that can be used by the service to determine the operation or function that needs to be performed.

activity identifier   A value, typically a GUID, that is used to identify an activity uniquely with WCF.

activity transfer   A step in the processing of an operation request at which the identifier for an activity on the client side of the request is sent to the service, where it becomes the identifier on the service side of the request.

ambient transaction   An established transaction that exists in the current thread or object context. It is available for use by any code that is interested in performing atomic operations.

authorization policy   Within WCF, a point in the request pipeline at which custom code can be injected to add claim sets to the request.

base address   For an endpoint, the foundational element of the address. The relative portion of the address is the piece that changes more frequently.

Basic Profile   A set of open Web service specifications used to promote interoperability between different implementations of Web service functionality. The full name is WS-I Basic Profile.

Callback channel   The channel the WCF plumbing must set up to enable the Duplex MEP, which involves two-way communication with the service calling back to the client.

Callback contract   The client-side Service contract a service uses to call back to its clients when it is engaged in a Duplex MEP.

ChannelFactory   A class offered by the WCF plumbing that can be used to create a proxy object dynamically, based on the service contract alone. Using only the Service contract and no explicitly defined proxy class, an instance of the *ChannelFactory* class can create a proxy object dynamically.

channel stack   The combination of layers involved in handling a WCF message. WCF uses a layer model to define how the client sends and receives information from the service. At each layer, processing can be performed to format and modify the message.

claim   An individual right or action that can be applied to a specific resource.

claim set   An order collection of claims that come from a single issuer.

client callback   The WCF mechanism that enables a WCF service to invoke a method that is implemented on the client.

command-line utility   Represents an application that executes within a command window and does not have a graphical user interface. The user interacts with the utility by typing commands directly inside the command window.

Common Log File System   A transactional logging subsystem built into a number of Microsoft Windows operating systems, starting with Microsoft Windows 2003 R2.

Data contract   Data contracts are the WCF mechanism for specifying the structure of the request documents being received by your service as well as the response documents the service sends back to its consumers.

declared SOAP fault   Operations in a WCF service decorated with a *FaultContract* attribute that has a *Type* parameter specified. (The constructor for the *FaultContract-Attribute* class takes a *Type* object as a parameter. This *Type* is the type that is declared as a possible SOAP fault value.)

Duplex   An MEP that involves two-way communication between a client and the service, thereby allowing the client to initiate sending messages to the client.

encoding   In terms of WCF, the process whereby a WCF message object—an object representing a SOAP message at the XML InfoSet level—is translated to a byte stream to be sent over the wire-level transport layer.

Fault contract   The part of a service's overall behavioral contract that tells consumers from which operations a service might issue a fault as well as which type of fault information it will send out.

fault exception   The WCF *Exception* class the plumbing uses to translate between the world of .NET exceptions and SOAP faults.

federation   Represents a collection of domains that have an established trust. The domains are part of a federated security architecture, which allows for a separation between the service and the authentication and authorization procedures.

globally unique activity identifier (gAId)   An activity identifier that is unique across all services and all systems.

Hypertext Transfer Protocol (HTTP)   Designed by the World Wide Web Consortium (W3C), this communication protocol provides a standard way to publish and retrieve hypertext pages over the Internet.

Internet Information Services (IIS)   Represents a set of Windows services that can host Web-based applications on HTTP. The services have gone through several versions, and the latest version is 7.0.

just-in-time-locking/as-soon-as-possible-releasing   A pattern that describes best practice for locking a scarce resource. The idea is that locking the resource should be delayed until just before the resource is required and that the resource should be unlocked as soon as possible after it has been used. The goal is to minimize the length of time the resource is locked as a way to minimize resource contention issues.

Kerberos   An authentication protocol that enables computers to authenticate one another across a nonsecured network. The protocol uses symmetric key cryptography and requires a third party to be available to provide authentication services.

local activity identifier (lAId)   An activity identifier that is unique only within the local system.

message body   The portion of the request that contains information used by the operation. It is a valid XML element and contains parameter values and, possibly, the name of the operation that is to be invoked.

Message contract   The part of a service's structural contract that specifies which custom SOAP header elements should be expected in its messages and how its SOAP messages will be structured.

Message Exchange Pattern (MEP)   A pattern that describes the protocol of message exchanges a consumer needs to engage in to converse properly with the service.

Message Inspection   The final point of extension on the proxy pipeline that occurs after the Message object has been created, and is typically used to perform functions that are not specific to one operation or service, but instead can apply to many different methods

Message Transmission Optimization Mechanism (MTOM)   Message encoding method used to optimize performance when transmitting large payloads.

message-based activation Indicates that a process will not begin until a message has been sent by one entity to another. In the world of WCF, the entity is a service, and services communicate by sending messages to each other. They can send messages to client applications as well.

metadata Data used to describe other data. In the case of WCF services, metadata represents the schema for message operations and the data they handle.

Microsoft Message Queue (MSMQ) services A set of services that enables applications to queue user requests and provide guaranteed message delivery along with efficient message routing.

named pipes Communication protocol used to facilitate multiple-process communication on the same computer.

OneWay A MEP that defines the situation wherein a client simply sends a message to a service without expecting any response. Only a one-way communication channel is set up.

one-way call A call made to a service with no expectation of a response.

peer-to-peer Represents a network architecture in which clients and services are equal and subscribe to the same network grid.

Plain old XML (POX) A term used to refer to messages that are sent between a client and service, using XML without any of the WS-* standards that are now commonplace.

policy alternative A collection of policy assertions that are grouped together for easier management and assignment.

policy assertion Within the WS-Policy standard, a description of a single capability, property, or behavior that is held or supported by either the client or the service in a distributed message exchange.

proxy An object you can use to encapsulate communication with a service. Method calls on these objects are translated (by the WCF plumbing) into operations on the remote service.

proxy class A class that, when instantiated, provides an object capable of acting as a proxy to a remote service.

relative addressing A technique in creating addresses for WCF endpoints by which the base address (which doesn't change) is combined with a variable portion (which is subject to frequent changes).

ReliableMessaging A mechanism by which all messages can be guaranteed to arrive at the intended destination. Some of the protocols used in WCF applications do not provide for guaranteed delivery of messages.

Request/Response A MEP that defines the situation wherein a client expects a response to its message. Either the request or the response could have an empty body, but both are part of the exchange nonetheless.

resource manager An application that keeps track of access to shared data. Typical examples include a database server and a message queue.

root scope The TransactionScope object associated with the first transaction in the group, the scope that initiated the transaction.

roundtripping A scenario in which data conforming to a newer Data contract (with new elements) is sent to an entity that knows only about an older Data contract and which sends the data back to the entity that knows of the newer contract. In a successful roundtripping scenario, no data is lost on the new-to-old-to-new trip.

scarce resource A resource that, because of its relative lack of availability, is a possible execution bottleneck.

Secure Sockets Layer (SSL) Uses certificates to secure communications across the network. The certificate is associated with a port and IP address.

security identifier (SID) A value used by Windows to identify security principals and groups.

serialization In WCF, the act of translating an object graph into a WCF message object, an object representing a SOAP message at the XML InfoSet level.

service agent A class of objects that aid communication with a service but offer some capabilities beyond what a proxy might offer. An agent class wraps access to a proxy and adds some additional capabilities, usually to cope with the service not being available and perhaps to cache some of the results retrieved from the service.

service authorization manager Provides authorization facilities to a service. This component is responsible for responding to any request for access made by the service. It will examine the execution context, including any existing claims, to determine whether a request should be allowed or denied.

service instance An instance of the class that contains the implementation of the service.

service object An instantiation of the class that implements the service interface for a WCF service. This object processes the incoming requests for a service. The number of service objects that are created depends on the *InstanceContextMode* property of the *ServiceBehavior* attribute.

service orientation A style of system design in which disparate systems execute as services that communicate only through messages.

service reference A term used in the context of Visual Studio to refer to references to a WCF service as opposed to an ASP.NET Web reference or a .NET assembly reference.

service type The WCF term for a class that implements a Service contract.

SOAP Designed by the World Wide Web Consortium (W3C), this transport protocol provides a standard way to send messages between applications, using XML.

svcutil A program used to generate a proxy class for use in a WCF client based on the metadata exposed by the WCF service.

thread affinity The need for a particular process to be executed on a specific thread. It occurs when the process has some special relationship with a thread, such as when thread local storage is used.

thread local storage A repository in .NET that stores information for the thread on which the current process is running. This information will follow the thread regardless of the class or method that is being executed.

thread-safe A situation in which multiple threads can access the properties and methods of a single instance without concern for deadlocking or causing an inconsistent state.

token authenticator Verifies the validity of a token that has been provided. In WCF, a security token can preserve user context across multiple interactions between the client and the service.

transaction coordinator Software responsible for coordinating the messages required for a transaction to take place. In a two-phase commit, this involves sending and receiving the messages between the various resource managers.

transaction manager Software that is responsible for coordinating the message required for a distributed transaction within a single physical computer.

transaction protocol A definition of the types and timing of messages that are required to perform a transaction.

Transmission Control Protocol (TCP) Efficient transport protocol used to exchange packets of data across computer boundaries.

two-phase commit A common protocol used to implement a distributed transaction.

virtual directory Indicates the path used to access files located on an IIS Web server. The Virtual directory maps to a physical directory located on the Web server.

WCF channel stack The collection of protocol, binding, and transport objects that interact with a request as it is being transmitted from the client to the service and back again.

WS-Addressing A standard that provides a transport-neutral mechanism to define addresses for Web service endpoints. Consideration is given to being able to route messages through various processing nodes, including endpoint managers, gateways, and other intermediaries.

WS-I The Web Services Interoperability Organization, an open industry organization whose charter is to promote Web Services interoperability across platforms, operating systems, and programming languages. For more information, see *http://www.ws-i.org/*.

WS-I Basic Profile The first profile defined by WS-I to maximize interoperability among the various Web services platforms. Specifically, the Basic Profile was intended to guide developers through SOAP, WSDL, and other landscapes so that they can make the choices among these technologies and standards that will help maximize their chances at interoperating successfully with other platforms.

WS-PolicyAssertions A WS-* standard that defines a common format for the expression of a policy by a service.

WS-SecureConversation A standard that describes a mechanism for establishing a secure context that can be used across multiple requests from the same client to a service.

WS-SecurityPolicy A standard that enables Web services to express their security requirements and capabilities by using a series of policy assertions.

Index

Additional Resources for Developers: Advanced Topics and Best Practices

Published and Forthcoming Titles from Microsoft Press

Code Complete, Second Edition
Steve McConnell • ISBN 0-7356-1967-0

For more than a decade, Steve McConnell, one of the premier authors and voices in the software community, has helped change the way developers write code—and produce better software. Now his classic book, *Code Complete*, has been fully updated and revised with best practices in the art and science of constructing software. Topics include design, applying good techniques to construction, eliminating errors, planning, managing construction activities, and relating personal character to superior software. This new edition features fully updated information on programming techniques, including the emergence of Web-style programming, and integrated coverage of object-oriented design. You'll also find new code examples—both good and bad—in C++, Microsoft® Visual Basic®, C#, and Java, although the focus is squarely on techniques and practices.

More About Software Requirements: Thorny Issues and Practical Advice
Karl E. Wiegers • ISBN 0-7356-2267-1

Have you ever delivered software that satisfied all of the project specifications, but failed to meet any of the customers expectations? Without formal, verifiable requirements—and a system for managing them—the result is often a gap between what developers think they're supposed to build and what customers think they're going to get. Too often, lessons about software requirements engineering processes are formal or academic, and not of value to real-world, professional development teams. In this follow-up guide to *Software Requirements*, Second Edition, you will discover even more practical techniques for gathering and managing software requirements that help you deliver software that meets project and customer specifications. Succinct and immediately useful, this book is a must-have for developers and architects.

Software Estimation: Demystifying the Black Art
Steve McConnell • ISBN 0-7356-0535-1

Often referred to as the "black art" because of its complexity and uncertainty, software estimation is not as hard or mysterious as people think. However, the art of how to create effective cost and schedule estimates has not been very well publicized. *Software Estimation* provides a proven set of procedures and heuristics that software developers, technical leads, and project managers can apply to their projects. Instead of arcane treatises and rigid modeling techniques, award-winning author Steve McConnell gives practical guidance to help organizations achieve basic estimation proficiency and lay the groundwork to continue improving project cost estimates. This book does not avoid the more complex mathematical estimation approaches, but the non-mathematical reader will find plenty of useful guidelines without getting bogged down in complex formulas.

Debugging, Tuning, and Testing Microsoft .NET 2.0 Applications
John Robbins • ISBN 0-7356-2202-7

Making an application the best it can be has long been a time-consuming task best accomplished with specialized and costly tools. With Microsoft Visual Studio® 2005, developers have available a new range of built-in functionality that enables them to debug their code quickly and efficiently, tune it to optimum performance, and test applications to ensure compatibility and trouble-free operation. In this accessible and hands-on book, debugging expert John Robbins shows developers how to use the tools and functions in Visual Studio to their full advantage to ensure high-quality applications.

The Security Development Lifecycle
Michael Howard and Steve Lipner • ISBN 0-7356-2214-0

Adapted from Microsoft's standard development process, the Security Development Lifecycle (SDL) is a methodology that helps reduce the number of security defects in code at every stage of the development process, from design to release. This book details each stage of the SDL methodology and discusses its implementation across a range of Microsoft software, including Microsoft Windows Server™ 2003, Microsoft SQL Server™ 2000 Service Pack 3, and Microsoft Exchange Server 2003 Service Pack 1, to help measurably improve security features. You get direct access to insights from Microsoft's security team and lessons that are applicable to software development processes worldwide, whether on a small-scale or a large-scale. This book includes a CD featuring videos of developer training classes.

Software Requirements, Second Edition
Karl E. Wiegers • ISBN 0-7356-1879-8

Writing Secure Code, Second Edition
Michael Howard and David LeBlanc • ISBN 0-7356-1722-8

CLR via C#, Second Edition
Jeffrey Richter • ISBN 0-7356-2163-2

For more information about Microsoft Press® books and other learning products,
visit: **www.microsoft.com/mspress** *and* **www.microsoft.com/learning**

Microsoft®
Press

Security Books for Developers
Published and Forthcoming Titles

The Security Development Lifecycle: Demonstrably More-Secure Software
Michael Howard and Steve Lipner
ISBN 9780735622142

Your software customers demand—and deserve—better security and privacy. This book is the first to detail a rigorous, proven methodology that measurably minimizes security bugs: the Security Development Lifecycle (SDL). Two experts from the Microsoft® Security Engineering Team guide you through each stage and offer best practices for implementing SDL in any size organization.

Developing More-Secure Microsoft ASP.NET 2.0 Applications
Dominick Baier
ISBN 9780735623316

Advance your security-programming expertise for ASP.NET 2.0. A leading security expert shares best practices, pragmatic instruction, and code samples in Microsoft Visual C#® to help you develop Web applications that are more robust, more reliable, and more resistant to attack. Includes code samples on the Web.

Writing Secure Code for Windows Vista™
Michael Howard and David LeBlanc
ISBN 9780735623934

Written as a complement to the award-winning book *Writing Secure Code*, this new reference focuses on the security enhancements in Windows Vista. Get first-hand insights into design decisions, and practical approaches to real-world security challenges. Covers ACLs, BitLocker™, firewalls, authentication, and other essential topics, and includes C# code samples on the Web.

Hunting Security Bugs
Tom Gallagher, Bryan Jeffries, Lawrence Landauer
ISBN 9780735621879

Learn to think like an attacker—with insights from three security testing experts. This book offers practical guidance and code samples to help find, classify, and assess security bugs *before* your software is released. Discover how to test clients and servers, detect spoofing issues, identify where attackers can directly manipulate memory, and more.

Writing Secure Code, Second Edition
Michael Howard and David LeBlanc
ISBN 9780735617223

Discover how to padlock applications throughout the entire development process—from designing applications and writing robust code to testing for security flaws. The authors—two battle-scarred veterans who have solved some of the industry's toughest security problems—share proven principles, strategies, and techniques, with code samples in several languages.

The Practical Guide to Defect Prevention
Marc McDonald, Robert Musson, Ross Smith
ISBN 9780735622531

Microsoft® Windows® Presentation Foundation Developer Workbook
Billy Hollis
ISBN 9780735624184

Developing Drivers with the Microsoft Windows Driver Foundation
Microsoft Windows Hardware Platform Evangelism Team
ISBN 9780735623743

Embedded Programming with the Microsoft .NET Micro Framework
Donald Thompson and Rob S. Miles
ISBN 9780735623651

See more resources at **microsoft.com/mspress**
and **microsoft.com/learning**

Additional Resources for C# Developers

Published and Forthcoming Titles from Microsoft Press

Microsoft® Visual C#® 2005 Express Edition: Build a Program Now!
Patrice Pelland • ISBN 0-7356-2229-9

In this lively, eye-opening, and hands-on book, all you need is a computer and the desire to learn how to program with Visual C# 2005 Express Edition. Featuring a full working edition of the software, this fun and highly visual guide walks you through a complete programming project—a desktop weather-reporting application—from start to finish. You'll get an unintimidating introduction to the Microsoft Visual Studio® development environment and learn how to put the lightweight, easy-to-use tools in Visual C# Express to work right away—creating, compiling, testing, and delivering your first, ready-to-use program. You'll get expert tips, coaching, and visual examples at each step of the way, along with pointers to additional learning resources.

Microsoft Visual C# 2005 *Step by Step*
John Sharp • ISBN 0-7356-2129-2

Visual C#, a feature of Visual Studio 2005, is a modern programming language designed to deliver a productive environment for creating business frameworks and reusable object-oriented components. Now you can teach yourself essential techniques with Visual C#—and start building components and Microsoft Windows®–based applications—one step at a time. With *Step by Step*, you work at your own pace through hands-on, learn-by-doing exercises. Whether you're a beginning programmer or new to this particular language, you'll learn how, when, and why to use specific features of Visual C# 2005. Each chapter puts you to work, building your knowledge of core capabilities and guiding you as you create your first C#-based applications for Windows, data management, and the Web.

Programming Microsoft Visual C# 2005 Framework Reference
Francesco Balena • ISBN 0-7356-2182-9

Complementing *Programming Microsoft Visual C# 2005 Core Reference*, this book covers a wide range of additional topics and information critical to Visual C# developers, including Windows Forms, working with Microsoft ADO.NET 2.0 and Microsoft ASP.NET 2.0, Web services, security, remoting, and much more. Packed with sample code and real-world examples, this book will help developers move from understanding to mastery.

Programming Microsoft Visual C# 2005 *Core Reference*
Donis Marshall • ISBN 0-7356-2181-0

Get the in-depth reference and pragmatic, real-world insights you need to exploit the enhanced language features and core capabilities in Visual C# 2005. Programming expert Donis Marshall deftly builds your proficiency with classes, structs, and other fundamentals, and advances your expertise with more advanced topics such as debugging, threading, and memory management. Combining incisive reference with hands-on coding examples and best practices, this *Core Reference* focuses on mastering the C# skills you need to build innovative solutions for smart clients and the Web.

CLR via C#, Second Edition
Jeffrey Richter • ISBN 0-7356-2163-2

In this new edition of Jeffrey Richter's popular book, you get focused, pragmatic guidance on how to exploit the common language runtime (CLR) functionality in Microsoft .NET Framework 2.0 for applications of all types—from Web Forms, Windows Forms, and Web services to solutions for Microsoft SQL Server™, Microsoft code names "Avalon" and "Indigo," consoles, Microsoft Windows NT® Service, and more. Targeted to advanced developers and software designers, this book takes you under the covers of .NET for an in-depth understanding of its structure, functions, and operational components, demonstrating the most practical ways to apply this knowledge to your own development efforts. You'll master fundamental design tenets for .NET and get hands-on insights for creating high-performance applications more easily and efficiently. The book features extensive code examples in Visual C# 2005.

Programming Microsoft Windows Forms
Charles Petzold • ISBN 0-7356-2153-5

CLR via C++
Jeffrey Richter with Stanley B. Lippman
ISBN 0-7356-2248-5

Programming Microsoft Web Forms
Douglas J. Reilly • ISBN 0-7356-2179-9

Debugging, Tuning, and Testing Microsoft .NET 2.0 Applications
John Robbins • ISBN 0-7356-2202-7

For more information about Microsoft Press® books and other learning products,
visit: **www.microsoft.com/books** *and* **www.microsoft.com/learning**

System Requirements

We assume that before using this training kit, you already have a working knowledge of Windows, Microsoft Visual Basic or C# (or both), and Extensible Application Markup Language (XAML).

Hardware Requirements

The following hardware is required to complete the practice exercises:

- A computer with a 1.6-gigahertz (GHz) or faster processor.
- A minimum of 384 megabytes (MB) of random access memory (RAM).
- A minimum of 2.2 gigabytes (GB) of available hard disk space is required to install Microsoft Visual Studio 2008. Additionally, 75 megabytes (MB) of available hard disk space is required to install the labs.
- A DVD-ROM drive.
- A 1024 × 768 or higher resolution display with 256 colors or more.
- A keyboard and Microsoft mouse or compatible pointing device.

Software Requirements

The following software is required to complete the practice exercises:

- One of the following operating systems:
  - ❑ Windows Vista (any edition except Windows Vista Starter)
  - ❑ Windows XP with Service Pack 2 or later (any edition except Windows XP Starter)
  - ❑ Windows Server 2003 with Service Pack 1 or later (any edition)
  - ❑ Windows Server 2003 R2 or later (any edition)
  - ❑ Windows Server 2008
- Microsoft Visual Studio 2008

What do you think of this book?

We want to hear from you!

Do you have a few minutes to participate in a brief online survey?

Microsoft is interested in hearing your feedback so we can continually improve our books and learning resources for you.

To participate in our survey, please visit:

www.microsoft.com/learning/booksurvey/

...and enter this book's ISBN-10 or ISBN-13 number (located above barcode on back cover*). As a thank-you to survey participants in the United States and Canada, each month we'll randomly select five respondents to win one of five $100 gift certificates from a leading online merchant. At the conclusion of the survey, you can enter the drawing by providing your e-mail address, which will be used for prize notification only.

Thanks in advance for your input. Your opinion counts!

* Where to find the ISBN on back cover

ISBN-13: 000-0-0000-0000-0
ISBN-10: 0-0000-0000-0

00000

0 000000 000000

Example only. Each book has unique ISBN.

***Microsoft*® Press**

No purchase necessary. Void where prohibited. Open only to residents of the 50 United States (includes District of Columbia) and Canada (void in Quebec). For official rules and entry dates see:

www.microsoft.com/learning/booksurvey/

Save 15%
on your Microsoft® Certification exam fee

Present this discount voucher to any participating test center worldwide, or use the discount code to register online or via telephone at participating Microsoft Certified Exam Delivery Providers. See microsoft.com/mcp/exams for locations.

Microsoft®

Microsoft® | Learning

Good for 15% off one exam fee in the Microsoft Certified Professional Program

Offer expires 12/31/2013

2V2B0NVZ3H

Your voucher discount code

exam voucher

Redeemable at Microsoft Certified Exam Delivery Providers worldwide. For locations, visit: www.microsoft.com/mcp/exams

Promotion Terms and Conditions

- Offer good for 15% off one exam fee in the Microsoft Certified Professional Program.
- Voucher code can be redeemed online or at Microsoft Certified Exam Delivery Providers worldwide.
- Exam purchased using this voucher code must be taken on or before December 31, 2013.
- Inform your Microsoft Certified Exam Delivery Provider that you want to use the voucher discount code at the time you register for the exam.

Voucher Terms and Conditions

- Expired vouchers will not be replaced.
- Each voucher code may only be used for one exam and must be presented at time of registration.
- This voucher may not be combined with other vouchers or discounts.
- This voucher is nontransferable and is void if altered or revised in any way.
- This voucher may not be sold or redeemed for cash, credit, or refund.

Part No. X15-02750